P9-CCX-032

LAURENCE STEINBERG
Temple University

McGRAW-HILL, INC.
New York St. Louis San Francisco Auckland Bogotá Caracas
Lisbon London Madrid Mexico City Milan Montreal New Delhi
San Juan Singapore Sydney Tokyo Toronto

FOR WENDY AND BENJAMIN

Adolescence

Copyright ©1996, 1993 by McGraw-Hill, Inc. All rights reserved. Copyright ©1989, 1985 by Alfred A. Knopf, Inc. All rights reserved. Printed in the United States of America. Except as permitted under the United States Copyright Act of 1976, no part of this publication may be reproduced or distributed in any form or by any means, or stored in a data base or retrieval system, without the prior written permission of the publisher.

Acknowledgments appear on pages 583–585 and on this page by reference.

This book is printed on acid-free paper.

1 2 3 4 5 6 7 8 9 0 DOW DOW 9 0 9 8 7 6 5

ISBN 0-07-061262-5

This book was set in Veljovic by The Clarinda Company.
The editors were Jane Vaicunas, Beth Kaufman, and James R. Belser;
the design was done by Circa 86, Inc.;
the production supervisor was Friederich W. Schulte.
The photo editor was Kathy Bendo;
the photo researcher was Elyse Rieder.
R. R. Donnelley & Sons Company was printer and binder.

Library of Congress Cataloging–in–Publication Data
Steinberg, Laurence D., (date).
Adolescence / Laurence Steinberg. —4th ed.
p. cm.
Includes bibliographical references and indexes.
ISBN 0-07-061262-5
1. Adolescent psychology. I. Title.
BF724.S75 1996
305.23′5—dc20 95-19666

ABOUT THE AUTHOR

Laurence Steinberg is Professor of Psychology at Temple University. He graduated from Vassar College in 1974 and received his Ph.D. in Human Development and Family Studies from Cornell University in 1977. A Fellow of the American Psychological Association's Division of Developmental Psychology, Professor Steinberg has taught previously at the University of California, Irvine and the University of Wisconsin–Madison. He is the author of numerous scholarly articles on adolescent development as well as the books *When Teenagers Work: The Psychological and Social Costs of Adolescent Employment* (with Ellen Greenberger), *Childhood* (with Roberta Meyer), *You and Your Adolescent: A Parent's Guide for Ages 10 to 20* (with Ann Levine), and *Crossing Paths: How Your Child's Adolescence Triggers Your Own Crisis* (with Wendy Steinberg).

CONTENTS IN BRIEF

CONTENTS

PREFACE

In 1976, the first time I was asked to teach a semester-long course in adolescent development, my graduate advisor, John Hill—who at that time had been teaching adolescent development for ten years—took me aside. "Getting them to learn the stuff is easy," John said, smiling. "Unfortunately, you'll only have about three weeks to do it. It'll take you ten weeks just to get them to *unlearn* all the junk they're sure is true."

He was right. I would present study after study documenting that turmoil isn't the norm for most adolescents, that most teenagers have relatively good relationships with their parents, that adolescence isn't an inherently stressful period, and so on, and my students would nod diligently. But five minutes later someone would tell the class about his or her cousin Billy, who had either run away from home, attempted to set his parents' bedroom on fire, or refused to say a word to either his mother or his father for eight years.

As most instructors discover, teaching adolescent development is both exhilarating and exasperating. Every student comes into class an expert; for many of them, adolescence wasn't very long ago. No good instructor wants to squelch the interest and curiosity most students bring with them when they first come into a class. But no conscientious teacher wants to see students leave with little more than the preconceptions they came in with and an even firmer conviction that social scientists who study human development are out of touch with the "real" world.

One of my other mentors, Urie Bronfenbrenner, once wrote that the science of child development had found itself caught between "a rock and a soft place"—between rigor and relevance. Teachers of adolescent development find themselves in the same boat. How do you present scientific research on adolescent development in ways students find interesting, believable, relevant, and worth remembering when the term is over? I hope this book will help.

ABOUT THE FOURTH EDITION

About the time of the publication of the first edition of *Adolescence* in 1985, the study of development during the second decade of the life cycle suddenly became a hot topic. New journals devoted exclusively to the study of adolescence began publication; established journals in the field of child development became deluged with submissions on adolescence; more and more well-trained scholars specializing in the study of adolescent development appeared on the scene. During the eight years between the publication of the first and third editions of this text, our understanding of adolescent development expanded dramatically, and this expansion has continued at a rapid pace since the last edition was published three years ago.

The fourth edition of this textbook reflects this new and more substantial knowledge base. Although the book's original organization has been retained, the material in each chapter has been significantly updated and revised. More than six hundred new studies have been cited since the third edition alone.

In some areas of inquiry, issues that were unresolved at the time of the earlier editions have been settled by newer and more definitive studies. In many cases, conclusions that had been tentatively accepted by the field were abandoned in favor of more contemporary views. For instance, when the first edition went to press, most scholars conceived of various aspects of problem behavior—drug use, unprotected sex, delinquency, for example—as being more or less independent phenomena, and theorists went out of their way to treat these issues under separate headings. In the past decade, however, our theories of adolescent problem behavior have changed substantially, because the weight of the evidence now indicates that many of the various problem behaviors associated with adolescence are indeed highly interrelated. New theories linking these problem areas to one another, and drawing a distinction between "internalizing" and "externalizing" problems, necessitated discussing them in a different fashion. Accordingly, *Adolescence* was revised to reflect this change in perspective, and Chapter 13, "Psychosocial Problems in Adolescence"—devoted entirely to psychosocial problems—was added to the third edition. This chapter has been retained and substantially updated in the current edition.

In yet other areas, our knowledge has expanded so dramatically that several altogether-new sections were added to the text. Readers will find expanded sections in this edition about hormonal influences on mood and behavior, physical health and adolescent health care, information processing and adolescent risk-taking, neighborhood and community effects on adolescent development, economic strain and adolescent development, the impact of parental remarriage and postdivorce custodial arrangements, the structure of peer crowds and gangs, adolescents' use of the mass media, ethnic identity, attachment and internal working models, AIDS, achievement attributions, violence and aggression, and eating disorders. These additions, corrections, and expansions are natural responses to the development of new knowledge in a dynamic growing scientific field.

Perhaps the greatest expansion of knowledge during the past decade has been about adolescents growing up in poverty and about adolescents from ethnic minority groups. This has permitted increased coverage of the ways in which the course of development during adolescence is affected both by economics and ethnicity. Instead of presenting this material in boxed inserts, however, I have incorporated this information into the text. More than one hundred new references on development within ethnic minority populations have been added to this edition.

This edition of *Adolescence* retains a feature that ran throughout the last two editions. A box entitled "The Sexes" in each chapter considers in detail whether a particular pattern of adolescent development is different for boys and for girls. I emphasize the word *whether* here, for in many instances the scientific evidence suggests that the similarities between the sexes are far more striking than the differences. Some of the topics I examine are whether there are sex differences in the impact of early pubertal maturation, in cognitive abilities, in rates of depression, in relations with mothers and fathers, in intimacy, and in the nature of the transition into adulthood.

A second set of boxed inserts was added to the current edition. Although most instructors (and virtually all students) who have used this text have enjoyed its "dejargonized" writing style, some felt that including more information about research design and methods would be useful. Each chapter now contains a boxed feature entitled "The Scientific Study of Adolescence," which examines in detail one particular study discussed in that chapter and teaches students about an important aspect of research methods, design, or statistics. Among the topics covered in this series are, for example, the meaning of a statistical interaction, how researchers use electronic beepers to study adolescents' moods, why correlation is not causation, statistical power, the Q-Sort procedure, and the use of meta-analysis in examining a research literature.

ADOLESCENT DEVELOPMENT IN CONTEXT

If there is a guiding theme to *Adolescence,* it is this. Adolescent development cannot be understood apart from the context in which young people grow up. Identity crises, generation gaps, and peer pressure may be features of adolescent life in contemporary society, but their prevalence has more to do with the nature of our society than with the nature of adolescence as a period in the life cycle. In order to understand how adolescents develop in contemporary society, students need first to understand the world in which adolescents live and how that world affects their behavior and social relationships. I have therefore devoted a good deal of attention in this book to the contexts in which adolescents live—families, peer groups, schools, and work and leisure settings—to how these contexts are changing, and to how these changes are changing the nature of adolescence.

ORGANIZATION

The overall organization of this book has not changed since the last edition. Specifically, the chapters about psychosocial development during adolescence are separate from those about the contexts of adolescence. In this way, the psychosocial concerns of adolescence—identity, autonomy, intimacy, sexuality, and achievement—are presented as central developmental concerns that surface across, and are affected by, different settings.

This book contains an introduction and thirteen chapters, which are grouped into three parts: *the fundamental biological, cognitive, and social changes of the period* (Part One); *the contexts of adolescence* (Part Two); and *psychosocial development during the adolescent years* (Part Three). The Introduction presents a model for studying adolescence that was developed by the late John Hill and that serves as the organizational framework for the text. I have found the framework to be extremely helpful in teaching adolescent development, and I highly recommend using it. However, if the model does not fit with your course outline or your own perspective on adolescence, it is possible to use the text without using the framework. Each chapter is self-contained, and so it is not necessary to assign chapters in the sequence in which they are ordered in the text. However, if you choose to use the model presented in the Introduction, it may be helpful to follow the text organization.

One slight change in organization concerns the placement of chapter summaries. Some students have told their instructor that the text was so engaging to read that they would come to the end of a chapter without having underlined or highlighted the material they needed to review for their examinations. After much deliberation about the mixed blessings of having written a "readable" text, I decided to drop the traditional end-of-chapter summaries in favor of a series of "RECAP" paragraphs inserted at key points in each chapter. These paragraphs review and summarize the material that has been covered in the preceding pages of the text.

THEORY AND METHODS

One of the things you will notice about *Adolescence* when you thumb through the contents is that the ubiquitous chapters about "theories of adolescence" and "research methods" are missing. The chapter titles are indeed missing, but the material isn't. After teaching adolescence for many years, I am convinced that students seldom remember a word of the chapters about theory and methods because the information in them is presented out of context. Therefore, although there is plenty of theory in this text, it is presented when it is most relevant, in a way that shows students how research and theory are related. At the beginning of the chapter on intimacy, for example, Sullivan's perspective on intimacy (and on psychosocial development in general) is presented, and then the relevant research is examined. Similarly, the research methods and tools employed in the study of adolescence are discussed in the context of specific studies that illustrate the powers—or pitfalls—of certain strategies. Many of these research issues are spotlighted in the boxed material on "The Scientific Study of Adolescence," which appears in each chapter. Overall, my approach has been to blend theory, research, and practical applications in a way that shows students how the three depend on each other. For students unfamiliar with theories in developmental psychology, I have included an Appendix that gives an overview of this material.

ACKNOWLEDGMENTS

Revising a textbook at a time when so much new information is available is a challenge that requires much assistance. Over the years my students have suggested many ways in which the text might be improved, and I have learned a great deal from listening to them. I am especially grateful to Elizabeth Cauffman, who ably tracked down and organized much of the new research published in the three years between editions; and to several colleagues, including Ailene Dean, California State University, Chico; Mary Ann Drake, Mercer University; Cynthia Edwards, Meredith College; Karen Howe, Trenton State College; Nancy Leffert, University of Minnesota; Pamela Manners, Troy State University; Judith Meece, University of North Carolina–Chapel Hill; Karla K. Miley, Black Hawk College; Christine A. Readick, Florida State University; Susan L. Rosenthal, Children's Hospital Medical Center, Cincinnati; Lee B. Ross, Frostburg State University; Nicholas R. Santilli, John Carroll University; and Jean A. Steitz, Memphis State University, who carefully reviewed the third edition and initial drafts of this edition and suggested a variety of ways in which the text might be revised. I also wish to thank my colleagues at McGraw-Hill, including Beth Kaufman, Michael Clark, James Belser, and Jane Vaicunas, who helped develop this edition of the book. Finally, my thanks to the many colleagues across the country who took the time to write during the past ten years with comments and suggestions based on their firsthand experiences using *Adolescence* in the classroom. They have improved the text with each edition.

Laurence Steinberg

ADOLESCENCE

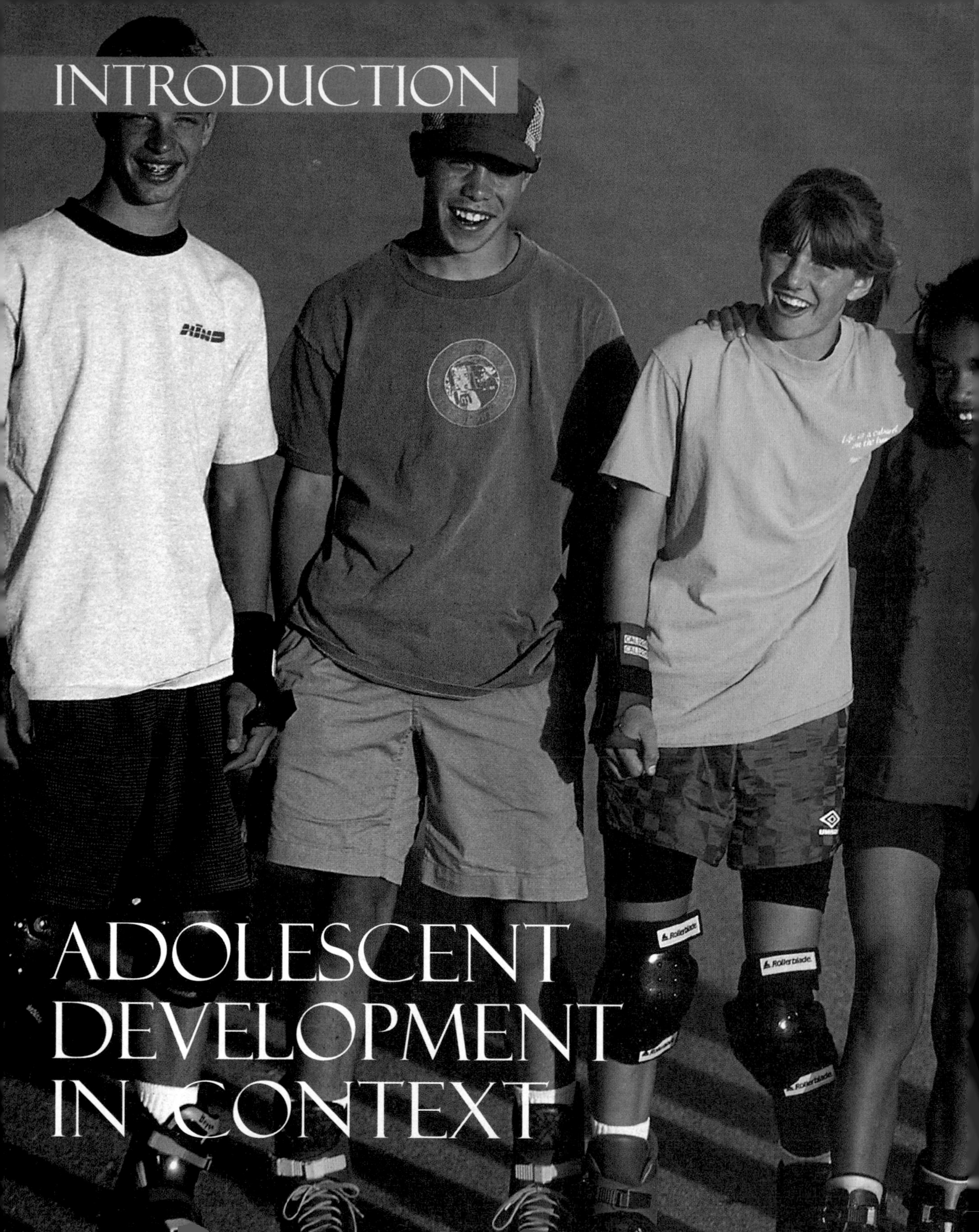

INTRODUCTION

ADOLESCENT DEVELOPMENT IN CONTEXT

THE SCIENTIFIC STUDY OF ADOLESCENCE

THE BOUNDARIES OF ADOLESCENCE

(Lori Adamski: Peek/Tony Stone)

In May of 1994, the *New York Times* published several gripping and worrisome front-page reports on the increasing rate of violence among American youth—many of whom are young adolescents (e.g., Wilkerson, 1994). In one incident described in the newspaper, for example, two boys—Damien, a 14-year-old, and Jacob, only 10—robbed and killed a pregnant mother of three as she was withdrawing cash from an automated teller machine. At 14, Damien was already an established neighborhood drug dealer, and he was in debt to one of his suppliers. Jacob, the older boy's younger "assistant," had the assignment of watching the cash machine and alerting Damien when a potential victim approached. After the woman was shot, the boys ran off with the cash. Jacob used his share of the money—$20—to buy a chili dog and some Batman toys.

The 10-year-old described in this incident is, of course, an exception. Despite the often-sensationalized coverage of adolescent violence in the mass media, it is still the case that the vast majority of young adolescents never commit a serious crime. Most are more similar to my son, Benjamin, who, like Jacob, is also 10. Ben's life revolves around doing well in school, spending time with his family, playing with Oscar, his springer spaniel, and relentlessly pursuing a perfect jump shot. Any serious violence in Ben's life is limited to what he sees on television and in the video games he plays with his friend Matt, a 14-year-old who lives across the street.

It is easy enough to identify the factors that contribute to the different adolescent experiences of youngsters like Jacob and Benjamin. Jacob, one of eight children, was raised in a crack house, where he watched his father beat his mother. He witnessed his sister's shooting death when he was only 4, and he lost his father to a bar fight soon after. He began smoking marijuana at the age of 9. Ben, in contrast, has enjoyed all the luxuries of a stable, suburban, middle-class upbringing—a life full of Little League, family vacations, and bike rides in the countryside with his two parents.

More difficult to see than these tremendous differences in experience, however, are the commonalities that unite Jacob and Ben—and, for that matter, most preadolescents. Both Jacob and Ben are fast approaching puberty, the period of physical and sexual maturation that unfolds early in adolescence. Each looks up to an older peer and yearns for the privileges and freedoms that he hopes will come with age. Over the next ten years, each will face a common set of psychological tasks that lead, ultimately, to becoming an adult member of society. Perhaps most important, Jacob and Benjamin each has hopes and dreams for the future. And each desperately needs the guidance and affection of caring adults in order for those hopes and dreams to be realized.

Perhaps you have heard stories about someone in your family's past whose adolescence was markedly different from your own. At the age of 13, for example, my grandfather left his family and smuggled himself in the back of a haywagon out of Russia and ultimately came to Ellis Island in New York City—without knowing a soul or a word of English. At the same age, I, on the other hand, growing up some fifty years later and less than 20 miles from Ellis Island, was worrying about such weighty matters as whether my classmates would laugh at the new braces on my teeth. Today, my own son faces yet a different set of challenges. While Ben, too, may worry about the braces on *his* teeth, he is coming of age in an era of AIDS, violence, and what sometimes seem like daily technological advances.

One of the goals of this book is to help you understand the universals and the particulars of the adolescent experience—the things all adolescents share in common and the things that differentiate them from one another. As you read on, think about what it is that defines the adolescent experience for all young people—regardless of the context in which they develop—and, at the same time, which factors make one young person's adolescence markedly different from that of his or her agemates growing up in other circumstances.

A MULTIDISCIPLINARY APPROACH TO ADOLESCENCE

What is the nature of adolescents' identity development in a changing world? How should society deal with problems of youth unemployment, adolescent AIDS, teenage pregnancy, or juvenile crime? What is the best way to prepare young people for the roles of adulthood? Should adolescents be required to obtain their parents' consent in order to receive contraceptives? How should the criminal justice system treat youthful offenders like Damien and Jacob?

Answering these questions requires a thorough understanding of adolescents' psychological development, and in this book we will examine how—and why—people's hopes and plans, their fears and anxieties, and their questions and concerns change as they grow into adulthood. But answering these difficult questions also requires knowledge of how individuals develop physically, how their relationships with parents and friends change, how young people as a group are viewed and treated by society, how adolescence in our society differs from adolescence in other cultures, and how the nature of adolescence itself has changed over the years. In other words, a complete understanding of adolescence in contemporary society depends on being familiar with biological, social, sociological, cultural, and historical perspectives on adolescence.

In this book, we look at adolescence from a *multidisciplinary* perspective—a perspective that draws on a variety of disciplines. Each provides a view of adolescence that helps, in its own way, to further our understanding of this period of the life cycle. We will look at contributions to the study of adolescence made by biologists, psychologists, educators, sociologists, historians, and anthropologists. The challenge ahead of us in this book is not to try to determine which perspective on adolescence is best but to find ways by which to integrate the contributions from different disciplines into a coherent and comprehensive viewpoint on the nature of adolescent development in contemporary society.

RECAP

A thorough understanding of adolescent development in contemporary society depends on being familiar with numerous perspectives on adolescence. Among the most important are those drawn from psychology, biology, history, sociology, education, and anthropology.

THE BOUNDARIES OF ADOLESCENCE

Let's begin with a fairly basic question. When does adolescence begin and end? Perhaps we can gain some insight into this question by examining the word itself.

The word *adolescence* is Latin in origin, derived from the verb *adolescere,* which means "to grow into adulthood." In all societies, adolescence is a time of growing up, of moving from the immaturity of childhood into the maturity of adulthood. **Adolescence** is a period of transitions: biological, psychological, social, economic. It is an exciting time of life. Individuals become interested in sex and become biologically capable of having children. They become wiser, more sophisticated, and better able to make their own decisions. Adolescents are permitted to work, to get married, and to vote. And eventually, adolescents are expected to be able to support themselves financially.

For the purposes of this book, adolescence is defined, roughly speaking, as the second decade of the life span. As you can see in the accompanying box, however, there are a variety of different boundaries that one might draw between childhood and adolescence and between adolescence and adulthood. Although it may seem frustrating, determining the beginning and ending of adolescence is more a matter of opinion than absolute fact. Whereas a biologist would place a great deal of emphasis on the attainment and completion of puberty, an attorney would look instead at important age breaks designated by law, while an educator might draw attention to differences between students enrolled in different grades in school. Is a biologically mature fifth-grader an adolescent or a child? Is a 20-year-old college student who lives at home an adolescent or an adult? It all depends on the boundaries one uses to define the period.

One significant aspect of the transition from childhood into adolescence is the young person's entry into the labor force. (LeDuc/Monkmeyer)

One recent study of individuals' conceptions of adolescence asked a sample of adolescents to designate the most important factors that they thought differentiated adolescence from adulthood (Scheer, Unger, and Brown, 1994). According to this group of respondents, psychological factors, such as "taking responsibility for my actions" or "making my own decisions," were generally seen as more important boundaries between adolescence and adulthood than were the more event-related transitions that we traditionally use to define the shift in status, such as getting married, completing school, or establishing one's own residence. The one event-related transition that was seen as a relatively important factor by the adolescents surveyed, interestingly, was having a job.

Rather than argue about which boundaries are the correct ones, it probably makes more sense to think of development during adolescence as involving a *series* of passages from

THE SCIENTIFIC STUDY OF ADOLESCENCE

THE BOUNDARIES OF ADOLESCENCE

One problem that students of adolescence encounter early is a fundamental one: deciding when adolescence begins and ends, or what the boundaries of the period are. Different theorists have proposed various markers, but there is little agreement on this issue. Here are some examples of the ways in which adolescence has been distinguished from childhood and adulthood that we shall examine in this book. Which boundaries make the most sense to you?

	When Adolescence Begins	When Adolescence Ends
Biological	Onset of puberty	Becoming capable of sexual reproduction
Emotional	Beginning of detachment from parents	Attainment of separate sense of identity
Cognitive	Emergence of more advanced reasoning abilities	Consolidation of advanced reasoning abilities
Interpersonal	Beginning of a shift in interest from parental to peer relations	Development of capacity for intimacy with peers
Social	Beginning of training for adult work, family, and citizen roles	Full attainment of adult status and privileges
Educational	Entrance into junior high school	Completion of formal schooling
Legal	Attainment of juvenile status	Attainment of majority status
Chronological	Attainment of designated age of adolescence (e.g., 13 years)	Attainment of designated age of adulthood (e.g., 20 years)
Cultural	Entrance into period of training for a ceremonial rite of passage	Completion of ceremonial rite of passage

immaturity into maturity. Some of these passages are long, and some are short; some are smooth, and others are rough. And not all of them occur at the same time. Consequently, it is quite possible—and perhaps even likely—that an individual will mature in some respects before he or she matures in others. The various aspects of adolescence have different beginnings and different endings for every individual. Every young person is a child in some ways, an adolescent in other ways, and an adult in still others.

RECAP

Adolescence is a transitional period. Rather than viewing adolescence as having a specific beginning and a specific ending, it makes more sense to think of the period as being composed of a series of passages—biological, psychological, social, and economic—from immaturity into maturity.

Early, Middle, and Late Adolescence

Although adolescence may span a ten-year period, most social scientists and practitioners recognize that so much psychological and social growth takes place during this decade that it makes more sense to view the adolescent years as comprising a series of phases rather than as being one homogeneous stage. The 13-year-old whose interests center on grunge rock and basketball, for example, has little in common with the 18-year-old who is contemplating marriage, worried about pressures at work, and beginning college.

Social scientists who study adolescence usually differentiate among **early adolescence,** which covers the period from about age 11 through age 14; **middle adolescence,** from about age 15 through age 18; and **late adolescence** (or *youth,* as it is sometimes known), from about age 18 through age 21 (Kagan and Coles, 1972; Keniston, 1970; Lipsitz, 1977). These divisions, as you may have guessed, correspond to how society groups young people in educational institutions; they are the approximate ages that customarily mark attendance at middle or junior high school, high school, and college. In discussing development during adolescence, we will need to be sensitive not only to differences between adolescence and childhood, and between adolescence and adulthood, but also

Social scientists who study adolescence usually differentiate among three periods: early adolescence (approximately 11 through 14 years of age), middle adolescence (15 through 18 years), and late adolescence (18 through 21 years). (David S. Strickler/Picture Cube; Rick Smolan/Stock, Boston)

to differences among the various phases of adolescence itself.

A FRAMEWORK FOR STUDYING ADOLESCENT DEVELOPMENT

In order to organize information from a variety of different perspectives, this book uses a framework that is based largely on a model suggested by the late psychologist John Hill (1983). The framework is organized around three basic components: the *fundamental changes* of adolescence, the *contexts* of adolescence, and the *psychosocial developments* during adolescence.

The Fundamental Changes of Adolescence

What, if anything, is distinctive about adolescence as a period in the life cycle? According to Hill, there are three features of adolescent development that give the period its special flavor and significance: (1) the onset of puberty, (2) the emergence of more advanced thinking abilities, and (3) the transition into new roles in society. We refer to these three sets of changes—biological, cognitive, and social—as the *fundamental changes of adolescence.* They are changes that occur universally; virtually without exception, all adolescents in every society go through them.

Biological Transitions. The chief elements of the biological changes of adolescence—which together are referred to as **puberty**—involve changes in the young person's physical appearance (including breast development in girls, the growth of facial hair in boys, and a dramatic increase in height for both sexes) and the attainment of reproductive capability—the ability to conceive children (Brooks-Gunn and Reiter, 1990).

Chapter 1 describes not only the biological changes that occur in early adolescence but also the impact of puberty on the adolescent's psychological development and social relations. Puberty requires adaptation on the part of the young people and of those around them. An adolescent's self-image, for example, may be temporarily threatened by marked changes in physical appearance. The body changes, the face changes, and not surprisingly, the way the adolescent feels about himself or herself changes. Relationships inside the family are transformed by the adolescent's greater need for privacy and by his or her interest in forming intimate relationships with peers. Girls may suddenly feel uncomfortable about being physically affectionate with their fathers, and boys may feel similarly about their mothers. And, of course, adolescents' friendships are altered by newly emerging sexual impulses and concerns.

Cognitive Transitions. The word *cognitive* is used to refer to the processes that underlie how people think about things. Memory and problem solving are both examples of cognitive processes. Changes in thinking abilities, which are dealt with in Chapter 2, constitute the second of the three fundamental changes of the adolescent period. The emergence of more sophisticated thinking abilities is one of the most striking changes to take place during adolescence. Compared with children, for example, adolescents are much better able to think about hypothetical situations (that is, things that have not yet happened but will, or things that may not happen but could), and they are much better able to think about abstract concepts, such as friendship, democracy, and morality (Keating, 1990).

The implications of these cognitive changes are also far-reaching. The ability to think more capably in hypothetical and abstract terms affects the way adolescents think about themselves, their relationships, and the world around them. We will see, for example, that teenagers' abilities to plan ahead, to argue with their parents, to solve chemistry problems, and to resolve moral dilemmas are all linked to changes in the way they think. Even the way that day-to-day decisions are made is affected. For the first time, individuals become able to think in logical ways about what their lives will be like in the future, about their relationships with friends and family, and about politics, religion, and philosophy.

The implications of the cognitive changes of adolescence are far-reaching. (Michelle Bridwell/PhotoEdit)

● ***Social Transitions.*** All societies distinguish between individuals who are thought of as children and those who are seen as ready to become adults. Our society, for example, distinguishes between people who are "under age," or minors, and people who have reached the age of majority. It is not until adolescence that individuals are permitted to drive, marry, and vote. Such changes in rights, privileges, and responsibilities—which are examined in Chapter 3—constitute the third set of fundamental changes that occur during adolescence: social changes. In some cultures, the social changes of adolescence are marked by a formal ceremony—a **rite of passage.** In others, the transition is less clearly demarcated. Still, a change in social status is a universal feature of adolescence (Ford and Beach, 1951).

Society's redefinition of the individual provokes reconsideration of the young person's capabilities and competencies. As the young person's treatment by society changes, so do relationships around the home, at school, and in the peer group. Changes in social status also permit young people to enter new roles and engage in new activities, such as marriage and work, which dramatically alter their self-image and relationships with others. Adolescents, on the verge of becoming adults, have choices to consider that previously did not exist for them.

RECAP

Three features of adolescence give the period its special flavor and distinctiveness: the biological changes of puberty, the emergence of more advanced thinking abilities, and the transition of the individual into new roles in society. These three sets of universal changes are referred to as the *fundamental changes* of adolescence.

THE THREE FUNDAMENTAL CHANGES OF ADOLESCENCE

BIOLOGICAL TRANSITIONS

COGNITIVE TRANSITIONS

SOCIAL TRANSITIONS

The Contexts of Adolescence

Although all adolescents experience the biological, cognitive, and social transitions of the period, the *effects* of these changes are not uniform for all young people. Puberty makes some adolescents feel attractive and self-assured, but it makes others feel ugly and self-conscious. Being able to think in hypothetical terms makes some youngsters thankful that they grew up with the parents they have, but it prompts others to run away in search of a better life. Reaching 18 years of age prompts some teenagers to enlist unhesitatingly in the army or to apply for a marriage license, but for others, becoming an adult is frightening and unsettling.

If the fundamental changes of adolescence are universal, why are their effects so varied? Why aren't all individuals affected in the same ways by puberty, by changes in thinking, and by changes in social and legal status? The answer lies in the fact that the psychological impact of the biological, cognitive, and social changes of adolescence is shaped by the environment in which the changes take place (Bronfenbrenner, 1979). In other words, psychological development during adolescence is a product of the interplay between a set of three very basic and universal changes and the context in which these changes are experienced.

Consider, for example, two 14-year-old girls growing up in neighboring communities. When Alice went through puberty, around age 13, her parents responded by restricting her social life because they were afraid that Alice would become too involved with boys and neglect her schoolwork. Alice felt that her parents were being unfair and also foolish, since she rarely had a chance to meet any boys she wanted to date, anyway. All the older boys went to the high school across town. Even though she was in the eighth grade, she was still going to school with fifth-graders. And she couldn't meet anyone through work, either. Her school would not issue work permits to any student under the age of 16.

Maria's adolescence was very different. For one thing, when she had her first period, her parents took her aside and discussed sex and pregnancy with her. They explained how different contraceptives worked and made an appointment for Maria to see a gynecologist in town in case she ever needed to discuss something with a doctor. Although she was still only 14 years old, Maria knew that she would begin dating soon, because in her community the junior and senior high schools had been combined into one large school, and the older boys frequently asked the younger girls out. In addition, since there was no prohibition at her school against young teenagers working, Maria decided to get a job; she knew she would need money to buy clothes if she were going to start dating.

Two teenage girls. Each goes through puberty, each grows intellectually, and each moves closer in age to becoming an adult. Yet each grows up under very different circumstances: in different families, in different schools, with different groups of peers, and under different work conditions. Both are adolescents, but their adolescent experiences are markedly different. As a result, each girl's psychological development will follow a different course.

Alice's and Maria's worlds may seem quite different from one another. Yet the two girls share many things in common, at least in comparison with two girls growing up in different parts of the world or in different historical eras. Imagine how different your adolescence would have been if you had grown up without going to high school and had had to work full time beginning at age 12. Imagine how different it would have been to grow up 100 years ago—or how different it will be to grow up 100 years from today. And imagine how different adolescence is for a youngster whose family is very poor and for one whose family is very rich. Even siblings growing up within the same family have different growing-up experiences, depending on their birth order within the family and various other factors (Daniels, Dunn, Furstenberg, and Plomin, 1985). You can see that it is impossible to generalize about the nature of adolescence without taking into account the surroundings and circumstances in which young people grow up.

For this reason, the second component of our framework is the *context of adolescence.* In modern societies, four main contexts affect the development and behavior of young people: families, peer groups, schools, and work and leisure settings. The nature and structure of these contexts dramatically affect the way in which the fundamental changes of adolescence are experienced. To the extent that one adolescent's world differs from another's, the two young people will have very different experiences during the adolescent years.

Although young people growing up in modern America share some experiences with young people all over the world, their development is distinctively different from that of young people in other societies, because their families, peer groups, schools, and work settings are different. In other words, the contexts of adolescence are themselves shaped and defined by the larger society in which young people live. In this book, we shall be especially interested in how the contexts of adolescence have changed in Western society, and in the implications of those changes for adolescent development.

As in discussions of young people's psychological development, it is important when discussing families, peer groups, schools, and work and leisure settings to differentiate among the phases of adolescence. Take adolescent peer groups, for example. During early adolescence, peer groups are usually composed of teenagers of the same sex. During middle adolescence, peer groups become a context in which males and females interact. And during late adolescence, the large peer groups of earlier phases begin to disintegrate.

Let us now briefly survey how the contexts of American adolescence have changed as our society has changed.

● ***Families.*** Frequent moves, high rates of divorce, increasing numbers of single-parent households, and more and more working mothers have become characteristic of family life in contemporary America (Furstenberg, 1990a). In Chapter 4, we look at these changes in family life and try to assess how they are affecting young people's psychological development.

● ***Peer Groups.*** Over the last 100 years, age-segregated peer groups—groups of people of the same age who spend most of their time together—have come to play an increasingly important role in the socialization and development of teenagers (Brown, 1990). But has the rise of peer groups been a positive or negative influence on young people's development? In Chapter 5, we discuss how peer groups have changed adolescence in contemporary America.

● ***Schools.*** Chapter 6 examines schools as a context for adolescent development. Since the 1930s, Americans have turned more and more to schools as a setting to occupy, socialize, and educate adolescents (Entwistle, 1990). But how good a job are schools doing? And how should schools for adolescents be structured? These are two of the many difficult questions we will examine.

● ***Work and Leisure.*** If you've been to a fast-food restaurant lately, you know that many of today's teenagers are working. But did you know that more adolescents are working now than at any other time in the last forty years (Fine, Mortimer, and Roberts, 1990)? In Chapter 7, we look at the world of adolescent work and at how part-time jobs are affecting young people's psychological development and well-being. We also take a look at adolescents' leisure pursuits—their involvement in extracurricular activities, their use of the mass media, and so forth.

RECAP

Although the fundamental changes of adolescence are universal, they occur in a given social context that varies from individual to individual and across space and time. The most important elements of the context of adolescent development are the family, the peer group, schools, and work and leisure settings.

THE FOUR CONTEXTS OF ADOLESCENCE

FAMILIES

PEER GROUPS

SCHOOLS

WORK AND LEISURE

● Psychosocial Development during Adolescence

Five sets of developmental issues are paramount during adolescence: **identity, autonomy, intimacy, sexuality,** and **achieve-**

As family life has changed, so has the context in which adolescents develop. (B. Daemmrich/Image Works)

ment. These five sets of **psychosocial** issues, as well as certain psychosocial problems that may arise during adolescence, constitute the third, and final, component of our framework. Theorists use the word *psychosocial* to describe aspects of development that are both psychological and social in nature. Sexuality, for instance, is a psychosocial issue because it involves psychological change (that is, changes in the individual's emotions, motivations, and behavior) as well as changes in the individual's social relations with others.

Of course, identity, autonomy, intimacy, sexuality, and achievement are not concerns that arise for the first time during the adolescent years; and psychological or social problems can and do occur during all periods of the life cycle. Nor do psychosocial concerns disappear when the adolescent becomes an adult. These five sets of issues are present throughout the entire life span, from infancy through late adulthood. They represent basic developmental challenges that all people face as they grow and change: discovering and understanding who they are as individuals (identity); establishing a healthy sense of independence (autonomy); forming close and caring relationships with other people (intimacy); expressing sexual feelings and enjoying physical contact with others (sexuality); and being successful and competent members of society (achievement).

Although psychosocial concerns are not new to the adolescent, development in each of these areas takes a special turn during the adolescent years. Understanding how and why such psychosocial developments take place during adolescence is a special concern of social scientists interested in this age period. We know that individuals form close relationships before adolescence, for example, but why is it during adolescence that intimate relationships with opposite-sex agemates first develop? We know that infants struggle with learning how to be independent, but why during adolescence do individuals need to be more on their own and make some decisions apart from their parents? We know that children fantasize about what they will be when they grow up, but why is it not until adolescence that these fantasies are transformed into serious concerns?

Part Three of this book (Chapters 8 to 13) discusses changes in each of the five psychosocial areas and examines several common psychosocial problems.

● ***Identity.*** Chapter 8 deals with changes in identity, self-esteem, and self-conceptions.

During adolescence, a variety of important changes in the realm of identity occur (Harter, 1990). The adolescent may wonder who he or she really is and where he or she is headed (Erikson, 1968). Coming to terms with these questions may involve a period of experimentation—a time of trying on different personalities in an attempt to discover one's true self. As you will read, the adolescent's quest for identity is a quest not only for a personal sense of self but also for recognition from others and from society that one is a special and unique individual.

● ***Autonomy.*** The struggle of adolescents to establish themselves as independent, self-governing individuals—in their own eyes and in the eyes of others—is a long and occasionally difficult process, not only for young people but also for those around them. Chapter 9 focuses on three sorts of concerns that are of special importance to developing adolescents: becoming less emotionally dependent on parents, becoming able to make independent decisions, and establishing a personal code of value and morals (Douvan and Adelson, 1966; Steinberg, 1990).

● ***Intimacy.*** During adolescence, important changes take place in the individual's capacity to be intimate with others, especially with peers. As we shall see in Chapter 10, friendships emerge for the first time during adolescence that involve openness, honesty, loyalty, and exchanging confidences, rather than simply sharing activities and interests (Savin-Williams and Berndt, 1990). Dating takes on increased importance, and as a consequence, so does the capacity to form a relationship that is trusting and loving.

● ***Sexuality.*** Sexual activity generally begins during the adolescent years. Becoming sexual is an important aspect of development during adolescence—not only because it transforms the nature of relationships between adolescents and their peers but also because it raises for the young person a range of trying and difficult questions. Chapter 11 discusses these concerns, including efforts to incorporate sexuality into a still-developing sense of self, the need to resolve questions about sexual values and morals, and coming to terms with the sorts of relationships into which one is prepared—or not prepared—to enter (Katchadourian, 1990). We also look at sex education, contraceptive use, the dangers of sexually transmitted diseases, and adolescent childbearing.

● ***Achievement.*** In Chapter 12, we examine changes in individuals' educational and vocational behavior and plans. Important decisions—many with long-term consequences—about schooling and careers are made during adolescence. Many of these decisions depend on adolescents' achievement in school, on their evaluations of their own competencies and capabilities, on their aspirations and expectations for the future, and on the direction and advice they receive from parents, teachers, and friends (Henderson and Dweck, 1990).

● ***Psychosocial Problems.*** In Chapter 13, we look at four sets of problems typically associated with adolescence: drug and alcohol use, delinquency, depression, and eating disorders. In each case, we examine the prevalence of the problem, the factors believed to contribute to its development, and approaches to prevention and intervention.

RECAP

Five sets of psychosocial concerns are paramount during adolescence. These issues involve self-discovery and self-understanding (identity), establishing a healthy sense of independence (autonomy), forming close and caring relationships with others (intimacy), expressing sexual feelings and enjoying physical contact with others (sexuality), and being successful and competent members of society (achievement). Although these are not new concerns in adolescence, development in each of these areas takes a special turn during the adolescent years. There are a number of specific psychosocial problems that we associate with adolescence, although they affect only a minority of young people. Among the most important are drug and alcohol use, delinquency, depression, and eating disorders.

THE PSYCHOSOCIAL ISSUES AND PROBLEMS OF ADOLESCENCE

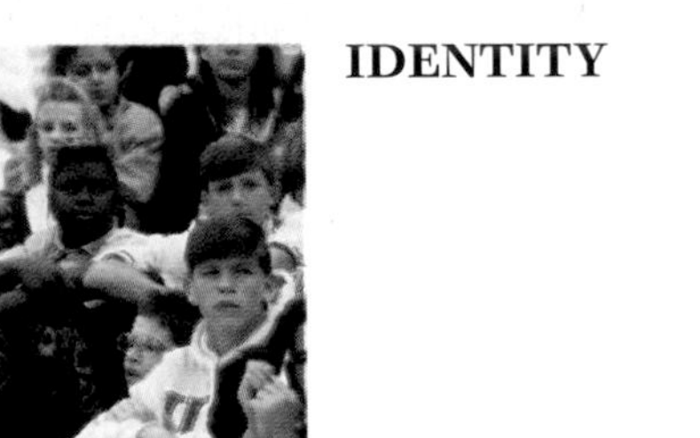

IDENTITY

AUTONOMY

INTIMACY

SEXUALITY

ACHIEVEMENT

PSYCHOSOCIAL PROBLEMS

The illustration below puts together the three pieces of the framework that we have been discussing: fundamental changes, contexts, and psychosocial development during adolescence.

A FRAMEWORK FOR STUDYING ADOLESCENT DEVELOPMENT

FUNDAMENTAL CHANGES

CONTEXTS

PSYCHOSOCIAL ISSUES AND PROBLEMS

Your experiences as a teenager were the product of a unique set of cultural and historical forces at work in the context in which you came of age. Long after he enters adulthood, this Moscow adolescent will forever remember having to hoard vegetables underneath the living room sofa during the Soviet food shortages of the 1990s. (Ursula Markus/Photo Researchers)

STEREOTYPES VERSUS SCIENTIFIC STUDY

One of the oldest debates in the study of adolescence is whether adolescence is an inherently stressful time for individuals. G. Stanley Hall, who is generally acknowledged as the father of the modern study of adolescence, likened adolescence to the turbulent transitional period in the evolution of the human species from savagery into civilization. "Adolescence is a new birth," Hall wrote. "Development is less gradual, suggestive of some ancient period of storm and stress" (1904, p. 6). Long before Hall, in the eighteenth century, the French philosopher Jean-Jacques Rousseau had described adolescence by drawing an analogy to a violent storm: "As the roaring of the waves precedes the tempest, so the murmur of rising passions announces the tumultuous change. . . . Keep your hand upon the helm," he warned parents, "or all is lost" (Rousseau, 1762/1911, pp. 172–173).

Although neither Hall nor Rousseau had any scientific evidence that adolescence was any more stormy than childhood or adulthood, their portrayal of teenagers as passionate, fickle, and unpredictable individuals persists today. For example, people still tend to think of adolescence as a difficult and stressful time. A 12-year-old girl once told me that her mother had been telling her that she was going to go through a difficult time when she turned 14—as though some magical internal alarm clock were set to trigger "storm and stress" on schedule.

The girl's mother wasn't alone in her view of adolescence, of course. Sometime this week, turn on the television, and note how teenagers are depicted. If they are not portrayed as juvenile delinquents—the usual role in which they are cast—adolescents are depicted as sex-crazed idiots (if they are male), mindless schoolgirls (if they are female), or tormented lost souls searching for their place in a strange, cruel world (if they aren't delinquent, sex-crazed, or mindless). Adolescents are one of the most stereotyped groups in America society, and as a consequence, they are one of the most misunderstood (Adelson, 1979). One recent study demonstrated that most of the undergraduates enrolled in an adolescent development course believed that adolescence was an inherently stressful period (Holmbeck and Hill, 1988). After completing the course, however—which, incidentally, used this textbook—the students were less likely to endorse this view.

No doubt you also have come into this course with many convictions about adolescence. These beliefs are based in part on your own experiences as a teenager and in part on the images of adolescents to which you have been exposed over the years—in books, on film, and on television. As one team of writers pointed out, even scientists' portrayal of teenagers is influenced by the broader social and historical context in which they work. During periods of economic downturns, for instance, scholars depict adolescents as immature, unstable, and in need of more schooling, whereas during periods of war, the same age group is portrayed as mature, responsible, and competent (Enright, Levy, Harris, and Lapsley, 1987). Presumably, these characterizations serve a broader, if hidden, agenda: During economic depressions, there are fewer jobs to go around, and adults may "need" to see adolescents as incapable of working, whereas the reverse is true during wartime, when even youngsters are needed to help in factories and on farms.

One of the goals of this book is to provide you with a more realistic understanding of adolescent development in contemporary society—an understanding that reflects the best scientific knowledge available. Some of the results of this scientific research will not mesh with your own experiences and beliefs; others will.

As you read the material, you should think about your personal experiences as an adolescent, but you should also try to look beyond them and be willing to question the "truths" about teenagers that you have grown accustomed to believing over the years. This does not mean that your experiences were invalid or that your recollections are inaccurate. Rather, your experiences as a teenager were the product of a unique set of forces that have made you the individual you are today. The person who sits next to you in class—or the person who right now, in some distant region of the world, is thinking back to his or her adolescence—was probably exposed to different forces than you were and probably had a different set of adolescent experiences as a consequence.

RECAP

Although it is commonly believed that adolescence is an inherently difficult time, there is little scientific support for this idea. Adolescence is a period of change, but not necessarily stress. One important goal of studying adolescence is to understand the factors that make the period difficult for some individuals but not for others.

KEY TERMS

achievement
autonomy
early adolescence
identity
intimacy
late adolescence
middle adolescence
psychosocial
puberty
rite of passage
sexuality

FOR FURTHER READING

Feldman, S., and Elliott, G. (Eds.). (1990). *At the threshold: The developing adolescent.* Cambridge, Mass.: Harvard University Press. An up-to-date collection of summaries of what is known about various aspects of adolescent development.

Kett, J. (1977). *Rites of passage: Adolescence in America, 1790 to the present.* New York: Basic Books. The history of adolescence in America, with an emphasis on how people's conception of this stage in the life cycle has changed.

Lerner, R. (Ed.). (1993). *Early adolescence: Perspectives on research, policy, and intervention.* Hillsdale, N.J.: Erlbaum. A collection of brief articles on various aspects of adolescent development, with an emphasis on applications of current research.

Spacks, P. (1981). *The adolescent idea.* New York: Basic Books. A thorough examination of how writers, philosophers, and scientists have looked at adolescence over the years.

Steinberg, L., and Levine, A. (1990). *You and your adolescent: A parent's guide for ages 10 to 20.* New York: Harper & Row. A practical, comprehensive discussion of adolescent development aimed at parents of teenagers.

PART ONE

THE FUNDAMENTAL CHANGES OF ADOLESCENCE

CHAPTER 1

BIOLOGICAL TRANSITIONS

(Tony Freeman/PhotoEdit)

According to an old joke, there are only two things in life that one can be sure of—death and taxes. To this brief list one might add puberty—the physical changes of adolescence—for, of all the developments that take place during the second decade of life, the only truly inevitable one is physical maturation. Not all adolescents experience identity crises, rebel against their parents, or fall head over heels in love; but virtually all undergo the biological transitions associated with maturation into adult reproductive capability.

Puberty, however, is considerably affected by the context in which it occurs. Physical development is influenced by a host of environmental factors, and the timing and rate of pubertal growth varies across regions of the world, socioeconomic classes, ethnic groups, and historical eras. Today, in contemporary America, the average girl reaches **menarche**—the time of first menstruation—between her twelfth and thirteenth birthdays. But among the Lumi people of New Guinea, the typical girl does not reach menarche until after 18 years of age (Eveleth and Tanner, 1976). Imagine how great a difference those five years make in transforming the nature of adolescence. Picture how different American high schools would be if sexual maturation did not occur until after graduation!

Physical and sexual maturation profoundly affect the way in which adolescents view themselves and the way in which they are viewed and treated by others. Yet the social environment exerts a tremendous impact on the meaning of puberty and on its psychological and social consequences; indeed, as you will read in this chapter, the social environment even affects the *timing* of puberty. In some societies, pubertal maturation brings with it a series of complex initiation rites that mark the passage of the young person into adulthood socially as well as physically. In other societies, recognition of the physical transformation from child into adult takes more subtle

Although puberty is a universal feature of adolescence, individuals develop physically at different ages and at different rates. (David Young-Wolff/PhotoEdit)

forms. Parents may merely remark, "Our little boy has become a man," when they discover that he needs to shave. Early or late maturation may be cause for celebration or cause for concern, depending on what is admired or derogated in a given peer group at a given point in time. In the fifth grade, developing breasts may be a source of embarrassment; but in the ninth grade, it may be just as embarrassing *not* to have developed breasts.

In sum, even the most universal aspect of adolescence—puberty—is hardly universal in its impact on the young person. In this chapter, we examine just how and why the environment in which adolescents develop exerts its influence even on something as fundamental as puberty.

PUBERTY: AN OVERVIEW

Puberty derives from the Latin word *pubertas,* which means "adult." Technically, the term refers to the period during which an individual becomes capable of sexual reproduction; that is, it denotes the series of biological changes leading up to reproductive capability. More broadly speaking, however, **puberty** encompasses all the physical changes that occur in the growing girl or boy as the individual passes from childhood into adulthood.

The following are the five chief physical manifestations of puberty (Marshall, 1978):

1. A *rapid acceleration in growth,* resulting in dramatic increases in both height and weight.
2. The *development of primary sex characteristics,* including the further development of the gonads, or sex glands, which are the testes in males and the ovaries in females.
3. The *development of secondary sex characteristics,* which involve changes in the genitals and breasts, and the growth of pubic, facial, and body hair, and the further development of the sex organs.
4. *Changes in body composition,* specifically, in the quantity and distribution of fat and muscle.
5. *Changes in the circulatory and respiratory systems,* which lead to increased strength and tolerance for exercise.

Each of these sets of changes is the result of developments in the endocrine and central nervous systems, many of which begin years before the external signs of puberty are evident—some occur even before birth.

RECAP

The term *puberty* refers to the physical changes that occur in the growing girl or boy as the individual passes from childhood into adulthood. The chief physical manifestations are the growth spurt, the further development of the gonads, the development of secondary sex characteristics, changes in body composition, and changes in circulation and respiration.

Onset and Termination of Puberty

Puberty may appear to be rather sudden, judging from its external signs, but in fact it is part of a gradual process that begins at conception (Petersen and Taylor, 1980). You may be surprised to learn that no new hormones are produced and no new bodily systems develop at puberty. Rather, some hormones that have been present since before birth increase, and others decrease.

Hormones play two very different roles in adolescent development; they perform both an

organizational role and an **activational role** (Coe, Hayashi, and Levine, 1988). Long before adolescence—in some cases, prenatally—hormones *organize* the brain in ways that may not be manifested in behavior until puberty. For example, sex differences in levels of certain hormones during the development of the fetus may predetermine different patterns of behavior for males and females that may not actually appear until adolescence. Studies of sex differences in adolescent aggression, for example, show that even though many of these differences may not appear until adolescence, they likely result from the impact of prenatal hormones, rather than from hormonal changes at puberty. In other words, the presence or absence of certain hormones early in life may "program" the brain and the nervous system to develop in certain ways later on. Because we may not see the resulting changes in behavior until adolescence, it is easy to conclude mistakenly that the behaviors result from hormonal changes specific to puberty. In reality, however, exposure to certain hormones before birth may set a sort of "alarm clock" that does not go off until adolescence. Just because the alarm clock "rings" at the same time that puberty begins does not mean that puberty caused the alarm to go off.

Other changes in behavior at adolescence occur, however, because of changes in hormone levels at puberty; these hormonal changes are said to *activate* the changes in behavior. For instance, the increase in certain hormones at puberty is thought to stimulate the development of secondary sex characteristics, such as the growth of pubic hair. Other hormonal changes at adolescence may stimulate an increase in individuals' sex drive.

Still other changes during puberty are likely to be results of an *interaction* between organizational and activational effects of hormones. Hormones that are present during the development of the fetus may organize a certain set of behaviors (for example, our brains may be set up to have us later engage in sexual behavior), but certain changes in those hormones at puberty may be needed to activate the pattern; that is, individuals may not become motivated to engage in sex until puberty.

The Endocrine System

The **endocrine system** produces, circulates, and regulates levels of hormones in the body. **Hormones** are highly specialized substances secreted by one or more endocrine glands. **Glands** are organs that stimulate particular parts of the body to respond in specific ways. Just as specialized hormones carry "messages" to particular cells in the body, so are the body's cells designed to receive hormonal messages selectively. For example, one of the many effects of the hormone adrenaline, secreted by the adrenal gland, is to stimulate the heart to increase its activity. The heart responds to adrenaline but not to all other hormones.

The endocrine system receives its instructions to increase or decrease circulating levels of particular hormones from the central nervous system, chiefly, the brain. The system works somewhat like a thermostat. Hormonal levels are "set" at a certain point, just as you might set a thermostat at a certain temperature. By setting your room's thermostat at 60°F, you are instructing your heating system to go into action when the temperature falls below this level. Similarly, when a particular hormonal level in your body dips below the endocrine system's **set point** for that hormone, secretion of the hormone increases; when the level reaches the set point, secretion temporarily stops. And, as is the case with a thermostat, the setting level, or set point, for a particular hormone can be adjusted up or down, depending on environmental or internal bodily conditions.

Such a **feedback loop** becomes increasingly important at the onset of puberty. Long before early adolescence—in fact, during infancy—a feedback loop develops involving the **pituitary gland** (which controls hormone levels in general), the **hypothalamus** (the part of the brain that controls the pituitary gland), and the **gonads** (in males, the **testes;** in females, the **ovaries**). The gonads release the "sex" hormones—**androgens** and **estrogens** (see Figure 1.1). Although one typically thinks of androgens as "male" hormones and estrogens as "female" hormones, both types of hormones are produced by each sex, and both are present in males and females at birth. During adolescence, however, the average male produces more androgens than estrogens, and the average female produces more estrogens than androgens (Petersen and Taylor, 1980).

FIGURE 1.1 *Levels of sex hormones are regulated by a feedback system composed of the hypothalamus, pituitary gland, and gonads.* (Grumbach et al., 1974)

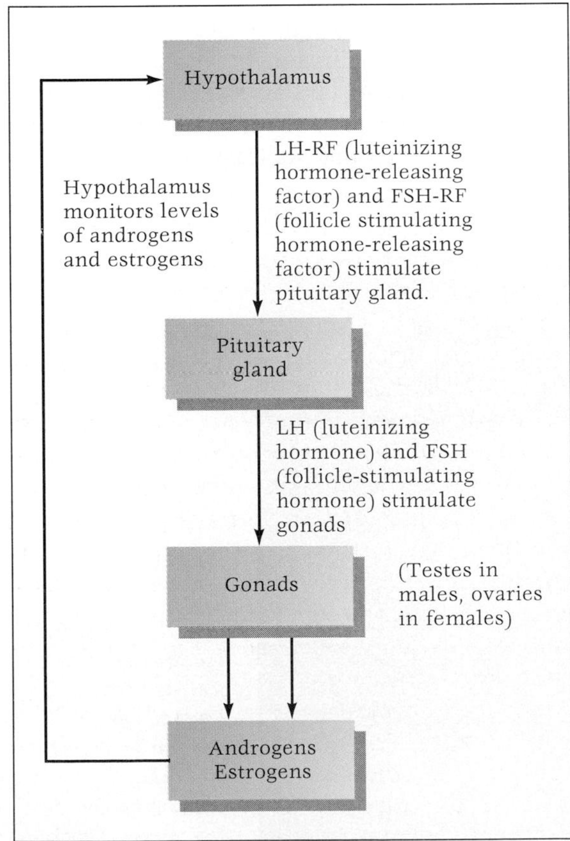

The hypothalamus responds to the levels of sex hormones circulating in the body. Your endocrine system is set to maintain certain levels of androgens and estrogens. When these levels fall below the set points, the hypothalamus no longer inhibits the pituitary, thus permitting it to stimulate the release of sex hormones by the gonads. When sex-hormone levels reach the set point, the hypothalamus responds by inhibiting its stimulation of the pituitary gland.

RECAP

The onset of puberty is regulated by a feedback loop in the endocrine system, involving the hypothalamus, the pituitary, and the gonads—ovaries in females, testes in males.

Endocrine Changes at Puberty

It is probably more accurate to say that the brain inhibits puberty before adolescence than to say that it stimulates puberty at adolescence (Brooks-Gunn and Reiter, 1990). During infancy, the set point for sex hormones is fixed so that very low levels of sex hormones will be maintained. But at puberty, there is a change in this feedback system. The hypothalamus appears to lose a certain degree of sensitivity to the sex hormones, and consequently it takes higher and higher levels of these substances to trigger the hypothalamus to inhibit the pituitary gland. It is as though a thermostat that had previously been set at 60°F were now set at 80°F and required a lot more fuel to reach the set point. Right before puberty, the hypothalamus begins to lose sensitivity to the sex hormones and, consequently, permits levels of these hormones to rise. As far as is known, this gradually decreasing sensitivity of the hypothalamus to sex hormones is the chief mechanism in initiating the onset of puberty. But the cause of this change in hypothalamic sensitivity is not well understood (Grumbach, Roth, Kaplan, and Kelch, 1974). Studies do show, however, that the onset of puberty is affected by the adolescent's psychological and physical health. Stress, illness, nutritional deficiencies, excessive exercise, and excessive thinness can all delay the onset of puberty (Frisch, 1983; McClintock, 1980).

At puberty, the pituitary also secretes hormones that act on the thyroid and on the adrenal cortex and hormones that stimulate overall bodily growth. The release of these substances is also under the control of the hypothalamus. The thyroid and adrenal cortex, in turn, secrete hormones that cause various physical (somatic) changes to take place at puberty.

SOMATIC DEVELOPMENT

The effects of the endrocrinological changes of puberty on the adolescent's body are remarkable. Consider the dramatic changes in physical appearance that occur during the short span of early adolescence. One enters puberty looking like a child but within four years or so has the physical appearance of a young adult. During this relatively brief period of time, the average individual grows nearly 12 inches taller, matures sexually, and develops an adult-proportioned body.

Changes in Stature and the Dimensions of the Body

The simultaneous release of growth hormone, thyroid hormones, and androgens stimulates rapid acceleration in height and weight. This dramatic increase in stature is referred to as the **adolescent growth spurt.** What is most incredible about the adolescent growth spurt

The timing of puberty is affected by experience as well as heredity. Rigorous or excessive exercise can delay the onset of puberty. (B. Daemmrich/Stock, Boston)

is not so much the absolute gain of height and weight that typically occurs but the speed with which the increases take place. Think for a moment of how quickly very young children grow. At the time of **peak height velocity**—the time at which the adolescent is growing most rapidly—he or she is growing at the same rate as a toddler. For boys, peak height velocity averages about 4.1 inches (10.5 centimeters) per year; for girls, it averages about 3.5 inches (9.0 centimeters) (J. Tanner, 1972).

Figure 1.2 shows just how remarkable the growth spurt is in terms of height. The graph on the left presents information on absolute height and indicates that, as you would expect, the average individual increases in height throughout infancy, childhood, and adolescence. As you can see, there is little gain in height after the age of 18. But look now at the right-hand graph, which shows the *average increase in height per year* over the same age span. Here you can see the acceleration in height at the time of peak height velocity.

Figure 1.2 also indicates quite clearly that the growth spurt occurs, on the average, about two years earlier among girls than among boys. In general, as you can see by comparing the two graphs, boys tend to be somewhat taller than girls before age 11; then girls tend to be taller than boys between ages 11 and 13; and finally boys tend to be taller than girls from about age 14 on. You may remember what this state of affairs was like during fifth

FIGURE 1.2 Left: *Height (in centimeters) at different ages for the average male and female youngster.* Right: *Gain in height per year (in centimeters) for the average male and female youngster. Note the adolescent growth spurt.* (Adapted from Marshall, 1978)

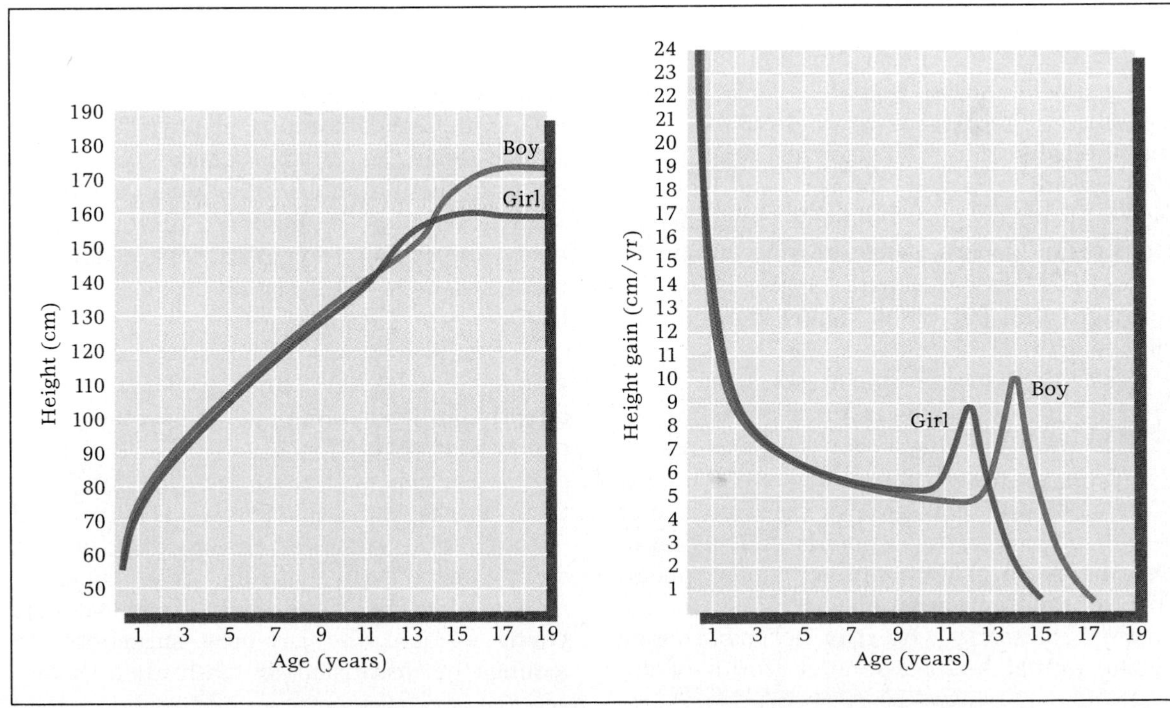

and sixth grades. Sex differences in height can be a concern for many young adolescents when they begin socializing with members of the opposite sex, especially if they are tall, early-maturing girls or short, late-maturing boys.

During puberty, the composition of the skeletal structure also changes; bones become harder, more dense, and more brittle. One marker of the conclusion of puberty is the closing of the ends of the long bones in the body, which terminates growth in height. Interestingly, there are ethnic differences in some of these skeletal changes, with bone density increasing significantly more during puberty among African-American than among white youngsters. Some experts believe that this ethnic difference in adolescence may account for the fact that, during adulthood, African-American women are less likely than white women to develop osteoporosis, and they have fewer bone fractures (Gilsanz, Roe, Mora, Costin, and Goodman, 1991).

Much of the height gain during puberty results from an increase in torso length rather than in leg length. The sequence in which various parts of the body grow is fairly regular. Extremities—the head, hands, and feet—are the first to accelerate in growth. Then accelerated growth occurs in the arms and legs, followed by torso and shoulder growth. In concrete terms, "a boy stops growing out of his trousers (at least in length) a year before he stops growing out of his jackets" (J. Tanner, 1972, p. 5).

Young adolescents often appear to be out of proportion physically—as though their noses or legs were growing faster than the rest of them. No, it's not an optical illusion. The parts of the body do not all grow at the same rate or at the same time during puberty. This **asynchronicity in growth** can lead to an appearance of awkwardness or gawkiness in the young adolescent, who may be embarrassed by the unmatched accelerated growth of different parts of the body. It is probably little consolation for the young adolescent to be told that an aesthetic balance probably will be restored within a few years; nevertheless, this is what usually happens.

The spurt in height during adolescence is accompanied by an increase in weight that results from an increase in both muscle and fat. However, there are important sex differences along these latter two dimensions. In both sexes, muscular development is rapid and closely parallels skeletal growth; but muscle tissue grows faster in boys than in girls (see Figure 1.3). Body fat increases for both sexes during puberty, but more so for females than for males, and at a somewhat faster rate for girls, especially during the years just before puberty. For boys, there is actually a slight decline in body fat just before puberty. The end result of these sex differences in growth is that boys finish adolescence with a muscle-to-fat ratio of about 3:1, but the comparable ratio for girls is approximately 5:4. This has important implications for understanding why sex differences in strength and athletic ability often appear for the first time during adolescence. According to one estimate, about half of the sex difference in physical performance during early adolescence results simply from the difference in body fat (Smoll and Schutz, 1990). Before puberty, there are relatively few sex differences in muscle development and only slight sex differences in body fat.

The rapid increase in body fat that occurs among females in early adolescence frequently prompts young girls to become overly concerned about their weight—even when their weight is within the normal range for their height and age (Smolak, Levine, and Gralen, 1993). Although the majority of girls diet unnecessarily during this time in response to the increase in body fat, the young women who are most susceptible to feelings of dissatisfaction with their bodies

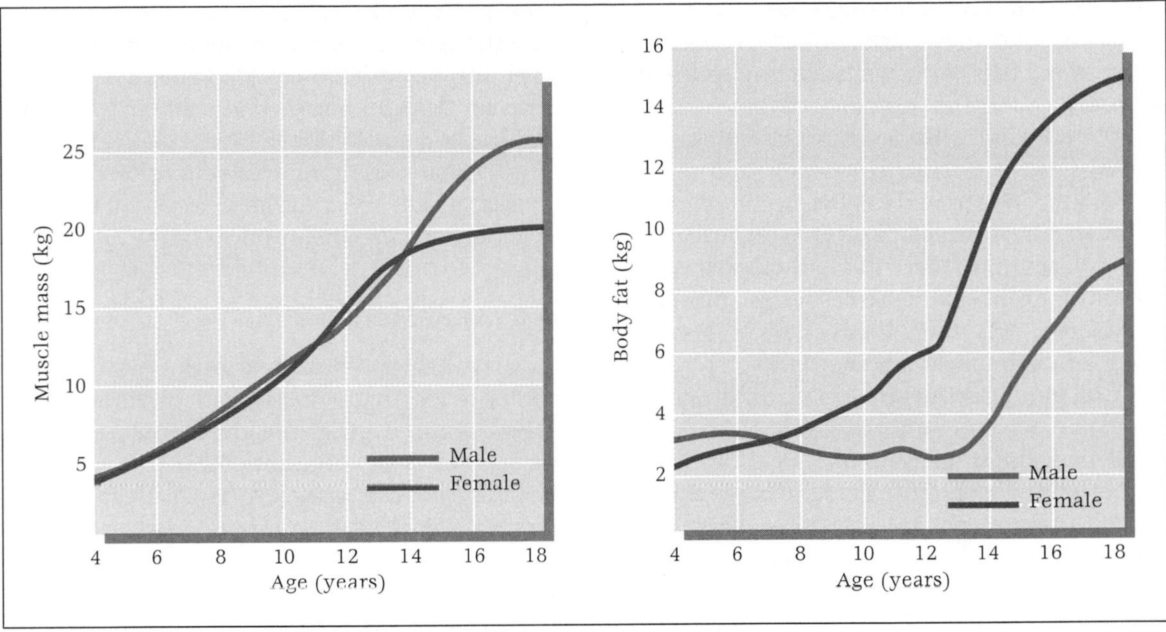

FIGURE 1.3 *During preadolescence, important sex differences emerge in body composition that continue through adolescence. Figures reflect muscle and body fat for individuals of average height at each age. Note the changes in muscle mass* (Left) *and body fat* (Right). (Adapted from Grumbach et al., 1974)

during this phase of development are those who mature early, begin dating early, and come from relatively more affluent families (Dornbusch, Carlsmith, Gross, Martin, Jennings, Rosenberg, and Duke, 1981; Smolak, Levine, and Gralen, 1993). African-American females seem less vulnerable to these feelings of body dissatisfaction than other girls, and consequently they are less likely to diet, presumably because of ethnic differences in conceptions of the ideal body type. Even among African-American youngsters, however, dieting is common in early adolescence (Halpern and Udry, 1994). As you will read in Chapter 13, many studies point to adolescence as the period of greatest risk for the development of eating disorders, such as anorexia and bulimia.

Accompanying the gains in strength that occur during early adolescence are increases in the size and capacity of the heart and lungs and, consequently, in exercise tolerance. In all these areas, the rate and magnitude of the gains favor males over females. By the end of puberty, boys are stronger, have "larger hearts and lungs relative to their size, a higher systolic blood pressure, a lower resting heart rate, a greater capacity for carrying oxygen to the blood, . . . a greater power for neutralizing the chemical products of muscular exercise, such as lactic acid," higher blood hemoglobin, and more red blood cells (Petersen and Taylor, 1980, p. 129).

It is tempting to attribute these sex differences purely to hormonal factors, because androgens, which increase during puberty in males at a much faster rate than in females, are closely linked to growth along these physical dimensions. But few studies have examined the role that sex differences in exercise patterns and diet may play. In fact, at least one study found that, with age, such environmental factors as diet and exercise become increasingly important influences on sex differences in physical performance (Smoll and Schutz, 1990). As Petersen and Taylor (1980) point out, there are strong social pressures on girls to curtail "masculine" activities—including some forms of exercise—at adolescence. Moreover, adolescent girls' diets are generally less adequate nutritionally than the diets of boys are. Both factors could result in sex differences in muscular development and exercise tolerance. Thus, sex differences in physical ability are influenced by a variety of factors, of which hormonal differences are but one part of an extremely complicated picture.

Along with many other of the body's organs, the brain changes in size and structure at puberty. Studies show that brain growth and maturation continue well into adolescence, with different regions of the brain undergoing growth "spurts" at different times during adolescence (Brooks-Gunn and Reiter, 1990). At one time it was believed that these spurts were linked to specific changes in thinking abilities. Some writers even proposed that early adolescents should not be taught demanding subject matter because their brains had not matured sufficiently! Careful studies have not substantiated this idea, however. Although important intellectual changes take place in adolescence, as you will read in Chapter 2, these developments do not seem linked in any one-to-one correspondence to specific changes in the brain's size or structure (Keating, 1990).

RECAP

The dramatic increase in stature that occurs during puberty is referred to as the adolescent growth spurt. On average, girls experience the growth spurt about two years earlier than boys. Important changes also take place in the relative proportions of body fat and muscle, and these changes leave boys relatively more muscular and with a lower proportion of body fat. Many girls react to the increase in body fat at puberty by dieting unnecessarily.

Sexual Maturation

Puberty brings with it a series of developments associated with sexual maturation. In both boys and girls, the development of the **secondary sex characteristics** is typically divided into five stages, often called **Tanner stages.**

Sexual Maturation in Boys. The sequence of developments in secondary sex characteristics among boys is fairly orderly (see Table 1.1). Generally, the first stages of puberty involve growth of the testes and scrotum, accompanied by the first appearance of pubic hair. Approximately one year later, the growth spurt in height begins, accompanied by growth of the penis and further development of pubic hair—now of a coarser texture and darker color. The five Tanner stages of penis and pubic hair growth in boys are shown in Figure 1.4.

The emergence of facial hair—first at the corners of the upper lip, next across the upper lip, then at the upper parts of the cheeks and in the midline below the lower lip, and finally along the sides of the face and the lower border of the chin—and body hair are relatively late developments in the pubertal process. The same is true for the deepening of the voice, which is gradual and generally does not occur until very late adolescence. During puberty, there are changes in the skin as well; the skin becomes rougher, especially around the upper arms and thighs, and there is increased development of the sweat glands,

TABLE 1.1 THE SEQUENCE OF PHYSICAL CHANGES AT PUBERTY

Boys		Girls	
Characteristic	**Age of First Appearance (years)**	**Characteristic**	**Age of First Appearance (years)**
1. Growth of testes, scrotal sac	10–13½	1. Growth of breasts	8–13
2. Growth of pubic hair	10–15	2. Growth of pubic hair	8–14
3. Body growth	10½–16	3. Body growth	9½–14½
4. Growth of penis	11–14½	4. Menarche	10–16½
5. Change in voice (growth of larynx)	About the same time as penis growth	5. Underarm hair	About 2 years after pubic hair
6. Facial and underarm hair	About 2 years after pubic hair appears	6. Oil- and sweat-producing glands (acne occurs when glands are clogged)	About the same time as underarm hair
7. Oil- and sweat-producing glands, acne	About the same time as underarm hair		

SOURCE: B. Goldstein. (1976). *Introduction to human sexuality*. Belmont, Calif.: Star.

which often gives rise to acne, skin eruptions, and increased oiliness of the skin.

During puberty there are slight changes in the male breast—to the consternation and embarrassment of many boys. Breast development is largely influenced by the estrogen hormones. As noted earlier, both estrogens and androgens are present in both sexes and increase in both sexes at puberty, although in differing amounts. In the male adolescent, the areola (the area around the nipple) increases in size, and the nipple becomes more prominent. Some boys show a slight enlargement of the breast, although in the majority of cases this development is temporary.

Other, internal changes occur that are important elements of sexual maturation. At the time that the penis develops, the seminal vesicles, the prostate, and the bilbo-urethral glands also enlarge and develop. The first ejaculation of seminal fluid generally occurs about one year after the beginning of accelerated penis growth, although this is often determined culturally, rather than biologically, since for many boys first ejaculation occurs as a result of masturbation (J. Tanner, 1972).

● ***Sexual Maturation in Girls.*** The sequence of development of secondary sex characteristics among girls (shown in Table 1.1) is somewhat less regular than it is among boys. Generally, the first sign of sexual maturation is the elevation of the breast—the emergence of the so-called breast bud. In about one-third of all

Penis and Scrotum

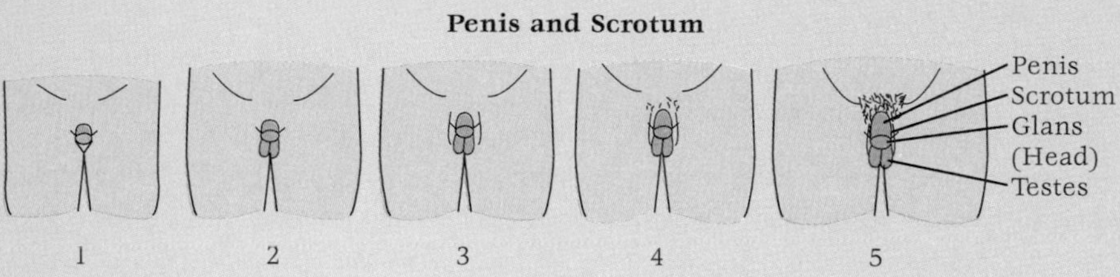

Stage 1: The infantile state that persists from birth until puberty begins. During this time the genitalia increase slightly in overall size but there is little change in general appearance.
Stage 2: The scrotum has begun to enlarge, and there is some reddening and change in texture of the scrotal skin.
Stage 3: The penis has increased in length and there is a smaller increase in breadth. There has been further growth of the scrotum.
Stage 4: The length and breadth of the penis have increased further and the glans has developed. The scrotum is further enlarged and the scrotal skin has become darker.
Stage 5: The genitalia are adult in size and shape. The appearance of the genitalia may satisfy the criteria for one of these stages for a considerable time before the penis and scrotum are sufficiently developed to be classified as belonging to the next stage.

Pubic Hair

1 2 3 4 5

Stage 1: There is no true pubic hair, although there may be a fine velus over the pubes similar to that over other parts of the abdomen.
Stage 2: Sparse growth of lightly pigmented hair, which is usually straight or only slightly curled. This usually begins at either side of the base of the penis.
Stage 3: The hair spreads over the pubic symphysis and is considerably darker and coarser and usually more curled.
Stage 4: The hair is now adult in character but covers an area considerably smaller than in most adults. There is no spread to the medial surface of the thighs.
Stage 5: The hair is distributed in an inverse triangle as in the female. It has spread to the medial surface of the thighs but not up the linea alba or elsewhere above the base of the triangle.

FIGURE 1.4 *The five pubertal stages for penile and pubic hair growth.*
(From Morris and Udry, 1980)

adolescent girls, however, the appearance of pubic hair precedes breast development. The development of pubic hair follows a sequence similar to that in males—generally, from sparse, downy, light-colored hair to more dense, curled, coarse, darker hair. Breast development often occurs concurrently and generally proceeds through several stages. In the bud stage, the areola widens, and the breast and nipple are elevated as a small mound. In the middle stages, the areola and nipple become distinct from the breast and project beyond the breast contour. In the final stages, the areola is recessed to the contour of the breast, and only the nipple is elevated. The female breast undergoes these changes at puberty regardless of changes in breast size. Changes in the shape and definition of the areola and nipple are far better indicators of sexual maturation among adolescent girls than is breast growth alone. The five Tanner stages of breast and pubic hair growth in girls are shown in Figure 1.5.

As is the case among boys, puberty brings important internal changes for adolescent girls that are associated with the development of reproductive capacity. In girls, these changes involve development and growth of the uterus, vagina, and other aspects of the reproductive system. In addition, there is enlargement of the labia and clitoris.

As is apparent in Table 1.1, the growth spurt is likely to occur during the early and middle stages of breast and pubic hair development. Menarche, the beginning of menstruation, is a relatively late development. Hence it is incorrect to use menarche as a marker for the onset of puberty among girls. A great deal of pubertal development has taken place long before the adolescent girl begins to menstruate. Generally, full reproductive function does not occur until several years after menarche, and regular ovulation follows menarche by about two years (Hafetz, 1976).

RECAP

One of the most important physical changes of puberty is the development of secondary sex characteristics—changes in outward appearance that signal the onset of reproductive maturity. These changes include the growth of pubic hair, changes in the appearance of the sex organs, and breast development.

TIMING AND TEMPO OF PUBERTY

You may have noted that, thus far, no mention has been made about the "normal" ages at which various pubertal changes are likely to take place. The truth is that the variations in the timing of puberty (the age at which puberty begins) and in the tempo of puberty (the rate at which maturation occurs) are so great that it is misleading to talk even about "average" ages.

Variations in the Timing and Tempo of Puberty

The onset of puberty can occur as early as 8 years in girls and $9^1/_2$ in boys, or as late as 13 in girls and $13^1/_2$ in boys. In girls, the interval between the first sign of puberty and complete physical maturation can be as short as a year and a half or as long as six years. In boys, the comparable interval ranges from about two years to five years (J. Tanner, 1972). Within a totally normal population of young adolescents, some individuals will have completed the entire sequence of pubertal changes before others have even begun. In more concrete terms, it is possible for an early-maturing, fast-maturing youngster to complete pubertal maturation by the age of 10

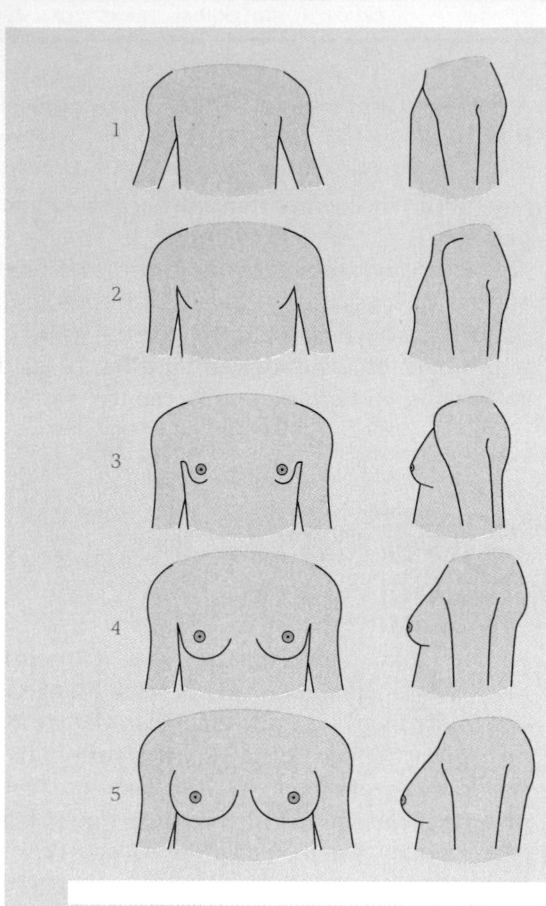

Breasts

1. No breast development.
2. The first sign of breast development has appeared. This stage is sometimes referred to as the breast budding stage. Some palpable breast tissue under the nipple, the flat area of the nipple (areola) may be somewhat enlarged.
3. The breast is more distinct although there is no separation between contours of the two breasts.
4. The breast is further enlarged and there is greater contour distinction. The nipple including the areola forms a secondary mound on the breast.
5. Size may vary in the mature stage. The breast is fully developed. The contours are distinct and the areola has receded into the general contour of the breast.

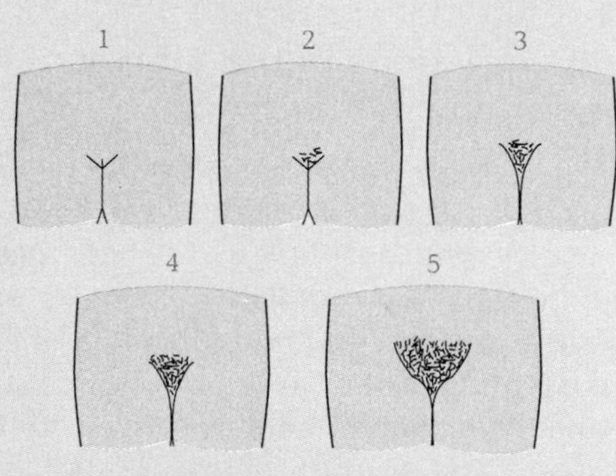

Pubic Hair

1. No pubic hair.
2. There is a small amount of long pubic hair chiefly along vaginal lips.
3. Hair is darker, coarser, and curlier and spreads sparsely over skin around vaginal lips.
4. Hair is now adult in type, but area covered is smaller than in most adults. There is no pubic hair on the inside of the thighs.
5. Hair is adult in type, distributed as an inverse triangle. There may be hair on the inside of the thighs.

FIGURE 1.5 *The five pubertal stages for breast and pubic hair growth.*
(From Marshall and Tanner, 1969)

or 11—two years before a late-maturing youngster has even begun puberty, and *seven years* before a late-maturing, slow-maturing youngster has matured completely!

There is no relation between the age at which puberty begins and the rate at which pubertal development proceeds. Furthermore, the timing of puberty has little to do with the ultimate adult stature or bodily dimensions of the individual. Late maturers, for example, attain the same average height as early maturers do (Marshall, 1978).

Many people believe that there are ethnic differences in pubertal maturation, although there is little scientific evidence to suggest that this is true, once differences in socioeconomic status are taken into account. For example, it is widely believed that youngsters of Asian descent mature later than white youngsters (perhaps because of the generally smaller and lighter stature of Asian individuals) and that youngsters of African descent mature earlier than white youngsters (perhaps because of the generally larger and heavier stature of African individuals). In general, though, once nutrition is adequate, rates of physical maturation are comparable across different ethnic groups (Brooks-Gunn and Reiter, 1990).

Genetic and Environmental Influences

What factors underlie the tremendous variations in the timing and tempo of puberty? Why do some individuals mature relatively early and others relatively late?

Researchers who study variability in the onset and timing of puberty approach the issue in two ways. One strategy involves the study of differences among individuals (that is, studying why one individual matures earlier or faster than another). The other involves the study of differences among groups of adolescents (that is, studying why puberty occurs earlier or more rapidly in certain populations that in others). Both sets of studies point to both genetic and environmental influences on the timing and tempo of puberty.

Individual Differences in Pubertal Maturation. Differences in the timing and rate of puberty among individuals growing up in the same general environment result chiefly, but not exclusively, from genetic factors. Comparisons between individuals who are genetically identical (identical twins) and individuals who are not reveal patterns of similarity in pubertal maturation indicating that the timing and tempo of an individual's pubertal maturation are largely inherited (Marshall, 1978).

Despite this powerful influence of genetic factors, the environment plays an important role. In all likelihood, every individual inherits a predisposition to develop at a certain rate and to begin pubertal maturation at a certain time. But this predisposition is best thought of as an upper and lower age limit, not a fixed absolute. Whether the genetic predisposition that each person has to mature around a given age is actually realized, and when within the predisposed age boundaries he or she actually goes through puberty, are subject to the influence of the environment. In this respect, the timing and rate of pubertal maturation are the product of an interaction between nature and nurture, between one's genetic makeup and the environmental conditions under which one has developed.

By far the two most important environmental influences on pubertal maturation are nutrition and health. Puberty occurs earlier among individuals who are better nourished throughout their prenatal, infant, and childhood years. Similarly, delayed puberty is more likely to occur among individuals with a history of protein and/or caloric deficiency. Chronic illness during childhood and adolescence is also associated with delayed puberty, as is excessive exercise. For example, girls in ballet companies or in other rigorous training programs often mature later than their peers (Frisch, 1983). Generally speaking, then, after genetic factors, an important determinant of the onset of puberty is the overall physical well-being of the individual from conception through preadolescence (Marshall, 1978).

Interestingly, a number of recent studies suggest that social as well as physical factors in the environment may influence the onset of maturation, especially in girls. Several studies, for example, have found that puberty may occur somewhat earlier among adolescents who have grown up in less cohesive, or more conflict-ridden, family environments (e.g., Ellis, 1991; Graber, Brooks-Gunn, and Warren, in press; Moffitt, Caspi, Belsky, and Silva, 1992; Steinberg, 1988). Another researcher found that girls who grow up in homes from which the father was absent—because of divorce or death, for example—mature at an earlier age than girls whose father was present (Surbey, 1990). In general, among humans and other mammals, living in proximity to one's close biological relatives appears to slow the process of pubertal maturation (Surbey, 1990). One explanation for the finding that distant family relations may accelerate pubertal maturation is that distance in the family may induce stress, which, in turn, may affect hormonal secretions in the adolescent (Graber et al., in press).

Although it may seem surprising that something as biological as puberty can be influenced by factors in our social environment, scientists have long known that our social relationships can indeed affect our biological functioning. One of the best-known examples of this is that women who live together—such as dormitory roommates—find that their menstrual periods begin to synchronize over time (Graham, 1991; McClintock, 1980).

● ***Group Differences in Pubertal Maturation.*** Researchers typically study group differences in puberty by comparing average ages of menarche in different regions. Most of *these* studies have indicated that genetic factors play an extremely small role in determining group differences in pubertal maturation (Eveleth and Tanner, 1976). Differences among countries in the average rate and timing of puberty are more likely to reflect differences in their environments than differences in their populations' gene pools.

The influence of the broader environment on the timing and tempo of puberty can be seen in more concrete terms by looking at three sorts of group comparisons: (1) compar-

The age at which adolescents mature physically varies around the world. On average, teenagers in highly industrialized countries, like Japan, mature earlier than their counterparts in developing nations, where health and nutritional problems slow physical growth. (R. M. Collins, III/Image Works)

isons of the average age of menarche across countries, (2) comparisons among socioeconomic groups within the same country, and (3) comparisons within the same population during different eras. (Although menarche does not signal the onset of puberty, researchers often use the average age of menarche when comparing the timing of puberty across different groups or regions.)

First, consider variations in the age of menarche across different regions of the world. Figure 1.6 presents median menarcheal ages throughout the world, across regions that vary considerably in typical dietary intake and health conditions. As you can see, the average age at menarche generally is lower in those countries where individuals are less likely to be malnourished or to suffer from chronic disease. For example, in Western Europe and in the United States, the median menarcheal age ranges from about 12.5 years to 13.5 years. In Africa, however, the median menarcheal age ranges from about 14 years to about 17 years. The range is much wider across the African

FIGURE 1.6 *The average menarcheal age of adolescent girls varies in different regions of the world.* (Adapted from Eveleth and Tanner, 1976)

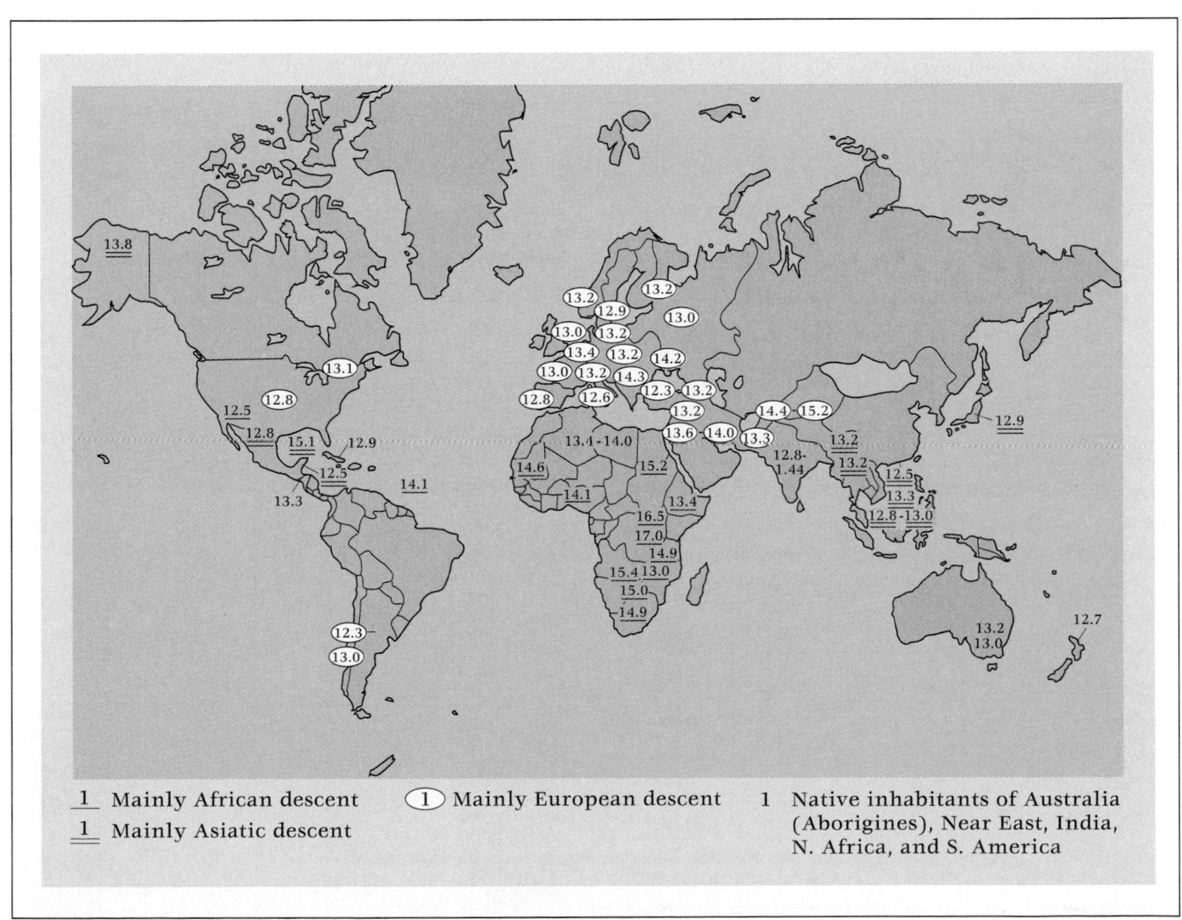

continent because of the much greater variation in environmental conditions there.

When we look *within* a specific region, we find that, almost without exception, girls from affluent homes reach menarche before economically disadvantaged girls. In comparisons of affluent and poor youngsters from the United States, Hong Kong, Tunis, Baghdad, and South Africa, for example, differences in the average menarcheal ages of economically advantaged and disadvantaged youngsters within each of these regions range from about 6 months to about 18 months.

Finally, we can examine environmental influences on the timing of puberty by looking at changes in the average age of menarche over the past two centuries. Because nutritional conditions have improved during the past 150 years, we would expect to find a decline in the average age at menarche over time. This is indeed the case, as can be seen in Figure 1.7. Generally, "children have been getting larger and growing to maturity more rapidly" (Eveleth and Tanner, 1976, p. 260). This pattern, referred to as the **secular trend,** is attributable not only to improved nutrition but also to better sanitation and better control of infectious diseases. In most European countries maturation has become earlier by about 3 to 4 months per decade. For example, in Norway 150 years ago, the average age of menarche may have been about 17 years. Today, it is about 13 years. Similar declines have been observed over the same time period in other

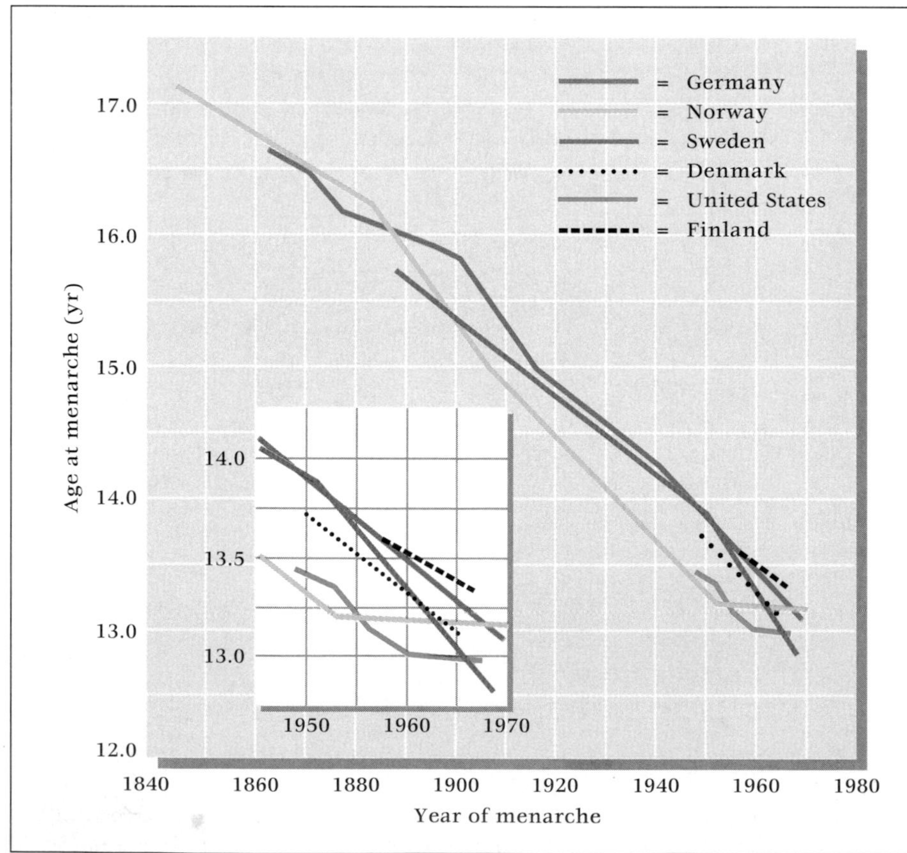

FIGURE 1.7 *The age at menarche has declined considerably over the past 150 years. This decline is known as the secular trend.* (Adapted from Eveleth and Tanner, 1976)

industrialized nations and, more recently, in developing countries as well.

The secular trend in pubertal maturation appears to be leveling off in most industrialized nations, however. This suggests that environmental conditions in these parts of the world have improved to the point where the average age of menarche is approaching its genetically bound lower limit. For example, no substantial changes in average menarcheal age have been reported during the past twenty-five years in Oslo, Norway, or London, England. You can lay to rest any fears you might have that children in future generations will go through puberty before they leave kindergarten. In all likelihood, the average age at menarche will not decline much below 12 years.

RECAP

There is considerable variation in the timing and tempo of puberty. As a result, a group of adolescents of the same chronological age will contain youngsters whose physical maturity varies considerably. The most important influence on the timing of maturation is genetic. But in addition, adolescents who have been well-nourished and healthy during childhood go through puberty earlier than their peers. Because of improvements in nutrition and health care, young people mature earlier today than they did centuries ago, a phenomenon known as the secular trend.

THE PSYCHOLOGICAL AND SOCIAL IMPACT OF PUBERTY

The psychosocial impact of puberty occurs through a cyclical, or reciprocal, process. Physical maturation affects the adolescent's self-image and behavior, and this in turn prompts changes in the behavior of others. For example, a boy who has recently gone through puberty may seek more privacy at home when he is dressing or bathing. He closes his door more often and is more modest around his parents than he used to be. If they are responsive to his discomfort, his parents will change their routines around the house. Before entering his room, they will knock and wait to see if he is dressed—something they did not have to do before.

The process works in the other direction as well. The adolescent's changed physical appearance may elicit new sorts of behavior from peers, parents, and others, and these new reactions may prompt the adolescent to adjust his or her behavior and self-image. An adolescent girl who has recently matured physically may find herself suddenly receiving the attention of older boys who had not previously paid her much heed. She may feel nervous about all the extra attention and may be confused about how she should respond to it. Moreover, she must now make decisions about how much time she wishes to devote to dating and how she should handle herself when out on a date.

Young people's reactions to the changes brought on by puberty, and others' reactions to them, are influenced by the broader social environment. Contemporary society's views of puberty and physical maturation are expressed through television commercials, newspaper and magazine advertisements, and depictions of young adolescents in films and other media. People cannot help but be influenced by these images, and the expectations they associate with puberty as well as the meaning they give it determine the reactions puberty brings out in them. Consider, for example, the treatment of menstruation in each of the advertisements reprinted on page 40. What sorts of reactions might each of the ads foster?

Researchers have generally taken two approaches to studying the psychological and social consequences of puberty. One approach is to look at individuals who are at various stages of puberty, either in a **cross-sectional study** (in which groups of individuals are compared at different stages of puberty) or in a **longitudinal study** (in which the same individuals are tracked over time as they move through the different stages of puberty). Studies of this sort examine the immediate impact of puberty on young people's psychological development and social relations. Researchers might ask, for example, whether youngsters' self-esteem is higher or lower during puberty than before or after.

A second approach compares the psychological development of early and late maturers. The focus of these studies is not so much on the absolute impact of puberty but on the effects of differential timing of the changes. Here, a typical question might be whether early maturers are more popular in the peer group than late maturers are.

One sign that attitudes toward menstruation have changed in the last twenty-five years is that advertisements for tampons and sanitary napkins have become far more explicit and far less mysterious. As a consequence, adolescent girls receive very different messages about the meaning of maturation today from twenty or thirty years ago. Here are two excerpts from magazine advertisements for sanitary napkins—one from 1951, the other from 1991. (KOTEX is a registered trademark of Kimberly-Clark Corporation. These advertisements reprinted by permission. All rights reserved)

The Immediate Impact of Puberty

Studies of the psychological and social impact of puberty indicate that physical maturation, regardless of whether it occurs early or late, affects the adolescent's self-image, mood, and relationships with parents. The short-term consequences of puberty may be more taxing on the adolescent's family, however, and less significant for the adolescent's self-perceptions or mood (Simmons and Blyth, 1987; Steinberg, 1987a).

Puberty and Self-Esteem. In a classic study of changes in self-esteem during the early adolescent years, sociologist Roberta Simmons and her colleagues found that going through puberty may lead to modest declines in self-esteem among adolescent girls but only when accompanied by other changes that require adaptation on the part of the young person (Simmons, Blyth, Van Cleave, and Bush, 1979). Among the nearly 800 youngsters who were studied, those who showed the greatest declines in self-esteem between sixth and seventh grade were girls who began menstruating, began dating, and had to change schools all during the same year. (Boys did not show the same adverse effects of going through puberty, but we should remember that few boys are likely to begin puberty during the transition into junior high school.)

This research suggests that puberty may be a potential stressor that has temporary adverse psychological consequences for girls, but only when it is coupled with other changes that necessitate adjustment. By itself, however, puberty appears to have only modest effects on girls' and boys' self-image (Simmons and Blyth, 1987). Indeed, recent studies suggest that the impact of puberty on adolescents' psychological functioning is to a great extent shaped by the social context in which puberty takes place (Brooks-Gunn and Reiter, 1990).

Adolescent Moodiness. Although an adolescent's self-image could be expected to be changed during a time of dramatic physical development, it could also be the case that self-esteem or self-image is a reasonably stable characteristic, with long and sturdy roots reaching back to childhood. For this reason, some researchers have turned their attention to the impact of puberty on more transient states, such as mood. One reason for this focus is that adolescents are thought to be moodier, on average, than either children or adults. One study, in which adolescents' moods were monitored repeatedly by electronic pagers, for example, showed that adolescents' moods fluctuate during the course of the day more than the moods of adults do (Csikszentmihalyi and Larson, 1984) (see Figure 1.8). Many adults assume that adolescent moodiness is directly related to the hormonal changes of puberty (Petersen, 1985). Is there any scientific evidence that the hormonal changes of puberty cause adolescents to be moody, or, for that matter, that these hormonal changes affect the adolescent's psychological functioning or behavior at all?

According to a recent comprehensive review of research on hormones and adolescent mood and behavior, the direct connection between hormones and mood, while apparent, is not very strong (Buchanan, Eccles, and Becker, 1992). When studies do find a connection between hormonal changes at puberty and adolescent mood or behavior, the effects are strongest early in puberty, when the system is being "turned on" and when hormonal levels are highly variable. For example, studies indicate that *rapid* increases in many of the hormones associated with puberty—such as testosterone, estrogen, and various adrenal androgens—especially when the increases take place very early in adolescence, may be associated with increased irritability, impulsivity, aggression (in boys), and depression (in girls). One interpretation of these findings is that it is

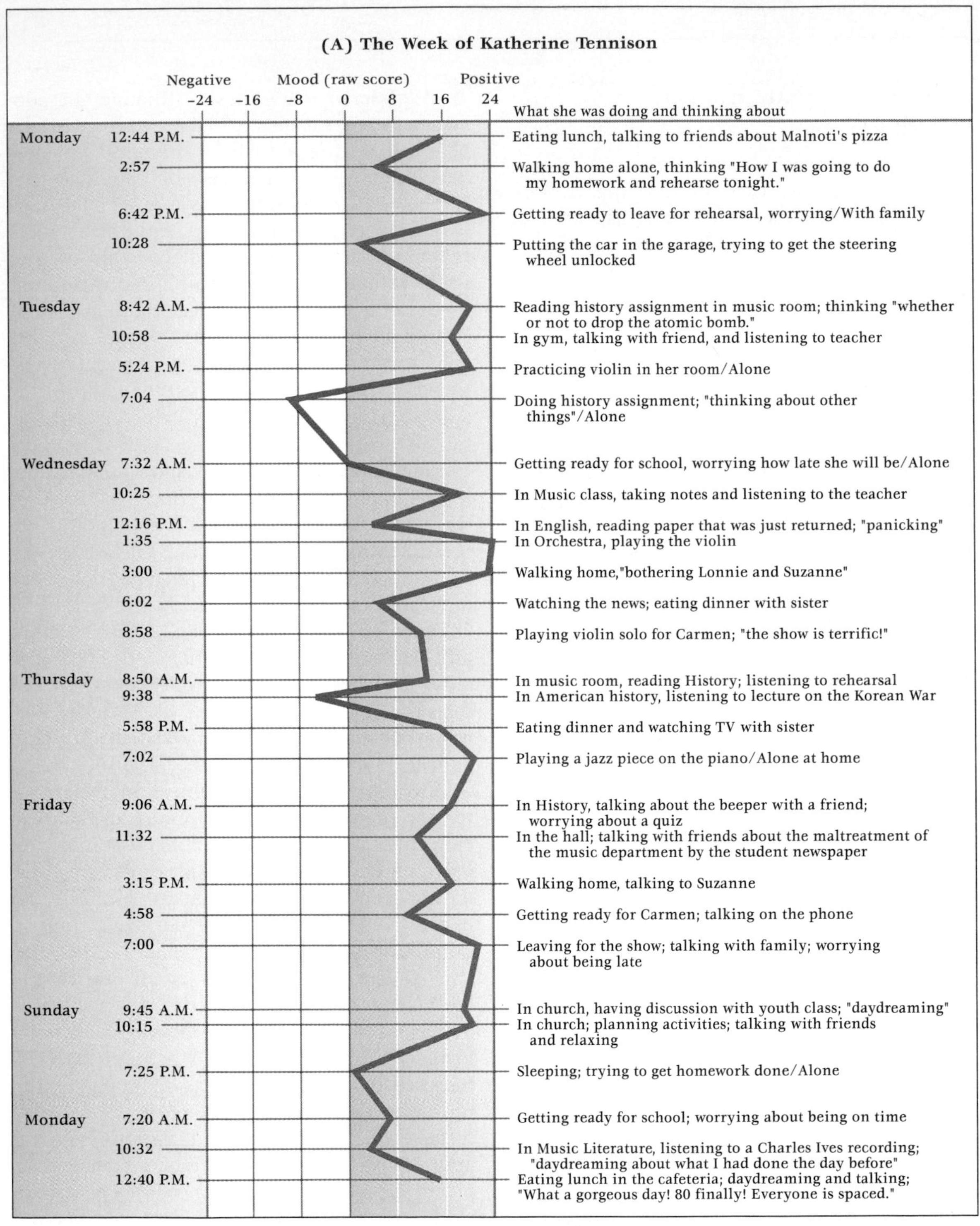

FIGURE 1.8 (A and B) *Fluctuations in two adolescents' moods over the course of a week.* (Csikszentmihalyi and Larson, 1984)

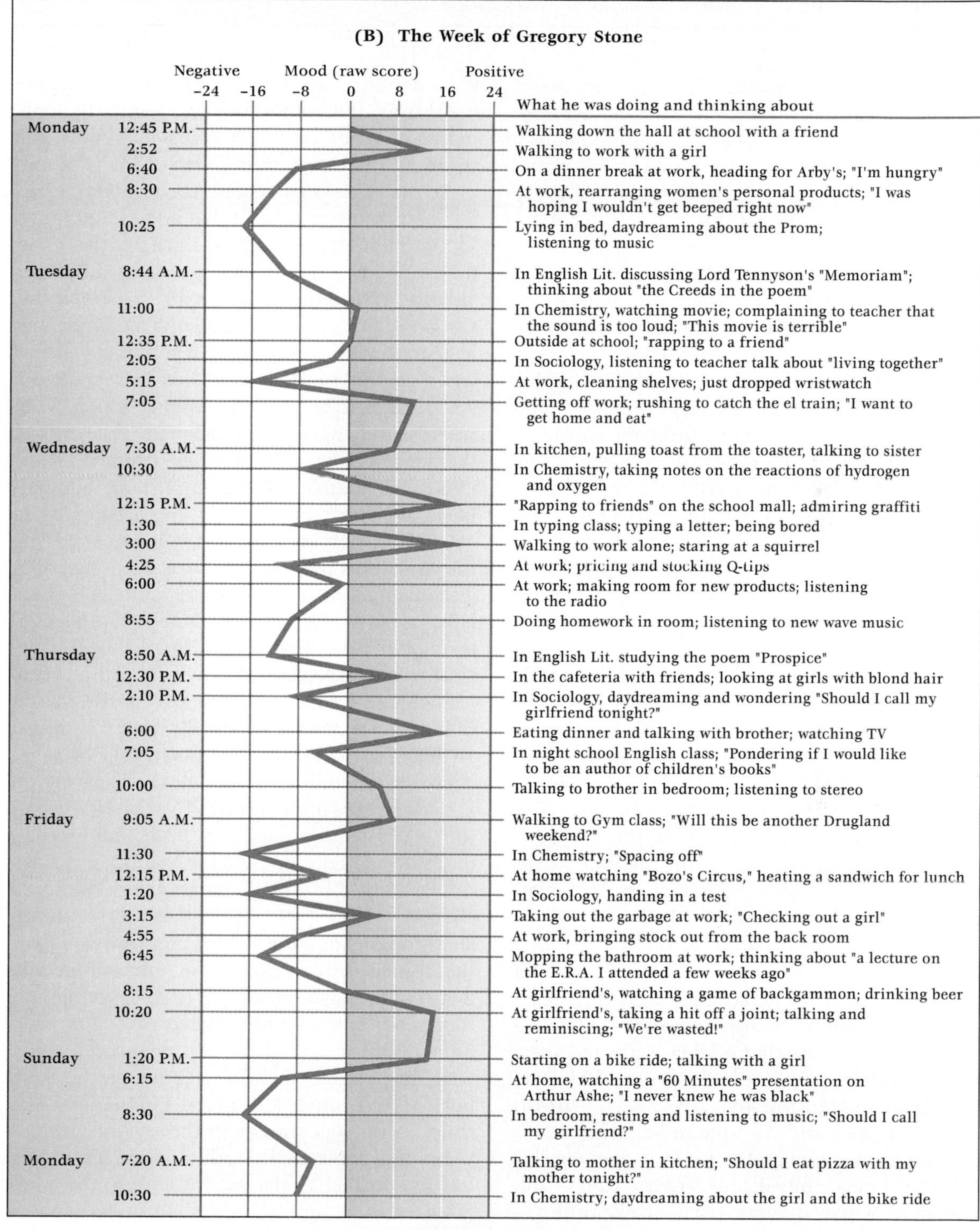
(B) The Week of Gregory Stone
Negative
Mood (raw score)
Positive
−24
−16
−8
0
8
16
24
What he was doing and thinking about
Monday 12:45 P.M. Walking down the hall at school with a friend
2:52 Walking to work with a girl
6:40 On a dinner break at work, heading for Arby's; "I'm hungry"
8:30 At work, rearranging women's personal products; "I was hoping I wouldn't get beeped right now"
10:25 Lying in bed, daydreaming about the Prom; listening to music
Tuesday 8:44 A.M. In English Lit. discussing Lord Tennyson's "Memoriam"; thinking about "the Creeds in the poem"
11:00 In Chemistry, watching movie; complaining to teacher that the sound is too loud; "This movie is terrible"
12:35 P.M. Outside at school; "rapping to a friend"
2:05 In Sociology, listening to teacher talk about "living together"
5:15 At work, cleaning shelves; just dropped wristwatch
7:05 Getting off work; rushing to catch the el train; "I want to get home and eat"
Wednesday 7:30 A.M. In kitchen, pulling toast from the toaster, talking to sister
10:30 In Chemistry, taking notes on the reactions of hydrogen and oxygen
12:15 P.M. "Rapping to friends" on the school mall; admiring graffiti
1:30 In typing class; typing a letter; being bored
3:00 Walking to work alone; staring at a squirrel
4:25 At work; pricing and stocking Q-tips
6:00 At work; making room for new products; listening to the radio
8:55 Doing homework in room; listening to new wave music
Thursday 8:50 A.M. In English Lit. studying the poem "Prospice"
12:30 P.M. In the cafeteria with friends; looking at girls with blond hair
2:10 P.M. In Sociology, daydreaming and wondering "Should I call my girlfriend tonight?"
6:00 Eating dinner and talking with brother; watching TV
7:05 In night school English class; "Pondering if I would like to be an author of children's books"
10:00 Talking to brother in bedroom; listening to stereo
Friday 9:05 A.M. Walking to Gym class; "Will this be another Drugland weekend?"
11:30 In Chemistry; "Spacing off"
12:15 P.M. At home watching "Bozo's Circus," heating a sandwich for lunch
1:20 In Sociology, handing in a test
3:15 Taking out the garbage at work; "Checking out a girl"
4:55 At work, bringing stock out from the back room
6:45 Mopping the bathroom at work; thinking about "a lecture on the E.R.A. I attended a few weeks ago"
8:15 At girlfriend's, watching a game of backgammon; drinking beer
10:20 At girlfriend's, taking a hit off a joint; talking and reminiscing; "We're wasted!"
Sunday 1:20 P.M. Starting on a bike ride; talking with a girl
6:15 At home, watching a "60 Minutes" presentation on Arthur Ashe; "I never knew he was black"
8:30 In bedroom, resting and listening to music; "Should I call my girlfriend?"
Monday 7:20 A.M. Talking to mother in kitchen; "Should I eat pizza with my mother tonight?"
10:30 In Chemistry; daydreaming about the girl and the bike ride

not so much the absolute increases in these hormones during puberty but their *rapid fluctuation* early in puberty that may affect adolescents' moods. Once the hormone levels stabilize at higher levels, later in puberty, their negative effects appear to wane (Buchanan et al., 1992).

Even still, most researchers agree that the impact of hormonal change on mood and behavior in adolescence is greatly influenced by environmental factors (Brooks-Gunn and Reiter, 1990). An excellent illustration of the way in which hormones and environment interact at puberty comes from the work of psychologist Jeanne Brooks-Gunn and her colleagues (Brooks-Gunn, 1987, 1989; Brooks-Gunn and Warren, 1989; Brooks-Gunn, Warren, and Rosso, 1991), who have been studying the development of psychological problems, such as depression and aggression, in young girls around the time of puberty. Although rapid increases in hormones early in puberty are associated with depressed mood in girls, it turns out that stressful life events, such as problems in the family, in school, or with friends, play a far greater role in the development of depression than do hormonal changes. Moreover, as she and others point out, it is quite possible that changes in the environment—in levels of stress, for instance—may affect hormonal activity, which in turn may affect adolescents' mood.

Interestingly, not only is there little evidence that adolescents' moodiness results from the "storm and stress" of "raging" hormones, but there is also research that questions the very idea that adolescents are inherently moodier than children. Psychologists Mihaly Csikszentmihalyi and Reed Larson (1984; Larson and Lampman-Petraitis, 1989) had teenagers carry electronic pagers similar to the ones physicians carry, and the researchers paged them periodically throughout the day. When the adolescents were paged, they filled out forms noting how they were feeling, what they were doing, where they were, and whom they were with. By looking at changes in mood across activities and settings, the researchers were able to determine the correlates of adolescent moodiness.

Their findings suggest that adolescent mood swings parallel their changes in activities. Over the course of a day, a teenager may shift from elation to boredom, back again to happiness, and then to anger. But this shifting appears to have more to do with shifts in activities—elated when seeing a girlfriend, bored in social studies class, happy when having lunch with friends, and angry when assigned extra work at the fast-food restaurant—than with internal, biological changes. More important, comparisons of youngsters between the ages of 9 and 15 did not show increases in moodiness during the transition into adolescence. Although adolescents may be moodier than adults, it is probably because they change activities and contexts more often than adults do.

How can we reconcile these scientific studies, which provide little support for the notion that adolescents are especially prone to mood swings, with the popular portrayals of teenagers as exceedingly moody? One suggestion is that there is a great deal of variability *within* the adolescent population in moodiness. In one study of adolescents, for example, five distinct patterns of mood change were identified (Bence, 1992) (see Table 1.2). One group showed considerable fluctuation in mood over the course of a week, but members typically were in a positive mood (these youngsters "bounced" back up to positive moods quickly after being in a bad mood). A second group was, on average, equally positive as the first, but showed much less mood fluctuation. The third group was similar to the second, in that members showed little fluctuation in mood; but in contrast to the second group, the third group was generally in a slightly bad mood. The fourth group, like the first, showed considerable fluctuation in mood but was gener-

TABLE 1.2 FIVE PATTERNS OF ADOLESCENT "MOODINESS"

Pattern	Size of Mood Change	Rate of Mood Change	Typical Mood	Intensity of Mood
I	Very large	Very fast	Positive	Very high
II	Small	Average	Positive	Low
III	Small	Slow	Negative	Very low
IV	Very large	Average	Negative	High
V	Average	Slow	Very negative	High

SOURCE: Bence, 1992.

ally in a bad mood (that is, members dropped back down to negative moods quickly after being in a positive mood). Finally, the fifth group was composed of youngsters whose mood did not fluctuate greatly but who were in an extremely negative mood most of the time.

One fascinating finding on hormones and behavior in adolescence concerns adolescents' sleep preferences. Many parents complain that their teenage children go to bed too late in the evening and sleep too late in the morning. It now appears that the emergence of this pattern—called a **delayed phase preference**—is directly related to the biological changes of puberty (Carskadon, Vieira, and Acebo, 1993). Thus, physically mature teenagers who are forced to maintain a sleep schedule similar to that of prepubertal individuals have biological "reasons" to feel energetic when it is time to go to bed and lethargic in the morning. When allowed to regulate their own sleep schedules (as on weekends), most teenagers will stay up until around 1 A.M. and sleep until about 10 A.M. It is therefore ironic that many school districts ask adolescents to report to school even *earlier* than younger children, since this demand clearly conflicts with the natural sleep preferences of adolescents. Indeed, one study found that adolescents were least alert between the hours of 8 and 9 A.M. (when most schools start) and were most alert after 3 P.M., when the school day is over (Allen and Mirabell, 1990).

● ***Puberty and Family Relations.*** Research into the impact of puberty on family relationships has pointed to a fairly consistent pattern, namely, that puberty appears to increase distance between parents and children; you should be aware, however, that few studies have examined puberty and family relations in nonwhite or in single-parent families (Paikoff and Brooks-Gunn, 1991; Steinberg, 1990). Several studies show that as youngsters mature from childhood toward the middle of puberty, distance between them and their parents increases, and conflict intensifies, especially between the adolescent and his or her mother (see Paikoff and Brooks-Gunn, 1991). The change that takes place appears to be more of an increase in "negatives" (e.g., conflict, complaining, anger) rather than a decrease in "positives" (e.g., support, smiling, laughter) (e.g., Holmbeck and Hill, 1991; Montemayor and Eberly, in press). Although negative interchanges may diminish after the adolescent growth spurt, adolescents and their parents do not immediately become as close as they were before the adolescents entered puberty. Interestingly, puberty increases distance between children and their parents in most species of monkeys and apes, and some writers have suggested that the pattern seen

Studies indicate that parent-adolescent conflict may increase during puberty.
(Billy E. Barnes/PhotoEdit)

in human adolescents may have some evolutionary basis (Steinberg, 1987b).

Because this connection between pubertal maturation and parent-child distance is not affected by the age at which the adolescent goes through puberty—in other words, the pattern is seen among early as well as late maturers—it suggests that something about puberty in particular may transform the parent-child bond. To date, we do not know whether this effect results from the hormonal changes of puberty, from changes in the adolescent's physical appearance, or from changes in adolescent psychological functioning that, in turn, affect family relationships. Moreover, because few studies of family relationships at puberty have examined multiple aspects of adolescent development simultaneously, it is difficult to say whether the patterns of change in family relationships that many studies have found do, in fact, result from puberty and not from some other change taking place at the same time in the adolescent or in the parent (Paikoff and Brooks-Gunn, 1991).

Whatever underlying mechanism that is involved, one interpretation of these studies is that developments occurring around the time of puberty can upset interpersonal "balances" that are established during childhood, causing temporary periods of disruption in the family system. During a son's or daughter's childhood, families develop patterns of relationships that are comfortable and workable, but they may find that puberty disrupts the patterns to which they have grown accustomed. They have developed a certain way of discussing things and a certain way of including the children in discussions. But as the children go through puberty, they may want to be treated more like adults and may want to have greater say in family decisions. Consequently, families may experience a temporary period of conflict or tension when sons and daughters enter early adolescence. It may take some time for the individual and the family to achieve a new equilibrium that takes into account the changes brought on by puberty.

Puberty may have an effect on relationships in the peer group, too. One study of adolescents' social networks—the people they are most likely to see and spend time with—found that adolescents who were physically mature were less likely than their less developed peers to name adults as people who were important to them, and they were more likely to name other adolescents (Garbarino, Burston, Raber, Russell, and Crouter, 1978). This finding suggests that pubertal maturation may be an important influence in shifting adolescents' interests and energies toward the peer group. Boys and girls who are physically mature are more likely than less mature agemates to be involved in cross-sex activities such as having a boyfriend or girlfriend or going out on dates (Crockett and Dorn, 1987), although this depends on the social norms of the adolescent's peer group and the prevailing expectations about the age at which teenagers should begin dating (Dornbusch, Carlsmith, Gross, Martin, Jennings, Rosenberg, and Duke, 1981; Gargiulo, Attie, Brooks-Gunn, and Warren, 1987).

The Impact of Menarche and First Ejaculation

Several studies have focused specifically on girls' attitudes toward and reactions to menarche and on boys' reactions to their first ejaculation. The onset of menstruation is "not just one of a series of physiological events during puberty, but is also a sociocultural event . . . imbued with special meaning" (Brooks-Gunn and Ruble, 1979, p. 1). Cultural beliefs concerning menarche and the specific information that a young woman receives from parents, teachers, friends, and health practitioners all influence how she greets and experiences menarche (Brooks-Gunn and Ruble, 1982).

In Western culture, many young women have developed a negative image of menstruation before reaching adolescence, and they enter puberty with ambivalent attitudes about menarche—a mixture of excitement and fear (Ruble and Brooks-Gunn, 1982). Adolescent girls' attitudes toward menarche are less negative today than they appear to have been in the past (Ruble and Brooks-Gunn, 1982; Greif and Ulman, 1982), a change that may be attributable to the more open and less mysterious presentation of information about menstruation in schools and in the media in recent years. In general, among today's adolescent girls, menarche is typically accompanied by gains in social maturity, peer prestige, and self-esteem—as well as by heightened self-consciousness (Brooks-Gunn and Reiter, 1990). As you will read later in this chapter, however, the impact of menarche on the young adolescent's psychological development depends in part on whether she matures early or late, relative to her peers.

Interestingly, one set of studies indicates that a strong negative bias toward menstruation before menarche may actually be associated with greater menstrual discomfort. Menstrual symptoms are reported to be more severe among women who expect menstruation to be uncomfortable, among girls whose mothers lead them to believe that menstruation will be an unpleasant or uncomfortable experience, and in cultures that label menstruation as an important event. In addition, girls who experience menarche early, relative to their peers, or who are otherwise unprepared for puberty report more negative reactions to the event (Rierdan, Kobb, and Stubbs, 1989; Ruble and Brooks-Gunn, 1982).

Far less is known about boys' reactions to their first ejaculation, an experience that we might consider analogous to menarche in girls. Although most boys are not very well prepared for this event by their parents or other adults, first ejaculation does not appear to cause undue anxiety, embarrassment, or fear. It is interesting to note, however, that in contrast to girls, who generally tell their mothers shortly after they have begun menstruating and tell their girlfriends soon thereafter, boys, at least in the United States, do not discuss their first ejaculation with either parents or friends (Gaddis and Brooks-Gunn, 1985). In other cultures, the event may be experienced somewhat differently. For example, one study of first ejaculation among adolescent boys in Nigeria found not only that boys were not upset by the event but also that they told their friends about the experience very soon after it occurred (Adegoke, 1993). Cultural differences in boys' responses to their first ejaculation are likely related to differences in how different cultures view masturbation.

RECAP

Although puberty may cause temporary disruption in the adolescent's social relationships, research has not shown that puberty is inherently stressful or associated with dramatic changes in mood or behavior. Puberty may be associated with increases in negative moods, but only during the very early stages of hormonal change, when hormone levels are fluctuating widely. More important than puberty itself is how puberty is viewed within the context in which the adolescent matures, and the extent to which the adolescent has been prepared psychologically for the biological changes of the era.

The Impact of Early or Late Maturation

Adolescents who mature relatively early or relatively late stand apart from their peers physically and may, as a consequence, elicit different sorts of reactions and expectations from those around them. Moreover, individual adolescents may be all too aware of whether they are early or late relative to their age-mates, and their feelings about themselves are likely to be influenced by their comparisons.

These adolescents are all the same chronological age, despite their markedly different physical appearances. Among boys, early maturation is associated with greater popularity and higher self-esteem. Although early-maturing girls are also more popular with their peers, they report more emotional difficulties than young women who mature later. (Alan Carey/Image Works)

Indeed, adolescents' *perceptions* of whether they are an early or a late maturer are more strongly related to their feelings about their physical maturation than whether they actually *are* early or late (Dubas, Graber, and Petersen, 1991). In short, early and late maturers may be treated differently by others, may view themselves differently, and may, as a result, behave differently. As we shall see, early and late maturation have different consequences in the immediate present and in the long run, different consequences in different contexts, and, most important, different consequences for boys and girls.

● ***Early versus Late Maturation among Boys.*** The first studies to compare early- and late-maturing boys suggested that it was an advantage to mature earlier than one's peers. Drawing on data collected as part of the Oakland Growth Study (a longitudinal study begun earlier this century), psychologist Mary Jones and her colleagues compared early- and late-maturing boys on a variety of psychological tests and measures of interpersonal relationships (Jones, 1957, 1965; Jones and Bayley, 1950; Mussen and Jones, 1957, 1958). They found that late maturers were seen by their peers as more childish and were less popular and less likely to have held leadership positions. On personality measures, late-maturing boys exhibited stronger feelings of inadequacy, higher needs for autonomy, more negative self-concepts, more childishness, less self-control, less responsibility, and less self-assurance.

Research conducted since these early studies has confirmed their findings, though with several modifications. With regard to self-image and popularity, early-maturing boys clearly have an advantage over their more slowly developing peers (Petersen, 1985). Consistent with this, a recent study of adolescents' daily moods indicates that boys who are more physically mature than their peers report more frequent feelings of positive affect, attention, strength, and being in love (Richards and Larson, 1993). With regard to *behavior,* however, studies conducted in America and Europe show that early maturers are more likely than their peers to get involved in antisocial or deviant activities, including truancy, minor delinquency, and problems at school (Duncan, Ritter, Dornbusch, Gross, and Carlsmith, 1985), and they are more likely to use drugs and alcohol (Andersson and Magnusson, 1990; Silbereisen, Kracke, and Crockett, 1990; Tschann, Adler, Irwin, Millstein, Turner, and Kegeles, 1991). One reasonable explanation is that boys who are more physically mature develop friendships with older peers and that these friendships lead them into activities that are problematic for the younger boys. Once involved with these older peer groups, the early maturers' higher rate of delinquency and substance use increases over time through their social contacts (Kracke, 1993). Thus, early puberty seems to play a role in the initiation, but not intensification, of substance use.

With regard to *mood,* one interesting reanalysis of old data by psychologist Harvey Peskin indicated that early-maturing boys may have more problems than the early research had indicated (Peskin, 1967). The researcher found that early and late maturers' moods were very similar when each group was examined one year before pubertal onset. But at the time of pubertal onset, and one year later as well, the late maturers showed significantly higher ratings on measures of intellectual curiosity, exploratory behavior, and social initiative. Interestingly, early maturers experienced more frequent and more intense temper tantrums during puberty (Livson and Peskin, 1980). Why should this be?

Late maturers, Peskin argued, have the advantage of a longer preadolescent period, giving them more time to "prepare" psychologically for the onset of puberty. This preparation may be important if, as noted earlier, rapid increases in hormones at puberty provoke changes in mood. Many theorists believe that the middle childhood and preadolescent years are extremely important periods for the development of coping skills—skills that prove valuable during adolescence and adulthood. Although puberty by no means marks the end of the growth of coping abilities, it does come as an abrupt interruption to the more relaxed preadolescent era. A later puberty, and hence a longer preadolescence, might allow for coping skills to develop more fully before adolescence. This may account in part for the apparently better coping skills demonstrated by late maturers—not only during puberty but, as you will read, later, as adults.

Do the psychological and interpersonal differences that are observed between early and late maturers during adolescence persist into adulthood? Do early-maturing boys remain more popular and more self-confident as adults, for example? In order to answer such questions, a series of follow-up studies that was conducted some twenty-five years later looked at the adult personalities of males who had been studied during adolescence (Livson and Peskin, 1980). At age 38, the early maturers were more responsible, more cooperative, more self-controlled, and more sociable. At first glance, it appeared as though the benefits of early maturation had carried over well into adulthood.

Yet the picture was not so clear-cut. By adulthood, some of the advantages had turned into disadvantages. True, the early maturers did appear more confident and more responsible. But they had also grown up to be more conforming, conventional, and humorless. Their peers who had been late maturers remained somewhat more impulsive and more assertive but turned out to be more insightful, more inventive, and more creatively playful. What had happened?

One interpretation is that because of their more adultlike appearance, the early-maturing boys had been pushed into adult roles earlier than their peers. They were more likely to be asked to assume responsibility, to take on leadership positions, and to behave in a more "grown-up" manner. But this early press toward adulthood may have come too soon and may have stifled a certain amount of creativity and risk taking.

Have you gone to any gatherings of former high school classmates? Did you discover that some of the people whom you had remembered as extremely mature and socially successful during high school have turned out to be not all that interesting a few years after graduation? Perhaps too much leadership, responsibility, social success, and "maturity" during the high school years interferes with the sort of psychological development that makes for interesting and creative adults. As we shall see in a later chapter, many psychologists believe that adolescents may benefit in the long run from having an extended period of time during which they are *not* being pushed into adulthood.

In short, success and social status may come too easily and too early for early-maturing boys, leaving them with less need to develop creative or flexible solutions to life's problems and less time to experiment with new roles and identities. In contrast, late-maturing youngsters, experiencing more difficulty in achieving social standing and recognition because of their immature physical appearance, may be forced to develop more inventive means of problem solving and greater cognitive and social flexibility. In other words, the greater difficulty that late maturers face as early adolescents may lead to their developing coping skills that prove useful when they reach adulthood. Unfortunately, however, at least one study of late-maturing boys indicates that heavy drinking may be one of the "coping" behaviors that persists into young adulthood (Andersson and Magnusson, 1990).

Early versus Late Maturation in Girls. The initial research on this issue, again conducted by researchers working on the Oakland Growth Study, suggested that, in contrast to boys, early-maturing girls were at a disadvantage—although the findings were far less consistent than they were in the studies of boys (Jones, 1949; Jones and Mussen, 1958). Early-maturing girls were found to be "less popular, less poised, less expressive, and more submissive, withdrawn, and unassured then [their] agemates" (Livson and Peskin, 1980, p. 71). Like the late-maturing boy, the early-maturing girl is out of step with her peers. And since girls mature about two years earlier than boys, the early-maturing girl is not only more physically advanced than her female peers but far more advanced than nearly all her male classmates as well. In these studies, the late-maturing girls were more likely to be seen as attractive, sociable, and expressive.

As is the case with research on early- and late-maturing boys, recent research on girls has tended to corroborate the findings of the earlier studies, but we have learned a good deal more about the development of early-maturing girls, in particular, in the ensuing years. A number of studies find that early-maturing girls have more emotional difficulties than do girls who mature on time or late, including lowered self-image and higher rates of depression, anxiety, eating disorders, and panic attacks (Aro and Taipale, 1987; Hayward, Killen, and Taylor, 1994; Simmons and Blyth, 1987), a finding that has been confirmed in several Western countries. These difficulties seem to have a great deal to do with girls' feelings about their weight, because early maturers are, almost by definition, heavier than their late-maturing peers (Petersen, 1988). In societies that define as physically attractive the thin, "leggy" woman, a late-maturing girl will look more like this image than an early-maturing girl will.

Whether earlier maturation has a negative effect on the young girl's feelings about herself appears to depend on the broader context in which maturation takes place, however. For example, studies of American girls generally find that early-maturing girls have lower self-esteem and a poorer self-image, because of our cultural preference for thinness and our national ambivalence about adolescent sexuality (Brooks-Gunn and Reiter, 1990). In Germany, however, where sex education is more open and attitudes toward adolescent sexuality are less conflicted, early-maturing girls are found to have *higher* self-esteem (Silbereisen, Petersen, Albrecht, and Kracke, 1989).

Interestingly, even *within* the United States, the impact of physical maturation appears to depend on the social context in which teenagers live. One study of suburban Chicago youngsters, for example, found that girls' body image was significantly higher in one community than in another—despite comparable levels of physical maturation between the two groups. One factor that differentiated the two communities was "cliquishness": In the more cliquish high school, girls were less satisfied with the way they looked, perhaps because cliquish girls place more emphasis on physical appearance in determining popularity (Richards, Boxer, Petersen, and Albrecht, 1990).

Although some early-maturing girls may have self-image difficulties, their popularity with peers is not jeopardized. Indeed, some studies indicate that early maturers are more popular than other girls, especially, as you would expect, when the index of popularity includes popularity with boys (Simmons, Blyth, and McKinney, 1983). Ironically, it may be in part because the early maturer is more popular with boys that she reports more emotional upset: At a very early age, pressure to date and, perhaps, to be involved in a sexual relationship may take its toll on the adolescent girl's mental health. Consistent with this,

THE SCIENTIFIC STUDY OF ADOLESCENCE

EARLY MATURATION AND GIRLS' PROBLEM BEHAVIOR—ACTIVATION OR ACCENTUATION?

As you know, researchers have observed for some time now that early physical maturation in both boys and girls is associated with higher rates of problem behavior, including delinquency, drug and alcohol use, and precocious sexual activity. But does early maturation by itself actually cause problem behavior to emerge at adolescence? Or are the two variables associated in some other fashion?

In order to examine this question, psychologists Avshalom Caspi and Terrie Moffitt drew upon data from an extensive study of 15-year-old New Zealand girls who had been studied since birth (Caspi and Moffitt, 1991). One of the interesting features of the data set used by the researchers was that measures of problem behavior had been gathered on the adolescents both during childhood, well before the onset of puberty (at age 9), and during adolescence, after puberty had begun (at ages 13 and 15). The researchers used age at menarche (first menstruation), as their indicator of early (menarche before age 13), on-time (menarche between 13 and 14), and late (menarche after age 14) maturation. They looked to see whether problem behavior increased between 13 and 15 to a greater degree among early maturers than among the other girls.

As hypothesized, and consistent with other studies, Caspi and Moffitt noted a larger increase in problem behavior between ages 13 and 15 among the early-maturing girls. But when they further broke down the early-maturing sample into two smaller groups—girls who had shown high rates of problem behavior before puberty and those who had not—they saw an interesting pattern: Early maturation was associated with an increase in problem behavior only among those girls who had a prior history of difficulties. As you can see in the accompanying figure, the discrepancy in problem behavior between early maturers and other girls is far more evident in the group of girls who had been rated "high" in problem behavior before adolescence. Indeed, within the group of girls who had been rated "low" in problem behavior at age 9, there were no differences at all between early- and on-time maturers in terms of problem behavior.

Does early maturation *cause* problem behavior during adolescence? Not entirely, then; rather, early maturation appears to accentuate, or magnify, differences between individuals that exist prior to adolescence. Why should this be so?

According to Caspi and Moffitt, early puberty is stressful, and stress, they suggest, tends to bring out differences between individuals. Although we tend to think of stress as something that

one team of researchers (Blyth, Simmons, and Zakin, 1985) found that early-maturing girls in schools with older peers (for example, sixth-graders who were in a school that had seventh- and eighth-graders, too) were psychologically worse off than early-maturing girls who were in the highest grade in their school (for example, sixth-graders who were in an elementary school). Again, we see the importance of context.

Like their male counterparts, early-maturing girls are also more likely to become involved in deviant activities, including delinquency and use of drugs and alcohol; are more likely to have school problems; and are more likely to experience early sexual intercourse

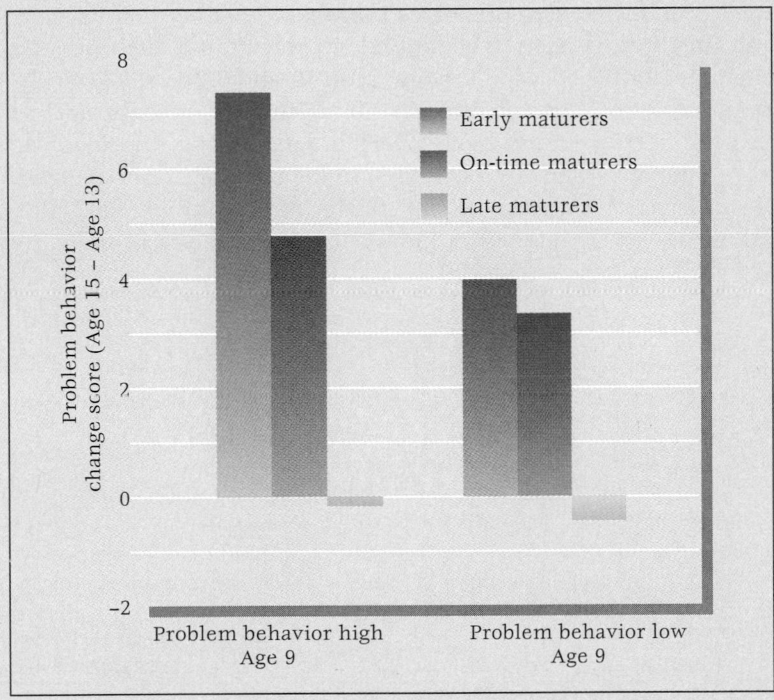

Early maturation is more likely to be associated with problem behavior among girls with a prior history of conduct problems. (Caspi and Moffitt, 1991)

changes people in dramatic ways, Caspi and Moffitt say that just the opposite is true: During times of stress, not only do we not change markedly but we also become even *more* like we were before the stress occurred.

Interestingly, in another paper, these and other researchers used the same data set to examine the possibility that problem behavior leads to early puberty, rather then the reverse (Moffitt, Caspi, Belsky, and Silva, 1992). Although, like other researchers, they found that earlier maturation was associated with higher levels of family conflict in childhood, they found no evidence that early puberty followed higher levels of behavior problems.

Source: Caspi, A., and Moffitt, T. (1991). Individual differences and personal transitions: The sample case of girls at puberty. *Journal of Personality and Social Psychology, 61,* 157–168.

(Aro and Taipale, 1987; Caspi and Moffitt, 1991; Magnusson, Statin, and Allen, 1986). This is true in Europe as well as in the United States (Silbereisen et al., 1989). These problems appear to arise because early-maturing girls are more likely to spend time with older adolescents, especially older adolescent boys, who initiate them into activities that might otherwise be delayed (Magnusson et al., 1986). Girls with a history of problem behavior prior to puberty appear most susceptible to the adverse effects of early maturation (Caspi and Moffitt, 1991) (see the accompanying box).

Interestingly, one set of studies indicates that girls' *perceptions* of their maturational timing (whether they *think* they are early, late, or on time) may be more important in influencing their behavior and their feelings about themselves than their actual maturational timing (Dubas, Graber, and Petersen, 1991; Petersen, Graber, and Sullivan, 1990). Adolescents who perceive themselves to be earlier maturers may see themselves as ready to engage in "adult" behaviors, such as smoking, drinking, and drug use. As you will read in a moment, although most of these behavioral differences disappear by the time the late-maturing girls have completed puberty, the earlier involvement of early-maturing girls in certain behaviors may have important long-term repercussions.

Again, however, it is important to consider the role of context in interaction with pubertal change. Although it is generally true that early-maturing girls are more likely to engage in delinquent behavior than their late-maturing peers, a recent study of New Zealand youngsters indicates that this may only hold true for girls who attend coeducational high schools (Caspi, Lynam, Moffitt, and Silva, 1993). Early-maturing girls in all-female schools are no more likely than late-maturers to be involved in delinquent activities, presumably because there are far fewer opportunities for delinquency in same-sex schools. Thus, while early

THE EFFECTS OF EARLY MATURATION

Researchers are still trying to make sense of the complicated pattern of findings that emerges from comparisons of early and late maturers, but one fact is clear: Early maturation brings many more disadvantages for girls than it does for boys. Psychologists have offered several explanations for this sex difference. The explanations all are compatible, but they derive from very different premises.

One explanation might be termed the "deviance" hypothesis (Simmons and Blyth, 1987). Simply put, youngsters who stand far apart from their peers—in physical appearance, for instance—may experience more psychological distress than adolescents who blend in more easily. Studies of adolescents who stand out physically in other ways—obese students or students who attend schools in which they are clearly in a racial minority—support the view that standing out too much can be an unfortunate disadvantage (Blyth, Simmons, Bulcroft, Felt, Van Cleave, and Bush, 1980; Simmons, Blyth, and McKinney, 1983). Because girls mature earlier than boys, on average, early-maturing girls mature much earlier than their male and female agemates. This makes them stand out at a time when they would rather fit in and, as a result, may make them more vulnerable. This explanation would also account for the lower self-esteem of late-maturing boys, who are "deviant" toward the other extreme.

A second explanation focuses on "developmental readiness." Here the notion is that psychological distress results when youngsters have experiences before they are psychologically "ready" for them (Simmons and Blyth, 1987). If puberty is a challenge that requires psychological adaptation by the adolescent, perhaps younger adolescents are less able to cope with the challenge than older ones. Because puberty occurs quite early among early-maturing girls (some may begin maturing at age 8 or 9 and may experience menarche at age 10), it may tax their psychological resources. Early maturation among boys, because it occurs at a much later age, would pose less of a problem. The developmental readiness hypothesis has been used to account for the finding that older youngsters (eighth-puberty may predispose girls toward more frequent and earlier deviance, this predisposition may be realized only in an environment that permits the behavior.

One study of the adult personalities of women who had been either early or late maturers suggests some interesting parallels between the personality development of early-maturing girls and late-maturing boys (Peskin, 1973). Both sets of youngsters may have self-esteem problems during adolescence, but both appear to be somewhat more psychologically advanced than their peers during adulthood. Like the late-maturing boys, early-maturing girls may be forced to develop coping skills during adolescence that have some long-term positive effects.

At the same time, however, more recent research indicates that the earlier involvement of early-maturing girls in problem behavior may adversely affect their long-term educational achievement. In one study of Swedish girls, for example, the researchers found that the school problems of early-maturing adolescent girls persisted over time, leading to the development of negative attitudes toward school and lower educational aspirations. In young adulthood, there were marked

graders) fare better during the transition from elementary to secondary school than do younger students (sixth-graders). This perspective also helps to account for the fact that, in puberty, late-maturing boys seem better able than early maturers to control their temper and their impulses (Peskin, 1967).

A final explanation concerns the cultural desirability of different body types (Petersen, 1988). Early maturation for girls means leaving behind the culturally admired state of thinness. As you read earlier, among girls, the ratio of fat to muscle increases dramatically at puberty, and many girls feel distressed when they mature, because they gain weight. Early maturers experience this weight gain at a time when most of their peers are still girlishly thin. One interesting study showed that in ballet companies—where thinness is even more important than in the culture at large—late maturers, who can retain the "ideal" shape much longer than earlier maturers, have fewer psychological problems than even on-time girls (Brooks-Gunn and Warren, 1985). In contrast, at puberty boys move from a culturally undesirable state for males (being short and scrawny) to a culturally admired one (being tall and muscular). Early maturers enjoy the special advantage of being tall and muscular before their peers and therefore are more likely to react well to puberty. The fact that the effects of early maturation on girls' self-esteem vary across cultures suggests that contextual factors need to be taken into account in explaining this pattern of sex differences.

Whatever the explanation, the fact that early-maturing girls are at heightened risk for temporary psychological problems, at least in the United States, is an important fact for parents and school counselors to bear in mind. Unfortunately, as long as our culture overvalues thinness and encourages the view that females should be judged on the basis of their physical appearance rather than their abilities, values, or personality, the risks of early puberty will probably persist. Adults can help by being supportive, by helping the early-maturing girl to recognize her strengths and positive features—physical and nonphysical alike—and by preparing her for puberty before it takes place.

differences between the early- and late-maturing girls' levels of education; for example, the late-maturing girls were twice as likely as early-maturing girls to continue beyond the compulsory minimum number of years of high school (Magnusson, Statin, and Allen, 1986).

RECAP

Psychologists have long been interested in the consequences of early versus late physical maturation. In general, early maturation brings with it more social advantages for boys and girls, but very early maturation may be somewhat of a psychological liability for girls, at least in the United States. For both sexes, however, early physical maturation is associated with more problem behavior, including drug and alcohol use, delinquency, and precocious sexual activity. This may be because early maturers see themselves as being more adult and, consequently, as being more entitled to engage in these activities. It is important to keep in mind, however, that early maturation has different effects in different social contexts.

PHYSICAL HEALTH IN ADOLESCENCE

Although puberty is undoubtedly the most important biological development of the adolescent decade, concerns about the physical health and well-being of young people are far broader than those involving reproductive maturation. In the last two decades, the field of **adolescent health** has grown rapidly, as health educators and health care practitioners have come to better understand that the health care needs of young people differ from those of children and adults in important respects (Slap and Jablow, 1994).

Adolescence is a paradox as far as physical health is concerned. On the one hand, adolescence is one of the healthiest periods in the life span, characterized by a relatively low incidence of disabling or chronic illnesses (e.g., asthma, cancer), fewer short-term hospital stays, and fewer days in which individuals stay home sick in bed. Moreover, in the past fifty years, rates of death and disability resulting from illness and disease during adolescence have decreased substantially, and new medical technologies and better health care delivery have improved the physical well-being of children, especially those with chronic illness and disabling medical conditions (Gans, 1990). In the United States, 1 in 15 adolescents is chronically ill, and the main causes of disability are mental disorders, such as depression; respiratory illnesses, such as asthma; and muscular and skeletal disorders, such as arthritis. Even so, however, teenagers with disabilities are better cared for today and live much longer than their counterparts did previously (Gans, 1990).

On the other hand, adolescence is a period of relatively great physical risk because of unhealthy behaviors (such as drug use), violence (both self-inflicted and inflicted by others), and risky activity (such as unprotected sexual intercourse). Moreover, adolescents are far less likely than adults to seek and receive medical and dental care (Millstein, Petersen, and Nightingale, 1993). In some senses, then, many of the improvements we have made in preventing and treating the traditional "medical" problems of the period—those having to do with chronic illnesses—have been offset by what some scientists call the "new morbidity and mortality" of adolescence (Hein, 1988a). Contributors to this new morbidity and mortality include accidents (especially automobile accidents), suicide, homicide, substance abuse (including tobacco and alcohol use), and sexually transmitted diseases (including AIDS).

The contrast between the "old" and "new" mortalities of adolescence is readily apparent. Although the death rate from natural causes (such as disease or illness) fell 90 percent between 1933 and 1985 among adolescents, the death rate from violence and injury remained stable—and even increased somewhat between 1950 and 1985. Fifty years ago, illness and disease accounted for more than twice as many deaths among teenagers as violence or injury, but the reverse is true today. According to recent estimates, nearly 40 percent of all teenage deaths result from car accidents (Hingson and Howland, 1993), and another 30 percent are a result of homicide, suicide, or some other violent act or injury (Gans, 1990). Adolescents are also more likely than other age groups to be injured as pedestrians and bicyclists in traffic accidents (Hingson and Howland, 1993).

Improving the health of young people is an especially important concern among those working with adolescents from ethnic minority groups, because these youngsters are at greater risk for many of the "new" morbidities and mortalities of adolescence. Nonwhite youngsters, for example, are relatively more likely than white youngsters to be obese or to have high blood pressure or high cholesterol levels (National Heart, Lung, and Blood Institute Growth and Health Study Research Group, 1992); to be physically inactive (Wolf, Gortmaker, Cheung, Gray, Herzog, and Colditz, 1993); to be victims of violent crimes (Earls, Cairns, and Mercy, 1993); to be infected with HIV, the AIDS virus (DiClemente, 1990); to die from drowning (Warneke and Cooper, 1994); or to be murdered (Sorenson, Richardson, and Peterson, 1993). Yet, despite their generally poorer health, minority youngsters are less likely to have access to sources of medical care, less likely to visit the doctor when ill, and less likely to have health insurance (Lieu, Newacheck, and McManus, 1993). The terrible combination of poor health and poor access to health care is even more concentrated among the 16 percent of adolescents who live in poverty, a disproportionate number of whom are from ethnic minority backgrounds (Klerman, 1993).

The consensus among health care experts is that the most significant threats to the health of today's youth arise from psychosocial rather than from natural causes (Gans, 1990; Millstein, 1989). Unlike many other periods of the life span (such as infancy or old age), when we are more vulnerable to disease and illness, most of the health problems of teenagers are preventable. As a result of this recognition, the focus in the field of adolescent health has shifted away from traditional medical models (in which the emphasis is on the assessment, diagnosis, and treatment of disease) toward more community-oriented, educational approaches (in which the emphasis is on the prevention of illness and injury and the promotion of good health). As a consequence, a major shift in the study of adolescent health care has been a focus on **health promotion** (Millstein, Petersen, and Nightingale, 1993; Susman, Koch, Maney, and Finkelstein, 1993).

In other words, instead of asking how we can best treat sick youngsters, experts in adolescent health care are now asking how we can encourage adolescents and children to take the steps necessary to prevent illness and disability. How can we help adolescents reduce **health-compromising behaviors,** such as drug use, unsafe driving, and unprotected sexual intercourse, and increase **health-enhancing behaviors,** such as eating properly, exercising adequately, and wearing seat belts? Current efforts include education about alcohol and other drug use, accident prevention, safe sex, and proper nutrition. Adolescent medicine expert Charles Irwin, Jr. (1993), has suggested that parents, practitioners, and educators who are interested in helping adolescents to live healthier lives keep in mind the "five *A*s" of successful health promotion:

Anticipatory guidance. (Establish a trusting relationship with the young person prior to adolescence.)

Ask. (Query adolescents directly about their health-enhancing and health-compromising behaviors.)

Advise. (Give advice about health promotion even if the young person doesn't ask for it.)

Assist. (Encourage the adolescent to participate in programs that promote health.)

Arrange. (Arrange follow-up visits or consultations to monitor the adolescent's progress.)

A variety of new, wide-reaching strategies for promoting adolescent health have been attempted in recent decades. Among the most popular of the latest wave involve **school-based health centers.** These are located in or adjacent to schools, and they provide such services as physical examinations, the treatment of minor injuries, health education programs, dental care, and counseling related to substance abuse, sexuality, and mental health. They often are set up to serve poor youth, who generally are less likely to receive medical and dental care than their more affluent counterparts.

School-based health centers became increasingly popular because they are positioned to address the most pressing problems in adolescent health care: the fact that most adolescent health problems are preventable, the fact that adolescents underutilize conventional medical services, and the fact that adolescents often want their health care needs to remain confidential. Although the development of these centers has generated controversy in a number of communities because some school-based health centers distribute contraceptives (a practice, that, as we shall see in a later chapter, upsets many adults), studies show that the vast majority of visits to these centers are for injuries, acute illnesses (e.g., influenza, strep throat), and mental health services (e.g., counseling). Visits for family planning services account for only 10 percent of visits to school-based clinics (Scales, 1991).

School-based health centers deliver important services to adolescents, including contraceptive information and counseling.
(J. Stettenheim/Saba)

How well are school-based clinics working? Recent evaluations of several school-based health programs—including those designed to improve adolescents' physical and mental health, those designed to reduce drug and alcohol use, and those designed to reduce teenage pregnancy—have been inconsistent. Although most programs have shown some success in increasing adolescents' understanding of health-related issues (e.g., how AIDS is spread) or knowledge about health risks (e.g., the dangers of cocaine use), few programs have been markedly successful in changing adolescents' *behavior,* particularly after the program was completed (see Millstein et al., 1993, for many examples). Why is this so? As is the case in studies of adults, studies of adolescents indicate that it is far easier to alter what individuals know than it is to change how they behave.

As many experts point out, health behavior is influenced by a large number of factors, of which knowledge is only one component (e.g., Leventhal and Keeshan, 1993). Changes in the *context* in which adolescents live (e.g., the accessibility of handguns, the availability of illicit drugs, the role models to which young people are exposed) must accompany changes in adolescents' knowledge and understanding if lasting health promotion is to be accomplished. For example, recent investigations of the impact of changing one element of the broader context of adolescent health—the legal drinking age—have found that raising the age leads to a significant decline in accidental death rates among young automobile drivers and pedestrians, as well as in the rates of unintentional injuries not involving cars and homicides (Jones, Pieper, and Robertson, 1992).

RECAP

Today, in contrast to fifty years ago, the most important physical health problems in adolescence have psychosocial rather than natural causes. This "new morbidity and mortality" of adolescence is caused by such preventable phenomena as automobile accidents, violence, substance abuse, and unprotected sex. New approaches to adolescent health care, emphasizing prevention and health promotion instead of treatment, are being studied. Among the most important innovations are school-based health centers.

KEY TERMS

activational role of hormones
adolescent growth spurt
adolescent health
androgens
asynchronicity in growth
cross-sectional study
delayed phase preference
endocrine system
estrogens
feedback loop
glands
gonads
health-compromising behaviors
health-enhancing behaviors
health promotion
hormones
hypothalamus
longitudinal study
menarche
organizational role of hormones
ovaries
peak height velocity
pituitary gland
puberty
school-based health centers
secondary sex characteristics
secular trend
set point
Tanner stages
testes

FOR FURTHER READING

Brooks-Gunn, J., and Reiter, E. (1990). The role of pubertal processes. In S. Feldman and G. Elliott (Eds.), *At the threshold: The developing adolescent.* Cambridge, Mass.: Harvard University Press. An excellent summary of the literature on the psychological consequences of puberty.

Buchanan, C., Eccles, J., and Becker, J. (1992). Are adolescents the victims of raging hormones? Evidence for activational effects of hormones on moods and behavior at adolescence. *Psychological Bulletin, 111,* 62–107. A comprehensive review of the literature on hormonal changes during puberty and their effects on adolescent mood and behavior.

Marshall, W. (1978). Puberty. In F. Faulkner and J. Tanner (Eds.), *Human growth,* Vol. 2. New York: Plenum. A good overview of the hormonal and somatic changes of puberty.

Millstein, S., Petersen, A., and Nightingale, E. (Eds.). (1993). *Promoting the health of adolescents: New directions for the twenty-first century.* New York: Oxford University Press. An excellent collection of chapters reflecting the latest thinking about adolescent health and its promotion.

Slap, G., and Jablow, M. (1994). *Teenage health care.* New York: Pocket Books. A comprehensive guide to the health care of adolescents, written for parents of teenagers.

CHAPTER 2

COGNITIVE TRANSITIONS

(Will McIntyre/Photo Researchers)

Changes in cognition, or thinking, represent the second in a set of three fundamental changes that occur during adolescence—the others being the biological changes of puberty and the transition of the adolescent into new social roles. Like developments in the other two domains, the cognitive transitions of adolescence have far-reaching implications for the young person's psychological development and social relations. Indeed, the expansion of thought during adolescence represents as significant an event and as important an influence on the adolescent's development and behavior as puberty.

CHANGES IN COGNITION

Most people would agree that adolescents are "smarter" than children. Not only do teenagers *know* more than children—after all, the longer we live, the more opportunities we have to acquire new information—but adolescents actually *think* in ways that are more advanced, more efficient, and generally more effective. This can be seen in five chief ways (Keating, 1990):

1. During adolescence individuals become better able than children to think about what is possible, instead of limiting their thought to what is real.
2. Adolescents become better able to think about abstract things.
3. During adolescence individuals begin thinking more often about the process of thinking itself.
4. Adolescents' thinking tends to become multidimensional, rather than being limited to a single issue.
5. Adolescents are more likely than children to see things as relative, rather than as absolute.

Let's look at each of these advantages—and some of their implications—in greater detail.

Thinking about Possibilities

The adolescent's thinking is less bound to concrete events than is that of the child. Children's thinking is oriented to the here and now—that is, to things and events that they can observe directly. But adolescents are able to consider what they observe against a backdrop of what is possible. Put another way, for the child, what is possible is what is real; for the adolescent, what is real is but one subset of what is possible. Children, for example, do not wonder, the way adolescents often do, about the ways in which their personalities might change in the future or the ways in which their lives might be affected by different career choices. For the young child, you are who you are. But for the adolescent, who you are is just one possibility of who you could be.

This does not mean that the child is incapable of imagination or fantasy. Even young children have vivid and creative imaginations. Nor does it mean that children are unable to conceive of things being different from the way they observe them to be. Rather, the advantage that adolescents enjoy over children when it comes to thinking about possibilities is that adolescents are able to move easily between the specific and the abstract, to generate alternative possibilities and explanations systematically, and to compare what they actually observe with what they believe is possible.

We can illustrate this development by looking at the following problem. How would you approach it?

> Imagine four poker chips, one red, one blue, one yellow, and one green. Make as many different combinations of chips, of any number, as you can. Use the notations R, B, Y, and G to record your answers. (Adapted from Elkind, Barocas, and Rosenthal, 1968)

How did you tackle this problem? Did you need to use real poker chips to solve the problem? Probably not. In all likelihood, you used some sort of system, beginning perhaps with the case of zero chips (don't worry, a lot of people forget this one) and then proceeding on to one-chip combinations (R, B, Y, G), two-chip combinations (RB, RY, RG, BY, BG, YG), three-chip combinations (RBY, RBG, RYG, BYG), and finally the single four-chip combination (RBYG). More important, you probably did not approach the problem haphazardly. You probably employed an abstract system for generating possibilities that you had in mind before being faced with the poker-chip problem—a system that you can apply across a variety of similar tasks. Although preadolescent children might be able to solve the problem correctly—in the sense that they might, with luck, generate all the possible combinations—children are far less likely than teenagers to employ a systematic approach (Neimark, 1975).

The adolescent's ability to reason systematically in terms of what is possible comes in handy in a variety of scientific and logical problem-solving situations. For instance, the study of mathematics in junior and senior high school (algebra, geometry, and trigonometry) often requires that you begin with an abstract or theoretical formulation—for example: "The square of a right triangle's hypotenuse is equal to the sum of the squares of the other two sides" (the Pythagorean theorem). This theorem, after all, is a proposition about the possible rather than the real. It is a statement about all *possible* right triangles, not just triangles that we might actually observe. In mathematics, we learn how to apply these theorems to concrete examples (that is, real triangles). Scientific experimentation—in biology, chemistry, and physics—also involves the ability to generate possibilities systematically. In a chemistry experiment in which you are trying to identify an unknown substance by performing various tests, you must first be able to imagine alternative possibilities for the substance's identity in order to know what tests to conduct.

The adolescent's use of this sort of thinking is not limited to scientific situations. We see it in the types of arguments adolescents employ, in which they are more able than younger children to envision and therefore anticipate the possible responses of an opponent and to have handy a counterargument or a series of counterarguments (Clark and Delia, 1976). Many parents believe that their children become more argumentative during adolescence. What probably happens in that their children become *better arguers.* An adolescent does not accept other people's points of view unquestioningly but instead evaluates them against other theoretically possible beliefs.

Related to the adolescent's increased facility with thinking about possibilities is the development of hypothetical thinking. Hypothetical thinking is what is sometimes called "if-then" thinking. In order to think hypothetically, you need to see beyond what is directly observable and you need to reason in terms of what might be possible.

The ability to think through hypotheses is an enormously powerful tool. Being able to plan ahead, being able to see the future consequences of an action, and being able to provide alternative explanations of events are all dependent on being able to hypothesize effectively.

Thinking in hypothetical terms also permits us to suspend our beliefs about something in order to argue in the abstract. Being capable of assuming a hypothetical stance is important when it comes to debating an issue, since doing so permits us to understand the logic behind the other person's argument, without necessarily agreeing with its conclusion. Playing devil's advocate, for example—as when you formulate a position contrary to what you really believe in order to challenge someone else's reasoning—requires the ability to think in hypothetical terms. Studies show that prior to adolescence, individuals have difficulty in dealing with propositions that are contrary to fact, unless they are part of a larger fictional story (Markovits and Valchon, 1989). So, for example, a 7-year-old boy would have trouble answering the question "Where would flying cows build nests?" He might say, "Cows don't fly," unless he had heard about flying cows in a story that was clearly fantasy-based.

Of course, hypothetical thinking also has implications for the adolescent's social behavior. It helps the young person to take the perspective of others by enabling him or her to think through what someone else might be thinking or feeling, given that person's point of view. ("If I were in that person's shoes, I would feel pretty angry.") Hypothetical thinking helps in formulating and arguing one's viewpoint, because it allows adolescents to think a step ahead of the opposition—a cognitive tool that comes in quite handy when dealing with parents. ("If they come back with 'You have to stay home and clean up the garbage,' then I'll remind them about the time they let Susan go out when she had chores to do.") And hypothetical thinking plays an important role in decision-making abilities, because it permits the young person to plan ahead and to foresee the consequences of choosing one alternative over another. ("If I choose to go out for the soccer team, then I am going to have to give up my part-time job.")

Thinking about Abstract Concepts

The appearance of more systematic, *abstract* thinking is the second notable aspect of cognitive development during adolescence. We noted earlier that children's thinking is more concrete and more bound to observable events and objects than is that of adolescents. This difference is clearly evident when we consider the ability to deal with abstract concepts—things that cannot be experienced directly through the senses.

For example, adolescents find it easier than children to comprehend the sorts of higher-order abstract logic inherent in puns, proverbs, metaphors, and analogies. When presented with verbal analogies, children are more likely than adolescents to focus on concrete and familiar associations among the words than on the abstract, or conceptual, relations among them.

Consider the following analogy, for example:

Sun : Moon : : Asleep : ?

a. Star
b. Bed
c. Awake
d. Night

Instead of answering "awake"—which is the best answer of the four given above—children would be more likely to respond with "bed" or "night," since both of these words have stronger associations with the word *asleep*. It is generally not until early adolescence that individuals are able to discern the abstract principles underlying analogies—in the one above, the principle involves antonyms—and therefore solve them correctly (Sternberg and Nigro, 1980).

The adolescent's greater facility with abstract thinking also permits the application of advanced reasoning and logical processes to social and ideological matters. This is clearly seen in the adolescent's increased facility and interest in thinking about interpersonal relationships, politics, philosophy, religion, and morality—topics that involve such abstract concepts as friendship, faith, democracy, fairness, and honesty. The growth of social thinking—generally referred to as *social cognition*—during adolescence is directly related to the young person's improving ability to think abstractly. Later in this chapter, we will examine the ways in which social thinking improves in adolescence.

Thinking about Thinking

A third noteworthy gain in cognitive ability during adolescence involves thinking about thinking itself, a process sometimes referred to as **metacognition.** Metacognition often involves monitoring one's own cognitive activity during the process of thinking—when you consciously use a strategy for remembering something (such as "*E*very *G*ood *B*oy *D*eserves *F*un," for the notes of the treble clef in music notation), or when you appraise your own comprehension of something you are reading before going on to the next paragraph. Studies show that using such strategies significantly aids adolescents in problem-solving situations (Chalmers and Lawrence, 1993).

Not only do adolescents "manage" their thinking more than children, but they are also better able to explain to others the processes they are using. For instance, in the poker-chip problem mentioned earlier, an adolescent would be able to describe the strategy to you ("First I took the single-chip possibilities, then I took the different pairs . . . "), whereas a child would probably just say "I thought of everything I could."

Another interesting way in which thinking about thinking becomes more apparent during adolescence is in increased introspection, self-consciousness, and intellectualization. When we are introspective, after all, we are thinking about our own emotions. When we are self-conscious, we are thinking about how others think about us. And when we intellectualize, we are thinking about our own thoughts. All three processes play an important role in the adolescent's psychological growth. As we shall see in Chapter 8, for example, these processes permit the sorts of self-examination and exploration that are important components of the young person's attempt to establish a coherent sense of identity.

These intellectual advances may occasionally result in problems for the young adolescent, particularly before he or she adjusts to having such powerful cognitive tools. Being able to introspect, for instance, may lead to periods of extreme self-absorption—a form of "adolescent egocentrism" (Elkind, 1967). Adolescent egocentrism results in two distinct problems in thinking that help to explain some of the seemingly odd beliefs and behaviors of teenagers (Goossens, Seiffge-Krenke, and Marcoen, 1992). The first, the **imaginary audience,** involves having such a heightened sense of self-consciousness that the teenager imagines that his or her behavior is the focus of everyone else's concern and attention. For example, a teenager who is going to a concert with 4,000 other people may worry about dressing the right way because "everybody will notice." Given the cognitive limitations of adolescent egocentrism, it is difficult indeed to persuade a young person that the "audience" is not all that concerned with his or her behavior or appearance.

A second related problem is called the **personal fable.** The personal fable revolves around the adolescent's egocentric (and erroneous) belief that his or her experiences are unique. For instance, a young man whose relationship with a girlfriend had just broken up might tell his sympathetic mother that she could not possibly understand what it feels like to break up with someone—even though breaking up is something that most people have experienced plenty of times during their adolescent and young adult years. Sometimes holding on to a personal fable can actually be quite dangerous, as in the case of a sexually active adolescent who believes that pregnancy simply won't happen to her or a careless driver who believes that he will defy the laws of nature by taking hairpin turns on a road at breakneck speed. Much of the risk-taking

Adolescent egocentrism can contribute to a heightened sense of self-consciousness. (Don Smetzer/Tony Stone)

behavior engaged in by adolescents can be explained partly in terms of the personal fable.

Although the concept of adolescent egocentrism rings true, several researchers have found it difficult to confirm that the various manifestations of adolescent egocentrism actually peak in early adolescence, as predicted (Gray and Hudson, 1984; Riley, Adams, and Neilsen, 1984). Instead, certain aspects of adolescent egocentrism, such as the personal fable and the imaginary audience, may remain present throughout the adolescent and adult years (Goossens et al., 1992; Quadrel, Fischoff, and Davis, 1993). Ask any *adult* cigarette smoker if he or she is aware of the scientific evidence linking cigarette smoking with heart and lung disease, and you'll see that it is quite common for adults to hold personal fables.

One problem with many of these studies of adolescent egocentrism is that they rely on fairly simple questionnaires to assess rather complicated belief systems invoked in real-life situations (Elkind, 1985). For example, it is easy to imagine that the same adolescent who worried about being seen by "everyone" at a rock concert might not appear so egocentric in his responses to a hypothetical dilemma posed in a questionnaire. This difference, of course, would raise doubts about whether adolescent egocentrism is an entirely cognitive phenomenon, since we would expect that cognitive deficiencies would show up in questionnaire assessments. It may be that Elkind is right about the increased prevalence of egocentrism during early adolescence but wrong about the processes that underlie it (Lapsley and Murphy, 1985). Indeed, one recent study found that adolescents' egocentrism was more closely tied to their interpersonal understanding than to their general cognitive ability (Jahnke and Blanchard-Fields, 1993). One guess is that adolescents are egocentric for emotional and social, not cognitive, reasons.

Thinking in Multiple Dimensions

A fourth way in which thinking changes during adolescence involves the ability to think about things in a multidimensional fashion. Whereas children tend to think about things one aspect at a time, adolescents can see things through more complicated lenses. For instance, when a certain hitter comes up to the plate in a baseball game, a preadolescent who knows that the hitter has a good home-run record might exclaim that the batter will hit the ball out of the park. An adolescent, however, would consider the hitter's record in relation to the specific pitcher on the mound and would weigh both factors, or dimensions, before making a prediction (perhaps this player hits homers against left-handed pitchers but strikes out against righties).

The ability to think in multidimensional terms is evident in a variety of different situations. Obviously, adolescents can give much more complicated answers than children to questions such as "Why did the Civil War begin?" or "How did Jane Austen's novels reflect the changing position of women in European society?" Thorough answers to these sorts of questions require thinking about several dimensions simultaneously.

But, as is the case with other gains in cognitive ability, the increasing capability of individuals to think in multiple dimensions has consequences for their behavior and thinking outside of academic settings, too. As you will read in a later section, adolescents describe themselves and others in more differentiated and complicated terms ("I'm both shy and extroverted") and find it easier to look at problems from multiple perspectives ("I know that's the way you see it, but try to look at it from her point of view"). Being able to understand that people's personalities are not one-sided, or that social situations can have different interpretations, depending on one's point of view, permits the adolescent to have far more sophisticated—and far more complicated—relationships with other people.

One interesting manifestation of adolescents' ability to look at things in multiple dimensions concerns the development of children's understanding of sarcasm. As an adult, you understand that the meaning of a speaker's statement is communicated by a combination of what is said, how it is said, and the context in which it is said. If I turned to you during a boring lecture, rolled my eyes, and said, in an exaggeratedly earnest tone, "This is the most interesting lecture I've ever heard," you would know that I actually meant just the opposite. But you only would know this if you paid attention to my inflection and to the context, as well as the content, of my statement. Only by attending simultaneously to multiple dimensions of speech can we distinguish between the sincere and the sarcastic. Because our ability to think in multidimensional terms improves during adolescence, we would predict improvements as well in our ability to understand when someone is being sarcastic.

In one study designed to look at this question, children, adolescents, and adults were presented with different stories, in which an interaction between two people was followed by a remark that was sincere, deliberately deceptive, or sarcastic (Demorest, Meyer, Phelps, Gardner, and Winner, 1984). The participants in the study were then asked what the true meaning and intent of the remark were. Before age 9, children had difficulty picking out sarcastic remarks. Individuals' understanding of sarcasm increased somewhat between 9 and 13, and it continued to increase during the adolescent years.

Adolescent Relativism

A final aspect of thinking during adolescence concerns the way in which adolescents look at things. Children tend to see things in absolute terms—in black and white. Adolescents, in contrast, tend to see things as relative. They are more likely to question others' assertions and less likely to accept "facts" as absolute truths.

This increase in relativism can be particularly exasperating to parents, who may feel as though their adolescent children question everything just for the sake of argument. Difficulties often arise, for example, when adolescents begin seeing parents' values that they had previously considered absolutely correct ("Moral people do not have sex before they are married") as completely relative ("Times change, Dad").

Adolescents' belief that everything is relative can become so overwhelming that they may begin to become extremely skeptical about many things (Chandler, 1987). In fact, once adolescents begin doubting the certainty of things that they had previously believed, they may come to feel as if everything is uncertain, or that no knowledge is completely reliable. Some theorists have suggested that adolescents pass through such a period of extreme skepticism on the way toward reaching a more sophisticated understanding of the complexity of knowledge.

RECAP

Changes in cognition, or thinking, are the second of three sets of fundamental changes that occur during adolescence. Adolescents show five main advantages in thinking over children: in thinking in terms of what is possible, not only what is real; in thinking about abstract things; in thinking about the process of thinking itself (referred to as metacognition); in thinking in multidimensional terms; and in seeing knowledge as relative, rather than as absolute.

THEORETICAL PERSPECTIVES ON ADOLESCENT THINKING

Although there is general agreement that adolescents' thinking is different and more advanced than children's in thc ways we have just described, there is far less consensus about the processes underlying the cognitive differences between children and adolescents. Part of the lack of agreement stems from the different points of view that theorists have taken toward the issue of cognitive development in general. Because researchers working from different theoretical perspectives have posed different research questions, used different tasks to measure cognitive growth, and emphasized some aspects of cognitive activity more than others, their studies provide different but theoretically compatible pictures of mental development during adolescence. The two theoretical viewpoints that have been especially important are the **Piagetian perspective** and the **information-processing perspective.** Although these two views of adolescent thinking begin from different assumptions about the nature of cognitive development in general, they each provide valuable insight into why thinking changes during adolescence.

The Piagetian View of Adolescent Thinking

Piaget's Theory of Cognitive Development. Generally, theorists who follow Piaget and take a **cognitive-developmental view** of intellectual development argue that cognitive development proceeds through a fixed sequence of qualitatively distinct stages, that adolescent thinking is fundamentally different from the type of thinking employed by children, and that during adolescence, individuals develop a special type of thinking that they use in a variety of situations.

According to Piaget, cognitive development proceeds through four stages: the **sensorimotor period** (from birth until about age 2), the **preoperational period** (from about age 2 until about age 5), the period of **concrete operations** (from about age 6 until early adolescence), and, finally, the period of **formal operations** (from adolescence through adulthood). These stages are presented in Table 2.1. Each stage is characterized by a particular type of thinking, with earlier stages of thinking being incorporated into new, more advanced, and more adaptive forms of reasoning. According to Piaget, transitions into higher stages of reasoning are most likely to occur at times when the child's biological readiness and the increasing complexity of environmental demands interact to bring about cognitive disequilibrium.

Given the emphasis that Piaget placed on the interaction between biological change and environmental stimulation in provoking intellectual growth, it comes as no surprise that early adolescence—a time of dramatic biological maturation and equally noteworthy changes in environmental demands—is viewed in Piagetian theory as an extremely important period in cognitive development.

Piaget believed that at the heart of formal-operational thinking was the use of an abstract system of **propositional logic**—a system based on theoretical, or formal, principles of logic (hence the term *formal* operations). Formal reasoning can be applied just as easily to hypothetical events as to real ones; is just as effective in dealing with abstract concepts as with concrete things; and is just as useful for thinking about alternatives to what really exists as it is for thinking about reality itself. Consider the significance of being able to understand the following example of propositional logic:

If A is true or B is true, then C is true.

This is a logical relationship that is encountered in all sorts of situations, ranging from scientific problem solving (for example, "If the solution turns blue or yellow, then it must contain the mineral copper") to understanding social relationships ("If Bob asks Susan out or if Judy calls me to do something this Friday night, then Bob and Judy must have broken up"). Once the *form* of the logic is understood—that *either* A or B is sufficient to demonstrate that C is true—it can be applied to all sorts of events (real as well as possible, concrete as well as abstract) merely by chang-

TABLE 2.1 THE FOUR STAGES OF COGNITIVE DEVELOPMENT ACCORDING TO PIAGET

Stage	Approximate Ages	Chief Characteristics
Sensorimotor	Birth–2 years	Discovery of relationships between sensation and motor behavior
Preoperational	2–7 years	Use of symbols to represent objects internally, especially through language
Concrete operations	7–11 years	Mastery of logic and development of "rational" thinking
Formal operations	11 years +	Development of abstract and hypothetical reasoning

ing what A, B, and C stand for. While concrete-operational thinkers are able to imagine alternative and hypothetical situations, they are unable to think about them in as systematic a way as formal-operational thinkers can.

Just because adolescents can employ propositional logic, however, does not mean that they are always consciously aware of doing so. In the example given above, for instance, we would hardly expect that an adolescent who is trying to figure out whether two friends are still "going steady" consciously runs through the As, Bs, and Cs of propositional logic. But you do not have to be aware of using propositional logic to use it effectively.

● ***The Growth of Formal-Operational Thinking.*** Piagetian theorists believe that the use of propositional logic—the foundation of formal-operational thinking—is the chief feature of adolescent thinking that differentiates it from the type of thinking employed by children. We noted before that adolescents' thinking can be distinguished from the thinking of children in several respects—among them, in thinking about possibilities, in thinking multidimensionally, and in thinking about abstract concepts. The connection between these types of thinking and the development of formal operations is clear: In order to think about alternatives to what really exists, in order to think in multidimensional terms, and in order to systematically think about concepts that are not directly observable, you must have a system of reasoning that works just as well in abstract, imagined, and complicated situations as it does in concrete ones. The system of propositional logic provides the basis for precisely this sort of reasoning.

The development of formal thinking appears to take place in two steps. During the first step, characteristic of early adolescence, formal thinking is apparent, but it has a sort of "now you see it, now you don't" quality to it. Young adolescents may demonstrate formal thinking at some times but at others may only be able to think in concrete terms; they may use formal operations on some tasks but not on others; they may reason formally under some but not all testing situations. Virtually all adolescents go through this period of "emergent formal operations" (Kuhn, Langer, Kohlberg, Haan, 1977). It is not until middle or even late adolescence that formal-operational thinking becomes consolidated and integrated into the individual's general approach to reasoning (Markovits and Valchon, 1990).

While virtually all adolescents have the potential to develop formal-operational thinking, and most can and do demonstrate it from time to time, not all adolescents (or, for that matter, all adults) employ formal-operational thinking regularly and in a variety of situations. One study suggests that adolescents who, as children, had more secure relationships with their parents are more likely to display formal thinking than their insecure peers, chiefly because the secure children were more self-confident (Jacobsen, Edelstein, and Hofmann, 1994). More important, the extent to which formal-operational thinking is displayed consistently depends a great deal on the conditions under which adolescents' reasoning is assessed. It is important, therefore, to differentiate between *competence* (i.e., what the adolescent is capable of doing) and *performance* (i.e., what the adolescent actually does in the assessment situation [Overton, 1990]).

The **competence-performance distinction** is nicely illustrated in a series of studies by Willis Overton and his colleagues (O'Brien and Overton, 1982; Overton, Ward, Noveck, Black, and O'Brien, 1987; Ward and Overton, 1990). The researchers find that adolescents' performance on sophisticated logical reasoning tasks varies as a function of both their underlying cognitive competence and the features of the task itself. Older adolescents have an easier time on reasoning tasks when the questions are personally relevant (e.g., questions about things that happen in schools) than when they are irrelevant (i.e., questions about things that happen to people when they retire from work), but younger adolescents have difficulty regardless of the relevance of the questions (see accompanying box). One interpretation of this is that having the underlying competence (as did the older, but not the younger, adolescents) is a necessary, but not sufficient, condition for performing well. Ultimate performance depends on contextual factors as well (Ward and Overton, 1990).

The Piagetian perspective on cognitive development during adolescence has stimulated a great deal of research on how young people think. Generally, the concept of formal operations as defined by Piaget and his followers appears to account for many of the changes in thinking observed during the adolescent years. Specifically, the theory of formal operations helps to explain why adolescents are better able than children to think about possibilities, to think multidimensionally, and to think about thoughts.

Where the Piagetian perspective on adolescent cognitive development appears to fall short is in its claim that cognitive development proceeds in a stagelike fashion and that the "stage" of formal operations is the stage of cognitive development characteristic of adolescence (Keating, 1990). Rather, research suggests that advanced reasoning capabilities (which may or may not be synonymous with what Piaget termed "formal operations") develop gradually and continuously from childhood through adolescence and beyond, probably in more of a quantitative fashion than was proposed by Piaget. Rather than talking about a "stage" of cognitive activity characteristic of adolescence, then, it appears to be more accurate to depict these advanced reasoning capabilities as skills that are employed by older children more often than by younger ones, by some adolescents more often than by other adolescents, and by individuals when they are in certain situations (especially, familiar situations) more often than when they are in other situations.

RECAP

Several theories have been proposed about the processes that underlie the development of more advanced thinking in adolescence. According to the Piagetian view, the development of more sophisticated thinking at adolescence results from the development of advanced logical abilities. Piaget believed that adolescence marked the transition into a qualitatively different way of reasoning—a stage of thinking based on "formal operations." In contrast to the concrete-operational child, the formal-operational adolescent is able to employ an abstract system of logic in a variety of social and scientific situations.

The Information-Processing View of Adolescent Thinking

During the past two decades, a different view of cognitive development during adolescence has emerged, partly in response to criticisms of the Piagetian perspective. Some scientists point out that the Piagetian approach has not been especially helpful in pinpointing exactly *what* it is that changes as individuals mature into and through adolescence. If we are left only with the conclusion that cognitive growth between childhood and adolescence reflects changes in "logical reasoning abilities," we have not moved a great deal closer to understanding which *specific* aspects of intellectual development during adolescence are the most important ones. Just what is it about the ways that adolescents think about things that makes

THE SCIENTIFIC STUDY OF ADOLESCENCE

SEPARATING COMPETENCE AND PERFORMANCE IN STUDIES OF ADOLESCENT REASONING

Experts agree that a complete understanding of the development of intellectual abilities in adolescence necessitates distinguishing between what adolescents *can* do and what they *do* do. This distinction, known as the competence-performance distinction, has been extensively investigated by Willis Overton and his colleagues in a series of studies of adolescent reasoning.

In these studies, adolescents are asked to solve a series of logical problems modeled after the *Wason selection task*. In the Wason selection task, individuals are presented with a series of logical problems similar to the following:

Running in school halls	Punished
Walking in school halls	Not punished

Each of the cards has information about a student attending school. On one side of the card is a student's behavior in school. On the other side of the card is whether or not the student has been punished for that behavior. Here is a rule: *If a student is caught running in the school halls, then the student must be punished.* Select the card or cards that you would definitely need to turn over to decide whether or not the rule is being broken.

Which card or cards would you need to turn over to decide if the rule is being broken? (The answer appears on the next page.)

Because some formal operational reasoning is needed to solve these problems, students' answers to a series of these problems can be scored for the presence and extent of formal reasoning. But how can the researchers disentangle students' formal reasoning *competence* from their formal reasoning *performance?* If a student does not solve the problem correctly, is that an indication of diminished competence or merely of diminished performance?

In one study (Ward and Overton, 1990) designed to examine this, the researchers presented adolescents with a mixture of problems that varied in their relevance to adolescents' lives. The most relevant problem concerned students' misbehavior in school; the least relevant problem concerned the situation of older individuals who had retired from work. The researchers hypothesized that having relevant problems to solve would improve adolescents' performance, but only among those adolescents who had the underlying competence to reason formally. In order to test this hypothesis, the problems were given to sixth-, ninth-, and twelfth-grade students. Presumably, if the hypothesis were correct, the relevance of the task would only affect the performance of the older students.

them better problem solvers than children? This question has been the focus of researchers working from a second theoretical vantage point: the information-processing perspective.

Information-processing researchers apply the same techniques to understanding human reasoning that computer scientists employ in writing programs. Suppose that you were asked to develop a computer program to solve

This is precisely what the researchers found, as you can see in the accompanying figure. Among the sixth-graders, only about 20 percent of the problems were solved correctly, regardless of whether the task was relevant. Among the ninth- and twelfth-graders, however, students were more than twice as successful when given relevant problems than when given less relevant ones. The researchers concluded from this study that the competence to reason deductively does not become available until early adolescence and that the relevance of the content of tasks used to assess logical reasoning is an important factor that influences adolescents' performance, once they have achieved the necessary level of competence.

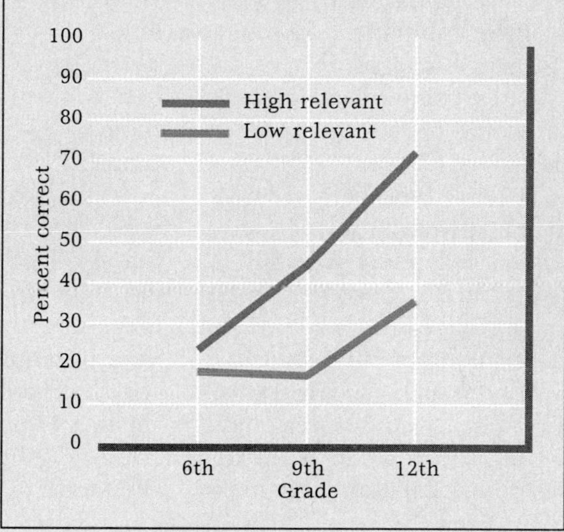

Percentage of correct solutions at each grade level for high- and low-relevant conditions. (Ward and Overton, 1990)

The fact that the relevance of the task had different effects at different grade levels is an example of what researchers call a **statistical interaction.** A statistical interaction is found when one factor (in this case, task relevance) affects some outcome variable (in this case, performance on the task) differently at different levels of another factor (in this case, grade level). If a researcher found that a certain teaching strategy affected boys' and girls' learning differently, that would be another example of a statistical interaction.

By the way, the correct solution to the problem is to turn over the first and fourth cards. Turning over both of these, but not the second and third ones, is necessary to determine whether the rule is being broken.

SOURCE: Ward, S., and Overton, W. (1990). Semantic familiarity, relevance, and the development of deductive reasoning. *Developmental Psychology, 26,* 488–493.

the poker-chip problem presented earlier in this chapter. A first step in the program might involve determining how many different-colored chips are contained in the set. But as you know if you have ever written a computer program, this first step is actually quite complicated when broken down into discrete tasks. It involves (1) taking the first chip and perceiving what color it is, (2) storing this information in memory, (3) considering the second chip and deciding what color it is, (4) storing this information in memory, (5) retrieving the color of the first chip from memory, (6) retrieving the color of the second chip from memory, (7) comparing these two bits of information, (8) determining whether the colors are the same or different, and (9) storing the results of the comparison in memory. And these nine steps take us only as far as comparing the first two chips. Imagine how involved a program would have to be in order to perform more complicated tasks!

Theorists like Robert Sternberg (1983), whose **componential approach** to the study of reasoning has been extremely influential, argue that it is possible to look at human intelligence in much the same way. When broken down into its component processes, human thinking involves such "subprograms" as paying attention to a stimulus, encoding information, retrieving information, comparing different pieces of information, and making decisions based on such comparisons. Obviously, deficiencies in any of these component functions will interfere with accurate problem solving. In the poker-chip problem, for example, perceiving the colors incorrectly will lead to mistakes in the solution. The ways in which component processes are combined also will affect the results. For example, if we try to compare the two chips' colors before storing the color of the first chip in memory, we will not be able to solve the problem.

Some arrangements of component processes are not only more accurate than others but also more efficient. Suppose you have successfully determined that the first two poker chips are, indeed, different in color. What is your next step? Do you compare the third chip with both the first and the second chips before moving on to the fourth chip, or do you compare the third with the first and then compare the fourth with the first?

Improvements in divided attention (left) and selective attention (right) abilities enable adolescents to tune out interference and focus on the task at hand. (Robert Brenner/PhotoEdit; Mary Kate Denny/PhotoEdit)

If you work this problem out, you will find that one approach is more efficient than the other.

● ***Changes in Information-Processing Abilities during Adolescence.*** Studies of changes in specific components of information processing have focused on five sets of gains that appear to occur during adolescence. Taken together, these gains help to explain why adolescents are better than children at abstract, multidimensional, and hypothetical thinking.

First, there are advances in individuals' ability to pay *attention.* Improvements are seen both in **selective attention,** in which adolescents must focus on one stimulus (such as a reading assignment) and tune out another (such as the electronic beeping of a younger brother's video game), and in **divided attention,** in which adolescents must pay attention to two sets of stimuli at the same time (such as studying while listening to music) (Higgins and Turnure, 1984; Schiff and Knopf, 1985). Improvements in attention mean that adolescents are better able than children to concentrate and stay focused on complicated tasks, such as reading and comprehending difficult material (Casteel, 1993).

Second, during adolescence our *memory* abilities improve. This is reflected both in **short-term memory** (being able to remember something for a brief period of time, such as 30 seconds) and in **long-term memory** (being able to recall something from a long time ago) (Keating, 1990). When we think of the importance of memory in problem solving, we typically think of having to retrieve facts that we deliberately have memorized—one aspect of long-term memory. For example, can you recall the name of the stage of thinking that precedes the stage of formal operations in Piaget's theory? (If not, refer to page 71.)

But short-term memory is extremely important in problem solving as well. For example, in order to solve multiple-choice questions

successfully, you need to be able to remember each alternative answer long enough to compare it with the other choices as you read them. Think for a moment of how frustrating it would be to solve a multiple-choice problem if, by the time you had read the final potential answer, you had forgotten the first one!

One illustration of how improvements in short-term memory might account for adolescents' advantages over children in problem solving comes from studies of individuals' solutions to problems involving analogies (Sternberg, 1977; Sternberg and Nigro, 1980; Sternberg and Rifkin, 1979). Through a series of experiments in which different types of analogies were presented to third-graders, sixth-graders, ninth-graders, and college students, Sternberg and his colleagues examined age differences in the use and organization of cognitive processes. The major difference between younger and older subjects concerned the incomplete nature of the younger ones' information processing. Although older and younger subjects appeared to use similar processes, the older ones employed them in a far more exhaustive fashion. For example, in determining the relation between pairs of terms, the third- and sixth-graders tended to curtail their information processing prematurely, before all possible relations had been considered.

The researchers attribute this premature termination to information overload in short-term memory. Because adolescents are able to hold more information in immediate memory than children can, they are more successful in the sorts of tasks (such as analogies) that require repeated comparisons between newly encoded information and information that has been stored previously. Running out of storage space before all necessary information has been encoded will result in information-processing errors.

A third component of information processing that may be closely related to the observed improvements in memory is an increase in the sheer *speed of information processing* (Hale, 1990; Kail, 1991a, 1991b). Regardless of the type of cognitive task employed, researchers find that older adolescents process the information necessary to solve the problem faster than early adolescents, who, in turn, process information faster than preadolescents. This fact would certainly help explain age differences in performance on timed tests (such as standardized achievement tests). Generally, the size of the improvement in the speed of information processing that occurs with age becomes smaller over the course of adolescence, so that the difference in speed between a 9-year-old and a 12-year-old is greater than that between a 12-year-old and a 15-year-old, which, in turn, is greater than that between a 15-year-old and an 18-year-old (Kail, 1991a). In fact, speed of processing does not appear to change very much between middle adolescence and young adulthood (Hale, 1990).

A fourth type of information-processing gain seen in adolescence involves improvements in individuals' *organizational strategies* (Siegler, 1988). Adolescents are more "plan-ful" than children—they are more likely to approach a problem with an appropriate information-processing strategy in mind. Psychologist Ann Brown (1975), for example, has suggested that the use of mnemonic devices and other organizational strategies helps to account for differences in the performance of older and younger children on tasks requiring memory and, moreover, that older children are better able to judge when the use of such strategies is likely to be helpful and when it is not. For instance, think for a moment about how you approach learning the information in a new textbook chapter. After years of studying, you are probably well aware of particular strategies that work well for you (underlining, highlighting, taking notes, writing in the margin of the textbook), and you begin a reading assignment with these strategies in mind.

Because children are not as "plan-ful" as adolescents, their learning is not as efficient.

Finally, individuals' *knowledge about their own thinking processes* improves during adolescence. We noted earlier that one of the most important gains to occur in adolescence is in the realm of metacognition—thinking about thinking. Adolescents are more likely than children to think about their own thoughts—a tendency, as we saw, that helps to explain their greater self-consciousness. But from an information-processing perspective, adolescents' heightened self-consciousness results from advances in basic metacognitive abilities. Self-consciousness may be more a cognitive than an emotional phenomenon: For the first time, the adolescent is capable of "thinking about thinking about thinking."

Of course, advances in metacognition are more a blessing than a curse. Because adolescents are better able to think about their own thoughts, they are much better at monitoring their own learning processes. For example, during the course of studying, adolescents are more able than children to step back from time to time and assess how well they are learning the material. Doing this enables them to pace their studying accordingly—to speed up and skim the material if they feel that they are learning it easily, or to slow down and repeat a section if they feel that they are having a hard time (e.g., Baker and Brown, 1984).

RECAP

Adolescent thinking also has been described from the information-processing perspective. According to this view, advances in thinking during adolescence result from quantitative increases in such skills as memory, attention, processing speed, organization, and metacognition. Information-processing theorists attempt to break down problem solving into its specific components in order to understand exactly what it is that develops as individuals mature intellectually.

New Directions for Theories about Adolescent Thinking

There is no doubt that many specific aspects of information processing improve during the adolescent years. What remains to be seen is whether and how understanding these specific cognitive gains can help account for the broader changes in thinking described at the beginning of this chapter—in abstraction, in hypothetical thinking, or in relativism, for example. To many theorists, the quantitative approach to thinking advocated by information-processing theorists leaves something out: the intuitive feeling that adolescents think in a way that is qualitatively different from children. Even if there is no evidence for a separate "stage" of thinking that is characteristic of adolescence, there may still be room for viewing adolescent thinking as different from—not simply more advanced than—that of children.

Several researchers have attempted to integrate findings on improvements in adolescents' information-processing abilities within a cognitive-developmental framework similar to Piaget's. One such theorist, the neo-Piagetian theorist Robbie Case (1985), for example, has argued, like Piaget, that cognitive development proceeds in discrete stages. Unlike Piaget, however, Case believes that the differences between stages can best be described not in terms of logical abilities but in terms of the cognitive components studied by information-processing theorists. For example, although Case, like information-processing theorists, believes that improvements in working memory or information-processing efficiency help explain gains in intellectual performance, he believes that these improvements occur in a stage-like fashion (Marini and Case, 1994). Moreover, Case has theorized that transitions from one stage to another are closely linked to physical changes in the brain.

With regard to adolescence, Case has argued that the gains in attention, memory, metacognition, and organization that are enjoyed during the adolescent years permit the individual to think in a more "automatic" way. For instance, think about how automatically you drive a car now in contrast to when you were first learning how. This **automatization** of thinking frees up cognitive resources for the adolescent that enables her or him to approach problems in a structurally more sophisticated way. In other words, as basic elements of information processing become more automatic—second nature, we might say—the adolescent is better able to devote conscious cognitive processes to more complicated tasks.

A different perspective has been suggested by Andreas Demetriou and his colleagues (Demetriou, Efklides, Papadaki, Papantoniou, and Economou, 1993). This view also integrates elements from both Piagetian and information-processing theories, but unlike Case's theory, Demetriou's is more similar to information-processing than to Piagetian approaches. According to this model, we can think of intellectual functioning as being organized around a series of very specialized cognitive structures, called **specialized structural systems,** that we draw on to solve different types of intellectual problems. (For example, these researchers distinguish among analytic thinking, experimental thinking, spatial thinking, and so forth.) Although a basic set of information-processing tools (such as memory or attention) are used in all these different structures (e.g., memory is used for solving analytic as well as verbal problems), and although there is an executive control system that coordinates activities across structures, the structures themselves develop at different rates and during different periods of childhood and adolescence. (As you will read on pages 82 and 83, this idea shares much in common with a theory of "multiple intelligences" proposed by psychologist Howard Gardner.) Although Demetriou suggests that there may be stages in the development of each structure, considered separately, he does not believe, as does Case, that there are overarching stages of intellectual development that cut across domains.

RECAP

Several recent theorists, such as Case and Demetriou, have attempted to integrate elements from Piagetian and information-processing approaches to adolescent cognitive development. These theorists suggest that changes in cognition in adolescence may be both stage-like *and* quantitative.

INDIVIDUAL DIFFERENCES IN INTELLIGENCE IN ADOLESCENCE

For the most part, theorists who have studied adolescent cognitive development from a Piagetian or information-processing framework have focused on the *universals* in adolescent intellectual growth. How does thinking change as individuals move into adolescence? What processes drive cognitive development as children become teenagers? What cognitive competencies do *all* adolescents share in common?

In contrast, other theorists have been more interested in studying individual differences in intellectual abilities. How can we account for different patterns of intellectual growth *within* the adolescent population? How large are individual differences in intelligence in adolescence? Are some adolescents "brighter" than others? If so, why, and in what ways?

● ***The Measurement of IQ.*** In order to answer questions about the relative intelligence of individuals, psychologists have had to devise ways of assessing intelligence, which has been no easy feat, since there is considerable disagreement over what "intelligence" really is. Today, the most widely used measures are intelligence tests, or IQ (for "intelligence quotient") tests. A variety of such tests exists, including the Stanford-Binet, the Wechsler Intelligence Scale for Children (WISC-R), and the Wechsler Adult Intelligence Scale (WAIS-R).

The IQ test is one of the most widely used—and most widely misused—psychological instruments ever developed. Initially developed by the French psychologist Alfred Binet in 1905, the first intelligence test was devised in response to the French government's interest in better predicting which children would profit from formal schooling. Thus although Binet's test—and the many others that would be developed over the years—was

Standardized intelligence tests, or IQ tests, are often used to study individual differences in cognitive abilities during adolescence. Critics of such tests argue that they measure just one type of intelligence—"school smarts"—and neglect other equally important skills, such as social intelligence, creativity, and "street smarts". (Arthur Grace/Stock, Boston)

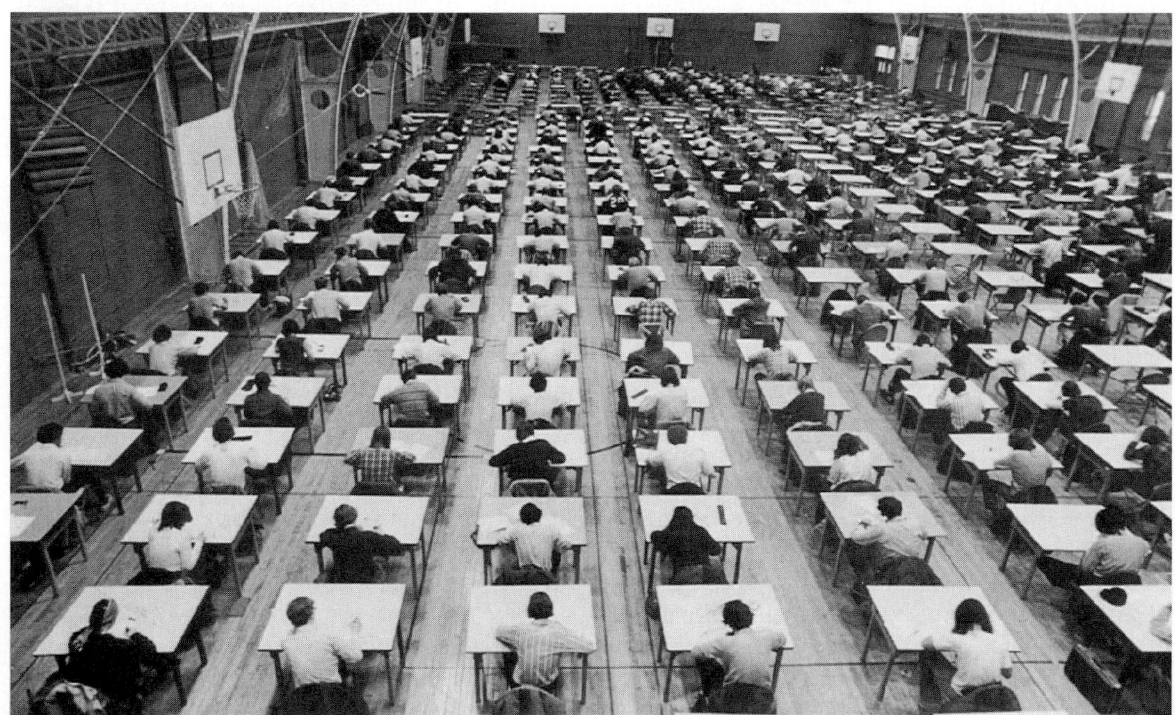

designed to yield a measure of "intelligence," the test was devised with a very specific type of intelligence in mind: the type of intelligence it takes to succeed in formal educational institutions. Even the best IQ tests used today measure only a very specific type of intelligence.

An individual's performance on an IQ test is usually presented not as a raw score but as a relative score in comparison to the scores of other individuals of the same age and from approximately the same **cohort** (a cohort is a group of people born during the same historical era). Comparison scores are collected every so often, so that the comparison group for individuals taking the test at any given time is valid, representative, and up to date. The score of 100 is used to designate the midway point: An IQ score below 100 indicates a poorer test performance than half of the comparison group; a score above 100 indicates a better performance than half the comparison group. In other words, the higher an individual's IQ, the smaller the number of agemates who perform equally or better on the same test.

Although an individual's score on an intelligence test is often reported in terms of his or her overall IQ, intelligence tests actually comprise a series of tests, and it is usually possible to look at performance in different areas independently. The WISC-R and the WAIS-R, for example, each contain two groups of tests: *verbal* tests, which include measures of vocabulary, general information, comprehension, and arithmetic abilities; and *performance* tests, which include block design, mazes, picture completion, and picture arrangement.

The IQ test represents only one of many ways of assessing intelligence in adolescence. Indeed, many theorists have argued that its exclusive focus on "school smarts"—the sorts of abilities that are related to scholastic success—yields a one-sided picture of what it means to be an intelligent person. Two of the more recent attempts to expand on this narrow definition come from the work of Robert Sternberg (1988) and Howard Gardner (1983).

● ***Sternberg's "Triarchic" Theory.*** Sternberg has proposed a **triarchic theory of intelligence.** He has argued that a thorough assessment of an individual's intellectual capabilities requires that we look at three distinct but interrelated types of intelligence: *componential intelligence,* which involves our abilities to acquire, store, and process information (as described in the previous section about information processing); *experiential intelligence,* which involves our abilities to use insight and creativity; and *contextual intelligence,* which involves our ability to think practically. Componential intelligence is closest to the type of intelligence measured on traditional intelligence tests. Experiential intelligence is closest to what we call creativity. Contextual intelligence is closest to what we might call "street smarts." All individuals have all three types of intelligence, but some individuals are stronger in one respect than in others. You probably can think of individuals who are good test takers but who are not particularly creative or sensible. According to Sternberg's model, these individuals would be high in componential intelligence but low in experiential and contextual intelligence.

More important, Sternberg's view forces us to look at individuals who are not good test takers, but who are creative or street smart, as being equally intelligent as individuals who score high on IQ tests—but intelligent in a different way. He argues that society needs individuals with all types of intelligence and that it is time we started assessing—and encouraging—experiential and contextual intelligence as much as we do componential intelligence.

● ***Gardner's Theory of "Multiple Intelligences."*** Howard Gardner's **theory of multiple intelligences** also stresses that there is more to being smart than being "book smart." He has proposed that there are seven types of intelligence: verbal, mathematical, spatial, kinesthetic (movement), self-reflective, interpersonal, and musical. According to his view, for example, outstanding athletes such as the basketball star Michael Jordan have a well-developed kinesthetic intelligence, which allows them to control their bodies and process the movements of others in extraordinarily capable ways. Although conventional tests of intelligence emphasize verbal and mathematical abilities, these are not the only types of intelligence that we possess—nor are they the only types that we should value.

● ***Culture and Intelligence.*** The problem of defining intelligence adequately is perhaps no more readily apparent than when issues of ethnic or racial differences in intelligence are raised. In general, studies find that within the United States, African-American and Hispanic-American youngsters typically score lower on standard IQ tests than do their white peers (Anastasi, 1988). But how are we to interpret this finding? Does this mean that minority youngsters are less "intelligent" than white youth? Or does it mean that the tests we use to assess intelligence are unfairly biased against minority children?

In recent years, experts have leaned toward the latter explanation. They point out that IQ tests, which were initially developed and standardized on populations of individuals of European descent, are loaded with questions that reflect the experiences and values of middle-class whites. These critics suggest that whites would do similarly poorly on intelligence tests designed by and for ethnic minority individuals (Miller-Jones, 1989). In addition, language differences between minority and nonminority youth (especially if English is not the minority youngster's first language) may lead to apparent differences in intelligence when the testing is performed in English.

These criticisms have lead to calls for **culture-fair tests**—intelligence tests that attempt to reduce sources of ethnic or cultural bias. Such tests tend to be based less on verbal skills (thus avoiding the language problems of many tests) and more oriented toward the sorts of items included on the performance scales of traditional IQ tests.

Even with the advent of culture-fair testing, the notion that there is such a "thing" as intelligence and that this "thing" is the same in all cultural and ethnic groups is difficult for many experts to swallow. The skills that contribute to intelligent behavior in a nonindustrialized farming and hunting community, or on the streets of an inner-city community, are likely very different from those that contribute to intelligence in a high school science class. Yet it is clear that the standard tests used in assessing intelligence place nearly exclusive emphasis on the intellectual skills that are chiefly helpful in educational settings. It is essential for practitioners to keep in mind that any assessment of a youngster's intelligence must take into account the nature and purpose of the test used, the circumstances of the assessment, and the background of the individual child.

● ***Intelligence Test Performance in Adolescence.*** Although ideas about the existence of different forms of intelligence have become popular in the last decade, most research in the psychometric tradition has employed traditional IQ tests to investigate the nature of intelligence during adolescence. Assessments based on IQ tests have been used to examine two seemingly similar but actually very different questions. First, how *stable* are IQ scores during adolescence? Second, do the sorts of mental abilities that are assessed via intelligence tests *improve* during adolescence?

It is easy to confuse these questions. At first glance, they seem to be asking the same thing. But consider this: Individuals' IQ scores remain remarkably stable during the adolescent years; yet, during the same time period, their mental abilities improve dramatically. Although this might seem contradictory, it is not. Studies of stability examine changes in individuals' *relative* standing over time, whereas studies of change examine changes in individuals' *absolute* scores.

Take height, for example. Children who are taller than their peers during middle childhood are likely to be taller than their peers during adulthood as well; children who are about average in height remain so throughout childhood and adulthood; and children who are shorter than their peers at one point in time are likely to be shorter than their peers later on. Height, therefore, is a very stable trait. But this does not mean that individuals don't grow between childhood and adolescence.

Like height, scores on intelligence tests are characterized by high stability and a good deal of change during childhood and adolescence. To the first question posed above—How stable are IQ scores during adolescence?—the answer, then, is very stable. Consider the pattern of correlations between an individual's intelligence test scores at various points during childhood and his or her score at age 18 (see Figure 2.1).

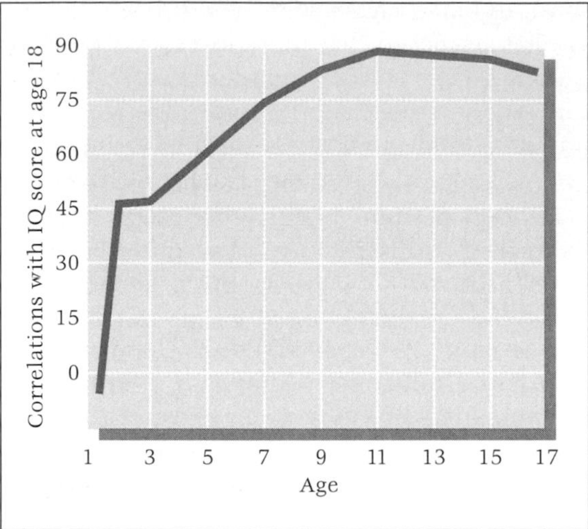

FIGURE 2.1 *Average correlations between individuals' intelligence test scores at various ages from 1 to 17 and their scores at age 18. By age 11, the correlation is over .90.* (Adapted from Bayley, 1949)

As you can see, from about age 1 to about age 5, intelligence test scores are not highly correlated with scores at age 18. Between ages 5 and 11, scores are moderately correlated with scores at age 18. From early adolescence on, however, scores are very highly correlated with scores at age 18. The pattern of correlations, then, indicates that intelligence test scores become increasingly stable during childhood and are remarkably stable during adolescence. To put it more concretely, youngsters who score higher than their peers on intelligence tests during early adolescence are likely to score higher throughout the adolescent years.

A 10-year-old boy whose score is average for his age would have an IQ of about 100. If his score were stable—that is, if he remained about average in comparison with his peers—his score would remain at about 100. Even if he became more intelligent over time, as any normal child would, his IQ score probably would not change very much, because the score would always reflect his performance *relative* to his peers. If his abilities increased at the same rate as his agemates', his relative standing would not change. In other words, when an individual's IQ scores are fairly stable, a graph of those scores over a period of time produces a relatively straight horizontal line.

For most individuals, this is indeed what happens. But some studies suggest that not everyone follows this pattern of high stability (McCall, Applebaum, and Hogarty, 1973; Moffitt, Caspi, Harkness, and Silva, 1993). After graphing many individuals' IQ scores during childhood and adolescence, one group of researchers was able to identify five different patterns—some very stable but others very unstable (McCall et al., 1973). Their findings are shown in Figure 2.2. As expected, most individuals fell into cluster number 1; that is, their scores were extremely stable over the 17-year period. But many youngsters' scores fluctuated considerably. In other words, although *most* adolescents' IQ scores remain stable throughout adolescence, not all do.

A recent study by Terrie Moffitt and her colleagues (Moffitt et al., 1993) indicates, however, that although some individuals show fluctuation in IQ scores between childhood and adolescence, ultimately most individuals end up with IQ scores as adolescents that are not very different from their scores as children. In this study, for example, the average amount of change over a seven-year period (from age 7 to age 13) among the individuals whose scores fluctuated at all was only 5 IQ points, which is not a change of much practical significance.

FIGURE 2.2 *For some individuals, IQ scores fluctuate very little during childhood and adolescence. But for others, variations of 20 or 30 points occur. Here are five common patterns of change in IQ scores during childhood and adolescence.* (Adapted from McCall et al., 1973)

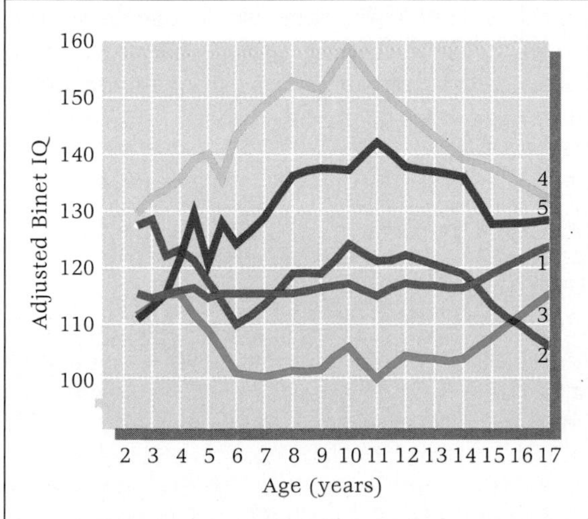

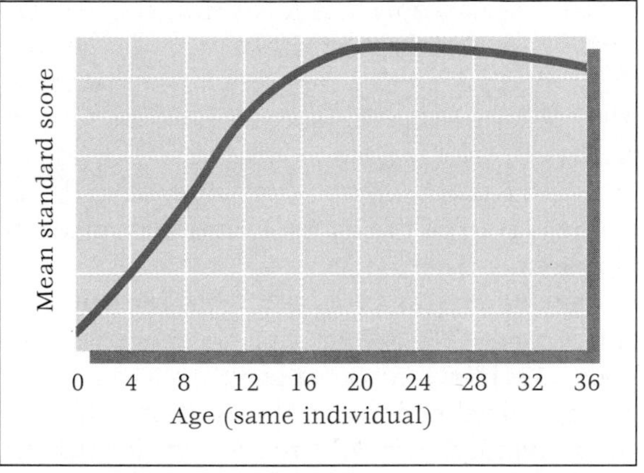

FIGURE 2.3 *The growth of mental abilities from birth to age 36.* (Adapted from Bayley, 1949)

In absolute terms, however, do mental abilities increase during adolescence? Figure 2.3 shows the growth of mental abilities as assessed by standardized tests. As you can see, abilities assessed by conventional IQ tests increase dramatically through childhood and adolescence, reaching a plateau sometime during early adulthood. Thus, despite the fact that IQ scores remain stable during adolescence, individuals do become smarter as they get older—a fact that argues strongly in favor of educational interventions designed to stimulate intellectual development during adolescence. In fact, at least one study shows that extended schooling enhances individuals' performance on standardized tests of intelligence (Shavit and Featherman, 1988). Whereas individuals who had dropped out of school early showed unchanging—and relatively lower—scores on intelligence tests during adolescence, students who remained in school, especially those in the more advanced tracks, showed impressive gains in verbal ability over time.

THE SEXES

ARE THERE DIFFERENCES IN MENTAL ABILITIES AT ADOLESCENCE (ANYMORE)?

For many years, social scientists had asserted that there were sex differences in mental abilities and that these differences emerge for the first time during adolescence (Maccoby and Jacklin, 1974). Although adolescent males and females did not show *overall* differences in IQ scores, studies showed that females enjoyed a small advantage in tests of verbal ability, whereas males had a small advantage in tests of spatial ability and, to a lesser extent, mathematics. What was especially interesting about the pattern, however, was that boys' and girls' scores on math and verbal tests were comparable before puberty.

Experts offered a number of explanations for this pattern of sex differences and, in particular, for their emergence in early adolescence. One explanation concerned the hormonal changes of puberty. As noted in Chapter 1, levels of androgens and estrogens change at puberty in different degrees for males and females. Because individuals with higher androgen levels score better on tests of spatial ability—this is true whether they are male or female—it has been argued that the male advantage in tests of spatial ability at adolescence may result from the higher level of androgens (Petersen and Taylor, 1980).

A second explanation focused on the fact that girls are more likely, on average, to mature earlier than boys. Researchers speculated that the development of certain brain functions was altered by the onset of puberty and, specifically, that the onset of puberty curtailed some developments in the structure of the brain that are related to spatial ability. Since girls mature earlier than boys, it was reasoned that their development of spatial abilities may be curtailed earlier (Waber, 1977). If this theory were true, however, one would expect that early maturers in general—whether male or female—would show worse spatial abilities than later maturers. But this turns out not to be the case, casting doubt on the idea that females' earlier maturation is the reason for their poorer performance on tests of spatial intelligence (Newcombe and Dubas, 1987).

A third account—that sex differences in mental abilities are social, not biological, in origin—actually has received the most support. The argument here is that boys and girls are rewarded for different interests and for showing different abilities. During elementary school, boys and girls take the same courses and would therefore be expected to show similar intellectual strengths and weaknesses. But once young people begin taking elective courses, males and females may be led down different educational paths by their guidance counselors, parents, and friends (Klebanov and Brooks-Gunn, 1992). Males, for example, are more likely to be encouraged to pursue advanced courses in math and science, whereas females are more likely to be steered away from these classes (Fennema and Sherman, 1977). Consistent with this explanation, one study found that differences in individuals' mathematical abilities are more closely related to their attitudes toward math and to prior knowledge of the content area (which reflects achievement, not ability) than to their gender (Byrnes and Takahira, 1993; Paulsen and Johnson, 1983). If, beginning in adolescence, girls are told, implicitly or explicitly, that math is not interesting, their performance in this area may decline.

Perhaps the clearest support for the idea that sex differences in mental abilities are socialized rather than biologically determined comes from several very recent examinations of males' and females' test scores. According to Carol Jacklin, who in 1974 had coauthored the initial study documenting reliable sex differences in mental abilities, by the end of the 1980s many of the differences in males' and females' performance either had vanished or diminished substantially (Jacklin, 1989). This is true with regard to both verbal and math abilities and to performance on various scales of achievement and intelligence tests (Feingold, 1993; Hyde and Linn, 1988; Marsh, 1989a). The fact that these more recent contrasts of males' and females' scores have shown much smaller sex differences than were found in earlier studies suggests to many experts that changes in sex roles and educational opportunities that have taken place in recent decades are now beginning to be reflected on measures such as the SAT (Feingold, 1988). Between 1987 and 1994, for example, the gender gap in math SAT scores declined by 20 percent.

Recent studies of sex differences in mental abilities have shown that the old gender gap in math abilities, favoring boys, has disappeared. Male and female adolescents also score equally well in tests of verbal ability. (Jean-Claude Lejeune)

It appears now that the only reliable sex difference in mental abilities during adolescence is in the area of spatial ability, but new research indicates that this is not a uniquely adolescent phenomenon. The male advantage on tests of spatial performance emerges before age 10 and is more or less constant during the adolescent years (Johnson and Meade, 1987). For reasons that predate adolescence, then—reasons that may be biological, social, or, most likely, both—boys score slightly higher than girls on tests measuring spatial intelligence. Even this difference is quite modest, however. And who knows? Five years from now, sex differences in spatial abilities may have gone the way of sex differences in math and verbal abilities.

● ***The Scholastic Aptitude Test.*** Another widely used—and equally controversial—measure of aptitude in adolescence is the Scholastic Aptitude Test, or SAT. (An **aptitude test** is designed to predict a student's future performance, not the student's current level of achievement.) Thus, the SAT was designed not to measure an adolescent's present level of accomplishment but to predict his or her likelihood of success in college. Like the IQ test, therefore, the SAT is a measure of "school smarts" (or, in Sternberg's framework, a measure of componential intelligence), and scores on this test should be so viewed. The SAT does not measure such important characteristics as insight, creativity, or practical intelligence.

Given that the SAT was created in order to predict high school students' college success, it is only fair that it be evaluated in this light. How well does the SAT predict success in college courses? The answer is, "well, but not perfectly." Knowing an individual's SAT scores helps to foretell how well he or she will do in college, but SAT scores are only one of many useful predictive factors. Because of this, most college admissions committees rely on many additional pieces of information about an applicant's academic record, including the difficulty of the student's high school curriculum and the student's class rank (Moll, 1986).

Interestingly, one recent study reported that scores on the mathematics section of the SAT may be a more valid predictor of college math grades for males than for females (Wainer and Steinberg, 1992). In this study, the researchers began with a sample of 47,000 college men and women who were then matched on their performance in college math classes (and on the difficulty of the math classes they took). If the SAT is an equally valid predictor of achievement for males and females, the researchers reasoned, then males and females who earn comparable grades in math classes should have had comparable SAT scores as high school students. This was not the case, however. Among college students earning As in math classes, for example, the men had scored 36 points higher on the mathematics subsection of the SAT than had the women. A college admissions committee who rejected a woman in favor of a man on the basis of their SAT mathematics scores would be making an ill-informed decision.

RECAP

Some researchers have focused on the measurement and assessment of individual differences in mental abilities during adolescence—in particular, differences in intelligence. In recent years, several theorists, like Sternberg and Gardner, have proposed alternatives to the view that intelligence can be adequately captured on standardized tests, arguing that true intelligence is defined by skills in addition to those assessed in tests of "school smarts," such as the IQ test or the SAT. Many critics have called for intelligence tests that are more "culture-fair."

ADOLESCENT THINKING IN CONTEXT

As our understanding of adolescent thinking has expanded, researchers have begun to look beyond laboratory experiments and standardized tests in an effort to examine how the cognitive changes of adolescence actually affect teenagers' day-to-day thoughts and actions. Do advances in propositional logic or information-processing abilities make a difference in the real world? In order to look at this issue, psychologists and educators have studied the practical side of adolescent thinking in three domains: in social situations, in risk-taking, and in the classroom.

Changes in Social Cognition

Many of the examples of adolescent thinking that we have looked at in this chapter have involved reasoning about scientific problems or physical objects. But the same sorts of gains in intellectual abilities that are observed in young people's thinking in these realms are apparent in their reasoning about social phenomena as well. **Social cognition** involves such cognitive activities as thinking about people, thinking about social relationships, and thinking about social institutions (Lapsley, 1989).

It is not difficult to imagine that adolescents' advanced abilities in thinking about possibilities, thinking in multiple dimensions, and thinking about abstract concepts make them more sophisticated when it comes to reasoning about social matters. Compared with those of children, adolescents' conceptions of interpersonal relationships are more mature, their understanding of human behavior is more advanced, their ideas about social institutions and organizations are more complex, and their ability to figure out what other people think is far more accurate. As we shall see in subsequent chapters, gains in the area of social cognition help to account for many of the psychosocial advances typically associated with adolescence—advances in the realms of identity, autonomy, intimacy, sexuality, and achievement.

Studies of social cognition during adolescence typically fall into three categories: studies of *impression formation,* which examine how individuals form and organize judgments about other people; studies of *social perspective taking,* which examine how, and how accurately, individuals make assessments about the thoughts and feelings of others; and studies of *morality and social conventions,* which examine individuals' conceptions of justice, social norms, and guidelines for social interaction.

Impression Formation. During preadolescence and adolescence, individuals' impressions of other people develop in five main directions (Hill and Palmquist, 1978). First, impressions become progressively more *differentiated.* Adolescents are more likely than children to describe people—themselves as well as others—in more narrowly defined categories and with more differentiated attributes. Whereas children tend to use fairly global descriptors, such as gender and age, adolescents are more likely to describe people in terms of such things as interests and personality characteristics. A second trend in the development of impression formation is toward *less egocentric* impressions. By this we mean that adolescents are more likely to be aware that their impressions of others are personal viewpoints and therefore are subject to disagreement. Third, impressions of other people become *more abstract;* that is, they become less rooted in such concrete attributes as physical characteristics or personal possessions and more tied to such abstract things as attitudes and motives. Fourth, individuals come to make *greater use of inference* in their impressions of others. Compared with children, adolescents are more likely to interpret the feelings of others and to infer the motives, beliefs, and feelings of others, even when specific information of this sort is not directly observable. Finally, adolescents' impressions of others are *more highly organized.* Adolescents are more likely than children, for example, to make judgments of others that link personality traits to the situations in which they are likely to be expressed ("She's impatient when she works with other people") and to reconcile apparently discrepant information about people into a more complex impression ("He's friendly toward girls but not at all friendly toward boys.")

Taken together, these gains in impression formation mark the beginning of the development of an **implicit personality theory**—a theory of why people are the way they are (Barenboim, 1981). As we shall see in Chapter 10, the development of this implicit personality theory has important implications for the development of intimate relationships.

● ***Social Perspective Taking.*** Related to these gains in impression-formation abilities are considerable improvements in the adolescent's **social perspective taking**—the ability to view events from the perspective of others. According to Robert Selman (1980), who has studied this development extensively, children become better able as they grow older to step back from their own point of view and to see that others may view an event from a different, but equally valid, perspective. Not only are adolescents more capable of discerning another person's perspective on some issue or event, but they are also better able to understand that person's perspective on their own point of view.

According to Selman, the development of social perspective taking progresses through a series of stages. During the preadolescent stage in the development of perspective taking, youngsters can put themselves in others' shoes but do not yet see how the thoughts and feelings of one person may be related to the thoughts and feelings of another. During early adolescence, with the progression into what Selman calls **mutual role taking,** the young adolescent can be an objective third party and can see how the thoughts or actions of one person can influence those of another. In thinking about two friends, for instance, an adolescent at this level would be able to look at the friends' relationship and see how each person's behavior affects the other's.

Later in adolescence, perspective taking develops an in-depth, societal orientation. The adolescent at this level understands that the perspectives which people have on each other

Advances in social cognition enhance adolescents' ability to reason with others. These teenagers are attempting to prevent their friend from getting into a fight. (Bob Daemmrich/Tony Stone)

are complicated, are often unconscious, and are influenced by larger forces than individuals can control—including each person's position in society or within a social institution. For example, you are able to understand that your perspective on the instructor teaching your class is influenced not only by your own personality and by the instructor's but also by forces inherent in the way the relationship of professor and student is defined.

Ultimately, an adolescent's gains in social perspective-taking abilities lead to improvements in communication, as he or she becomes more capable of formulating arguments in terms that are more likely to be understood by someone whose opinion is different. One study (Clark and Delia, 1976), for example, looked at how well youngsters of different ages were able to persuade other people to do something for them—such as convincing their parents to buy them a new stereo, for instance. The researchers found that adolescents were more likely to use reasoning that pointed out advantages to their parents ("If I have my own stereo in my room, you won't be bothered by my music.") than to use reasoning that simply stated the case from their own point of view ("I really need to have my own stereo. All the other kids do."). A major shift in reasoning took place during early adolescence, coinciding with the transition into the stage of "mutual" role taking. Although one might think that parents might find it more difficult to deal with a teenager who is more persuasive, studies suggest that when adolescents are able to take their parents' perspective in an argument, family communication becomes more effective and more satisfying (Silverberg, 1986).

● ***Conceptions of Morality and Social Convention.*** The realization that individuals' perspectives vary, and that their opinions may differ as a result, leads to changes in the ways that issues regarding morality and social convention are approached. Changes in moral reasoning during adolescence have been investigated extensively, and we examine this body of research in detail in Chapter 9. Briefly, during childhood, moral guidelines are seen as absolutes emanating from such authorities as parents or teachers; judgments of right and wrong are made according to concrete rules. During adolescence, however, such absolutes and rules come to be questioned, as the young person begins to see that moral standards are subjective and are based on points of view that are subject to disagreement. Later in adolescence comes the emergence of reasoning that is based on such moral principles as equality, justice, or fairness—abstract guidelines that transcend concrete situations and can be applied across a variety of moral dilemmas (Kohlberg, 1976).

The development of individuals' understanding of **social conventions**—the social norms that guide day-to-day behavior—follows a similar course (Turiel, 1978). During middle childhood, social conventions—such as waiting in line to buy movie tickets—are seen as arbitrary and changeable, but adherence to them is not; compliance with such conventions is based on rules and on the dictates of authority. When you were 7 years old, you might not have seen why people had to wait in line to buy movie tickets, but when your mother or father told you to wait in line, you waited. By early adolescence, however, conventions are seen as arbitrary and changeable in both their origins and their enforcement; conventions are merely social expectations. As an adolescent, you begin to realize that people wait in line because they are expected to, not because they are forced to. Indeed, young adolescents often see social conventions as *nothing but* social expectations and, consequently, as insufficient reasons for compliance. You can probably imagine youngsters in their midteens saying something like this: "Why wait in a ticket line simply because other people are lined up? There isn't a *law* that forces you to wait in line, is there?"

Gradually, however, adolescents begin to see social conventions as means used by society to regulate people's behavior. Conventions may be arbitrary, but we follow them because we all share an understanding of how people are expected to behave in various situations. In fact, high schoolers see conventions as so ingrained in the social system that individuals follow them partly out of habit. We wait in line for theater tickets not because we want to comply with any "rule" but because it is something we are accustomed to doing.

Ultimately, individuals come to see that social conventions serve a function in coordinating interactions among people. Social norms and expectations are derived from and maintained by individuals' having a common perspective and agreeing that, in given situations, certain behaviors are more desirable than others, because such behaviors help society and its institutions to function more smoothly. Without the convention of waiting in line to buy movie tickets, the pushiest people would always get tickets first. The older adolescent can see that waiting in line not only benefits the theater but also preserves everyone's right to a fair chance to buy tickets. In other words, we wait in line patiently because we all agree that it is better if tickets are distributed fairly.

Table 2.2 summarizes some of the important differences in social cognitive abilities between preadolescents and adolescents. As you can see, across all four domains, thinking becomes more abstract, more hypothetical, and more relativistic between childhood and adolescence.

Taken together, these gains in social cognitive abilities help to account for gains in individuals' social competence during adolescence. As you will read in Chapter 10, adolescents who have more sophisticated social cognitive abilities (i.e., more advanced perspective-taking abilities and more sophisticated impression-formation skills) actually behave in more socially competent ways

TABLE 2.2 DIFFERENCES BETWEEN PREADOLESCENT AND ADOLESCENT THINKING IN FOUR SOCIAL COGNITIVE DOMAINS

Domain	Preadolescent Thought	Adolescent Thought
Impressions of others (*e.g., Barenboim)*	Impressions are global, egocentric, concrete, disorganized, and haphazard	Impressions are differentiated, objective, abstract, and organized into coherent whole
Role taking *(e.g., Selman)*	Child is able to put self in other's shoes but has difficulty seeing how one person's perspective affects another's	Adolescent is able to take "third-party" perspective (mutual) and to see the bigger, societal picture
Moral reasoning *(e.g., Kohlberg)*	Morals are based on concrete rules handed down by authorities	Morals come out of agreements between people or out of abstract principles
Social conventions *(e.g., Turiel)*	Conventions are based on the rules and dictates of authorities	Conventions are based on expectations or grow out of social norms

(Ford, 1982). Although there is more to social competence than social cognition, being able to understand social relationships in a more advanced way is an important component of being able to behave in a more advanced way.

RECAP

The cognitive developments of adolescence are reflected in young people's behavior in real-world situations as well as in laboratory experiments. One area of inquiry that has received a good deal of attention is the development of social cognition. Studies show that thinking about social relationships and social institutions—like thinking in general—becomes more abstract, more multidimensional, and more relativistic throughout the adolescent period.

Adolescent Risk-Taking

A second practical application of research into adolescent thinking involves the study of adolescent risk-taking. In Chapter 1, we noted that many of the health problems of the adolescent period are the result of behaviors that can be prevented—behaviors such as substance abuse, reckless driving, or unprotected sex. One recent study of young adolescents in San Francisco found that nearly 80 percent of boys and 60 percent of girls take unnecessary risks while skateboarding or riding bikes; that more than one-third of both sexes have been passengers in cars driven by intoxicated drivers; that two-thirds of sixth-graders have experimented with alcohol, and half have smoked cigarettes; and that one-fifth of seventh-graders were sexually active (with less than half using contraception) (Millstein, Irwin, Adler, Cohn, Kegeles, and Dolcini, 1992). Nor is risk-taking prevalent only among American youth: A recent study of Danish

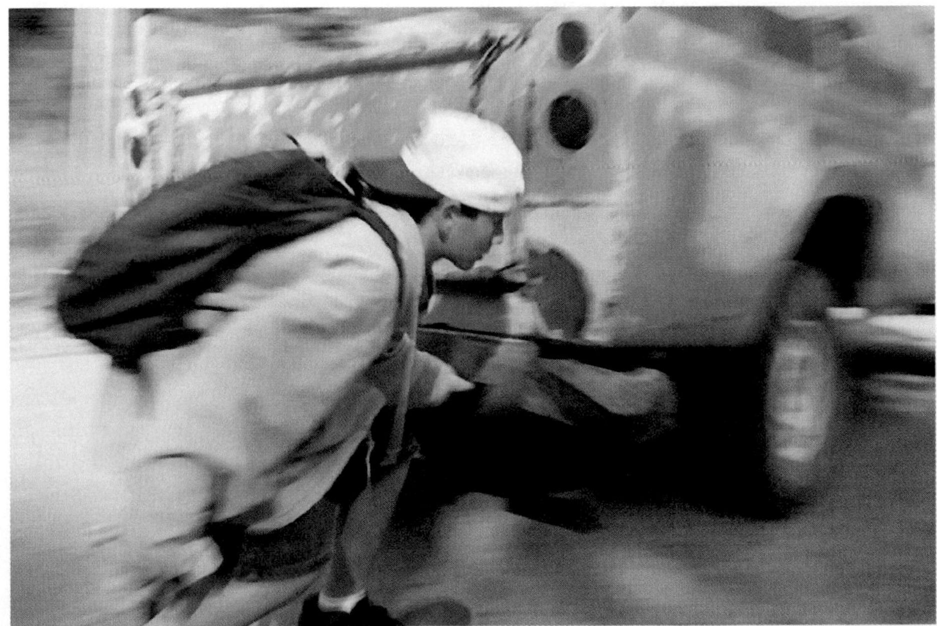

Research on cognitive development during adolescence has been aimed at understanding the thought processes behind adolescent risk-taking. (Dugald Bremner/Tony Stone)

adolescents found that half of all 14- to 15-year-olds had driven a bicycle while intoxicated, that one-fifth were regular cigarette smokers, and that one-sixth had sexual intercourse without using contraception (Arnett and Balle-Jensen, 1993).

Some writers have suggested that we look at these behaviors as resulting from decisions that adolescents make—for instance, decisions to drink alcohol, to drive fast, or to have intercourse without using contraception—and that we need to better understand the cognitive processes behind such decision making. One line of research has attempted to examine whether adolescents make risky decisions because of deficiencies in their developing cognitive abilities (Furbey and Beyth-Marom, 1992).

A number of writers have looked at adolescent risk-taking from a perspective called **behavioral decision theory** (Fischoff, 1988; Kahneman, Slovic, and Tversky, 1982). According to this theory, all behaviors can be analyzed as the outcome of a process that involves (1) identifying alternative choices, (2) identifying the consequences that follow each choice, (3) evaluating the desirability of each possible consequence, (4) assessing the likelihood of each possible consequence, and (5) combining all this information according to some decision rule (Beyth-Marom, Austin, Fischoff, Palmgren, and Jacobs-Quadrel, 1993).

So, for example, an adolescent girl who is trying to decide whether to smoke cigarettes for the first time at a party would (1) identify the choices (to smoke or not to smoke); (2) identify the consequences ("Smoking may make me appear 'cooler' in my friends' eyes, but if my parents find out, they will ground me"); (3) evaluate the desirability of each consequence ("Appearing cooler to my friends is good, but being grounded would be terrible"); (4) assess the likelihood of each consequence ("My friends probably won't really change their opinion of me just because I smoke, and my parents probably will smell cigarette smoke on my clothes and find out"); and (5) combine all the information according to some decision rule ("All things considered, I think I won't try smoking right now").

From the perspective of behavioral decision theory, then, it is important to ask whether adolescents use different processes than adults in identifying, estimating, and evaluating various behavioral options and consequences. If risky decisions are the result of faulty information processing—in attention, memory, metacognition, or organization, for example—perhaps it would make sense to train adolescents in these basic cognitive abilities as a means of lessening their risk-taking.

According to most studies, however, adolescents make decisions using the same basic cognitive processes as adults use (Beyth-Marom et al., 1993; Furbey and Beyth-Marom, 1992). This is true even regarding issues as complicated as deciding whether to abort a pregnancy (Lewis, 1987). The major gains in information processing appear to occur between childhood and adolescence rather than between adolescence and adulthood (Keating, 1990).

A second possibility that is often suggested is that adolescents are more likely to feel "invulnerable"—more likely, that is, to subscribe to the personal fable that they will not be harmed by potentially harmful experiences. However, as you read earlier, there is no evidence for the widely held belief that adolescents are more likely to subscribe to personal fables than are adults (Quadrel, Fischoff, and Davis, 1993). More important, studies indicate that adolescents are no more likely than adults to perceive themselves as invulnerable. *Both* age groups are equally likely to underestimate their likelihood of being harmed by potentially harmful experiences (Quadrel et al., 1993).

If adolescents use the same decision-making processes as adults, and if adolescents are no more likely than adults to think of themselves as invulnerable, why, then, do adolescents behave in ways that are excessively risky? The answer may involve the different ways in which adolescents and adults evaluate the desirability of different consequences.

For example, an individual's decision to try cocaine at a party may involve evaluating a number of different consequences, including the legal and health risks, the pleasure the drug may induce, and the way in which one will be judged by the other people present (judged both positively and negatively). Whereas an adult and an adolescent may both consider all these consequences, the adult may place relatively more weight on the health risks of trying the drug, while the adolescent may place relatively more weight on the social consequences of not trying. Although an adult may see an adolescent's decision to value peer acceptance more than health as "irrational," an adolescent may see the adult's decision as equally incomprehensible. Behavioral decision theory reminds us that all decisions—even risky ones—can be seen as "rational" once we understand how an individual estimates and evaluates the consequences of various courses of action.

A nice illustration of this comes from a recent study of adolescents' perceptions of the costs and benefits of engaging in various risky behaviors (Small, Silverberg, and Kerns, 1993). This study asked adolescents of different ages to rate the costs and the benefits of such behaviors as using alcohol or engaging in sexual intercourse. Interestingly, adolescents' perceptions of the benefits of engaging in the risky behaviors were not nearly as predictive of how they behaved as were their perceptions of costs. Adolescents' perceptions of *costs* were highly predictive of their behavior, however; the more costly an adolescent thought engaging in a given behavior would be, the less likely he or she was to engage in that behavior. A similar case has been made for understanding why adolescents risk exposing themselves to HIV infection by having unprotected sex: Many adolescents do not believe that the costs of unprotected sex are sufficiently great to avoid the risky behavior (Gardner and Herman, 1990).

In all likelihood, of course, neither adolescents' nor adults' decisions are always made in as straightforward or rational a way as suggested by behavioral decision theory. Nevertheless, this approach has opened up a new way of thinking about adolescent risk-taking. Instead of looking at "risky" decisions as the result of irrational or faulty judgment, experts are now trying to understand where and how adolescents obtain the information they use in reaching their conclusions, and how accurate the information is. If, for example, adolescents underestimate the likelihood of getting pregnant following unprotected sex, sex education efforts might focus on teaching teenagers the actual probability.

We should also keep in mind that emotional and contextual factors, as well as cognitive ones, contribute to adolescent risk-taking. With respect to emotional factors, studies show that individuals who are high in **sensation-seeking** (that is, individuals who enjoy novel and intense experiences) are more likely to engage in various types of risky behaviors than those who are low in sensation-seeking. It has also been suggested that sensation-seeking is higher during adolescence than during other periods of the life cycle (Arnett and Balle-Jensen, 1993). If this is indeed true, it may provide one explanation for the higher rate of risk-taking in adolescence (although it is not clear why sensation-seeking should be higher during adolescence than before or after it).

With respect to contextual factors, some research indicates that different contexts provide different *opportunities* for risky behavior. Adolescents living in large cities, for example, have more opportunities for risk-taking because they are less closely monitored by parents and other adults. As well, risk-taking may be less prevalent in settings that attempt to limit opportunities for risky behavior through legal or institutional means, such as having a higher legal drinking age or a higher legal driving age (Arnett and Balle-Jensen, 1993). More research is needed on how these various cognitive, emotional, and contextual factors interact in shaping risk-taking behavior.

RECAP

Researchers also have examined adolescent risk-taking from a cognitive point of view. Contrary to popular wisdom, which holds that adolescents are "bad" decision makers, recent studies suggest that adolescents make decisions in much the same way that adults do. Research also indicates that adolescents are no more likely than adults to suffer from feelings of "invulnerability." The current consensus is that young people sometimes behave in risky ways not because of faulty decision making but because they evaluate the possible consequences of their actions differently than adults do.

Adolescent Thinking in the Classroom

Given the sorts of changes in thinking that occur during the adolescent years, one would hope that schools and teachers adapt their methods and curricula to better mesh with the developing cognitive abilities of their students. In theory, adolescents' ability to think in more advanced ways—whether in terms of abstraction, multidimensionality, relativism, or some other dimension—should permit them to think more critically about a wide range of issues. Yet, the prevalence of **critical thinking** among American high school students—thinking that is in-depth, analytical, and discriminating—has been less than staggering, as we shall see in later chapters about school and achievement. Most assessments of adolescent achievement in recent years indicate that American youth have difficulty thinking in the sophisticated ways that our theories and research suggest they ought to be capable of. Part of the reason, some critics contend, is that adolescents are rarely asked to think in this fashion (Linn and Songer, 1991).

To what can we attribute this gap between theory and practice? According to some writers, our educational system does not encourage or stimulate the type of thinking that adolescents have the potential for. Although research indicates that it is possible, for example, to stimulate the development of formal-operational thinking (e.g., Danner and Day, 1977; Siegler, Liebert, and Liebert, 1973), few junior or senior high school classes are set up to do so. Rather than encouraging adolescents to think in abstract or relativistic ways, for instance, most secondary school classes reward the rote memorization of concrete facts and the parroting back of the teacher's "correct" answer. According to one expert, opportunities for real give-and-take in adolescents' schools account for less than 10 percent of the total time spent on instruction. At a time when individuals are becoming capable of seeing that most issues are too complicated to have one "right" answer, an educational program that stifles this developing ability works against adolescents' developmental inclinations. Although attempts have been made to make the instruction of adolescents more compatible with our understanding of their cognitive development, these efforts have not been widespread. Yet, studies show that teaching that takes advantage of adolescents' developing reasoning abilities can result in a more sophisticated understanding of the subject matter, especially in science classes (Linn and Songer, 1991, 1993).

The gap between what adolescents can do (i.e., their *competence*) and their actual school achievement (i.e., their *performance*) may be especially large among youth who attend English-speaking schools but who speak another language or dialect when not in school, as one study of native Hawaiian youth indicates (Feldman, Stone, and Renderer, 1990). Although the students in this research attended schools where the instruction was in Standard English, they spoke Hawaiian Creole-English at home and with their friends. The researchers found that even though students were functioning at a high cognitive level, they were uncomfortable speaking in class because of their language background, and this lack of verbal engagement interfered with their learning. One hypothesis is that speaking in class aids in the process of encoding the information, which facilitates learning. Presumably, all groups of youngsters whose in-school and out-of-school languages may be very different are at risk for this disadvantage.

Criticisms also have been leveled against schools' lack of attempts to deliberately enhance adolescents' information-processing skills. As our society becomes more information-dependent—some social commentators have talked about information "overload"—it is important that adolescents learn how to better manage and utilize this wealth of data. A number of writers have argued that schools can and should teach adolescents ways of focusing attention, improving short- and long-term memory, organizing information, and monitoring thought processes (Baron and Sternberg, 1987; Gagne, 1985; Glazer and Bassok, 1989). In other words, these experts believe that information-processing skills can be taught and that educators should make a more conscious effort to do so. Moreover, they point to recent advances in research on adolescent information-processing as providing the foundation for an overhaul of our secondary school curricula.

RECAP

Research on cognitive development in adolescence suggests a number of ways that schools might change in order to better match classroom instruction to the developing capabilities of adolescent students. Unfortunately, however, little has been done to change the way that adolescents are taught, and few high school programs are designed to stimulate the development of formal operations or more sophisticated information-processing skills.

KEY TERMS

aptitude test
automatization
behavioral decision theory
cognitive-developmental view
cohort
competence-performance distinction
componential approach
concrete operations
critical thinking
culture-fair tests
divided attention
formal operations
imaginary audience
implicit personality theory
information-processing perspective
long-term memory
metacognition
mutual role taking
personal fable

Piagetian perspective
preoperational period
propositional logic
selective attention
sensation-seeking
sensorimotor period
short-term memory
social cognition
social conventions
social perspective taking
specialized structural systems
statistical interaction
theory of multiple intelligences
triarchic theory of intelligence

FOR FURTHER READING

Baron, J., and Sternberg, R. (1987). *Teaching thinking skills: Theory and practice.* New York: Freeman. Applications of our understanding of information-processing to classroom instruction.

Elkind, D. (1978). Understanding the young adolescent. *Adolescence, 13,* 127–134. In this classic article, Piagetian theorist David Elkind explains how adolescents' social behavior can be understood in terms of their cognitive development.

Furbey, M., and Beyth-Marom, R. (1992). Risk-taking in adolescence: A decision-making perspective. *Developmental Review, 12,* 1–44. An overview of research and theory on adolescent risk-taking that emphasizes the contribution of behavioral decision theory.

Keating, D. (1990). Adolescent thinking. In S. Feldman and G. Elliott (Eds.), *At the threshold: The developing adolescent.* Cambridge, Mass.: Harvard University Press. A comprehensive overview of what is known about the development of thinking during the adolescent years.

Lapsley, D. (1989). Continuity and discontinuity in adolescent social cognitive development. In R. Montemayor, G. Adams, and T. Gullota (Eds.), *Advances in adolescence research,* Vol. 2. Beverly Hills, Calif.: Sage. A solid review of research on the development of social cognition in adolescence.

CHAPTER 3

SOCIAL TRANSITIONS

(Jose Carrillo/PhotoEdit)

Among the Thonga, an agrarian society in the southeastern region of Africa, at the time of her first menstruation, the adolescent girl goes to an older woman of her choosing and announces that she has come of age (Ford and Beach, 1951). At this point, a seclusion period of one month commences, and

> three or four girls, undergoing the initiation ceremony together, are shut up in a hut, and when they come out, must always wear over their face a veil consisting of a very dirty and greasy cloth. Every morning they are led to the pool, and their whole body is immersed in the water as far as the neck. Other initiated girls or women accompany them, singing obscene songs, and drive away with sticks any man who happens to be on the road, as no man is allowed to see a girl during this period. . . . When the cortege of women accompanying the initiated has returned home, the nubile girls are imprisoned in the hut. They are teased, pinched, scratched by the adoptive mothers or by other women; they must also listen to the licentious songs which are sung to them. . . . They are also instructed in sexual matters, and told that they must never reveal anything about the blood of the menses to a man. . . . At the end of the month the adoptive mother brings the girl home to her true mother. She also presents her with a pot of beer. A feast takes place on this occasion. (Junod, 1927, cited in Ford and Beach, 1951, p. 175)

Along with the biological changes of puberty and changes in thinking abilities, changes in social roles and status constitute yet another universal feature of development during adolescence. All societies differentiate among individuals on the basis of how old they are (although not all use chronological age as the defining criterion).

In all societies, adolescence is a period of social transition for the individual. Over the course of the adolescent years, the individual ceases to be viewed by society as a child and comes to be recognized as an adult. Although the specific elements of this social passage from childhood into adulthood vary across time and space, the presence during adolescence of some sort of recognition that the individual's status has changed—a **social redefinition** of the individual—is universal.

The process of social redefinition at adolescence is certainly less vivid and less ceremonial in contemporary America than it is among the Thonga. We do not seclude young people from the rest of society at the onset of puberty, nor, with the exception of certain religious ceremonies, do we mark the passage into adulthood with elaborate rituals. But just because the social transition of adolescence is less explicit in contemporary society than it is in many traditional cultures does not mean that the passage is any less significant. Indeed, some theorists have argued that the nature of adolescence is far more influenced by the way in which society defines the economic and social roles of young people than by the biological or cognitive changes of the period.

The study of social transitions at adolescence provides an interesting vehicle through which we can compare adolescence across different cultures and historical epochs. Although certain features of the social passage from childhood into adulthood are universal, considerable differences exist between the processes of social redefinition in industrialized society and in more traditional cultures, and between different cultural groups within contemporary society. In examining some of these differences, you will come to understand better how the way in which society structures the transition of adolescents into adult roles influences the nature of psychosocial development during the period.

Because young people go through puberty earlier today than 100 years ago, and because they tend to stay in school longer, the adolescent period has been lengthened and the transition into adulthood prolonged. Today, young people are caught between the world of childhood and the world of adulthood for an extremely long time, with only a vague sense of when—and how—they become adults. Indeed, in the minds of many social scientists who study adolescence in modern society, the social passage of young people into adult roles is too long, too vague, and too rocky (Nightingale and Wolverton, 1993). And, as we shall see, the passage from adolescence into adulthood is especially difficult among young people growing up in poverty.

RECAP

Changes in social definition make up the third set of fundamental transformations that define adolescence as a period of development. Although the specific elements of the social passage from childhood into adulthood vary from one society to another, all societies recognize that the social status of the individual changes during the adolescent period.

SOCIAL REDEFINITION AND PSYCHOSOCIAL DEVELOPMENT

Like the biological and cognitive transitions of adolescence, the social transitions have important consequences for the young person's psychosocial development. Indeed, from a sociological or anthropological perspective, it is social redefinition at adolescence—rather than, for example, puberty—that has the most profound impact on the individual's development and behavior. In the realm of *identity,* for example, attainment of adult status may transform a young woman's self-concept, causing her to feel more adultlike and to think more seriously about future work and family roles. Doing for the first time such things as reporting to work, going into a bar, or registering to vote all make us feel older and more mature. In turn, these new activities and opportunities may prompt self-evaluation and introspection.

Becoming an adult member of society, accompanied as it is by shifts in responsibility, independence, and freedom, also has an impact on the development of *autonomy.* In contrast to the child, the adolescent-turned-adult is permitted to make a wider range of decisions that may have serious long-term consequences. A young man who has reached the drinking age, for example, must decide how he should handle this new privilege. Should he go along with the crowd and drink every weekend night, or should he follow his parents' example and abstain from drinking? And in return for the privileges that come with adult status, adolescents are expected to behave in a more responsible fashion. Receiving a driver's license carries with it the obligation of driving safely. Thus the attainment of adult status provides chances for the young person to exercise autonomy as well as chances to develop a greater sense of independence.

Changes in social definition often bring with them changes in the sorts of relationships and interpersonal behaviors that are permitted and expected. Social redefinition at adolescence is therefore likely to raise new questions and concerns for the young person about *intimacy*—including, in particular, such matters as dating and marriage. Many parents prohibit their children from dating until they have reached an "appropriate" age. And not until the **age of majority** (the legal age for adult status) are individuals allowed to marry without first gaining their parents' permission. In certain societies, young people may even be *required* to marry when they reach adulthood, entering into a marriage that may have been arranged while they were children.

Changes in status at adolescence may also affect development in the domain of *sexuality.* In contemporary society, for example, laws governing sexual behavior (such as the definition of statutory rape) typically differentiate between individuals who have and have not attained adult status. By becoming an adult in a legal sense, the young person may be confronted with the need for new and different decisions about sexual activity. One problem currently facing society is whether sexually active individuals who have not yet attained adult legal status should be able to make independent decisions about such "adult" matters as abortion and contraception.

Finally, reaching adulthood often has important implications in the realm of *achievement.* For instance, in contemporary society, it is not until adult status is attained that one can enter the labor force as a full-time employee. Not until young people have reached a designated age are they permitted to leave school of their own volition. In less industrialized societies, becoming an adult typically entails entrance into the productive activities of the community. Taken together, these shifts are likely to prompt changes in the young person's skills, aspirations, and expectations.

ADOLESCENCE AS A SOCIAL INVENTION

Because so many of the psychological changes of adolescence are linked to the changes that accompany society's redefinition of the individual, many writers have argued that adolescence, as a period in the life cycle, is mainly a social invention (e.g., Lapsley, Enright, and Serlin, 1985). These **inventionists** point out that, although the biological and cognitive changes characteristic of the period are important in their own right, adolescence is defined primarily by the ways in which society recognizes (or does not recognize) the period as distinct from childhood or adulthood.

Many of our images of adolescence are influenced by the fact that we draw lines between adolescence and childhood (for instance, the boundary between elementary and secondary school) and between adolescence and adulthood (for instance, the age at which one can hold a job). Inventionists stress that it is because we *see* adolescence as distinct that it in fact exists as such. They point to other cultures and other historical periods in which adolescence either is not recognized at all or is viewed very differently. Many of these theorists view the behaviors and problems characteristic of adolescence in contemporary society as having to do with the particular way that adolescence is defined by society, rather than the result of the biological or cognitive givens of the period. This is an entirely different view than that espoused by writers such as G. Stanley Hall, for example, who saw the psychological changes of adolescence as driven by puberty and, as a result, by biological destiny.

RECAP

Some writers, called "inventionists," have argued that adolescence is more a social invention than a biological or cognitive phenomenon. They suggest that our conception of adolescence—whether it exists as a separate period and what its nature is—is determined largely by forces in the broader social environment. Changes in the broader environment, therefore, can change the very nature of adolescence.

According to the inventionist view, the origins of adolescence as we know it in contemporary society are closely linked to the industrial revolution of the middle of the nineteenth century. Prior to that time, in the agricultural world of the sixteenth or seventeenth century, children were treated primarily as miniature adults, and people did not make precise distinctions among children of different ages (the term *child* referred to anyone under the age of 18 or even 21). Children provided important labor to their families, and they learned early in their development the roles they were expected to fulfill later in life. The main distinction between children and adults was not based on their age or their abilities but on whether they owned property (Modell and Goodman, 1990). As a consequence, there was little reason to label some youngsters as "children" and others as "adolescents"—in fact, the term *adolescent* was not widely used before the nineteenth century.

With industrialization, however, came new patterns of work and family life. Adolescents were among the most dramatically affected by these changes. First, because the economy was changing so rapidly, away from the simple and predictable life known in agrarian society, the connection between what individuals learned in childhood and what they would need to know in adulthood became increasingly uncertain. Although a man may have been a farmer, his son would not necessarily follow in his footsteps. One response to this uncertainty was that parents, especially in middle-class families, encouraged adolescents to spend time preparing for adulthood within societal institutions, such as schools. Instead of working side by side with their parents and other adults at home, as was the case before industrialization, nineteenth-century adolescents were increasingly more likely to spend their days with peers of the same age, preparing for the future.

Inventionists have been quick to point out that the redefinition of adolescence as a time of preparation, rather than participation, suited society's changing economic needs as well. One initial outcome of industrialization was a shortage of job opportunities, because machines were used to replace workers. Although adolescents provided inexpensive labor, they were competing with adults for a limited supply of jobs. One way of protecting adults' jobs was to remove adolescents from the labor force, by turning them into full-time students. In order to accomplish this, society needed to begin discriminating between individuals who were ready for work and those who were not. And although there was very little factual basis for the distinction, society began to view adolescents as less capable and as more in need of guidance and training—as a way of rationalizing what was little more than age discrimination. Individuals who earlier in the century would have been working side by side with adults were now seen as too immature or too unskilled to carry out similar tasks. As noted in the introductory chapter, society's view of adolescents' capability and maturity has changed dramatically when their labor has been sorely needed, such as during wartime (Enright, Levy, Harris, and Lapsley, 1987).

A less cynical view of the events of the late nineteenth century emphasizes the genuine desire of some adults to protect adolescents from the dangers of the new workplace, rather than the selfish desire to protect adults' jobs from teenagers. Industrialization brought with it worrisome changes in community life, especially in the cities. Many factories were dangerous working environments, filled with new and unfamiliar machinery. The disruption of small farming communities and the growth of large urban areas because of the shift from agriculture to industry was accompanied by increases in crime and in "moral degeneracy." **Child protectionists** argued that young people needed to be kept away from the labor force for their own good. In addition to the rise of schools during this time, the early twentieth century saw the growth of many organizations aimed at protecting young people, such as the Boy Scouts and similar adult-supervised youth clubs (Modell and Goodman, 1990).

For whatever the reason, it was not until the late nineteenth century—about 100 years ago—that adolescence came to be viewed as we view it today: a lengthy period of preparation for adulthood, in which young people, in need of guidance and supervision, remain economically dependent on their elders. This view started within the middle class—where parents had more to gain by keeping their children out of the labor force and educating them for a better adulthood—but it spread quickly throughout much of society. Because the workplace has continued to change in ways that make the future uncertain, the idea of adolescence as a distinctive period of preparation for adulthood has remained intact.

Two other modifications of the definition of adolescence also gave rise to new terminology and ideas. The first of these concerns the use of the term **teenager,** which was not employed until about fifty years ago. In contrast to the term *adolescent, teenager* suggests a more frivolous and lighthearted age, during which individuals concern themselves with such things as cars and cosmetics. An important social change that led to the invention of the "teenager" was the increased affluence and economic freedom enjoyed by American adolescents during the late 1940s and early 1950s. Advertisers recognized that these young people represented an important consumer group and, with the help of the new publications such as *Seventeen* magazine, began cultivating the image of the happy-go-lucky teenager as a means of targeting ad campaigns toward the lucrative adolescent market (Greenberger and Steinberg, 1986).

A second term whose acceptance grew as a result of social change is **youth,** which was used long before *adolescent.* But, prior to industrialization, *youth* had a very vague and imprecise meaning and could refer to someone as young as 12 or as old as 24 (Modell and Goodman, 1990). Gradually, and during the 1960s in particular, the growth of the college population and the rise in student activism across the country focused attention on individuals who were somewhere between adolescence and young adulthood—those in the 18- to 22-year-old range. Many adults referred to the changes

Although adolescence was "invented" during the late nineteenth century, it was not until the middle of this century that our present-day image of the "teenager" was created. An important contributor to this image was the mass media—magazines such as Seventeen *cultivated the picture of the happy-go-lucky teenager as a way of targeting advertisments toward the lucrative adolescent market.* (Courtesy of Seventeen Magazine. Photographed exclusively for Seventeen by Francesco Scavullo)

they saw in attitudes and values among college students as the "youth movement." One theorist went so far as to argue that "youth" is a separate stage in the life cycle, psychologically as well as chronologically distinct from adolescence and adulthood (Keniston, 1970). Indeed, many college students are unsure about whether they are adolescents or adults, since they may feel mature in some respects (e.g., keeping up an apartment, being involved in a serious dating relationship) but immature in others (e.g., having to depend on parents for economic support, having to have an advisor approve class schedules). The lengthening of formal schooling in contemporary society has altered the social definition of adolescence, because the majority of young people continue their education past high school and are forced to delay their transition into many adult work and family roles.

It is important to note that when we say that adolescence (or the teenager, or youth) is in part a social invention, we do not mean that its significance is in any way diminished or that it is somehow less real than if it were an entirely biological phenomenon. "Democracy," after all, is a social invention, too, but its creation and development have had profound effects on the way that we live. As with other social inventions, the notion that there should be a distinct period of adolescence has endured over time and has had important and very concrete repercussions. But as with other social constructs, the nature of adolescence changes over time, and it will continue to change as we revise our notions of what it means to grow from childhood into adulthood.

RECAP

Adolescence as we know it in contemporary society has its roots in the industrial revolution of the nineteenth century. Prior to that time, children were viewed as miniature adults, and adolescents provided important labor for their families. With industrialization, however, new patterns of work and family life led to the exclusion of young people from the labor force and to the lengthening of formal schooling and adolescents' economic dependence on their elders.

CHANGES IN STATUS

"The most casual survey of the ways in which different societies have handled adolescence makes one fact inescapable," wrote anthropologist Ruth Benedict in her classic work *Patterns of Culture.* "[E]ven in those cultures which have made the most of the trait, the age upon which they focus their attention varies over a great range of years. . . . The puberty they recognize is social, and the ceremonies are a recognition in some fashion or other of the child's new status of adulthood. . . . In order to understand [adolescence] . . . we need . . . to know what is identified in different cultures with the beginning of adulthood and their methods of admitting to the new status" (Benedict, 1934, p. 25).

Changes in social definition at adolescence typically involve a two-sided alteration in status. On the one hand, the adolescent is given certain privileges and rights that are typically reserved for the society's adult members. On the other hand, this increased power and freedom generally are accompanied by increased expectations for self-management, personal responsibility, and social participation.

We can find examples of this double shift in social status in all societies, across a variety of interpersonal, political, economic, and legal arenas.

Changes in Interpersonal Status

In many societies, individuals who have been recognized as adults are usually addressed with adult titles. They also are expected to maintain different sorts of social relationships with their parents, with the community's elders, and with young people whose status has not yet changed. On holidays such as Thanksgiving, for example, some large families set two tables: a big table for the adults and a smaller, "children's" table. When a young person is permitted to sit at the big table, it is a sign that he or she has reached a new position in the family. These interpersonal changes are typically accompanied by new interpersonal obligations—for example, being expected to take care of and set a proper example for the younger members of the family.

Changes in Political Status

With the attainment of adult status, the young person is often permitted more extensive participation in the community's decision making. Among the Navaho, for example, it is only following a formal initiation ceremony that adolescents are considered members of the Navaho People and are permitted full participation in ceremonial life (Cohen, 1964). In contemporary America, attaining the age of majority brings the right to vote. But in return for this increased power usually come new obligations. In most societies, young adults are expected to serve their communities in cases of emergency or need. And in many cultures, training for warfare is often demanded of young people once they attain adult status (Benedict, 1934).

Changes in Economic Status

Attaining adult status also has important economic implications that again entail obligation as well as privilege. In some societies, only adults may own property and maintain control over their income (N. Miller, 1928). In many American states, for example, any income that a youngster earns before the age of 16 is technically the property of the young person's parents.

Entrance into certain work roles is also restricted to adults. In most industrialized societies, employment is regulated by child labor laws, and the attainment of a prescribed age is a prerequisite to employment in certain occupations. Among the Tikopia (Melanesia), one of the first privileges accorded boys when they reach adolescence is accompanying older males on fishing expeditions (Fried and Fried, 1980). In most communities, however, once they have attained the economic status and rights of adults, young people are expected to contribute to the economic well-being of their community. They are depended on to participate in the community's productive activities and to carry out the labor expected of adults. In contemporary society, the young adult's economic responsibilities to the broader community may entail having to pay taxes for the first time. In some families, adolescents who are permitted to work must contribute to their family's support.

Changes in Legal Status

In most societies, not until adult status is attained is the young person permitted to participate in a variety of activities that are typically reserved for adults. Gambling, purchasing alcoholic beverages, and driving are but three of the many privileges we reserve in America for individuals who have reached the legal age of adulthood. In many cultures, the eating of certain foods is restricted to individuals who have been admitted to adult society (Mead, 1928).

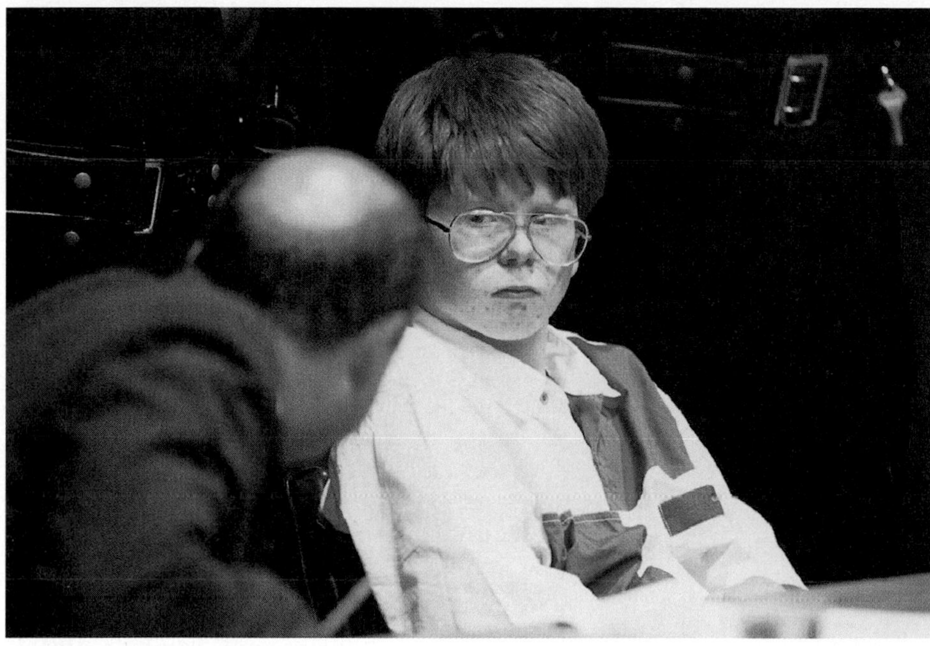

During the mid-1990s, many adults demanded that juveniles accused of violent crimes be tried as adults. This 14-year-old was tried as an adult and found guilty of murdering a preschooler. (Karen Garver/Sipa Press)

Once an adolescent is designated as an adult, however, he or she is also subject to a new set of laws and must expect to be treated differently by the legal institutions of the society, compared with how he or she was treated as a child. In the United States, for example, crimes by young adolescents are generally adjudicated in a separate **juvenile justice system,** which operates under different rules and principles from the system that applies to adults.

Unfortunately, development during the adolescent years is so rapid and so variable that it is difficult to know at what chronological age a line should be drawn between legally viewing someone as an adult and viewing someone as a child (Gold and Petronio, 1980). In one recent study, it was found that American jurors were significantly more likely to recommend the death penalty for an individual convicted of first-degree murder if he were 16 or older than if he were 15 or younger, suggesting that many people "draw the line" at 16. Interestingly, this is where the U.S. Supreme Court has drawn the line as well (Britner, Crosby, and Jodl, 1994).

Many other issues surrounding the legal status of adolescents remain vague and confusing. Two recent U.S. Supreme Court cases indicate just how inconsistent our views of adolescents' status are (Moshman, 1993). In one case, *Hazelwood v. Kuhlmeier,* the Court ruled that a public high school may censor articles written by students for their school newspaper, on the grounds that adolescents were "immature" enough to need the protection of "wiser" adults. Yet the same Court also ruled, in *Board of Education v. Mergens,* that students who wanted to form a Bible study group had the right to meet on campus because high school students were "mature" enough to understand that a school could permit the expression of ideas that it did not necessarily endorse!

There are many other examples of this sort of inconsistency. For example, courts have ruled that teenagers have the right to obtain contraceptives without their parents' approval. But they also have upheld laws forbidding adolescents access to cigarettes or to magazines that, although vulgar, were not considered so obscene that they were outlawed among adults (Zimring, 1982). Is there a pattern to this inconsistency? In general, legal decisions have tended to restrict the behavior of adolescents when the behavior in question is viewed as potentially damaging to the young person (buying cigarettes, for example) but have supported adolescent autonomy when the behavior is viewed as having potential benefit (using contraceptives).

RECAP

Changes in the individual's social definition at adolescence typically revolve around changes in status in four domains: interpersonal, political, economic, and legal (see Table 3.1). In each of these domains, individuals are given greater privileges but are expected to take increased responsibility for self-management and social participation.

THE PROCESS OF SOCIAL REDEFINITION

Social redefinition during adolescence is not a single event but a series of events that may occur over a relatively long time. In contemporary America, the process of redefinition typically begins at the age of 15 or 16, when the young person is first permitted to drive, to work, and to leave school. But in most states, the social redefinition of the adolescent continues well into the young adult years. Some privileges, such as voting, are not conferred until the age of 18, and others, such as purchasing alcoholic beverages, are not conferred until the age of 21, five or six years after the redefinition process begins. Even in societies that mark the social redefinition of the young person with a dramatic and elaborate **initiation ceremony,** the social transformation of the individual from a child into an adult may span many years, and the initiation ceremony may represent just one element of the transition. In fact, the initiation ceremony usually marks the beginning of a long period of training and preparation for adulthood, rather than the adolescent's final passage into adult status (Cohen, 1964).

In many cultures, the social redefinition of young people occurs in groups. That is, the

TABLE 3.1 SOME CONSEQUENCES OF ATTAINING ADULT STATUS

	In Traditional Societies	In Contemporary Societies
Interpersonal	Addressed with "adult" title by other members of community	Permitted to sit with grownups for special occasions
Political	Permitted to participate in community decision making	Eligible to vote
Economic	Permitted to own property	Permitted to work
Legal	Permitted to consume certain foods	No longer dealt with in a separate juvenile justice system

young people of a community are grouped with peers of approximately the same age—a *cohort*—and move through the series of status transitions together. One of the results of such age-grouped social transitions is that very strong bonds are formed among youngsters who have shared certain rituals. In many American high schools, for example, attempts are made to create "class spirit" or "class unity" by fostering bonds among students who will be graduated together. In many Latino communities, adolescent girls together participate in an elaborate sort of "coming-out" celebration, called the **quinceañera.** On college campuses, fraternities and sororities may conduct group initiations that involve difficult or unpleasant tasks, and special ties may be forged between "brothers" or "sisters" who have pledged together.

The timetable for the process of social definition is highly variable within and across societies, and it is affected by economics, politics, and culture. For instance, research on rural youth growing up in America (e.g., Elder, Conger, Foster, and Ardelt, 1992; Schonert-Reichl and Elliott, 1994) points to the tremendous impact that the farm crisis of the 1980s had on youngsters' hopes and plans, which in turn affected their transition into adult roles. One recent study of German adolescents after the unification of Germany found that youngsters who were recent immigrants from Eastern Europe had age expectations for various transitions (such as drinking alcohol without adults present, and falling in love for the first time) that were, on average, about two years later than were the expectations of their West German–born counterparts or immigrants who had been living in unified Germany for a longer period of time (Schmitt-Rodermund and Silbereisen, 1993). Another study found that adolescents of European descent from the United States, Australia, and Hong Kong have faster timetables than do those of Asian descent (Feldman and Rosenthal, 1994).

Common Practices in the Process of Social Redefinition

Although the specific ceremonies, signs, and timetables of social redefinition during adolescence vary from one culture to another, several general themes characterize the process in all societies.

First, social redefinition usually entails the *real or symbolic separation of the young person from his or her parents.* In traditional societies, this may take the form of **extrusion:** During late childhood, children are expected to begin sleeping in households other than their own. Youngsters may spend the day with their parents, but they spend the night with friends of the family, with relatives, or in a separate residence reserved for preadolescent youngsters (Cohen, 1964). In America, during earlier times, it was customary for adolescents to leave home temporarily and live with other families in the community, either to learn specific occupational skills (i.e., as apprentices) or to work as domestic servants (Kett, 1977). Interestingly, the "placing out" of adolescents from their parents' home often coincided with puberty (Katz, 1975). In contemporary societies, the separation of adolescents from their parents takes somewhat different forms. They are sent to summer camps, to boarding schools, or, as is more common, to live at college.

A second aspect of social redefinition during adolescence entails the *accentuation of physical and social differences between males and females* (Ford and Beach, 1951; Schlegel and Barry, 1991). This accentuation of differences occurs partly because of the physical changes of puberty and partly because adult work and family roles are generally highly sex-differentiated. Many societies separate males and females during religious ceremonies, have individuals begin wearing sex-specific articles of clothing (rather than clothing permissible for either gender), and keep males and females apart during initiation ceremonies. Some traditional societies employ a practice that is called **brother-sister avoidance:** After puberty, a brother and sister may not have any direct contact or interaction until one or both are married (Cohen, 1964).

The separation of males and females is not limited to social redefinition in traditional societies. In earlier times in America (and to a certain extent in many other industrialized societies today), males and females were separated during adolescence in educational institutions, either by excluding adolescent girls from secondary and higher education, grouping males and females in different schools or different classrooms, or having males and females follow different curricula. In present-day America, many of these practices have been discontinued, but some elements of accentuated sex differentiation and sex segregation during adolescence still exist: in residential arrangements, in styles of dress, in athletic activities, and in household chores (Hill and Lynch, 1983; Medrich, Roizen, Rubin, and Buckley, 1982; White and Brinkerhoff, 1981). And many contemporary ceremonies designed to recognize the young person's passage into adulthood are either limited to one sex or the other (e.g., debutante balls or the quinceañera, each of which is for young women) or somehow differentiate between males and females (e.g., the **Bar Mitzvah** and the **Bas Mitzvah** ceremonies for Jewish males and females, respectively).

Formal rites of passage from childhood into adolescence or from adolescence into adulthood are rare in contemporary society. Certain religious ceremonies, such as the Confirmation or the Bar Mitzvah (pictured here), are as close as we come to initiation rites in contemporary America. (Peter Southwick/Stock, Boston)

Third, social redefinition during adolescence typically entails the *passing on of cultural, historical, and practical information* from the adult generation to the newly inducted cohort of young people. This information may concern (1) matters thought to be important to adults but of limited utility to children (for example, information about the performance of certain adult work tasks); (2) matters thought to be necessary for adults but unfit for children (for example, information regarding sex); or (3) matters concerning the history or rituals of the family or community (for example, how to perform certain ceremonies). In traditional societies, initiates are often sent to some sort of "school" in which they are instructed in the productive activities of the community (hunting, fishing, farming). Following puberty, boys and girls receive instruction about sexual relations, moral behavior, and societal lore (Fried and Fried, 1980; N. Miller, 1928).

In contemporary society, too, adolescence is a time of instruction in preparation for adulthood. Elementary school students, for example, are generally not taught a great deal about sexuality, work, or financial matters; such coursework is typically reserved for high school students. We also restrict entrance into certain "adult" activities (such as sexually explicit movies) until the adolescent is believed to be old enough to be exposed to them.

Because formal initiation ceremonies are neither very common nor very meaningful in modern society, students sometimes overlook important similarities between the processes of social redefinition in traditional and contemporary societies. Practices like extrusion, brother-sister avoidance, and **scarification** (the intentional creation of scars on some part or parts of the body, often done as part of an initiation ceremony) are alien and seem odd to us. But if we look beneath the surface, at the meaning and significance of each culture's practices, we find many common threads. In contemporary society, for example, our own form of "brother-sister avoidance" begins at puberty: Once adolescents have reached puberty, brothers and sisters are more likely to seek privacy from each other when dressing or bathing. And while we do not practice anything as "alien" as scarification, we do have our share of body rituals which often are not seen until adolescence and which might seem equally alien to someone unfamiliar with our society: the punching of holes in earlobes or other parts of the body (ear or body piercing), the scraping of hair from faces or legs (shaving), the permanent decoration of skin (tattoos), and the application of brightly colored paints to lips, eyes, and cheeks (putting on makeup).

RECAP

Certain themes are common to the process of social redefinition across many societies. These include the real or symbolic separation of young people from their parents; the accentuation of differences between males and females; and the passing on of cultural, historical, or practical information deemed important for adulthood.

Variations in Social Transitions

Different societies recognize and orchestrate the passage into adult status at different times and in different ways. In this respect, although the presence of social redefinition in a general sense is a universal feature of adolescent development, there is considerable diversity in the nature of the transition. Examining social redefinition from cross-cultural and historical perspectives provides a valuable means of contrasting the nature of adolescence in different social contexts. Two very important dimensions along which societies differ in the process of social redefinition are in the explicitness, or *clarity,* of the transition and in the smoothness, or *continuity,* of the passage.

Variations in Clarity. Initiation ceremonies are in many ways religious ceremonies. As such, they are most often employed in societies in which a shared religious belief unites the community and structures individuals' daily experiences. Universal, formal initiation ceremonies therefore have never been prevalent in American society, largely because of the diversity of the population and the general separation of religious experience from everyday affairs.

There are, however, factors other than the presence of formal rites of passage that determine how clear the transition into adult status is to the young person and society. One such factor concerns the extent to which various aspects of the status change occur at about the same time for an individual and during the same general time period for adolescents growing up together (Elder, 1980). When transitions into adult work, family, and citizenship roles occur close in time, and when most members of a cohort experience these transitions at about the same age, the passage into adulthood takes on greater clarity. If all young people were to graduate from high school, enter the labor force, and marry at the age of 18, this age would be an implicit boundary between adolescence and adulthood, even without a formal ceremony. But when different aspects of the passage occur at different times, and when adolescents growing up in a similar environment experience these transitions in different order and along different schedules, the boundary between adolescence and adulthood is made more cloudy.

The clarity of social redefinition in contemporary society. When did you become an adolescent? When did you (or when will you) become an adult? If you are like most individuals in contemporary society, your answers to these questions will not be clear-cut. We have no formal ceremonies marking the transition from childhood into adolescence, nor do we have any to mark the passage from adolescence into adulthood. Although in many religious, cultural, and social groups the young American adolescent may undergo an initiation ceremony of sorts—the confirmation, the Bar Mitzvah, the quinceañera, and the "coming-out" parties of debutantes are some examples—rarely does such a rite have much significance outside the youngster's family, circle of friends, or religious community. School graduation ceremonies perhaps come the closest to universal rites of passage in contemporary society, but school graduation does not bring with it many meaningful or universal changes in social status, responsibilities, or privileges. As a result, social redefinition in contemporary society does not give the adolescent any clear indication of when his or her responsibilities and privileges as an adult begin.

Attaining adult status is essentially an individual matter in contemporary society, and the absence of clear-cut and universal markers of the passage make the process confusing. It is often difficult for young people to tell when they have reached adulthood. In many states, for example, the age for starting employment is 15; for leaving high school, 16; for attending restricted (R-rated) movies without parents, 17; for voting, 18; and for drinking, 21. We have few universal markers of adulthood—adolescents are treated as adults at different times by different people in different contexts. A young person may be legally old enough to drive, but his parents may feel that 16 is too early and may refuse to let him use the family car. Another may be treated like an adult at work, where she works side by side with people three times her age, but she may be treated like a child at home. A third may be viewed as an adult by her mother but as a child by her father. It is little wonder, in light of the mixed and sometimes contradictory expectations facing young people, that for many adolescents the transition into adult roles is a difficult passage to navigate. According to social psychologist Kurt Lewin (1948), the adolescent in modern society is a **marginal man,** caught in a transitional space between childhood and adulthood.

The clarity of social redefinition in traditional cultures. Unlike the case in contemporary society, social redefinition during adolescence is clearly recognized in most traditional cultures. Typically, the passage from childhood into adolescence is marked by a formal initiation ceremony, which publicly proclaims the young person's entrance into a new position in the community (Ford and Beach, 1951). For boys, such ceremonies may take place at the time of puberty, at the attainment of a designated chronological age, or at a time when the community decides that the individual is ready for the status change. For girls, initiation is more often linked to puberty and, in particular, to the onset of menstruation. In both cases, the initiation ceremony serves to ritualize the passing of the young person out of childhood and, if not directly into adulthood, into a period of training for it.

In many initiation ceremonies, the adolescent's physical appearance is changed, so that other members of the community can distinguish between initiated and uninitiated young people. For example, new types of clothing may be worn following initiation; or some sort of surgical operation or scarification may be performed to create a permanent means of marking the individual's adult status. In most traditional societies, there is no mistaking which individuals are adults and which still children.

The clarity of social redefinition in previous eras. The transition into adulthood may actually have been then even more disorderly and cloudy during the early nineteenth century than it is today. According to historian Joseph Kett (1977), many young people at that time moved back and forth between school, where they were viewed as children, and work, where they were viewed as adults. Moreover, timetables for the assumption of adult roles varied considerably from one individual to the next, because they were highly dependent on family and household needs rather than on generally accepted age patterns of school, family, and work transitions. An adolescent might have been working and living away from home, but if his family needed him—because, let's say, someone became ill—he would leave his job and move back in with his parents. During the middle of the nineteenth century, in fact, many young people were neither enrolled in school nor working, occupying a halfway stage that was not quite childhood but not quite adulthood (Katz, 1975). As we noted earlier, industrialization excluded many young people from the labor force, and only those adolescents from affluent families were able to afford private school. Descriptions of adolescent idleness during the era are strikingly reminiscent of descriptions of unemployed, out-of-school youth today. Indeed, concern about juvenile misbehavior was one factor that encouraged the development of public high schools.

One study comparing adolescents' transitions today with those of their counterparts 100 years ago indicates that the passage into adulthood may have been more prolonged as well as less clearly defined during the nineteenth century than it is today. Using census data and historical documents, social historian John Modell and his colleagues compared the timing and patterning of adolescents' transitions in 1970 with those in 1880 (Modell, Furstenberg, and Hershberg, 1976). The researchers examined five transitions, all of which can be thought of as indicators of the passage into adulthood: exit from school, entry into the labor force, departure from home, first marriage, and the establishment of an independent household. They were interested in the extent to which these transitions were negotiated along a common timetable and clustered around a narrow age period.

Compared with contemporary youth, adolescents living in the late nineteenth century underwent family-related transitions (leaving home, getting married, and setting up an independent household) somewhat later, and they made school- and work-related transitions (leaving school and entering the labor force) much earlier. In other words, the passages into adulthood were much more spread out over time. Over time, however, the timing of family-related and nonfamily-related transitions have converged, and the age range during which young people make these transitions is narrower and more universal now than it was 100 years ago (Modell and Goodman, 1990). Interestingly, though, there are some sex differences in the way in which different elements of the transition are ordered, as the box on page 118 describes.

In this respect, it appears as though the transition into adult status today has greater uniformity, if not greater clarity, than it did during much of the nineteenth century. As Modell and his colleagues suggest, those "who see today's period of youth as extended, normless, [and] lacking bounds" would do well to compare the structure of the adolescent passage as it exists today with that of 100 years ago (Modell et al., 1976, p. 31).

RECAP

The process of social definition varies from society to society in its clarity. In some societies, as well as within certain religious and cultural groups, adolescence is marked by a formal initiation ceremony and specific rites of passage, which clearly mark the redefinition of the individual. In others, however, the transition from childhood into adulthood is vague and poorly defined. This absence of clarity is especially the case in contemporary industrialized societies.

● ***Variations in Continuity.*** A second way in which the process of social redefinition varies across cultural and historical contexts is along the dimension of *continuity*—the extent to which the adolescent's transition into adulthood is gradual or abrupt (Benedict, 1934). Gradual transitions, in which the adolescent assumes the roles and status of adulthood bit by bit, are referred to as **continuous transitions.** Transitions that are not so smooth, and in which the young person's entrance into adulthood is more sudden, are referred to as **discontinuous transitions.** Children who grow up working on the family farm and continue this work as adults have a continuous transition into adult work roles. In contrast, children who do not have any work experience while they are growing up and who enter the labor force for the first time when they graduate from college have a discontinuous transition into adult work roles.

The continuity of the adolescent passage in contemporary society. In contemporary society, we tend to exclude young people from the world of adults; we give them little direct training for adult life and then thrust them rather abruptly into total adult independence. Transitions into adulthood in contemporary society are therefore more discontinuous than in other cultural or historical contexts. Consider, for example, three of the most important roles of adulthood that individuals are expected to carry out successfully—the roles of worker, parent, and citizen. In all three cases we find that adolescents in contemporary society receive little preparation for these positions.

For instance, young people are segregated from the workplace throughout most of their childhood and early adolescent years and receive little direct training in school relevant to the work roles they will likely find themselves in as adults. The transition into adult work roles, therefore, is fairly discontinuous—and often difficult—for most young people in industrialized society. And according to former U.S. Secretary of Labor Ray Marshall, writing with his colleague, Robert Glover, "America has the worst approach to school-to-work transition of *any* industrialized nation" (Glover and Marshall, 1993, p. 588, italics added).

During the early 1990s, and with the enthusiastic backing of President Clinton, many educators and policy-makers began calling for changes in our educational system in order to improve the **school-to-work transition** (e.g., Kazis, 1993; Rosenbaum, Stern, Hamilton, Hamilton, Berryman, and Kazis, 1992;

Stern, Finkelstein, Stone, Latting, and Dornsife, 1994). These writers have argued that many individuals have difficulty making this transition successfully because there really exists only one acceptable way of making this passage—through higher education—and not all individuals can, or want to, make the transition via this route. Moreover, this transition is inherently discontinuous, which makes it harder to negotiate.

But is it possible to create a route from high school to adult work that doesn't involve college? Many critics of the American educational system say that there is. They point out that in other industrialized countries many different possibilities for high school students exist other than going to college, including, most importantly, the option of taking a formal **youth apprenticeship;** this provides structured, work-based learning that will likely lead to a high-quality job. Typically, a high school student would combine time in an apprenticeship with time in school as he or she gradually made the transition from school to work. Among the most successful models of youth apprenticeships are those developed in Germany, in which young people during their last few years of high school can spend 1 or 2 days per week in school and the remainder of the week at a job supervised by master workers. Unlike American high school students, who have difficulty finding good jobs after graduation, German graduates who complete a youth apprenticeship program usually enter a high-quality job within a few days of finishing school (Rosenbaum et al., 1992). Although some writers have questioned whether the German model can be directly copied in the United States, there is hope that some version of an apprenticeship system can be developed successfully in America.

Actually, the transition of young people into adult family roles is even more abrupt than is their transition into work roles. Before actually becoming a parent, most young people have little training in child rearing or other related matters. Families are relatively small today, and youngsters are likely to be close in age to their siblings; as a result, few opportunities exist for participating in child-care activities at home. Schools generally offer little if any instruction in family relationships and domestic activities. And with childbirth generally taking place in hospitals rather than at home, few young people today have the opportunity of observing a younger sibling's birth.

Passage into adult citizenship and decision-making roles is also highly discontinuous in contemporary Western society. Adolescents are permitted few opportunities for independence and autonomy in school and are segregated from most of society's political institutions until they complete their formal education. Young people are permitted to vote once they turn 18 years old, but they have received little preparation for participation in government and community roles before this time.

Some fifty years ago, anthropologist Ruth Benedict (1934) pointed out that the degree of stress individuals experience at adolescence is related to the degree of continuity they experience in making the transition into adulthood; the more discontinuous the passage, the more stressful it is likely to be. Benedict's view suggests that adolescent turmoil, if it exists, is more likely a consequence of environmental than biological factors.

It is little surprise, then, that some young people today have difficulty in assuming adult roles and responsibilities. Instead of being gradually socialized into work, family, and citizenship positions, adolescents in modern society typically are segregated from activities in these arenas during most of their childhood and youth. Yet young people are supposed to be able to perform these roles capably on reaching the age of majority. With little preparation in meaningful work, adolescents are

THE SEXES

SIMILARITIES AND DIFFERENCES IN THE TRANSITION INTO ADULTHOOD

The transition from adolescence to adulthood in America is marked by several related changes in social roles. Among the most important events in this transition are the completion of formal schooling, entrance into the full-time labor force, marriage, and parenthood. One way to think about the transition into adulthood, therefore, is to think about the transition out of one role (that of student) and into three other roles (worker, spouse, and parent) (Marini, 1984).

Because these four transitions do not occur simultaneously, it is interesting to ask how they might be related to one another over time. Do most individuals finish school before taking on a full-time job, or does entry into the world of work precede leaving school? How do transitions into family roles, such as spouse and parent, link up with nonfamily transitions? For instance, do individuals become "adults" in nonfamily roles (that is, by leaving school and entering the workforce) before or after they become adults with respect to family roles? Is one sequence more common than another?

Sociologist Margaret Marini has examined these questions by looking at the way in which role transitions during young adulthood are ordered in contemporary America. Using data collected as a part of a longitudinal follow-up of individuals who had been high school students during the late 1950s, Marini was able to look at the relations among the role transitions out of school and into work, marriage, and parenthood. Although Marini found that about half of all males and females followed one particular sequence of role transitions, she also found several important differences between males' and females' patterns that have implications for understanding sex differences in educational and occupational attainment.

The most common sequence followed for both sexes was (1) exit from school, (2) entrance into work, (3) entrance into marriage, and (4) entrance into parenthood. But half of all the individuals did not follow this "normative" path toward adulthood. One-fifth of the women and nearly one-third of the men had taken a full-time job before finishing school; some worked while in school, and others left school for a time and returned later. One-fifth of the women and nearly one-quarter of the men married before finishing school, and about 1 in 10 men and women had married and become parents before their education was finished.

In general, the longer an individual stayed in school, the less likely he or she was to follow the expected sequence—primarily because longer schooling made it more likely that one or another of the transitions would occur before education was completed. At the turn of the century, for example, the average age by which the majority of individuals had completed school was still a few years younger than the average age by which even the

expected to find, get, and keep a job immediately after completing their schooling. With essentially no training for marriage or parenting, they are expected to form their own families, manage their own households, and raise their own children soon after they reach adulthood. And without any previous involvement in community activities, they are expected on reaching the age of majority to vote, pay taxes, and behave as responsible citizens.

The continuity of the adolescent passage in traditional cultures. The high level of discontinuity found in contemporary Amer-

youngest members of the generation had married. By 1930, however, individuals were staying in school longer and marrying earlier, so that there were large numbers of individuals who were leaving school and marrying at about the same age. By 1960, these trends had continued to the point where substantial numbers of individuals were marrying *before* finishing their education. Although between 1960 and 1980 the tendency toward younger and younger marriages that had characterized the first half of the century began to reverse itself, the average age at which individuals completed their education continued to increase. As a result, the time frame within which individuals finished school and got married remained fairly narrow (Modell and Goodman, 1990).

A similar pattern is found when we look at individuals' entrance into the labor force. Although individuals are staying in school longer than they did 100 years ago, they have barely delayed their entry into the labor force. These findings counter the widely held belief that entering into work or family commitments before finishing school necessarily impedes educational attainment. As Marini notes, we need more research on the long-term occupational experiences of students who marry or work before completing school.

Why were men somewhat more likely than women to interrupt or combine their schooling with work or family commitments? Women who went on to higher levels of education were especially likely to delay taking on family roles. Marini suggests that women's traditional family roles—and, in particular, their greater involvement in domestic responsibilities—make it more difficult for them to move between student and nonstudent roles and make marriage and parenthood "less compatible with the continuation of education for women than for men" (Marini, 1984, p. 78). As she writes, "Although for men the continuation of education does not permit direct fulfillment of the traditional male role of provider, because of its future payoff for the well-being of the family, it is viewed as an investment in the family's future. Women's educational and occupational pursuits tend to be viewed as secondary to those of their husbands" (p. 78). Put simply, men find it easier than women to become both spouse and parent while still in school.

Because becoming a spouse and parent interrupts the process of educational attainment more for women than for men, it may be more important for women to delay taking on family roles until after they have finished school, or they risk compromising their careers. Indeed, Marini has pointed out that the earlier transition into parenthood among women than men and its greater educational cost for women are main factors in the generally lower occupational attainment of women. Although it is possible for men and women to marry and become parents before they stop being students, the costs of deviating from the "normative" sequence are not equal for the two sexes.

ica is not characteristic of adolescence in traditional societies. Consider the socialization of young people in Samoa, for example. From early childhood on, youngsters are involved in work tasks that have a meaningful connection to the work they will perform as adults. They are involved in the care of younger children, in the planting and harvesting of crops, and in the gathering and preparation of food. Their entrance into adult work roles is gradual and continuous, with work tasks being graded to children's skills and intelligence. Young people are charged with the socialization of their infant brothers and sisters, particularly during

In societies in which hunting, farming, and fishing are the primary work activities, young people often are taught the skills they will need as adult workers by accompanying—and observing—their elders in daily activities rather than by attending school. (Owen Franken/Stock, Boston)

middle childhood, when they are not yet strong enough to make a substantial contribution to the community's fishing and farming activities. Gradually, young people are taught the fundamentals of weaving, boating, fishing, building, and farming. By the time they have reached late adolescence, Samoan youngsters are well trained in the tasks they will need to perform as adults (Mead, 1928).

Such continuity is generally the case in societies in which hunting, fishing, and farming are the chief work activities. As Margaret Mead (1928) observed, the emphasis in these societies is on informal education in context rather than on formal education in schools. Children are typically not isolated in separate educational institutions, and they accompany the adult members of their community in daily activities. Adolescents' preparation for adulthood, therefore, comes largely from observation and "hands-on" experience in the same tasks that they will continue to carry out as adults. Typically, boys learn the tasks performed by adult men, and girls learn those performed by adult women. When work activities take adults out of the community, it is not uncommon for children to travel with their parents on work expeditions (N. Miller, 1928).

The continuity of the adolescent passage in previous eras. During earlier periods in American history, the transition into adult roles and responsibilities began at an earlier age and proceeded along a more continuous path than generally is the case today. This is especially true with regard to work. During the eighteenth century, of course, and well into the early part of the nineteenth century, when many families were engaged in farming, a good number of adolescents were expected to work on the family farm and to learn the skills necessary to carry on the enterprise. Some youngsters, generally boys, accompanied their fathers on business trips, learning the trades of salesmanship and commerce (Kett, 1977)—a pattern reminiscent of that found in many traditional societies.

Many other young people left home relatively early—some as early as age 12—to work for nonfamilial adults in the community or in nearby villages (Katz, 1975; Kett, 1977). Even as recently as the midnineteenth century, it was common for young adolescents to work as apprentices, learning skills and trades in preparation for the work roles of adulthood; others left home temporarily to work as servants or to learn domestic skills. The average nineteenth-century youngster left school well before the age of 15 (Modell, Furstenberg, and Hershberg, 1976).

However, census data and historical documents—such as letters, diaries, and community histories—indicate that although adolescents of 100 years ago took on full-time employment earlier in life than they typically do today, they were likely to live under adult supervision for a longer period than is usual in contemporary society. That is, although the transition into work roles may have occurred earlier in the nineteenth century than in the twentieth century, this transition was made in the context of semi-independence rather than complete emancipation (Katz, 1975; Kett, 1977; Modell and Goodman, 1990). This semi-independent period—which for many young people spanned the decade from about ages 12 to 22, and even beyond—may have increased the degree of continuity of the passage into adulthood by providing a time during which young people could assume certain adult responsibilities gradually (Katz, 1975). The semi-independence characteristic of adolescence in the nineteenth century had largely disappeared by 1900, however (Modell and Goodman, 1990).

Socialization for family and citizenship roles may also have been more continuous in previous historical eras. Living at home during the late-adolescent and early-adult years, particularly in the larger families characteristic of households 100 years ago, contributed to the preparation of young people for future family life. It was common for the children in a family to span a wide age range, and remaining at home undoubtedly placed the older adolescent from time to time in child-rearing roles (President's Science Advisory Committee, 1974). As opposed to today's adolescents, who typically have little experience with infants, adolescents 100 years ago were more likely to have fed, dressed, and cared for their younger siblings. They were also expected to assist their parents in maintaining the household (Modell et al., 1976), and this experience probably made it easier for young people to manage when they eventually established a home separate from their parents. One recent study indicates that leaving one's parents' home earlier and living independently before marriage encourages young women to develop less traditional attitudes, values, and plans than their counterparts who live with their parents as young adults (Waite, Goldscheider, and Witsberger, 1986). Interestingly, individuals from single-parent homes, stepfamilies, adoptive families, and foster homes tend to leave home at an earlier age than do their peers whose biological parents remain married (Aquilino, 1991; Mitchell, Wister, and Burch, 1989).

Recent reports of changes in home-leaving are noteworthy, however, and suggest that this aspect of the transition into adulthood may be changing: On average, individuals are living with their parents longer today than was the case 30 years ago; more than half of all 20- to 24-year-olds either live with or are supported by their parents—up from 40 percent in 1960 (Kutner, 1988). Most experts attribute this trend to the increased cost of housing, which makes it difficult for individuals to move out of their parents' home (or give up their parents' financial support) and establish a separate residence.

The current impact of the economy on adolescents' home-leaving reaffirms the importance of looking at the broader context in defining what "normal" adolescence is. In 1960, because it was the exception to live at home past high school, we tended to view individuals who did so as being less independent or less mature than their peers. But now that living at home has become the norm, we no longer view it as an index of maturity.

Major historical events, such as the Great Depression, may temporarily alter the transition to adulthood. During the Depression, many adolescent boys had to leave school and enter the workforce full-time at an unusually early age. Many adolescent girls also were forced to leave school early, in order to assume adult responsibilities at home. (Bettmann Newsphotos)

Above all, we need to keep in mind that, because adolescence is in part defined by society, its nature changes along with society.

Indeed, some massive historical events such as the 1991 war in the Persian Gulf or the economic recession of the early 1980s may temporarily alter the nature of the adolescent passage and may produce exceptions to general historical trends. One such event was the Great Depression of the early 1930s. Sociologist Glen Elder, Jr., has examined the impact of growing up during this era on adolescents' behavior and development (Elder, 1974), and many of his findings are relevant to the issue of continuity in the adolescent passage. Elder looked at the data collected during the Depression as part of a longitudinal study of individuals living in Oakland, California. The group Elder focused on was born between 1920 and 1921 and thus were preadolescents during the worst years of the Depression.

Elder found that youngsters whose families experienced economic hardship during these years were more likely to be involved in adult-like tasks at an earlier age than were their more privileged peers. Boys, for example, were more likely to work and to help support their families; girls were more likely to play a major role with household chores. And both boys and girls were more likely to marry and enter into full-time employment relatively early. Thus, some aspects of the semi-independent stage of adolescence that had become uncommon by 1930 may have reappeared during the Great Depression. For many youngsters growing up during this time period, the adolescent passage may have resembled that of an earlier era.

Research on contemporary German and Polish youngsters by Rainer Silbereisen and his colleagues (Silbereisen, Schwarz, Nowak, Kracke, and von Eye, 1993) indicates that, still today, growing up under adversity is associated with an earlier transition into adult roles and behaviors. Whether "earlier" means "better" is a matter of some debate, however; as you will read in Chapter 8, some writers believe that adolescents profit psychologically from having a relatively long period of time to develop without being burdened by adult responsibilities.

RECAP

In addition to the clarity of the adolescent passage, societies also vary in the extent to which the passage is continuous or discontinuous. In a continuous passage, the adolescent assumes the roles and status of adulthood bit by bit, with a good deal of preparation and training along the way. In a discontinuous passage, the adolescent is thrust into adulthood abruptly, with little prior preparation. Contemporary industrialized societies generally are characterized by a discontinuous passage into adulthood.

THE TRANSITION INTO ADULTHOOD IN CONTEMPORARY SOCIETY

We do not know for certain whether the discontinuity characteristic of the passage into adulthood today impedes the adolescent's psychosocial development and responsible assumption of adult roles. But many social scientists have speculated that these consequences may result. Identity development, to take one example, is probably made more difficult by the higher levels of confusion and inconsistency that surround the social passage into adulthood in modern society. Erik Erikson (1968) and other theorists view identity development during adolescence as the result

THE SCIENTIFIC STUDY OF ADOLESCENCE

DOES LEAVING HOME TOO EARLY CAUSE PROBLEMS FOR ADOLESCENTS?

Scientists often have difficulty in determining whether two factors that are associated with each other, or *correlated,* have any causal connection to each other. For example, we might find that smart people eat a great deal of fish (i.e., that intelligence and eating fish are correlated), but it wouldn't necessarily be correct to conclude on the basis of this finding that eating fish *causes* people to become smarter. It might be the case, instead, that smart people are more aware of the nutritional benefits of eating seafood and choose to eat seafood more often—in which case we might be correct in saying that being smart "causes" people to eat more fish. Or it might be the case that some other factor—living near the ocean, for example—is associated both with being smart and with eating fish, making it only *appear* that intelligence and fish-eating are independently related. It is far more difficult to demonstrate that one thing causes another than to show that the two are merely correlated. A nice example of the difference between correlation and causation is found in a study of early home-leaving and problem behavior (Stattin and Magnusson, 1994a).

The researchers had been following a sample of urban youth from Solna, a community near Stockholm, from birth onward. The individuals were all born between 1955 and 1958. Data were collected each year during the children's first 18 years of life and again at the ages of 21, 25, and 36 years. The median age for leaving home in this sample was 18 for girls and 20 for boys (a **median** is a type of average, defined as the score above and below which there are equal numbers of people in a sample) (see accompanying figure). In the study of home-leaving, the researchers focused their attention on females.

When the researchers computed the correlation between age of leaving home and various indicators of the women's behavioral adjustment, they discovered that earlier home-leaving was associated, in young adulthood, with earlier marriage, more childbearing, and lower educational attainment, measured in terms of years of school completed. But did leaving home early *cause* these outcomes? Before you conclude that it did, think about the difference between correlation and causation.

Because the researchers had collected data throughout the women's lives, they were able to examine the correlation between various indicators of adjustment during childhood and early adolescence and the age of leaving home later on. The results showed that young women who chose to leave home earlier than their peers may have been dif-

of the interplay between the young person's growing self-awareness and society's changing view of him or her. It is not difficult to see, then, how an "identity crisis" might be intensified by not knowing whether one is an adult or a child or when the change in social definition takes place.

In recent years, observers of adolescence in America have suggested that the discontinuity in the passage into adulthood has become so great that many youngsters, especially those not bound for college, are having tremendous problems negotiating the passage into adult roles (Hamburg, 1986; Kazis, 1993; National Research Council, 1993; William T. Grant Foundation, 1988). One national commission found that society had so neglected the needs of noncollege-bound adolescents that its report called them "The Forgotten Half" (William T. Grant Foundation, 1988). Another ferent from their agemates long before leaving home. Women who left home relatively early had shown, throughout childhood and early adolescence, more strained family relations, poorer adjustment, more impulsivity, more aggression, higher rates of school problems, lower educational aspirations, more drug and alcohol use, earlier sexual activity, and more sexual partners. Instead of early home-leaving *causing* lower educational attainment, then, it appears as though having more modest educational plans precedes early home-leaving. In other words, girls who have lower educational aspirations by mid-adolescence may complete less school *and* may also choose to leave home early. By the same token, girls who are more sexually active than their peers may marry earlier *and* may also choose to leave home early.

As the old social science maxim goes, "Correlation is not causation."

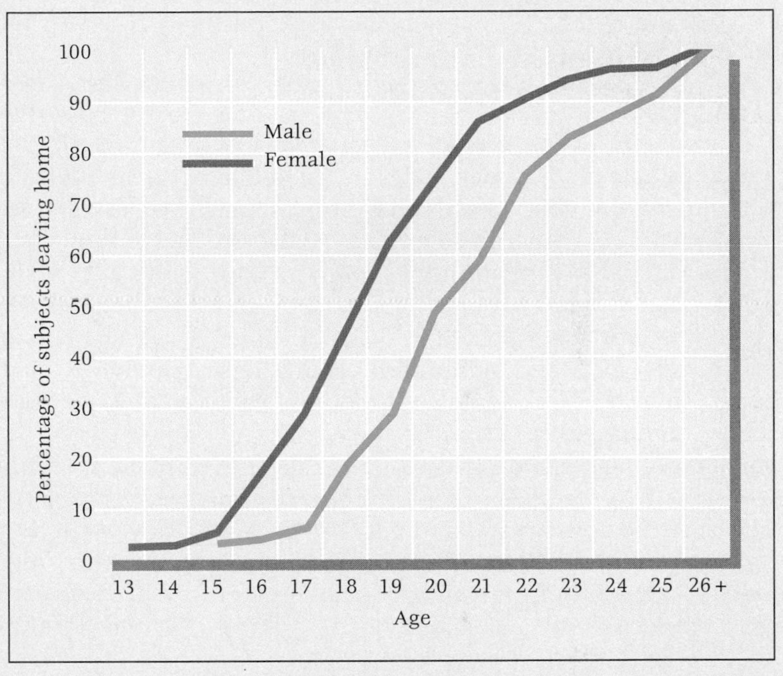

SOURCE: Stattin, H., and Magnusson, C. (1994a, February). *Behavioral and interpersonal antecedents behind the age at leaving home, and the future consequences for parent-child relations.* Paper presented at the biennial meetings of the Society for Research on Adolescence, San Diego.

prestigious panel, in a disheartening volume, estimated that nearly seven million young Americans—about one-quarter of adolescents 10- to 17-years-old—are at risk of failing to achieve productive adult lives (National Research Council, 1993).

These observers point to problems many young people experience in developing a coherent sense of identity, establishing a healthy sense of autonomy, and making informed decisions about commitments to family and work. They note that the lack of clarity and continuity in the transition into adulthood may contribute to some of the problems faced by adolescents in contemporary society and may also contribute to some of the problems faced by contemporary society in dealing with young people. Many social scientists believe that our relatively high rates of divorce, family violence, youth unemployment, juvenile delinquency, and teenage alcoholism stem in part from the confusing and contradictory nature of the passage into adulthood in modern society (National Research Council, 1993).

Special Transitional Problems of Poor and Minority Youth

No discussion of the transitional problems of young people in America today is complete without noting that youngsters from some minority groups—African-American, Hispanic-American, and American Indian youth, in particular—have more trouble negotiating the transition into adulthood than do their white and Asian-American counterparts. Youngsters from minority backgrounds make up a substantial and growing portion of the adolescent population in America. By the end of this century, about 15 percent of the youth population will be African-American, and another 13 percent will be Hispanic-American. Approximately 4 percent of the youth population will be composed of Asian-American, Pacific Islander, and American Indian youth. In other words, about one-third of the youth population in the year 2000 will be from minority groups (Wetzel, 1987) (see Figure 3.1). By the year 2020, minority children will account for nearly half of all U.S. children (Pallas, Natriello, and McDill, 1989).

The Effects of Poverty on the Transition into Adulthood. Growing up in poverty may profoundly impair youngsters' ability to move easily between adolescence and adulthood. Poverty is associated with failure in school, unemployment, and out-of-wedlock pregnancy, all of which contribute to transition difficulties (Edelman and Ladner, 1991; National Research Council, 1993). Because minority youngsters are more likely than other teenagers to grow up in poverty, they are more likely than other youths to encounter transitional problems during middle and late adolescence (see Figure 3.2). Poverty is especially high among adolescents living in single-parent families, in the South, and in urban and rural (as opposed to suburban) communities (Sum and Fogg, 1991).

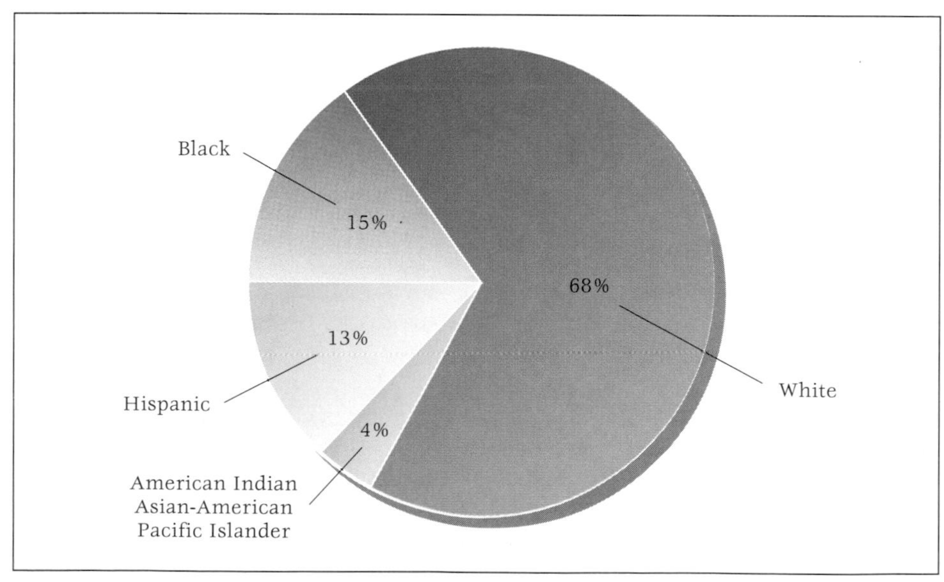

FIGURE 3.1
By the end of this century, youngsters from minority backgrounds will compose about one-third of the U.S. adolescent population. (Wetzel, 1987)

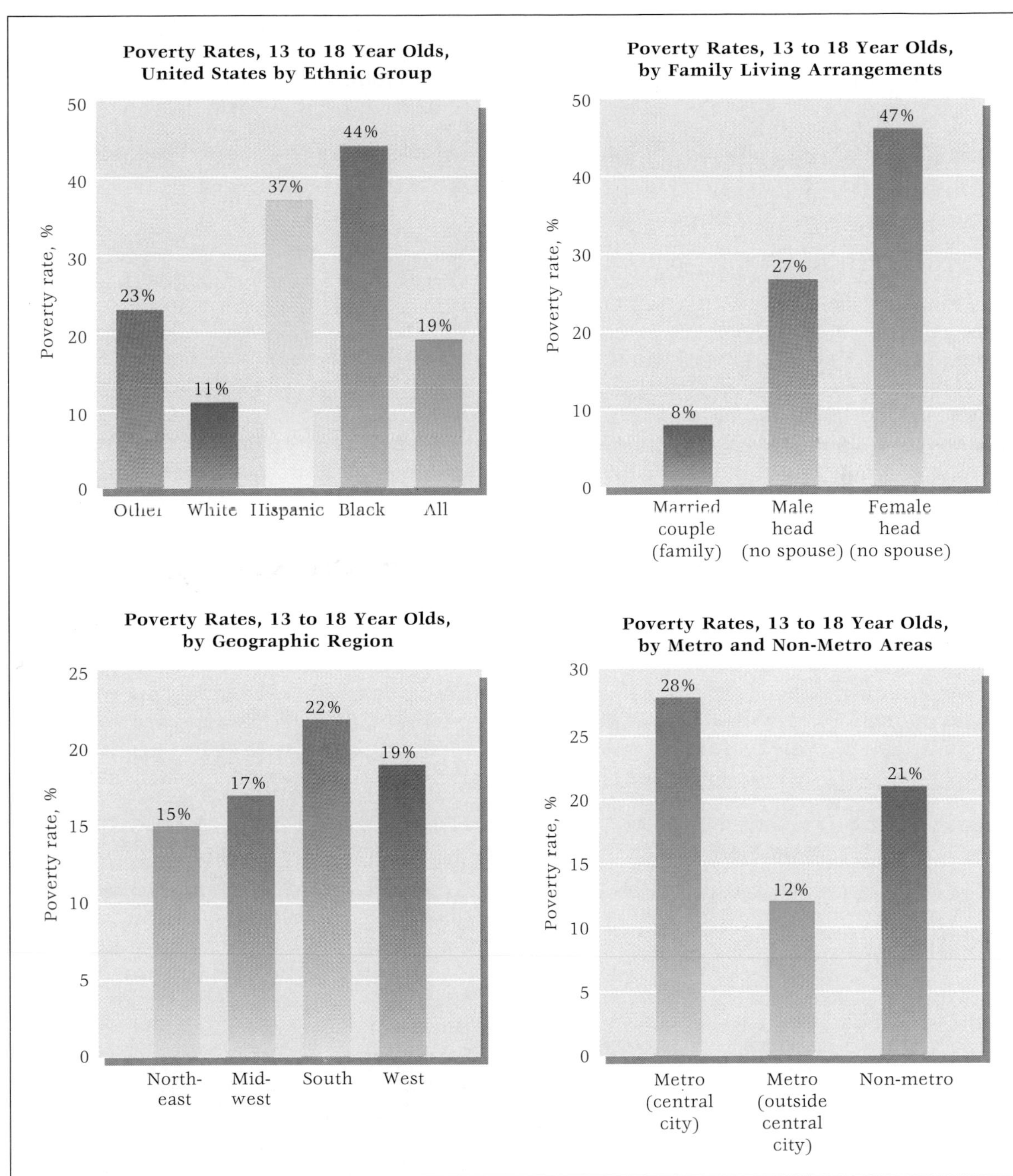

FIGURE 3.2 *Poverty rates among adolescents in the United States vary by ethnicity, family living arrangement, geographic region, and urbanicity.* (Sum and Fogg, 1991)

As you will read in later chapters, school dropout rates are much higher among Hispanic-American and American Indian teenagers than among other groups, and college enrollment is lower among African-American, Hispanic-American, and American Indian youth. Unemployment is much higher among African-American, Hispanic-American, and American Indian teenagers. African-American and Hispanic-American youth are more likely to be victimized by crime. And rates of out-of-wedlock births are higher among African-American and Hispanic-American teenagers than among white teenagers (Wetzel, 1987). All these factors disrupt the transition into adulthood by limiting individuals' economic and occupational success. Poverty impedes the transition to adulthood among all teenagers, regardless of race, of course; but because minority youth are more likely to grow up poor, they are more likely to have transition problems.

As William Julius Wilson documented in his widely cited book *The Truly Disadvantaged,* the situation is particularly grave for poor minority youngsters growing up in the inner city (Wilson, 1987). Many of these young people grow up without knowing a single adult "whose stable employment supports an even modest standard of family life" (Wilson, cited in Nightingale and Wolverton, 1993, p. 480). As two writers for the Carnegie Council on Adolescent Development noted with depressing clarity:

> Those who have succeeded in attaining a solid standard of living often have moved away from the city to the suburbs, further depriving young people of role models. Such young people have no experience working or living among people with . . . different kinds of jobs and their choices are limited to poorly paying and unrewarding jobs or quick money from drug running. Often the only role models available in areas of concentrated poverty are gang members or drug dealers, who appear to have what adolescents desperately want, respect and money.
>
> In these neighborhoods, often adult women were adolescent mothers themselves. Their daughters, in turn, may see a child of their own as the only hope for affection and respect, and perhaps even stability. However, the babies quickly become demanding toddlers. Usually the fathers of these children do not marry or provide family support. Too early child-bearing can have disastrous consequences for both mother and child, including dropping out of school and long-term unemployment for the mother, and low birth-weight and other health problems for the child. (Nightingale and Wolverton, 1993, p. 480)

● ***The Effects of Growing Up in a Poor Neighborhood.*** One factor contributing to the especially worrisome situation of poor youth is that poverty became much more concentrated during the 1970s and 1980s, with greater and greater clustering of poor families into economically and racially segregated communities. In response to this, and taking the lead from Wilson's ideas about the devastating impact of "concentrated" poverty outlined in *The Truly Disadvantaged,* a number of researchers have turned their attention to the study of adolescents in poor neighborhoods. Their aim is to see whether *neighborhood* poverty, in addition to *family* poverty, is predictive of adolescents' transition difficulties (e.g., Brooks-Gunn, Duncan, Klebanov, and Sealand, 1993; Coulten and Pandy, 1992). These researchers hypothesize that living in a community that has a high proportion of poor families affects adolescents for the worse, regardless of their own family's situation.

For instance, even if an adolescent lives in a economically stable, supportive household, he or she may be adversely affected by growing up in a community that has a high unemployment rate (because there will be fewer employed role models with whom to identify), few resources (like parks and libraries), and a high crime rate (as is often the case in poor

Gang membership is common among adolescents who grow up in poverty. (Bob Daemmrich/ Tony Stone)

neighborhoods) (National Research Council, 1993). Exposure to concentrated poverty is an especially prevalent problem among nonwhite adolescents. Close to 90 percent of all residents of the poorest neighborhoods in the United States are from ethnic minority groups (National Research Council, 1993).

Studies of neighborhood poverty and its impact are just now beginning to appear, but there appears to be growing evidence that coming of age amidst concentrated poverty has negative effects on the transition to adulthood, and these effects are above and beyond those attributable to growing up in a poor family. Adolescents growing up in impoverished communities are more likely than their peers from equally poor households, but better neighborhoods, to bear children as teenagers and to drop out of high school—two factors that, as you will read in later chapters, seriously interfere with the successful transition into adulthood (Brooks-Gunn et al., 1993; Crane, 1991). Interestingly, it seems to be the *absence of affluent neighbors,* rather than the *presence of poor neighbors,* that places adolescents in impoverished communities at greatest risk.

How might concentrated neighborhood poverty adversely affect the behavior and development of adolescents? At least two mechanisms have been suggested. First, some writers (e.g., Crane, 1991) suggest that social problems are contagious; they are spread from one adolescent to another in a pattern not unlike a medical epidemic. To the extent that poverty increases behavior problems, adolescents living in poor neighborhoods will come into contact with deviant peers all the more often. Second, poverty in neighborhoods breeds social isolation, which, in turn, leads to ineffective parenting (Brooks-Gunn et al., 1993; Sampson and Lamb, 1994). When parents are not effective in supervising and monitoring their teenagers, for example, the teenagers are more likely to get into trouble.

Growing up amid concentrated poverty is a risk factor for young people all over the world, of course. According to recent estimates, approximately 100 million children and adolescents are growing up on the streets of large cities worldwide (Campos, Raffaelli, Ude, Greco, Ruff, Rolf, Antunes, Halsey, Greco, and the Street Youth Study, 1994). One recent study of street youth in Brazil, for example, compared youngsters "on" the street (that is, youth who were working and contributing to the welfare of their families) with youngsters "of" the street (youth who were homeless and without stable adult supervision); as you might expect, the homeless youngsters were at great risk for involvement in crime, drug use, violent victimization, and dangerous sex (Campos et al., 1994).

What Can Be Done to Ease the Transition?

A variety of suggestions have been offered for making the transition into adulthood smoother for all young people, especially those who are not college-bound, including restructuring secondary education, expanding work and volunteer opportunities, and improving the quality of community life for adolescents and their parents. Some groups have called for expanded opportunities in the workplace as a way of making the high school years more of a "bridge" between adolescence and adulthood (Kazis, 1993). Other groups have suggested that adolescents be encouraged to spend time in voluntary, nonmilitary service activities—such as staffing day-care centers, working with the elderly, or cleaning up the environment—for a few years after high school graduation so that they can learn responsibility and adult roles (Children's Defense Fund, 1989). Still others have pointed out that adolescents cannot come of age successfully without the help of adults and that programs are needed to strengthen families and communities and bring adolescents into contact with adult mentors (National Research Council, 1993). Overall, most experts agree that a comprehensive approach to the problem is needed and that such an approach must simultaneously address the educational, employment, interpersonal, and health needs of adolescents from all walks of life (Dryfoos, 1990).

RECAP

Many social commentators have argued that the vague and discontinuous nature of the adolescent passage in contemporary society has contributed to numerous psychological and behavioral problems among today's youth. These difficulties are more severe among adolescents who are not bound for college, and especially so among poor, minority youth living in pockets of concentrated poverty within the inner city. Most experts agree that a comprehensive approach to the problem is needed and that such an approach must simultaneously address the educational, employment, interpersonal, and health needs of adolescents from all walks of life.

KEY TERMS

age of majority
Bar (Bas) Mitzvah
brother-sister avoidance
child protectionists
continuous transitions
discontinuous transitions

extrusion
initiation ceremony
inventionists
juvenile justice system
marginal man
median
quinceañera
scarification
school-to-work transition
social redefinition
teenager
youth
youth apprenticeship

FOR FURTHER READING

Hamilton, S. (1990). *Apprenticeship for adulthood.* New York: Free Press. A thoughtful discussion of the school-to-work transition in the United States and abroad, with an emphasis on the European apprenticeship system.

Kett, J. (1977). *Rites of passage: Adolescence in America, 1790 to the present.* New York: Basic Books. An extensive discussion of how adolescence in America has changed over the last two centuries.

Mead, M. (1928). *Coming of age in Samoa.* New York: Morrow. Margaret Mead's classic discussion of adolescence in the South Pacific and what we can learn about our own society by studying a more traditional one.

Modell, J., and Goodman, M. (1990). Historical perspectives. In S. Feldman and G. Elliott (Eds.), *At the threshold: The developing adolescent.* Cambridge, Mass.: Harvard University Press. An excellent overview of the recent history of adolescence, with an emphasis on its definition in the United States and the United Kingdom.

National Research Council. (1993). *Losing generations.* Washington, D.C.: National Academy Press. The report of a panel of the National Academy of Sciences on the transition problems of high-risk adolescents.

Schlegel, A., and Barry, H. (1991). *Adolescence: An anthropological inquiry.* New York: Free Press. A recent anthropological study of adolescence, with an emphasis on gender differences in the social definition of the individual.

PART TWO

THE CONTEXTS OF ADOLESCENCE

CHAPTER 4

FAMILIES

(Frank Siteman/Picture Cube)

In the eyes of many, the American family by 1990 had become an endangered species, and children and adolescents were bearing the costs of the family's demise. According to some observers, the all-too-familiar problems of young people—low achievement test scores, high rates of alcohol and drug use, sexual precocity, violence in the schools—reflected the progressive fragmentation of the family (e.g., Uhlenberg and Eggebeen, 1986).

Others, less pessimistic, argued that the family had not died but changed. They noted that although the family of the 1950s—two parents (with mother at home), three children, and a station wagon—had become less common, new forms of family life, commendable in their own right, were emerging. The family of the 1950s, these observers pointed out, was not very well suited for life in the 1990s, and there was little reason to lament its disappearance.

There is no question that, in America and in many comparably industrialized countries, the family has undergone a series of profound changes during the past quarter-century. Rising rates of divorce, increases in maternal employment, a changing international economy, and accelerating geographic mobility all have dramatically altered the world in which children and adolescents grow up. And, although some of the most striking trends in family life slowed during the 1980s, they did not reverse, by any means. Between 1980 and 1990, for example, the number of American single parents grew by 41 percent, and the number of divorced mothers grew at a rate of nearly 2 percent per year (*New York Times,* 1991). Nevertheless, qucstions about whether these changes have weakened the family's influence over young people or, in one way or another, have harmed young people are difficult to answer. Yes, the family has changed—but so has society. This chapter and the three that follow focus on the changing nature of adolescence in contemporary society. As you will see, it is not only the family that has changed.

Amid all this talk of change, it is important to bear in mind two fundamental points about young people and their families that have not changed very much at all. First, the family remains an extremely important influence on adolescent development. As an influence on the development of identity, autonomy, and achievement, for example, few forces are as significant as the young person's family. And second, regardless of the family's structure or composition—one parent or two, natural or reconstituted, employed mother or unemployed father—having positive and warm family relationships stands out as one of the most powerful predictors and correlates of healthy psychosocial growth during the adolescent years. In this chapter, we take a close look at families during adolescence and at why they exert such an important influence on development.

THE ADOLESCENT'S FAMILY TODAY

Just how dramatic have the changes in American family life been over the past forty years? Consider four of the most important shifts: increases in the rate of divorce, increases in the number of single parents, increases in the rate of mothers' employment, and increases in the proportion of families living in poverty. These shifts have transformed the nature of family life for many young people.

As you can see from Figure 4.1, the rate of divorce had increased markedly since 1950 and rose steadily, and at times rapidly, until 1980. (The divorce rate increased most dramatically after 1965 and peaked around 1980.) By 1979, the divorce rate in the United States was the highest in the world (Hetherington,

1981). Between 1980 and 1995, the rate of divorce remained more or less constant, rising somewhat in some years but falling in others. **Demographers** (social scientists who study changes in the composition of the population) estimate that two-thirds of all first marriages are likely to disrupt, and that nearly half of all American children born during the late 1970s and the 1980s—today's teenagers—will experience their parents' divorce and will spend approximately five years in a single-parent household (Martin and Bumpass, 1989). In addition, a sizable percentage of youngsters will spend time in a single-parent household from birth, since they are born outside of marriage (Furstenberg, 1990a). When youngsters live with only one of their natural parents, either in single-parent or in two-parent households, it is nearly always with the mother; only about 10 percent of children whose parents have been divorced live with the father (Furstenberg, 1990).

There are important racial and ethnic differences in these patterns, however. African-American youngsters are far more likely than other youngsters to experience parental divorce and to be born outside of marriage, but they are far less likely to experience their parents' remarriage (Furstenberg, Peterson, Nord, and Zill, 1983). As Figure 4.2 indicates, whereas two-thirds of all African-American children at any given time are residing with a single parent, the ratio is about 1 in 3 among Hispanic-American adolescents and about 1 in 4 among white youngsters (Furstenberg, 1990a). Among children born in 1980—the adolescents of the 1990s—70 percent of whites and nearly 95 percent of African-American youngsters will have spent some time in a single-parent family by the age of 17 (Scales, 1991).

Because more than 75 percent of divorced parents remarry, the majority of youngsters whose parents separate also experience living in a stepfamily at some time. And, because the rate of divorce is higher for second marriages than first marriages, the majority of youth whose parents remarry will experience yet a second divorce. Moreover, because divorces generally occur faster in remarriages,

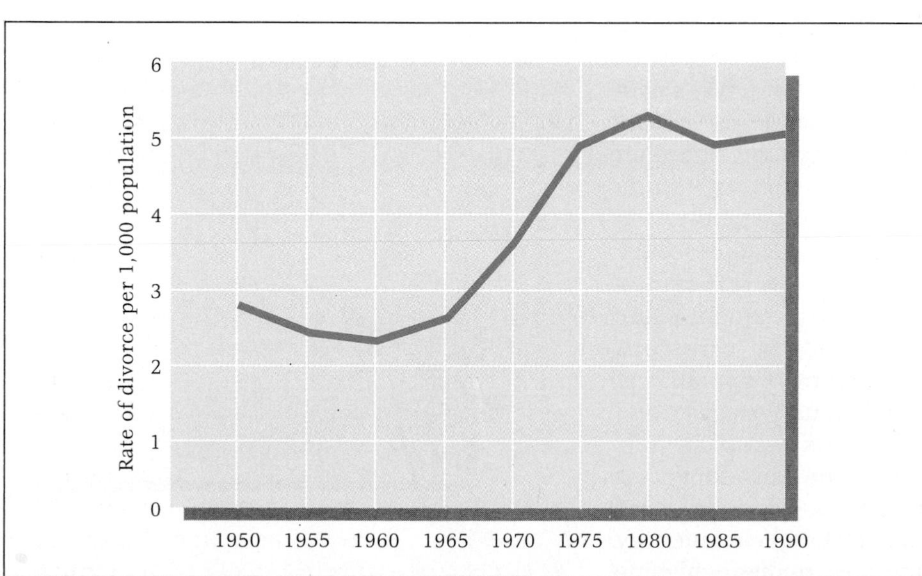

FIGURE 4.1
The divorce rate rose dramatically between 1960 and 1980 and has more or less leveled off since then.

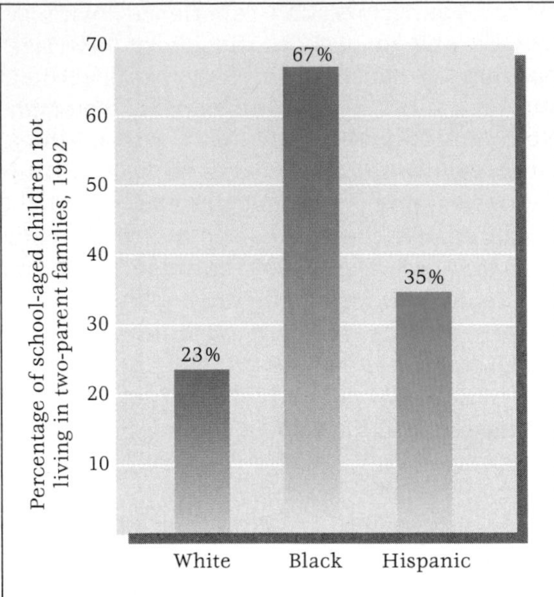

FIGURE 4.2 *The proportion of youngsters living in single-parent households varies a great deal across racial and ethnic groups.* (Statistical Abstract of the United States, 1993)

many children must confront a second divorce before they have finished adapting to having a stepparent (Furstenberg, 1990a).

Our recognition of the fact that today's adolescents often experience a series of household reorganizations during their development has changed the way social scientists study adolescence and the changing family. As Mavis Hetherington, an expert on adolescence and divorce, has written, "Divorce and remarriage should not be viewed as single static events but as part of a series of transitions modifying the lives and development of children" (Hetherington, Stanley-Hagan, and Anderson, 1989, p. 303). As we shall see, much of the recent work on this topic has examined how young people adapt to these family transitions and has sought to identify the factors most important in distinguishing between adolescents who do, and do not, show ill effects.

Another trend worth noting concerns maternal employment. Figure 4.3 indicates that, among women with school-aged children, full-time employment has increased steadily since 1950 (Masnick and Bane, 1980). Today, over three-quarters of all married women with school-aged children are employed outside the home. And the rate, not surprisingly, is even higher among single mothers, over 80 percent of whom work. Among elementary school children, 2 out of 3 have mothers in the labor force (Hofferth, 1992).

Finally, between the mid-1970s and the mid-1980s, there was a substantial increase in the proportion of families living below the poverty line. Today, approximately 20 percent of all young people grow up in poor families (Huston, McLoyd, and Garcia Coll, 1994). Poverty, as we noted in Chapter 3, is much more likely

FIGURE 4.3 *The employment of mothers with school-aged children has increased steadily since 1950.*

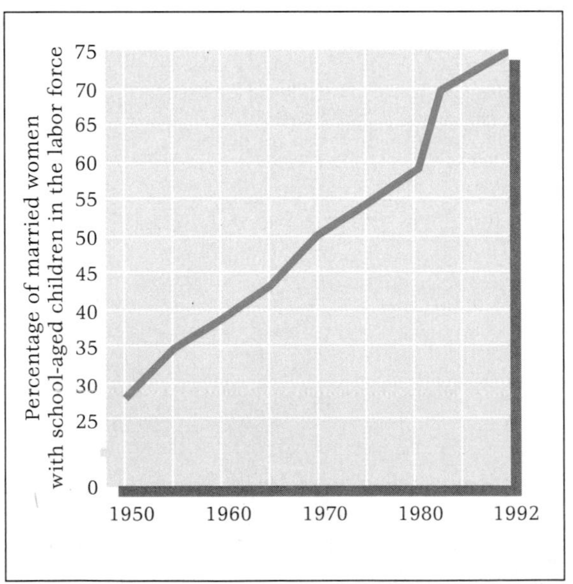

to touch the lives of nonwhite children; between 40 and 50 percent of African-American and Hispanic-American children grow up in poverty in the United States. Among the many contributors to the increase in poverty during recent decades has been the rise in single-parent families (40 percent of white single-mother households and 60 percent of nonwhite single-mother households are poor); the erosion of blue-collar jobs; and a decline in government benefits for families, such as Aid for Families with Dependent Children (Huston et al., 1994). One reason for the large disparity in poverty rates between white and nonwhite children, in fact, is the racial disparity in rates of single parenthood: Because nonwhite children are more likely to be raised in single-parent homes, they are more likely to be poor (Eggebeen and Lichter, 1991).

In summary, few adolescents live in the idealized—perhaps even romanticized—family structure that was common before 1960: the two-parent family with the father as the only wage earner. In fact, less than 15 percent of all adolescents live in this sort of arrangement. Today, more adolescents live in single-parent households, almost invariably with their mothers; and in most cases those mothers work. Of the young people living in two-parent families, a substantial number—close to 15 percent—live with only one of their natural parents (Furstenberg, 1990a). And a shockingly high number of adolescents grow up under severe economic disadvantage.

RECAP

Four of the most important changes that have occurred among American families with adolescents are the increase in the rate of divorce, the increase in the prevalence of single-parent households, the increased participation of mothers in the labor force, and the increase in the proportion of families living in poverty. Half of all children who will become teenagers during the 1990s will experience their parents' divorce, and more than half of these youngsters will experience living in a stepfamily. The vast majority of all children born in the early 1980s will spend at least part of their childhood or adolescence in a single-parent household. Three-quarters will have mothers who are employed outside the home. And one-fifth of all adolescents will grow up in poverty; poverty is especially common among ethnic minority families.

ADOLESCENT DEVELOPMENT AND THE CHANGING FAMILY

To what extent has the changed nature of the American family changed the nature of adolescent development? How do divorce, absent fathers, working mothers, and economic stress affect adolescents' development?

Many individuals are certain that the answer to these questions is, "For the worse." But before we jump to this conclusion, it is important to raise two considerations. First, although increases in adolescents' problems over the period between 1950 and 1980—as indexed by such indicators as drug use, suicide, and poor school achievement, for example—occurred alongside many of these shifts in family life, it is difficult to say that the family changes *caused* the changes in adolescent behavior. Social scientists who have argued that the decline in family life has led to these problems (e.g., Uhlenberg and Eggebeen, 1986) have had a hard time explaining why adolescents' psychological and behavioral well-being took a turn for the *better* in the early 1980s, despite the continued "demise" of the family (see Furstenberg, 1990a). Moreover, the one group of young people whose psychological and behavioral profile improved most markedly in the past ten years—poor, minority youngsters—experienced the most dramatic "decline" in family life during this time.

Second, because the conditions under which divorce, father absence, and maternal employment take place vary tremendously from family to family, it is hard to generalize about their effects on adolescents. (In contrast, it is relatively easy to generalize about the effects of poverty on adolescents, which are almost always negative.) To some young people, divorce may bring a welcome end to family conflict and tension; to others, it may be extremely disruptive psychologically. Some young people living with their mothers see their fathers more often than do their peers who live in homes where the father ostensibly is present. And although, for some adolescents, having an employed mother may mean curtailed family time and less contact with her, for others a mother who is employed may provide an important role model and added opportunities to take on responsibility around the household. In other words, the variations *within* different family structures are likely to be more important than the differences *among* them. This is readily apparent when we look at how adolescents are affected by parental divorce and remarriage.

Divorce

The recognition that divorce and remarriage can be better understood as family transitions than as static events has focused researchers' attention on adolescents' adaptation to these changes over time and on the identification of factors that seem to make a difference. In general, most studies show that the period of greatest difficulty for most children and adolescents is, as you would think, right around the time of the disruption itself. Although many young people show signs of difficulty immediately after the divorce or remarriage—among them, problems in school, more behavior problems, and more anxiety—by the time two years have passed, the majority of children whose parents have divorced or remarried have adjusted to the change and behave comparably to their peers whose parents have remained married (Hetherington, Stanley-Hagan, and Anderson, 1989).

Most researchers believe that this temporary period of disturbance reflects a combination of factors, including the exposure of the children to marital conflict (Amato and Keith, 1991a; Borrine, Handal, Brown, and Searight, 1991; Forehand, Wierson, Thomas, Fauber, Armistead, Kemptom, and Long, 1991); disorganization or dramatic changes in parenting practices (Fauber, Forehand, McCombs, and Wierson, 1990; Forehand, Thomas, Wierson, Brody, and Fauber, 1990; Hetherington, Clingempeel, Anderson, Deal, Hagan, Hollier, and Lindner, 1992); or marked increases in the degree of economic stress experienced by the household (Furstenberg, 1990a). One reason we suspect these factors is that children living in intact families (i.e., families in which no divorce has occurred) are also harmed by marital conflict, disrupted parenting (especially parenting that is too lenient, too harsh, or inconsistent), and family stress, such as loss of income. In other words, the adverse temporary effects of divorce or remarriage on youngsters' well-being appear to reflect the heightened conflict, disorganization, and stress surrounding the event, not the divorce or remarriage per se. Once the family has had a chance to establish a calmer, more organized, and more secure routine, many of the problems diminish. In fact, adolescents in divorced, single-parent families describe their parents as friendlier than do adolescents whose parents are married (Asmussen and Larson, 1991), and adolescents and their parents argue less often in divorced households, perhaps because single parents tend to be more permissive in their child-rearing, which may make for less parent-adolescent conflict (Smetana, Yau, Restrepo, and Braeges, 1991).

There are interesting differences among children in how vulnerable they are to the short-term effects of divorce, however. Some children show more difficulty than others. In general, immediate problems are relatively more common among boys, younger children, children with a difficult temperament, children who do not have supportive relationships with adults outside the immediate family, children who end up in the custody of a parent of the opposite sex, and youngsters whose parents divorce during childhood or preadolescence. Taken together, studies indicate that young boys who live with their mother following a divorce have the roughest time, particularly if they have a difficult temperament to begin with (Hetherington, 1991, 1993). Especially interesting, if somewhat disheartening, is the finding that contact after the divorce between the child and his or her noncustodial father does *not* seem to reduce the adverse effects of marital dissolution. Financial support from fathers, however, does seem to be associated with less problem behavior (Furstenberg, Morgan, and Allison, 1987).

A recent study of African-American youth indicates that social support from relatives outside the family may be an important buffer for children growing up in single-parent homes (Taylor, Casten, and Flickinger, 1993). Support from kin appears to increase single parents' effectiveness in child-rearing, and this, in turn, tends to limit adolescents' misbehavior. This support can come from relatives living apart from, or within, the adolescent's household. For example, one study of African-American youngsters found that children growing up in homes headed by their mother and grandmother fared significantly better than did those growing up in single-parent homes or in stepfamilies (Barbarin and Soler,

Contact with members of one's extended family may play an especially important role in the socialization of African-American youth. (Bill Bachman/PhotoEdit)

1993). These studies, as well as others, remind us that relatives other than parents may play an extremely important role in adolescents' lives, especially within ethnic groups that historically have placed a great deal of importance on maintaining close ties to the extended family. Single parenthood and extensive contact with the extended family have been salient features of African-American family life for more than 100 years (Ruggles, 1994).

Although divorce is often associated with short-term difficulties for the adolescent, several studies show that at least some of the differences between adolescents from divorced versus nondivorced homes were present *before* the parents divorced (e.g., Cherlin, Furstenberg, Chase-Lansdale, Kiernan, Robins, Morrison, and Teitler, 1991; Elliott and Richards, 1991). One study of British youngsters found, for example, that 7-year-olds whose parents *eventually* divorced had more educational and behavioral problems than did 7-year-olds whose parents did not divorce (Elliott and Richards, 1991). One explanation for this is that the children in the future-divorce house-

THE SCIENTIFIC STUDY OF ADOLESCENCE

PARENTAL DIVORCE AND THE WELL-BEING OF ADOLESCENTS

Research into the impact of divorce on adolescent development burgeoned during the 1980s, with dozens of studies appearing in the scientific literature in a relatively short period of time. When so many studies on one topic appear so quickly, the overall pattern of results frequently appears inconsistent and contradictory, with some studies showing significant effects and others not. This happened in the early years of research on the long-term impact of divorce; some scientists concluded that children from divorced homes were at a psychological disadvantage, while others argued that they were not.

Apparent inconsistency in research findings is especially likely when the **effect size** under consideration is small—that is, when the absolute size of the difference between comparison groups (e.g., adolescents from divorced versus nondivorced homes) is not very large. In order for a small effect to be statistically significant, the study sample needs to be sufficiently large. For example, a correlation of .25 (which most social scientists would consider a small-to-moderate effect), would be statistically significant in a sample of sixty cases but not in a sample of fifty cases. (A **correlation** is a measure of the strength of an association between two variables, which can range from −1.0 to 1.0, with a correlation of .00 indicative of no association whatsoever.) Two researchers studying the same phenomenon could come to opposite conclusions (i.e., one saying a finding is significant, and the other saying it is not) simply because they had different sample sizes. The size of one's sample affects one's power to detect an effect.

How do social scientists make sense of a literature in which many studies with varying sample sizes have been reported? One useful way is to statistically combine the results of different studies through a procedure called **meta-analysis.** In a meta-analysis, the researchers track down all the scientifically acceptable research published on a topic and essentially calculate the average effect observed across the many different studies. They then interpret this average effect size relative to the total number of adolescents who have been participants in the studies.

holds were exposed to higher levels of marital unhappiness and conflict, which are known to increase children's difficulties. Girls may be especially susceptible to the ill effects of predivorce marital conflict (Doherty and Needle, 1991).

Social scientists have also looked at the longer-term (more than two or three years) consequences of divorce. These studies, for example, might look at elementary school children whose parents had divorced when their child was in preschool, or at adolescents whose parents had split up during the youngster's elementary school years. Presumably, if the adverse effects of divorce are solely attributable to the immediate problems of adjusting to a new household structure, these effects would dissipate by the time a few years had elapsed.

Research on the longer-term consequences of parental divorce has yielded very interesting findings, and in recent years psychologists have changed their tune a bit. Initially, studies of children whose parents divorced early in life suggested that most of the adverse effects disappeared within three years. Research on

Sociologists Paul Amato and Bruce Keith did just this in a meta-analysis of studies of divorce and children's well-being (Amato and Keith, 1991a). They examined the results of ninety-two different studies that collectively involved over thirteen thousand children. The studies compared youngsters from divorced versus nondivorced homes on a wide range of outcomes, including academic achievement, behavior problems, psychosocial adjustment, and family relations. Amato and Keith were able to break the studies down by various characteristics of the samples studied, so that they could examine separately the effects of divorce on girls versus boys, children versus adolescents, and so on.

The researchers concluded that, although divorce clearly diminishes youngsters' well-being, the average effect size is quite small. Thus, although there are significant differences between children from divorced versus nondivorced homes in school achievement, behavior problems, psychosocial adjustment, and family relations—all favoring individuals from nondivorced homes—the absolute difference in the groups' scores was seldom substantial. The largest effects were observed in studies of behavior problems and father-child relations, whereas the differences observed in studies of psychosocial adjustment were trivial. (Studies of other outcomes fell somewhere between these two extremes.)

In general, the reported effects tended to be stronger for school-aged individuals than for preschoolers or college students; interestingly, the effects were comparable for boys and girls. One especially intriguing finding is that the effects of divorce seem to be smaller among youngsters from the United States than among those from other countries. The explanation: Divorce is more common in the United States than abroad, and, as a consequence, children from divorced homes are less likely to be stigmatized and more likely to have access to psychological services (such as counseling) that may attenuate the negative impact of family disruption.

SOURCE: Amato, P., and Keith, B. (1991a). Parental divorce and the well-being of children: A meta-analysis. *Psychological Bulletin, 110,* 26–46.

elementary school children whose parents had divorced earlier indicated that, after a few years, the children were functioning essentially as well as children whose parents had remained married (e.g., Hetherington, 1981).

More recent research, however, indicates that this conclusion may have been somewhat optimistic. Specifically, some studies show that individuals whose parents divorce during preadolescence continue to demonstrate adjustment difficulties during early adolescence, even after two or three years (e.g., Hetherington, 1993). And others find that adolescents whose parents divorced early in the child's life may show adjustment problems as teenagers that were not present earlier (Wallerstein and Blakeslee, 1989).

The problems typically seen in greater frequency among adolescents from divorced homes include higher rates of drug and alcohol use, more behavior problems, and poorer school performance (Allison and Furstenberg, 1989; Astone and McLanahan, 1991; Sandefur, McLanahan, and Wojtkiewicz, 1992; Zimiles and Lee, 1991); poorer interpersonal relationships with members of the opposite sex in late adolescence and young adulthood, including higher rates of divorce (McLanahan and Bumpass, 1988; Wallerstein and Blakeslee, 1989); and, with the exception of African-American and Hispanic-American males, lower levels of occupational attainment as adults (Amato and Keith, 1991b). These effects do not appear to be ameliorated by parental remarriage; adolescents from stepfamilies score similarly on measures of adjustment as do adolescents from single-parent, divorced homes (Allison and Furstenberg, 1989; Dornbusch, Carlsmith, Bushwall, Ritter, Liederman, Hastorf, and Gross, 1985; Steinberg, 1987c). Interestingly, these longer-term studies do not find sex differences in adjustment problems.

To what can we attribute these "sleeper" effects—effects of divorce that may not be apparent until much later in the child's development? Two possible explanations come to mind. The first is that the ways in which adjustment difficulties might be expressed may not surface until adolescence. For example, social scientists believe that increased drug use and higher rates of early pregnancy are consequences of the lower level of parental monitoring found in divorced homes (e.g., Dornbusch et al., 1985; McLanahan and Bumpass, 1988). But because younger children—even poorly monitored ones—are unlikely to use drugs or be sexually active, no matter what their family background, the effect of the poor monitoring is not seen until adolescence, when individuals might begin using drugs and having sex.

A second explanation concerns the particular developmental challenges of adolescence (Sessa and Steinberg, 1991). Adolescence is a time during when individuals first begin experimenting with intimate, sexual relationships. If having one's parents divorce or being exposed to marital conflict early in life affects one's conceptions of relationships or views of commitment (Belsky, Steinberg, and Draper, 1991; Franklin, Janoff-Bulman, and Roberts, 1990), it makes sense that some of the effects of early parental divorce will not be manifested until the adolescent begins dating and getting seriously involved with others of the opposite sex. These initial forays into intimate relationships may recall old and difficult psychological conflicts that had remained latent for some time (Wallerstein and Blakeslee, 1989).

Custody following Divorce

In recent years several researchers have turned their attention to the question of custodial arrangements. That is, after a divorce, do adolescents fare better or worse in different kinds of living arrangements?

Although research on this is just beginning, studies to date indicate that it is the nature of the relationship between the adolescent's divorced parents, and not which one he or she lives with, that makes a difference. In the years immediately following a divorce, children may fare a bit better in the custody of the parent of the same sex, but these effects are not long-lasting; over time, it appears that both male and female adolescents fare equally well either in dual custody or in the sole custody of their mother (Buchanan and Maccoby, 1990; Donnelly and Finkelhor, 1992). More important, especially for adolescents who have dual residences, are two factors: (1) whether the ex-spouses continue to fight and place the child between them and (2) whether the adolescent's discipline is consistent across the two households. Adolescents whose parents have a congenial, cooperative relationship and who receive consistent discipline from both homes report less emotional difficulty and fewer behavioral problems than those whose parents fight or are inconsistent with each other (Buchanan, Maccoby, and Dornbusch, 1992; Donnelly and Finkelhor, 1992).

RECAP

Research on divorce indicates that the period of greatest difficulty is the time immediately after the event. Hardest hit by divorce are young boys in the custody of their mother. Although most youngsters ultimately adapt to parental divorce, new research indicates that certain adjustment or behavior problems may appear or reappear in adolescence. These include academic problems, increased drug and alcohol use, and difficulties in romantic relationships. It is important to remember, however, that differences between adolescents from divorced versus nondivorced homes tend to be small in size; moreover, there is considerable variability within the population of adolescents whose parents have divorced.

Remarriage

Although it is difficult to make sweeping generalizations about the impact of divorce, single parenthood, or maternal employment on the development of the adolescent, several recent studies indicate that adolescents growing up in stepfamilies—especially if the remarriage has occurred during early adolescence rather than childhood—may have more problems than their peers (Zill, 1984). For example, youngsters growing up in single-parent homes are more likely than those in intact homes to be involved in delinquent activity, but adolescents in stepfamilies are even more at risk for this sort of problem behavior than are adolescents in single-parent families (Dornbusch et al., 1985; Steinberg, 1987c).

The short-term effects of remarriage also appear to vary among children, although not necessarily in the same ways as the short-term effects of divorce. In general, girls show more difficulty in adjusting to remarriage than boys do, and older children have more difficulty than younger children (Hetherington, 1993; Lee, Burkham, Zimiles, and Ladewski, 1994; Needle, Su, and Doherty, 1990; Vuchinich, Hetherington, Vuchinich, and Clingempeel, 1991; Zimiles and Lee, 1991). One explanation for this is that both boys and younger children have more to gain from their mother's remarriage than do girls or older children, who may have become accustomed to having a single mother (Hetherington, 1991). In the case of remarriage, as in the case of divorce, temperamentally more difficult youngsters have a harder time than more easy-going ones (Hetherington, 1993).

Remarriage during the adolescent years may be extremely stressful when families are unable to accommodate the new stepparent relationship. Given what we know about family reorganization and change during adolescence, having to integrate a new type of relationship into a family system that is already undergoing a great deal of change may be more than some families can cope with. Many adolescents find it difficult to adjust to a new authority figure's moving into the household, especially if that person has different ideas about rules and discipline. This appears to be especially true when the adolescent in question is already somewhat vulnerable, either because of previous psychological problems or because of a very recent divorce or other stressful event.

By the same token, many stepparents find it difficult to join a family and not be accepted immediately by the children as the new parent. Stepparents may wonder why love is not forthcoming from their stepchildren, who often act critical, resistant, and sulky (Vuchinich et al., 1991). In extreme cases, relationships between adolescents and stepparents can become so strained that family violence results. Although many stepfathers and their adolescent stepchildren do establish positive relations, the lack of a biological connection between stepparent and stepchild—coupled with the stresses associated with divorce and remarriage—may make this relationship especially vulnerable to problems.

According to E. Mavis Hetherington, a psychologist who has done extensive research on family disruption in adolescence, it may be helpful if stepfathers build a close relationship with their stepchildren slowly, and if they defer in matters of discipline to the children's biological mother early on: "In the beginning of a remarriage, stepdads should be like polite strangers in their new wife's home and talk to the teen-age kids, but not intervene or exercise too much control over their lives. There's too much hostility in the kids who at that age want independence, not control" (quoted in Nordheimer, 1990, p. C6).

The findings of this research underscore the need—particularly as remarriage becomes a more common part of American family life—to understand the special problems that may arise in the course of family reorganization. Several studies indicate that children's adjustment declines somewhat *each time* they must cope with a change in their family's organization (e.g., Capaldi and Patterson, 1991; Kurdek, in press), presumably, because parenting may become less effective during each family transition (Forgatch, DeGarmo, and Knutson, 1994; Kurdek and Fine, 1993). As our understanding of stepfamily relationships grows, it should become easier to anticipate stepfamily problems before they occur, to prepare families in the process of reorganization for the transition they are about to make, and to provide special services for families who need help.

One factor that seems to make a difference in the adjustment of children in stepfamilies is the nature of the relationship they have with their *noncustodial* parent—that is, the biological parent with whom they do *not* live. Children in stepfamilies fare better when there is consistency in discipline between their custodial and noncustodial parents and when they have a good relationship with the noncustodial parent, especially in the years immediately following the remarriage (Anderson, 1992; Bray, Berger, Touch, and Boethel, 1993; Buchanan and Maccoby, 1993; Gunnoe, 1994). Having a close relationship with the noncustodial parent does not appear to undermine the relationship with the custodial parent (Buchanan and Maccoby, 1993).

RECAP

Because adolescents' mental health suffers somewhat each time their family situation changes, young people growing up in stepfamilies may be at even greater risk than their peers in single-parent, divorced homes. In general, girls show more difficulty in adjusting to remarriage than boys do, and older children have more difficulty than younger children. One factor that seems to make a difference in adolescents' adjustment to remarriage is the quality of the relationship they maintain with the noncustodial biological parent.

Parental Employment and Adolescent Adjustment

The increase in women's participation in the labor force has prompted a good deal of research on the effects of maternal employment on adolescent development. This label *maternal employment* is a misnomer, of course, because most children whose mothers work have fathers who are employed as well. It is important to remember that most studies of "maternal employment" are really studies of the impact of having *both* parents employed, not simply studies of the impact of having an employed mother. We do not know what the impact of "paternal employment" by itself is, because there are too few families with employed mothers and nonemployed fathers to make a comparison.

Adolescents whose mothers are employed differ from those whose mothers are not, in several respects. In general, maternal employment during adolescence has quite positive effects on daughters but more mixed or negligible effects on sons, especially in middle-class and professional families (Bronfenbrenner and Crouter, 1982). Not surprisingly, in these social classes, girls whose mothers work outside the home have higher career aspirations than do girls whose mothers do not work, but this is not necessarily the case for boys (Hoffman, 1974). Because daughters are more likely than sons to identify with their mother, girls' occupational plans are more influenced by having a mother work than are boys' plans.

One especially interesting finding concerns the impact of maternal employment on adolescents' academic achievement. A number of studies have found that in middle-class and upper-middle-class homes, full-time maternal employment during the high school years is associated with lowered school performance among boys, but not among girls (Bogenschneider and Steinberg, 1994; Bronfenbrenner and Crouter, 1982). This effect is not found in homes where mothers work part time, nor is it found in working-class or lower-class households. Presumably, the added income from mother's work in poorer families

Maternal employment has quite positive effects on the development of adolescent females, who have higher career aspirations than girls whose mothers are not employed. The impact of maternal employment on sons is mixed, however, especially in middle-class or professional families. (Spencer Grant/Stock, Boston)

makes up for any negative effects it has on boys' schooling.

Researchers have been puzzled by this sex difference. Why are boys, but not girls, adversely affected in school by full-time maternal employment? One explanation concerns the impact of maternal employment on parental monitoring, in general, and in relation to school, in particular (Bogenschneider and Steinberg, 1994; Crouter, MacDermid, McHale, and Perry-Jenkins, 1990). We know that boys are more adversely affected by less vigilant parental monitoring than girls are, because boys tend to be more active and more prone to get into trouble. We also know that children who are monitored more carefully by their parents tend to do better in school than their peers do (Steinberg, Elmen, and Mounts, 1989). If one effect of having two parents work full time is to interfere with parental monitoring, it may have a more negative effect on boys than on girls.

A second explanation concerns the effect on adolescents' family relationships when two parents work. At least one study finds that boys whose mothers work have more arguments with their mothers and with their siblings than do boys whose mothers are not employed (Montemayor, 1984). Interestingly, this does not appear to be related to mothers' work stress (Galambos and Maggs, 1991) but, instead, to the increased demands for household work placed on the children of working mothers (Montemayor, 1984). Boys may react more negatively than girls to having to help out around the house, and this may contribute to family arguments. If conflict at home depresses school performance, this may help explain why boys whose mothers work full time do less well in school.

Above all, however, studies indicate far more similarities than differences in the daily experiences of adolescents with employed versus nonemployed mothers (Richards and Duckett, 1994). Experts believe that the most important factor may be the way in which the family *perceives* the mother's employment, rather than her employment per se. Children whose mothers are happily employed are much more likely to benefit from the experience than are children whose mothers would prefer not to work or who have jobs with which they are unhappy. When a mother is happy to be working, and her spouse and family are appreciative of it, her youngster is more likely to develop self-reliance and independence (Hoffman, 1974). In contrast, adolescent girls who perceive their mothers to have been held back occupationally are more likely than their peers to report depression and psychosomatic distress (Silverstein, Perlick, Clauson, and McKoy, 1993).

RECAP

Research on maternal employment indicates that the effects depend on the sex of the adolescent and the attitude of the mother, and other family members, toward her work. Maternal employment has positive effects on daughters but mixed effects on sons, especially where school performance is concerned. Children whose mothers are happy with their employment are more likely to benefit than are children whose mothers don't wish to work or dislike their jobs. All in all, however, research suggests that the daily experiences of adolescents whose mothers are employed are not significantly different from those of adolescents whose mothers are not employed.

Economic Stress and Poverty

Although many psychologists have focused their attention on the effects of maternal employment on adolescent development, in recent years there has been an upsurge in interest in the relation between parents' *un*employment and adolescents' well-being and, in particular, in the ways in which adolescents' mental health is affected by changes in their family's financial situation. Much of this research was stimulated by the economic recession of the early 1980s, during which many adults became unemployed and many families lost substantial income.

To date, the studies of family income loss and adolescent adjustment suggest a number of parallels with the research on divorce and remarriage. Like divorce, income loss tends to be associated with disruptions in parenting, which in turn lead to increases in adolescent problem behaviors, including irritability, academic difficulties, and delinquency (Elder, van Nguyen, and Caspi, 1985; Elder, Caspi, and van Nguyen, 1986; Lempers, Clark-Lempers, and Simmons, 1989). But, as is the case with divorce, the sex of the adolescent seems to play an important moderating role. For girls, financial difficulty is likely to lead to more demands for maturity and increased responsibility around the house (perhaps to take over some of mother's duties while she works or looks for employment) (Elder, 1974; Flanagan, 1990). This may contribute to their developing more pessimistic expectations about their own occupational futures, since they may develop more traditional views and find it difficult to envision a satisfying career outside the home (Galambos and Silbereisen, 1987). For boys, in contrast, disruptions in family finances seem to lead to more frequent conflict, especially with fathers (Elder, van Nguyen, and Caspi, 1985; Flanagan, 1990). Boys whose fathers have been laid off may lose respect for them and challenge their authority. The resulting disruption in family functioning may lead to more involvement in problem behavior and more irresponsibility.

A recent series of studies of rural families during the American farm crisis of the 1980s by sociologists Rand Conger and Glen Elder sheds light on some of the processes through which economic strain on the family can adversely affect adolescents' psychological development (Conger, Conger, Elder, Lorenz, Simons, and Whitbeck, 1992, 1993; Conger, Ge, Elder, Lorenz, and Simons, 1994; Elder, Conger, Foster, and Ardelt, 1992) (see Figure 4.4). Financial strain increases mothers' and fathers' feelings of depression, worsens parents' marriages, and causes conflicts between parents and adolescents over money. These consequences, in turn, make parents more irritable, which adversely affects the quality of their parenting. Studies show that parents under economic strain are less involved, less nurturant, harsher, and less consistent in their discipline.

The family climate created by economic strain puts adolescents at risk for a wide variety of problems. As you will read later in this chapter, adolescents who are exposed to harsh, uninvolved, and inconsistent parenting are at greater risk for a wide range of psychological and behavioral problems. When adolescents are repeatedly exposed to marital conflict—especially when it is not resolved—they are more likely to become aggressive and depressed (Cummings, Ballard, El-Sheikh, and Lake, 1991). And when adolescents themselves are the recipients of aggressive parenting, they are likely to imitate this behavior in their relationships with siblings (Conger, Conger, and Elder, 1994) and also later, when they themselves have children (Simons, Whitbeck, Conger, and Chyi-In, 1991).

Researchers have also studied the impact on adolescents of growing up amidst *chronic* economic disadvantage (Brody, Stoneman, Flor, McCrary, Hastings, and Conyers, 1994; Felner et al., in press; McLoyd, Jayaratne, Ceballo, and Borquez, 1994; Sampson and Laub, 1994), a condition disproportionately likely to characterize the lives of African-American and Hispanic-American youth, especially those living in inner-city or rural

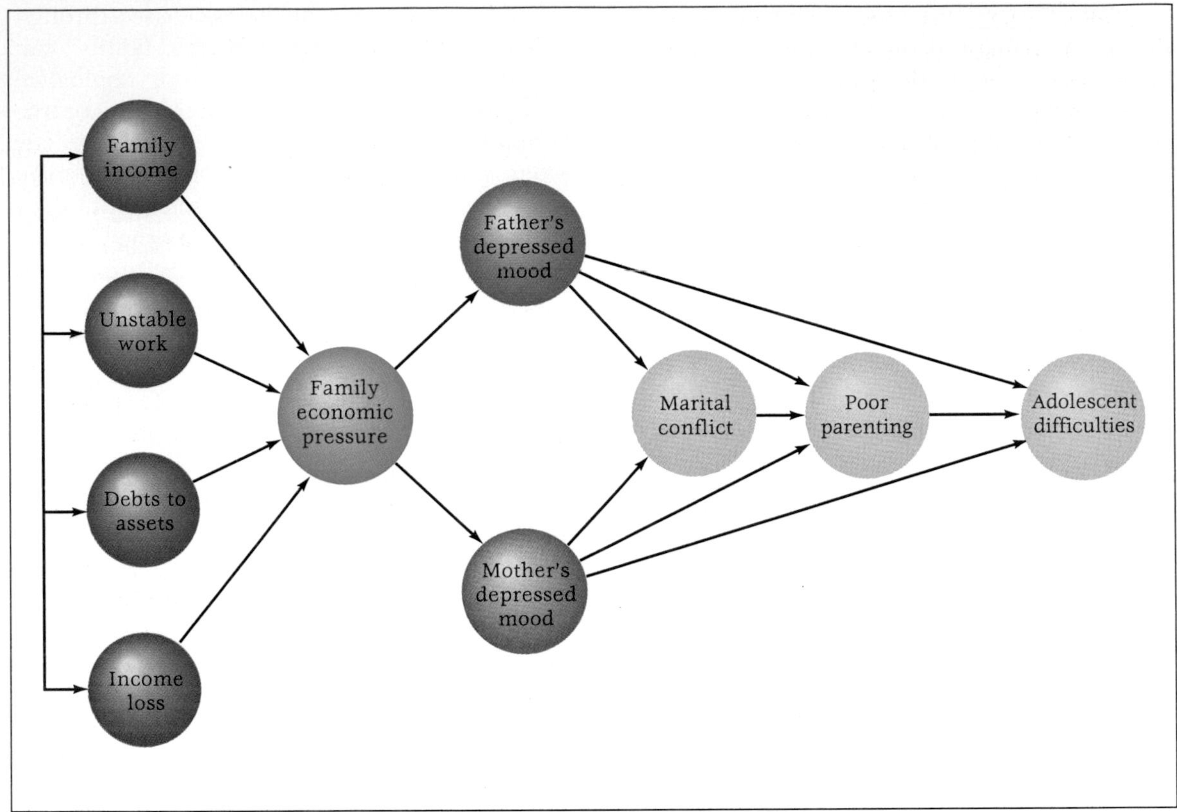

FIGURE 4.4 *How economic strain affects adolescent adjustment.*
(Conger et al., 1993)

communities. In general, persistent poverty, like temporary economic strain, undermines parental effectiveness, making mothers and fathers harsher, more depressed, less vigilant, and, if married, more embroiled in marital conflict. These consequences all have negative effects on adolescent adjustment, which are manifested in increases in anxiety and depression, more frequent conduct problems, and diminished school performance.

Growing up poor affects adolescents' mental health through other means as well. Poor children, especially minority youngsters, are more likely to be victims of violence, which is associated with higher rates of depression (Fitzpatrick, 1993); to feel more alienated from school (Felner et al., in press); and to be exposed to high levels of stress (Felner et al., in press; Masten, Miliotis, Graham-Bermann, Ramirez, and Neeman, 1993). Although few scientific studies have been conducted on homeless adolescents, research suggests that these youngsters share many of the same problems with other youth who experience chronic poverty, including higher rates of depression, academic difficulties, and behavior problems (Masten et al., 1993; Zima, Wells, and Freeman, 1994).

Studies of families living under poverty also tell us what parents living in poor neighborhoods can do to help protect their children from the adverse consequences of growing up in a poor neighborhood (Early and Eccles, 1994; Elder and Ardelt, 1992; Furstenberg, 1990b; McCarthy, Lord, Eccles, Kalil, and Furstenberg, 1992). Two sets of strategies are tried by parents in poor neighborhoods: *promotive* strategies, which attempt to strengthen the adolescent's competence through effective child rearing within the home environment or through involving the child in positive activities outside the home; and *restrictive* strategies, which attempt to minimize the child's exposure to dangers in the neighborhood (Elder and Ardelt, 1992). Although much of this research is still in a preliminary stage, studies seem to indicate that promotive strategies as well as moderately (but not overly) restrictive strategies may be beneficial to adolescent development. Although adolescents in poor neighborhoods benefit from consistent parental monitoring, they do not thrive when their parents exercise control that is excessive (McCarthy et al., 1992).

RECAP

Adolescents whose families have suffered severe economic losses, or who live in chronic poverty, are at heightened risk for psychological difficulties and problem behavior. Research on economic strain and its impact on the adolescent indicates that the main effects of financial stress are transmitted to the adolescent through the negative impact they have on parents' mental health and marital relations. Parents under financial strain are harsher, more inconsistent, and less involved as parents, which, in turn, leads to problems for their children.

THE "GENERATION GAP"

One of the most frequently asked questions in the study of families during adolescence concerns **intergenerational conflict,** or as it is more commonly known, the **generation gap.** In what sense is there a "gap" between adolescents and their parents, and how wide is it? In order to answer these questions, it is important to distinguish among family relationships, values and attitudes, and personal tastes. In some of these respects, there is indeed a schism between the generations. But in others, there is not.

If we consider the quality of adolescents' *relationships* with their parents, we find that there is very little gap between young people and their elders. Study after study on this issue has shown that, although some adolescents and their parents have serious interpersonal problems, the overwhelming majority of adolescents feel close to their parents, respect their parents' judgment, feel that their parents love and care about them, and have a lot of respect for their parents as individuals (Steinberg, 1990). In one study, for example, three-quarters of the adolescent respondents agreed with the statements "I can count on my parents most of the time" and "When I grow up and have a family, it will be in at least a few ways similar to my own" (Offer, Ostrov, and Howard, 1981). If intergenerational conflict exists, it is not of the sort that seriously affects the quality or closeness of most adolescents' family relationships.

To be sure, there are times when adolescents and parents have their problems. But so are there times when younger children and their parents have problems and when adults and their parents do also. To date, no studies demonstrate that family problems are any more likely to occur during adolescence than at other times in the life span. Most systematic studies indicate that among the 25 percent of teenagers and parents who report having problems, about 80 percent had problematic relations during childhood (Rutter, Graham, Chadwick, and Yule, 1976). Thus only about 5 percent of families who enjoy positive relations during childhood can expect to develop serious problems during adolescence.

When we look at intergenerational differences in *values and attitudes,* we also find little evidence in support of a generation gap—or at least, of a schism as large as many people have been led to believe exists. Adolescents and their parents have similar beliefs about the importance of hard work, about educational and occupational ambitions, and about the personal characteristics and attributes that they feel are important and desirable (Gecas and Seff, 1990). Indeed, when it comes to more basic values—concerning religion, work, education, and the like—diversity within the adolescent population is much more striking than are differences between the generations. Socioeconomic background, for instance, has a much stronger influence on individuals' values and attitudes than does age, and adolescents are more likely to share their parents' values than those of other teenagers who are from a different background. Wealthy adolescents growing up in affluent suburbs, for example, have educational and career plans that resemble their parents' plans for them, and their plans are very different from those of poor adolescents growing up in less prosperous areas. Interestingly, there is some evidence that adolescents' and parents' values may be closer today than they were in recent decades (Gecas and Seff, 1990).

In matters of *personal taste* there is often a gap between the generations, however. It is

One source of conflict between teenagers and parents involves the different ways that they define the same issues. Making sure that the adolescent's bedroom is tidy often is seen by parents as an area over which they have "jurisdiction." Teenagers, however, tend to see their rooms as their own private space and decisions about neatness as matters of personal choice. (Joan Albert/Image Works)

most clearly seen in styles of dress, preferences in music, and patterns of leisure activity. Adolescents are more likely to be influenced by their friends than by their parents in these matters, and, as a consequence, disagreements and differences in opinion between old and young often result. Indeed, it is over these matters that much of the bickering that occurs in families takes place (Montemayor, 1983). A mother and her daughter may argue about such things as the daughter's curfew, how the daughter spends her spare time, whether the daughter keeps her room clean enough, or what sorts of clothes the daughter wears. Unlike values, which develop gradually over time and are shaped from an early age, preferences and tastes are far more transitory and subject to the immediate influences of the social environment. Because adolescents spend a great deal of time with their friends (and because a good deal of that time is spent in social activities in which taste in clothes, music, etc. is especially important), teenagers' tastes are likely to be shaped to a large measure by forces outside the family. Conflict between adolescents and parents is generally less frequent in ethnic minority than in nonminority families, although the topics of disagreement are similar across ethnic groups (Barber, 1994; Kupersmidt, Burchinal, Leff, and Patterson, 1992).

A recent series of studies helps illuminate the causes of these conflicts between parents and teenagers over mundane issues, such as household chores, clothing, and the adolescents' choice of friends. We saw in earlier chapters that this sort of bickering and squabbling between parents and teenagers was more likely to occur during early adolescence than during any other period (Steinberg, 1990). What is it about *early* adolescence that may explain this pattern?

According to research by Judith Smetana (1988a, 1988b, 1989; Smetana and Asquith, 1994), a major contributor to adolescent-parent arguments is the fact that teenagers and their parents define the issues of contention very differently. Parents are likely to see these as issues of "right" and "wrong"—not in a moral sense, but as matters of custom or convention. For instance, a mother who disapproved of her daughter's outfit may say, "People just don't dress that way to go to school." Adolescents, in contrast, are likely to define these same issues as matters of personal choice. The daughter may respond by saying, "*You* might not dress this way for school, but *I* do."

Smetana believes that teenagers and their parents often clash more over the definition of the issue (that is, as a matter of custom versus a matter of personal choice) than over the specific details. The struggle, then, is over who has the authority—and whose "jurisdiction" the issue falls into. Because early adolescence is a time during which adolescents' reasoning abilities are changing—recall the dramatic cognitive developments discussed in Chapter 2—there are changes in the ways that individuals understand family rules and regulations. A boy who is willing to accept his parents' views of right and wrong—who doesn't question his mother when she says, "We do not leave clothes on the floor"—grows into an adolescent who understands that some issues are matters of personal choice, rather than social convention ("It's my room, so why should it bother you?").

Obviously, if parents and teenagers define day-to-day issues differently to begin with, resolving conflicts is going to be quite difficult. According to some experts, it is important for parents and teenagers to begin by trying to understand each other's point of view and attempting to jointly define the disagreement as a problem that both sides are eager to resolve, bypassing the question of whose "authority" it is. This is far more effective than struggling through a battle of wills, particularly because the adolescent and parent are beginning from entirely different premises. Parents and teenagers can work through many of these disputes by working together to find solutions that both parties can live with ("I'll pick up my clothes twice a week and whenever company is coming over, and I'll keep my bedroom door closed when the room is messy; in return, you won't nag me about my room") (Steinberg and Levine, 1990).

RECAP

The notion that a wide gap exists between the generations is largely a myth. When parents and adolescents disagree, it tends to be over mundane, day-to-day issues, not over major values or priorities. Many disagreements between parents and teenagers stem from the different perspectives that they bring to the discussion: Parents typically see the issues as matters of "right" or "wrong," whereas adolescents see them as matters of personal choice.

FAMILY RELATIONSHIPS AT ADOLESCENCE

Although it is incorrect to characterize adolescence as a time of conflict in most families, it is important to keep in mind that adolescence is a period of change and reorganization in family relationships. It is to these processes of change and reorganization in the adolescent's family that we now turn.

The Family as a System

You may remember from high school science classes that living organisms and their environments function as systems. The family is a system, too—a system in which relationships change in response to the changing needs and concerns of family members and in response to changes in the family's relationship with the larger society (Minuchin, 1974). And like other systems, families attempt to maintain a sense of equilibrium, or balance, in their relationships. Certain implicit understandings develop within families—concerning which family members have decision-making power, how much privacy different individuals can expect to have, how much freedom and control each family member has, and the like—and these understandings form the unwritten rules according to which the system operates. Family members may not be aware of the rules under which their family works, but outsiders are usually able to see what sorts of principles and norms a family system follows.

The tendency for family systems to try to maintain their established patterns of behavior is challenged from time to time by changes to which they must adapt. When someone new moves into the household, the members of the system must find a way to reorganize and reestablish workable types of relationships and patterns of activity. (This is one of the difficulties families have following a divorce or remarriage, for example.) And when a family member changes in one way or another—psychologically or emotionally, for example—the change usually has reverberations throughout the family system.

Often, following a change in a family system, the family goes through a period of imbalance, or "disequilibrium," before it adjusts to the change. These periods of disequilibrium can be difficult for families. They may sense that old ways of relating to one another are no longer working, but they may not realize why. Establishing new ways of dealing with one another may take some time (Steinberg, 1990). Only after a new and different equilibrium is established may the family feel comfortable again.

Relationships in families change most dramatically during those times when individual family members are changing or when the family's circumstances are changing, since it is during these times that the family's previously established equilibrium will be upset. During these times, it is healthy for family relationships to change, for through such changes families restore balance to the system. Not surprisingly, one period in which family relationships usually change a great deal is adolescence.

The Life Cycle of Families

A family in its "infancy" is different from a family in its "adolescence." Like individuals, families move through a life cycle, a family life cycle—that is, various developmental phases in which new issues arise and different concerns predominate (Rodgers, 1973). Each stage of the family life cycle is different from the stages that came before and the stages that will follow.

The concerns and issues characteristic of families at adolescence arise not just because of the changing needs and concerns of the young person but also because of changes in the adolescent's parents and because of changes in the needs and functions of the family as a unit. Consequently, in order to understand the changing nature of family relationships during the adolescent years, we must take into account not only characteristics of the developing young person but characteristics of the adolescent's parents and of families at this stage as well.

The Adolescent's Parents

Today, the typical parent is close to 40 years old when his or her first child enters early adolescence. It is important therefore to consider psychological development during this period of adulthood and ask how the concerns characteristic of this age may contribute to the changing nature of family relationships at adolescence. A growing body of evidence suggests that the period surrounding age 40 can be a potentially difficult time for many adults. Indeed, some theorists have gone so far as to describe it as a time of **midlife crisis** (Farrell and Rosenberg, 1981; Levinson, 1978).

If we look at the nature of these midlife crises in some detail, we find that the developmental concerns of parents and adolescents are complementary (Steinberg and Steinberg, 1994). First, consider the issue of biological change. At the same time that adolescents are entering into a period of rapid physical growth, sexual maturation, and, ultimately, the period of the life span that society has labeled one of the most physically attractive, their parents are beginning to feel increased concern about their own bodies, about their physical attractiveness, and about their sexual appeal (R. Gould, 1972).

A second overlap of crises concerns perceptions of time and the future. At the same time that adolescents are beginning to develop the capability to think systematically about the future and do, in fact, begin to look ahead, their parents are beginning to feel that the possibilities for change are limited. While adolescents' ideas about the future are becoming more expansive, their parents' ideas are probably becoming more limited. Bernice Neugarten, who has studied adult personality development extensively, suggests that an important shift in time perspective takes place during midlife: Before this phase in the life cycle, we tend to measure time in terms of how long we have been alive; after midlife, we are more likely to see things in terms of how much longer we have to live (Neugarten and Datan, 1974). One reason for this shift may be that midlife adults are reminded of their mortality because they see their own parents aging.

For many adults, midlife is a time of heightened introspection and personal reevaluation. Because many parents are at this stage in the life cycle when their children are teenagers, the so-called "midlife crisis" of adulthood may coincide with the "identity crisis" of adolescence. (Ellis Herwig/Stock, Boston)

Finally, consider the issue of power, status, and entrance into the roles of adulthood. Adolescence is the time when individuals are on the threshold of gaining a great deal of status. Their careers and marriages lie ahead of them, and choices seem limitless. For their parents, in contrast, many choices have already been made—some successfully, others perhaps less so. Most adults reach their occupational plateau—the point at which they can tell how successful they are likely to be—during midlife, and many must deal with whatever gap exists between their early aspirations and their actual achievements (R. Gould, 1972). In sum, for adolescents, this phase in the family life cycle is a time of boundless horizons; for their parents, it is a time of coming to terms with choices made when they were younger.

This overlap of crises is likely to have an impact on family relationships (Steinberg and Steinberg, 1994). A father who is worried about his own physical health suddenly feels uncomfortable about playing tennis each weekend with his growing son, as they did for years when the son was younger. They may have to find new activities that they can share together. An adolescent girl with big plans for the future finds it difficult to understand why her father seems so cautious and narrow-minded when she asks him for advice. She may react by turning to her friends more often. An adolescent boy finds his mother's constant attention annoying; he doesn't see that, to her, his interest in independence signifies the end of an important stage in her career as a parent. In fact, the adolescent's desire for autonomy in particular may be especially stressful for parents (Small, Eastman, and Cornelius, 1988). Although none of these situations may cause family conflict, each requires a period of adjustment on the part of parents and their children.

This generalization must be tempered by the fact that recent decades have seen important changes in both the age at which individuals marry and the age at which they have their first child. The average age at marriage has increased by several years since 1970, for both men (who now tend to marry in their late 20s) and women (who tend to marry in their mid-20s). And whereas it had been common in the past for couples to begin having children soon after marriage, proportionately more couples today are delaying child-bearing until they have become established in their careers. As a consequence of both of these changes, adults tend to be older today when their children reach adolescence than was the case two decades ago. Although psychologists have studied the impact of this change on parents' relationships with their infants (e.g., Parke, 1988), we do not know how being an older parent affects relationships during adolescence.

Adjusting to adolescence may take more of a toll on the mental health of parents than on the mental health of adolescents (Steinberg and Steinberg, 1994). One study found that nearly two-thirds of mothers and fathers described adolescence as the most difficult stage of parenting (Pasley and Gecas, 1984), and several studies have found this period in the family life cycle to be a low point in parents' marital and life satisfaction (Gecas and Seff, 1990).

Parents may be especially adversely affected by the transition of their child into adolescence if the child is of the same sex. Mothers of daughters and fathers of sons, for example, show more psychological distress, report less satisfaction with their marriage, and experience more intense midlife identity concerns as their children begin to mature physically, get involved in dating relationships, and distance themselves from their parents emotionally. Parents who are deeply involved in work outside the home or who have an especially happy marriage may be buffered against some of these negative consequences, however, whereas single mothers may be especially vulnerable to these effects (Kalil and Eccles, 1993; MacDermid and Crouter, in press; Silverberg and Steinberg, 1987, 1990; Steinberg and Silverberg, 1987; Steinberg and Steinberg, 1994).

Along similar lines, studies also show that parents who have high self-esteem have better relationships with their adolescents than do parents who think more poorly of themselves (Small, 1988). Mothers with high self-esteem, in particular, grant their adolescent more autonomy and communicate more effectively, and this, in turn, contributes to greater satisfaction on the part of the teenager. When adolescents are more satisfied with the degree of autonomy their parents grant them, they are less likely to challenge their parents, and their parents report less stress at home as a result.

● Changes in Family Needs and Functions

It is not only individual family members who undergo change during the family's adolescent years. The family as a unit changes as well in its economic circumstances, its relationship to other social institutions, and its functions. One of the most important changes undergone by the family during adolescence is financial: Family finances are likely to be strained during adolescence. Children grow rapidly during puberty, and clothing for adolescents is expensive. Keeping up with the accoutrements of the peer culture—the CDs, cosmetics, and high-priced home video, computer, and stereo equipment—may push a family budget to the limit. Many families also begin saving money for large anticipated expenditures, such as the adolescent's college education. And in some families, parents may find themselves having to help support their own parents at a time when their children are still economically dependent. These financial demands require adjustment on the part of the family system.

In addition to these financial pressures, the adolescent's family must cope with the increasing importance of two new contexts in which the young person spends time and invests energy: the peer group and, later in adolescence, the workplace (Larson and Richards, 1994). During the early stages of the life cycle, the child's social world is fairly narrow, and the family is the central setting. As the child grows, the school begins to take on increased significance, and relationships and concerns revolving around school must be balanced with those revolving around the family. During late childhood and early adolescence, however, the peer group becomes a setting in which close ties are formed. Families may have a tough time adjusting to the adolescent's increasing interest in forgoing family activities for peer activities. They may have arguments about the teenager's reluctance to give up time with his or her friends for family outings.

Finally, important changes in family functions also take place during adolescence. During infancy and childhood, the functions and responsibilities of the family are fairly clear: nurturance, protection, and socialization. While all these roles are still important during adolescence, adolescents are more in need of support than nurturance, of guidance more than protection, of direction more than socialization. Making the transition from the family functions of childhood to the family functions of adolescence is not necessarily easy, for the shift often upsets the equilibrium established during childhood. The transition is further complicated in contemporary society, where preparation for adulthood—one of the chief tasks of adolescence that was once carried out primarily by the family—is increasingly done by other institutions, such as the school. Many families may feel at a loss to figure out just what their role during adolescence is. A 16-year-old girl once told the author that she wasn't sure whether she needed her parents any more, now that she could drive and had a job at the local fast-food restaurant.

● Transformations in Family Relations

Together, the biological, cognitive, and social transitions of adolescence, the changes experienced by adults at midlife, and the changes undergone by the family during this stage in the family life cycle set in motion a series of transformations in family relationships. Think for a moment about the difference between the relationship between parents and a 12-year-old and that between parents and an 18-year-old. In most families, there is a movement during adolescence from patterns of influence and interaction that are asymmetrical and unequal to ones in which parents and their adolescent children are on a more equal footing. And there is some evidence that early adolescence—when this shift toward more egalitarian relationships first begins—may be a time of temporary disequilibrium in the family system.

Studies of family interaction suggest that early adolescence may be a time during which young people begin to try to play a more forceful role in the family but when parents may not yet acknowledge the adolescents' input. As a result, young adolescents may interrupt their parents more often but have little impact. By middle adolescence, however, teenagers act and are treated much more like adults. They have more influence over family decisions, but they do not need to assert their opinions through interruptions and similarly immature behavior.

Increases in the assertiveness and influence of adolescents as they get older are consistent with their changing needs and capabilities. It is adaptive for families to permit these changes to happen, because it is through such changes that adolescents learn to be more mature and independent. In fact, there is some evidence that families who resist making changes in their patterns of interaction during adolescence are more likely to experience such problems as juvenile delinquency (Alexander, 1973). This further corroborates the idea that family systems must be able to adapt when changes in family members or family circumstances make such adaptation necessary.

In order to adapt successfully to the changes triggered by the child's entrance into adolescence, family members must have some shared sense of what they are experiencing and how they are changing. Yet studies show that, in many families, parents and children live in "separate realities," perceiving their day-to-day experiences in very different ways (Larson and Richards, 1994). A mother and son, for example, may have a "conversation" about the boy's schoolwork, and while she may experience the conversation as a serious discussion, he may perceive it as an argument. Studies show that families have more difficulties when individual members have more divergent perceptions of family life (Larson and Richards, 1994; Paikoff, Carlton-Ford, and Brooks-Gunn, 1993).

The adolescent's biological and cognitive maturation may play a role in unbalancing the family system during early adolescence. Several researchers have demonstrated that family relationships change during puberty, with conflict between adolescents and their parents increasing slightly, and closeness between adolescents and their parents diminishing (Holmbeck and Hill, 1991; Paikoff, Brooks-Gunn, and Warren, 1991; Susman, Inhoff-Germain, Nottlemann, Loriaux, Cutler, and Chrousos, 1987; Steinberg, 1981, 1987a). Although puberty seems to distance adolescents from their parents, it is not associated with familial "storm and stress," and rates of outright conflict between parents and children are not dramatically higher during adolescence than before or after (Laursen and Collins, 1994). Rather, disagreements between parents and teenagers are more likely to take the form of bickering over day-to-day issues such as household chores than outright fighting. Similarly, the diminished closeness is more likely to be manifested in increased privacy on the part of the adolescent and diminished physical affection between teenagers and parents, rather than any serious loss of love or respect between parents and children (Montemayor, 1983, 1986). Research suggests that the distancing effect of puberty is temporary, though, and that relationships may become less conflicted and more intimate during late adolescence. In any event, it does appear that early adolescence, at least in white families, may be a somewhat more strained time for the family than earlier or later. Part of the problem may be that conflicts between teenagers and parents tend to be resolved not through compromise but through submission (i.e., giving in) or disengagement (i.e., walking away), neither of which enhances the quality of their relationship (Laursen and Collins, 1994). Interestingly, one study found that in Asian-American households, the increase in conflict did not occur until later in adolescence (Greenberger and Chen, 1994), consistent with the finding, discussed in Chapter 3, that the timetable for the development of independence may be slower in Asian than in non-Asian households.

Other researchers have emphasized changes in the adolescents' cognitive abilities and how these changes may reverberate throughout the family. We noted earlier in this chapter that changes in the ways adolescents view family rules and regulations may contribute to increased conflict between them and their parents (Smetana, 1989). Research also indicates that early adolescence is a time of changes in youngsters' views of family relationships and in family members' expectations of each other. For example, one study asked adolescents of different ages to characterize their actual and "ideal" families in terms of how close and dominant different family members were (Feldman and Gehring, 1988). With age, the gap between adolescents' actual and "ideal" portraits widened, indicating that as they became older, adolescents became more aware of their families' shortcomings—at least in comparison to what they believed a perfect family was like. This realization does not necessarily lead adolescents to reject their parents, but it does lead to a more balanced, and probably more accurate, appraisal of them (Youniss and Smollar, 1985).

Psychologist W. Andrew Collins (1988, 1990) has studied the changes in children's and parents' expectations for each other that take place during adolescence and how "violations" of these expectations can cause family conflict. A child may enter adolescence expecting that it will be a time of great freedom, for example, whereas the parents may view the same period as one in which tighter reins are necessary. Alternatively, another child, perhaps influenced by television sitcoms portraying happy families, may imagine that adolescence will be a time of increased closeness and shared activities in the family, only to be disappointed to find that his or her parents have been looking forward to having time to themselves. It is easy to see how differences in expectations about what adolescence is going to be like can escalate into arguments and misunderstandings. For this reason, psychologists have been studying the sorts of beliefs that children and parents have about adolescence and where they turn for sources of information (Steinberg, 1990).

RECAP

Adolescence is a time of renegotiation in family relationships, with adolescents gaining increasingly more power and becoming increasingly more assertive. These transformations in family relations are sparked by the biological, cognitive, and social maturation of the adolescent. Many of the changes in family relations that occur at adolescence affect the psychological well-being of the adolescent's middle-aged parents as well as the teenager; indeed, in some regards, adolescence may be a more difficult time for the parents than for the teenager. In general, parents who have some strong interests outside the family and who have a positive sense of self-esteem cope better with the changes of adolescence than do other parents.

FAMILY RELATIONSHIPS AND ADOLESCENT DEVELOPMENT

Thus far we have looked at the sorts of issues and concerns faced by most families during the adolescent years. We have seen that adolescence is not usually a time of dire conflict in most households, but we have also seen that families must be able to adapt to the social and psychological changes that arise at this time in the family life cycle.

In our focus on those experiences that all families share, however, we have not addressed the very important questions of how relationships differ from family to family and whether these differences have important consequences for the developing adolescent. Some parents are stricter than others. Some adolescents are given a great deal of affection, while others are treated more distantly. In some households, decisions are made through open discussion and verbal give-and-take; in other households, parents lay down the rules, and children are expected to follow them. To what extent are different patterns of family relationships associated with different patterns of adolescent development? Are some styles of parenting more likely to be associated with healthy development than others? In this section, we look at variations in parenting practices and their correlates in adolescent behavior.

It is important to bear in mind that although our tendency is to see child behavior as the result of parent behavior, socialization is actually a two-way, not a one-way, street (Bell, 1968). It is a known fact, for example, that parents who employ physical punishment (spanking, hitting, etc.) are more likely to have aggressive adolescents (Bandura and Walters, 1959). But we cannot be sure whether (1) physical punishment leads to adolescent aggression; (2) adolescent aggression leads to parents' using physical punishment; (3) some other factor is correlated with parents' using physical punishment and with adolescent aggression (a genetic predisposition to behave aggressively that adolescents inherit from their parents); or (4) some combination of these causal and correlational factors is at work. Thus when we look at the findings concerning parenting practices and adolescent development, we must remember that just as parents affect their adolescents' behavior, so do adolescents affect their parents' behavior, thereby playing a role in shaping their own development (Felson and Zielinski, 1989; Lerner, Castellino, and Perkins, 1994).

Parenting Styles and Their Effects

There are a variety of ways to characterize parents' behavior toward their children. One of the most useful approaches derives from the work of psychologist Diana Baumrind (1978). According to her work and that of others in this vein, two aspects of the parent's behavior toward the adolescent are critical: parental responsiveness and parental demandingness (Maccoby and Martin, 1983). **Parental responsiveness** refers to the degree to which the parent responds to the child's needs in an accepting, supportive manner. **Parental demandingness** refers to the extent to which the parent expects and demands mature, responsible behavior from the child. Parents vary on each of these dimensions. Some are warm and accepting, while others are unresponsive and rejecting; some are demanding and expect a great deal of their child, while others are permissive and demand very little.

Because parental responsiveness and demandingness are more or less independent of each other—that is, it is possible for a parent to be very demanding without being responsive and vice versa—it is possible to look at various combinations of these two dimensions (see Figure 4.5). Many studies of parents and children indicate that the fourfold classification scheme presented in Figure 4.5 is very important in understanding the impact of parents' behavior on the child, and psychologists have given labels to the four different prototypes presented in the figure.

A parent who is very responsive but not at all demanding is labeled *indulgent,* whereas one who is equally responsive but also very

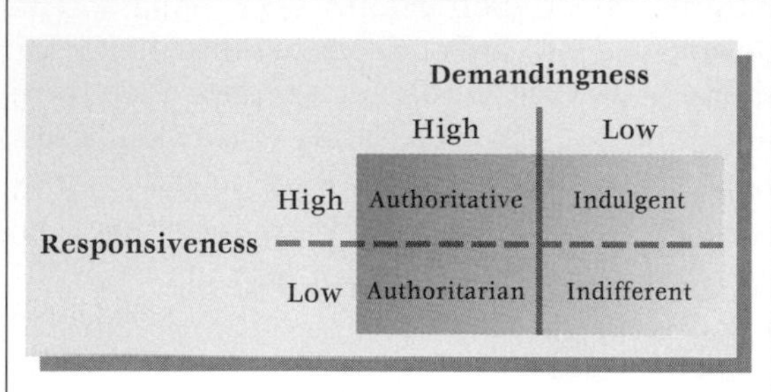

FIGURE 4.5 *A scheme for classifying parenting types.* (Maccoby and Martin, 1983)

demanding is labeled *authoritative.* Parents who are very demanding but not responsive are *authoritarian;* parents who are neither demanding nor responsive are labeled *indifferent.* These four general patterns are described below.

Authoritative parents are warm but firm. They set standards for the child's conduct but form expectations that are consistent with the child's developing needs and capabilities. They place a high value on the development of autonomy and self-direction but assume the ultimate responsibility for their child's behavior. Authoritative parents deal with their child in a rational, issue-oriented manner, frequently engaging in discussion and explanation with their children over matters of discipline.

Authoritarian parents place a high value on obedience and conformity. They tend to favor more punitive, absolute, and forceful disciplinary measures. Verbal give-and-take is not common in authoritarian households, because the underlying belief of authoritarian parents is that the child should accept without question the rules and standards established by the parents. They tend not to encourage independent behavior and, instead, place a good deal of importance on restricting the child's autonomy.

Indulgent parents behave in an accepting, benign, and somewhat more passive way in matters of discipline. They place relatively few demands on the child's behavior, giving

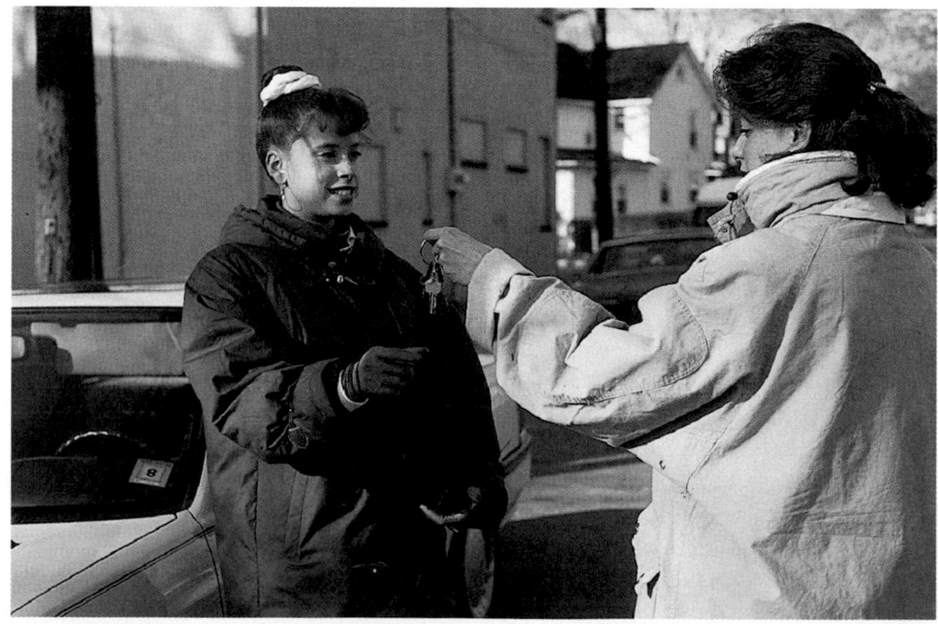

Authoritative parents are warm, firm, and fair in exercising their authority over the adolescent while granting an appropriate degree of independence. (Rhoda Sidney/Stock, Boston)

the child a high degree of freedom to act as he or she wishes. Indulgent parents are more likely to believe that control is an infringement on the child's freedom that may interfere with the child's healthy development. Instead of actively shaping their child's behavior, indulgent parents are more likely to view themselves as resources which the child may or may not use.

Indifferent parents try to do whatever is necessary to minimize the time and energy that they must devote to interacting with their child. In extreme cases, indifferent parents may be neglectful. They know little about their child's activities and whereabouts, show little interest in their child's experiences at school or with friends, rarely converse with their child, and rarely consider their child's opinion when making decisions. Rather than raising their child according to a set of beliefs about what is good for the child's development (as do the other three parent types) indifferent parents are "parent centered"—they structure their home life primarily around their own needs and interests.

The categorization proposed by Baumrind provides a useful way of summarizing and examining some of the relations between parenting practices and adolescent psychosocial development. Generally speaking, young people who have been raised in authoritative households are more psychosocially competent than peers who have been raised in authoritarian, indulgent, or indifferent homes: Adolescents raised in authoritative homes are more responsible, more self-assured, more adaptive, more creative, more curious, more socially skilled, and more successful in school. Adolescents raised in authoritarian homes, in contrast, are more dependent, more passive, less socially adept, less self-assured, and less intellectually curious. Adolescents raised in indulgent households are often less mature, more irresponsible, more conforming to their peers, and less able to assume positions of leadership. Adolescents raised in indifferent homes are often impulsive and more likely to be involved in delinquent behavior and in precocious experiments with sex, drugs, and alcohol (Fuligni and Eccles, 1993; Kurdek and Fine, 1994; Lamborn, Mounts, Steinberg, and Dornbusch, 1991; Pulkkinen, 1982; Steinberg, Lamborn, Darling, Mounts, and Dornbusch, 1994). In general, the effects of parental nonresponsiveness tend to be slightly worse among girls than boys, whereas the effects of parental nondemandingness tend to be slightly worse among boys than girls. Although occasional exceptions to these general patterns have been noted, the evidence linking authoritative parenting and healthy adolescent development is remarkably strong, and it has been found in studies of a wide range of ethnic and socioeconomic groups (Dornbusch, Ritter, Liederman, Roberts, and Fraleigh, 1987; Maccoby and Martin, 1983; Steinberg, Mounts, Lamborn, and Dornbusch, 1991). There is some evidence, however, that adolescents in stepfamilies may profit more from somewhat more distant relations with their parents than is the case for adolescents from nondivorced homes (Lyons and Barber, 1992).

A number of researchers have attempted to "unpack" authoritative parenting into its core components in an effort to understand how different aspects of authoritativeness are related to adolescent adjustment (Steinberg, 1990). Most researchers agree that authoritative parenting is composed of three main components: *warmth* (the degree to which the adolescent is loved and accepted), *structure* (the degree to which the adolescent has expectations and rules for his or her behavior), and *autonomy support* (the degree to which parents accept and encourage the adolescent's individuality) (Barber, 1992; Connell and Wellborn 1991; Steinberg, Elmen, and Mounts, 1989). In general, parental warmth is associated with adolescent competence overall; the presence of structure is associated with fewer behavior problems; and the presence of autonomy support is associated with fewer symptoms of psychological distress, such as depression or anxiety (Barber, Olsen, and Shagle, 1994; Steinberg, 1990).

Why is authoritative parenting associated with healthy adolescent development? First, authoritative parents provide a nice balance between restrictiveness and autonomy, which on the one hand provides the young person with opportunities to develop self-reliance but on the other hand sets the sorts of standards, limits, and guidelines that developing individuals need. The authoritative family is more able than other families to adjust to new stages of the family life cycle. Because authoritative parents are flexible in their approach to parenting, they tend to shape and tailor their demands and expectations to suit the changing needs and competencies of the adolescent, a process that is likely to help the young person's continued development (Hill, 1980). Authoritative parents, for instance, are more likely to give children more independence gradually as they get older, which helps children develop self-reliance. One study, for example, found that authoritative parenting led to the development of psychological maturity, which in turn led to school success (Steinberg et al., 1989).

Second, because authoritative parents are more likely to engage their children in verbal give-and-take, they are likely to promote the sort of intellectual development that provides an important foundation for the development of psychosocial competence. Authoritative parents, for example, are less likely than other parents to assert their authority by turning adolescents' personal decisions (e.g., over what type of music is listened to) into "moral" issues (Smetana and Asquith, 1994). Family discussions in which decisions, rules, and expectations are explained help the child to understand social systems and social relationships. This understanding plays an important part in the development of reasoning abilities, role taking, moral judgment, and empathy (Baumrind, 1978). The extensive discussion characteristic of authoritative households stimulates the adolescent's thinking.

Third, because authoritative parenting combines moderate control with a good deal of warmth, children are more likely to identify with their parents. In fact, one of the strongest predictors of identification between children and their parents is warmth in the parent-child relationship. We are more likely to identify with and imitate people who treat us with warmth and affection. A child raised warmly by parents who value self-direction will imitate his or her mother and father and display a similar preference for independence (Hill, 1980).

Finally, the child's own behavior may play a role in shaping authoritative parenting practices (Lewis, 1981a). Children who are responsible, self-directed, curious, and self-assured elicit from their parents warmth, flexible guidance, and verbal give-and-take. In contrast, children who are aggressive, dependent, or less psychosocially mature in other ways may provoke parents' behavior that is excessively harsh, passive, or distant. Parents may enjoy being around children who are responsible and independent, for example, and may treat them more warmly. In contrast, children who are continually "acting up" make their parents short-tempered, impatient, or distant. In other words, the relationship between adolescent competence and authoritative parenting may be the result of a reciprocal cycle in which the child's psychosocial maturity leads to authoritative parenting, which in turn leads to the further development of maturity (Lerner, Castellino, and Perkins, 1994; Steinberg et al., 1989).

Ethnic Differences in Parenting Practices

A number of researchers have asked whether parents from different ethnic groups vary in their child rearing and whether the relation between parenting and adolescent outcomes is the same across different ethnic groups. These, of course, are two different questions: The first concerns average differences between groups in their approaches to parenting (e.g., whether ethnic minority parents are stricter than white parents), whereas the second concerns the correlation between parenting practices and adolescent adjustment in different groups (e.g., whether the effect of strictness is the same in ethnic minority families as it is in white families).

In general, researchers find that authoritative parenting, as defined earlier in this chapter, is less prevalent among African-American, Asian-American, or Hispanic-American families than among white families, no doubt reflecting the fact that parenting practices are often linked to cultural values and beliefs (Dornbusch et al., 1987; Steinberg et al., 1991; Steinberg, Dornbusch, and Brown, 1992). Nevertheless, even though authoritative parenting is less common in ethnic minority families, its effects on adolescent adjustment are beneficial in all ethnic groups (Steinberg et al., 1992). In other words, ethnic minority youngsters for the most part benefit just as much from parenting that is responsive and demanding as do their nonminority peers.

Research has also indicated that authoritarian parenting (high in demandingness but low in responsiveness) is more prevalent among ethnic minority than among white families, even after taking ethnic differences in socioeconomic status into account (Chao, 1994; Dornbusch et al., 1987; Steinberg, Lamborn, Dornbusch, and Darling, 1992). As opposed to research on authoritative parenting, however, research on authoritarian parenting indicates that the adverse effects of this style of parenting may be greater among white youngsters than among their ethnic minority counterparts (Chao, 1994; Dornbusch et al., 1987; Steinberg, Lamborn, Darling, Mounts, and Dornbusch, 1994). Several explanations have been offered for this finding.

Research indicates important ethnic differences in parenting practices during adolescence. In general, Asian-American parents are stricter than their counterparts from other cultures. (Michael Newman/PhotoEdit)

First, some writers have suggested that because ethnic minority families are more likely to live in dangerous communities, authoritarian parenting, with its emphasis on control, may not be as harmful and may even carry some benefits. Second, as psychologist Ruth Chao (1994) has pointed out, the concept of "authoritative" or "authoritarian" parenting may not make a great deal of sense when applied to parents from other cultures, especially those from Asian backgrounds. Specifically, she notes that European-American researchers may mislabel traditional Asian approaches to child "training" (which appear very controlling, but which are neither aloof nor hostile) as authoritarian. Asian parents are more likely than non-Asian parents to combine a high degree of strictness with a high degree of warmth (Rohner and Pettengill, 1985).

ARE THERE SEX DIFFERENCES IN ADOLESCENTS' FAMILY RELATIONSHIPS?

One question frequently asked by researchers is whether and in what ways there may be sex differences in patterns of family relationships. Do daughters and sons have different sorts of relationships with their mothers and fathers? Now that several studies have been completed, we have a tentative answer to this question, and it is a surprising one.

In general, differences between the family relations of sons and daughters are minimal (Silverberg, Tennenbaum, and Jacob, 1992). Although there are occasional exceptions to the rule, sons and daughters report similar degrees of closeness to their parents, similar amounts of conflict, similar types of rules (and disagreements about those rules), and similar patterns of activity (Hill and Holmbeck, 1987; Montemayor and Brownlee, 1987; Youniss and Ketterlinus, 1987). Observational studies of interactions between parents and adolescents indicate that sons and daughters interact with their parents in remarkably similar ways (Cooper and Grotevant, 1987; Hauser, Book, Houlihan, Powers, Weiss-Perry, Follansbee, Jacobson, and Noam, 1987).

Does this mean that sex differences in the family are absent? Not entirely. These same studies also indicate that the sex of the adolescent's *parent* may be a more important influence on family relationships than the sex of the adolescent. A recent review of studies of adolescent-parent relations indicates that teenagers—males and females alike—relate very differently to mothers and to fathers (Collins and Russell, 1991). Adolescents tend to be closer to their mother, to spend more time alone with their mother, and to feel more comfortable talking to their mother about problems and other emotional matters. Fathers are more likely to be perceived as relatively distant authority figures who may be consulted for "objective" information (such as help with homework) but who are rarely sought for support or guidance (such as help for problems with a boyfriend or girlfriend). Interestingly, adolescents also fight more often with their mothers than with their fathers, but this higher level of conflict does not appear to jeopardize the closeness of the mother-adolescent relationship. It seems safe to say that relationships between adolescents and their mothers are more emotionally intense in general, and that this intensity has both positive and negative manifestations (Apter, 1990; Larson and Richards, 1994).

One of the most interesting findings to emerge from these

Autonomy and Attachment in the Adolescent's Family

Several recent studies of conversations between adolescents and their parents have examined factors in the nature of parent-adolescent communication that contribute to healthy adolescent development. In these studies, families are asked to discuss a problem together, and their interaction is taped and later analyzed. Generally speaking, families with psychologically competent teenagers interact in ways that permit family members to express their autonomy while remaining attached, or connected, to other family members (Silverberg, Tennenbaum, and Jacob, 1992). In these families, verbal give-and-take is the norm, and adolescents (as well as parents) are encouraged to express their own opinions, even if this sometimes leads to dis-

studies concerns the father-daughter relationship in particular. Most researchers have found that this relationship is especially distant (Larson and Richards, 1994), although we are not quite sure of the reasons. Some theorists have speculated that unconscious taboos against incest may make it difficult for fathers and daughters to remain close after puberty, while others have suggested that the general emotional inexpressiveness of fathers may put daughters off more than sons (Youniss and Ketterlinus, 1987). Yet it seems clear that this relationship is the flattest, emotionally speaking, in the family. Whether and in what ways this may affect the daughter's development is not known.

Why should mothers and fathers have such different sorts of relationships with their adolescent children? One explanation concerns differences in the socialization of men and women. We know, for example, that women in Western cultures are socialized to be more emotionally expressive than men, and this may give them talents and capabilities that permit them to form closer relationships with their children. Growing up in a household in which mothers are emotionally accessible and fathers are emotionally distant only furthers this tendency, for this provides role models for adolescents to imitate. A somewhat different explanation concerns differences in the maternal and paternal roles. The mother's role in this culture traditionally has included more of an "expressive," or emotional, component, whereas the father's role may be more "instrumental" (Parsons, 1949). Moreover, until relatively recently, patterns of work and family life were so different for mothers and fathers that it may have been difficult for fathers—whatever their socialization—to form close relationships with their children. Mothers may be closer than fathers simply because they spend more time with their children as their children develop, and time together may foster and strengthen emotional bonds.

Whatever the explanation, however, the consistency with which studies of parents and adolescents uncover different patterns of relations for mothers and fathers is striking—especially in light of changes that have taken place in sex roles in contemporary society. Although we cannot be sure of the origins of these differences, we are fairly confident that they exist, even in today's families. In discussing the parent-adolescent relationship, we clearly need to pay attention to sex differences—not necessarily the differences between sons and daughters, however, but the differences between mothers and fathers.

agreement. At the same time, however, the importance of maintaining close relationships in the family is emphasized, and individuals are encouraged to consider how their actions may affect other family members. Indeed, a series of studies by Joseph Allen and his collaborators demonstrates that adolescents who are permitted to assert their own opinions within a family context that is secure and loving develop higher self-esteem and more mature coping abilities. Adolescents whose autonomy is squelched are at risk for developing feelings of depression, and those who do not feel connected are more likely than their peers to develop behavior problems (Allen, Hauser, Bell, and O'Conner, 1994; Allen, Hauser, Eickholt, Bell, and O'Conner, in press).

Other researchers have also found that healthy adolescent development is associated with particular patterns of verbal interaction. Psychiatrist Stuart Hauser and his colleagues (Hauser, Powers, and Noam, 1991) have drawn a distinction between "enabling" and "constraining" patterns of interchange in the family. **Enabling interactions** include explanation, problem solving, and empathy. **Constraining interactions** are distracting, judgmental, or devaluing of a family member's opinion. Not surprisingly, adolescents who grow up in homes in which the family tends to interact in enabling ways score higher on measures of psychological development than do those who grow up in relatively more constraining families. One recent study found as well that adolescents' needs for autonomy can be especially frustrated when their parents form strong coalitions with one another (Vuchinich, Vuchinich, and Wood, 1993).

Rather than viewing attachment and autonomy as opposites, these studies of family interaction indicate that the path to healthy psychological development during adolescence is likely to combine the two. In other words, adolescents appear to do best when they grow up in a family atmosphere that permits the development of individuality against a backdrop of close family ties (Cooper, Grotevant, and Condon, 1983; Grotevant and Cooper, 1986). In these families, conflict between parents and adolescents can play a very important and positive role in the adolescent's social and cognitive development, because individuals are encouraged to express their opinions in an atmosphere that does not risk severing the emotional attachment (Cooper, 1988). In Chapter 10, we will look more closely at the nature of attachment between parents and adolescents.

RECAP

Psychologists have identified four basic styles of parenting during adolescence: authoritative, authoritarian, indulgent, and indifferent. In general, adolescents from authoritative homes fare the best on measures of psychological adjustment, whereas adolescents from indifferent homes fare worst. Authoritative parenting, which has been shown to benefit adolescents from a variety of ethnic backgrounds, is composed of three main factors: warmth, structure, and autonomy support. Studies of parent-adolescent interaction show, as well, that the healthiest families are those that permit the adolescent to develop a sense of autonomy while staying emotionally attached to the family at the same time.

Adolescents' Relationships with Siblings

Far more is known about adolescents' relations with their parents than about their relations with brothers and sisters. In general, studies suggest that sibling relationships may have characteristics that set them apart from both other family relationships (such as those between adolescents and their parents) and other relationships with peers (such as those between adolescents and their close friends) (Furman and Buhrmester, 1985; Raffaelli and Larson, 1987). In one study, for example, young adolescents were asked to rate several different types of relationships (for example, with parents, siblings, friends, grandparents) along similar dimensions. As you can see in Figure 4.6, sibling relationships were rated like those with parents for companionship and importance, but they were rated more like friendships with respect to power, assistance, and how satisfying the relationship is.

Over the course of adolescence, adolescents' relationships with siblings, and especially with younger siblings, become more egalitarian but more distant and less emotionally intense (Anderson and Starcher, 1992; Buhrmester and Furman, 1990). Despite these changes over time, there is considerable stability in the quality of sibling relationships between childhood and adolescence, and siblings who are relatively closer during middle childhood are relatively closer as young adolescents (Dunn, Slomkowski, and Beardsall, 1994). Having a close sibling relationship can partially ameliorate the negative effects of not having friends in school (East and Rook, 1992).

One striking difference between sibling and other types of relationships involves conflict; adolescents report far higher levels of conflict with brothers and sisters than they do with anyone else. Because siblings live in proximity to each other, they may have added opportunities for both positive and negative interaction. One study finds that in poorly functioning families aggressive interchanges between unsupervised siblings may provide a "training ground" within which adolescents learn, practice, and perfect antisocial behavior (Bank, Reid, and Greenley, 1994). Negative interactions between siblings are especially common in families under economic stress (Conger, Conger, and Elder, 1994).

One topic of interest to researchers who study adolescents and their siblings concerns how closely siblings resemble each other in intelligence, personality, and interests. Because siblings share some genetic influences (because they have the same parents) and at least some environmental influences (because they have grown up in the same household), you might think that they would be more alike than different. But new research suggests that adolescents growing up in the same family are actually quite different from each other—far more than would be expected given their supposedly similar genetic and environmental influences. For example, siblings' scores on standard measures of personality traits are virtually uncorrelated (Plomin and Daniels, 1987). Indeed, the findings concerning differences between siblings are so consistent that one team of investigators wrote recently that "two children in the same family are as different from one another as are pairs of children selected randomly from the population" (Plomin and Daniels, 1987, p. 1).

Why might siblings be so different from each other, even when they grow up in the same home? Three explanations come to mind. First, unless they are identical twins, siblings only share a portion of their genes in common. (The average overlap between two siblings with the same biological parents is 50 percent, but the actual overlap can be much lower or much higher.) To the extent that certain traits are influenced by genetic factors, siblings who have very different genetic makeups will have different personalities.

Second, although siblings may grow up in the same family, they may experience their family environment very differently (Hoffman, 1991; Plomin and Daniels, 1987). One brother may describe his family as very close knit, while another may have experienced it as very distant. One girl describes her family

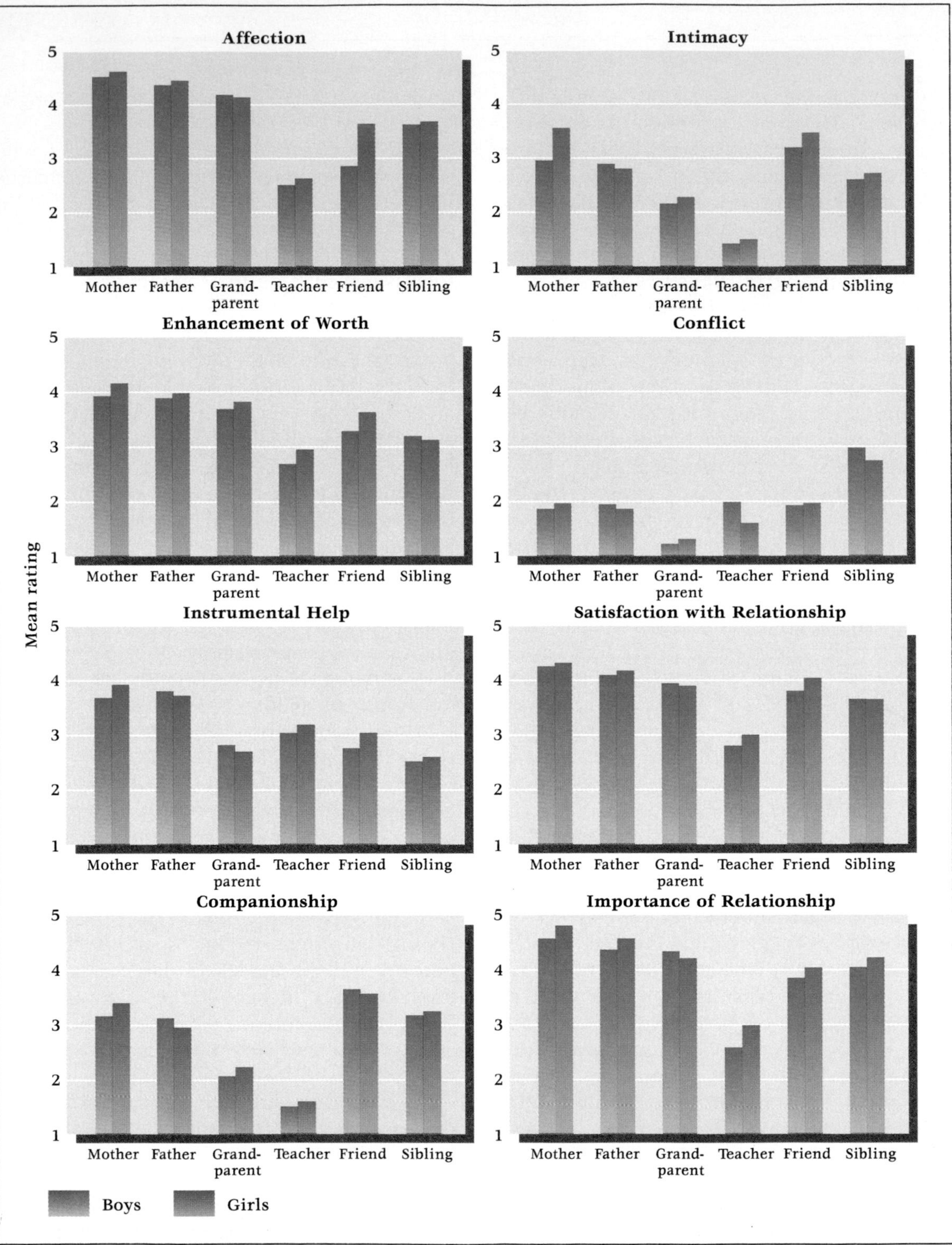

FIGURE 4.6 *These graphs show similarities and differences among adolescents' relationships with parents, friends, siblings, and significant others.* (Furman and Buhrmester, 1985)

Because siblings live in close proximity to each other, they have added opportunities for both positive and negative interaction. (© Ken Lax)

life as plagued with argument and conflict; her sister describes it as peaceful and agreeable. In other words, even though we may assume that children growing up in the same family have shared the same environment, this may not really be the case.

Siblings may experience the same family environment differently for a variety of reasons. First, parents may treat their children differently because of their own conscious and unconscious preferences, because of differences in their children's temperaments, or because of changes in their child-rearing philosophies over time. Second, the family may itself be at different stages in its own development, and this may affect children differently. For instance, it may be different to be raised by older parents than by younger ones, and children born later in the family's history may have parents who treat them differently because of this. Finally, differences in the family's circumstances at different times may affect the way that siblings are raised. A child who is raised during a time of financial strain may have very different experiences from a sibling who grows up when the family is more comfortable.

Studies show that siblings actually do describe their upbringings as being very different and, moreover, that these differences in experiences are related to different patterns of development. In general, better-adjusted adolescents were more likely than their siblings to report that their relationship with their mother was close, that their relations with brothers or sisters were friendly, that they were involved in family decision making, and that they were given a high level of responsibility around the house (Daniels, Dunn, Furstenberg, and Plomin, 1985).

The third explanation for sibling differences is that even if they are exposed to similar environments within the family, and even if they have similar genetic makeups, siblings may have very different experiences outside the family—at school, with friends, in the neighborhood. To the extent that factors other than the family environment shape adolescent development and behavior, siblings may turn out very different if they have divergent experiences outside the home. In the next chapter, we'll look at one potentially influential context outside the family—the adolescent's peer group.

RECAP

In general, adolescents' relations with siblings are different from those with parents or with friends. Over the course of adolescence, adolescents' relationships with siblings—and especially with younger siblings—become more equal but more distant and less emotionally intense. Interestingly, research suggests that adolescents are often quite dissimilar from their brothers and sisters, despite the strong genetic and environmental influences they share. Among the reasons for dissimilarity between siblings are that siblings may have very different experiences both within and outside the family.

KEY TERMS

authoritarian parents
authoritative parents
constraining interactions
correlation
demographers
effect size
enabling interactions
generation gap
indifferent parents
indulgent parents
intergenerational conflict
meta-analysis
midlife crisis
parental demandingness
parental responsiveness

FOR FURTHER READING

Furstenberg, F., Jr. (1990a). Coming of age in a changing family system. In S. Feldman and G. Elliott (Eds.), *At the threshold: The developing adolescent.* Cambridge, Mass.: Harvard University Press. An extensive overview of the implications of recent trends in family life in the United States for adolescent development.

Hetherington, E. M. (1993). An overview of the Virginia longitudinal study of divorce and remarriage with a focus on early adolescence. *Journal of Family Psychology, 7,* 39–56. A summary of findings from the best and most extensive study of divorce and remarriage conducted to date.

Silverberg, S., Tennenbaum, D., and Jacob, T. (1992). Adolescence and family interaction. Pp. 347–370 in V. Van Hasselt and M. Hersen (Eds.), *Handbook of social development: A lifespan perspective.* New York: Plenum. A thorough review of the literature on parent-adolescent interaction and relationships.

Steinberg, L., and Steinberg, W. (1994). *Crossing paths: How your child's adolescence triggers your own crisis.* New York: Simon & Schuster. An investigation of the "intersection" of adolescence and middle age and its implications for parents' mental health.

CHAPTER 5

PEER GROUPS

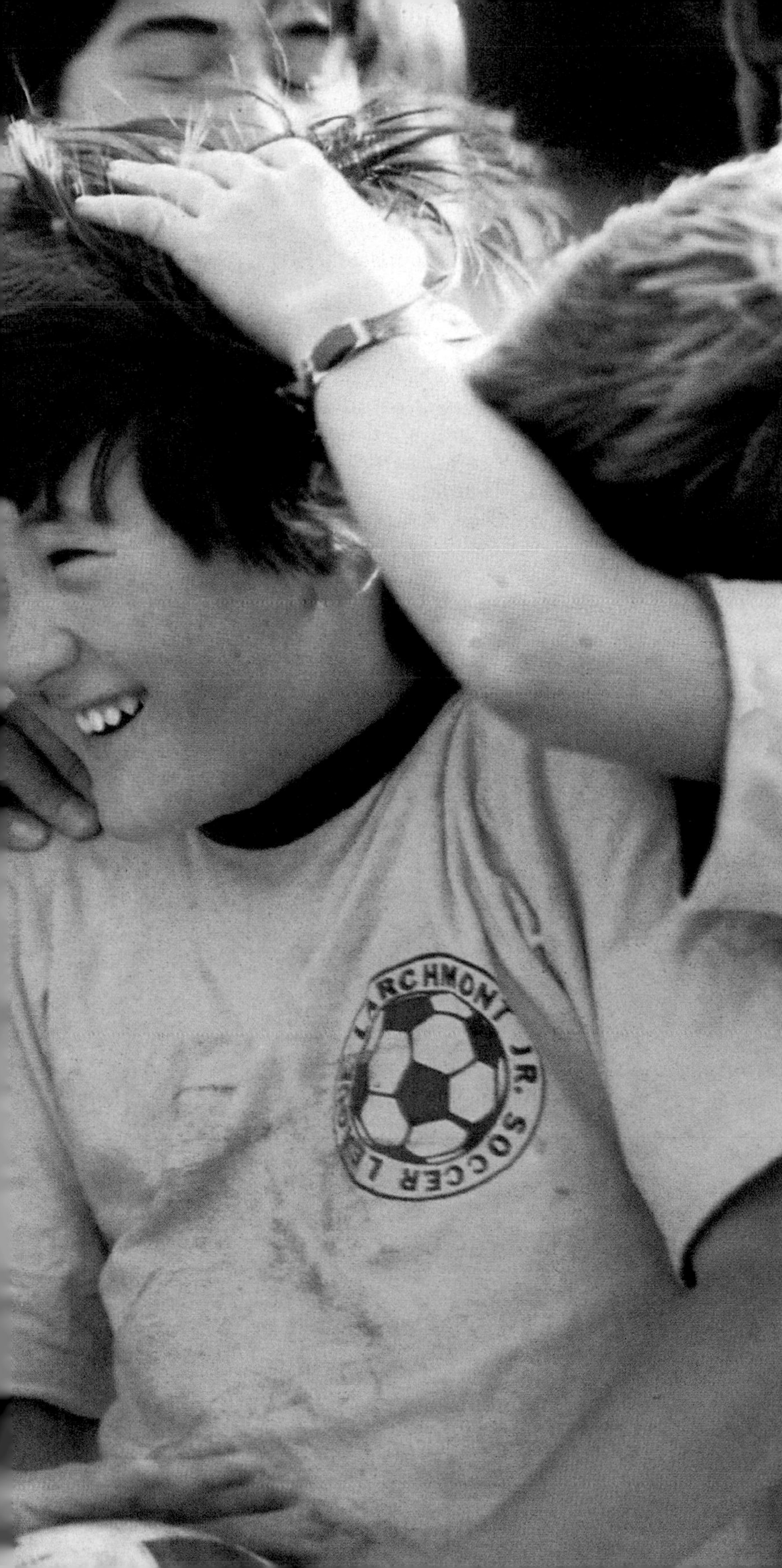

(Richard Hutchings/Photo Researchers)

It is about 8:30 in the morning. A group of teenagers congregates in the hallway in front of its first-period classroom. The teens are discussing their plans for the weekend. As the first-period bell sounds, they enter the classroom and take their seats. For the next four hours (until there is a break in their schedule for lunch) they will attend class in groups of about thirty—thirty adolescents to one adult.

At lunch, the clique meets again to talk about the weekend. They have about forty-five minutes until the first afternoon period begins. After lunch, they spend another two hours in class—again, in groups of about thirty. The school day ends, and the clique reconvenes. They are going over to someone's house to hang out for the rest of the day. Everyone's parents are working. They are on their own. At about 6 in the evening, they disperse and head home for dinner. A few will talk on the phone that night. Some will get together to study. They will see one another first thing the next morning.

When you stop to think about it, adolescents in modern society spend a remarkable amount of time with their peers. In fact, American teenagers spend more time talking to their friends each day than in any other single activity (Csikszentmihalyi, Larson, and Prescott, 1977). High school students spend twice as much of their time each week with peers as with parents or other adults—even discounting time in class (Brown, 1990). Virtually all adolescents spend most of each weekday with their peers while at school, and the vast majority also see or talk to their friends in the afternoon, in the evening, and over the weekend (Medrich, Roizen, Rubin, and Buckley, 1982). Even when adolescents work in part-time jobs, they are more likely to work with people their own age than with adults (Greenberger and Steinberg, 1986). And studies show that adolescents' moods are most positive when they are with their friends, and that time spent with friends becomes more rewarding over the course of adolescence (Larson, 1983; Larson and Richards, 1991).

American society is very age segregated. From the time youngsters enter school at the age of 5 until they graduate at age 18 or so, they are grouped with children their own age. They have little contact with people who are older or younger, outside of relatives. Because schools play such an important role in determining children's friendships, age grouping carries over into after-school, weekend, and vacation activities. Little League, scouting, church groups—all are structured in a way that groups people together by age.

In contemporary society, **peer groups** (groups of people who are roughly the same age) have become an increasingly important context in which adolescents spend time. Modernization has led to more and more age segregation—in schools, in the workplace, and in the community. Today's teenagers spend far more time in the exclusive company of their peers than their counterparts did in the past. Indeed, the rise of peer groups in modern society gives adolescence in contemporary America some of its most distinctive features. And the role of peers in shaping adolescent psychosocial development has become increasingly important.

For these reasons, understanding how adolescent peer groups form and what takes place within their boundaries is critical to understanding adolescent development in contemporary society. No discussion of adolescent identity development is complete without an examination of how and why teenagers derive part of their identity from the group they spend time with. No discussion of adolescent friendship is complete without an examination of teenagers' cliques and how they are formed. And no discussion of adolescent sexuality is complete without an examination of how, and when, peer groups change from same-sex groups to mixed-sex groups.

THE ORIGINS OF ADOLESCENT PEER GROUPS IN CONTEMPORARY SOCIETY

Contact between adolescents and their peers is found in all cultures. But not all societies have peer groups that are as narrowly defined and age segregated as those in modern-day America. Although adolescent peer relationships are universal, age-segregated peer groups are not. In earlier times, for example, interactions among youngsters occurred largely in the context of mixed-age groups composed of infants, children, and adolescents (Hartup, 1977). And much interaction among children occurred in the presence of their parents, because adults and children were not isolated from one another during the day. Even today, in societies that are less industrialized, young people spend a good part of the day in contact with their elders.

In contemporary America, however, age segregation is the norm. The reasons have to do with the ways in which our schools, our work, and our population are structured.

The physical separation of teenagers and adults has increased during the past four decades, due to changing patterns of housing and employment. In contemporary society, many adolescents spend a good deal of their free time without contact with adults. (Paul Conklin/ Monkmeyer)

The Educational Origins of Adolescent Peer Groups

Educators first developed the idea of free public education, with students grouped by age (a practice called **age grading**), in the middle of the nineteenth century (President's Science Advisory Committee, 1974). In so doing, they established an arrangement that would eventually touch all American youngsters and encourage the development and maintenance of age-segregated peer groups.

It was not until the second quarter of this century that most *adolescents* were directly affected by educational age grouping, however. Attending elementary school may have been common, but, until 1930 or so, high school was a luxury available only to the very affluent. In other words, adolescent peer groups based on friendships formed in school were not prevalent until the second quarter of this century.

What about adolescents growing up before 1930? Did they have peer groups similar to those that adolescents have today? We do not know for sure. But we can be fairly certain that the forces encouraging adolescents to associate almost exclusively with people of exactly the same age were not as strong at the beginning of the century as they are today. Youngsters who were not in school were generally working and living at home, where they were likely to have a good deal of contact with adults and children (Modell, Furstenberg, and Hershberg, 1976). Even those youngsters from families wealthy enough to send their children to high school typically attended academies where children of different ages were mixed together, and it was not uncommon during the nineteenth century for "peer groups" to be composed of individuals ranging in age from 14 to 20 (President's Science Advisory Committee, 1974). Today, in contrast, virtually all American adolescents spend the years between ages 10 and 16 in age-graded schools, and fewer than 25 percent leave school before graduating at the age of 17 or 18 (William T. Grant Foundation, 1988).

The impact of this educational age grading on adolescents' social life has been staggering. In one survey, in which seventh- through tenth-grade students were asked to list the people who were important to them, over two-thirds of the same-sex peers they mentioned were from the same grade in their school (Blyth, Hill, and Thiel, 1982). Participation in organized activities outside of school also contributes to age segregation. One study found that close to 80 percent of sixth-graders are involved in at least one nonschool club, extracurricular activity group, or youth organization in which they are likely to have contact only with peers of the same age (Medrich et al., 1982).

Work, Family Life, and Adolescent Peer Groups

A second set of factors related to the rise of adolescent peer groups concerns changes in the workplace, or more precisely, changes in the relationship between work and other aspects of daily life. With industrialization came more stringent and more carefully monitored child labor laws, which restricted adolescents' participation in the world of work (Bakan, 1972; Modell and Goodman, 1990). Because the implementation of tougher child labor laws coincided with the rise of secondary education, adolescents and adults (who had once shared the same daily activity—work) went their separate ways. Adolescents spent the day in school, and adults were at work.

The segregation of adolescents from adults also has been fueled by the rise in maternal employment. For example, the proportion of employed mothers of children between the ages of 6 and 17 rose from about 25 percent in 1948 to more than 75 percent today. The movement of mothers out of the home and into the workplace furthered the trend—already set in motion by suburbanization—toward the development of residential neighborhoods dominated by young people during weekday mornings and afternoons. Today, between 2 million and 6 million school-aged youngsters come home from school to houses with no adults present, and an additional half-million care for themselves in the morning, before school begins (Berman, Winkleby, Chesterman, and Boyce, 1992; Richardson, Radziszewska, Dent, and Flay, 1993). Later in this chapter we examine how the changing nature of adolescents' after-school environment may affect their behavior and development.

Changes in the Population

Perhaps the most important factor influencing the rise of adolescent peer groups in recent years was the rapid growth of the teenage population between 1955 and 1975, a trend which is now repeating itself during the 1990s. Following the end of World War II, many parents wanted to have children as soon as possible, creating what has come to be called the postwar **baby boom.** The products of this baby boom became adolescents during the 1960s and early 1970s, creating an "adolescent boom" for about 15 years. As you can see from Figure 5.1, the size of the population from ages 15 to 19 nearly doubled between 1955 and 1975 and, more important, rose from less than 7 percent of the total population to over 10 percent. During the mid-1970s, 1 out of every 7 Americans was a teenager. One reason for the growth of peer groups, therefore, was the sheer increase in the number of peers that young people had.

This trend, as you can see, turned downward in 1975, and the relative size of the adolescent population decreased until 1990. But during the last decade of this century—when the products of the baby boom have adolescents of their own—the size of the teenage population has been increasing once again. In the year 2000, the population of 15- to 19-year-olds in the United States will number about 23 million, or more than 8 percent of the nation's entire population. An additional 23 million individuals will be young adolescents at that time, meaning that as we enter the twenty-first century, approximately 1 in 6 individuals in this country will be adolescents (Scales, 1991).

Social scientists are interested in tracking the size of the adolescent population for several reasons. First, changes in the size of the adolescent population may warrant changes in the allocation of funds for social services, educational programs, and health care, since adolescents' needs are not the same as those of children or adults.

Second, changes in the size of the adolescent population have implications for understanding the behavior of cohorts. A cohort is a group of individuals born during a given era, such as the "baby boomers" (born in the

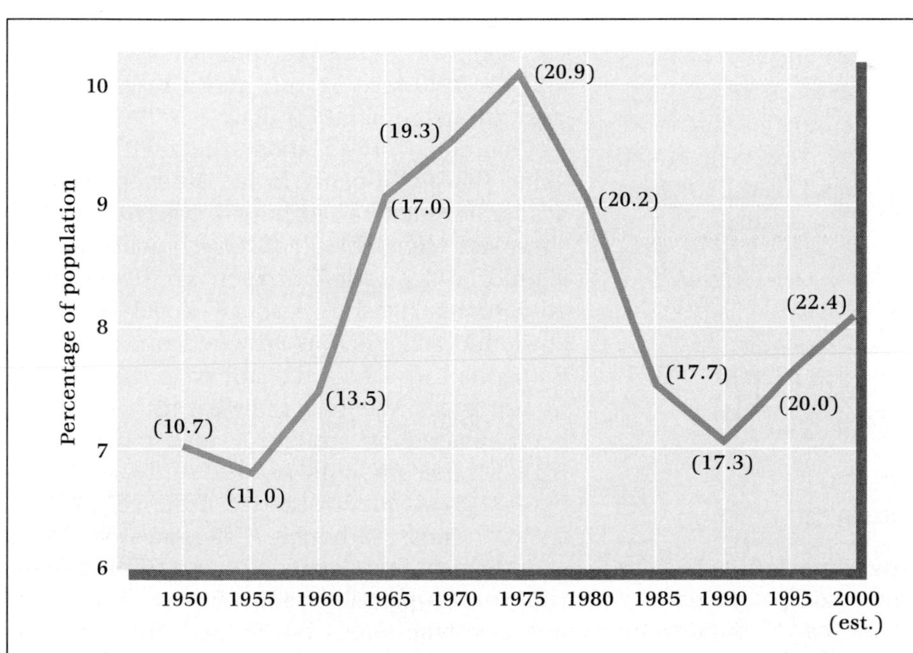

FIGURE 5.1 *The percentage of the U.S. population comprising 15- to 19-year-olds reached its highest level in 1975. It began to increase again in 1990. Figures in parentheses indicate the number of 15- to 19-year-olds, in millions.* (From Scales, 1991; United Nations Population Division, 1976)

late 1940s and early 1950s) or "Generation X" (born in the early 1970s). Baby-boomers, many of whom were adolescents in the early and mid-1970s, for example, were members of a very "crowded" cohort, which meant that they encountered a relatively high degree of competition from each other for places in college, jobs, and so on. The size of this cohort also meant that it could attract a great deal of public attention, from politicians to advertisers. In contrast, members of Generation X, who were adolescents in the late 1980s and early 1990s, were members of a much smaller cohort, with less competition among individuals but with far less clout in the larger society.

RECAP

In contemporary society, adolescents spend a great deal of time with agemates, or peers. Many factors contributed to the rise of peer groups in the last century, including the spread of compulsory secondary education, changes in the workplace that segregated young from old, and changes in the relative size of various cohorts of adolescents.

THE ADOLESCENT PEER GROUP: A PROBLEM OR A NECESSITY?

Is the rise of peer groups in modern society a problem that needs to be remedied, or is it an inevitable—perhaps even necessary—part of life in contemporary America? This question has sparked some of the hottest arguments in the study of adolescence during the past twenty-five years (Brown, 1990). On one side are those who say that age segregation has led to the development of a separate **youth culture,** in which young people maintain attitudes and values that are different from—even contrary to—those of adults. On the other side are those who argue that industrialization and modernization have made peer groups more important, that adults alone can no longer prepare young people for the future, and that peer groups play a vital and needed role in the socialization of adolescents for adulthood. Let's look at both sides of the debate.

Is There a Separate Youth Culture?

The belief that age segregation has fueled the development of a separate—and troublesome—youth culture was first expressed by sociologist James Coleman, whose book *The Adolescent Society* (1961) presented the findings of an extensive study of the social worlds of ten American high schools. Even though this book was published some thirty-five years ago, its influence on our views of adolescent peer groups remains strong.

Coleman worried about the relatively low value the adolescents in his study placed on academic success. Although the parents he surveyed felt that academic achievement should be a priority for their youngsters, the adolescents lived in a social world in which academic success was frowned on, in which doing well in school did not earn the admiration of peers. Whereas their parents may have been pleased by straight-A report cards, the high school students in the study said that being a good student carried little weight with their friends. Although Coleman's study is about thirty-five years old, its findings still ring true. It probably is fair to say that academic achievement is not valued any more by American teenagers today than it was four decades ago. Indeed, there are some indica-

Studies show that in most high schools, athletic and social success are more reliable routes to popularity with peers than is academic success. (Polly Brown/Picture Cube)

tions that, if anything, it is valued even less (Meyer, 1994).

What should we make of the fact that adolescents do not, relative to adults, place a great deal of emphasis on doing well in school? According to some observers, age segregation has so strengthened the power of the peer group that American adolescents have become alienated and unfamiliar with the values of adults. No longer are young people interested in the things their parents wanted for them, these commentators say. In fact, teenagers have become separated from adult society to such an extent that they have established their own society—a separate youth culture that undermines parents' efforts to encourage academic excellence and instead emphasizes sports, dating, and partying.

According to this view, problems such as youth unemployment, teenage suicide, juvenile crime and delinquency, drug and alcohol use, and premarital pregnancy can be attributed to the rise of peer groups and the isolation of adolescents from adults. Many observers of the adolescent scene have noted that all these problems increased dramatically after 1940, as peer groups became more prominent and age segregation became more prevalent (e.g., Bronfenbrenner, 1974). The argument, then, is that the rise in adolescents' problems can be directly linked to the rise in the power of adolescent peer groups. Although this view is widely held among adults, at least one study indicates that it may not be entirely true.

In this study, the researcher contrasted the peer orientation of young people at three different points in time. Identical questionnaires assessing how much adolescents looked to their parents and friends for advice on a range of issues were given to groups of teenagers from the same community in 1963, 1976, and 1982 (Sebald, 1986). As might have been predicted, between 1963 and 1976 adolescents became more oriented toward their peers and less toward their parents. Between 1976 and 1982, however—a period of time during which rates of adolescent problems increased—this trend reversed itself somewhat, as adolescents' orientation toward their peers diminished. During this later period, boys' orientation toward their parents increased, but girls' continued to decline, although at a less dramatic rate. And, as we noted in Chapter 4, studies indicate that adolescents' values were more similar to those of their parents during the early 1980s than they were during the late 1960s and early 1970s (Gecas and Seff, 1990).

As B. Bradford Brown (1990), an expert on adolescent peer groups, has noted, the nature and strength of adolescent peer influence varies a great deal from one historical period to the next. We must be cautious about generalizing images of adolescent peer pressure derived from one point in time to all generations of young people. The strength of peer influence also may vary from one context to another. One study of Canadian adolescents, for example, found that the majority of students preferred to be remembered as outstanding students (rather than as great athletes or popular adolescents), and other studies have found that students' preferences for how they will be remembered vary a great deal by sex, age, and where they fit into the social structure of the school (Brown, 1990).

These cautions notwithstanding, it seems obvious to even the most casual observer that peers play a more important role in the lives of adolescents in modern society than they did in previous eras. But has the rise of adolescent peer groups in modern society really caused so many problems?

Unfortunately, this question is very difficult to answer. While it is true that age segregation has increased over the last fifty years, society has changed in other ways during this same time—ways that may also have contributed to increases in such problems as crime and drug use. In many regards, the world is a far more stressful place to grow up in now than it was in the past. Families move every few years. Divorce is commonplace. Adolescents experience enormous pressures from parents, peers, and the mass media (Meyer, 1994). The health of the economy seems to change from month to month, and competition to get a good job is fierce. Is it any wonder that problems such as suicide and alcohol abuse are on the rise?

To be sure, contemporary adolescents spend more *time* in peer groups than adolescents did in past eras. But we do not know if today's young people are any more susceptible to the influence of their friends than their counterparts were previously, nor do we know if teenagers are any worse off because peer groups have come to play a more prominent role in modern society. In fact, studies of peer pressure indicate that most teenagers feel that their friends are likely to pressure them *not* to use drugs or to engage in sexual activity. Adolescents do, however, report a good deal of pressure to drink alcohol, and this pressure increases during the adolescent years (Brown, Clasen, and Eicher, 1986), and few adolescents report that their friends pressure them to do well in school (Steinberg, Darling, Fletcher, Brown, and Dornbusch, in press). Thus, adolescents exert *both* positive and negative influences on each other, and it is incorrect to describe the peer group as a monolithic, negative influence. More to the point, some theorists have suggested that peer groups—regardless of how they influence adolescent behavior—are inevitable and *necessary* byproducts of modernization. Let's now look at their point of view.

The Need for Peer Groups in Modern Society

In less industrialized societies, political, economic, and social institutions revolve around the family. Occupation, choice of spouse, place of residence, treatment under society's laws, and participation in governing the community are all tied to who one's relatives are. Individuals' family ties determine whom they can trade with and how much they pay for various commodities. In short, how adults are expected to behave depends on which family they come from.

Because not all adults are expected to behave in the same way in these kinship-based societies, it is not possible to educate or socialize all young people in one large group, since they all have to learn somewhat different sets of norms. When norms for behavior vary from person to person, they are called **particularistic norms.** Suppose, for example, that the rules for driving were particularistic—that the rules of the road were different for every person. Perhaps people from families who had lived in the community for a long time would be allowed to drive at 75 miles an hour, but people from families who were new to the area would have to drive at 55. Under a particularistic system such as this, having driver education courses for high school students wouldn't make much sense, because each student would have to learn a different set of rules.

In societies in which norms are particularistic, grouping adolescents by age and sending them off to school is not an effective strategy for socializing them for adulthood, since their family ties, not their age, determine what their rights and responsibilities are. The socialization of adolescents in kinship-based societies is best accomplished in family groups, where elders can pass on the family's particular values and norms to their younger relatives.

In contemporary societies, things are quite different. Modernization has eroded much of the family's importance as a political, social, and economic unit. Generally speaking, in modern society, all individuals are expected to learn the same set of norms, because the rules governing behavior apply equally to all members of the community. These norms are called **universalistic norms.** When you walk into a department store to buy something or when you go into a voting booth to vote, it generally makes no difference who your relatives are. Whom you may marry, what kind of work you do, where you live, and how you are treated under the law are not based on family lineage. The norms that apply to you apply to everyone.

Under these circumstances, it is not wise to limit the socialization of adolescents to the family, because doing so does not ensure that all youngsters will learn the same set of norms. In societies that require individuals to learn universalistic norms, it is more efficient to group together by age all the individuals who are to be socialized (Eisenstadt, 1956). Teaching is better done in schools than left up to individual families. One of the reasons we have driver education classes, for example, is that our rules for driving are universalistic—the same for everyone—and we need to make sure that individuals learn a common set of regulations, not simply the ones their parents teach them.

As the family has become a less important political and economic institution, universalistic norms have come to replace particularistic ones. And this has required a change in the way in which adolescents are prepared for adulthood. Not only has modernization created age groups—it has made them absolutely necessary. Without systematic age grouping in schools, it would be impossible to prepare young people for adulthood. And because age grouping in schools carries over into activities outside of school, the need for universal school-based education has created age-segregated peer groups.

Some theorists do not see this as a bad thing. They feel that as society has become more technologically advanced, adolescents have come to play a valuable role in preparing one another for adulthood. According to

In postfigurative societies, cultural change is slow. As a result, the socialization and education of adolescents is performed almost exclusively by their elders. In cofigurative societies, such as ours, where cultural change takes place at a faster rate, much of the socialization and education of adolescents is performed by peers. (George Bellrose/Stock, Boston; Harry Wilkes/Stock, Boston)

the anthropologist Margaret Mead ([1928] 1978), the way in which young people are best socialized for adulthood depends on how fast their society is changing. In some cultures, cultural change is so slow that what a child needs to know to function as an adult changes very little over time. Mead called these **postfigurative cultures;** they socialize children almost exclusively through contact with the culture's elders, because the way in which older generations have lived is almost identical to the way in which subsequent generations will live.

Imagine, for a moment, growing up in a world in which you had to know only what your grandparents knew in order to survive. In this age of laptop computers, CD-ROM, satellites, and space shuttles, growing up in a world in which very little changes over fifty years seems almost impossible to imagine. Fifty years ago, television had barely been on the market. Yet, strange as it may seem to us now, most societies until fairly recently have been postfigurative—and they still are, in much of the developing world. In other words, until fairly recently, adolescents could learn exclusively from their elders what they needed to know to be successful adults.

During the past 100 years, contemporary societies have shifted away from being postfigurative cultures. They have become **cofigurative cultures,** in which socialization of young people is accomplished not merely through contact between children and their elders but through contact between people of the same age. In cofigurative cultures, society changes so quickly that much of what parents are able to teach their children may be outdated by the time their children become adults. Today, we live in a cofigurative society. For adolescents in contemporary America, peers have become role models as important as parents and grandparents. As a result of such rapid change, adolescents increasingly need to turn to members of their own generation for advice, guidance, and information.

If you were a teenager living in a postfigurative culture, you might ask your grandfather for advice about how to hunt or farm. But if you were a teenager in today's cofigurative culture, to whom would you turn for advice about how to use a CD-ROM drive on a computer? Would you turn to your friends, who probably have grown up with computers in their homes and schools, or to your grandparents, who may never even have used a computer?

Mead believed that as cofigurative cultures changed even more rapidly, they would be replaced by **prefigurative cultures,** in which young people would become adults' teachers. We already may be living in a prefigurative culture. Instead of parents asking, "Why can't Johnny read?" teenagers ask, "Why can't Mom and Dad program the VCR?"

Do these analyses mean that the adolescents of the future will cease to profit from having close relationships with adults? Of course not. Young people will always need the support, affection, and advice of their elders. But understanding how peer groups have been made necessary by modernization casts the issue of age segregation in a new light. Despite whatever problems may have been caused by the rise of peer groups in contemporary society, there may be little we can do to make adolescent peer groups less important.

RECAP

Social scientists have long debated whether the prominent role played by peer groups in the socialization of young people is cause for concern or celebration. On the one side are commentators who suggest that the rise of peer groups has contributed to the development of a separate youth culture that is hostile toward adult values. On the other side are those who point to the necessary and valuable educational role played by peer groups in quickly changing societies like ours.

After-School Activities and Adolescent Peer Groups: How Are Adolescents Affected by Self-Care?

Adults' concerns about the problems associated with adolescent age-segregation change from era to era. During the 1960s, adults worried that the separation of young from old had given rise to "antiestablishment" political ideas. During the 1970s, concerns were not so much about the youth culture's politics but about its morals (or lack of them), as adults were alarmed by young people's apparent tolerance for drug use and their permissive attitudes toward sex. (Forget, for the time being, that adults themselves became more tolerant toward drugs and permissive toward sex during the 1970s, too.) During the past decade, the segregation of young people from their elders has once again emerged as a social issue warranting public attention (e.g., Carnegie Council on Adolescent Development, 1992). This time the concern is couched in debates about adolescents in self-care, or as they are sometimes called, "latchkey" youngsters.

Changes in patterns of work and family life have resulted in a large number of young people who are not supervised by their parents after school. Affluent, suburban, and white children are most likely to be home alone. (Myrleen Ferguson Cate/PhotoEdit)

As noted earlier, changes in patterns of work and family life have resulted in a large number of young people—somewhere between 2 million and 6 million school-aged youngsters—who are not supervised by their parents after school. While some of these youngsters are involved in school- or community-based programs that provide adult supervision, others spend their after-school hours away from adults, in their homes, with friends, or simply "hanging out" in neighborhoods and shopping malls (Carnegie Council on Adolescent Development, 1992). Affluent, suburban, and white children are most likely to be home unsupervised, and poor, minority, and urban and rural children are least likely (U.S. Bureau of the Census, 1994).

Psychologists have debated whether latchkey youth are profiting from these opportunities for self-management (e.g., Rodman, Pratto, and Nelson, 1988) or potentially are heading for trouble (Richardson et al., 1989, 1993). In general, most studies show that children who care for themselves after school are not different from their peers when it comes to psychological development, school achievement, and self-conceptions (e.g., Galambos and Garbarino, 1985; Vandell and Corasaniti, 1988). These studies argue against the view that having to care for oneself contributes in positive ways to the development of self-reliance or personal responsibility. In addition, several studies, including a study of nearly four thousand youngsters from a variety of ethnic backgrounds (Richardson et al., 1993), suggest that children in self-care are more socially isolated, more depressed, more likely to be involved in problem behavior, and more likely use more drugs and alcohol than children who are supervised after school by adults (Carnegie Council on Adolescent Development, 1992; Galambos and Maggs, 1991; Richardson et al., 1989, 1993; Steinberg, 1986). Taken together, these studies seem to suggest that latchkey arrangements may have more costs than benefits.

One limitation of studies of latchkey youth is that they typically lump together all children who take care of themselves after school, even though there are important differences *within* the latchkey population (Steinberg, 1986). Several studies that have recognized these differences have shown, for example, that the setting in which adolescents care for themselves makes a difference: Latchkey youngsters who go straight home after school are far less likely to engage in problem behavior than their peers who go to a friend's house or who just hang out (Galambos and Maggs, 1991; Richardson et al., 1993; Steinberg, 1986). In addition, latchkey youngsters who are raised effectively by their parents and who are monitored by their parents from a distance—via telephone check-ins, for example—are no more susceptible to problem behavior than are children whose parents are home with them (Galambos and Maggs, 1991; Steinberg, 1986; Vandell and Ramanan, 1991).

Taken together, these studies suggest that self-care after school probably does not hold great benefits for youngsters, and, in fact, may cause problems if adolescents' parents do not promote the development of responsible behavior when they are with their child. What should parents who have no choice but to leave their youngsters in self-care do? Experts advise parents to provide clear instructions about the child's after-school activities and whereabouts, asking the child to check in with an adult as soon as he or she gets home, and teaching the child how to handle emergencies, should they arise (Steinberg and Levine, 1990).

RECAP

Somewhere between 2 million and 6 million school-aged American youngsters are not supervised by their parents after school. Studies suggest that self-care after school probably does not hold great benefits for youngsters, and, in fact, may cause problems if adolescents' parents do not promote the development of responsible behavior when they are with their child.

THE NATURE OF ADOLESCENT PEER GROUPS

Changes in Peer Groups during Adolescence

Visit any elementary school playground and you will readily see that peer groups are an important feature of the social world of childhood. But even though peer groups exist well before adolescence, during the teenage years they change in significance and structure. Four specific developments stand out (Brown, 1990).

First, as we noted earlier, *there is a sharp increase during adolescence in the sheer amount of time individuals spend with their peers* and in the relative time they spend in the company of peers versus adults. If we count school as being a setting in which adolescents are mainly with agemates, well over half of the typical adolescent's waking hours are spent with peers, as opposed to only 15 percent with adults—including parents (a good deal of the remaining time is spent alone or with a combination of adults and agemates). Indeed, during the transition into adolescence, there is a dramatic drop in the amount of time adolescents spend with parents; for boys, this is mainly replaced by time spent alone, whereas for girls, this is replaced by time alone and by time with friends (see Figure 5.2) (Larson and Richards, 1991).

When asked to list the people in their life who are most important to them—what psychologists call their **significant others**—nearly half the people adolescents mention are people of the same age. By sixth grade, adults other than parents account for less than 25 percent of the typical adolescent's social network—the people he or she interacts with most regularly. And among early-maturing teenagers, this figure is only about 10 percent (Brown, 1990).

Second, during adolescence, *peer groups function much more often without adult supervision* than they do during childhood (B. Brown, 1990). Groups of younger children typically play where adults are present, or in activities that are organized or supervised by adults (e.g., Little League, Brownies), whereas adolescents are granted far more independence. A group of teenagers may go off to the mall on their own, or to the movies, or will deliberately congregate at the home of someone whose parents are out.

Third, during adolescence *increasingly more contact with peers is with opposite-sex friends.* During childhood, peer groups are highly sex segregated, a phenomenon known as **sex cleavage.** This is especially true of children's peer activities in school and other settings organized by adults, although somewhat less so of their more informal activities, such as neighborhood play (Maccoby, 1990). During adolescence, however, an increasingly larger proportion of an individual's significant others are opposite-sex peers, even in public settings (Brown, 1990). As we shall see in a later section, this movement toward opposite-sex peers seems to stimulate changes in the structure of the peer group.

Finally, whereas children's peer relationships are limited mainly to pairs of friends and relatively small groups—three or four children at a time, for example—*adolescence marks the emergence of larger collectives of peers, or "crowds."* (Adolescents still have close friendships, of course, which we shall look at in Chapter 10.) In junior high school cafeterias, for example, the "popular" crowd sits in one section of the room, the "brains" in another, and the "druggies" in yet a third (see Eder, 1985). These crowds typically develop their own minicultures, which include particular styles of dressing, talking, and behaving. Studies show that it is not until early adolescence that individuals can confidently list the different crowds that characterize their schools and reliably describe the stereotypes that distinguish the different crowds from each other (Brown, 1990).

These changes in peer relations have their origins in the biological, cognitive, and social transitions of adolescence. Puberty, as we have seen, stimulates adolescents' interest in opposite-sex relationships and serves to distance them from their parents, which helps to explain why adolescents' social networks increasingly include more opposite-sex peers and fewer adults. The cognitive changes of adolescence permit a more sophisticated under-

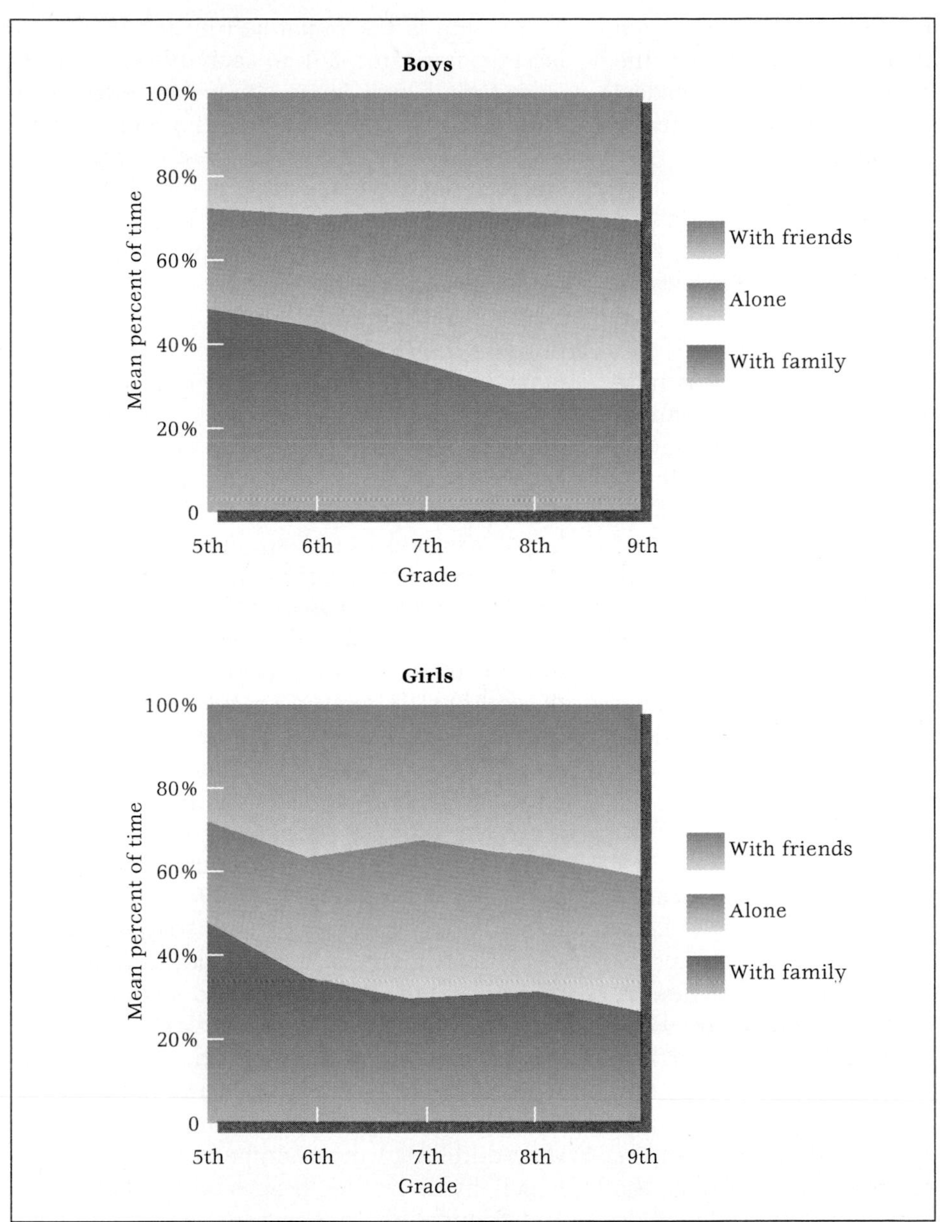

FIGURE 5.2
Changes in how individuals spend leisure time during early adolescence.
(Larson and Richards, 1991)

standing of social relationships, an understanding which may allow the sort of abstract categorization that leads to grouping individuals into crowds. And changes in social definition may stimulate changes in peer relations as a sort of adaptive response: The larger, more anonymous social setting of the secondary school, for instance, may force adolescents to seek out individuals whom they perceive as having common interests and values, perhaps as a way of recreating the smaller, more intimate groups of childhood

(Brown, 1990). Instead of floundering in a large, impersonal high school cafeteria, the adolescent who belongs to the "cheerleader" crowd, or even the "nerds," may head directly for her or his place at a familiar table.

RECAP

The structure of peer groups changes as individuals move into adolescence. First, there is an increase in the amount of time individuals spend in the exclusive company of their peers. Second, peer groups function outside adult supervision more during adolescence than before. Third, during adolescence increasingly more time is spent with the opposite-sex peers. Finally, during adolescence larger collectives of peers, called crowds, begin to emerge. These transformations are linked to the biological, cognitive, and social transitions and definitional changes of adolescence.

Cliques and Crowds

In order to better understand the significance of peer relations during adolescence, it is helpful to think of adolescents' peer groups as organized around two related, but different, structures (Brown, 1990). **Cliques** are small groups of between two and twelve individuals—the average is about five or six—generally of the same sex and, of course, the same age (Dunphy, 1969; Hollingshead, 1975). Cliques can be defined by common activities (e.g., the "drama" group, a group of students who study together regularly, etc.) or simply by friendship (e.g., a group of girls who have lunch together every day or a group of boys who have known each other for a long time). The importance of the clique, whatever its basis, is that it provides the main social context in which adolescents *interact* with each other. The clique is the social setting in which adolescents hang out, talk to each other, and form close friendships. Some cliques are more open to outsiders than others (i.e., the members are less "cliquish"), but virtually all cliques are small enough so that the members feel that they know each other well and appreciate each other more than people outside the clique do (Brown, 1990).

Cliques are quite different in structure and purpose than crowds. **Crowds** are "large, *reputation-based* collectives of similarly stereotyped individuals who may or may not spend much time together" (Brown, 1990, p. 177). In contemporary American high schools, typical crowds are "jocks," "brains," "nerds," "populars," "druggies," and so on. The labels for these crowds may vary from school to school ("jocks" versus "sportos," "populars" versus "trendies"), but their generic presence is commonplace, and you can probably recognize these different types of crowds from your own school experience. In contrast to cliques, crowds are not settings for adolescents' intimate interactions or friendships but, instead, serve three broad purposes: to locate adolescents (to themselves and to others) within the social structure of the school, to channel adolescents into associations with some peers and away from others, and to provide contexts that reward certain lifestyles and disparage others (Brown, Mory, and Kinney, 1994).

Membership in a crowd is based mainly on reputation and stereotype, rather than on actual friendship or social interaction. This is very different from membership in a clique, which, by definition, hinges on shared activity and friendship. In concrete terms—and perhaps ironically—an adolescent does not have to actually have "brains" as friends, or to hang around with "brainy" students, to be a member of the "brain" crowd. If he dresses like a "brain," acts like a "brain," and takes honors courses, then he is a "brain," as far as his crowd membership goes. The fact that crowd membership is based on reputation and stereotype can be very difficult for individual adolescents, who—if they do not change their reputation early on in high school—may find themselves stuck, at least in the eyes of their peers, in a crowd that they do not wish to belong to (or that they do not see themselves as a part of) (Brown, Freeman, Huang, and Mounts, 1992). This also means that some individuals can be members of more than one crowd simultaneously, if their reputation is such (Mory, 1994).

The images adolescents have of various crowds in their schools are often highly stereotyped and caricatured, and adolescents tend to inflate the positive qualities of their own crowd while exaggerating the negative qualities of others (Mory, 1992). In one study (cited in Brown et al., 1994), in which teenagers were asked about the crowds in their school, responses such as these were given:

> Oh, yeah; they all wear these tight-fitting jeans and sit around the commons in between classes like they own the place!
>
> You'd be crazy to walk down the B-wing by yourself because the headbangers, they, like, attack you.
>
> They all wear glasses and "kiss up" to teachers, and after school they all tromp uptown to the library, or they go over to somebody's house and play some stupid computer game until 9:00 at night—and then they go right to bed, 'cause their mommies make 'em!

Whether each and every "popular" wears tight-fitting jeans, each and every "headbanger" stalks other adolescents, or each and every "nerd" goes to sleep at 9 P.M. doesn't really matter. What is more important, perhaps, is that their peers believe that they do.

Although an adolescent's closest friends are almost always members of the same clique, some of them may belong to a different crowd, especially when one crowd is close in lifestyle to the other. Thus, for example, a "brain" will have some friends who are also "brains" and some who are "nerds" but few, if any, who are "druggies" (Brown et al., 1994).

More important, crowds are not simply clusters of cliques; the two different structures serve entirely different purposes. Because the clique is based on activity and friendship, it is the important setting in which the adolescent learns social skills—how to be a good friend to someone else, how to communicate with others effectively, how to be a leader, how to enjoy someone else's company, or even how to break off a friendship that is no longer satisfying. These and other social skills are important in adulthood as well as in adolescence. In contrast, because crowds are based on reputation and stereotype, and not interaction, they probably contribute more to the adolescent's sense of identity and self-conceptions—for better and for worse—than to his or her actual social development.

RECAP

Social scientists distinguish between crowds and cliques. Crowds are larger and more vaguely defined groups that are based on reputation. Contrary to the stereotype of a homogeneous youth culture, research has indicated that the social world of adolescents is composed of many distinct subcultures. In order to understand how peers influence adolescent development, it is essential to know which peer group a youngster is a part of.

Changes in Clique and Crowd Structure over Time

Studies of the structure of adolescents' peer groups often make use of a research technique called **participant observation.** In this approach, the researcher establishes rapport with a group of individuals in order to infiltrate and eventually join the group. In *Inside High School* (Cusick, 1973), for example, the author pretended to be a newcomer to the community and attended high school for a year to learn more about the adolescents' social world. As an observer who is also a participant, the researcher can observe the group's behavior under conditions that are more natural and more private than would otherwise be the case. Overhearing a ten-minute conversation in a high school locker room can be more informative than interviewing a student for three hours, if the student feels uncomfortable or uneasy.

Observational studies of young people indicate that there are important changes in the structure of cliques and crowds during the adolescent years (e.g., Dunphy, 1963). During early adolescence, adolescents' activities revolve around same-sex cliques. Adolescents at this stage are not yet involved in parties and typically spend their leisure time with a small group of friends, playing sports, talking, or simply hanging around.

Somewhat later, as boys and girls become more interested in one another—but before dating actually begins—boys' and girls' cliques come together. This is clearly a transitional stage. Boys and girls may go to parties together, but the time they spend there actually involves interaction with peers of the same sex. When youngsters are still uncomfortable about dealing with members of the opposite sex, this setting provides an opportunity in which adolescents can learn more about opposite-sex peers without having to be intimate and without having to risk losing face. It is not unusual, for example, at young adolescents' first mixed-sex parties, for groups of boys and girls to position themselves at opposite sides of a room, watching each other but seldom interacting.

The peer group then enters a stage of structural transformation, generally led by the clique leaders. As youngsters become inter-

By late adolescence, same-sex peer groups have mainly disintegrated. Adolescents are more likely to spend their leisure time as members of couples. (Tom McCarthy/ Unicorn Stock Photos)

ested in dating, part of the group begins to divide off into mixed-sex cliques, while other individuals remain in the group but in same-sex cliques. The shift into dating is usually led by the clique leaders, with other clique members following along. For instance, a clique of boys whose main activity is playing basketball may discover that one of the guys they look up to has become more interested in going out with girls on Saturday nights than in hanging out at the schoolyard. Over time, they will begin to follow his lead, and their clique at the schoolyard will become smaller and smaller.

During middle adolescence, mixed-sex cliques become more prevalent. In time, the peer group becomes composed entirely of heterosexual cliques. One clique might consist of the drama students—male and female students who know each other from acting together in school plays. Another might be composed of four girls and four boys who like to drink on the weekends. The staff of the school yearbook might make up a third.

Finally, during late adolescence, the peer group begins to disintegrate. Pairs of dating adolescents begin to split off from the activities of the larger group. The larger peer group is replaced by loosely associated sets of couples. Couples may go out together from time to time, but the feeling of being in a crowd has disappeared. This pattern—in which the couple becomes the focus of social activity—persists into adulthood.

When viewed from a structural point of view, the peer group's role in the development of intimacy is quite clear. Over time, the structure of the peer group changes to become more in keeping with adolescents' changing needs and interests. As we shall see in Chapter 10, the adolescent's capacity for close relationships develops first through friendships with peers of the same sex. Only later does intimacy enter into opposite-sex relationships. Thus the structure of the peer group changes during adolescence in a way that parallels the adolescent's development of intimacy: As the adolescent develops increasing facility in close relationships, the peer group moves from the familiarity of same-sex activities to contact with opposite-sex peers but in the safety of the larger group. It is only after adolescent males and females have been slowly socialized into dating roles—primarily by modeling their higher-status peers—that the safety of numbers is no longer needed and adolescents begin pairing off.

There also are changes in peer crowds during this time. Many of these changes reflect the growing cognitive sophistication of the adolescent, as we described in Chapter 2. For example, as adolescents mature intellectually, they come to define crowds more in terms of abstract and global characteristics (i.e., "preppies," "nerds," "jocks") than in terms of concrete, behavioral features (i.e., "the ballet crowd," "the Nintendo crowd," "the kids who play basketball on Arcadia Street") (O'Brien and Bierman, 1988). As you know, this shift from concrete to abstract is a general feature of cognitive development in adolescence. In addition, as adolescents become more cognitively capable, they become more consciously aware of the crowd structure of their school and their place in it (Brown, 1990).

Over the course of adolescence, the crowd structure also becomes more differentiated, more permeable, and less hierarchical, which allows adolescents more freedom to change crowds and enhance their status (Kinney, 1993). For example, in a study of peer crowds in one small Midwestern city, the researcher found that, over the course of adolescence, the crowd structure shifted between middle school, early high school, and late high school. During middle school, there was a clear, small in-group ("trendies") and a larger out-group ("dweebs"). During early high school, there was one high-status crowd ("trendies"), two other socially acceptable crowds ("headbangers" and "normals"), and two less desirable groups ("grits" and punkers"). And during late high school, the status differences among "trendies," "normals," and "headbangers" were negligible and "hybrid" crowds (e.g., "grit-headbangers") were common (see Figure 5.3). As the accompanying box illustrates, this change over time permitted some individuals who were low in status during middle school to "recover" during high school.

As crowds become increasingly more salient influences on adolescents' view of their social world, they come to play an increasingly important role in structuring adolescent social behavior (O'Brien and Bierman, 1988). By ninth grade, there is nearly universal agreement among students in a school about their school's crowd structure, and students' assessment of the strength of peer group influence is very high. Between ninth and twelth grade, however, the significance of the crowd structure begins to decline, and the salience of peer pressure wanes. As we shall see in Chapter 9, this pattern of an increase and then a decline in the salience of peer crowds parallels developmental changes in adolescents' susceptibility to peer pressure. In other words, as crowds become more important in defining the teenager's social world—

FIGURE 5.3 *Developmental changes in crowd structure. Line widths indicate the degree of impermeability between crowds. Vertical location indicates each crowd's position in the school's peer-status hierarchy.* Note: G/H = "Grit-Headbangers." (Brown, Mory, and Kinney, 1994)

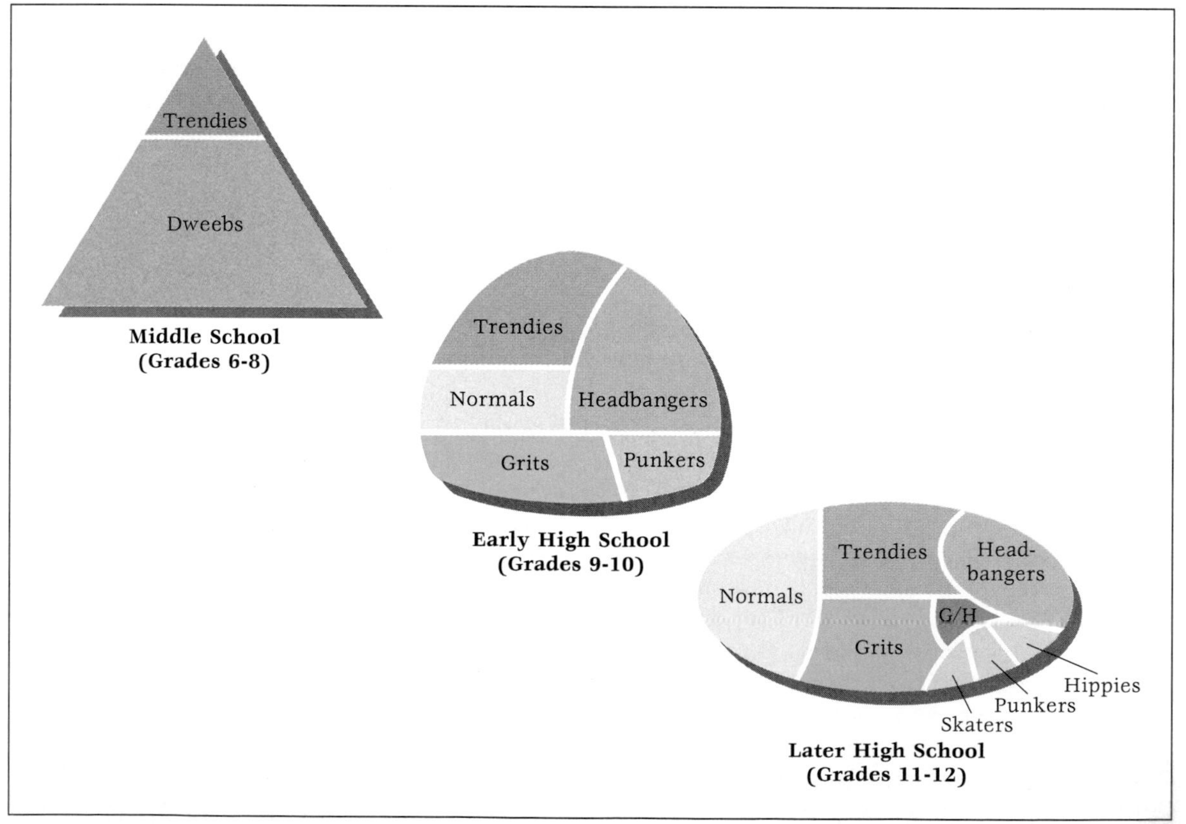

between early and middle adolescence—adolescents become more likely to accede to their influence. As crowds become less important, however—between middle adolescence and late adolescence—their influence over the individual adolescent's behavior weakens as well (Brown, 1990; Gavin and Furman, 1989).

Just as the changes in the structure of cliques play a role in the development of intimacy during adolescence, changes in the salience of crowds over the adolescent years play an important role in adolescent identity development. In Chapter 8, we shall see that adolescence is frequently a time for experimentation with different roles and identities. During the early adolescent years, before adolescents have "found" themselves, the crowd provides an important basis for self-definition (Newmann and Newmann, 1976). By locating themselves within the crowd structure of their school—through style of dress, language, or choice of hangouts—adolescents wear "badges" that say, "This is who I am." At a time when adolescents may not actually know just "who" they are, associating with a crowd provides them with a rudimentary sense of identity.

As adolescents become more secure about their identity as individuals, however, the need for affiliation with a crowd diminishes. Indeed, by the time they have reached high school, older adolescents are likely to feel that remaining a part of a crowd *stifles* their sense of identity and self-expression (Larkin, 1979; Varenne, 1982). The breakup of the larger peer group in late adolescence may both foreshadow and reflect the emergence of each adolescent's unique and coherent sense of self (Brown, 1990).

RECAP

Social scientists have charted changes in the structure of cliques and crowds over the course of adolescence. Cliques, which begin as same-sex groups of individuals, gradually merge to form larger, mixed-sex groups, as adolescents begin dating and socializing with peers of the opposite sex. In late adolescence, these groups begin to break down, as adolescents' social lives start to revolve more around couple-based activities. Crowds, which peak in importance during the midadolescence years, become more differentiated and more permeable during high school, and their influence becomes less salient.

ADOLESCENTS AND THEIR CROWDS

The Social Map of Adolescence

We noted earlier that the idea of a single "youth culture" has not held up very well in recent research. Most ethnographic studies of high schools indicate that the social world of adolescents is far more multifaceted than this (e.g., Cusick, 1973). One helpful scheme for mapping the social world of adolescent crowds was suggested by Rigsby and McDill (1975) and later modified by Brown (1990).

According to this model, adolescents' crowds can be placed along two dimensions: how involved they are in the institutions controlled by adults, such as school and extracurricular activities; and how involved they are in the informal, peer culture (see Figure 5.4). "Jocks" and "populars," for example, are quite involved in the peer culture, but they are also very involved in the institutions valued by adults (sports and school organizations, for example). "Brains" and "nerds," in contrast, are also involved in adult-controlled organizations (in their case, academics), but they tend to be less involved in the peer culture. "Partyers" are on the opposite side of the map from

THE SCIENTIFIC STUDY OF ADOLESCENCE

HOW "NERDS" BECOME "NORMALS"

"Popular films and television shows about adolescents and schools," writes sociologist David Kinney, "usually include a certain type of teenager who is frequently ridiculed and rejected by his or her peers. These adolescents are often portrayed as awkward, intelligent, shy, unattractive social outcasts with unfashionable hair and dress styles. . . . They are called 'nerds,' 'dweebs,' 'dorks,' 'geeks,' 'brainiacs,' and 'computer jocks' " (1993, p. 21). What happens to nerds as they move through adolescence? One surprising finding from Kinney's research is that many individuals who are "nerds" early in adolescence become "normals" by the end of high school.

In order to study the day-to-day experiences of "nerds" and their interactions with other students, Kinney conducted an **ethnography** of the social interaction and peer culture in a high school in a small Midwestern city. In contrast to survey or experimental research, which is typically quantitative in nature (that is, the data collected can be quantified), ethnographic research is qualitative. The researcher spends a considerable amount of time observing interactions within the setting, interviewing many adolescents, and writing up field notes, much as an anthropologist would do to study a foreign culture. Ethnographic approaches can be extremely useful in studying social relationships, because they provide rich, descriptive data. Indeed, in the study of adolescent peer culture, we have learned a great deal more from qualitative research than from quantitative studies.

How do ethnographers go about establishing themselves in the setting? As Kinney explains:

> I attempted to carve out a neutral identity for myself at the school by making and maintaining connections with students in a wide variety of peer groups and by being open to their different viewpoints. During my initial contacts with the students and before I conducted the interviews, I stressed that I would be the only one to listen to the audiotapes and that neither the school nor any individual students would be identified. . . . I also distanced myself from adult authority figures by dressing in jeans and casual shirts and by emphasizing my status as a college student writing a paper about teenagers' high school experiences. (1993, p. 25)

At the time, Kinney was a graduate student collecting data for his doctoral dissertation. Kinney asked students to recall their middle school experiences. Here is an excerpt of an interview he conducted with two students, "Ross" and "Ted," who had been "nerds":

> Ross: And middle school—
>
> Ted: We were just *nerds.* I mean—
>
> Ross: Yeah—
>
> Ted: people hated us.
>
> Ross: Well, they didn't hate us, but we weren't—

"nerds": These adolescents are very involved in the peer culture but are not involved in adult institutions. "Toughs" and adolescents who are members of delinquent gangs are not involved in either the peer culture or adult institutions. Other crowds, such as "normals" or "druggies," fall somewhere between these extremes. This conceptualization points to an important limitation of Coleman's view of a monolithic adolescent society: His description

Ted: popular. Which was either you were popular or you weren't.

Ross: In middle school it's very defined. There's popular people and unpopular people. It's just very—rigid. You were popular or unpopular. That's it.

Ted: And there wasn't people that were in between.

Ross: Oh no!

Ted: You just had one route [to becoming popular], and then there was the other. And we were the other, and—basically you were afraid of getting laughed at about anything you did because if you did one thing that was out of the ordinary, and you weren't expected to do anything out of the ordinary, then you were laughed at and made fun of, and you wouldn't fit the group at all, and then, of course, you were excluded and then you didn't even exist.

Ross: You got "nuked," so to speak. (Kinney, 1993, p. 27)

Kinney discovered, however, that many individuals who had been unpopular in middle school had managed to transform themselves from "nerds" into "normals" sometime during high school. For some, this transition was accomplished because the high school peer structure was more differentiated and more permeable. As opposed to middle school, where there were only two groups—the popular and the unpopular—in high school, there were more socially acceptable groups with which to affiliate. For others, the transition to "normal" came about through gains in self-assurance that came with physical and social development. And for others still, the transformation was facilitated by the development of a more cognitively sophisticated, confident view of the social hierarchy—one that permitted them to reject the premise that whatever the "trendies" valued was necessarily desirable. As one woman put it:

> If you have confidence, you can overlook people who put you down 'cause there are always people who are going to put you down. And [when you have confidence], you don't have to worry about what I think are the more trivial things in life, like appearance or being trendy (Kinney, 1993, p. 33).

In essence, the transformation of "nerds" to "normals" was enabled by a combination of factors both within the context (e.g., the increasing differentiation and permeability of the peer crowd system) and within the adolescent (e.g., the physical, cognitive, and social maturation of the individual). Kinney's study reminds us of the potential for growth and change during the adolescent years, even for individuals who begin the period at a social disadvantage.

Source: Kinney, D. (1993). From nerds to normals: The recovery of identity among adolescents from middle school to high school. *Sociology of Education, 66*, 21–40.

of adolescents as fun-loving and anti-intellectual accurately described one segment of the adolescent society—a segment known in some schools as "partyers"—but not all young people in general.

Crowds as Reference Groups

Knowing where an adolescent fits into the social system of the school can often tell us a fair amount about the individual's behavior

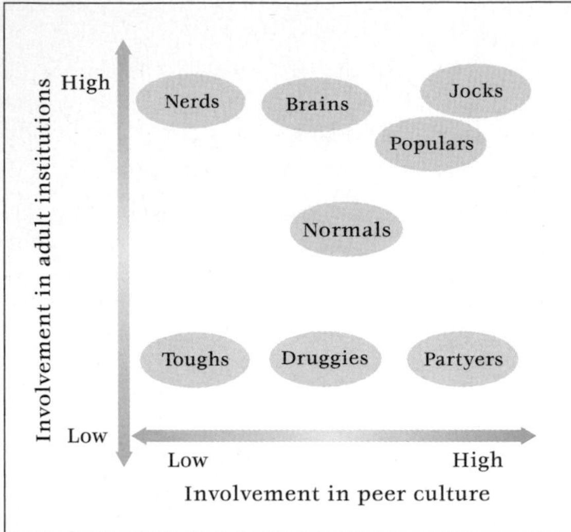

FIGURE 5.4 *A model for mapping the social world of adolescent peer groups.* (From Brown, 1990)

and values. This is because crowds contribute to the definition of norms and standards for such things as clothing, leisure, and tastes in music. Being a "jock" means more than simply being involved in athletics; it means wearing certain types of clothes, listening to certain types of music, spending Saturday nights in certain hangouts, and using a particular slang. These adolescents accept many of the values of the adults around them but also value many elements of the contemporary peer culture.

Another way of putting this is that adolescents' crowds serve as **reference groups.** They provide their members with an identity in the eyes of other adolescents. Adolescents judge one another on the basis of the company they keep. Individuals become branded on the basis of whom they hang around with. Such labels as "jocks," "brains," "socies," "druggies," and "leathers" serve as shorthand notations—accurate or inaccurate—to describe what someone is like as a person and what he or she holds as important.

Crowd membership is important not only because crowds are used by adolescents when talking about one another but also because membership in a crowd is often the basis for an adolescent's own identity. A girl who runs with the "preppies" identifies herself as such by wearing their "uniform," shopping in their stores, and speaking their language. After a while, "preppiness" becomes part of her own self-concept; she wouldn't think of dressing or talking in a different way. Or consider the boys whose clique is held together by a dislike of school. Since this attitude toward school is continuously reinforced by the clique, each boy's feelings about school become strengthened, and not liking school becomes part of each boy's identity. Even if something very positive happens at school, it becomes difficult for someone in the clique to admit that it makes him feel good about himself. Doing well on a test or receiving a compliment from a teacher is likely to be dismissed as unimportant.

Because the adolescent's peer group plays such an important role as a reference group and a source of identity, the nature of the crowd with which an adolescent affiliates is likely to have an important influence on his or her behavior, activities, and self-conceptions. Brown and his colleagues have studied how peer group membership—that is, *which* peer group the adolescent affiliates with—may affect the adolescent's development and behavior. Although most adolescents feel pressure from their friends to behave in ways that are consistent with their crowd's values and goals, the specific nature of the pressure varies from one crowd to another. Adolescents who are part of the "druggie" crowd report much more peer pressure to engage in misconduct, for example, than do adolescents from the "jock" crowd (Clasen and Brown, 1985).

Crowd membership can also affect the way adolescents feel about themselves. Adolescents' self-esteem is higher among students who are identified with peer groups that have relatively more status in their school. In the high schools that Brown has studied, the "jocks" and "socies" were highest in status, and the "druggies" and "toughs" were lowest. Students who were identified with the higher-status groups had higher self-esteem than did those who were identified with the lower-status groups (Brown and Lohr, 1987). As the authors wrote: "Crowds are not merely fertile grounds for bolstering self-esteem through identity testing or building supportive social relationships. Crowd labels also provide one feedback on one's comparative standing among peers, which in turn may enhance or depreciate self-esteem" (1987, p. 53).

Researchers do not know how the social structure of adolescent crowds differs for minority and nonminority adolescents, because most of the research to date has been conducted in predominantly white high schools. Some research indicates that at least some of the basic distinctions among crowds that were found in studies of predominantly white high schools (e.g., academically oriented crowds, partying crowds, deviant crowds, trendy crowds) also exist among adolescents from ethnic minority groups (e.g., Brown and Mounts, 1989; Fordham and Ogbu, 1986). There is some evidence, however, that in multiethnic high schools, the adolescents may divide first across ethnic lines and then into the more familiar adolescent crowds within ethnic groups. Thus, in a large urban high school there may be separate groups of African-American "jocks" and white "jocks," of Hispanic-American "populars" and African-American "populars," and so on. Interestingly, in multiethnic schools, adolescents from one ethnic group are less likely to see crowd distinctions within other ethnic groups than they are in their own group. Thus, to white students all Asian-American adolescents are part of the "Asian" crowd, whereas the Asian-American students see themselves as divided into "brains," "populars," and so on (Brown and Mounts, 1989).

In multiethnic high schools, peer groups often divide along ethnic lines. (Mary Kate Denny/PhotoEdit)

There is also reason to believe that the meaning associated with belonging to different crowds may vary among ethnic groups. According to one team of researchers, for example, in predominantly African-American high schools, adolescents who are in the "brain" crowd are ridiculed (Fordham and Ogbu, 1986). In the inner-city schools they studied, students who were high achievers were labeled "Brainiacs" and were ostracized for "acting white." Similarly, in some schools it may be admirable to be a "jock," while in others it may be frowned upon. Thus, the values we associate with being in one crowd as opposed to another may not be constant across all school contexts.

RECAP

Although the specific crowd names may differ from school to school, and from one ethnic group to the next, most high schools have relatively similar crowd structures with some version of "jocks," "populars," "brains," "nerds," and "toughs." Adolescents' crowds can be mapped on two distinct dimensions: how involved they are in adult institutions, like school; and how involved they are in the peer culture. Because they often serve as reference groups, crowds play an important role in the adolescent's identity development.

ADOLESCENTS AND THEIR CLIQUES

What draws adolescents into one clique and not another? Because cliques serve as a basis for adolescents' friendships and play an important role in their social development, many researchers have studied the determinants of clique composition.

Similarity among Clique Members

The most important influence on the composition of cliques is similarity. Adolescents' cliques typically are composed of people who are of the same age and the same race, from the same socioeconomic background, and—at least during early and middle adolescence—of the same sex.

Age Segregation. Age grouping in junior and senior high schools makes it unlikely for an individual to have friends who are substantially older or younger. A tenth-grader who is enrolled in tenth-grade English, tenth-grade math, tenth-grade history, and tenth-grade science simply does not have many opportunities to meet adolescents who are in different grades. Age segregation in adolescents' cliques does, indeed, appear to result mostly from the structure of schools (Shrum, Cheek, and Hunter, 1988). When an adolescent's friends come from a different school, those friends are just as likely to be younger or older as they are to come from the same grade (Blyth, Hill, and Thiel, 1982).

Sex Segregation. During the early and middle adolescent years, cliques also tend to be composed of adolescents of the same sex. This so-called sex cleavage begins in childhood and continues through most of the adolescent years, although it is stronger among white students than among African-American students (Hallinan, 1981; Sagar, Schofield, and Snyder, 1983), and it weakens later in adolescence (Shrum et al., 1988). The causes of sex segregation in adolescents' cliques are more interesting than the causes of age segregation, because schools do not separate boys and girls into different classes. Why, then, do adolescent males and females separate themselves into different cliques? Psychologist Eleanor Maccoby, an expert on gender and development, has suggested several reasons (Maccoby, 1990).

First, cliques are formed largely on the basis of shared activities and interests. Generally speaking, preadolescent and early adolescent boys and girls are interested in different things. It is not until adolescents begin dating that boys' cliques and girls' cliques mix, presumably because dating provides a basis for common activity.

A second reason for the sex cleavage in adolescent peer groups concerns young adolescents' sensitivity about sex roles. Over the course of childhood, boys and girls become increasingly concerned about behaving in ways that are judged to be sex-appropriate. When boys show an interest in dolls, they are often told either explicitly (by parents, friends, and teachers) or implicitly (by television, books, and other mass media), "Little boys don't play with dolls. Those are for girls." And when girls start wrestling or roughhousing, they are often reprimanded and told to "act like ladies."

As a consequence of these continual reminders that there are "boys' activities" and "girls' activities," early adolescents—who are trying to establish a sense of identity—are very concerned about acting in sex-appropriate ways. This makes it very difficult for an adolescent girl to be part of a boys' clique, in which activities are likely to be dominated by athletics and other physical pursuits, or for a boy to be a part of a girls' clique, in which activities are likely to revolve around clothing, grooming, and talking about boys (Schofield, 1981). Adolescents who go against prevailing sex-role norms by forming friendships with members of the opposite sex may be teased about being "fags" or may be ostracized by their peers because they are "perverts." Ironically, once dating becomes the norm, adolescents who *don't* have relationships with peers of the opposite sex become the objects of equally strong suspicion and social rejection.

● ***Social-Class Segregation.*** One of the most important studies ever undertaken of adolescents' peer groups is *Elmtown's Youth* (Hollingshead, [1949] 1975). In this study of adolescents in the Midwestern community of "Elmtown," sociologist August Hollingshead examined the relation between the social position of adolescents' families and the composition of teenagers' cliques. He was interested in determining whether adolescents' cliques were segregated along class lines.

Hollingshead used such indicators as income, residence, and reputation in the community to sort families into five different **social-class groups.** In the highest class were families who were very affluent, lived in the best neighborhoods, and were known in the community as powerful and respected families. These "upper-class" families had lived in the community for a long time and belonged to all the exclusive clubs and organizations. In the "lower class" were families who were poor, lived on the "wrong" side of town, and were not highly regarded in the community. Between these extremes were three groups of families: the hard-working but not very well off "working-class" families; the comfortable but not especially affluent "middle-class" families; and the "upper-middle-class" families, who had money but did not quite have the reputation and prestige of the families in the highest class.

Hollingshead found that adolescents do, in fact, associate chiefly with peers from the same social class. More than 60 percent of each adolescent's close friendships in Elmtown High School were between teenagers from the same background. Of the remaining clique relationships, the vast majority were between adolescents of adjacent social classes (for example, between middle-class adolescents and upper-middle-class adolescents). Almost never did adolescents from one social class associate with students from a class that was two steps higher or lower.

Hollingshead found similar patterns when he looked at adolescents' best friends and dating relationships: Rarely were social-class lines crossed, and, when they were, it was virtually always between adolescents of adjacent classes. Moreover, adolescents became even more class conscious as they got older.

Social class was also important in shaping the status hierarchy of the school. Hollingshead asked the adolescents to list those students who were the leaders in extracurricular and social activities and those who were shunned by most of their classmates. Over 40 percent of the leaders came from the two highest social classes, even though only 9 percent of the student body were from these social groups. Only 14 percent of the leaders came from the two lowest classes, even though over half the students in the school were from these social groups. And adolescents from the lower classes were far more likely to be among those who were shunned—in fact, students from the two lowest classes constituted virtually all of this group.

Several other studies that were conducted since the time of *Elmtown's Youth* have confirmed the importance of social class in influencing an adolescent's status in the peer group of the high school. But subsequent research has shown the pattern to be somewhat different from that suggested by Hollingshead. In *The Adolescent Society* (1961), the study of the "youth culture" in ten different high schools that was discussed early in the chapter, Coleman also looked at some of the same questions examined in *Elmtown's Youth*. Overall, as in "Elmtown," adolescents from wealthier backgrounds were proportionately more likely to occupy leadership positions in their schools. The student government leaders, the team captains, the presidents of different clubs and activities, and the students who were in the leading crowd usually came from the more affluent families. But this pattern was more characteristic of some schools than of others. Specifically, Coleman found that the dominance of high school activities by middle- and upper-middle-class students is most likely to occur in communities with a high proportion of middle- and upper-middle-class families. In communities dominated by working-class families, however, middle-class adolescents have less of an advantage over the other students. In this respect, then, the social structure of the high school mirrors the social structure of the broader community in which the high school is found.

This finding has important implications for understanding how the location of an adolescent's school can have an impact on his or her social life and psychosocial development. A youngster from a poor family probably has less of a chance to become a leader in a middle-class school than in a school located in a working-class or poor neighborhood. Opportunities to develop responsibility, leadership skills, and self-confidence are more restricted for poor youngsters than they are for their affluent peers, particularly in schools dominated by middle-class families.

● ***Race Segregation.*** Race is not a strong determinant of clique composition during childhood, but, like social class, it becomes increasingly powerful as youngsters get older (Shrum et al., 1988). By middle and late adolescence, adolescents' peer groups typically are racially segregated. This appears to be the case, although somewhat less so, even within desegregated schools (Schofield, 1981).

There are several explanations for racial separation in adolescents' peer groups. First, because adolescents' cliques are often segregated along socioeconomic lines, peer groups that appear to be segregated because of race actually may be separated on the basis of class, since disproportionately higher numbers of minority youngsters come from economically poorer families. This explanation helps to account for the race cleavage in desegregated schools, which often bring together youngsters not only of different racial backgrounds but from varying economic backgrounds and neighborhoods as well. Even among adolescents who do have cross-racial friendships at school, few report seeing those friends outside of school (Dubois and Hirsch, 1990).

Another reason for the strong racial split in adolescents' cliques appears to be the differential levels of academic achievement of white and African-American adolescents (Schofield, 1981). Adolescents who are friends usually have similar attitudes toward school, similar educational aspirations, and similar school achievement levels (Savin-Williams and Berndt, 1990). Racial differences in school achievement may lead to racial separation in adolescent peer groups through tracking and other mechanisms (Hallinan and Williams, 1989).

A third reason for racially segregated peer groups—according to one study of adolescents in a recently desegregated school—is attitudinal. In this school, the white adolescents perceived their African-American peers as aggressive, threatening, and hostile. The black students felt that the white students were conceited, prejudiced, and unwilling to be friends with them. These perceptions, which fed on each other, made the formation of interracial peer groups unlikely. The more the white students felt that the African-American students were hostile, the more the white students acted distant and kept to themselves. But the more the white students acted this way, the more likely the black students were to feel rejected, and the more hostile they became. In many schools, adolescents' lack of familiarity with youngsters from other racial groups results in misperceptions of the others' attitudes and motives, and this misunderstanding limits interracial interaction (Schofield, 1981). In general, white students are less apt to initiate contact with African-American students than vice versa (Sagar et al., 1983).

One way out of this cycle of misunderstanding is to bring white and black youngsters together from an early age, before they have had time to build up prejudices and stereotypes. Interracial school busing, for example, has been far more successful in communities that began such programs during elementary school than in districts that implemented them for the first time at the high school level. If white and black children grow up together from an early age, they are less likely to misunderstand each other and less likely to go off into separate peer groups purely on the basis of race.

Common Interests among Friends

Thus far we have seen that adolescents' cliques are usually composed of adolescents who are the same age, in the same grade in school, from the same social class, and of the same race. But what about factors beyond these? Do adolescents who associate with one another also share certain interests and activities? Generally speaking, they do. Three factors appear to be especially important in determining adolescent clique membership and friendship patterns: orientation toward school, orientation toward the teen culture, and involvement in antisocial activity. In general, this is true for both white youth (e.g., Berndt, 1982) and nonwhite youth (e.g., Tolson, Halliday-Scher, and Mack, 1994).

Orientation toward School. Adolescents and their friends tend to be similar in their attitudes toward school, in their school achievement, and in their educational plans (Berndt, 1982; Epstein, 1983a). Adolescents who earn high grades, study a great deal, and plan to go on to college usually have friends who share these activities and aspirations. One reason for this is that how much time a student devotes to schoolwork affects his or her involvement in other activities. Someone who is always studying will not have many friends who are out late at night partying, because the two activities conflict. By the same token, someone who wants to spend afternoons and evenings out having fun will find it difficult to remain friends with someone who prefers to stay home and study. Stu-

WHY ARE THERE SEX DIFFERENCES IN INTERRACIAL CONTACT?

Two findings from studies of adolescent peer groups emerge over and over again. First, a strong sex cleavage limits the interaction between adolescent boys and girls—at least, until dating begins. And second, adolescents have very little contact with peers from other races, even when they attend desegregated schools that have been developed to increase cross-racial interaction.

One curiosity that has been uncovered, as noted in this chapter, is that, although the race cleavage seems to characterize boys' as well as girls' interaction, it is much stronger among adolescent girls than boys. Specifically, although boys and girls alike are likely to interact more often with adolescents of the same race, the likelihood of white boys interacting with black boys is much greater than the likelihood of white girls interacting with black girls. Indeed, several studies suggest that cliques of young adolescent black girls are among the most socially isolated of all adolescent groups (Damico and Sparks, 1986). This isolation seems to work both ways: White students of both sexes are less likely to talk to black girls than to any other group, and black girls are less likely than any other group to initiate contact with whites.

No one is quite sure why black females face this predicament, but at least three hypotheses may be offered. One researcher has suggested that a special tension exists between white and black girls that does not exist between white and black boys (Schofield, 1981). She suggests that as sex and romance become more important during early adolescence, students become increasingly competitive for the attention of opposite-sex students. Although both boys and girls seek this attention, it may be more important for girls, who may rely more on the prestige derived from dating popular boys as an index of their social status in school. Boys, in contrast, may look more to athletics for status and may be slightly less concerned about getting the attention of girls in their classes. The heightened concern for male attention introduces a greater level of competition into adolescent girls' social relations, and this competition may underlie white and black girls' reluctance to interact.

An alternative explanation concerns the special role that white girls may play in the communication network of the school. One team of researchers has suggested that from an early age white girls try to develop personalized relationships with their teachers (Damico and Sparks, 1986). By junior high school, these girls may have become an important source of "inside information" for students in the school about teachers and classes. Thus white girls may find themselves more centrally located within the school's social network than black girls. Black girls may receive fewer social overtures from other students because they are perceived as less tied into the school's network.

Finally, sex differences in the degree to which peer interaction is racially segregated may be based on differences between the activity patterns of girls and boys in general. As you will read in Chapter 10, adolescent boys are more likely than girls to spend time in large-group activities, such as sports, and girls are more likely to spend time talking in pairs or in small groups. The large-group activities of boys may simply provide greater opportunities for cross-racial interaction to take place—as when white and black students are on the same team, for example. In contrast, the focus of adolescent girls on more intimate peer relations may make them less likely to interact with individuals whom they perceive—correctly or not—to have different values and norms for behavior. In other words, sex differences in the structure of adolescent peer activities may make cross-racial contact easier for boys than for girls.

dents also may influence each other's academic performance. Given two students with similar records of past achievement, the student whose friends do better in school is likely to achieve more than the student whose friends do worse (Epstein, 1983a).

● ***Orientation toward the Teen Culture.*** Adolescents and their friends generally listen to the same type of music, dress similarly, spend their leisure time in similar types of activities, and have similar patterns of drug use (Berndt, 1982). It would be very unlikely, for example, for a "jock" and a "druggie" to be part of the same clique, because their interests and attitudes are so different. In most high schools, it is fairly easy to see the split between cliques—in how people dress, where they eat lunch, how much they participate in the school's activities, and how they spend their time outside of school.

● ***Involvement in Antisocial Activity.*** A number of studies, involving both boys and girls from different ethnic groups, indicate that antisocial, aggressive adolescents may gravitate toward each other, forming deviant peer groups (Bukowski, Peters, Sippola, and Newcomb, 1993; Cairns, Cairns, Neckerman, Gest, and Gariepy, 1988; Dishion, Patterson, Stoolmiller, and Skinner, 1991). That is, contrary to the popular belief that antisocial adolescents do not have friends, these studies show that such youngsters do have friends but that their friends tend also to be antisocial. Although one would not necessarily want to call these peer groups "delinquent," since they are not always involved in criminal activity, understanding the processes through which antisocial peer groups form provides some insight into the development of delinquent peer groups, or gangs.

According to an extensive study of antisocial peer groups by Tom Dishion and his colleagues (Dishion et al., 1991), the process of antisocial peer group formation begins in the home. Problematic parent-child relationships that are coercive and hostile lead to the development of an antisocial disposition in the child, and this disposition contributes, in elementary school, to school failure and rejection by classmates. (As you will read in a later section of this chapter, aggression in elementary and middle school often leads to peer rejection.) Rejected by the bulk of his classmates, the aggressive boy "shops" for friends and finds that he is accepted only by other aggressive boys. Once these friendships are formed, the boys, like any other adolescents, reward each other for participating in a shared activity—in their case, antisocial behavior.

On the surface, these antisocial peer groups look like other types of cliques—they are groups of adolescents who are similar in background and orientation and who share common interests. But a recent study of Puerto Rican male adolescents from New York City suggests that the actual relationships that antisocial adolescents have with their cliquemates may be less satisfying than are those between other adolescents and their friends (Pabon, Rodriguez, and Gurin, 1992). This study found that although antisocial peers spent a great deal of time together, they did not describe their relationships as emotionally close or intimate. Rather, most of the boys felt estranged from each other. As the researchers point out, this finding has implications for the design of interventions aimed at controlling delinquency by involving antisocial peer groups in positive activities; in the absence of their shared interest in antisocial activities, delinquent peers may have little reason to maintain their friendship.

Similar findings on the role of the family in friendship choice have been reported in studies of crowd selection (Brown, Mounts, Lamborn, and Steinberg, 1993). That is, parents play a role in socializing certain traits in their children, and these orientations, whether toward aggression or academic achievement, predispose adolescents toward choosing certain friends or crowds with which to affiliate. Once in these cliques or crowds, adolescents are rewarded for the traits that led them there in the first place, and these traits are strengthened. Thus, a child who is raised to value academics will perform well in school and will likely select friends who share this orientation. Over time, these friends will reinforce the youngster's academic orientation and strengthen his or her school performance.

Because antisocial activities seem to be such a strong determinant of clique composition, many adults have expressed concern over the influence of peers in the socialization of delinquent activity and drug and alcohol use. Parents often feel that if their youngster runs with the wrong crowd, he or she will acquire undesirable interests and attitudes. They express concern, for instance, when their child starts spending time with peers who seem to be less interested in school or more involved with drugs. But which comes first, joining a clique or being interested in a clique's activities? Do adolescents develop interests and attitudes because of who their friends are, or is it more the case that people with similar interests and tastes are likely to become friends?

This question has been examined by social psychologist Denise Kandel (1978) in a longitudinal statewide study of New York high school students. Students completed a battery of questionnaires once during the beginning weeks of a school year and again toward the end of the year. They answered questions concerning a range of activities and interests, including delinquency, drug use, and educational aspirations. In addition, through the use of an intricate coding system that kept information anonymous and confidential, respondents provided the identities of their close friends. By examining patterns of attitudinal and behavioral change over the course of the school year and comparing these shifts with patterns of friendship formation and change, Kandel was able to determine whether adolescents were attracted to one another because of their initial similarity or whether they became similar as a result of the friendship.

Kandel found that both *selection* (choosing a friend on the basis of similarity) and *socialization* (becoming more similar as a result of the friendship) are at work. Moreover, on almost every dimension studied—including delinquency, drug use, and attitudes toward school—selection and socialization operated with about equal weight. In other words, similarity among adolescent friends about equally results from their selecting one another as friends to begin with and from their influencing one another after they become friends.

How stable are adolescents' friendships over time? In general, adolescents' cliques show only moderate stability over the course of the school year—with some members staying in the clique, others leaving, and new ones joining—although cliques become more stable during the later years of high school (Cairns, Leung, Buchanan, and Cairns, 1994; Degirmencioglu, Tolson, and Urberg, 1993). Although the actual composition of adolescents' cliques may shift over time, the defining characteristics of their cliques do not, however (Hogue and Steinberg, 1995; Neckerman, Cairns, and Cairns, 1993). That is, even though some members of an adolescent's clique may leave and may be replaced by others, the new members are likely to have attitudes and values that are quite similar to the former members'. Even best friends are likely to change during the school year: One study found that only about one-third of junior and senior high school students who were surveyed in the fall of a school year renamed the same best friend in the spring (Degirmencioglu et al., 1993).

RECAP

Cliques are small groups of adolescents who are friends and who see each other regularly. For this reason, cliques play an important role in the development of social skills and intimacy. Although clique members influence each other's behavior and values, research has also shown that adolescents select their friends to begin with on the basis of similarity. Generally, adolescents form cliques with peers who are similar in background, in orientation toward school, in orientation toward the peer culture, and in their level of involvement in antisocial activities.

POPULARITY AND REJECTION IN ADOLESCENT PEER GROUPS

Thus far, our discussion has focused on how and why crowds and cliques serve as the basis for adolescents' social activities. But what about the *internal* structure of peer groups? Within a clique or a crowd, what determines which adolescents are popular and which ones are disliked?

The chief determinant of a youngster's popularity during adolescence is his or her social skill. Popular adolescents act appropriately in the eyes of their peers, are skilled at perceiving and meeting the needs of others, and are confident without being conceited. Additionally, popular adolescents are friendly, cheerful, good natured, humorous, and—you may be surprised to learn—intelligent (Hartup, 1983; Hollingshead, 1975). (Contrary to myth, popular adolescents are more intelligent than unpopular ones. This is because intelligent individuals are better at figuring out how to behave in ways that will get them liked. Remember also that being intelligent is not the same as being a "brain.") Interestingly, the determinants of popularity in adolescent peer groups are the same for boys and for girls and are the same for older and for younger individuals. People of all ages like to be around others who make them feel good, who know how to have a good time, and who are able to communicate well. Popular adolescents are more knowledgeable specifically about what it takes to make and keep friends than are adolescents who are less well accepted by their peers (Wentzel and Erdley, 1993).

An interesting ethnographic study of early adolescent girls provides insight into the dynamics of popularity. Ethnographer Donna Eder (1985) spent two years in a middle school observing interactions among early adolescent girls in various extracurricular and informal settings (in the cafeteria, in the hallway, at school dances). In this school, the cheerleaders were considered the elite crowd, and girls who made the cheerleading squad were immediately accorded social status. Other girls then attempted to befriend the cheerleaders as a means of increasing their own status. This, in turn, increased the cheerleaders' popularity within school, since they became the most sought-after friends. The girls who were successful in cultivating friendships with the cheerleaders then became a part of this high-status group and themselves became more popular.

This popularity had a price, however, as one eighth-grader explained to the researcher:

> A lot of times, people don't talk to the popular kids because they're kind of scared of them and they don't know their real personality. So that's kind of a bummer when you're considered to be popular because you don't usually meet a lot of other people because they just go, "Oh." (Eder, 1985, p. 162)

Paradoxically, popularity in many cases led to these girls' being disliked. As Eder explains:

> There are limits to the number of friendships that any one person can maintain. Because popular girls get a high number of affiliative offers, they have to reject more offers of friendship than other girls. Also, to maintain their higher status, girls who form the elite group must avoid associations with lower-status girls. . . . These girls are likely to ignore the affiliative attempts of many girls, leading to the impression that they are stuck-up. . . . Shortly after these girls reach their peak of popularity, they become increasingly disliked. (Eder, 1985, p. 163)

Social scientists believe that it is important to distinguish among three types of unpopular, or disliked, adolescents (Hymel, Bowker, and Woody, 1993; Olweus, in press; Parkhurst and Asher, 1992). One set of unpopular adolescents is overly *aggressive;* they are likely to get into fights with other students, are more likely to be involved in antisocial activities, and often are involved in bullying. A second set of unpopular adolescents are *withdrawn;* these adolescents are exceedingly shy, timid, and inhibited and, interestingly, are themselves more likely to be the victims of bullying. A third group of unpopular youngsters are *aggressive-withdrawn.* Like other aggressive youngsters, aggressive-withdrawn children have problems controlling their hostility; but like other withdrawn children, they tend to be nervous about initiating friendships with other adolescents.

Being unpopular has negative consequences for adolescents' mental health and psychological development—peer rejection is associated with subsequent depression, behavior problems, and academic difficulties (Kupersmidt and Coie, 1990; Morison and Masten, 1991; Olweus, in press; Parker and Asher, 1987; Patterson and Stoolmiller, 1991). But studies show that the specific consequences of peer rejection may differ among rejected youth who are aggressive versus those who are withdrawn. As discussed earlier, aggressive children who are rejected are often likely to end up in peer groups with other aggressive youngsters, and they are at risk for conduct problems and involvement in antisocial activity. In contrast, rejected, withdrawn children are likely to feel exceedingly lonely and are at risk for low self-esteem and diminished social competence. Adolescents who are both aggressive and withdrawn are at the greatest risk of all (Morison and Masten, 1991; Parkhurst and Asher, 1992; Rubin, LeMare, and Lollis, 1990).

Many psychologists believe that unpopular youngsters lack some of the social skills and social understanding necessary to be popular with peers. According to findings from an extensive program of research by Kenneth Dodge and his colleagues, unpopular aggressive children are more likely than their peers to think that other children's behavior is deliberately hostile, even when it is not (Dodge, 1986; Dodge and Coie, 1987). When accidentally pushed while waiting in line, for instance, unpopular aggressive children are more likely than others to believe that the person who did the pushing did it on purpose and, consequently, to retaliate. A recent study of African-American adolescents finds that deficits in **social information processing** may characterize overly aggressive black youngsters as well (Graham, 1993).

Not surprisingly, the inferences that adolescents draw from the behavior of others vary in part as a function of their ethnic and cultural background. In one fascinating study, the reactions of African-American and Mexican-American adolescents to videotapes of different social situations were compared (Rotheram-Borus and Phinney, 1990). In one situation, for example, a boy was rejected for a team. Whereas the African-American adolescents who saw the videotape said that, in a similar situation, they would get angry or leave, the

Mexican-American youngsters said that they would feel hurt but would not leave. In another vignette, two teenagers were working at a table on which the necessary supplies were close to one adolescent but not to the other. In response to this video, the Mexican-American adolescents were more likely to say simply that the adolescent who was closer to the supplies should hand them to the other teenager, whereas the African-American adolescents were more likely to say that if they were the adolescent farther from the supplies, they would be upset and would reach over and get what they needed. These differences in social information processing likely reflect cultural differences in the emphases placed on group solidarity and cooperation—two things that tend to be highly valued in Mexican-American families.

What about unpopular withdrawn children? What are their social skills deficits? In general, research shows that unpopular withdrawn children are excessively anxious and uncertain around other children, often hovering around the group without knowing how to break into a conversation or activity (Rubin et al., 1990). Their hesitancy and lack of confidence makes other children feel uncomfortable, and their submissiveness makes them easy targets for bullying (Olweus, in press). Unfortunately, the more these children are teased and rejected, the more hesitant they feel, which only compounds their problem (Hymel, Rubin, Rowden, and LeMare, 1990).

Can unpopular adolescents be helped? In recent years, several teams of psychologists have experimented with different sorts of interventions designed to improve the social skills of unpopular adolescents. These social competence training programs have focused on three different strategies. One type of program has been designed to teach social skills—self-expression, questioning others about themselves, and leadership (Kelly and de Armaa, 1989; Repinski and Leffert, 1994). These social skills intervention programs have been shown to improve adolescents' abilities to get along with peers. A second approach has been to have unpopular adolescents participate in group activities with popular ones under the supervision of psychologists. Programs like this have been shown to improve adolescents' self-conceptions and their acceptance by others (Bierman and Furman, 1984). Finally, some social competence programs focus on a combination of behavioral and cognitive abilities, including social problem solving. Psychologist Roger Weissberg and his colleagues (Weissberg, Caplan, and Sivo, 1989) developed a social problem-solving program designed to improve young adolescents' abilities to judge social situations and figure out acceptable ways of behaving. In Weissberg's program, for example, adolescents are taught to calm down and think before they react, to decide what the problem is, to figure out what their goal is, and to think of positive approaches toward reaching that goal. Instead of lashing out at a classmate who grabbed the last basketball from a gym closet, for example, a hot-tempered boy who had been through this sort of social skills program might calm himself down, tell himself that his goal is to play basketball rather than get into a fight, and approach another student to ask if he can get into a game.

RECAP

Popular adolescents tend to be socially skilled, intelligent, humorous, and friendly. Unpopular adolescents tend to fall into three categories: aggressive adolescents, withdrawn adolescents, and aggressive-withdrawn adolescents. In general, adolescents who are rejected by their peers are at risk for a wide variety of psychological and behavioral problems, including academic failure, conduct problems, and depression. Numerous interventions have been designed to improve adolescents' social competence, including those that focus on improving unpopular adolescents' social skills and their social understanding.

THE PEER GROUP AND PSYCHOSOCIAL DEVELOPMENT

Regardless of the structure or norms of a particular peer group, peers play an extremely important role in the psychological development of adolescents. Problematic peer relationships are associated with a range of serious psychological and behavior problems during adolescence and adulthood. Individuals who are unpopular or who have poor peer relationships during adolescence are more likely than their socially accepted peers to be low achievers in school, to drop out of high school, to have a range of learning disabilities, to show higher rates of delinquent behavior, and to suffer from an array of emotional and mental health problems as adults (Savin-Williams and Berndt, 1990). Although it is likely that poorly adjusted individuals have difficulty making friends, there is now good evidence that psychological problems result from—as well as cause—problems with peers (Hymel et al., 1990; Kupersmidt and Coie, 1990; Parker and Asher, 1987).

Peers also play a crucial role in promoting (or hindering) normal psychosocial development. In the realm of identity, peers provide the sorts of models and feedback that adolescents cannot get from adults. In the context of the peer group, young people can try on different roles and personalities and can experiment with different identities with greater ease than at home. And, as we saw earlier, the peer group may serve as a way station in the development of identity as adolescents begin to develop a separate sense of self that is differentiated from the family (Brown et al., 1986). Experience in the peer group also can be an important influence on adolescents' self-image.

Experience in the peer group also is vital for the development and expression of autonomy. The process of developing more mature and more independent relationships with parents is accompanied by the establishment of more mature relationships with peers. In addition, the peer group provides a context for adolescents to test out decision-making skills in an arena where there are no adults present to monitor and control their choices (Hill and Holmbeck, 1986).

Intimacy and sexuality, of course, are much more common between peers than between adolescents and adults, for a variety of reasons. Perhaps most critical is that both intimacy and sexuality require interaction between two individuals who are relative equals. Moreover, sexual relationships and close intimacy within the family context would be likely to disrupt important functions of family relationships (Hartup, 1977). It is therefore the adolescent's peer group that generally plays the central role in socializing youngsters in appropriate sexual behavior and in developing the capacity for intimate friendship (Sullivan, 1953a).

Finally, peers are an important influence on adolescent achievement. Although they may play a less influential role than parents or teachers in influencing adolescents' long-term educational and occupational plans, peers are a significant influence on adolescents' day-to-day school behaviors and feelings, including how much they value school, how much effort they devote to their studies, and how well they perform in class (Epstein, 1983b; Steinberg, Darling, Fletcher, Brown, and Dornbusch, in press). Peers seem to be an

In general, popularity in the adolescent peer group is associated with social competence—popular teenagers are friendly, cheerful, and humorous. Status in the peer group, in contrast, has more to do with leadership and capability in highly valued activities. (Richard Hutchings/Photo Researchers)

especially important influence on the achievement of ethnic minority youth (Steinberg, Dornbusch, and Brown, 1992).

Adolescents consider the time they spend with peers to be among the most enjoyable parts of the day (Csikszentmihalyi and Larson, 1984). One reason is that activities with friends are typically organized around having a good time, in contrast to activities with parents, which are more likely to be organized around household chores and the enforcement of parental rules (Larson, 1983; Montemayor, 1982). Rather than being competing institutions, the family and peer group seem to provide contrasting opportunities for adolescent activities and behaviors. The family is organized around work and other tasks, and it may be important in the socialization of responsibility and achievement. The peer group provides more frequent opportunity for interaction and leisure, which contributes to the development of intimacy and enhances the adolescent's mood and psychological well-being.

KEY TERMS

age grading
baby boom
cliques
cofigurative cultures
crowds
ethnography
participant observation
particularistic norms
peer groups
postfigurative cultures
prefigurative cultures
reference groups
sex cleavage
significant others
social-class groups
social information processing
universalistic norms
youth culture

FOR FURTHER READING

Asher, S., and Coie, J. (Eds.). (1990). *Peer rejection in childhood.* New York: Cambridge University Press. An excellent collection of articles about the factors that lead children and adolescents to be rejected by their peers.

Brown, B. (1990). Peer groups. Pp. 171–196 in S. Feldman and G. Elliott (Eds.), *At the threshold: The developing adolescent.* Cambridge, Mass.: Harvard University Press. A thorough review of the literature on the structure and significance of peer groups in adolescence.

Eder, D. (1985). The cycle of popularity: Interpersonal relations among female adolescents. *Sociology of Education, 58,* 154–165. A fascinating ethnography of social interactions at the cheerleaders' table in a middle school cafeteria.

Fine, G. (1987). *With the boys.* Chicago: University of Chicago Press. A wonderful ethnographic study of preadolescent boys, reported by a researcher who spent a season observing a Little League team.

Mead, M. ([1928] 1978). *Culture and commitment.* Garden City, N.Y.: Anchor. The late eminent anthropologist's compelling analysis of the important role played by peers in rapidly changing societies.

CHAPTER 6

SCHOOLS

SECONDARY EDUCATION IN AMERICA
The Origins of Compulsory Education
The Rise of the Comprehensive High School

SCHOOL REFORM: PAST AND PRESENT

THE SOCIAL ORGANIZATION OF SCHOOLS
School Size and Class Size
Approaches to Age Grouping
Tracking
School Desegregation
Public Schools versus Private Schools

THE IMPORTANCE OF SCHOOL CLIMATE

BEYOND HIGH SCHOOL
The College Bound
The "Forgotten Half"

SCHOOLS AND ADOLESCENT DEVELOPMENT

THE SEXES
ABILITY GROUPING, COEDUCATION, AND SEX DIFFERENCES IN MATHEMATICS ACHIEVEMENT

THE SCIENTIFIC STUDY OF ADOLESCENCE
TEACHER EXPECTATIONS AND STUDENT PERFORMANCE

(Bob Daemmrich/Stock, Boston)

The study of schools is important to social scientists and policy-makers who are interested in influencing adolescent development, because it is through educational institutions that the greatest number of young people can most easily be reached. During the 1950s, for example, when politicians felt that the United States had lost its scientific edge to the Soviet Union, schools were called upon to see to it that students took more courses in math and science (Conant, 1959). When policy-makers felt that society ought to do something to close the economic gap between the races—as they did in the 1960s—schools were called upon to implement desegregation programs so that all individuals would have equal schooling and equal economic opportunity (Coleman, Campbell, Hobson, McPartland, Mood, Weinfeld, and York, 1966). When social scientists felt that adolescents were growing up unfamiliar with the world of work—as they did in the 1970s—schools were asked to provide opportunities for work-study programs and classes in career education (President's Science Advisory Committee, 1974). When economists felt that America was losing its competitive edge in the world economy—as they did in the 1980s—schools were called upon to return to the "basics" and to become more academically demanding (National Center on Education and the Economy, 1990). And today, as society grapples with a broad array of social problems affecting and involving youth—problems such as violence, AIDS, and poverty—we are once again looking to schools for assistance (Dryfoos, 1993).

Because of the important role it has come to play in modern society, the educational system has been the target of a remarkable amount of criticism, scrutiny, and social science research. Parents, teachers, educational administrators, and researchers debate what schools should teach, how schools should be organized, and how schools might best teach their students. They debate such issues as whether high schools should stick to instructing students in the basics—reading, writing, and arithmetic—or should offer a more diverse range of classes and services designed to prepare young people for adulthood socially and emotionally, as well as intellectually. They ask such questions as whether early adolescents should be schooled in separate junior high schools, whether students should be grouped by ability ("tracked"), and whether certain classroom atmospheres are preferable to others.

These questions have proved difficult to answer. Nevertheless, they remain extremely important. Virtually all American adolescents under the age of 16 and the vast majority of 16- and 17-year-olds are enrolled in school. More than half of all youth now continue their education beyond high school graduation—in technical schools, colleges, and universities. During most of the year, the typical student spends more than one-third of his or her waking hours each week in school or in school-related activities. Not only are schools the chief educational arena for adolescents in America, but they also play an extremely important role in defining the young person's social world and in shaping the adolescent's developing sense of identity and autonomy. It is therefore crucial that we understand how best to structure schools.

SECONDARY EDUCATION IN AMERICA

Consider the data presented in Figure 6.1. Today, virtually all young people from ages 14 to 17 are enrolled in school. In 1930, only about half of this age group were students, and at the turn of the century only 1 in 10 attended school (D. Tanner, 1972; William T. Grant Foundation, 1988).

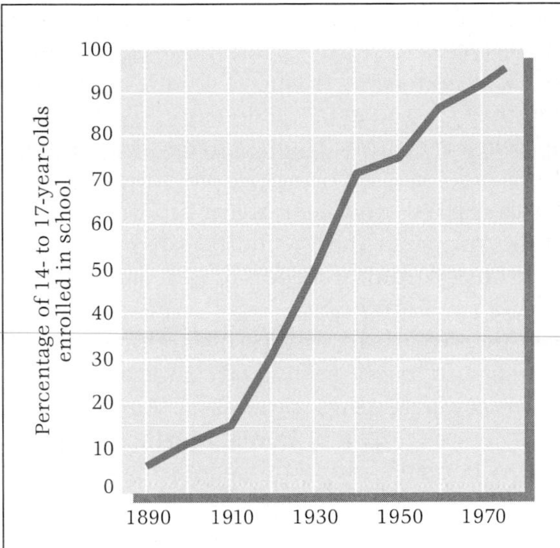

FIGURE 6.1 *The proportion of the 14- to 17-year-old population enrolled in school increased dramatically between 1910 and 1940. Today, nearly 95 percent of individuals this age are in school.* (D. Tanner, 1972; William T. Grant Foundation, 1988)

Not only are there considerably more youngsters enrolled in school today than there were fifty years ago, but today's students also spend more days per year in school. In 1920, for example, the average school term was 162 days, and the average student attended only 121 days, or 75 percent of the term. By 1968, however, the school term had been lengthened to nearly 180 days; which is still the national average today, and the typical student attends 90 percent of term (National Education Commission on Time and Learning, 1994; President's Science Advisory Committee, 1974). In many European countries, the school year is even longer. In England, for example, high school students spend 220 days in school each year (National Commission on Excellence in Education, 1983).

Although some critics of American schools have called for lengthening our school year (National Commission on Excellence in Education, 1983), others have pointed out that simply expanding the school year, without changing what takes place in school, may be misguided (Boyer, 1983; National Education Commission on Time and Learning, 1994). For example, although today the typical school offers a six-period day, with about 5.6 hours of classroom time, studies show that students spend only 40 percent of their time on such core academic subjects as math, English, history, and science (National Education Commission on Time and Learning, 1994). Clearly, it would be possible to increase the amount of time students spend on academic matters considerably without lengthening the school day at all.

Adolescents also remain in school for more years now than they did in past eras. In 1924, fewer than one-third of all youngsters entering the fifth grade eventually graduated from high school; today, about 75 percent of all fifth-graders will eventually graduate on time, and a substantial number of those who do not graduate on schedule eventually get their diploma through equivalency programs or continuation schools. Over the course of the twentieth century, then, schools have become increasingly prominent settings in the life of the average American adolescent.

RECAP

Schools play an extremely important role in structuring the nature of adolescence in modern society. In the United States, virtually all individuals between 14 and 17 years old are enrolled in school. One hundred years ago, fewer than 10 percent of this age group were students. Now, the average American adolescent's school year consists of 180 six-hour days.

The Origins of Compulsory Education

The rise of secondary education in America was the result of several historical and social trends at the turn of the century. Most important were industrialization, urbanization, and immigration.

Following widespread industrialization during the late nineteenth century, the role of children and young adolescents in the workplace changed dramatically. With the economy expanding, many families who at one time had needed their children in the labor force for financial reasons were able to make ends meet without the labor of their young. Furthermore, as the nature of the workplace changed, employers recognized that they needed workers who were more skilled and more reliable than youngsters. The few unskilled jobs that remained required strength beyond the capacity of many youth (Church, 1976). Social reformers also expressed concerns about the dangers children faced working in factories, and organized labor—an increasingly powerful force during the early 1900s—sought to protect not only the welfare of children but also the security of their own employment. Child labor laws narrowed and limited the employment of minors (Bakan, 1972). Together, these changes in the workplace have kept many youngsters out of the labor force.

During this same period, the nature of life in American cities was also changing markedly. Industrialization brought with it urbanization and, along with the rising rate of immigration during the early twentieth century, new problems for urban centers. The effects of a rapidly expanding economy were seen in the tenements and slums of America's cities: poor housing, overcrowded neighborhoods, crime. Eager to improve living conditions for the urban masses, social reformers envisioned education as a means of improving the life circumstances of the poor and working classes. And eager to ensure that the problems of cities did not get out of hand, many saw compulsory secondary education as a means of social control. High schools would take thousands of idle young people off the streets, it was argued, and keep them in a social institution in which they could be supervised and kept out of trouble. Eager, too, to see that foreign-born immigrants were well socialized into the American way of life, reformers presented universal secondary education as a necessary part of the process of "Americanization": It was a way of homogenizing a population characterized by increasing—and to many, increasingly uncomfortable—ethnic and cultural diversity (Church, 1976; D. Tanner, 1972). By 1915, the idea of universal compulsory education for adolescents had gained widespread acceptance.

The Rise of the Comprehensive High School

Prior to the early twentieth century, before secondary education became compulsory, high schools were designed for the elite. In curriculum, staff, and student composition, they were similar to the colleges of the day, the emphasis being for the most part on classical liberal arts instruction (Church, 1976; D. Tanner, 1972).

By 1920, however, educators saw a need for curricular reform. Compulsory secondary education had changed the social composition of the schools; many educators argued for a corresponding diversification in the secondary school curriculum. Now that secondary education was aimed at the masses, schooling was seen not merely as a means of intellectual training but also as a way of preparing youth for life in modern society. It was argued that education, especially for the majority, should include preparation for work and citizenship roles.

The 1920s marked the birth of what came to be known as the **comprehensive high school,** an educational institution that promised to meet the needs of a diverse and growing population of young people. Classes in general education, college preparation, and vocational education were all housed under one roof. As can be seen in Figure 6.1, the proportion of high school-aged individuals enrolled in school jumped dramatically in the years between World War I and World War II—from 32 percent in 1920 to over 73 percent in 1940. This was also a time of tremendous change in the high school curriculum. During these years, new courses were added in music, art, family life, health, physical education, and other subjects designed to prepare adolescents for family and leisure as well as work roles.

The high school had come a long way from its exclusive focus at the turn of the century on the intellectual development of the economic elite. By the 1950s, its concern had broadened to include the social and intellectual development of all young people. And today, despite all the questioning and criticism that have been aimed at it over the years, the comprehensive high school remains the cornerstone of the American system of secondary education.

RECAP

A number of social forces combined to lead the development of compulsory education for adolescents in America. Among the most important were industrialization, immigration, and urbanization. During the 1920s, the high school as we know it today—the comprehensive high school—was born. By 1940, nearly three-fourths of high school-aged individuals were enrolled in school.

SCHOOL REFORM: PAST AND PRESENT

Suppose you were asked to make a list of the things you think young people need to know in order to function as competent, responsible, and satisfied adults. Which items on your list should be the responsibility of high schools? Should high school curricula be limited to the traditional academic subjects, or should schools play a broader role in preparing young people for adulthood by providing instruction more directly relevant to work, family, leisure, and citizenship? Should students receive instruction only in English, mathematics, science, and social studies, or should they take courses as well in "general education"—in subjects such as art, home economics, health, sex education, driver education, and personal finance? Which courses should be required, and which should be left as electives? If you were to discuss these questions with your classmates, you would probably find little agreement.

In recent years, politicians and parents have sounded the cry for schools to scale down their general education offerings and place greater emphasis on the traditional academic subjects: English, mathematics, science, social studies, and a new "basic"—computer science (National Commission on Excellence in Education, 1983; National Education Commission on Time and Learning, 1994). Several social commentators have argued that educators—in high schools and colleges alike—have lost sight of the common core of knowledge and values that serves as the intellectual foundation of our society (Bloom, 1987).

To observers who are unfamiliar with the history of America's high schools, this plea for limiting the high school curriculum to the "essentials" sounds like a fresh and timely idea. But although returning to the basics

During the second quarter of this century, high schools began to play an increasingly important role in the lives of American adolescents. (Culver)

may, indeed, be seen as a welcome change, this is by no means the first time that education critics have called for a more rigorous and more focused curriculum. Similar calls were heard during the 1950s, in response to the perceived threat of the former Soviet Union's space program.

Actually, the current cry for more rigor in our schools is in part a reaction to curricular changes that took place some twenty-five years ago. During the early 1970s, education reformers claimed that schools were not preparing young people for the roles they would encounter as adults (Church, 1976). They felt that adolescents should spend less time in school and more time in community and work settings. Programs such as career education and experiential education were implemented in many school districts so that young people could receive "hands-on" experience in the "real world" (President's Science Advisory Committee, 1974). During this time period, students also became more vocal and demanded more courses in relevant and practical subject areas. Schools began to offer an increasingly wide range of electives for students to choose among.

The students of the 1970s clearly took advantage of these opportunities. By the late 1970s, over 40 percent of all high school students were taking a general—rather than a college preparatory or vocational—course of study, and 25 percent of their educational credits came from work experience outside of school, from remedial coursework, and from courses aimed at personal growth and development (National Commission on Excellence in Education, 1983). As we noted earlier, still today less than half of the school day is spent on core academic subjects, a carryover from the 1970s focus on relevance (National Education Commission on Time and Learning, 1994).

During the 1980s, however, the pendulum swung back toward the "basics." Why? The achievement test scores of American high school students had been falling steadily. Cross-cultural comparisons of student achievement consistently placed American youngsters at or near the bottom of the international list. As one team of investigators put it:

> A close examination of American children's academic achievement rapidly dispels any notion that we face a problem of limited scope. The problem is not restricted to a certain age level or to a particular academic subject. Whether we look at the average scores for schools or at the scores for individuals, we find evidence of serious and pervasive weakness. (Stevenson and Stigler, 1992, p. 50)

Partly in response to these worrisome findings, several proposals called for more demanding curricula (e.g., National Commission on Excellence in Education, 1983). One set of writers bemoaned what they called the "shopping-mall high school," where students were given too much freedom in choosing courses and schools were more concerned with keeping students happy than with seeing that genuine and important learning took place (Powell, Farrar, and Cohen, 1985). Noting that America was losing its competitive edge in the world market, education reformers called for more academic rigor in the schools as a means of preparing young people for the workplace of the future. One group, for example, called for schools to implement more demanding academic requirements, tougher standards for graduation, and longer school days (National Commission on Excellence in Education, 1983). Another recommended that schools spend at least 5.5 hours daily on instruction in core academic subjects (National Education Commission on Time and Learning, 1994). Whereas school reformers of the 1970s had demanded more relevant curricula, reformers of the 1980s demanded more rigorous ones.

During the late 1980s, yet another type of school reform received widespread attention. This time, however, the focus shifted from the content of the curriculum to the process of learning. Education reformers called for more emphasis in the classroom on higher-order thinking—whether in the teaching of basics or in the teaching of electives (Newmann, 1992). **Higher-order thinking** is stimulated when students are encouraged to interpret, analyze, and evaluate information, rather than simply memorizing or applying it in a routine way. In social studies, for example, asking students to discuss why political revolts occur may stimulate higher-order thinking, whereas asking them simply to memorize (and regurgitate) the dates of important political revolutions probably will not.

The stimulation of higher-order thinking sounds like an admirable goal. But as with all educational reforms, the reasons behind this goal are embedded in a particular historical and economic context. Why, in the 1990s, would education reformers suddenly become interested in restructuring the curriculum toward the promotion of higher-order thinking? Beginning in the late 1980s it had become apparent that American adolescents were sorely deficient in skills requiring in-depth analysis, which did not bode well for our country's competitiveness in an international economy that was increasingly centered on high-skilled jobs.

For example, one national assessment found declines during the 1970s and 1980s in

Higher-order thinking is stimulated when students are encouraged to interpret, analyze, and evaluate information, rather than simply memorize or apply it in a routine way. (Sven Martson/Comstock)

the proportion of 17-year-olds who could synthesize and learn from advanced reading materials, solve multistep math problems, and use detailed scientific knowledge to draw conclusions. Improvements during this same time period were found among younger adolescents, but these improvements were limited to fairly basic skills, such as reading comprehension, addition and subtraction, and knowledge of everyday science facts. Consider these grim conclusions of a blue-ribbon report issued by the National Assessment of Educational Progress in 1990 (Mullis, Owen, and Phillips, 1990):

> Students are learning facts and skills, but few show the capacity for complex reasoning and problem solving. . . . Most of the gains in achievement over the past two decades appear to have occurred in lower-level skills and basic concepts. . . . In contrast, most of the declines have occurred in the area of higher-level applications. (p. 33)

Nowhere is the problem of low student achievement—and its implications for the future of the labor force—more severe than in inner-city public schools. As one recent review pointed out, despite all the educational reforms and improvements implemented during the past twenty-five years, urban schools remain in a state of crisis:

> [A]chievement in inner-city schools continues to lag behind national norms, and dropout rates in inner-city high schools (especially among African-American and Hispanic youth) remain distressingly high, while many of those who do graduate are often so poorly prepared they cannot compete successfully in the labor market. One recent report on urban education concluded that because of the continued failure to

educate city children, many people now dismiss urban schools "as little more than human storehouses to keep young people off the streets." (Kantor and Brenzel, 1992, pp. 278–279)

Why has school reform failed in so many urban schools? Experts point to several reasons. First, the increasing concentration of poverty into certain inner-city communities (see Chapter 3) has produced a population of students with very grave academic and behavioral problems—problems which few schools are equipped or able to address. In one recent study of two inner-city junior high schools, for example, the researchers found that one-fourth of all males had carried a gun to school and that nearly one-half of all males and more than one-third of all females had carried a knife (Webster, Gainer, and Champion, 1993). Second, many urban school districts are burdened by huge administrative bureaucracies that often impede reform and stand in the way of educational innovation. Finally, the erosion of job opportunities in inner-city communities has left many students with little incentive to remain in school or to devote a great deal of effort to academic pursuits (Kantor and Brenzel, 1992).

RECAP

Educators have long debated the nature of the high school curriculum. During the 1970s, educators clamored for "relevance." During the 1980s, the pendulum swung "back to basics." During the 1990s, the fashion is "higher-order thinking." In general, efforts to reform school curricula are closely linked to economic and political concerns. The current concern with higher-order thinking is a response to worries about the competitiveness of the United States in an international economy that increasingly is reliant on high technology and high-skilled jobs. Special concerns have been raised about the degree to which inner-city schools are preparing students for this new labor market.

By the early 1990s, it had become evident to economists that merely training our students in "basics" was not going to help build a competitive workforce for the next century (Jackson and Hornbeck, 1989; National Center on Education and the Economy, 1990). According to one commission, the world's workplace had become split into two markedly different sectors: One was composed of low-paying jobs that required little skill or training, while the other was composed of high-paying jobs that required advanced training and well-developed intellectual skills, including higher-order thinking abilities. Most industrialized countries have made a concerted effort to expand the high-skill sector of their workplace, because these jobs are more lucrative for their economy as well as for their workers. But in order to maintain this expansion, it is necessary to develop a steady pool of highly skilled workers. In the words of this commission, America's choice was clear: "High skills or low wages" (National Center on Education and the Economy, 1990). This recognition has fueled much of the current debate about how best to reform America's schools. Proposals have been put forth by both the Bush and Clinton administrations aimed at overhauling America's schools by the year 2000.

What directions would these reforms likely take? In the past decade, consensus about the characteristics of a good school for adolescents has emerged among experts (Linney and Seidman, 1989). First and foremost, good schools emphasize intellectual activities. They create this atmosphere in different ways, depending on the nature and size of the student body, but in these good schools a common purpose—

quality education—is valued and shared by students, teachers, administrators, and parents. Learning is more important to students than school athletics or social activities are, and seeing that students learn is more important to teachers and administrators than seeing that they graduate.

Second, good schools have teachers who are committed to their students and who are given a good deal of freedom and autonomy by the school administration in the way that this commitment is expressed in the classroom. In all schools, of course, teachers have curricular requirements that they must fulfill. But in good schools, teachers are given relatively more authority to decide how their lessons are planned and how their classes are conducted. When teachers are given this sort of say in school governance, they may find it easier to make a commitment to the shared values of the institution.

Third, good schools constantly monitor themselves and their students in order to become even better. Rather than viewing questions and concerns about school policies and practices as threatening, principals and other administrators welcome opportunities for dialogue and discussion. When school personnel encourage flexibility, openness to change, and the exchange of ideas, they set a tone for the entire school that may even affect the classroom and may result in more stimulating student-teacher interaction.

Fourth, good schools are well integrated into the communities they serve. Active attempts are made to involve parents in their youngsters' education. Links are forged between the high school and local colleges and universities, so that advanced students may take more challenging and more stimulating courses for high school credit. Bridges are built between the high school and local employers, so that students begin to see the relevance of their high school education to their occupational futures.

Finally, and perhaps obviously, good schools are composed of good classrooms. In good classrooms, students are active participants in the process of education, not passive recipients of lecture material. The atmosphere is orderly but not oppressive. Innovative projects replace rote memorization as a way of encouraging learning. Students are challenged to think critically and to debate important issues, rather than being asked simply to regurgitate yesterday's lessons.

RECAP

Experts agree that good schools are those that (1) emphasize intellectual activities, (2) have committed teachers who are given autonomy, (3) monitor their own progress, (4) are well integrated into their community, and (5) have a high proportion of classrooms in which students are active participants in their education.

THE SOCIAL ORGANIZATION OF SCHOOLS

In addition to debating curricular issues, social scientists who have been interested in school reform have also discussed the ways in which secondary schools should be organized. In this section we examine the research on five aspects of school organization: (1) school and classroom size; (2) different approaches to age grouping and, in particular, how young adolescents should be grouped; (3) tracking, or the grouping of students in classes according to their academic abilities; (4) school desegregation; and (5) public versus private schools.

School Size and Class Size

When it comes to schools, is bigger better? The most extensive data about the effects of *school size* on adolescents come from a series of classic studies conducted by ecological psychologist Roger Barker and his colleagues (Barker and Gump, 1964). These researchers were interested in how the size of a school influences the variety of classes and extracurricular activities available to students as well as the students' participation in them.

Large schools offer more varied instruction than do small schools. But the variety of courses offered in a school increases substantially only when the size of the school increases dramatically. While a school with 2,000 students might offer fifty different classes, a school with 4,000 students might offer only sixty.

Perhaps the most interesting findings, however, concern participation in nonacademic activities. One might expect that, in addition to providing a more varied curriculum, large schools would be able to offer a more diverse selection of extracurricular activities to their students, and indeed they do. Large schools can afford to have more athletic teams, after-school clubs, and student organizations. In fact, Barker found that nearly four times as many nonacademic activities were available to students attending very large high schools as were available to students in small schools.

But because the large schools also contained so many more students, actual participation in different activities was only half as high in the large schools as in the smaller schools. In Barker's terminology, the large schools were "overmanned"—they had many more students per activity than necessary. As a result, students tended more often to be observers than participants in school activities. For instance, during the fall, a small school and a large school might each field teams in football, soccer, and cross-country running, together requiring a total of 100 students. An individual's chances of being 1 of those 100 students are greater in a school that has only 500 students than in a school with an enrollment of 4,000.

Because students in small schools are more likely than students in large schools to be active in a wider range of activities, they are more likely to report doing things that help them develop their skills and abilities, that allow them to work closely with others, and that make them feel needed and important. In a small school, chances are that, sooner or later, most students will find themselves on a team, in the student government, or in an

Generally speaking, research has shown that adolescents in large classes learn just as much as adolescents in small ones. An important exception, however, is remedial education: Here, adolescents benefit from smaller classes and one-on-one instruction. (Meri Houtchens-Kitchens/Picture Cube)

extracurricular organization. Students in small schools also are more likely to be placed in positions of leadership and responsibility, and they more often report having done things that made them feel confident and diligent. School size especially affects the participation of students whose grades are not very good. In large schools, academically marginal students often feel like outsiders; they rarely get involved in school activities. In small schools, however, these students feel a sense of involvement and obligation equal to that of more academically successful students.

At least two studies of American high schools have echoed this sentiment (Boyer, 1983; Goodlad, 1984). Although large schools may be able to offer more diverse curricula or provide greater material resources to their students, the toll that school size may take on student learning and engagement appears to exceed the benefits of size. Experts now agree that the ideal size of a school for adolescents is between 500 and 1,000 students (Entwisle, 1990).

In contrast to studies of school size, studies of *class size* indicate that variations within the typical range of classroom sizes—from twenty to forty students—do not generally affect students' scholastic achievement (Rutter, 1983). Without changes in instruction, changes in class size alone are unlikely to have an effect on students (Bennett, 1987). Students in classes with forty students learn just as much as students in classes with twenty students. However, in situations that call for highly individualized instruction or tutoring, smaller classes appear to be more effective. For example, in remedial education classes, where teachers must give a great deal of attention to each student, small classes are valuable. As Michael Rutter (1983) points out, one important implication of these findings is that it may be profitable for schools that maintain regular class sizes of twenty-five or thirty students to increase the sizes of these classes by a student or two in order to free instructors and trim the sizes of classes for students who need specialized, small-group instruction.

Approaches to Age Grouping

A second issue that social scientists have examined in the study of school structure and organization concerns the way in which schools group students of different ages. Early in this century, most school districts separated youngsters into an elementary school (which had either six or eight grades) and a secondary school (which had either four or six grades). However, many educators felt that the two-school system was unable to meet the special needs of young adolescents. During the early years of compulsory secondary education, the establishment of separate schools for young adolescents began, and the **junior high school** was born (Hechinger, 1993). In more recent years, the **middle school**—a three- or four-year school housing the seventh and eighth grades with one or more younger grades—has gained a certain popularity, replacing the junior high school in some districts. Proponents of middle schools point to the earlier maturation of young people today and the greater similarity of fifth- and sixth-graders to their older peers than to their younger ones.

What is known about the differential effects of these various arrangements? From the point of view of the developing adolescent, are some organizational schemes superior to others? One recent review suggests that the evidence, although sparse, favors the middle school arrangement (Entwisle, 1990). Middle schools are typically smaller and less departmentalized, which probably means that young adolescents are less likely to feel "lost" in them. In addition, teachers in middle schools are more likely to engage in team teaching, to teach only one grade level, and to teach in their area of specialization. For these reasons, middle schools are likely to be better environments both academically and socially than are junior high schools.

Although most experts now agree that middle schools are preferable to junior high schools, there is still considerable room for improvement in existing middle schools. One well-publicized report on this subject was issued by the Carnegie Corporation's Council on Adolescent Development (1989). Among the most important recommendations made were to divide middle schools into units of between 200 and 500 students in order to reduce students' feelings of anonymity, to hire teachers who have special training in adolescent development, and to strengthen ties between schools and the communities in which they are located.

Researchers also have compared school arrangements in which students remain in elementary school until eighth grade with arrangements in which they move from elementary school into middle or junior high school and, later, into high school. The most comprehensive study was conducted by sociologists Roberta Simmons and Dale Blyth (1987). These researchers studied youngsters in the Milwaukee public schools for a five-year period. Some of these students were in school districts organized around the 8-4 arrangement, while others were in schools using a 6-3-3 plan. The researchers were interested in the impact of having to change schools at different ages. They compared shifts in adolescents' self-esteem, grade-point averages, participation in extracurricular activities, and feelings of anonymity as the students moved through each of the two arrangements. In the 8-4 arrangement, students change schools only once, whereas in the 6-3-3 arrangement, they must make two transitions.

As shown in Figure 6.2, adolescent boys' and girls' self-esteem is affected quite differently by the two school arrangements. For boys, self-esteem rises throughout the years between sixth and tenth grades, with the exception of the year between ninth and tenth grades for those in a 6-3-3 arrangement, during which self-esteem remains essentially unchanged. For girls, self-esteem rises throughout the five years in the 8-4 arrangement—as with the boys in this arrangement. But the girls in the 6-3-3 arrangement show two dramatic drops in self-esteem, during each of the transitions into a new school (that is, between the sixth and seventh grades and between the ninth and tenth grades).

The data on youngsters' participation in extracurricular activities again favored the 8-4 arrangement, this time for both boys and girls. Over the five-year period, extracurricular participation decreased slightly for boys in the 6-3-3 plan, whereas it increased slightly for boys in the 8-4 plan. For girls, the differences were more striking. Although sixth-graders in both types of schools participated in the same number of extracurricular activities, in the eighth grade, girls who were in the 8-4 arrangement participated in about twice as many activities as did girls in the 6-3-3 organization; and in the tenth grade, they participated in nearly three times as many. The findings concerning students' grade-point averages and feelings of anonymity paint a somewhat different picture. Students' grades declined whenever they had to change schools, regardless of the timing of the transition. Similarly, whenever students changed schools, their feelings of anonymity increased for a time.

The researchers concluded that, while all school transitions may have a temporary negative impact on adolescents' psychological well-being and social participation, changing schools may be harder—and consequently may have a more deleterious impact—the earlier it occurs during adolescence. This view is consistent with Simmons and Blyth's "developmental readiness" hypothesis, which we examined in Chapter 1. There we saw evidence that

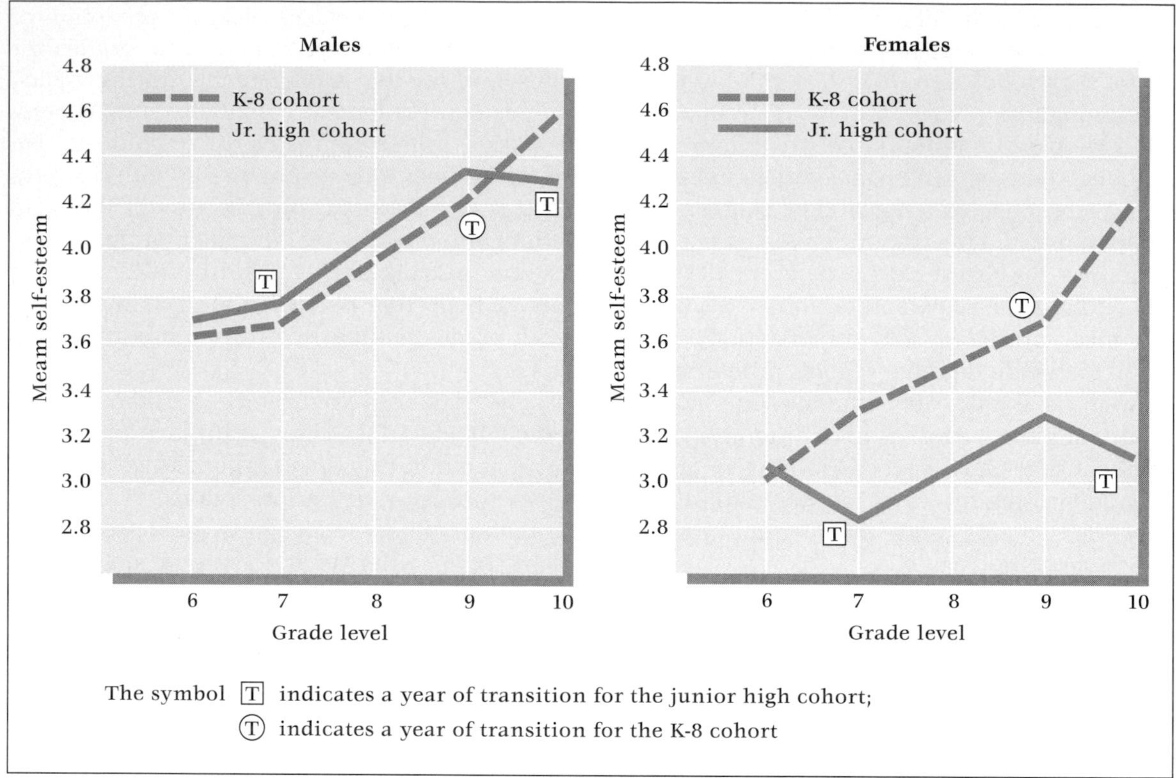

FIGURE 6.2 *For boys and girls, self-esteem is affected differently by different school arrangements.*

puberty, too, may be more disruptive if it occurs early. These researchers also contend that the impact of several simultaneous changes is worse than the impact of any one change alone. Thus the early school transition is particularly hard for girls, because changing schools following the sixth grade often coincides with the onset of puberty and with their initiation into dating (Simmons, Burgeson, Carlton-Ford, and Blyth, 1987). Although the effects for boys do not seem as severe, there is evidence that for them, too, the 8-4 arrangement may be preferable to the 6-3-3 plan.

An alternative explanation for these findings has been suggested by psychologist Jacquelynne Eccles and her colleagues (Eccles, Lord, and Midgley, 1991; Eccles, Midgley, Wigfield, Buchanan, Reuman, Flanagan, and Mac Iver, 1993). Eccles has argued that the classroom environment in the typical junior high school is quite different from that in the typical elementary school. Not only are junior high schools larger and less personal, but junior high school teachers also hold different beliefs about students than do elementary school teachers—even when they teach students of the same chronological age. For example, teachers in junior high schools are less likely to trust their students and more likely to emphasize control and discipline. They also tend to be more likely to believe that students' abilities are fixed and not easily modified through instruction. Eccles points out that it is little surprise that students experience a drop in self-esteem and in achievement motivation when they enter junior high school, given the change in environments they experience and given the mismatch between what adolescents need developmentally and what the typical junior high school context provides. The issue, according to her, is not that the adolescents must make a transition; it is the nature of the transition they must make. Indeed, although students' self-esteem drops during the transition into junior high school, it increases somewhat during the early junior high school years, suggesting that the initial decline reflects students' temporary difficulties in adapting to the new environment (Wigfield, Eccles, Mac Iver, Reuman, and Midgley, 1991). Consistent with this, junior high school students attending more personal, less departmentalized schools do better in school than their peers in more rigid and more anonymous schools (Lee and Smith, 1993).

Why do junior high school teachers differ from those who teach elementary school? At this point, the answer is not clear-cut. It does not seem that the individuals who choose to become junior high teachers differ all that much from those who choose to teach younger grades. Rather, Eccles has suggested that the organization and anonymity of junior high schools have a negative effect on the teachers who work in them, which in turn affects the way they interact with students. This is consistent with a large body of evidence that students are more engaged in school when their teachers themselves are more engaged in their work (Louis and Smith, 1992).

Eccles also points out that cultural stereotypes about adolescence may have a negative influence on junior high school teachers' beliefs. As we saw in the Introduction to this book, many adults believe that adolescence is an inevitably difficult time—not only for teenagers themselves but also for those who work with them. To the extent that teachers come into the classroom with negative images of adolescence as a stage in the life cycle—that teenagers are inherently unruly, or unteachable, or perplexing—their preconceptions may interfere with their work as educators (Midgley, Feldlaufer, and Eccles, 1988). As we shall see in a later section of this chapter, one of the most important influences on the adolescent's experience in school is the climate of the classroom.

The fact that many teachers of young adolescents have negative, or even erroneous, perceptions of this stage in the life cycle is not at all surprising, given the lack of specialized training in early adolescence that most teachers of middle grades have received. According to a recent report, only about one-third of middle school principals report that the teachers in their school had specialized college coursework that focused on middle-grades education and that only about one-third had done student teaching at this grade level. Even among teachers who *had* received specialized middle-grades training, half felt that their training was poor or inadequate (Scales and McEwin, 1994).

It is important to remember that although some aspects of the transition into secondary school may be difficult for students to negotiate, not all students experience the same degree of stress during the transition. The Simmons and Blyth studies indicate that students who experience the transition earlier in adolescence have more difficulty with it than those who experience it later. Eccles's research shows that the environment that students move into makes a big difference. And other studies indicate that adolescents who have close friends before and during the transition into secondary school adapt more successfully to the new school environment (Berndt, 1987). Consistent with this, students who have more academic and psychosocial problems before the transition into middle or junior high school—that is, during elementary school—cope less successfully with the transition (Safer, 1986).

Evidently, then, the transition into secondary school is not the sort of stressor that has uniform effects on all students. More vulnerable adolescents, adolescents with fewer sources of social support, and adolescents moving into more impersonal schools may be more susceptible to the adverse consequences of this stressor than their peers are. Not surprisingly, a recent study of poor, inner-city youngsters found significant negative effects of the school transition on adolescents' self-esteem, achievement, classroom preparation, perceptions of the school environment, reports of social support, and participation in extracurricular activities (Seidman, Allen, Aber, Mitchell, and Feinman, 1994). Another study of Texas adolescents found that African-American and, especially, Mexican-American youngsters were more likely than their white peers to experience a variety of difficulties during the transition out of elementary school—including receiving poor grades, getting into trouble with teachers, or being hassled by other students (Munsch and Wampler, 1993).

One recent report from a team of investigators at the University of Vermont suggests that low-income students' adjustment to middle school may be enhanced as a result of an intervention targeted at their *parents* (Bronstein, Duncan, Clauson, Abrams, Yannett, Ginsburg, and Milne, 1994). The researchers had parents participate in an eleven-week program designed to increase their understanding of adolescent development and their effectiveness as parents. The children whose parents had participated in the program were functioning better psychologically and behaviorally, both immediately after the program and one year later, than were their counterparts whose parents had not participated. Moreover, the children whose parents had participated did not show the decline in functioning that often is associated with the transition into middle school.

RECAP

Educators have long debated how best to structure schools for young adolescents. Middle schools seem slightly preferable to junior high schools, but research on the transition from elementary school into secondary school (whether a middle school or a junior high school) indicates that this transition is difficult for many students. Researchers point to features of the middle school environment that may be problematic and, more generally, to a mismatch between the middle school environment and the developmental needs of young adolescents.

Tracking

In some schools, students with different academic abilities and interests do not attend classes together. Some classes are designated as more challenging and more rigorous and are reserved for students who are identified as especially capable. Other classes in the same subject area are designated as average classes and are taken by most students. Still others are designated as remedial classes and are reserved for students having academic difficulties. The process of separating students into different levels of classes within the same school is called **tracking.** Not all high schools use tracking systems. In some schools, students with different abilities take all their classes together.

Even among schools that use tracking, there are important differences in the implementation of the tracking system. Some schools are more inclusive in their tracking, permitting a relatively high proportion of students into the highest track (even, perhaps, some students whose abilities do not warrant such placement). Other schools are more exclusive, limiting the places in the highest track to a privileged few (even if this means placing some high-ability students in the lower tracks). And still other schools are "meritocratic," placing students in tracks that match their abilities. In general, *inclusive tracking* is found in schools where principals have confidence in their students, where teachers influence track placement, and where there is open communication between students and teachers. *Exclusive tracking* is more likely to be found in smaller, more affluent schools where principals lack confidence in their students, where teachers have high "professional" standards, and where there is little information flow between staff and students. *Meritocratic tracking* is found more often in larger schools (Kilgore, 1991).

Educators have debated the pros and cons of tracking for years (Rutter, 1983). On the positive side, tracking allows teachers to design class lessons that are more finely tuned to students' abilities. Tracking may be especially useful at the high school level, where students must master certain basic skills before they can learn such specialized subjects as science, math, or foreign languages.

Unfortunately, however, tracking creates problems of its own. Students who are placed in the remedial track are likely to be labeled by their peers as "slow" or "stupid." Their self-esteem may suffer, and they may eventually come to see themselves as failures (Rutter, 1983). What is more, because schools play such an important role in influencing adolescents' friendships, when students are tracked, they tend to socialize only with peers from the same academic group (Rosenbaum, 1976). Tracking can thereby contribute to the polarization of the student body into different subcultures that feel hostile toward each other. The students in the advanced track may feel academically superior and may look down on other students, and the students in the remedial track may feel angry and resentful. Finally, some critics of tracking point out that decisions about track placements often discriminate against poor and minority students and may hinder rather than enhance their academic progress (Rosenbaum, 1976). Some school counselors assume, for example, that minority or poor youngsters are not capable of handling the work in advanced classes and may assign them to average or remedial classes, where less material is covered and the work is less challenging (Vanfossen, Jones, and Spade, 1987). Other studies, however, indicate that a student's ability has a stronger influence on track placement than his or her background has (Alexander and Cook, 1982).

Recent research on tracking in high schools indicates quite clearly that students in different tracks have markedly different opportunities to learn (Gamoran, 1987). Students in the more advanced tracks receive more challenging instruction and better teaching, and they are more likely to engage in classroom activities that emphasize higher-order thinking rather than rote memorization. Being placed in a more advanced track has a positive influence on school achievement (how much is actually learned over time), on subsequent course selection (the curriculum to which a student is exposed), and on ultimate educational attainment (how many years of schooling a student completes) (Gamoran and Mare, 1989; Lee and Bryk, 1989; Natriello, Pallas, and Alexander, 1989).

In many respects, then, early track placements set in motion a sort of educational "trajectory" that is often difficult to change, once in place (Alexander and Cook, 1982; Dornbusch, 1994; Hallinan, 1992). Junior high track placements, for example, determine

ABILITY GROUPING, COEDUCATION, AND SEX DIFFERENCES IN MATHEMATICS ACHIEVEMENT

According to most reviews, differences in the mathematics achievement of boys and girls, which favor boys, are well documented (Fennema and Peterson, 1985). Although elementary school girls generally outscore boys on tests of math achievement, junior and senior high school boys are more likely to take math classes and are more likely to outperform girls. These sex differences are important, because students emerging from high school with little preparation in mathematics are unlikely to be able to enter certain college programs (such as engineering) or to pursue certain occupations (such as scientist) that require training in math. Decisions that young women make early in their education therefore may have important long-term implications for their educational and occupational futures.

Many psychological explanations have been offered for the flip-flop in math achievement during early adolescence, including (1) that girls come to see math achievement as part of the masculine role and develop negative attitudes toward math as a consequence; (2) that girls have fewer role models of successful mathematicians or scientists and, consequently, are less likely to aspire to enter these fields; and (3) that girls receive pressure from their male peers not to excel in math class (Hallinan and Sorensen, 1987). We examine some of these explanations in Chapter 12 as part of our discussion of adolescent achievement. As Hallinan and Sorensen point out, however, psychological explanations of sex differences in math achievement ignore organizational aspects of schools that may have important effects. In particular, they suggest that tracking biases in the math curriculum operate against the assignment of girls to high-ability math classes.

These researchers examined mathematics ability-group assignments in a large sample of fourth-through seventh-graders. They were interested in whether assignment to the high-ability group was influenced by the student's math ability, by his or her gender, or by a combination of both. They found, not surprisingly, that a student's ability weighed heavily in the assignment process, with more able students being more likely to be assigned to the high-ability group. But they also found that high-ability girls were less likely to be assigned to the high-ability group than were boys of comparable talent (Hallinan and Sorensen, 1987).

Even within math classes, teachers interact differently with males and females. Teachers are more likely to communicate to girls who are having difficulty that their problem is related to a lack of ability, whereas they are

which sorts of courses a student is eligible to take in high school, which in turn determine which colleges he or she may apply to. Moreover, because students are assigned to different tracks initially on the basis of test scores and other indicators of aptitude, and because students in the lower tracks receive an inferior education, the net effect of tracking over time is to increase preexisting differences among students. The students who need the most help are assigned to the tracks in which the quality of instruction is the poorest. In other words, in a school that uses tracking, the academically "rich get richer, and the poor get more likely to communicate to boys who are having difficulty that their problem results from a lack of effort. As a consequence, girls may be more likely than boys to develop feelings of helplessness when it comes to learning math, and they may emerge with negative perceptions of their own abilities (Henderson and Dweck, 1990).

Moreover, the biased assortment of youngsters into math tracks has long-term implications for future course selection. An adolescent girl who is not assigned to a high-ability math class—despite her talent—may come to develop more negative attitudes toward math than she might have otherwise and may miss opportunities to pursue certain careers that require advanced mathematics training. Indeed, girls are less likely than boys to receive advice, encouragement, and counseling to take advanced courses in math or to prepare for careers that would require these courses (Lee, Marks, and Byrd, 1994).

Is this sort of sexism diminished in single-sex schools? One recent investigation involving sixty private schools—twenty coeducational, twenty boys' schools, and twenty girls' schools—says "not necessarily." The researchers observed classes in these schools and carefully noted both subtle and blatant forms of sexism, such as a teacher's ignoring a young woman's interest in science or providing female students with less challenging math instruction than was warranted. Somewhat surprisingly, these sorts of practices existed even in girls' schools, despite the hope that girls might encounter less sexist instruction in a single-sex environment. Although a number of academically demanding girls' schools were less sexist than the norm, there was considerable variation among the girls' schools studied. For example, the researchers observed teachers in girls' schools "talking down to girls, making academic activities more palatable by 'wrapping calculus in a nontechnical package,' setting up expectations that students would have difficulty with assignments by offering help before it was required or requested, or promulgating an attitude that 'trying hard is as important as succeeding' with difficult undertakings" (Lee et al., 1994, p. 114). In contrast, boys' schools were more likely to use an aggressive style of teaching that encouraged students to state their views assertively and to expect the intense scrutiny of their teachers and peers. Sexism was just as pronounced in coeducational schools, however, especially in science classes. In one chemistry class that was observed, for example, the female teacher responded positively to boys who spoke out without raising their hands, and yet she reprimanded girls for the exact same behavior. Another chemistry teacher at a different coeducation school told the researchers that he believed that "girls are not suited to 'do' science" (Lee et al., 1994, p. 108).

poorer." Although students in the lower tracks get the short end of the educational stick, there are some exceptions—for example, schools in which classes in the lower tracks are taught by strong teachers who insist on maintaining high standards (Gamoran, 1993; Hallinan, 1994).

Even in schools that do not have formal tracking, of course, teachers may group students within the same class into ability groups. In such an arrangement, students may have a wider range of peers with whom to compare themselves than they would in separate tracks, since their classes are much more diverse in composition. The impact of this comparison process on both students and teachers is quite interesting. For high-ability students, within-classroom ability grouping raises their expectations for achievement and raises their teachers' evaluations of them; for low-ability students, the opposite is true: The students have lowered expectations and get worse grades from their teachers (Reuman, 1989). Presumably, both adolescents and teachers make their evaluations based on unstated comparisons, and in mixed classes with ability groups, the high-ability students look better, and the low-ability students look worse, than they would in a conventionally tracked school or in a school in which ability grouping is not used. As is the case with tracking, within-classroom ability grouping also exposes students in different groups to different levels of educational quality, with students in the high-ability groups receiving more challenging instruction and more engaging learning experiences (Catsambis, 1992).

Related to the issue of tracking are questions concerning the placement of individuals who are considered **gifted students** and of those who have a **learning disability.** Adolescents who are gifted score 130 or higher on an intelligence test. Adolescents with a learning disability are those whose actual performance is significantly poorer than their expected performance (based on intelligence tests and the like) and whose difficulty with academic tasks cannot be traced to an emotional problem, such as coping with a parental divorce, or sensory dysfunction, such as a visual or hearing impairment. Most learning disabilities are presumed to be neurological in origin (Lovitt, 1989).

Educators have debated whether gifted students and those with learning disabilities are best served by instruction in separate classes (for example, in enriched classes for gifted students or in special education classes for students with a learning disability) or by **mainstreaming,** the integration of all students with special needs into regular classrooms. Pros and cons of each approach have been identified. On the one hand, separate special education programs can be tailored to meet the specific needs of students and can target educational and professional resources in a cost-effective way. On the other hand, however, segregating students on the basis of their academic ability may foster social isolation and stigmatization—either for being "stupid" or for being a "brainiac."

Generally speaking, educators have tended to favor mainstreaming over separate classrooms for adolescents with special needs. (Mainstreaming, whenever possible, is required by federal law in the case of adolescents with disabilities.) Their argument has been that the psychological costs of separating adolescents with special academic needs from their peers outweigh the potential academic benefits. One study of gifted youngsters found, for example, that those who were integrated into regular classrooms scored higher on measures of self-conception than did those in special classes (Schneider, Clegg, Byrne, Ledingham, and Crombie, 1989). Even with mainstreaming, adolescents who have learning disabilities may suffer psychological consequences related to their problems in school. Compared with average-achieving students, adolescents with learning disabilities report more social and behavioral difficulties and, not surprisingly, more problems in coping with school. They are also more likely than other adolescents to have poor peer relations, are less likely to participate in school-based extracurricular activities, and are more likely to drop out of school (Lovitt, 1989). Given the tremendous importance society places on school success, it is not difficult to see why students who have difficulties learning would suffer psychological, as well as scholastic, problems.

RECAP

In general, educational research does not favor grouping students by ability, or tracking. Students placed in the lower tracks or in low-ability groups within classrooms receive a markedly inferior education than do those in the higher tracks or groups; and once a student is placed in a lower track, it is very difficult for the student to move up. Tracking also may contribute to the polarization of the student body into different subcultures that feel hostile toward each other. Even in the case of gifted adolescents or adolescents with learning disabilities, educators generally recommend mixing students of different ability levels instead of separating them.

School Desegregation

Since the landmark U.S. Supreme Court rulings in *Brown v. Board of Education of Topeka* (1954, 1955), many of the nation's school districts have enacted changes aimed at desegregating their schools. Underlying the Court's rulings was the belief that segregation in schools impedes the academic and economic progress of students from racial minorities and, in addition, fosters hostility and misunderstanding between individuals of different backgrounds. Even if racially segregated schools appear equivalent on various indices of quality (for example, the amount of money spent on educational materials and programs), segregated schools are "inherently unequal," the Court argued, because "to separate [African-American youngsters] from others solely because of their race generates a feeling of inferiority as to their status in the community that may affect their hearts and minds in a way unlikely ever to be undone" (*Brown v. Board of Education of Topeka,* 1954). Since the Court's rulings, many school districts have adopted measures designed to create voluntary desegregation (for example, permitting families to choose among different schools within a large catchment area rather than assigning students to specific schools on the basis of their residence). Others have enacted policies aimed at mandatory desegregation (assigning students of different racial backgrounds to specific schools in order to create predetermined racial balances) (Bradley and Bradley, 1977).

Despite the clear legal basis for desegregation, research into the effects of desegregation programs on high school students has not been overwhelmingly encouraging. Several sets of studies point to this disappointing conclusion. First, research indicates that desegregation has surprisingly little impact on the achievement levels of either minority or white youngsters (Entwisle, 1990). Second, there is some evidence that minority youngsters' self-esteem is higher when they attend schools in which they are in the majority—a phenomenon true not only for African-American youth but for all youth (Rosenberg, 1975). Third, as we saw in Chapter 5, interracial contact, even in desegregated schools, is rare, largely because of the reluctance on the part of white students to form cross-racial friendships (Hallinan and Teixeira, 1987). Fourth, studies indicate that immediately following the imposition of a desegregation program, white enrollment in a school declines as white families move or withdraw their children from the public school (although the high rate of "white flight" appears to be most pronounced during the first year of a desegregation program and slows shortly thereafter) (Wilson, 1985).

As sociologist Jomills Braddock (1985) points out, however, focusing on the short-term impact of desegregation may provide only a very narrow means of assessing its costs and benefits. He notes that African-Americans who have attended desegregated high schools—

especially boys—are more likely to graduate and to continue their education in desegregated institutions. Because African-Americans graduating from predominantly white colleges earn more when they enter the labor force than those who attend predominantly minority colleges, it seems that youngsters who attend desegregated high schools may reap advantages in the labor force later on, as young adults. Moreover, African-American graduates of predominantly white schools are more likely to work in integrated environments and to live in integrated neighborhoods during adulthood. Taken together, these studies suggest that desegregated high school programs do benefit minority youth but that the benefits may not be apparent until adulthood. Furthermore, these studies suggest that desegregation during high school does appear to help break down racial barriers in society at large.

It also may not be advisable to make generalizations about the impact of school desegre-

Research on the presumed positive effects of school desegregation has not been encouraging. One reason is that many desegregated schools are integrated in theory but not in practice. In many so-called integrated schools, segregation continues through tracking and other structural arrangements. (Peter Southwick/Stock, Boston)

gation without looking further at the processes inside the school and how they are affected (or not affected) by its racial composition. De facto segregation may be maintained even in "desegregated" schools through tracking, seating assignments, ability grouping within classrooms, and class scheduling (Entwisle, 1990). To assess the situation, one would need information about how the school's policies and procedures were changed and about how students, teachers, and administrators responded to the changes. Not all desegregated schools are the same (Campbell, 1977). Consider, for example, the differences between two desegregated schools. Each has achieved racial balance. But in one school, minority and white students are taught in different classes; in the other, the classes are all integrated. Obviously, it makes little sense to view these schools as having similar environments merely because they are both classified as "desegregated."

Finally, not all children and families respond in the same way to changes in the racial composition of their school. Some parents and students are enthusiastic about such changes, whereas others are apprehensive. Thus in any comprehensive study of the effects of school desegregation, it would be important to know how children of different ages are affected, how children from different racial and socioeconomic backgrounds are affected, how parents' attitudes toward desegregation affect the child's reaction, and so forth. These and other factors are likely to mediate the impact of desegregation on the adolescent (St. John, 1975).

Although social scientists disagree over their interpretation, studies show that adolescents attending parochial schools generally achieve at a higher level than those attending public schools. (Mimi Forsyth/Monkmeyer)

● Public Schools versus Private Schools

While the vast majority of students attending secondary school in America are enrolled in public schools, a substantial minority attend private schools, either parochial (i.e., with a religious affiliation) or "independent." In the past, researchers cared little about studying differences between private and public schools. But during the late 1980s, many education policy-makers suggested that one way to improve schools would be to give parents more of a choice in determining where their child was enrolled, in order to force schools to compete with each other for the best students. One concrete suggestion was that states should provide parents with vouchers that could be used to "purchase" education at the school of their choice—private or public. In light of these suggestions, researchers became interested in studying whether some types of schools produced more high-achieving students than others.

Initial investigations of this by sociologist James Coleman and his colleagues (e.g., Coleman, Hoffer, and Kilgore, 1982; Coleman and Hoffer, 1987) pointed to clear advantages for students attending private high schools, and especially for those attending Catholic schools. The studies found that students from private schools achieved more, even after taking into account preexisting differences between public and private students that could explain their achievement differences. (For example, we know that IQ scores are positively correlated with social class and that wealthier families can better afford private school; and even within social classes, parents may be more likely to invest money in the education of more capable students.) The better achievement of students in private schools was especially clear in comparisons of juniors and seniors (Entwisle, 1990).

Social scientists disagree about the interpretation of this finding. According to Coleman, the chief reason for the advantages enjoyed by Catholic school students has to do with the close links between their schools and families. He has argued that a Catholic school is a part of a **functional community**—a community in which parents, teachers, and students all share similar values and attitudes. Students profit from this because the lessons taught in Catholic school are reinforced at home, at church, and in the neighborhood. In addition, private schools are typically more orderly and more disciplined, and they assign more homework as well (Coleman et al., 1982). Other researchers, however, have suggested that the curricula and tracking practices of private and public schools are very different (e.g., Lee and Bryk, 1988). Students at Catholic schools, for example, take more academic courses in school and are less likely to be tracked into general or vocational classes, even if their prior records are not strong. Given what we examined in the preceding section about the negative effects of being placed in lower tracks, it makes sense that schools that have less tracking will have overall higher levels of achievement.

THE IMPORTANCE OF SCHOOL CLIMATE

Thus far we have seen that certain elements of the school's social organization—size, age grouping, tracking, and so forth—can affect students' behavior and achievement. But these factors are important mainly because they influence what takes place in classrooms and in other school settings. Indeed, most social scientists and educators now agree that the school-related factors which are most important in influencing learning and psychosocial development during adolescence concern the more immediate environment of the school and classroom. As noted earlier, in good schools the classroom environments encourage dialogue between teachers and students and among students, and learning is emphasized over memorization. According to Michael Rutter (1983), various aspects of the **school climate** have important effects on youngsters' learning and achievement. Specifically, the way teachers interact with students, the way classroom time is used, and the sorts of standards and expectations that teachers hold for their students are all more important than the size of the school, the way that age groups are combined, or the racial composition of the school. One reason that tracking makes a difference, for example, is that it affects the school climate.

What sort of climate brings out the best in students? Considered together, the results of several studies indicate that the same factors which promote psychosocial development in the home—warmth, high standards, and moderate control—also promote positive behavior in the classroom. Students and teachers are more satisfied in innovative than in control-oriented classes and in classes that combine a moderate degree of structure with high student involvement and high teacher support. In these classes, teachers encourage their students' participation but do not let the class get out of control. Classes that are too task oriented—particularly when they also emphasize teacher control—tend to make students feel anxious, uninterested, and unhappy (Moos, 1978). The pattern of classroom variables that is associated with positive student behavior and attitudes, then, is reminiscent of the *authoritative* family environment (see Chapter 4). Similarly, an overemphasis on control in the classroom in the absence of support is reminiscent of the *authoritarian* family, while a lack of clarity and organization is reminiscent of both the *indulgent* family and the *indifferent* family—and these styles may affect adolescents detrimentally. Students do best when their teachers spend a high proportion of time on lessons (rather than on setting up equipment or dealing with discipline problems) and when teachers begin and end lessons on time, provide clear feedback to students about what is expected of them and about their performance, and give ample praise to students when they perform well (Rutter, 1983). A good high school teacher, in other words, bears a striking resemblance to a good parent.

This general pattern of findings has been replicated in several other studies. In an extensive program of research on young adolescents in London schools, for example, Michael Rutter and his colleagues (Rutter, Maugham, Mortimore, and Ouston, 1979) found that after controlling for differences in students' backgrounds and in their abilities before entering secondary school, school climate was significantly associated with students' performance, attendance, and delinquency. Generally speaking, schools in which teachers were supportive but firm and maintained high, well-defined standards for behavior and academic work had fewer problems, higher rates of attendance, lower rates of delinquency, and higher scores on tests of achievement. This pattern is remarkably similar to that uncovered in studies comparing public and private high schools (Coleman, Hoffer, and Kilgore, 1982). In these studies, too, students' achievement was higher in schools that were somewhat more structured and demanding—no matter whether the school was public or private.

As Rutter (1983) explains, being an effective teacher entails two distinct processes: gaining and maintaining students' attention and instructing students in the subject matter. A teacher who is a good lecturer will not be an effective teacher if he or she lacks classroom management skills. Managing a classroom effectively entails more than merely knowing how to discipline students once they become unruly, however. In fact, teachers who spend too much time on disciplining the few students who misbehave run the risk of losing the interest of the rest of the class. Especially in junior high school classrooms, where young adolescents may not yet have developed a high level of self-control in the absence of guidelines from adults, maintaining students' attention depends on having well-organized lesson plans, teaching in a way that involves and engages the whole class, and using creative and innovative approaches to instruction. As most experienced teachers know, disorganized lesson plans and frequent interruptions for discipline can quickly lead to chaos in the classroom. The National Commission on Excellence in Education (1983), for example, recommended that schools adopt and enforce firm disciplinary codes and that continually disruptive students be removed from classrooms in order to permit teachers to spend more time on teaching and less on discipline.

Recently, education researcher Fred Newmann (1992) has suggested that if we want to understand the impact of classroom climate on student achievement, we need to better understand how to enhance student **engagement,** or the extent to which students are psychologically committed to learning and mastering the material rather than simply completing the assigned work. Newmann believes that the make-work, routinized, rigid structure of most classrooms, in which teachers lecture at students rather than engaging them in discussion, alienates most students from school and undermines their desire to achieve. As one student explains:

> What do I like least about school? Basically, it's boring. Like English. What we do in there—we're supposed to read something, and then maybe do something in your notebook, when you could do everything at home. So I don't really have to show up. So, I'd say that class could be about 10 minutes long. (Cited in Brown, Lamborn, and Newmann, 1992)

Think back to your own high school experience. What distinguished the good classes from the tedious ones? Newmann (1992) suggests a number of factors that contribute to engagement. First, teachers need to provide opportunities for students to genuinely display their competencies. Second, schools should try to facilitate students' feelings of belonging to their school. Finally, and most important, teachers should assign work that is "authentic"—work that is interesting, fun, and relevant to the real world. There is nothing more alienating to a student than being asked to perform tasks that are boring, colorless, and irrelevant.

Several studies also point to the importance of teachers' expectations of students. When teachers expect more of their students, the students actually learn more; when teachers expect less, they learn less. This phenomenon is known as the **self-fulfilling prophecy** (Rosenthal and Jacobson, 1968) (see the accompanying box). Unfortunately, research suggests that teachers are likely to base their expectations in part on students' ethnic and socioeconomic background. In much the same way that these factors may influence tracking decisions, as we saw earlier, they may consciously and unconsciously shape teachers' expectations, which, in turn, affect students' learning. Thus, for example, teachers may call on poor or minority students less often than they call on affluent or white students—conveying a not-so-subtle message about whose responses the teacher believes are more worthy of class attention (Good and Brophy, 1984). It is not difficult to see how years of exposure to this sort of treatment can adversely affect a student's self-concept and interest in school. Indeed, teachers' biases against lower-class children may make it difficult for students from lower socioeconomic groups to attain a level of academic accomplishment that would permit upward mobility.

RECAP

Researchers agree that the climate of the school is more important than its organization or structure. Effective teachers are similar to effective parents: warm, firm, and fair. Students are also more likely to be engaged in school when they have opportunities for developing their competencies, feel attached to the school as an institution, and are engaged in authentic work, rather than make-work.

Teachers and school personnel, of course, are not the only influences on adolescents' behavior in school. Several writers have noted that the peer group's values and norms also

THE SCIENTIFIC STUDY OF ADOLESCENCE

TEACHER EXPECTATIONS AND STUDENT PERFORMANCE

Although researchers have documented a link between teachers' expectations for their students and their students' performance, it is not clear whether this connection exists because teacher expectations create self-fulfilling prophecies that ultimately influence student achievement or, instead, because teachers' expectations are genuinely accurate reflections of students' ability. One recent study of nearly two thousand early adolescents in Michigan attempted to disentangle these two explanations.

Psychologists Lee Jussim and Jacquelynne Eccles gathered information from teachers and students at several points in time in order to look at the over-time relation between teacher expectations and student performance. A *longitudinal* design, in which the same students were followed over time, was necessary for this research because a *cross-sectional* study, in which one might examine the correlation at one point in time between teacher expectations and student performance, would not reveal which came first (that is, whether expectations preceded performance or performance preceded expectations). Because the researchers had information about student achievement both before and after the assessment of teacher expectations, they were able to look at both possible pathways.

Data about student achievement were gathered at the end of fifth grade and right at the beginning of sixth grade and, again, at the end of sixth grade and the beginning of seventh grade. Data about teacher expectations were gathered during October of the students' sixth grade. If teachers' expectations are accurate, the researchers argued, there should be a correlation between student achievement before sixth grade and teacher expectations in October. If teachers' expectations really influence students' achievement, the researchers reasoned, the October expectations should predict student performance later in the year, even after taking into account student performance *before* teacher expectations were measured.

The researchers found support for both possibilities. The teachers' expectations were accurate, in that student achievement in the fifth grade predicted both teacher expectations in the sixth grade and student achievement in the sixth grade. Yet, these very expectations in turn further influenced student performance, because teacher expectations in October predicted whether and how much student achievement changed over the course of the year. Which pathway was more powerful? Based on the size of the various correlations they computed, the researchers concluded that about 80 percent of the connection between teacher expectations and student achievement results from teachers' having accurate perceptions, whereas about 20 percent is an effect of the self-fulfilling prophecy.

Even though the self-fulfilling-prophecy effect was relatively small, it may be quite powerful, as the researchers point out, when accumulated over years of schooling. If teachers' expectations are unfairly based on characteristics such as students' gender, ethnicity, or socioeconomic background, the over-time effect of having teachers with low expectations may be quite substantial.

SOURCE: Jussim, L., and Eccles, J. (1992). Teacher expectations II: Construction and reflection of student achievement. *Journal of Personality and Social Psychology*, *63*, 947–961.

exert an important influence. In *The Adolescent Society* (1961), for example, James Coleman found that high schools vary a great deal in the extent to which the prevailing peer culture emphasizes academic success as a route toward status and popularity. In schools in which academic success is not valued by the student body, students are less likely to achieve grades that are consonant with their tested ability. In other words, a bright student who attends a school in which getting good grades is frowned upon by other students will actually get lower grades than he or she would in a school in which scholastic success is generally admired.

As we noted in Chapter 5, however, cliques and crowds differ enormously in the extent to which they encourage or discourage academic success (Clasen and Brown, 1985). It therefore is misleading to generalize about the impact of peer groups on adolescents' engagement in school without knowing more about the specific peer group in question. Some peer groups (e.g., the "brains") may place a great deal of pressure on their members to succeed in school and may engage in behaviors (e.g., studying together) that promote academic success. Other groups, in contrast, may actively discourage scholastic efforts and success. An especially telling example of this is seen in a recent ethnographic study of African-American male peer groups in an inner-city school (Fordham and Ogbu, 1986). In the peer groups studied, pressure was put on the group members *not* to achieve, because succeeding in school was seen as "acting white" and breaking from the group's ethnic identity. Thus those students with high aspirations found themselves having to choose between succeeding in school and keeping their friends, a position that few adolescents of any race or ethnicity would want to find themselves in.

Other researchers have focused on adolescents' experiences outside of school—at home, at work, and in extracurricular activities—and on the impact of those experiences on their school achievement and engagement. This research demonstrates that the impact of school on adolescent achievement cannot be understood in isolation. Studies show, for example, that students whose parents are involved in school activities (such as parent-teacher conferences and "back-to-school" nights), who encourage and emphasize academic success, and who use authoritative parenting practices (see Chapter 4) do better in secondary school than their peers (Dornbusch, Ritter, Liederman, Roberts, and Fraleigh, 1987; Seginer, 1983; Steinberg, Lamborn, Dornbusch, and Darling, 1992; Stevenson and Baker, 1987). In Chapter 7, we shall look more closely at the effects of employment and extracurricular participation on school achievement; suffice it to say here that students who overextend themselves on the job or the playing field may inadvertently jeopardize their school performance (Brown, Lamborn, and Newmann, 1992; Steinberg and Dornbusch, 1991).

BEYOND HIGH SCHOOL

The College Bound

The early part of the twentieth century was an important time in the development not only of secondary schools but also of postsecondary educational institutions in the United States. Although colleges and, to a lesser extent, universities had existed for some time previously, not until the latter part of the nineteenth century did diversity in institutions of higher education begin to develop. Early postsecondary institutions were typically small, private liberal arts academies, often with a strong theological emphasis. But during a relatively brief period bridging the nineteenth and twentieth centuries, these colleges were joined by a host of other types of institutions, including large private universities, technical colleges, professional schools, publicly financed state universities, land-grant colleges, urban universities, and two-year community colleges (Brubacher and Rudy, 1976).

Although postsecondary educational institutions multiplied and became more varied during the early part of this century, enrollment in college was still a privilege enjoyed by very few young people. In 1900, only 4 percent of the 18- to 21-year-old population was enrolled in college; and by 1930, the proportion had grown only to 12 percent. Even as recently as 1950, fewer than 1 in 5 young people were enrolled in college (Church, 1976). During the first half of the twentieth century, then, colleges and universities were not prominent in the lives of most American youth.

How different the state of affairs is today! Paralleling the rise of secondary education between 1920 and 1940, postsecondary education grew dramatically between 1950 and 1970 (see Figure 6.3). By 1960, one-third of all young people were entering college directly after high school graduation. College enrollments, which numbered about 1 million in 1930, had risen to more than 3 million by 1960 and to nearly 8.5 million by 1970. Today, nearly half of the 18- to 19-year-old population, and well over half of the high school graduates of this age group, are enrolled in college (U.S. Bureau of the Census, 1993). Although there were large increases in the enrollment of minority youth during the 1970s, the proportion of minority youth enrolled in higher education fell during the early 1980s (Wetzel, 1987). The proportion of African-American high school graduates enrolled in college has increased in recent years, but the proportion of Hispanic-American high school graduates in college has continued to decline (U.S. Bureau of the Census, 1993).

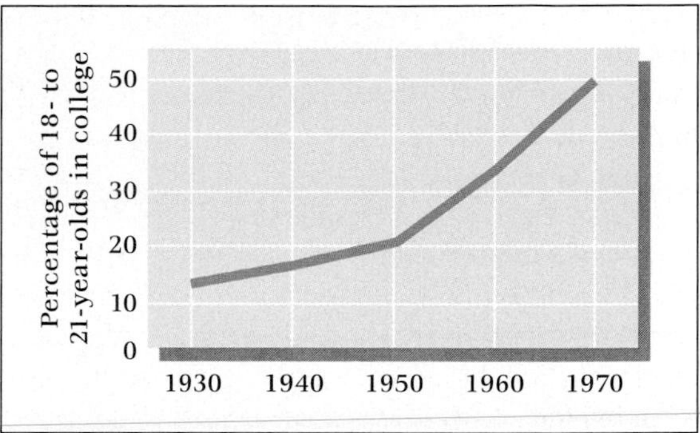

FIGURE 6.3 *Between 1950 and 1970, U.S. college enrollments expanded markedly. They have remained reasonably stable since then.*

If there are two dominant characteristics that distinguish the development of postsecondary education in contemporary America from that in other parts of the world, they are diversity and accessibility (Brubacher and Rudy, 1976). In countries other than the United States, postsecondary education is likely to be monopolized by monolithic public universities, and fewer adolescents continue their formal education beyond high school (President's Science Advisory Committee, 1974). Individuals are often separated into college- and noncollege-bound tracks early in adolescence, typically on the basis of standardized national examinations. In fact, rather than housing all high school students in comprehensive high schools such as those found in the United States, many European nations separate students during early adolescence into schools for college-bound youngsters and schools designed to provide vocational and technical education.

Although the accessibility and diversity of its postsecondary educational institutions have been commended by many, the American system of higher education has not been

Well over half of today's high school graduates enter college. These individuals are touring the University of Virginia. (Bohdan Hrynewych/Stock, Boston)

without its critics (Brubacher and Rudy, 1976). Some observers have suggested that educational diversity has been gained at the expense of quality. With so many different options and electives for young people to choose among, it has been hard for colleges to ensure that all students receive a high-quality education. Others have pointed out that it is difficult for many young people to obtain adequate information about the range of alternatives open to them and that students are often poorly matched with the colleges they enter (Boyer, 1986). The large enrollments of high schools make it difficult for school counselors to give each student individualized advice.

In some respects, the transition from high school to college parallels the transition from elementary to secondary school. For many students, going to college means entering an even-larger, more formidable, and more impersonal environment. For some, the transition may coincide with other life changes, such as leaving home, breaking off or beginning an important relationship, or having to manage one's own residence or finances for the first time.

As a consequence of all of these factors, although many more young people enroll in college today than in previous years, a very large number do not graduate. Perhaps as a consequence of increasing accessibility, poor matching, and a lack of "consumer" knowledge among college applicants, rates of college attrition are high: Only 4 of every 10 students who enter college in the United States graduate from the same college four years later. Of the 60 percent of students who leave the school they entered, about half eventually finish college, either returning to that particular college or transferring to another. Half, however, never obtain a college degree. Of the students who drop out of college, about half do so during their first year (Pantages and Creedon, 1978). In other words, although a great deal has been done to make college entrance more likely, rates of college graduation lag far behind.

The "Forgotten Half"

The problems associated with moving from high school to college pale in comparison, however, with the problems associated with not going to college at all. In general, college graduates earn substantially more income over their lifetime than do individuals who attend college but do not graduate, and these individuals in turn earn much more than students who do not attend college at all (William T. Grant Foundation Commission on Work, Family, and Citizenship, 1988). Individuals who drop out of high school before graduation suffer a wide range of problems, which we examine in detail in Chapter 13.

One of the unfortunate by-products of our having made postsecondary education so accessible—and so expected—is that we have turned our backs on individuals who do not go to college, even though they compose about half of the adolescent population—approximately 20 million individuals (William T. Grant Foundation Commission on Work, Family, and Citizenship, 1988). This so-called **Forgotten Half** was the subject of a lengthy and detailed study conducted in the late 1980s by a prestigious national commission.

The report concluded that our secondary schools are geared almost exclusively toward college-bound youngsters. We noted earlier that opportunities for learning and for higher-order thinking are much greater in college-prep classes than in the general or vocational tracks. In addition to this, the commission noted that students who are not headed for college—some by choice, others by unavoidable circumstance—find that their high schools have not prepared them at all for the world of work. Even those who complete school and earn a diploma—who have done what they were "supposed" to do as adolescents—may have a hard time finding employment and a nearly impossible time finding a satisfying, well-paying job. As a consequence, many individuals who make up the Forgotten Half spend their early adult years floundering between periods of part-time work, underemployment (working at a job that is less challenging than one would like), and unemployment. By the time they are 25 or so, most have found steady, if low-paying, employment. But they may have spent six or seven years living very close to the edge, if not in genuine poverty.

Noncollege graduates have always fared worse economically than their peers who have continued their education past high school. But the gap between the "haves" and the "have-nots" widened considerably during the 1980s. For instance, in the United States, the "real" annual earnings (that is, earnings adjusted for changes in the cost of living) of young adult men fell between 1973 and 1986. But whereas the drop in income was about 6 percent for college graduates during this time period, the drop for high school graduates was more than 28 percent; and for high school dropouts, income fell 42 percent. In other words, the typical high school graduate without college experience must survive on one-third less income today than his counterpart in the early 1970s (William T. Grant Foundation Commission on Work, Family, and Citizenship, 1988).

One important contributing factor to the declining fortunes of the Forgotten Half has been the change in the world of work mentioned earlier in this chapter: As manufacturing jobs began to be replaced by minimum-wage service jobs, the chances of making a decent living without college experience worsened appreciably. Today, young adults without college experience often must try to make ends meet on minimum-wage jobs—jobs that offer little in the way of promotion or advancement. The economic problems faced by noncollege-bound youth have been compounded by the escalating costs of such essentials as housing and health care.

Given the high dropout rate already characteristic of most colleges, the answer to the problems of the Forgotten Half does not seem to be simply to encourage more individuals to continue their education past high school. Obviously, for those who want post-secondary education, we should make every attempt to see that they can obtain and afford it. But what about those adolescents who just are not interested in a college degree? How can these individuals be helped?

Experts believe that one potential answer involves strengthening the links between the worlds of school and work during high school, as we discussed in Chapter 3. In most other industrialized countries, noncollege-bound youth begin apprenticeships during their last two years of compulsory school, so that by the time they have completed their formal schooling, they are well trained to take on skilled jobs (Hamilton, 1990). Instead of just "dumping" such adolescents into the labor force at graduation, as we do in America, schools and communities provide training, career counseling, and job placement services throughout high school. In most contemporary American high schools, counseling is geared toward helping college-bound students continue their education. Some critics have suggested that we should spend just as much time helping the other 50 percent of adolescents make their transition into adulthood as smooth as possible.

RECAP

About half of all American adolescents go on to some form of education beyond high school, but only two-thirds of these students eventually receive a degree. Many students drop out after their first year of postsecondary education, probably because of mismatch between their needs and the school environment. More worrisome, perhaps, is the experience of adolescents who are not interested in attending college. Many social critics believe that high schools as they are presently structured do not serve noncollege-bound adolescents very well. As a result, half of the country's adolescents—the so-called Forgotten Half—leave high school without adequate preparation for the world of work they hope to enter.

SCHOOLS AND ADOLESCENT DEVELOPMENT

Whatever the shortcomings of schools may be, staying in school is preferable to dropping out, not only in terms of earnings but in terms of cognitive development as well. One study contrasted the performance of dropouts and graduates on a battery of standardized tests of achievement administered during late adolescence (Alexander, Natriello, and Pallas, 1985). The study took into account differences in achievement levels that existed before the dropouts had left school (two years before the assessment was conducted), because dropouts are more likely than graduates to show achievement problems early in their education. Compared with the dropouts, adolescents who stayed in school gained far more intellectually over the two-year interval in a variety of content areas. More important, the results showed that the adverse effects of dropping out were most intense among socioeconomically disadvantaged students. Paradoxically, then, those students who are most likely to leave school prior to graduation may be most harmed by doing so.

One other way of assessing the contribution of schools to adolescents' intellectual development is by comparing early adolescents' intellectual gains during the school year with their gains during the summer. An ingenious study by Heyns (1982) did just this. Using information about the academic progress of students measured at three points in time—the beginning of the school year, the end of the school year, and the beginning of the next year—she was able to see how the academic progress of students during the summer compared with their academic progress during the school session. Her results were surprising and point once again to the importance of school for minority and disadvantaged youth. Among white students, rates of academic progress during the school year and during the summer were comparable. Among African-American students, however, the pattern was different. Although rates of progress during the school year were more or less equal to those of white students, during the summer months African-American students' scores actually declined. In other words, if it were not for the effects of school on cognitive development, the discrepancy between white and African-American youngsters' achievement scores would be much greater than it currently is.

Far less is known about the impact of schools on the psychosocial development of adolescents. Some observers have noted that most schools are not structured to promote psychosocial development, with their excessive focus on conformity and obedience and their lack of encouragement for creativity, independence, and self-reliance (Friedenberg, 1967). But there are very many good schools in which students not only learn the academic material taught in classes but also learn about themselves, their relationships with others, and their society. Schools differ from each other, and it may be difficult to generalize about the impact of schools on adolescent development without knowing more about the particular school in question.

It is also important to recognize that, despite adults' intentions and objectives, students do not view school solely in terms of its academic agenda. In one study, the researchers asked a sample of seventh- through twelfth-graders to list the best and worst things about school. The best things? "Being with my friends" and "Meeting new people." The worst? Homework, tests, and the restrictive atmosphere of the school (Brown, Lamborn, and Newmann, 1992). Adults may evaluate schools in terms of their contribution to adolescents' cognitive and career development, but for the typical adolescent school is the main setting for socializing. When we ask about the consequences of leaving school early, we must take into account the impact this would have on the individual's social, as well as cognitive, development.

Studies also show that students' experiences within a school can vary widely according to the track they are in, the peer group they belong to, and the extracurricular activities in which they participate. It seems safe to say that academically talented and economically advantaged students have a more positive experience in school than their less capable or less affluent counterparts do—positive not only with respect to what they learn in class but also with respect to the impact of school on their feelings about themselves as individuals. Their teachers pay more attention to them, they are more likely to hold positions of leadership in extracurricular organizations, and they are more likely to experience classes that are engaging and challenging. In other words, the structure of a school—its size, its tracking policy, its curricula—provides different intellectual and psychosocial opportunities for students who occupy different places within that structure. Not surprisingly, a recent study of Swedish adolescents found a great deal of variability in students' feelings about school: About 25 percent enjoyed school a great deal, about 25 percent detested school (and felt that their friends in school were their only salvation), and the remainder felt ambivalent (Andersson, 1994). The best answer to the question "How do schools affect adolescent development?" then, is another question: "Which schools, which adolescents, and in what respects?"

RECAP

It is difficult to generalize about the role of schools in adolescent development, since different students may have markedly different experiences within the same school. Research indicates, above all, that academically and economically advantaged adolescents have a more positive experience in school than do their less capable or less affluent counterparts. One worrisome theme that has emerged from studies of high schools is that schools, as they are presently structured, seem to work best for those students who need the least help.

KEY TERMS

comprehensive high school
engagement
Forgotten Half
functional community
gifted students
higher-order thinking
junior high school
learning disability
mainstreaming
middle school
school climate
self-fulfilling prophecy
tracking

FOR FURTHER READING

Church, R. (1976). *Education in the United States.* New York: Free Press. A comprehensive history of the development of schools in America.

Entwisle, D. (1990). Schools and the adolescent. Pp. 197–224 in S. Feldman and G. Elliott (Eds.), *At the threshold: The developing adolescent.* Cambridge, Mass.: Harvard University Press. A review of research on schools and adolescent development.

Lee, V., Marks, H., and Byrd, T. (1994). Sexism in single-sex and coeducational independent secondary school classrooms. *Sociology of Education, 67,* 92–120. A study of the subtle and not-so-subtle ways that sexism creeps into classrooms.

Newmann, F. (Ed.). (1992). *Student engagement and achievement in American high schools.* New York: Teachers College Press. A collection of articles on the factors that influence students' interest and performance in high school.

Stevenson, H., and Stigler, J. (1992). *The learning gap: Why our schools are failing and* *what we can learn from Japanese and Chinese education.* New York: Simon & Schuster. A highly readable report of a cross-cultural study of achievement and education in the United States, Japan, and China.

William T. Grant Foundation Commission on Work, Family, and Citizenship. (1988). *The forgotten half: Non-college youth in America.* Washington, D.C.: William T. Grant Foundation Commission on Work, Family, and Citizenship. A discussion of the special problems of noncollege-bound youth.

CHAPTER 7

WORK AND LEISURE

(Rashid/Monkmeyer)

Most discussions of the contexts of adolescence are limited to those that we have looked at in the past three chapters: the peer group, the family, and the school. There is no question that these settings exert a profound influence on the development and behavior of the young person. Yet it may surprise you to learn that today's teenagers spend more time in leisure activities than they do in the "productive" activities of school, more time alone than with members of their family, about four times the number of hours each week on a part-time job as on homework, and considerably more time "wired" to music, videotapes, or television than "tuned into" the classroom (Carnegie Council on Adolescent Development, 1992; Csikszentmihalyi and Larson, 1984). In this chapter, we look at these other important contexts of adolescence—the contexts of work and leisure.

Social scientists are just now beginning to study the ways in which work and leisure influence adolescent development (Fine, Mortimer, and Roberts, 1990). Perhaps because we historically have considered school to be the most important activity of adolescence in contemporary society, we have paid far less attention to what adolescents do in their "spare" time—even though their spare time occupies more of their waking hours than does their time in school. As you know, however, one of the hallmarks of life in industrialized society is that adolescents have considerable amounts of time and money to devote to activities of their choosing. Among the most popular are working at a part-time job, participating in an after-school extracurricular activity, shopping and hanging out with friends, and enjoying one or more of the mass media, including television, videotapes, radio, recorded music, and movies.

Just as adolescents are affected by the family, friends, and school, they are also influenced by work and leisure.

WORK AND LEISURE IN CONTEMPORARY SOCIETY

The tremendous significance of discretionary, or free, time in the lives of contemporary adolescents has had several origins. Ironically, one of the most important contributors was the development of compulsory schooling. Prior to this, adolescents were expected to work full time, and most maintained schedules comparable to adults, working long hours each week. With the spread of high schools during the early decades of this century, however, adolescents were in effect barred from the labor force; the part-time jobs familiar to us today simply did not exist in large numbers, making after-school employment relatively rare. One indirect effect of compulsory high school, then, was to increase the amount of free time available to the young person—time that previously would have been occupied by work. Indeed, adults were so worried about the free time available to adolescents that they began to organize various youth clubs and activities—such as the Boy Scouts or organized sports, for example—in order to occupy their "idle hands" (Modell and Goodman, 1990). In some respects, organized leisure became an institutionalized part of adolescence as a supplement to school and a replacement for full-time employment.

A second influence on the rise of free time for adolescents in contemporary society was the increased affluence of Americans following the World War II. As we noted in Chapter 3, the invention of the "teenager"—and, more important, the discovery of the teenager by those in advertising and marketing—changed the nature of adolescence in modern society. As adolescents gained more autonomy, they came to be recognized as consumers with plenty of discretionary income, an image that persists today. This week, notice the commercials and advertisements aimed at teenagers in popular television shows, teen magazines, or on rock stations. You'll see that much of the advertising aimed at young people concerns leisure expenditures: music, movies, eating out, athletic equipment, and even, unfortunately, cigarettes and alcohol. The cultivation of adolescents as consumers has played an important role both in shaping their leisure tastes and in drawing them into the part-time labor force. As we shall see later in this chapter, today's adolescent cannot afford such "necessities" as a personal stereo, designer clothes, or inflatable sneakers without taking on an after-school job.

How much time do adolescents spend in various leisure activities? According to one study, in which adolescents were asked to monitor their time use with electronic pagers, the typical American adolescent spends about 29 percent of his or her waking hours in "productive" activities, such as attending class or studying; about 31 percent in "maintenance" activities, such as grooming, eating, or running errands; and about 40 percent in "leisure" activities, such as socializing, watching TV, or playing sports (Csikszentmihalyi and Larson, 1984) (see Figure 7.1). As you can see, younger adolescents spend relatively more time in productive activities and relatively less time in maintenance activities; they spend about the same amount of time in discretionary activities (Timmer, Eccles, and O'Brien, 1985). There are some important dif-

FIGURE 7.1 *How younger and older adolescents spend their time. What similarities and differences do you see in the patterns?* (SOURCES: Younger adolescents: Timmer, Eccles, and O'Brien, 1985; Older adolescents: Csikszentmihalyi and Larson, 1984)

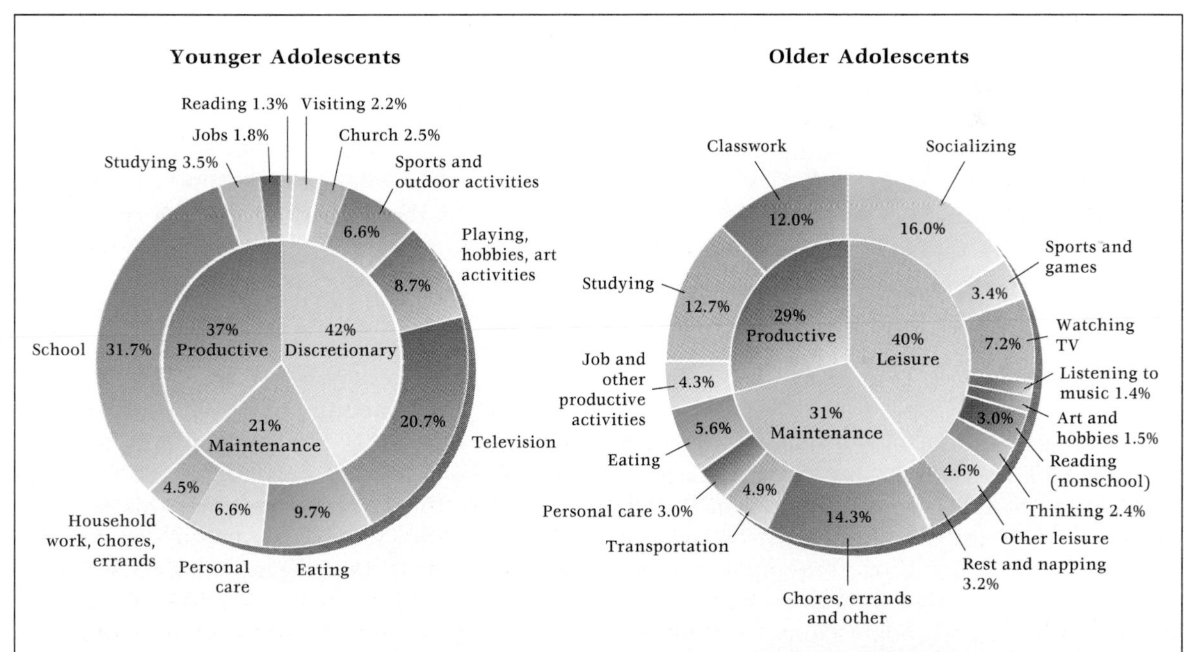

ferences in time use between younger and older adolescents, however. Younger adolescents spend far more time on television and far less time socializing. Interestingly, American adolescents spend far more time on leisure, and far less time on schoolwork, than do their counterparts in other countries. For instance, the average American high school student spends fewer than five hours per week on homework; in Japan, the average is close to five hours per day (Greenberger and Steinberg, 1986). And whereas most Chinese and Japanese students are assigned homework over summer vacation, almost no American students are (Stevenson and Stigler, 1992).

What is the effect of all this "free" time on adolescents' behavior and development? Are they learning about the "real world" from their part-time jobs? Are their extracurricular activities as "character-building" as adults believe they are? Are they being driven toward sex and violence by the mass media? Are teenagers really affected by the lyrics of rock music, the images of MTV, or the violence of many video games? These are some of the questions we examine in this chapter. We begin with one of the most controversial issues in the study of contemporary adolescents: how teenagers are affected by after-school employment.

RECAP

The rise of compulsory schooling and the affluence of the adolescent population have contributed to the increased importance both of part-time employment and of leisure activities in the lives of contemporary adolescents. Having large amounts of free time is one hallmark of adolescence in modern society.

ADOLESCENTS AND WORK

The participation of adolescents in the world of work has gone through a number of dramatic changes during the past 100 years. Today, it is commonplace to see teenagers working in restaurants and retail stores. Indeed, most youngsters who were enrolled in high school during the 1990s held part-time jobs at one time or another during the school year. More than 75 percent of today's high school students will have worked before graduating (Steinberg and Cauffman, 1995). But although working while attending high school may currently be the norm, only recently has part-time employment become prevalent among American adolescents. In fact, the widespread employment of students represents an important break from past eras, in which going to school and working were mutually exclusive activities. In order to understand how and why the state of affairs has changed, we need to begin with a look at school and work early in this century.

● School and Work in the Early Twentieth Century

Before 1925—when continuing on in high school was the exception, not the rule—most teenagers entered the workforce by the time they turned 15 years old. Teenagers from all but the most affluent families left school between the ages of 12 and 15 and became full-time workers (Horan and Hargis, 1991; Modell, Furstenberg, and Hershberg, 1976). Adolescents were either students or workers, but not both.

During the second quarter of this century, however, the school began to replace the workplace as the setting in which most adolescents spent their weekdays. As secondary education grew and became more widespread among different social and economic seg-

In previous eras, adolescents played an important role in farming. Early work experience of this sort readied young people for the work they would perform during adulthood. (Bettmann)

ments of American society, more youngsters remained in school well into middle and late adolescence, and fewer elected to work. Compulsory education laws were passed in most states that required youngsters to remain in school until at least the age of 16, and part-time jobs were not plentiful. Furthermore, a variety of child labor laws were enacted to restrict youngsters' employment (Kett, 1977).

As a result of these social and legislative changes, the employment of American teenagers in the formal labor force declined steadily during the first four decades of this century. As labor force expert Beatrice Reubens points out:

> It is true that a tradition has long existed in the United States that it was respectable, even praiseworthy to work one's way through school, but [before 1940] the numbers [of students who worked] were not large. Prior to World War II, attending school and holding a . . . job were

almost exclusive activities. (Reubens, Harrison, and Rupp, 1981, p. 296)

An incredible reversal has taken place in a period of about twenty-five years. Early in the century, most adolescents were workers, not students. By the middle of the century, most adolescents had become students, not workers. In 1940, only 5 percent of 16- and 17-year-old male high school students worked during the school year. Less than 2 percent of female students of this age were employed (U.S. Department of Commerce, 1940).

The Emergence of the Student-Worker

The situation began to change again between 1940 and 1950. The rise of a separate workplace, composed almost exclusively of adolescents, was under way. Examining this phenomenon in detail provides a nice example of how changes in society can transform the nature of adolescence.

Following the end of World War II, sectors of the American economy that needed large numbers of part-time employees expanded rapidly (Ginzberg, 1977). In particular, the postwar period was a time of tremendous growth in retail stores and restaurants. Between 1950 and 1976, the retail trade sector of the economy (which includes all jobs in which people sell finished products to consumers) expanded by 96 percent, and the service sector (which includes all jobs in which people provide services to others) increased by 172 percent. More than 3 out of every 5 new jobs created between 1950 and 1977 were in retail trade or services, where many jobs are part time. Employers, particularly in businesses such as fast-food restaurants, needed workers who were willing to work part time for relatively low wages and for short work shifts. Many employers looked to teenagers to fill these jobs. Consequently, over the past twenty-five years or so, 1 out of every 3 new entrants into the labor force has been a young person (Ginzberg, 1977).

Another reason for the phenomenal rise of the adolescent workplace is the dramatic increase during the last thirty years in the cost of living for the typical American teenager. Although inflation took its toll on people of all ages, it hit teenagers especially hard. For example, the cost of being a teenager rose more than 20 percent in the four-year period between 1975 and 1979; it rose more than 15 percent in 1979 alone. In both periods, the rate of inflation on typical teen items, such as records and movie tickets, rose considerably faster than did the rate of inflation overall. But unlike many adults, who receive cost-of-living salary increases commensurate with the rate of inflation, many adolescents rely on a weekly allowance from their parents, which usually does not rise as economic indicators change. As prices rose and allowances held steady, adolescents who were looking for spending money were drawn into the world of work (Rotbart, 1981).

As shown in Figure 7.2, the proportion of high school students holding part-time jobs rose dramatically from 1940 on. By 1980, according to a nationwide survey conducted for the National Center for Education Statistics (Lewin-Epstein, 1981), about two-thirds of all high school seniors and about half of all high school sophomores held part-time jobs during the week prior to the survey. More recent estimates indicate that the proportion of working high school students has not changed appreciably since this time (Bachman, Bare, and Frankie, 1986; Barton, 1989). By current estimates, at any one time during the school year, well over 6 million American high school students are working.

In less than half a century, adolescence had undergone a remarkable change. In 1940, it was virtually unheard-of for a high school student to hold a regular part-time job during the

A large proportion of employed high school students work in fast-food restaurants. (L. Kolvoord/Image Works)

school year. Today, it is almost unheard-of for a high school student *not* to work.

In the past it was young people from less affluent families who were more likely to work; today the opposite is true. Working during high school is slightly more common among middle- and upper-middle-class teenagers than among poor youth, presumably because these youngsters have an easier time finding employment. Jobs in the adolescent workplace are more likely to be located in suburban areas, where the more affluent families reside. Working is also more common among white than among nonwhite students, with employment rates being lowest for African-American youth. Male and female adolescents are equally likely to be employed (Steinberg and Cauffman, 1995).

Not only are more high school students working today than ever before, but those who do work are working for considerably more hours than adolescents have in the past (Greenberger and Steinberg, 1986). The average high school sophomore puts in close to fifteen hours per week at a job, and the average senior works about twenty hours per week (Bachman et al., 1986; Barton, 1989; Lewin-Epstein, 1981; Steinberg and Cauffman, 1995). Considering that the average school day runs for about six hours, today's typical working adolescent is busy with school or work commitments for close to fifty hours a week.

Although youngsters in contemporary America do not enter the formal labor force until the age of 15 or 16, many individuals have worked on an informal basis during childhood, when most boys and girls are assigned chores around the house (White and Brinkerhoff, 1981). Typically, they help in the kitchen, help care for younger siblings, and help in such tasks as yard work and cleaning. And by early adolescence, many youngsters

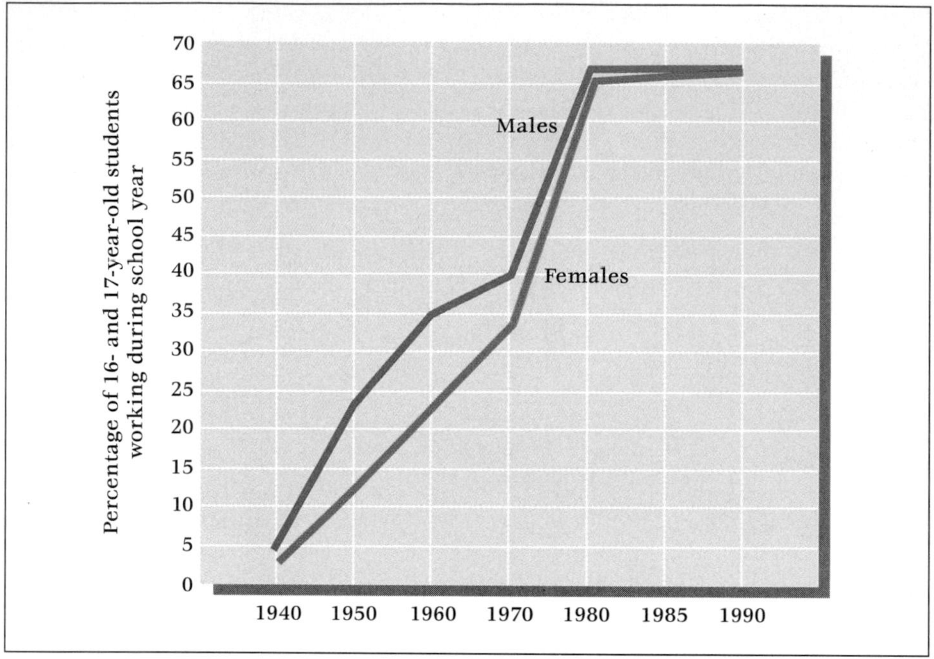

FIGURE 7.2 *More U.S. high school students are working during the school year now than at any other time in recent history.*

begin to take on informal employment outside the home for other family members or neighbors. Babysitting is a common source of income for many young adolescents, as are gardening, house cleaning, and newspaper delivery (Greenberger and Steinberg, 1983).

Teenage Employment in America and in Other Nations

The extent and nature of teenage employment vary considerably from country to country. In most nonindustrialized societies, work life and family life are not as distinct as they are in contemporary America, and youngsters are typically integrated into the world of work before they reach adolescence (Whiting and Whiting, 1975). If the society subsists on farming, children are taught how to farm at an early age. If the society subsists on hunting, children are taught how to hunt. Although young people who are still acquiring work skills may be given tasks that are more elementary than those performed by their elders, adolescents and adults work side by side, and a distinct adolescent workplace—such as that in the United States—is not usually found. Whereas we draw a distinction between schooling and work in contemporary society, in many traditional societies, the two activities are essentially the same.

In developing nations, where industrialization is still in a relatively early stage and a large percentage of the population is poor, adolescents generally leave school early—at least by American standards. In these countries, most adolescents enter into full-time employment by the time they are 15 or 16, in jobs similar to the ones they will hold as adults. Very often, adolescents work for their families. The pattern in these countries closely resembles America during an earlier stage in its industrialization: school for adolescents of the extremely affluent, and work for the majority of teenagers.

Other comparably industrialized countries provide the most interesting contrast, for we can see that the high school student-worker is a distinctively American phenomenon. In most highly industrialized countries other than the United States, adolescents are more likely to defer employment until their education is completed. In the early 1980s, for example, over two-thirds of all American 16- and 17-year-old adolescents were working while attending school; but in Canada, only about 37 percent of this group was employed; in Sweden, only about 20 percent; and in Japan, less than 2 percent (Reubens et al., 1983). Although more recent systematic cross-national comparative data are not available, anecdotal evidence suggests that student employment is more common in other industrialized countries today than it was fifteen years ago, but it is still far less prevalent abroad than in the United States. In other industrialized countries, young people generally move from school directly into full-time employment without an intervening period of formal part-time work. In the United States today, it is more common for youngsters to move from full-time school with no formal employment (during early adolescence), to a combination of school and part-time work (during middle and late adolescence), to full-time work (sometime during late adolescence or early adulthood).

Although European adolescents are less likely than their American counterparts to hold paying part-time jobs during the school year, they are more likely to work in school-sponsored or government-sponsored apprenticeships (Hamilton, 1990). In many countries, such as Germany, these apprenticeships play an extremely important role in preparing adolescents for the transition into adult employment, especially for students who are not bound for college. It is important to remember as you read this chapter that the studies of teen employment in the United States are typically studies of students who are working in part-time jobs that have little to do with the careers they hope to pursue after they complete their education. In contrast, in Europe, students' work experience is much more continuous with the roles they will enter as adults.

How can we account for these differences between the United States and other industrialized countries? First, part-time employment opportunities are not as readily available elsewhere as they are in America. Fast-food restaurants, although increasingly popular in other countries, are not seen on every major street. Second, the scheduling of part-time jobs in other countries is not well suited to the daily routines of students. In Europe, for example, the school day lasts well into the late afternoon, and relatively few shops are open in the evenings. In the United States, many adolescents leave school early in the afternoon and go straight to their part-time jobs, where they work until 9 or 10 o'clock in the evening. Third, in most other industrialized countries, the employment of children is associated with being poor, and there is a strong stigma attached to having one's children work. Many middle-class parents do not feel that it is appropriate for their children to have jobs while attending school. Fourth, schools in countries other than the United States demand much more out-of-school time; it is not uncommon for a European high school student to be assigned four or five hours of homework nightly (Reubens et al., 1981). Finally, as we noted in Chapter 6, American schools have not done a very good job of anticipating the needs of adolescents who do not intend to go to college. As a result, formal apprenticeship programs, such as those found in most other industrialized countries, are quite rare in the United States.

SEX DIFFERENCES IN THE ADOLESCENT WORKPLACE

One topic that social scientists who are interested in work have studied extensively concerns sex differences in the labor force. It is well documented that men and women typically work in different types of jobs and that men generally are paid higher wages—even when they do the same work as women. This disparity has been an important concern to many people who feel that such sex differences in patterns of work are unfair and serve to maintain economic inequities between the sexes. Are the same sorts of disparities found in teenagers' jobs? The answer seems to be yes (Greenberger and Steinberg, 1983; Lewin-Epstein, 1981).

We know that today boys and girls are equally likely to be employed during the school year but, generally speaking, that they work at very different jobs. Boys are more likely to work as manual laborers, skilled laborers, gardeners, busboys, janitors, and newspaper deliverers. Girls are more likely to be employed as food servers, house cleaners, and babysitters. Moreover, boys almost never work as secretaries, receptionists, babysitters, nurses' aides, or house cleaners; and girls almost never work as "busgirls," dishwashers, gardeners, manual laborers, janitors, or newspaper deliverers (see accompanying figure). A study of over three thousand adolescents in southern California revealed that boys work longer hours than girls and that "boys'" jobs pay better than "girls'" jobs. In fact, the average hourly wage for boys is about 15 percent higher than it is for girls (Greenberger and Steinberg, 1983).

These findings are important because they indicate that youngsters are exposed to the sort of sex differences characteristic of the adult workplace long before they reach adulthood. However, one question that cannot be answered is whether sex differences in adolescents' work experience result from the different preferences of boys and girls (that is, whether boys and girls choose to work in different kinds of jobs) or from discrimination in the labor force (that is, whether employers choose boys for some jobs and girls for others). Could it be that sex differences in job preferences are established even before adolescence? In order to answer this question, one needs to look at patterns of work during childhood.

Were you expected to do household chores when you were growing up? If you had a sibling of the opposite sex, did you each do the same chores, or did you have different chores? Recent research suggests that in most families the separation of "boys'" work and "girls'" work begins early in childhood and that chores become even more sex-typed as children get older. Among young children, for example, boys and girls are equally likely to be given the chore of washing dishes. By the time children are a little older, however, dishwashing has become a "girls'" job. The opposite is true for various sorts of manual labor around the house, such as yard work, which becomes more and more a "boys'" job as children get older (White and Brinkerhoff, 1981).

On the basis of these studies, it seems that young people learn lessons about the sex-appropriateness of various work roles at an early age. And these lessons have important implications for the subsequent occupational development of males and females. Adolescent males and females aspire to different jobs and expect to enter different occupations. Early work experience, it appears, reinforces and readies adolescent boys and girls for the sex roles they will be likely to encounter in the workplace as adults.

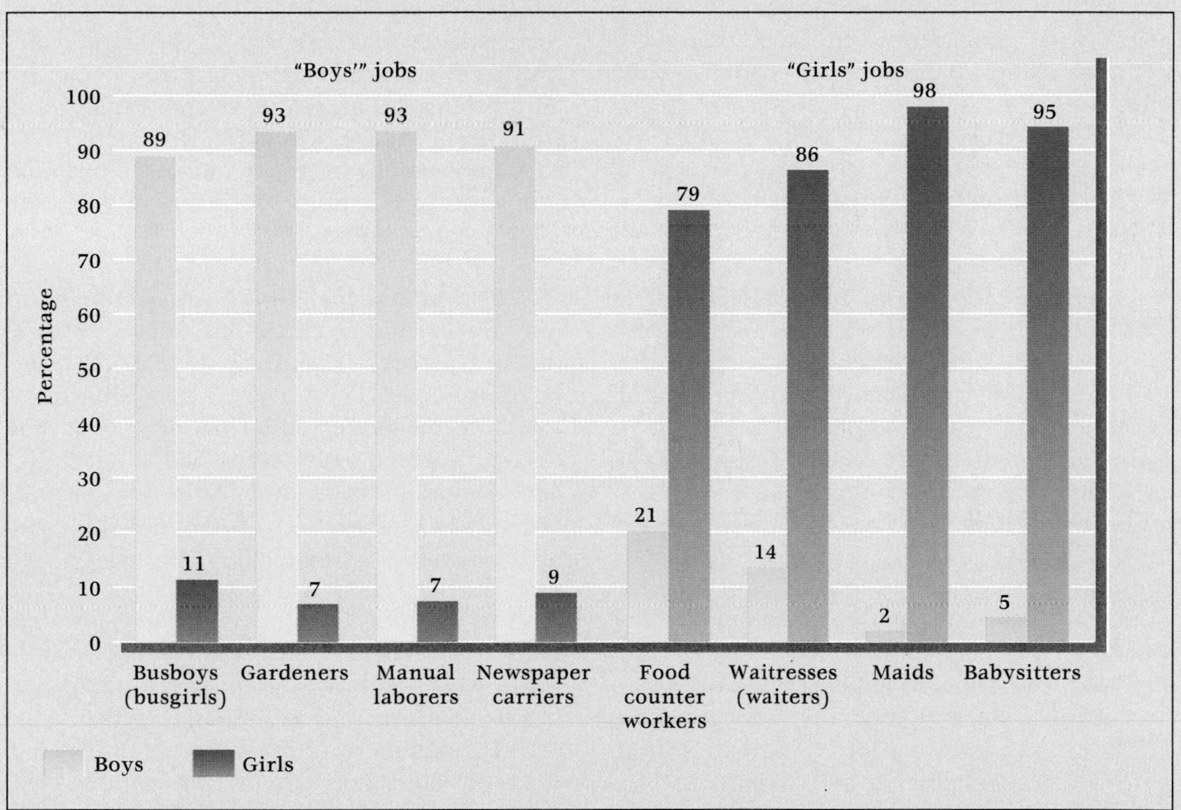

Percentage of boys versus girls in common adolescents' jobs. Some jobs are almost always held by boys, whereas others are almost always held by girls.

RECAP

Today, the majority of American teenagers hold part-time jobs during the school year, and many work more than fifteen or twenty hours weekly. This is an important departure from the recent past, when it was unlikely for students to work. This is also a departure from the case in most other industrialized countries, where student employment is quite rare. Students in other countries are more likely to gain work experience through structured apprenticeship programs in career-related jobs.

The Adolescent Workplace Today

Common Adolescent Jobs. The range of jobs open to American adolescents who wish to work in the formal labor force is rather limited, and surveys indicate that the proportion of adolescents who hold challenging or interesting jobs is very, very small. Most studies of contemporary youth indicate that the vast majority are employed in the retail and service industries, although, as one would expect, there are important differences as a function of region, age, and gender. In general, older working students are more likely to hold formal jobs (e.g., retail or food service work) than are younger working students, who are more likely to hold informal jobs (e.g., babysitting, yard work) (Greenberger and Steinberg, 1986; Mortimer, Finch, Shanahan, and Ryu, 1992; Schneider and Shouse, 1991). As expected, working teenagers who live in rural areas are more likely to be employed in agricultural occupations than are their urban or suburban counterparts. Also, boys are more likely to work in manual labor than are girls, who are more likely than boys to work in service positions (Greenberger and Steinberg, 1986).

These differences notwithstanding, it is important to recognize that a very small number of different sorts of jobs accounts for a very large proportion of today's student workers. According to data from a recent government survey, nearly 60 percent of employed eighth-graders worked in one of two jobs: babysitting or lawn work (Schneider and Shouse, 1991). And job opportunities appear to be just as restricted for older workers: According to a recent study, restaurant work (such as a counter worker in a fast-food restaurant) and retail sales work (such as a cashier in a clothing store) accounted for nearly 60 percent of all working students (Steinberg, Fegley, and Dornbusch, 1993). Unlike in previous eras, very few teenagers today are employed on farms or in factories (Charner and Fraser, 1987; Lewin-Epstein, 1981).

The Adolescent Work Environment. In one series of studies of adolescents who work, the researchers examined teenagers' work environments. They were especially interested in collecting information about the degree to which adolescents had contact with adults on their jobs and about the sorts of tasks teenagers were given (Greenberger and Steinberg, 1981; Greenberger, Steinberg, and Ruggiero, 1982). If working is going to be a positive influence on youngsters' development, they reasoned, it is likely to be so only if the work environment provides opportunities for learning and self-reliance. Most of the workers studied were employed in one of five types of work: food service (for example, fast-food counter worker); clerical (file clerk in an office); retail (cashier in a store); manual labor (gardener); and skilled labor (assistant automobile mechanic). Using an elaborate coding system to record on-the-job activities, the researchers observed what went on in the work settings. They recorded the tasks that the adolescents performed (for example, "cleans table"), the things they said ("May I help you?"), and the people with whom they interacted (an adult customer). They also interviewed the adolescent workers and had them complete a series of questionnaires about their experiences at work.

The results were surprising. Unlike adolescents in traditional societies, whose work typically brings them into extensive contact with adults, the young people who were observed in these studies spent as much time on the job interacting with other adolescents as they did with their elders. In the typical fast-food restaurant, for example, nearly all the workers were teenagers, the supervisor was usually not much older, and the customers were often young people, too. Few of the teenage workers surveyed reported having formed close relationships with adults at work. They were unlikely to see their adult supervisors or co-workers outside of work; they felt reluctant to go to the adults at work with personal problems; and generally they reported feeling less close to adults at work than to other people in their lives (Greenberger and Steinberg, 1981).

The studies also indicate that most teenagers' jobs are pretty dreary. Few jobs permit adolescents to behave independently or make decisions; the adolescents receive little instruction from their supervisors, and they are rarely required to use the skills they have been taught in school (Greenberger and Steinberg, 1986). As an illustration of this point, consider the following contrast: The average adolescent worker spends less than 6 percent of time on the job in such activities as reading, writing, or arithmetic; but he or she spends more than 25 percent of the time cleaning or carrying things.

With occasional exceptions, most teenagers' jobs are repetitive, monotonous, and unlikely to be intellectually stimulating. Some are even highly stressful, requiring that youngsters work under intense time pressure without much letup (Greenberger and Steinberg, 1986).

RECAP

Most employed U.S. adolescents work in retail jobs or in restaurants. Studies suggest that the work they do is highly routine and uninteresting and that male and female adolescents work in very different jobs.

● Working and Adolescent Development

● ***The Development of Responsibility.*** Most people believe that working builds character, teaches adolescents about the "real" world, and helps young people prepare for adulthood. Like many of the widely held views about adolescence that have gone unquestioned over the years, these assumptions are not entirely supported by research on teenagers and work. Indeed, recent studies indicate that working during adolescence may even have some costs to young people's development.

Actually, one study that supports the view that work is character-building examined the impact of employment on young people growing up during the Great Depression. The researchers found that boys who took on part-time jobs outside the home became more adultlike as a result: "Boys . . . who were employed showed a much greater interest in adults and spent more time with them . . . than other children. . . . Economic hardship and jobs increased their desire to associate with adults, to 'grow up' and become adult. This adult orientation is congruent with other behavioral correlates of roles in the household economy, including the responsible use of money . . . energetic or industrious behavior . . . and social independence" (Elder, 1974, pp. 81–82). Because very few girls worked outside the home during the Depression (most remained home and performed household labor so that their mothers could enter the labor force), the impact of employment on the development of responsibility among girls was not studied.

Studies of more contemporary youth, however, generally do not support the view that holding a job makes adolescents become more personally responsible (Mortimer et al., 1990, 1993; Steinberg and Dornbusch, 1991; Steinberg et al., 1993). This suggests that the impact of work on the development of responsibility may depend on the broader economic context in which adolescents live. Working may help adolescents become more responsible when their work makes a genuine contribution to their family's welfare. This condition may not characterize the situation of most contemporary middle-class adolescents, however, who work mainly to secure their own spending money.

Some researchers have asked whether working makes adolescents more *socially* responsible. Generally, these studies find that working does not enhance adolescents' feelings of social obligation, social tolerance, or social belongingness (Greenberger and Steinberg, 1986). Working does not make adolescents feel more concern for the well-being of others. If anything, working seems to make youngsters more individualistic. Moreover, adolescents who have jobs are more likely to express cynical attitudes toward work and to endorse unethical business practices. For example, it has been found that workers are more likely than nonworkers to agree with such statements as "People who work harder at their jobs than they have to are a little crazy" (an item from a scale designed to measure cynicism toward work) and "In my opinion, it's all right for workers who are paid a low salary to take little things" (an item from the scale measuring tolerance of unacceptable business practices; see Table 7.1) (Steinberg, Greenberger, Garduque, Ruggiero, and Vaux, 1982). Another study found that adolescents who work long hours (twenty-plus hours weekly) are less satisfied with their lives than are adolescents who work fewer hours (Fine, Mortimer, and Roberts, 1990).

What can we make of these findings? Why would working make youngsters more self-reliant but at the same time more cynical about work, less concerned about the welfare of others, and less satisfied with their lives? Perhaps the answer has something to do with the nature of the work most adolescents perform. Think for a moment about the job environment of most teenagers. Their work is dull, monotonous, and often stressful. Even if you have never worked in such a job, you can certainly imagine that working under these conditions could make people feel cynical and protective of their own interests above all else.

● ***Money and Its Management.*** One specific aspect of responsibility that working is believed to affect is money management. Because the average working teenager earns around $300 each month, holding a job may provide many opportunities for learning how to budget, save, and use money responsibly. Although about half of all adolescents are given an allowance by their parents (most often, these are younger adolescents who are not employed), parents appear to exert more control over purchases made from allowances than they do over purchases made from job earnings (Greenberger and Steinberg, 1986; Miller and Yung, 1990). Research indicates, however, that few teenagers exercise a great deal of responsibility when it comes to managing their earnings. One national survey, for example, showed that the majority of working teenagers spent most of their earnings on their own needs and activities (Johnston, Bachman, and O'Malley, 1982). Few adolescents who work save a large percentage of their income for their education, and fewer still use their earnings to help their families with household expenses. Instead, the picture

TABLE 7.1 SCALES USED TO MEASURE "CYNICISM TOWARD WORK" AND "TOLERANCE OF UNETHICAL BUSINESS PRACTICES"

Sample Items from the "Cynicism toward Work" Scale	Sample Items from the "Tolerance of Unacceptable Business Practices" Scale
People who work harder at their jobs than they have to are a little crazy.	People who break a few laws to make a profit aren't doing anything I wouldn't do in their position.
Most people today are stuck in dead-end, go-nowhere jobs.	Workers are entitled to "call in sick" when they don't feel like working.
Hard work really doesn't get you much of anything in this world.	It doesn't matter if a businessman bends the law a little to make a profit.
There's no such thing as a company that cares about its employees.	In my opinion, it's all right for workers who are paid a low salary to take little things.
If I had the chance, I'd go through life without ever working.	It's acceptable to me if a teenage worker cheats a little on the amount of income tax he or she pays the government.
People who take their work home with them probably don't have a very interesting home life.	

SOURCE: Steinberg et al., 1982.

of the contemporary working teenager that emerges from these studies is one of self-indulgent materialism. Wages are spent on designer clothing, expensive stereo equipment, movies, and eating out (Steinberg et al., 1993). A fair proportion of the earnings are spent on drugs and alcohol (Greenberger and Steinberg, 1986).

According to one social scientist, today's working teenagers may suffer from **premature affluence** (Bachman, 1983). As he put it, in an article entitled "Do High School Students Earn Too Much?":

> A fairly popular assumption these days is that students should have a great deal of freedom in spending their part-time earnings, so that in making their own choices and occasionally their own mistakes they will get some reality experiences and "learn the value of a dollar." . . . The problem is that the "reality" faced by the typical high school student with substantial part-time earnings is just not very realistic. In the absence of payment for rent, utilities, groceries, and the many other necessities routinely provided by parents, the typical student is likely to find that most or all of his/her earnings are available for discretionary spending. . . . It seems likely that some will experience what I've come to call "premature affluence"—affluence because $200 or more per month represents a lot of "spending money" for a high school student, and premature because many of these individuals will not be able to sustain that level of discretionary spending once they take on the burden of paying for their own necessities. (p. 65)

What might be some of the effects of premature affluence? According to one team of researchers, some of the consequences may be increased cynicism about the value of hard work and a lack of interest in working harder than is absolutely necessary, increased interest in buying drugs and alcohol, and the tendency to develop more materialistic attitudes

Few adolescents who work save a large percentage of their income for their education, and fewer still use their earnings to help their families with household expenses. More often than not, wages are spent on clothing, cars, entertainment, and eating out. (Felicia Martinez/PhotoEdit)

(Greenberger and Steinberg, 1986). The very experience that many adults believe builds "character" may, in reality, teach adolescents undesirable lessons about work and the meaning of money.

RECAP

Contrary to widespread belief, employment in today's adolescent workplace is unlikely to contribute to healthy psychological development or to the growth of desirable attitudes toward work. Rather, part-time employment is more likely to lead to cynicism about the value of hard work and to the development of "premature affluence."

● ***Work and Deviance.*** It comes as no surprise to learn that some adolescents, like some adults, behave at work in ways that would certainly upset their employers—if their employers knew. Do adolescents who are cynical about working actually do things at work to retaliate for their unpleasant working conditions? There is not a great deal of research on this question, but one study that has examined **occupational deviance** in the adolescent workplace revealed relatively high rates of misconduct among adolescent workers, even in the early months of their first jobs (Ruggiero, Greenberger, and Steinberg, 1982). Adolescent workers completed a questionnaire that examined several categories of occupational deviance. The workers, who were assured that their responses would remain confidential and anonymous, were asked to check whether and how often they had committed each of nine acts (see Figure 7.3). After nine months on the job, more than 60 percent had committed at least one "deviant" act. About 38 percent of working teenagers in the sample were "nonoffenders," about 38 percent were "occasional offenders," and about 24 percent were "relatively frequent offenders."

Because comparisons between adolescent and adult workers were not made, it would be erroneous to conclude that adolescents necessarily make bad or untrustworthy workers. Furthermore, it is not clear from the study whether adolescents learned these deviant behaviors in the workplace or merely used the work setting as a context in which to display behaviors learned elsewhere. Nevertheless, the findings challenge the idea that the workplace is invariably a positive influence on the socialization of young people.

Some studies have also examined the time-honored belief that having a job deters youngsters from delinquent and criminal activity.

FIGURE 7.3 *Some first-time workers do things on the job that their employers would not be pleased about.* (Ruggiero, Greenberger, and Steinberg, 1982)

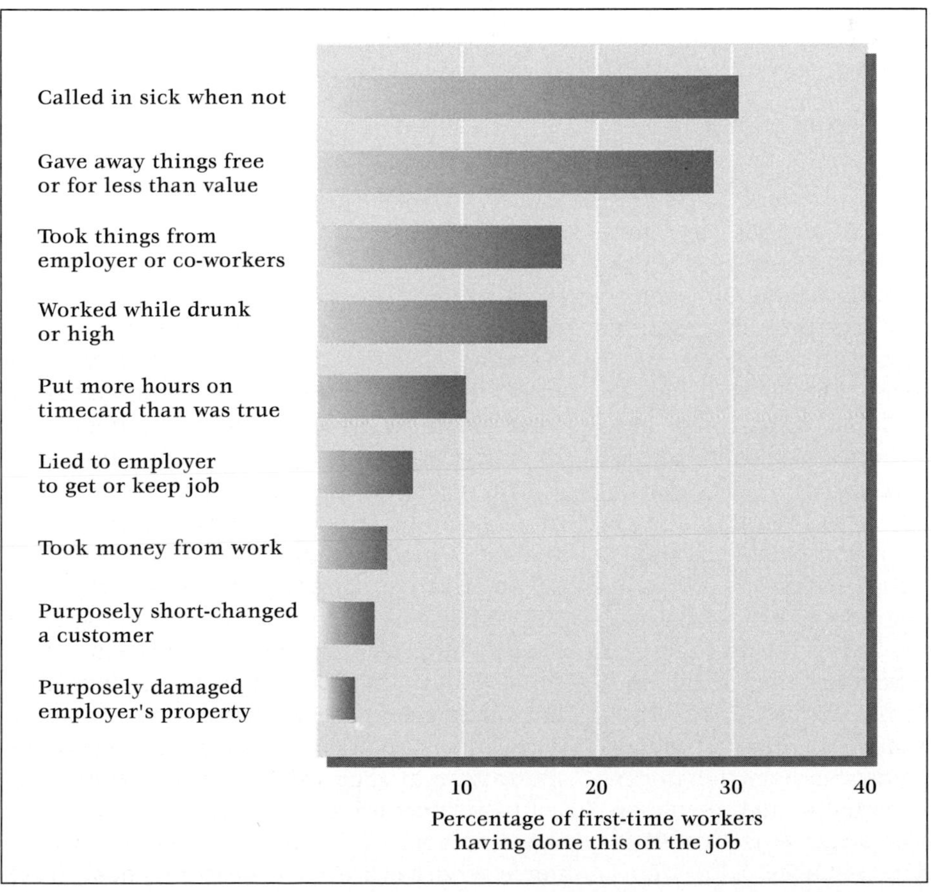

Contrary to popular belief, however, employment during adolescence does not deter delinquent activity (Gottfredson, 1985). Indeed, several studies suggest that working may actually be associated with *increases* in deviance, including aggression; in school misconduct; and in minor delinquency, including petty theft, joyriding, carrying a weapon, and buying stolen goods (Steinberg and Cauffman, 1995).

Several studies also have found that drug and alcohol use is higher among workers than nonworkers, especially among students who work long hours (e.g., Bachman and Schulenberg, 1993; Elliott and Wofford, 1991; Greenberger, Steinberg, and Vaux, 1981; Mortimer et al., 1993; Steinberg and Dornbusch, 1991; Steinberg et al., 1993). Although some writers have proposed that adolescents who are already inclined toward using drugs and alcohol are more likely to choose to work long hours (e.g., Bachman and Schulenberg, 1993), recent analyses suggest that this is not, in fact, the case. Rather, increases in work hours precede increases in drug and alcohol use (Mortimer et al., 1993; Steinberg et al., 1993). The impact of extensive employment on adolescent drug and alcohol use probably reflects the fact that adolescents who work long hours have more discretionary income and, hence, greater opportunity to purchase drugs and alcohol. In addition, drug and alcohol use is higher among adolescents who work under conditions of high job stress than it is among their peers who work for comparable amounts of time and money but under less stressful conditions (Greenberger, Steinberg, and Vaux, 1981).

The connection between working and antisocial behavior comes as a surprise, especially in light of many theories of delinquency, which link antisocial behavior to disenfranchisement, rolelessness, and alienation from adult institutions (e.g., Hirschi, 1969). Why should employment make adolescents more delinquent? One explanation is that workers' antisocial behavior is the consequence of extensive employment in menial, repetitive, unchallenging work that is largely done in the absence of close adult supervision (Steinberg et al., 1993). An alternative account is that working long hours does not so much *cause* increases in drug use or deviance as it *reflects* a common underlying problem, such as disengagement from school, "pseudomaturity" (see also Greenberger and Steinberg, 1986), or "precocious" development (see also Bachman and Schulenberg, 1993).

● ***Work and Its Impact on School.*** Many experts now believe that working more than twenty hours a week may jeopardize adolescents' schooling. Youngsters who work long hours are absent from school more often, are less likely to participate in extracurricular activities, report enjoying school less, spend less time on their homework, and earn lower grades. These results occur both because youngsters who are less interested in school choose to work longer hours and because working long hours leads to disengagement from school (Steinberg and Cauffman, 1995). In some regards, then, working long hours most threatens the school performance of those students who can least afford to have their grades decline.

The adverse impact of working long hours on schooling is especially troublesome in light of studies pointing to achievement problems of American youngsters (see Chapters 6 and 12). Not only does working long hours seem to lead to increased absenteeism and decreased time spent on homework and school activities, but intensive involvement in a part-time job early in a student's education—during sophomore year in high school, for example—may actually increase the likelihood of dropping out of school (Damico, 1984). Moreover, students who work a good deal have less ambi-

Participation in extracurricular activities, such as working on the school yearbook, is less frequent among students who work long hours at a part-time job. (Tony Freeman/PhotoEdit)

tious plans for further education while in high school, and they complete fewer years of college (Mortimer and Finch, 1986).

Although the degree of impact that working has on students' grades and achievement test scores is small (Barton, 1989), several studies indicate that extensive employment during the school year may take its toll on students in ways that are not revealed by looking only at grade-point averages. One recent study, for example, found that students who work a great deal report paying less attention in class, exerting less effort on their studies, and skipping class more frequently (Steinberg and Dornbusch, 1991). Additionally, when students work a great deal, they often develop strategies for protecting their grade-point averages. These strategies include taking easier courses, "cutting corners" on homework assignments, copying homework from friends, and cheating (Greenberger and Steinberg, 1986; McNeil, 1984; Steinberg and Dornbusch, 1991). And teachers have responded to the influx of students into the workplace by assigning less homework and by using class time for students to complete assignments that otherwise would be done outside of school (McNeil, 1984).

RECAP

Recent studies indicate that working long hours may increase adolescent deviance and take a toll on youngsters' schooling. Teenagers who work in excess of fifteen to twenty hours weekly are more likely to use drugs and alcohol, are less engaged in school, and are more likely to "protect" their grades by taking easier classes and expending less effort on their schoolwork.

Youth Unemployment

Although the employment of teenagers has become commonplace in contemporary America, a sizable minority of young people who wish to work are nevertheless unable to find jobs. Many of these young people are poor, minority youth who reside in inner-city neighborhoods. Much attention has been given to the problem of **youth unemployment** over the past two decades, but there remains a good deal of controversy over the nature of the problem and possible solutions to it.

Most young people in this country ultimately find full-time employment after they graduate from high school or college. For example, one team of researchers, using data collected by the U.S. Department of Labor, found that more than 90 percent of all teenage boys were in school, or working, or both. Only 5 percent were out of school, unemployed, and looking for full-time work (Feldstein and Ellwood, 1982). Much of the unemployment of young people is attributable to their involvement in other productive activities, such as school, rather than to deficiencies in job skills or constraints in the labor force (Mare, Winship, and Kubitschek, 1984). The situation is similar even among slightly older individuals. According to the U.S. Census (1993), in 1991, for example, about half of all 18- to 21-year-olds were enrolled in school (either in high school or college); of the remaining half who were not in school, two-thirds were employed. Overall, then, about 15 percent of 18- to 21-year-olds were "roleless"—not in school and unemployed (see Figure 7.4).

Moreover, those young people who are out of school and out of work are unemployed for only short periods of time. Nearly half of the unemployed youth in the survey mentioned above had been out of work for one month or less; only 10 percent had been unemployed for as long as six months. An important con-

FIGURE 7.4 *Percentages of 18- to 21-year-olds in various roles.* (U.S. Bureau of the Census, 1993)

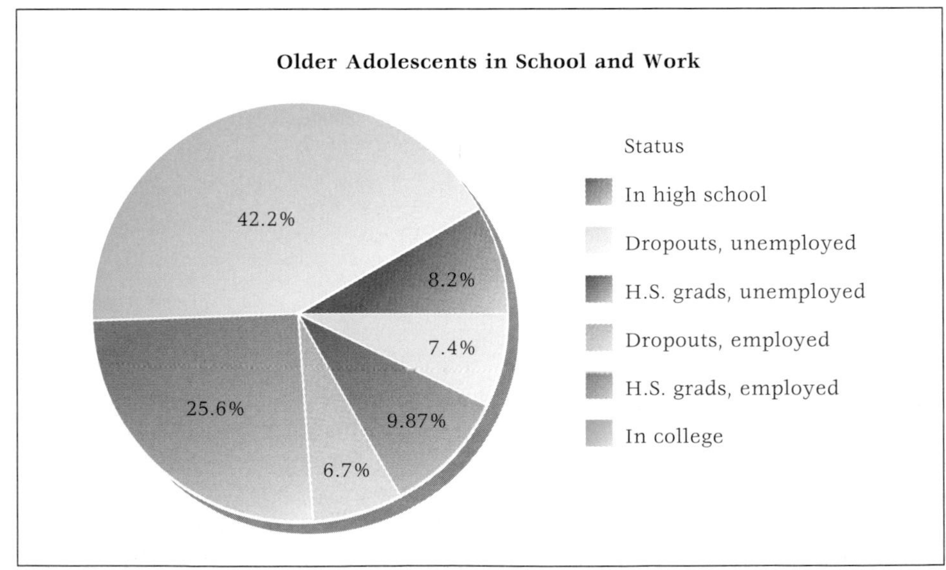

clusion to keep in mind, therefore, is that long-term unemployment is a problem that afflicts a very small minority of young people.

It is also important to note that the majority of unemployed youth are high school dropouts. In 1991, for example, whereas nearly 75 percent of noncollege 18- to 21-year-olds who had graduated from high school were employed, less than half of the high school dropouts were. And, although high school dropouts constitute only about 14 percent of the population of 18- to 21-year-olds, they account for about half of the unemployed people in this age bracket.

Minority youth are far more likely to experience unemployment than white youth are. Among the reasons for this are the relatively higher proportion of minority youth who drop out of high school (dropout rates are especially high among Hispanic-American youth) and the relatively lower proportion of minority high school graduates who attend college. In 1991, for example, nearly half of all white youth were in college, compared with only one-fourth of minority youth. And, whereas fewer than 1 in 10 noncollege white youth were unemployed, about one-third of noncollege African-American youth were (U.S. Bureau of the Census, 1993).

Unemployment also is more common among teenagers who come from low-income families and who live in areas that have high overall unemployment rates where competition for available employment is severe (Freeman and Wise, 1982). Their unemployment problems may have more to do with poverty and related factors than with youth or inexperience. Most studies show that unemployment during adolescence and young adulthood results primarily from a combination of economic and social factors, rather than from a lack of motivation on the part of unemployed individuals.

It is important to keep in mind, however, that the consequences of unemployment during adolescence and young adulthood appear to be worse in the short term than in the long run. Unemployment is not a condition that stays with a person throughout his or her life. Researchers have found that most people who have been unemployed as teenagers are eventually able to secure stable full-time employment. Youth unemployment is a problem among individuals not in school mostly because it is associated with higher rates of crime, drug abuse, and violence (Freeman and Wise, 1982).

Nevertheless, for the minority of youngsters who experience long-term difficulty in finding and holding a full-time job, chronic unemployment is an onerous condition filled with hopelessness. Because of the serious effects of chronic unemployment during young adulthood on individuals' later lives, many different approaches have been taken over the years in trying to solve the youth unemployment problem.

One set of proposals comes out of concern for the Forgotten Half—the nearly 50 percent of all adolescents who do not go on to college. As we have noted in this chapter and in Chapter 6, our secondary schools do little to prepare noncollege-bound youngsters for the world of work. These youngsters, of course, are far more likely to experience unemployment. Many experts therefore believe that the youth unemployment problem is attributable mainly to the lack of clear linkages between school and work. They point out that there are so many "cracks" in the transition from school to work that it is easy for students who are not in school—and who are carried along by inertia—to fall into periods of unemployment.

Several suggestions have been made to combat this problem (William T. Grant Foundation Commission on Work, Family, and Citizenship, 1988). Many commentators have argued that expanding opportunities for **community service** will help integrate adolescents into the community, enhance their feelings of confidence and responsibility, and put them in touch with adult role models. It is hoped that these sorts of efforts will help unemployed young people ultimately find paid, full-time employment.

A second suggestion is that communities improve their services for young people and strengthen youth organizations. In Europe, for example, local communities provide much better employment services for youth—including job placement—than is the case in the United States. Such services would also help with career counseling, college counseling, summer employment, and placement in volunteer activities. In most high schools, guidance counselors are so busy counseling students for college that they rarely pay attention to noncollege-bound students.

Finally, it has been proposed that American schools experiment with apprenticeship programs modeled after those found in Europe (Hamilton, 1990). These programs would introduce young people to the world of work early in high school and would gradually move them from full-time school into a mixture of school and work and finally into full-time employment. Instead of working in the dead-end jobs of the adolescent workplace, teenagers would combine schooling and on-the-job training with employers who are likely to offer them full-time, career-oriented jobs after graduation.

What about the substantial proportion of adolescents who do not graduate from high school, who, as you have seen, are at the greatest risk of experiencing unemployment? To date, many different types of interventions have been tried, but few have succeeded (Smith, 1993). Despite some thirty years of government programs designed to train unemployed youth and place them in the labor force, most evaluations of these efforts find that high school dropouts who participate in such programs are no more likely to find full-time employment than are dropouts who do not participate in the programs. This is quite disconcerting, since the programs that were evaluated have tried a wide array of approaches, including work experience, job training, job placement, and instruction in labor market skills (such as interviewing, job seeking, and so on). In light of this evidence, most experts believe that efforts should be concentrated on helping youngsters who are at-risk for dropping out of school to stay in school.

RECAP

Although extensive part-time employment during the school year may be a problem among working- and middle-class adolescents, many social commentators have worried about the high rate of youth unemployment, especially among poor, minority youth who have dropped out of high school, but also among high school graduates who do not attend college. Among the suggestions offered for combating youth unemployment are increasing adolescents' opportunities for community service, strengthening counseling and career services for high school students, encouraging the development of apprenticeship programs like those found in Europe, and, above all, encouraging all adolescents to complete high school.

ADOLESCENTS AND LEISURE

Although adolescents devote considerable time each week to school, and many also commit a good number of hours to a part-time job, leisure occupies more of the typical adolescent's waking hours (about 40 percent) than do school and work combined (about 30 percent) (Fine et al., 1990). Leisure activities include socializing with friends, playing sports and games, watching television and listening to music, working on hobbies, and just plain "kicking back." One important difference between leisure and other activities is that adolescents choose their leisure activities, whereas their time at school and work is dictated by others (teachers, supervisors, etc.). Perhaps as a consequence, studies show that adolescents report being in a better mood during leisure activities than during school or work (Csikszentmihalyi and Larson, 1984).

Adults have mixed feelings about adolescents' leisure. On the positive side, adults take pride in watching teenagers' organized sports and creative activities and believe that these "productive" uses of leisure help build character and teach important skills, such as teamwork and perseverance (consider, for example, all the movies you have seen about the character-building benefits of team sports). On the other hand, adults view many adolescent leisure activities as wasted time, or worse, as preludes to trouble: They worry about groups of teenagers "cruising" the mall, they poke fun at groups of girls sequestered in front of a mirror trying on an array of cosmetics, and they cringe at the image of an adolescent plugged into his stereo, wildly playing an "air guitar."

This mixed view of adolescent leisure reflects an interesting paradox about the nature of adolescence in modern society. Because industrialized society has "given" adolescents a good deal of free time, adults expect them to "use" it productively. But by definition, leisure is supposed to be time that can be used for purposes other than production. As you will read in Chapter 8, some theorists of adolescence believe that the existence of large blocks of uncommitted time is one feature of adolescence in modern society that has the potential to contribute in positive ways to young people's development (e.g., Erikson, 1968).

Nevertheless, it seems difficult for adults to resist the temptation to worry that leisure activities are *displacing* the more "important" tasks of adolescence, such as school. This is generally referred to as the **displacement hypothesis.** Interestingly, however, studies show that intensive involvement in the "productive" activity of part-time work has a more consistently negative impact on school performance than does comparable involvement in extracurricular activities (Lamborn et al., 1992). And, although adults believe that television viewing has a negative effect on adolescents' academic performance, studies do not always support this conclusion. It is more likely that poor school performance leads to increased television viewing than the reverse. More often displaced by television viewing than schoolwork are more marginal activities, such as daydreaming or "goofing off" (Fine et al., 1990).

By valuing adolescents' leisure only when it is "free" time that is used productively, however, adults may misunderstand the important functions that leisure serves in the psychosocial development of the young person. For example, studies show that a moderate amount of solitude (during which daydreaming is a central activity) is positively related to high school students' psychological well-being (Csikszentmihalyi and Larson, 1984). As we shall see in subsequent chapters, leisure plays an important role in helping young people to develop a sense of themselves, to explore their relationships with each other, and to learn about the society around them.

Participation in Extracurricular Activities

For many adolescents, school-sponsored extracurricular activities provide the context for much of their leisure activity. According to recent surveys, about two-thirds of American high school students participate in one or more extracurricular activities, although the participation rate varies greatly from school to school. The most popular type of extracurricular activities are athletics, in which nearly half of all adolescents participate. The other two sets of activities in which many adolescents participate are those related to music (such as band, chorus, orchestra, or glee club; about one-fourth of all adolescent students participate in these) and those related to academic or occupational interests (such as science clubs, language clubs, or clubs oriented toward certain careers; about one-fifth of all adolescent students participate in these) (Berk, 1992).

Participation in extracurricular activities is influenced by a number of factors. In general, participation is somewhat more prevalent among adolescents from middle-class families, among students who earn better grades, and among students from smaller schools and smaller, more rural communities, where school activities often play a relatively more central role in the lives of adults and adolescents alike (e.g., where an entire community may turn out for a school's Friday night basketball or football game). African-American students are somewhat more likely to participate than white students; and whereas boys are more likely than girls to participate in athletic activities, the reverse is true in the case of nonathletic activities (Berk, 1992).

Researchers have spent considerable time studying the impact of extracurricular participation on adolescent development, but it has been difficult to draw any firm conclusions, because few studies separate cause and effect. For example, although researchers generally find that participants have higher self-esteem than nonparticipants, it isn't clear whether students with high self-esteem are more likely to go out for extracurricular activities to begin with, or whether participation makes students feel better about themselves. The few longitudinal studies that have tried to get at cause and effect suggest, however, that participation in an extracurricular activity seems to improve students' performance in school, to reduce the likelihood of dropping out, to deter delinquency and drug use, and to enhance students' psychological well-being. Extracurricular activities may also provide greater opportunities for cross-racial friendship than does the regular school day, and African-American adolescents in integrated schools who participate in extracurricular activities especially show better mental health as a result. Extracurricular participation in high school also seems to be linked to extracurricular participation in college and to community involvement in adulthood—people who are "do-ers" as adolescents tend to remain so in young and middle adulthood.

The generally positive picture that emerges of extracurricular participation is especially interesting in light of the research reviewed earlier regarding after-school jobs. Whereas employment tends to hurt school performance, increase delinquency, and heighten drug and alcohol use, participating in school-sponsored extracurricular activities seems to have reverse effects. Researchers speculate that this is because extracurricular activities increase students' contact with teachers and other school personnel who may reinforce the value of school (as when a coach or advisor counsels a student about plans for college) and because participation itself may improve students' confidence and self-image. Some educators believe that extracurricular participation also helps bond students to their school, especially in the case of adolescents who are not achieving much academically; for many of them, their extracurricular activity is what keeps them coming to school each day (Berk, 1992).

Leisure Activities and Socialization for Adulthood

Despite adults' feelings to the contrary, leisure serves a number of important functions during adolescence. Many leisure activities—especially those organized and controlled by adults—are structured to socialize adolescents into adult roles, including, quite often, traditional sex roles. Donna Eder and Stephen Parker (1987), for example, have studied how high school extracurricular activities socialize males and females in different ways. In an extensive ethnographic study of a secondary school, the researchers examined how different extracurricular activities were viewed within the school, and they studied the values that were communicated to adolescents through activities.

In the school they studied, as in many others, athletics were the chief route to popularity and status for boys. But which values were communicated through team sports? An analysis of interactions during practice and during other free periods (e.g., lunch time) revealed that the culture of boys' athletics emphasizes achievement, toughness, dominance, and competition—all traits that society has traditionally valued in the socialization of adult males. Consider, for example, the following observation taken from the researchers' field notes during football practice:

> A player came up to a coach as practice was just beginning and complained that another player was starting a fight with him. The coach seemed aggravated at having to deal with this and told him to "knock his socks off in practice." This player was not particularly satisfied with the suggestion but realized that was all he could get from Coach James. (Eder and Parker, 1987, p. 205)

In contrast, although aggression and competitiveness were valued within girls' sports, athletics were not a route toward popularity or status for girls in the school, and, as a consequence, these traits were less likely to be socialized among girls. For instance, on days when "big" games were to be played by the boys' teams, team members wore their athletic jerseys to school so that they would be recognized by their peers. On days when the girls' teams had "big" games, however, team members did not wear their jerseys. One reason was that being a member of an athletic team *detracted* from a girl's popularity.

The main route toward popularity for girls in this school was through cheerleading. Are the traits that were valued in this activity the ones traditionally stressed in the socialization of adult women? Consider the following observation recorded during cheerleading tryouts:

Many of the articles and advertisements contained in magazines read by adolescent girls convey the message that physical beauty is the road to true happiness. (Photo Works)

> At one point, Mrs. Tolson started to tell them what they were going to be judged on, saying they would get 10 points (out of 50) for a "sparkle," which was their smile, personality, bubbliness, appearance, attractiveness—not that all cheerleaders had to be attractive, but it was important to have a clean appearance, not to be sloppy, have messy or greasy hair, because that doesn't look like a cheerleader. (Eder and Parker, 1987, p. 207)

These traits—appearance, neatness, and "bubbliness"—are all characteristics traditionally socialized in women. In essence, the popularity accorded male athletes rewarded boys for behaving in ways stereotypical for men, while the popularity accorded female cheerleaders rewarded girls for behaving in ways stereotypical for women.

You may well be thinking that this difference in emphasis makes perfect sense, because football requires aggression and toughness and cheerleading requires "sparkle." But as the researchers point out, it is "interesting that neatly combed hair was emphasized [in cheerleading tryouts], given the physical nature of this activity, which includes cartwheels and backflips. It is also interesting to compare the focus on neatness during cheerleading with the absence of this concern during male and female athletics" (p. 207). According to these researchers, an important reason for the difference between the emphases of football and cheerleading concerns the function of extracurricular activities in the socialization of male and female gender roles. Along similar lines, male and female athletes are more likely to be admired when they participate in "sex-appropriate" sports (Holland and Andre, 1994).

Similar results emerged from an analysis of the content of leading magazines aimed at adolescent girls (Evans et al., 1990). The majority of articles in these magazines focused on dating and heterosexual relationships, and most emphasized the importance of physical attractiveness for young women. According to the researchers, the articles and advertisements contained in these magazines conveyed a clear message that attracting males by being physically beautiful was the road to true happiness. In contrast, little space was devoted to issues of education, to self-improvement in other than physical ways, or to matters of ethics. As in cheerleading, the emphasis in teen magazines that are aimed at girls is on cultivating that superficial "sparkle." Another analysis, of the fiction appearing in *Seventeen* magazine, found that in the majority of the stories the main character did not solve her own problems but depended on someone else to solve them for her. In these stories, as well, occupations were portrayed in traditionally sex-stereotyped terms (Pierce, 1993).

Although many of the messages teenagers receive from the mass media reinforce traditional stereotypes, some do not. One analysis of the content of popular television shows about families found that the portrayal of families on television was markedly different from reality. On these shows, nonconventional families (single-parent homes, families with adopted children, families composed of children and nonparental guardians) were greatly overrepresented on television and that men were depicted as being much more involved in family roles than is generally the case. Difficult issues like poverty, family conflict, divorce, and stress were generally sidestepped (Moore, 1992). Another analysis, of the presentation of work on television, found that television shows overrepresent and glamorize more prestigious, exciting, and adventurous jobs (e.g., lawyers, doctors, entertainers). Interestingly, adolescents who watch a great deal of television are more likely to aspire to such jobs and to believe that such jobs are easy and lucrative and permit one to take long vacations (Signorelli, 1993).

RECAP

Leisure occupies more of an adolescent's time than do school and work combined. Although adults are prone to see leisure as "wasted" time, leisure serves a number of important functions during adolescence. It socializes adolescents for adult roles and, in the case of participation in school-sponsored extracurricular activities, may enhance adolescents' well-being and strengthen their attachment to school.

Leisure and the Mass Media

Not all of the socialization that occurs in adolescents' leisure activities is aimed at teaching about adult roles; indeed, if this were the case, adults would rarely complain about how adolescents spend their free time. Leisure activities also play an important role in exposing adolescents to elements of the popular culture in general, and to elements of the youth culture in particular. It is in this respect that adolescent leisure activity has generated the most controversy.

Researchers estimate that adolescents spend between one-half and one-third of their waking hours with one or another of the mass media, including television, radio, and print. Sometimes the media are the focus of the teenager's activity; often, they are in the background. (Interestingly, when teenagers and adults listen to music while doing something else and then they are asked to say what they are doing, teenagers are more likely than adults to list listening to music as the primary activity [Larson, 1994].) Although there is considerable variation within the adolescent population in the amount of time spent in front of the television, contemporary adolescents view, on average, between two and four hours of television daily (Fine et al., 1990). This does not include music video, which is typically grouped along with other types of music media in studies of adolescent media use, or prerecorded movies on videotape, which is typically considered along with other film viewing. In general, TV viewing peaks during early adolescence, and then it declines over the high school years.

One reason for the decline of television viewing during adolescence is that it is displaced by time spent with other media. By middle adolescence, the typical American teenager listens to music from four to six hours daily, either via radio, recorded music, or music video. As teenagers get older, more attend movies (about half of all teenagers report going to the movies at least monthly) and spend considerable time watching videocassettes—studies of VCR use report teenagers watching between five and ten hours weekly. Use of print media also increases during adolescence: Between 60 percent and 80 percent of late adolescents report at least some daily newspaper reading, one-third report daily magazine reading, and one-fifth report daily reading of nonschool books. According to a recent review, when time devoted to all media is combined—even figuring that some time is spent engaged in more than one activity simultaneously, such as reading while listening to music—it appears that the average adolescent spends about eight hours each day with some form of mass media (Fine et al., 1990).

According to psychologist Reed Larson (1994), one of the reasons that television viewing declines, and listening to music increases, is that television viewing is far less satisfying to the adolescent as far as his or her developmental needs are concerned. Television, he argues, is created by adults for a general audience, while many types of popular music (e.g., rap, heavy metal) are created specifically for adolescents. Not surprisingly, studies of teenagers' emotional states indicate that they often feel vacant while watching television but

THE SCIENTIFIC STUDY OF ADOLESCENCE

THE EXPERIENCE SAMPLING METHOD

Many of the questions that psychologists who study adolescence are interested in are difficult to answer through the conventional methodologies of observational or questionnaire research. Questions concerning adolescents' emotional states, for instance, are especially tricky, because individuals' emotions change during the day and may not be, at the time of a researcher's assessment, reflective of their moods at other points in the day. Suppose a researcher wanted to know how adolescents' moods were affected by various activities—such as attending school, watching television, or having dinner with the family. Although it would be possible to interview respondents and ask them to *recall* their moods at different points in the day, we cannot be sure whether their recollections are entirely accurate.

One of the most interesting innovations to shape the scientific study of adolescence in recent years was designed to overcome this and other sorts of methodological problems. Using the **Experience Sampling Method (ESM),** researchers can collect much more detailed information about adolescents' experiences over the course of the day, and scientists using this method have illuminated many different aspects of the adolescent experience. The ESM has been used to chart adolescents' moods, to monitor their social relationships, and to catalog their activities in far greater detail than has been previously available.

The use of the ESM in the study of adolescent development has been pioneered by psychologist Reed Larson and his colleagues (Larson and Lampman-Petraitis, 1989; Larson and Richards, 1989, 1991). In studies using this method, adolescents "carry electronic pagers and report on their activities, companionship, and internal states at random times when signaled by the pagers" (Larson and Richards, 1991). In one study, for example, Larson had nearly five hundred adolescents between the ages of 9 and 15 carry pagers and booklets of self-report forms for one week and asked the adolescents to fill out a form each time they were signaled. The form contained a series of questions about companionship ("Who were you with [or talking to on the phone]?"), location ("Where were you?"), activity ("What were you doing?"), and affect (the adolescents used a checklist to report their moods). The adolescents were "beeped" seven times each day, once within every two-hour block between 7:30 A.M. and 9:30 P.M. By examining the adolescents' many reports, the researchers were able to chart changes in activities, companionship, and mood over the course of the week and to relate variations in activity, companionship, and mood to one another. Thus, the method permitted the researchers to ask how activities, companionship, and mood varied as a function of age; how mood varied as a function of what the adolescent was doing; and how both activity and mood varied as a function of whom the adolescent was with.

One of the questions asked in the study was how adolescents' moods varied as a function of whom they were with (parents, peers, or no one) and whether the connection between mood and companionship changed with age. The results are presented in the accompanying figure.

As you can see, adolescents' moods are generally most positive when they are with their friends and least positive when they are alone; their moods when with their family fall somewhere in between. More interesting, perhaps, is that between grades 5 and 9, adolescents' moods while with friends become more positive, whereas their moods while with their family follow a **curvilinear pattern,** which either can be *U*-shaped or can look like an inverted *U*. That is, their moods while with their family become more negative between elementary and middle school (i.e., between grades 5 and 7) and then rise between middle school and high school (between grades 8 and 9). As Larson and Richards point out, this dip parallels findings from other research on family relations (see Chapter 4) that points to early adolescence as a time of somewhat heightened strain in the parent-child relationship.

The data about these adolescents' moods when they were alone are somewhat surprising. Given the fact that adolescents spend increasingly more time alone as they get older, one might expect that solitude would be associated with more positive—not more negative—affect. Although the researchers could not explain this finding easily, one hypothesis is that, when alone, adolescents spend a good deal of their time thinking about themselves and working through the events of the day (Larson, 1990). Some of the time spent alone is spent listening to music, and some of the music adolescents listen to may have sad or depressing themes (unrequited love, broken relationships, etc.). Interestingly, other studies using the ESM (e.g., Csikszentmihalyi and Larson, 1984) find that adolescents feel *better* after being alone and that, with age, solitude tends to become associated with more positive feelings (Larson, 1990). Taken together, these findings suggest that periods of solitude may be associated with negative mood in the short term but with positive mood in the long term.

SOURCE: Larson, R., and Richards, M. (1991). Daily companionship in late childhood and early adolescence: Changing developmental contexts. *Child Development*, *62*, 284–300.

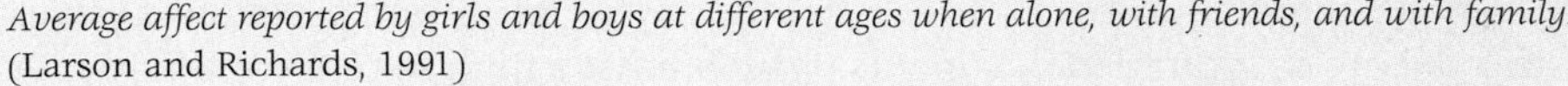

Average affect reported by girls and boys at different ages when alone, with friends, and with family. (Larson and Richards, 1991)

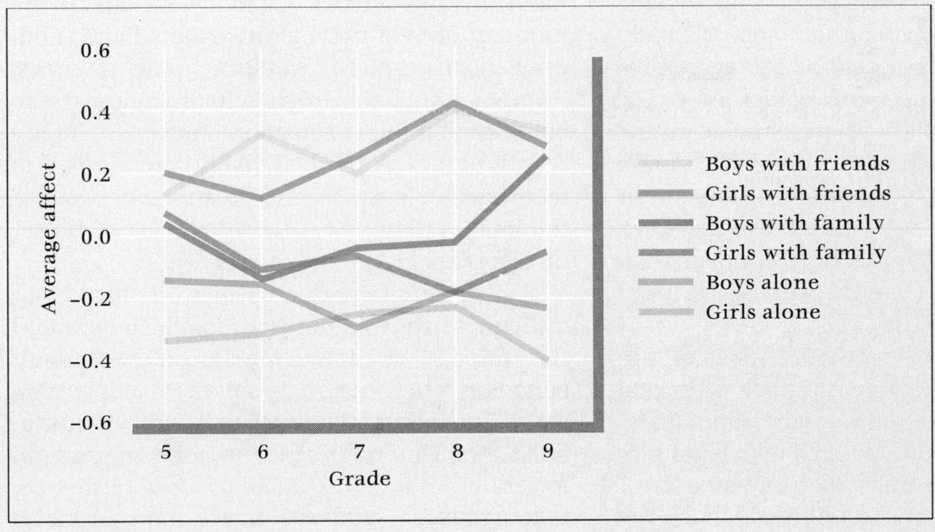

are more aroused (either positively or negatively) while listening to music (Larson, 1994). In addition, Larson finds that television tends to link adolescents with their families (in part because adolescents, especially young adolescents, often watch television with other family members), whereas listening to music is often a solitary activity. (Watching television with parents becomes less frequent during adolescence, however [Sang, Schmitz, and Tasche, 1993].) Indeed, the typical teenager spends 13 percent of waking hours in the bedroom—second only to time spent at school—and much of that time is spent listening to music (J. Brown, 1994). Over the course of adolescence, there is a substantial increase in the amount of time adolescents spend alone, although this increase is greater for boys than for girls (Larson and Richards, 1991; Wong and Csikzentmihalyi, 1991; see accompanying box).

Given the considerable amount of time adolescents spend in the presence of mass media, it is not surprising to find that the impact of the media on teenagers' behavior and development has been the subject of much debate. Unfortunately, little of the debate is grounded in scientific research. Although some adults have expressed worry that the sexually explicit lyrics of rock music or the aggressive images of MTV corrupt the values of young people (e.g., Gore, 1987), there is no scientific evidence that teenagers are influenced in any systematic way by what they listen to or watch (Fine et al., 1990). Adults read more sex and violence into the lyrics of rock music than adolescent listeners actually pick up (Prinsky and Rosenbaum, 1987).

It is clear, however, that teenagers are exposed to a considerable number of sexual messages through the mass media. One analysis of teenagers' top-ten favorite television programs found, for example, that one-quarter of all the interactions between individuals on the shows contained sexual content (Ward, in press). In some shows, among the most popular, more than half of all interactions between individuals contained sexual content (see Figure 7.5). The most common messages concerned men seeing women as sex objects ("Look at the body on that chick"; "In case she's a dog, I can fake a heart attack"); sex being viewed as a defining aspect of masculinity ("I slept with ten girls last week"; "Oh, that's one afternoon for me"); sex as a competition ("You're supposed to be keeping score, not trying to score"); and sex as fun and exciting ("It's so romantic, all that passion, when you have to make love every minute of the day"). Similar messages are carried in most MTV videos, in which men are shown as aggressive and dominant, and women are seen as the subservient objects of men's sexual advances (Sommers-Flanagan, Sommers-Flanagan, and Davis, 1993).

Although we are not sure that exposure to these sorts of messages alters adolescents' *behavior,* repeated exposure likely affects their beliefs. For example, one study found that college students who frequently watched soap operas (which have a high sexual content) gave higher estimates than nonviewers did of the number of real-life extramarital affairs, children born out of wedlock, and divorces. Another found that high school students who believed that television characters enjoy highly satisfying sex were less likely themselves to feel that sex is satisfying, presumably because the images they had seen on television had set up false expectations (Roberts, 1993).

For a number of reasons, it has been difficult to draw definitive conclusions about the impact of mass media on adolescent behavior. One major problem is separating cause and effect: Although it has been speculated that violent images provoke aggression, for example, it is just as likely, if not more so, that aggressive adolescents are more prone to choose to watch violent images. If sexual

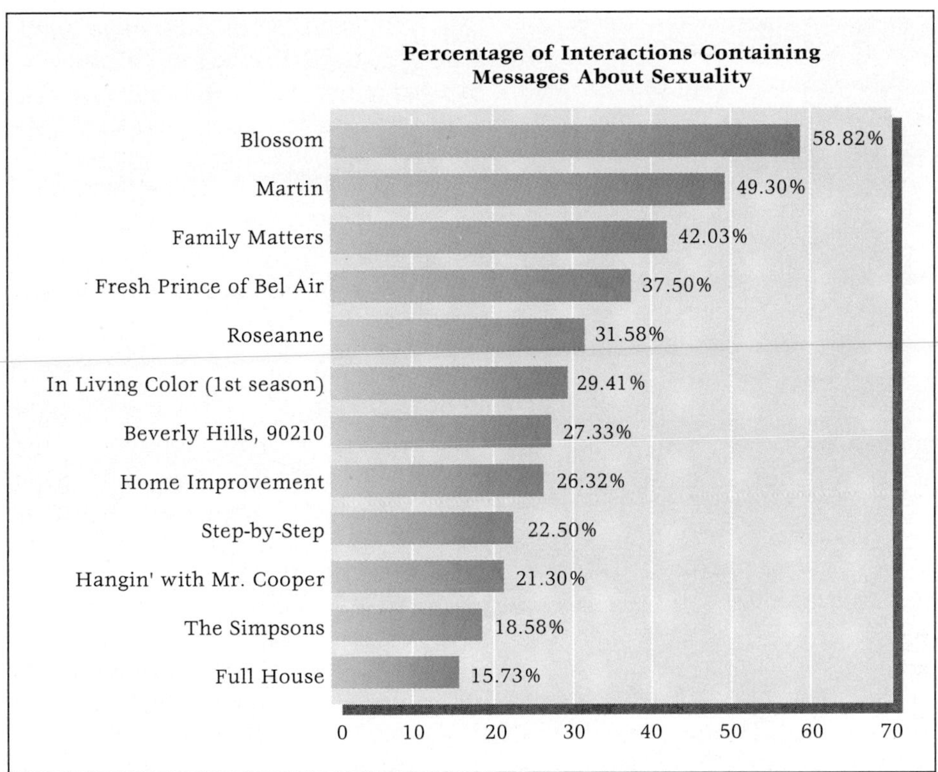

FIGURE 7.5 *Percentage of interactions with sexual content in ten television shows popular with teenagers.* (Ward, in press)

behavior is correlated with listening to "sexy" music, it is impossible to say which causes which.

Researchers also have found that adolescents use the different media under different social circumstances. As noted above, television is often viewed with other members of the family, whereas radio is often listened to alone, and movies are typically viewed with other teenagers (Fine et al., 1990; Larson, Kubey, and Colletti, 1989). Whereas music videos are more attention-getting than audiotape, they provoke less use of the imagination than audio recordings do (Greenfield, Bruzzone, Koyamatsu, Satuloff, Nixon, Brodie, and Kingsdale, 1987). It is quite difficult, in light of all this, to separate the effects of media *content* from those of media *context*.

Finally, and most important, we often fail to distinguish between what adolescents actually perceive and remember and what adults believe adolescents see and remember. After all, media are not simply viewed or heard—they are interpreted. Adolescents are not exposed to the mass media as blank slates; rather, they bring preexisting values, beliefs, and expectations to the experience of watching or listening, and these preexisting states influence what they perceive and remember (Leming, 1987). One extensive study of girls'

Many adults are concerned about the images that adolescents are exposed to in music videos. More often than not, men are shown as aggressive and dominant, and women as the subservient objects of men's sexual advances. (Photo Works)

responses to sexual media content found, for instance, that some girls were disinterested in sexual media, others were intrigued, and still others resisted the sexual imagery to the point of criticizing it. When asked to comment on what she had been watching on television, for example, a disinterested girl wrote:

> I was watching Moonlighting tonight. . . . Maddie takes off her clothes (you don't see anything) and says, "Sam, I can't marry you because I love David, but for tonite, hold me. Make love to me." I thought it was kind of gross. (Brown, White, and Nikopoulou, 1993, p. 182)

This lack of interest in sexual matters was not seen among other girls, however, who were more intrigued with the sexual content of media messages, if still somewhat confused. One such girl had written the following about a popular song:

> This song was about sex. This song was saying basically "Come over to my house so we can do it!" This represents sex as being O.K. Later I heard "Let's Wait Awhile" by Janet Jackson. Which basically says, "Let's not rush into it." It's kind of hard as a teenager to decide which is right. The guy who was talking about it as being good seemed happy with a carefree sound. Janet

> sounded sad and depressed. Even though I know it's better "to wait awhile" the other song was more appealing. It seemed harmless. They talk about it like, "come over and have ice cream." . . . I really know which way is the right way but sometimes the way the media talks about it you really begin to wonder. (p. 187)

Finally, some of the girls in the study actively resisted, even criticized, the sexual messages conveyed in the popular media. Here, one comments on the movie *Top Gun:*

> Everyone went to see it because of Tom Cruise, they didn't go see it because it was a movie. They came back saying Tom Cruise looked so good and when I asked what it was about, they said, "Oh, flying or something." I didn't like it because of the relationship. They were just using each other at different times for different things. (p. 192)

And, of a magazine ad for perfume, the same girl wrote:

> This is a very BAD sketch of part of an ad for Obsession by Calvin Klein—the whole idea portrayed is SEX, SEX, SEX—people are so goddamned hypocritical. They go all out against pornography and probably some of them buy this perfume. . . . (p. 189)

RECAP

Much of adolescents' leisure time involves one or more of the mass media. Whereas television viewing declines during adolescence, use of music media, movies, and print media all increase. The average adolescent is exposed to the mass media about eight hours daily. Although adults have worried about the corrupting influence of media such as television or rock music, it has been difficult to document such alleged effects. Nevertheless, many observers of the adolescent scene are concerned about the high level of adolescents' exposure to sexual messages through the mass media.

Leisure and the Economy

A final, and very important, function of adolescent leisure activity is economic. Both the size of the adolescent population and the fact that adolescents save less than any other age group make young people an attractive target for a variety of businesses (Fine et al., 1990). In 1993, teenagers spent $61 billion, not counting the $24 billion their parents gave them to spend on groceries and the estimated $127 billion in purchases by others whom they influence. The average young adolescent has nearly $150 per month in spending money; the average high school student has more than $300. Not surprisingly, virtually all of adolescents' money is spent on purchases related to leisure activities. According to recent surveys, girls spend money on clothes, food, and cosmetics, in that order; boys use their money for food, clothes, and saving for big-ticket items, like cars or stereo equipment (Meyer, 1994).

One can certainly debate the merits of cultivating such strong consumer urges among the young and impressionable (see Greenberger and Steinberg, 1986). But it is important to recognize that the segments of our economy which are devoted to leisure and recreation depend on the adolescent market. Among the most important industries are those connected with movies, music, sports, and television. Teenagers make up a large, and therefore influential, segment of the consumers of these products—as a glance at the local movie or television listings or a trip through a music store will readily attest.

Students of adolescent consumerism have been quick to point out the strong influence that teenagers have on each other when it comes to purchases. It is important to point out, however, that the influence of the adolescent market extends well beyond the youth cohort—as evidenced by the uncanny predictability with which adult tastes in clothing and music often follow those of teenagers, albeit in a toned-down fashion. Interestingly, the power of adolescents as consumers has increased in recent decades, owing to the growth in the proportion of single-parent and dual-worker households. In many such homes, adolescents influence both day-to-day and major purchases—in part because adolescents themselves may do a fair amount of the family's shopping (Graham, 1988).

KEY TERMS

community service
curvilinear pattern
displacement hypothesis
Experience Sampling Method (ESM)
occupational deviance
premature affluence
youth unemployment

FOR FURTHER READING

Berk, L. (1992). The extracurriculum. In P. Jackson (Ed.), *Handbook of research on curriculum.* New York: Macmillan. A thorough review of the literature on the nature, antecedents, and consequences of extracurricular participation.

Fine, G., Mortimer, J., and Roberts, D. (1990). Leisure, work, and the mass media. Pp. 225–252 in S. Feldman and G. Elliott (Eds.), *At the threshold: The developing adolescent.* Cambridge, Mass.: Harvard University Press. A review of research on work and leisure in adolescence.

Greenberg, B., Brown, J., and Buerkel-Rothfuss, N. (Eds.). (1993). *Media, sex, and the adolescent.* Creskill, N.J.: Hampton Press. A collection of articles on sexual images in the mass media and how adolescents are affected by them.

Larson, R., and Richards, M. (Eds.). (1989). The changing life space of early adolescence. *Journal of Youth and Adolescence, 18(6).* A special issue of the journal devoted to a series of studies, using the Experience Sampling Method, of how adolescents spend their time.

Steinberg, L., and Cauffman, E. (1995). The impact of employment on adolescent development. In R. Vasta (Ed.), *Annals of Child Development,* Vol. 11. A comprehensive review of research on teenagers and their jobs.

PART THREE

PSYCHOSOCIAL DEVELOPMENT DURING ADOLESCENCE

CHAPTER 8

IDENTITY

(Paul Conklin/PhotoEdit)

What am I like as a person? Complicated! I'm sensitive, friendly, outgoing, popular, and tolerant, though I can also be shy, self-conscious, and even obnoxious. Obnoxious! I'd *like* to be friendly and tolerant all of the time. That's the kind of person I *want* to be, and I'm disappointed when I'm not. I'm responsible, even studious every now and then, but on the other hand I'm a goof-off too, because if you're too studious, you won't be popular. I don't usually do that well at school. I'm a pretty cheerful person, especially with my friends, where I can even get rowdy. At home I'm more likely to be anxious around my parents. They expect me to get all A's. It's not fair! I worry about how I probably *should* get better grades. But I'd be mortified in the eyes of my friends. So I'm usually pretty stressed-out at home, or sarcastic, since my parents are always on my case. But I really don't understand how I can switch so fast. I mean, how can I be cheerful one minute, anxious the next, and then be sarcastic? Which one is the *real* me? Sometimes I feel phony, especially around boys. Say I think some guy might be interested in asking me out. I try to act different, like Madonna. I'll be flirtatious and fun-loving. And then *everybody,* I mean everybody else is looking at me like they think I'm totally weird! Then I get self-conscious and embarrassed and become radically introverted, and I don't know who I really am! Am I just trying to impress them or what? But I don't really care what they think anyway. I don't *want* to care, that is. I just want to know what my close friends think. I can be my true self with my close friends. I can't be my real self with my parents. They don't understand me. What do *they* know about what it's like to be a teenager? They treat me like I'm still a kid. At least at school people treat you more like you're an adult. That gets confusing, though. I mean, which am I, a kid or an adult? It's scary, too, because I don't have any idea what I want to be when I grow up. I mean, I have lots of *ideas.* My friend Sheryl and I talk about whether we'll be stewardesses, or teachers, or nurses, veterinarians, maybe mothers, or actresses. I know I don't want to be a waitress or a secretary. But how do you decide all of this? I really don't know. I mean, I think about it a lot, but I can't resolve it. There are days when I wish I could just become immune to myself! (Harter, 1990, pp. 352–353)

As you may recall from your own adolescence, there are few experiences that can be as trying—or as exhilarating—as questioning who you really are and, more important, who you would like to be. Some, but not all, adolescents share the feelings of self-consciousness and confusion expressed in the statement above by a 15-year-old girl. For these young people, adolescence is a time of "identity crisis." For other adolescents, though, this period is one of more gradual and more subtle change.

Because changes—whether gradual or abrupt—take place during adolescence in the way young people view and feel about themselves, the study of identity development has been a major focus of research and theory on adolescents. In this chapter, we examine whether adolescence is indeed a time of major changes in identity and how the course of adolescent identity development is shaped by the nature of life in contemporary society.

IDENTITY AS AN ADOLESCENT ISSUE

Changes in the way in which we see and feel about ourselves occur throughout the life cycle. You have probably heard and read about the so-called "midlife crisis," for example—an identity crisis thought to occur during middle age. And certainly there are important changes in self-conceptions and in self-image throughout childhood. When a group of 4-year-olds and a group of 10-year-olds are asked to describe themselves, the older children provide a far more complex self-portrait. While

For some young people, like those portrayed in the television show My So-Called Life, *adolescence is a time of "identity crisis." For other adolescents, the period is one of more gradual and subtle change.* (Photofest)

young children restrict their descriptions to lists of what they own or what they like to do, older children are more likely to tell you also about their personality.

If, in fact, changes in identity occur throughout the life cycle, why have researchers who are interested in identity development paid so much attention to adolescence? One reason is that the changes in identity which take place during adolescence involve the first substantial reorganization and restructuring of the individual's sense of self at a time when he or she has the intellectual capability to appreciate fully just how significant the changes are. Although important changes in identity certainly occur during childhood, the adolescent is far more self-conscious about these changes and feels them much more acutely.

Another reason for the attention that researchers and theorists have given the study of identity development during adolescence concerns the fundamental biological, cognitive, and social changes characteristic of the period. Puberty, as we saw in Chapter 1, brings with it dramatic changes in physical appearance and alters the adolescent's self-conceptions and relationships with others. It is not hard to see why puberty plays an important role in provoking identity development during adolescence. When you change the way you look—when you have your hair cut in a different way, lose a great deal of weight, or dramatically change the way you dress—you sometimes feel as though your personality has changed, too. During puberty, when adolescents are changing so dramatically on the *outside,* they understandably have questions about changes that are taking place on the *inside.* For the adolescent, undergoing the physical changes of puberty may prompt fluctuations in the self-image and a reevaluation of who he or she really is.

Just as the broadening of intellectual capabilities during early adolescence provides new ways of thinking about problems, values, and interpersonal relationships, it also permits adolescents to think about themselves in new ways. We saw in Chapter 2 that it is not until adolescence that the young person is able to think in systematic ways about hypothetical and future events. For this reason, it is not until adolescence that individuals typically begin to wonder, "Who will I become?" "What possible identities are open to me?" or "What am I really like?" Because the preadolescent child's thinking is concrete, it is difficult for him or her to think seriously about being a different person. But the changes in thinking that take place during adolescence open up a whole new world of alternatives.

Finally, we saw in Chapter 3 that the changes in social roles that occur at adolescence open up a new array of choices and decisions for the young person that were not concerns previously. In contemporary society, adolescence is a time of important decisions about work, marriage, and the future. Facing these decisions about our place in society does more than provoke questions about who we are and where we are headed—it necessitates the questions. At this point in the life cycle, young people must make important choices about their careers and their commitments to other people, and thinking about these questions prompts them to ask more questions about themselves: "What do I *really* want out of life?" "What things are important to me?" "What kind of person would I *really* like to be?" Questions about the future, which inevitably arise as the adolescent prepares for adulthood, raise questions about identity.

Identity development is complex and multifaceted. Actually, it is better understood as a *series* of interrelated developments—rather than one single development—that all involve changes in the way we view ourselves in relation to others and in relation to the broader society in which we live. Generally speaking, researchers and theorists have taken three different approaches to the question of how the individual's sense of identity changes over the course of adolescence. Each approach, examined in detail later in this chapter, focuses on a different aspect of identity development.

The first approach emphasizes changes in *self-conceptions*—the ideas that individuals have of themselves as regards various traits and attributes. An entirely different approach focuses on adolescents' *self-esteem,* or self-image—how positively or negatively individuals feel about themselves. Finally, a third approach emphasizes changes in the *sense of identity*—the sense of who one is, where one has come from, and where one is going.

RECAP

Although changes in the way we see and feel ourselves occur throughout the life cycle, the study of identity development has been a prominent issue in the field of adolescent development in particular. One reason for this attention concerns the impact that the biological, cognitive, and social definitional changes of adolescence have on the young person's ability to engage in self-examination, and on his or her interest in doing so. Researchers have traditionally distinguished among three aspects of identity development in adolescence: changes in self-conceptions, changes in self-esteem, and changes in the sense of identity.

CHANGES IN SELF-CONCEPTIONS

During adolescence, important shifts occur in the way individuals think about and characterize themselves—that is, in their **self-conceptions.** As individuals mature intellectually and undergo the sorts of cognitive changes described in Chapter 2, they come to conceive of themselves in more sophisticated and more differentiated ways. As we saw in that chapter, adolescents are much more capable than children of thinking about abstract concepts. This intellectual advantage affects the way in which individuals characterize themselves. Compared with children, who tend to describe themselves in relatively simple, concrete terms, adolescents are more likely to employ complex, abstract, and psychological self-characterizations (Harter, 1990).

Self-conceptions change in structure as well as in content during the transition from childhood into and through adolescence. Structurally, self-conceptions become *more differentiated and better organized* (Livesley and Bromley, 1973; Marsh, 1989a; Montemayor and Eisen, 1977).

Consider first the movement toward greater differentiation. In answer to the question "Who am I?" adolescents are more likely than children to link traits and attributes that describe themselves to specific situations, rather than using them as global characterizations. While a preadolescent child might say, "I am nice" or "I am friendly" and not specify when or under what conditions, an adolescent is more likely to say, "I am nice *if* I am in a good mood" or "I am friendly *when* I am with people I have met before." The realization that one's personality is expressed in different ways in different situations is one example of the increased differentiation that characterizes the self-conceptions of youngsters as they mature toward adulthood.

There is another way in which self-conceptions become more highly differentiated at adolescence. As opposed to characterizations provided by children, adolescents' self-descriptions take into account *who* is doing the describing (Livesley and Bromley, 1973). Teenagers differentiate between their own opinions of themselves and the views of others. Suppose you asked a group of youngsters to describe how they behaved when they were with other people. Instead of saying, "I am shy" or "I am outgoing," an adolescent would be more likely to say, "People think I'm not at all shy, but most of the time, I'm really nervous about meeting other kids for the first time." Adolescents also recognize that they may come across differently to different people, another type of differentiation in self-conceptions that does not appear until this point in time: "My parents think I'm quiet, but my friends know I really like to party a lot."

With this shift toward increased differentiation in self-conceptions comes better organization and integration (Harter, 1990; Marsh, 1989a). When children are asked to describe themselves, the traits and attributes they list remain somewhat disparate, like items haphazardly placed on a grocery list. Adolescents, however, are likely to organize and integrate different aspects of their self-image into a more logical, coherent whole. Whereas a younger child may list a sequence of several traits that appear to be contradictory ("I am friendly. I am shy."), an adolescent will attempt to organize apparently discrepant bits of information into more highly organized statements ("I am shy when I first meet people, but after I get to know them, I'm usually pretty friendly.")

Although it does not appear that self-conceptions become even more differentiated after early adolescence (Marsh, 1989a), the movement toward more abstract and more psychological self-conceptions continues well into the high school years, as the 15-year-old's self-description at the beginning of this chapter clearly indicates. Interestingly, however, the increased abstraction and psychological complexity of self-conceptions may present some difficulties for middle adolescents, who may be able to recognize—but not yet quite understand or reconcile—inconsistencies and contradictions in their personality. The proportion of adolescents who give opposite traits in self-descriptions, who feel conflicts over such discrepancies, and who feel confused over such discrepancies increases markedly between seventh and ninth grades, and then it declines somewhat after (Harter and Monsour, 1992). For example, one 15-year-old girl, when asked about her contention that she was happy with friends but depressed with her family, said, "I really think of myself as a happy person, and I want to be that way with everyone because I think that's my true self, but I get depressed with my family and it bugs me because that's not what I want to be like" (Harter and Monsour, 1992, p. 253).

In one study, when asked to reflect on contradictions in their personalities, early, middle, and late adolescents responded in very different ways, as in the following examples (cited in Harter, 1990, p. 358):

> I guess I just think about one thing about myself at a time and don't think about the other until the next day. (11–12 years old)
>
> I really think I am a happy person and I want to be that way with everyone, but I get depressed with my family and it really bugs me because that's not what I want to be like. (14–15 years old)
>
> You can be shy on a date, and then outgoing with friends because you are just different with different people; you can't always be the same person and probably shouldn't be. (17–18 years old)

In another study, psychologists Susan Harter and Ann Monsour asked adolescents to characterize their personalities by placing various traits (which were written on a series of gummed labels) on a series of concentric circles, indicating those traits that were more central and those that were less important. Figure 8.1 shows the diagram constructed by a 15-year-old girl. As you can see, the diagram illustrates a number of conflicting traits, some of which are based on the girl's description of herself as being one way in a certain setting (e.g., outgoing with friends) but the opposite in another (e.g., shy in romantic relationships).

Although the recognition that one's personality is multifaceted—even contradictory—may initially cause some distress, in the long run it probably has a number of advantages. For example, adolescents who have more complex self-conceptions are less likely to be depressed (Evans, 1993). One additional advantage of having a more differentiated self-concept is that the adolescent is now able to distinguish among his or her actual self (who the adolescent really is), ideal self (who the adolescent would like to be), and feared self (who the adolescent most dreads becoming). According to one view, being able to make these distinctions provides a motive for the adolescent to improve—either to bring his or her actual self more into line with the ideal self or to strive to become one's ideal self and avoid becoming one's feared self (Markus and Nurius, 1986; Oyserman and Markus, 1990). One important aspect of having a healthy self-concept is having an ideal self to balance a feared self. One study found, for example, that delinquent adolescents were less likely than nondelinquent youth to have this sort of balanced view; although delinquent adolescents might dread becoming criminals, for instance, they may not have a positive hoped-for self (e.g., to be successfully employed) to balance this fear (Oyserman and Markus, 1990). Interestingly, adolescents tend to imagine more similarity between their present and future

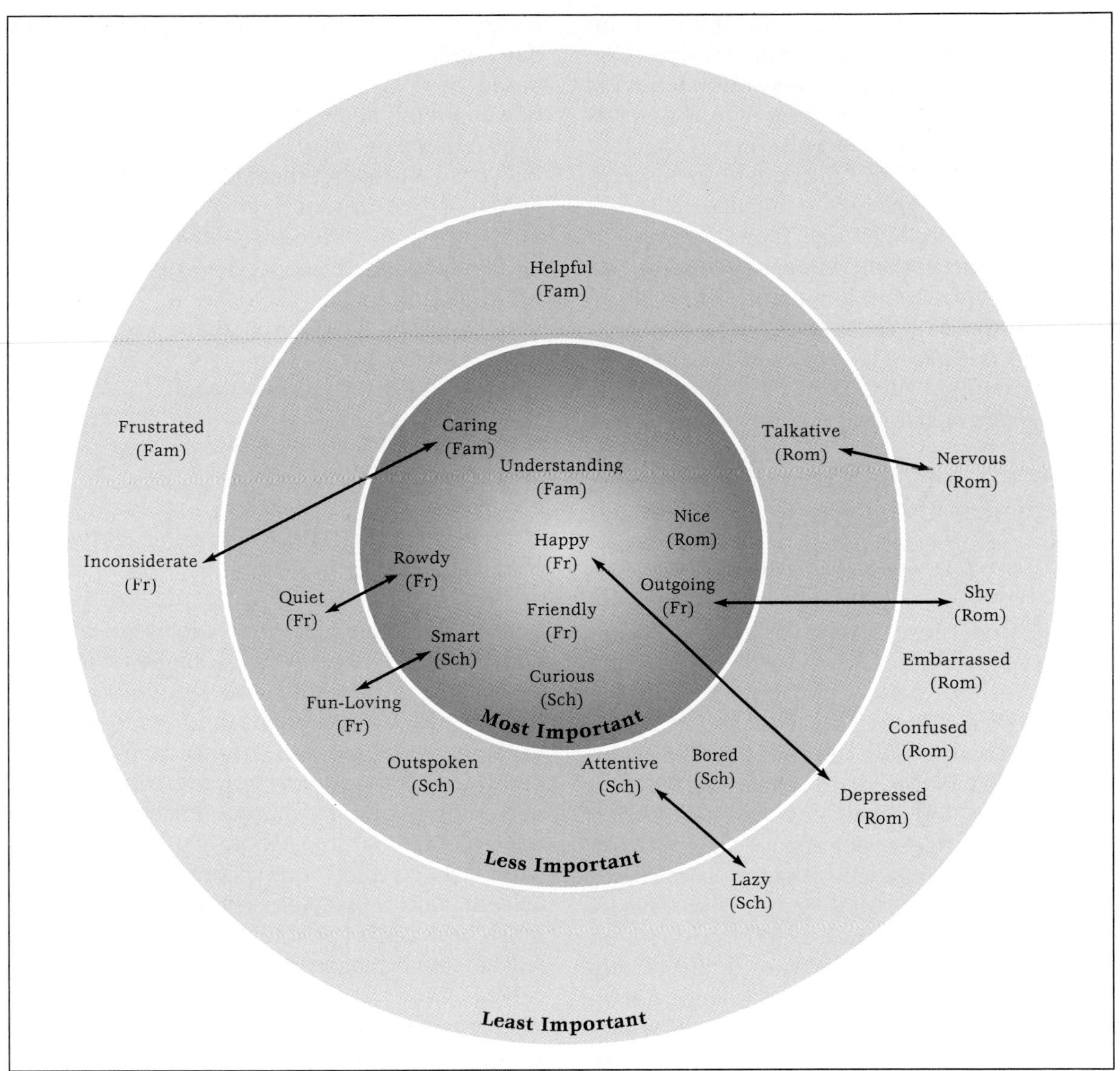

FIGURE 8.1 *The psychological self-portrait of a ninth-grade girl.* Note: Fam = family; Rom = romantic relationship; Fr = friends; Sch = school.
(Harter and Monsour, 1992)

selves than they say exists between their past and present selves (Hart, Fegley, and Brengelman, 1993).

Another interesting consequence of adolescents' recognition that they are not always consistent in their personality relates to their ability to distinguish between their true and false selves (i.e., their authentic and inauthentic selves). Adolescents are most likely to behave inauthentically in romantic and dating situations and with classmates, and they are least likely to put on a false front with close friends. Interestingly, **false-self behavior** occurs less often with parents than with dates but more often with parents than with close friends (Harter, 1990). Although adolescents sometimes say that they dislike false-self behavior, they also say that there are times in which it is acceptable, such as when one is trying to impress another person or trying to hide an aspect of his or her personality that others do not like. You can well imagine how the ability to put on a false front would come in handy on a date, at school, or with one's parents.

Adolescents differ, of course, in the degree to which they present false fronts and in their reasons for doing so. In general, adolescents who report less emotional support from parents and peers, those who have low self-esteem, and those who are relatively more depressed and hopeless than their peers are more likely to engage in false-self behavior. Whereas some adolescents engage in false-self behavior *because* they are low in self-esteem, others experience a drop in self-esteem *because* they knowingly put on a false front. Depression and hopelessness are highest among adolescents who engage in false-self behavior because they genuinely devalue their true self, in contrast to those who put on a false front because they want to please others or because they are experimenting with different personalities (Harter, Marold, Whitesell, and Cobbs, in press).

Understanding how self-conceptions change during adolescence helps to explain why issues of identity begin to take on so much importance at this time in the life span. As self-conceptions become more abstract and as individuals become more able to see themselves in psychological terms, young people become more interested in understanding their own personalities and why they behave the way they do. The distress caused by recognizing one's inconsistencies may spur identity development. You may recall having wondered as a teenager about your personality development, about the influences that shaped your character, about how your personality had changed over time. "Am I more like my father or like my mother? Why do my sister and I seem so different? Will I always be so shy?" Although these sorts of questions may seem commonplace to you now, in all likelihood you did not think about these things until adolescence, when your own self-conceptions became more abstract and more sophisticated.

RECAP

During the transition into adolescence, self-conceptions become increasingly complex, abstract, and psychological. In addition, adolescents' self-conceptions are more differentiated and better organized than those of children. Although having more complex self-conceptions initially may be unsettling to the adolescent, it ultimately provides for a more sophisticated and more accurate view of oneself. In addition, adolescents are able to distinguish between their actual and their imagined selves, and between their authentic and false selves.

Dimensions of Personality in Adolescence

While many researchers have studied adolescent personality development by examining young people's views of themselves, others have attempted to assess personality by administering standardized inventories designed to assess the most important aspects of personality. Most personality researchers now approach the study of personality using the **Five-Factor Model** (McCrae and John, 1992), which is based on the observation that there are five critical personality dimensions, often referred to as the **Big Five:** *Extraversion* (how outgoing and energetic a person is), *Agreeableness* (how kind or sympathetic someone is), *Conscientiousness* (how responsible and organized someone is), *Neuroticism* (how anxious or tense someone is), and *Openness to Experience* (how curious and imaginative someone is). Although the Five-Factor Model was developed through research on adults, it has been successfully applied to adolescents as well. For example, delinquent adolescents are more likely than their peers to score high on the Extraversion dimension and low on the Agreeableness and Conscientiousness dimensions, whereas adolescents who are high achievers in school score high on the Conscientiousness and Openness dimensions (John, Caspi, Robins, Moffitt, and Stouthamer-Loeber, 1994). In general, the structure of personality appears comparable across groups of adolescents from different ethnic backgrounds (Rowe, Vazsonyi, and Flannery, 1994).

Researchers point to both genetic and environmental influences on individual differences in personality traits (e.g., Rose, 1988). Individuals may inherit temperamental predispositions (such as a high activity level or an inclination to be sociable), which are observable early in life, and these predispositions may "harden" and become organized into personality traits partially in response to the environment (John et al., 1994). Thus, an active and sociable child who enjoys interacting with others may be rewarded for doing so and, over time, may become extraverted. Longitudinal studies show that both temperament and personality become increasingly stable as we grow older, in part because we tend to spend time in environments that reward and reinforce the traits that draw us to these settings (Guerin and Gottfried, in press).

RECAP

There are five critical personality dimensions in adolescence and adulthood, often referred to as the Big Five: Extraversion, Agreeableness, Conscientiousness, Neuroticism, and Openness to Experience. In general, these traits are influenced by a combination of genetic and environmental factors and are highly stable over time.

CHANGES IN SELF-ESTEEM

As noted in the Introduction to this book, ever since G. Stanley Hall initially suggested that adolescence was a time of "storm and stress," researchers and theorists have asked whether adolescence is a more difficult time for the developing person than are earlier or later periods in the life span. For many years, in fact, the idea that adolescence is inherently stressful for the individual was accepted without question. One of the manifestations assumed to result from the stress of adolescence involves problems in the adolescent's **self-esteem**—how the individual feels about himself or herself.

Research has not supported the view that adolescence is a time of tumultuous upheaval in personality, however, nor is adolescence the time of "rebirth" that philosophers once cast it as being. As one team of researchers put it, "The person who enters adolescence is basically the same as that who exits it" (Dusek and Flaherty, 1981, p. 39). There is also a good deal of evidence that many personality traits, such as aggressiveness, are quite stable between childhood and adolescence. Although the external manifestations of these traits may change with age (for example, anxiety may appear as bed wetting in early childhood but as nervous talkativeness in adolescence), basic, underlying traits are quite stable over time. For example, studies show that individuals who have displayed relatively higher levels of aggression in preadolescence, temper tantrums during childhood, or negative emotions during infancy are more likely to behave aggressively as adolescents (Cairns, Cairns, and Neckerman, 1989; Caspi, Elder, and Bem, 1987; Lerner, Herzog, Hooker, Hassibi, and Thomas, 1988).

Adolescents' feelings about themselves may fluctuate somewhat, particularly during the very early adolescent years (late elementary school and junior high school). From about eighth grade on, however, self-esteem remains stable; individuals with high self-esteem as children are likely to have high self-esteem as adolescents. Nor is there any apparent loss of self-esteem during adolescence. If anything, over the course of middle and late adolescence, and between late adolescence and young adulthood, self-esteem either remains at about the same level or increases (Block and Robins, 1993; Harter, 1990; Nottelmann, 1987; O'Malley and Bachman, 1983; Rosenberg, 1986; Savin-Williams and Demo, 1984). In general, self-esteem tends to become increasingly more stable with age, suggesting that adolescents' feelings about themselves gradually consolidate over time and become less likely to fluctuate in response to different experiences (Alasker and Olweus, 1992).

Just as the "storm-and-stress" view of adolescence is not supported in studies of family relations, neither does it appear to apply to adolescent self-esteem. There is some evidence, however, that for a brief and temporary period during early adolescence, minor problems in self-image may arise. Roberta Simmons and her colleagues have completed a series of studies that shed light on when and why these problems in self-image are likely to occur. These researchers (Simmons, Rosenberg, and Rosenberg, 1973) employed an extensive questionnaire to assess three aspects of adolescents' self-image: their **self-esteem** (how positively or negatively they feel about themselves), their **self-consciousness** (how much they worry about their self-image), and their **self-image stability** (how much they feel that their self-image changes from day to day). They hypothesized that young adolescents would show the lowest levels of self-esteem, the highest levels of self-consciousness, and the shakiest self-image.

Consistent with their expectations, these researchers found that fluctuations in the self-image are most likely to occur between the ages of 12 and 14. Compared with older adolescents (15 years and older) and with preadolescents (8 to 11 years old), early adolescents have lower self-esteem, are more self-conscious, and have a more unstable self-image than other youngsters. Generally speaking, the small but reliable differences between the preadolescents and the early adolescents are greater than those between the younger and the older adolescents, which indicates that the most marked fluctuations occur during the transition into adolescence, rather than over the course of adolescence itself (Simmons, Rosenberg, and Rosenberg, 1973). How can we reconcile these findings about fluctuations in self-esteem with studies indicating that self-esteem is quite stable during adolescence?

According to sociologist Morris Rosenberg (1986), it is important to differentiate between two aspects of self-perceptions in looking at studies of self-esteem. **Barometric self-esteem** refers to the extent to which our feelings about ourselves shift and fluctuate rapidly, from moment to moment. Perhaps you can remember times as a teenager—or even as an adult—when you entered a room full of people and were feeling confident but you suddenly felt nervous and insecure—only to engage in a pleasant interaction with someone an hour later and to feel confident once again. You were experiencing fluctuations in your barometric self-esteem.

Baseline self-esteem, in contrast, is less transitory and less likely to fluctuate from moment to moment. This aspect of self-image is relatively stable over time and is unlikely to be easily shifted by immediate experiences. Even if you feel momentarily insecure when entering a room full of new people, your integral, or baseline, self-esteem has not shifted. Indeed, individuals with high baseline self-esteem would readily dismiss transient feelings of insecurity as having more to do with the situation than with themselves.

Studies that report very high stability in self-esteem over adolescence are likely tapping the individual's baseline self-esteem, which is unlikely to change dramatically over time. This may be because the determinants of baseline self-esteem are themselves relatively stable factors such as social class (middle-class adolescents have higher self-esteem than do less affluent peers); sex (boys have higher self-esteem than girls); birth order (oldest or only children have higher self-esteem); and academic ability (more able adolescents have higher self-esteem) (Bachman and O'Malley, 1986; Savin-Williams and Demo, 1983). In contrast, studies that show fluctuation and volatility in self-image during early adolescence are probably focusing on the barometric self-image, which, by definition, is more likely to fluctuate. It seems safe to say, therefore, that although individuals' baseline self-image does not change markedly over adolescence, early adolescence is a time of increased volatility in the barometric self-image (Rosenberg, 1986). In other words, young adolescents are more likely than children or older adolescents to experience moment-to-moment shifts in self-esteem. Interestingly, the extent to which an individual's barometric self-esteem is volatile is itself a fairly stable trait; that is, young adolescents whose self-image fluctuates a lot from moment to moment are likely to develop into older adolescents who experience the same thing (Savin-Williams and Demo, 1983).

Although an individual's baseline self-image is probably a better overall indicator of how the person feels about him- or herself, fluctuations in barometric self-image can be distressing and uncomfortable—as most of us know well (Rosenberg, 1986). Consistent with this, studies indicate that young adolescents report higher levels of depression than preadolescents or older teenagers do (Simmons, Rosenberg, and Rosenberg, 1973). Moreover, young adolescents with the most volatile self-image report the highest levels of anxiety, tension, psychosomatic symptoms, and irritability (Rosenberg, 1986).

Volatility in barometric self-image during early adolescence probably reflects several interrelated factors. First, the sort of egocentrism common in early adolescence, discussed in Chapter 2, may make the young adolescent painfully aware of others' reactions to his or her behavior. Second, as individuals become more socially active, they begin to learn that people play games when they interact, and consequently they learn that it is not always possible to tell what people are thinking on the basis of how they act or what they say. This ambiguity may leave the young adolescent—who is relatively unskilled at this sort of "impression management"—puzzled and uncomfortable about how he or she is *really* viewed by others. Finally, because of the increased importance of peers in early adolescence, young adolescents are especially interested in their peers' opinions of them. For the first time, they may have to come to terms with contradictions between the messages they get from their parents ("I think that hairstyle makes you even more beautiful") and the messages they get from their peers ("You'd better wear a hat until your hair grows back!"). Hearing contradictory messages probably generates a certain degree of uncertainty about oneself (Rosenberg, 1986).

Some researchers have argued that the question of whether self-esteem is stable during adolescence is a poor one. According to one recent study (Hirsch and DuBois, 1991), some adolescents show very high stability in self-esteem over time, whereas others do not. These researchers identified four dramatically different self-esteem trajectories followed by youngsters during the transition into junior high school (see Figure 8.2). Approximately one-third of the adolescents were classified as consistently high in self-esteem, and approximately one-sixth were classified as chronically low. Half the sample, however, showed impressive patterns of change over just a two-year period: About one-fifth were categorized as steeply declining, and nearly one-third showed a small but significant increase in self-esteem. This pattern is reminiscent of one we encountered in Chapter 2, in which we saw that while most youngsters demonstrated stability in IQ scores over time, a substantial minority showed marked fluctuations. These studies remind us that focusing only on general tendencies may mask important individual differences in developmental trajectories. One recent study indicates that boys may be disproportionately overrepresented in the group whose self-esteem increases, whereas girls may be overrepresented in the group whose self-esteem declines—even though the majority of boys *and* girls show stability, rather than dramatic change, in self-esteem during adolescence (Block and Robins, 1993).

FIGURE 8.2 *Research indicates that individuals follow different self-esteem trajectories during early adolescence.* (Adapted from Hirsch and DuBois, 1991)

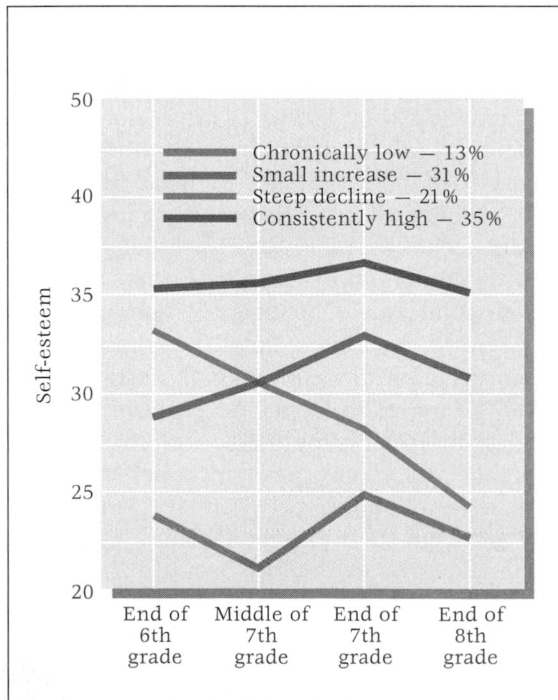

A second criticism of studies about the stability of self-esteem in adolescence questions the validity of examining self-esteem in such a global, or general, sense. Although most research on adolescent self-esteem has focused on teenagers' overall feelings about themselves, most researchers today believe that self-esteem is multidimensional and that young people evaluate themselves along several different dimensions (Cauce, 1987; Harter, 1990; Lau, 1990). As a consequence, it is possible for an adolescent to have high self-esteem when it comes to academic abilities, low self-esteem when it comes to athletics, and moderate self-esteem when it comes to physical appearance. The following passage, taken from a study of adolescent self-esteem by Susan Harter (1990, pp. 364–365), is fairly typical:

> How much do I *like* the kind of person I am? Well, I like some things about me, but I don't like others. I'm glad that I'm popular since it's really important to me to have friends. But in school I don't do as well as the really smart kids. That's OK, because if you're too smart you'll lose your friends. So being smart is just

Today, most researchers believe that self-esteem is multidimensional, and that young people evaluate themselves along several different dimensions simultaneously. As a consequence, it is possible for an adolescent to have high self-esteem when it comes to athletic abilities, but low self-esteem when it comes to academics. (Larry S. Voight/Photo Researchers)

not that important. Except to my parents. I feel like I'm letting them down when I don't do as well as they want. But what's really important to me is how I look. If I like the way I look, then I really like the kind of person I am. Don't get me wrong. I mean, I don't exactly look like Madonna even though I try to act like her. But compared to the other girls in my school, I'm sort of good-looking. There's another thing about how much I like the kind of person I am. It matters what other people think, especially the other kids at school. It matters whether they like you. I care about what my parents think about me too. I've also changed. It started when I went to junior high school. I got really depressed. I thought it was going to be so great, like I'd feel so grown-up, and then I saw all of these new, older kids who really had it together and I didn't. So I felt terrible. There was this one day when I hated the way I looked, and I didn't get invited to this really important party, and then I got an awful report card, so for a couple of days I thought it would be best to just end it all. I mean, why bother getting up the next morning? What's the point? Who cares? I was letting my parents down, I wasn't good-looking anymore, and I wasn't that popular after all, and things were never going to get better. I talked to Sheryl, my best friend, and that helped some, but what does she really know? I mean, she's my best friend, so of course she likes me! I mean, her opinion doesn't really count. It's what all the other kids think and want that counts. It was a lot easier for my brother. He got involved in this gang and just decided that what they thought was what was really important, and he stopped caring about the kids in school, or my parents, or even society. That's what he did, and he likes himself fine. But I really don't, not right now.

THE SCIENTIFIC STUDY OF ADOLESCENCE

ETHNIC DIFFERENCES IN SELF-ESTEEM: STUDYING MEANS VERSUS STUDYING CORRELATIONS

Social scientists who study adolescence often rely on two very different types of statistical tests to draw conclusions about adolescent development. One set of tests searches for *mean differences* in a variable of interest between one or more groups. Do boys have higher self-esteem than girls? Do adolescents who attend coeducational schools have more positive self-esteem than their peers who attend single-sex schools? Do 8-year-olds score higher on measures of self-esteem than 11-year-olds? All these questions ask whether the mean score of a certain group (boys, students from coed schools, 8-year-olds) is significantly different from the mean score of some comparison group (girls, students from single-sex schools, 11-year-olds).

Usually, social scientists compare mean scores using a statistical procedure called the **analysis of variance (ANOVA),** which tests whether the differences between people from different groups are greater than the differences among people within each group. Typically, we refer to the variable used to create the groups as the **independent variable** and the variable on which we compare the groups as the **dependent variable** (because scores on this variable are assumed to "depend" on what group a person is in). In the three examples above, self-esteem is always the dependent variable, whereas the independent variables is sex, type of school, or age.

Different sorts of tests are used to answer questions about whether scores on two variables are correlated with each other. Does higher self-esteem go hand in hand with academic achievement? Is there a link between parental warmth and adolescent self-esteem? Is low self-esteem predictive of involvement in delinquent activity? In each of these cases, we want to know whether variations in the value of one score are systematically linked to variations in the value of the other score and, if so, how strong the link is. Typically, a researcher who is interested in a question of this sort would compute a **correlation coefficient** (which can range from 1.0 to −1.0) and then test whether the correlation was significantly different from 0. The larger the correlation (that is, the closer the correlation is to 1.0 or −1.0), the stronger the link. A correlation close to 0 would indicate that scores on the two variables are unrelated.

It is important to understand the differences between the sorts of questions these two approaches are designed to answer and the sorts of conclusions one can draw from each sort of test. A nice illustration comes from the study of ethnic differences in self-esteem. Many studies report that African-American adolescents report higher self-esteem than their white peers (Harter, 1990). As explained in this chapter, one common explanation for this finding is that African-American adolescents receive especially high levels of support from family members and from kin and that

Do some aspects of self-esteem contribute more to an adolescent's overall self-image than others? The answer appears to be yes. In general, adolescents' physical self-esteem—how they feel about their appearance—is the most important predictor of overall self-esteem, followed by self-esteem about acceptance by peers (Harter, 1990). Less important are self-esteem about academic ability, athletic ability, or moral conduct.

this support contributes positively to youngsters' self-image. Studies documenting the higher self-esteem of African-American adolescents typically rely on some form of analysis of variance to examine the data. The test, as explained above, would ask whether the difference in self-esteem *between* the ethnic groups studied is significantly greater than differences in self-esteem *within* the groups.

The test of the difference between the two means does not tell us whether the *correlates* of self-esteem among African-American and white adolescents are different, however. In order to examine this question, one would need to look at the relation between self-esteem and some other variable—family support, for example—and compare the two correlation coefficients to see if they are significantly different from each other. Unfortunately, social scientists use this technique much less often than they should in the study of ethnic differences in development, focusing instead on mean differences between ethnic groups.

One exception to the typical approach is a recent article by David Rowe and his colleagues (Rowe, Vazsonyi, and Flannery, 1994), entitled "No More Than Skin Deep: Ethnic and Racial Similarity in Developmental Processes." Instead of asking whether there are ethnic differences in mean levels of various psychological traits (including self-esteem), Rowe asked whether the pattern of relations among different psychological variables (e.g., self-esteem, school achievement, self-efficacy, parental warmth, drug use) was comparable across different ethnic groups. (This study included Hispanic-American, Asian, African-American, and white youngsters.) In order to do this, he divided samples of adolescents into ethnic groups and then calculated the correlations among the variables separately within each group. Rowe then tested to see whether the observed patterns of relations were different from one ethnic group to another.

The analyses showed quite clearly that the correlations were not different. That is, although there may have been mean differences in the ethnic groups' scores on some of the variables of interest (e.g., Asian-Americans tend to have higher school achievement, and white adolescents tend to use more drugs), there were no differences in the relations among these variables (e.g., in all ethnic groups, school achievement was negatively correlated with drug use and positively correlated with parental warmth).

The answer to the question "Are there ethnic differences in self-esteem?" is a complicated one. Yes, there are differences, in that adolescents from different ethnic groups report different levels of self-esteem. But no, there are not, in that the predictors of self-esteem—doing well in school, having parents who love you, and having friends who support you—seem to be the same among adolescents of all colors.

SOURCE: Rowe, D., Vazsonyi, A., and Flannery, D. (1994). No more than skin deep: Ethnic and racial similarity in developmental processes. *Psychological Review, 105,* 396–413.

It is important to note both that physical self-esteem is a more important influence on overall self-esteem among girls than among boys (Harter, 1990) and that girls' physical self-esteem is, on average, lower than boys' (e.g., Wright, 1989). Taken together, these findings help to explain why there are sex differences in the extent to which adolescents' experience self-image difficulties and depression (see Chapter 13).

RECAP

Researchers have differed in their approach to the study of self-esteem. While some have studied adolescents' general, or global, feelings about themselves, others have stressed the multidimensional nature of self-esteem. In general, during adolescence global self-esteem is quite stable and, contrary to popular belief, increases slightly. During early adolescence, however, individuals' self-image may fluctuate more than during other periods.

Sex, Class, and Ethnic Differences in Self-Esteem

Not all adolescents undergo the same degree of fluctuation in self-esteem, nor are all adolescents' levels of self-esteem comparable. Several studies have shown that early adolescent girls, especially white girls, are more vulnerable to disturbances in the self-image than any other group of youngsters. Specifically, their self-esteem is lower, their degree of self-consciousness higher, and their self-image shakier than is the case for boys (Rosenberg and Simmons, 1972; Simmons, Brown, Bush, and Blyth, 1978; Simmons and Rosenberg, 1975). They are more likely to say negative things about themselves, to feel insecure about their abilities, and to worry about whether other people like being with them.

Why would girls have greater difficulty during early adolescence than boys? The answer may be related to the special significance of physical self-esteem and self-esteem about acceptance by peers, as discussed earlier. Compared with other youngsters, young girls seem to worry a great deal about their looks and about dating and being popular in school. Yet they are also worried about doing well academically. Other adolescents care about these things, of course, but they have a more casual, less worried attitude. Adolescent girls may feel caught in a bind between pressures to do well academically and pressures to do well socially, especially as they move into secondary school. As we saw in Chapter 5, getting good grades in school is at the bottom of the list of attributes which adolescent girls feel are important for being accepted into the leading crowd (Coleman, 1961). Several studies have shown that adolescents who worry a lot about being popular are most likely to feel self-conscious and are most likely to have unstable views of themselves (Simmons and Rosenberg, 1975). Because young girls appear to be more concerned than boys about physical attractiveness, dating, and peer acceptance, they may experience a greater number of self-image problems.

Studies also indicate that an adolescent's social class—as indexed by his or her parents' occupations, education, and income—is an important determinant of self-esteem, especially as the individual moves into middle and later adolescence. In general, middle-class youngsters have higher self-esteem than their less-affluent peers, and this discrepancy grows greater over the course of adolescence. One explanation for this is that middle-class youngsters do better in school than their less affluent peers, and this success leads to enhanced self-esteem (Demo and Savin-Williams, 1983).

Researchers have only recently systematically studied ethnic variations in adolescent self-esteem. To date, most of this research has focused on African-American youngsters. Although early studies suggested that African-American children suffered from a poor self-image, more recent research indicates that the self-esteem of African-American adolescents is comparable to, or greater than, that of their majority peers (Harter, 1990). A number of researchers have asked why this is, given the prevalence of prejudice in American society and the generally disadvantaged

Youngsters who attend schools in which they are in the racial minority may suffer greater self-esteem problems than their peers who attend schools in which they are in the majority. Although desegregation may have a positive impact on minority youngsters' academic achievement, this benefit may be counterbalanced by the apparently negative impact of desegregation on minority youngsters' self-image. (Rick Smolan/Stock, Boston)

position of African-Americans in the workplace and in school, two institutions where individuals' performance is believed to influence their self-image. Two main explanations for the relatively high self-esteem of African-American adolescents have been offered.

First, some writers have argued that, despite their encounters with racism and prejudice, African-American teenagers benefit from the support and positive feedback of adults in the African-American community, especially in the family (Barnes, 1980). This is not surprising, given the wealth of research showing that the approval of others is an especially powerful influence on adolescents' self-esteem (e.g., Felson and Zielinski, 1989; Robinson, in press). Second, other researchers suggest that all teenagers—minority and otherwise—tend to shift their priorities over time so that they come to value those activities at which they excel. In doing so, adolescents are able to protect their self-esteem by focusing on areas of strength instead of weakness. For example, a boy who is an outstanding artist but who feels physically unattractive and has not been doing well in school will likely derive positive self-esteem from his artwork and not restrict his self-evaluation to his looks or grades in school (Hunt and Hunt, 1977).

The context in which adolescents develop has a substantial impact on the self-image, however. Some research indicates, for example, that high school–aged youngsters who live in a social environment or go to a school in which their ethnic or socioeconomic group is in the minority are more likely to have self-image problems than those who are in the majority (Rosenberg, 1975). This seems to be true with regard to religion, socioeconomic status, race, and family structure (single-parent or two-parent home). African-American teenagers, for example, have a higher opinion of themselves when they go to schools in which African-American students are a majority than when they attend predominantly white schools, where they may feel out of place and under pressure to play down their cultural heritage. By the same token, Jewish adolescents have higher self-esteem in schools in which there are many other Jewish students than in schools in which Jews compose a small minority of the student body. Similarly, levels of maladjustment are higher among both Hispanic and non-Hispanic youngsters when they are in the minority in their school (Kaufman, Gregory, and Stephan, 1990).

Research into changes in self-image during adolescence has helped paint a new picture of adolescence as a developmental period. In contrast to views that prevailed even as recently as twenty-five years ago, adolescence is now viewed as a time of gradual rather than tumultuous change in the individual's self-image. Instead of adhering to the view that adolescence is an inevitably difficult time for all young people, researchers are coming to understand that certain factors seem to worsen stress during adolescence and that some youngsters are more susceptible to its adverse effects.

Antecedents and Consequences of High Self-Esteem

Several researchers have examined the link between self-esteem and adolescent behavior, in an attempt to see whether certain sorts of experiences contribute—either positively or negatively—to adolescents' feelings about themselves. Others have posed the question in reverse: Does having high (or low) self-esteem lead adolescents to behave in particular ways?

Regarding the first question, studies find that self-esteem is enhanced by having the approval of others, especially of parents and peers, and by having success in school (Bachman and O'Malley, 1986; Bohrnstedt and Felson, 1983; Hoge, Smit, and Hanson, 1990; Liu, Kaplan, and Risser, 1992). These correlates of high self-esteem have been found in virtually all ethnic and cultural groups, although the self-esteem of Asian-American youngsters seems especially influenced by their academic success (e.g., Szesulski, Martinez, and Reyes, 1994). Adolescents whose self-esteem is *too* wrapped up in the approval of others—especially the approval of peers—may be at risk for developing self-image problems, however, since peer acceptance may fluctuate over time, leading to temporary drops in self-esteem (Harter, Stocker, and Robinson, in press).

What about the reverse question? How does having high self-esteem influence adolescents' adjustment and behavior? Although it once was believed that enhanced self-esteem leads to school success, there actually is little evidence for this and a good deal of evidence for the opposite (e.g., Liu et al., 1992; Rosenberg, Schooler, and Schoenback, 1989). That is, academic success leads to improvements in the way that adolescents feel about themselves, not the other way around. These findings cast doubt on the logic behind programs designed to raise teenagers' school performance by increasing their self-esteem. High self-esteem does enhance adolescents' well-being, however, whereas low self-esteem leads to involvement in deviant activity and psychological distress (Liu et al., 1992; Rosenberg et al., 1989). Interestingly, adolescents with low self-esteem who engage in delinquency actually may experience an *increase* in self-esteem as a result, perhaps because their involvement in delinquency gets them approval from certain peers (Rosenberg et al., 1989).

RECAP

Generally speaking, males, middle-class adolescents, and African-American adolescents have higher self-esteem than females, less affluent youth, or white adolescents. Across all demographic groups, however, high self-esteem is related to parental approval, peer support, and success in school.

THE ADOLESCENT IDENTITY CRISIS

One of the most wonderful and memorable stories of an adolescent's struggle to find her identity is told in Carson McCullers's novel *The Member of the Wedding* (1946). Set in the South during the mid-1940s, the story revolves around the identity development of Frankie Addams, a 12-year-old girl who has her first encounter that summer with the sort of self-examination and introspection that we have come to associate with the adolescent years. Here is Frankie speaking to her confidante, Berenice:

> Listen. . . . What I've been trying to say is this. Doesn't it strike you as strange that I am I, and you are you? I am F. Jasmine Addams. And you are Berenice Sadie Brown. And we can look at each other, and touch each other, and stay together year in and year out in the same room. Yet always I am I, and you are you. And I can't ever be anything else but me, and you can't ever be anything else but you. Have you ever thought of that? And does it seem to you strange? (p. 109)

If you were asked to talk about your own identity development, what sorts of things would *you* mention? Perhaps you would talk about the development of a sense of purpose, or the clarification of your long-term plans and values, or the growing feeling of knowing who you really are and where you are headed. If these are the sorts of things that come to mind when you think about identity development, you are thinking about an aspect of development that psychologists refer to as the **sense of identity.** The dominant view in the study of adolescent identity development emphasizes precisely these aspects of psychosocial development, and the theorist whose work has been most influential in this area is Erik Erikson.

Erikson's Theoretical Framework

Erikson's (1959, 1963, 1968) theory developed out of his clinical and cross-cultural observations of young people at various stages of development. He viewed the developing person as moving through a series of eight psychosocial crises over the course of the life span. Each crisis, although present in one form or another at all ages, takes on special significance at a given period of the life cycle because biological and social forces interact to bring the crisis into prominence. Erikson believed that the establishment of a coherent sense of identity is the chief psychosocial crisis of adolescence.

In Erikson's model, each psychosocial crisis defines an "age" or "stage" of the life span (see Figure 8.3). Each crisis is a sort of challenge that the individual must resolve. The crises are *normative,* in the sense that they are an inevitable part of being alive and growing older. Erikson described each of the eight crises as a continuum with positive and negative poles. The crisis of infancy, for example, is labeled "trust versus mistrust." By this Erikson meant that during infancy, the child must be able to establish a feeling of trust, or security, with his or her caregivers. Resolving each crisis, though, does not entail coming through the crisis either entirely positively or entirely negatively, nor does it mean resolving the issue once and for all. "It is instead a matter of tipping the balance more in one direction (i.e., toward one end of the continuum) than in another" (Gallatin, 1975, p. 175). In other words, it is important that the infant come through the

FIGURE 8.3 *The eight stages of development and their corresponding psychosocial crises, according to Erikson (1959).*

I Infancy	Trust vs. mistrust							
II Early childhood		Autonomy vs. shame, doubt						
III Play age			Initiative vs. guilt					
IV School age				Industry vs. inferiority				
V Adolescence					Identity vs. identity diffusion			
VI Young adult						Intimacy vs. isolation		
VII Adulthood							Generativity vs. self- absorption	
VIII Mature age								Integrity vs. disgust, despair

first stage of development feeling more secure than insecure.

In Erikson's view, each crisis builds on the previous ones. Specifically, the successful resolution of each challenge depends on the healthy resolution of the challenges that have preceded it. An infant who has not successfully resolved the crisis of trust versus mistrust, for example, will have a difficult time with the crises encountered through the rest of the life cycle. Such individuals may always be somewhat hesitant about becoming close with other people because, deep down inside, they fear that others will let them down. With respect to adolescent identity development, then, Erikson believed that the successful resolution of the crisis of "identity versus identity diffusion" depends on how the individual has resolved the previous crises of childhood. Without a healthy sense of trust, autonomy, initiative, and industry, it is difficult to establish a coherent sense of identity. Moreover, the way in which the adolescent resolves the crisis of identity will have an impact on his or her struggle with the crises of adulthood. Far from seeing adolescence as a separate period of the life cycle, Erickson believed that what takes place during adolescence is much intertwined with what has come before and what will follow.

Identity versus Identity Diffusion

Before adolescence, the child's identity is like patches of fabric that have not yet been sewn together. But by the end of adolescence, these patches will be woven into a patchwork quilt that is unique to the individual. This process of integration is at the center of the fifth psychosocial crisis described by Erikson: the crisis of **identity versus identity diffusion.** As Erikson described it, "From among all possible and imaginable relations, [the young person] must make a series of ever-narrowing selections of personal, occupational, sexual, and ideological commitments" (1968, p. 245). The maturational and social forces that converge at adolescence force young people to reflect on their place in society, on the ways that others view them, and on their options for the future. Achieving a balanced and coherent sense of identity is an intellectually and emotionally taxing process. According to Erikson, it is not until adolescence that one even has the mental or psychological capacity to tackle this task.

The key to resolving the crisis of identity versus identity diffusion, argued Erikson, lies in the adolescent's interactions with others. Through responding to the reactions of people who matter, the adolescent selects and chooses from among the many elements that could conceivably become a part of his or her adult identity. The other people with whom the young person interacts serve as a mirror that reflects back to the adolescent information about who he or she is and who he or she ought to be. As such, the responses of these important others shape and influence the adolescent's developing sense of identity. Through others' reactions, we learn whether we are competent or clumsy, attractive or ugly, socially adept or tactless. Perhaps more important—especially during periods when our sense of identity is still forming—we learn from others what it is we do that we ought to keep doing, and what it is we do that we ought not to do.

Forging an identity, therefore, is a social as well as mental process. Erikson placed a great deal of weight on the role of the young person's society (and, especially, on those individuals who have influence over the adolescent) in shaping the adolescent's sense of self. The adolescent's identity is the result of a mutual recognition between the young person and society: The adolescent forges an identity, but at the same time society identifies the adolescent.

The Social Context of Identity Development

The social context in which the adolescent attempts to establish a sense of identity exerts a tremendous impact on the nature and outcome of the process. Clearly, if adolescents' identities are forged out of a recognition on the part of society, society will play an important role in determining which sorts of identities are possible alternatives; and of those identities that are genuine options, society will influence which are desirable and which are not.

As a consequence, the course of identity development will vary in different cultures, among different subcultures within the same society, and over different historical eras (Kroger, 1993). For example, the career options open to women in contemporary American society have changed dramatically in the past thirty years and, consequently, so has the nature of adolescent girls' identity development. In the past, most young women assumed that their adult identity would be exclusively tied to marriage and family life. But today far more alternative identities are open to women. As a result, the process of choosing among different alternatives has become more complicated than it once was.

The social context in which an adolescent develops also determines to a large extent whether the youngster's search for self-definition will take the form of a full-blown crisis or whether it will be a more manageable challenge. Generally speaking, the more alternatives available to the young person and the more arenas in which decisions must be made, the more difficult establishing a sense of identity will be. Growing up in contemporary America, where adolescents have a range of careers to decide among, for example, is far more likely to provoke an occupational identity crisis than is growing up in a small agrarian community in which each young person continues farming the family's land. The rapid rate of social change in the United States has raised new and more complicated sets of questions for young people to consider—questions not only about occupational plans but also about values, lifestyles, and commitments to other people. No longer are all young people expected to follow the same narrow path into adulthood: marriage and children for all, work for men, and homemaking for women. Today, male and female adolescents alike must ask themselves *if* they want to remain single, live with someone, or marry; *if* and *when* they want to have children; and *how* they plan to incorporate these choices into their career plans. Consequently, the likelihood of going through a prolonged and difficult identity crisis is probably greater today than it has ever been.

The Psychosocial Moratorium. The complications inherent in identity development in modern society have created the need, Erikson argued, for a **psychosocial moratorium**—a time-out during adolescence from the sorts of excessive responsibilities and obligations that might restrict the young person's pursuit of self-discovery. Adolescents in contemporary America are given a moratorium of sorts by being encouraged to remain in school for a long time, where they can think seriously about their plans for the future without making irrevocable decisions.

During the psychosocial moratorium, the adolescent can experiment with different roles and identities, in a context that permits and encourages this sort of exploration. The experimentation involves trying on different postures, personalities, and ways of behaving—sometimes to the consternation of the adolescent's parents, who may wonder why their child's personality seems so changeable. One week, an adolescent girl will spend hours putting on makeup; the next week she will insist to her parents that she is tired of caring so much about the way she looks. An adolescent boy will come home one day wearing boots and a leather jacket and acting tough, and a few weeks later he will discard the tough-guy image for that of a serious student. Sometimes, parents describe their teenage children as going through "phases." Much of this behavior is actually experimentation with roles and personalities.

Having the time to experiment with roles is an important prelude to establishing a coherent sense of identity. But role experimentation can take place only in an environment that allows and encourages it (Gallatin, 1975). Without a period of moratorium, a full and thorough exploration of the options and alternatives available to the young person cannot occur, and identity development will be somewhat impeded. In other words, according to Erikson, adolescents must *grow* into adulthood—they should not be forced into it prematurely.

It is clear, however, that the sort of moratorium Erikson described is an ideal; indeed, some might even consider it to be a luxury of the affluent. Many young people—perhaps even most—do not have the economic freedom to enjoy a long delay before taking on the responsibilities of adult life. For many youngsters, alternatives are not open in any realistic sense, and introspection only interferes with the more pressing task of survival. Does the 17-year-old who must drop out of school to work a full-time factory job go through life without a sense of identity? Do youngsters who cannot afford a psychosocial moratorium fail to resolve the crisis of identity versus identity diffusion?

Certainly not. But from an Eriksonian point of view, the absence of a psychosocial moratorium in some adolescents' lives—either because of restrictions they place on themselves or restrictions placed on them by others or because of their life circumstances—is truly lamentable. The price these youngsters pay is not in failing to develop a sense of identity but in lost potential. You may know people whose parents have forced them into prematurely choosing a certain career or who have had to drop out of college and take a job they really did not want because of financial pressures. According to Erikson, without a chance to explore, to experiment, and to choose among options for the future, these young people may not realize all that they are capable of becoming. In theory, these individuals should encounter difficulties in resolving the subsequent crises of intimacy, generativity, and integrity.

Resolving the Identity Crisis

Is establishing a sense of identity a consciously felt achievement? According to Erikson, it is. It is experienced as a sense of well-being, a feeling of "being at home in one's body," a sense of knowing where one is going, and an inner assuredness of recognition from those who count. It is a sense of sameness through time—a feeling of continuity between the past and the future.

Establishing a coherent sense of identity is a lengthy process. Most writers on adolescence and youth believe that identity exploration continues well into young adulthood. But rather than thinking of the adolescent as going through an identity crisis, it probably makes more sense to view the phenomenon as a series of crises that may concern different aspects of the young person's identity and that may surface—and resurface—at different points in time throughout the adolescent and young adult years. As Erikson wrote, "A sense of identity is never gained nor maintained once and for all . . . it is constantly lost and regained, although more lasting and more economical methods of maintenance and restoration are evolved and fortified in late adolescence" (1959, p. 118). During adolescence, the feeling of well-being associated with establish-

Role experimentation during adolescence often involves trying different looks, images, and patterns of behavior. According to theorists such as Erik Erikson, having time to experiment with roles is an important prelude to establishing a coherent sense of identity. (M. B. Duda/Photo Researchers)

ing a sense of identity is somewhat fleeting. Ultimately, however, the identity crisis of adolescence, when successfully resolved, culminates in a series of basic life commitments: occupational, ideological, social, religious, ethical, and sexual (Bourne, 1978a).

RECAP

The predominant influence on the study of identity development in adolescence comes from the work of Erik Erikson. Erikson suggested that the major psychosocial issue of adolescence revolves around the "identity crisis"—coming to terms with who one is and where one is headed. In order to resolve this crisis successfully, the young person needs some time out from excessive responsibilities—a psychosocial moratorium—in order to engage in identity exploration and experimentation.

● Problems in Identity Development

Given the wide variations in developmental histories that individuals bring to adolescence and the wide variations in the environments in which adolescence is experienced, it is not surprising to find differences in the ways in which individuals approach and resolve the crisis of identity versus identity diffusion. Problems in identity development can result when an individual has not successfully resolved earlier crises or when the adolescent is in an environment that does not provide the necessary period of moratorium. Three sorts of problems received special attention from Erikson. They are labeled identity diffusion, identity foreclosure, and negative identity, respectively.

● ***Identity Diffusion.*** **Identity diffusion,** or **identity confusion,** is characterized by an incoherent, disjointed, incomplete sense of self. Identity diffusion can vary in degree from a mild state of not quite knowing who you are while in the midst of an identity crisis to a more severe, psychopathological condition that persists beyond a normal period of exploration. It is marked by disruptions in the individual's sense of time (some things seem to happen much faster than they really do, while others seem to take forever); excessive self-consciousness, to the point that it is difficult to make decisions; problems in work and achievement-related activities; difficulties in forming intimate relationships with others; and concerns over sexuality. Identity confusion is reflected not only in problems of identity but also in the areas of autonomy, intimacy, sexuality, and achievement.

A classic example of an adolescent in the throes of identity diffusion is Holden Caulfield in the 1951 novel *The Catcher in the Rye.* He has flunked out of several prep schools, has severed most of his friendships, and has no sense of where he is headed. At one point in the book, for example, walking up Fifth Avenue in New York City, Holden says: "Every time I came to the end of a block and stepped off the goddam curb, I had this feeling that I'd never get to the other side of the street. I thought I'd just go down, down, down, and nobody'd ever see me again. Boy, did it scare me" (Salinger, [1951] 1964, pp. 197–198).

● ***Identity Foreclosure.*** Some young people bypass—either willingly or unwillingly—the period of exploration and experimentation that precedes the establishment of a healthy sense of identity. Instead of considering a range of alternatives, these adolescents prematurely commit themselves to a role, or series of roles, and settle upon a certain identification as a final identity. In essence, these individuals are not given—or do not take advantage of—a psychosocial moratorium. For example, a college freshman who made up his mind about becoming a doctor at the age of 13 may enroll in a rigid pre-med curriculum without considering other career possibilities. The circumvention of the identity crisis is called **identity foreclosure.**

Typically, the roles adopted in the process of identity foreclosure revolve around the goals set for the young person by parents or other authority figures. The adolescent may be led into these roles directly or may be forced into them indirectly by being denied a true period of psychosocial moratorium. Perhaps the parents of the would-be doctor have arranged their child's school schedule and summer vacations so that all of his or her spare time is spent taking extra science courses. No time is left for role experimentation or introspection. Individuals who have bypassed the identity crisis have made commitments, but they have not gone through a period of experimentation before making them. Identity foreclosure can be viewed, then, as a kind of interruption of the identity development process, an interruption that interferes with the individual's discovery of his or her full range of potentials.

● ***Negative Identity.*** Occasionally, adolescents appear to select identities that are obviously undesirable to their parents and their community. The examples are familiar: the daughter of the local police chief who repeatedly gets into trouble with the law; the son of prestigious and successful parents who refuses to go to college; the child of a devoutly religious family who insists that he or she is a confirmed atheist. Because the establishment of a healthy sense of identity is so intimately tied to the recognition of the adolescent by those who count in his or her life, the adoption of a so-called **negative identity** is a sign that problems in identity development have arisen. The adolescent who adopts a negative identity is, indeed, recognized by those around him or her but not in a way that fosters healthy development.

Usually, selecting a negative identity is an attempt to forge some sense of self-definition in an environment that has made it difficult for the young person to establish an acceptable identity. This appears to be especially likely when, after repeatedly trying and failing to receive positive recognition from those who are important in their lives, adolescents turn to a different, perhaps more successful, route to being noticed—adopting a negative identity. Consider this example: The son of successful parents is a good student but not quite good enough to please his excessively demanding parents. He feels he is a nobody in his parents' eyes. So the boy drops out of school to play guitar in a band—something his parents vehemently oppose. To paraphrase Erikson, this adolescent, like most youngsters, would rather be somebody "bad" than nobody at all.

RECAP

Some adolescents have difficulty in successfully resolving the identity crisis. Among the three most common problems described by Erikson are identity diffusion, identity foreclosure, and negative identity. Problems in identity development can result when an individual has not successfully resolved earlier crises or when the adolescent is in an environment that does not provide the necessary period of psychosocial moratorium.

RESEARCH ON IDENTITY DEVELOPMENT

Determining an Adolescent's Identity Status

In order to determine an individual's identity status, researchers have used an approach developed by James Marcia (1966, 1976), which focuses on identity exploration in three areas—occupation, ideology, and interpersonal relations. Based on responses to an interview or questionnaire, individuals are rated on two dimensions: (1) the degree to which they have made commitments and (2) the degree to which they engaged in a sustained search in the process (see Figure 8.4). On the basis of these ratings, the researchers assign young people to one of four categories: identity achievement (the individual has established a coherent sense of identity—that is, has made commitments after a period of crisis and experimentation); moratorium (the individual is in the midst of a period of crisis and experimentation); identity foreclosure (the individual has made commitments but without a period of crisis or experimentation); and identity diffusion (the individual does not have firm commitments and is not currently trying to make them).

Generally speaking, research employing this approach has supported Erikson's theory. For example, identity achievers are psychologically healthier than other individuals on a variety of measures: They score highest on measures of achievement motivation, moral reasoning, intimacy with peers, reflectiveness, and career maturity. Individuals in the moratorium category score highest on measures of anxiety, show the highest levels of conflict over issues of authority, and are themselves the least rigid and least authoritarian. Individuals classified as being in the foreclosure group have been shown to be the most authoritarian and to have the highest need for social approval, the lowest level of autonomy, and the greatest closeness to their parents. Individuals in a state of identity diffusion display the

FIGURE 8.4 *Identity status categories derived from Marcia's (1966) measure.*

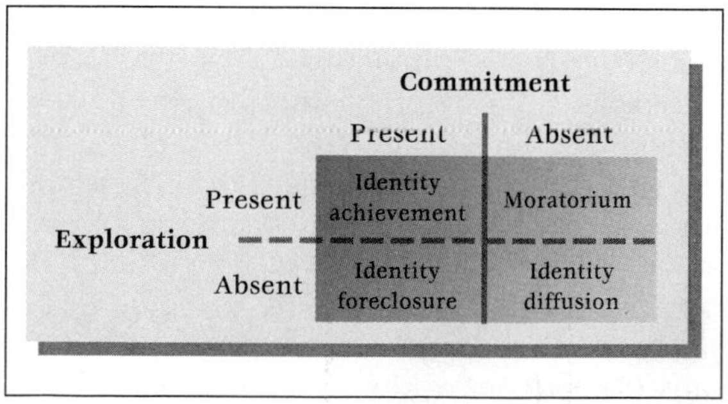

		Commitment: Present	Commitment: Absent
Exploration	Present	Identity achievement	Moratorium
	Absent	Identity foreclosure	Identity diffusion

highest level of psychological and interpersonal problems: They are the most socially withdrawn and show the lowest level of intimacy with peers (Adams, Gullotta, and Montemayor, 1992; Wallace-Broscious, Serafica, and Osipow, 1994).

A recent study attempted to link classifications based on a measure of identity development with scores on the personality dimensions tapped within the Five-Factor Model of personality discussed earlier (Clancy and Dollinger, 1993). As expected, adolescents who were classified as identity achievers were higher in extraversion and less neurotic than other adolescents; foreclosed adolescents were less open; and diffused adolescents were more neurotic, less open, and less agreeable. It was not clear from this study whether different personality constellations led to different patterns of identity development or, alternatively, whether different patterns of identity development influenced subsequent personality. Given what we know about the childhood antecedents of personality traits, however, it would seem that the former explanation (that personality affects identity development) is more likely than the latter.

What sorts of parenting practices are associated with these different identity statuses? Generally speaking, individuals whose identity development is healthy are more likely to come from homes characterized by warm, not excessively constraining relations (Grotevant and Cooper, 1986). As we saw in Chapter 4, individuals who grow up in these environments are encouraged to assert their individuality but to remain connected to their families at the same time. Typically, the absence of parental warmth is associated with problems in making commitments—the most extreme case being identity diffusion—whereas the absence of parental encouragement of individuality is associated with problems in engaging in extensive exploration (Campbell, Adams, and Dobson, 1984).

Studying Identity Development over Time

In order to examine the development of a sense of identity, researchers have done both cross-sectional studies (comparing individuals of different ages) and longitudinal studies (following the same individuals over a period of time). Perhaps the most significant finding to emerge from this line of research is that establishing a coherent sense of identity generally does not occur much before age 18 (Marcia, 1980). In general, when comparisons are made among groups of youngsters of different ages over the span from ages 12 to 24, differences in identity status are most frequently observed between groups in the 18- to 21-year-old range. Few consistent differences emerge in comparisons of teenagers in the middle adolescent years, suggesting that, although self-examination may take place throughout adolescence, the consolidation of a coherent sense of identity does not begin until very late in the period (Adams and Jones, 1983; Archer, 1982). The late teens and early twenties appear to be the critical times for the crystallization of a sense of identity.

The movement toward identity achievement that occurs between ages 18 and 21 among college students appears to be primarily in the area of occupational commitments. Alan Waterman and his associates (Waterman, Geary, and Waterman, 1974; Waterman and Goldman, 1976; Waterman and Waterman, 1971), who followed samples of college students for several years, found that during the college years vocational plans solidify but that religious and political commitments are not as clearly established. More specifically, individuals emerge from college with more clearly defined occupational plans but no firm religious or political commitments (Waterman, 1982). In fact, college seems to undermine students' "traditional" religious beliefs—the beliefs that they acquired from their parents—without replacing them with others. Students who enter college as devout Catholics, for example, may graduate having lost some of their commitment to Catholicism but without having developed any new religious commitments instead. This pattern may not hold for adolescents from all religious groups, however. One study of Mormon adolescents, for example, found that these youngsters were much more likely than their peers to maintain a strong—even foreclosed—commitment to their religious upbringing (Markstrom-Adams, Hofstra, and Dougher, in press).

A study by Raymond Montemayor and his colleagues supports the idea that the freshman year of college may be an important time in the process of identity development. A group of students was assessed before entering college and again toward the end of the freshman year. Before entering college, half of the adolescents were judged to be in a state of identity diffusion and 40 percent were judged to be in a state of moratorium—consistent with the notion that the identity crisis is unlikely to be resolved during high school. Another 8 percent were in the identity achievement status, and the rest were judged to be foreclosed.

During the college years, many individuals begin to develop clearer vocational identities. Many colleges sponsor career days and offer job counseling services. (Stu Rosen/Stock, Boston)

What happened to these individuals as college freshmen? Over the first year of college, the most common pathway was either remaining diffused or in a state of moratorium or moving from one of the "committed" statuses (identity achievement or identity foreclosure) to one of the "noncommitted" statuses (diffusion or moratorium). In other words, while freshman year may "shake up some students and cause them to reexamine previously held commitments, students who are uncertain to begin with . . . remain so. . . . The freshman year appears to produce uncertainty in many students but does not help to resolve it" (Montemayor, Brown, and Adams, 1985, p. 7).

Do young people need to go to college in order to develop a clear sense of identity? Unfortunately, because there are so few developmental studies among noncollege youth, we have little way of answering this question. But the results of one study comparing identity development in college and noncollege youth are quite interesting. Gordon Munro and Gerald Adams (1977) compared a sample of college students with a same-aged sample (18 to 21) of noncollege working youths. The working youths were actually *more likely* to have established a sense of identity—more in the area of ideological commitments than in vocational commitments. This finding suggests that for many young people, college may prolong the psychosocial moratorium, especially in matters of political and religious beliefs.

Shifts in Identity Status

As you will recall, Erikson theorized that the sense of identity that is developed during adolescence is constantly lost and regained, that the identity challenge is not resolved once and for all at one point in time. If, according to Erikson's model, identity crises surface and resurface throughout the life cycle, we ought to find that individuals move from one identity status to another, particularly during the adolescent and young adult years.

This appears to be precisely the case. In one study that followed students over a one-year period (Adams and Fitch, 1982), nearly 60 percent of the students who were classified as experiencing identity diffusion at the beginning of the study were no longer in this category one year later. Changes in status also occurred for half of the students who initially were placed in the moratorium category. In two other longitudinal studies, each spanning a four-year period (Waterman et al., 1974; Waterman and Goldman, 1976), the degree of shifting was 50 percent in one study and 33 percent in the other for students who had been classified as experiencing identity diffusion, and 91 percent and 100 percent for students who initially had been classified as being in the midst of a moratorium.

These sorts of shifts are not surprising, of course, since both the diffusion and moratorium categories are, theoretically, unstable ones. But in these same longitudinal studies, about one-third of each of the identity achievement and foreclosure groups *also* shifted status over the course of one year; and over the course of four years, more than half of the students who had been classified as foreclosed and one-third of those who had been classified as identity achievers moved into a different group. In other words, some individuals who at one point had apparently resolved the identity crisis (had been classified as identity achievers) actually had not resolved it—at least, not in any final sense. The weight of the evidence collected to date, therefore, suggests that identity status classifications made during adolescence and young adulthood probably represent short-term, temporary states rather than long-term, enduring traits. As Erikson has suggested, revising and maintaining one's sense of self-definition is a challenge that continues beyond adolescence.

RECAP

Research on identity development from Erikson's theoretical perspective has generally supported his model. Most studies indicate, however, that the major developments in this domain occur in late adolescence and young adulthood, rather than earlier during the adolescent decade.

THE DEVELOPMENT OF ETHNIC IDENTITY

For all individuals, but especially for those who are not part of the white majority, integrating a sense of **ethnic identity** into their overall sense of personal identity is likely to be an important task of late adolescence, perhaps as important as establishing a coherent occupational, ideological, or interpersonal identity (Phinney and Alipuria, 1987). To date, far more is known about the development of ethnic identity among African-Americans than among other ethnic groups, but research on Hispanic-American, American Indian, and Asian-American youth is beginning to appear at a rapid pace (Phinney, 1990; Spencer and Markstrom-Adams, 1990). Studies are beginning to differentiate among adolescents *within* major ethnic categories as well (e.g., between black youth of Caribbean versus African ancestry [Biafora, Taylor, Warheit, Zimmerman, and Vega] or among Asian-American youth whose families come from different Asian countries [e.g., Fletcher and Steinberg, 1994]).

The Process of Ethnic Identity Development

According to several writers (Cross, 1978; Kim, 1981, cited in Phinney and Alipuria, 1987), the process of ethnic identity development follows in some respects the process of identity development in general, with an unquestioning view of oneself being displaced or upset by a crisis. Following the crisis, the individual may become immersed in his or her own ethnic group and may turn against the white majority culture. Eventually, as the value and importance of having a strong ethnic identity become clear, the individual establishes a more coherent sense of personal identity that includes this ethnic identity and, with growing confidence, he or she attempts to help others deal with their own struggles with ethnic identity.

Some research indicates that moving through the early stages of ethnic identity development may be speeded up somewhat when parents take a more deliberate approach to ethnic socialization (Marshall, 1994). **Ethnic socialization** refers to the process through which parents attempt to teach their children about their ethnic identity and about the special experiences they may encounter within the broader society, given their ethnic background (Thornton, Chatters, Taylor, and Allen, 1990). According to one model, ethnic socialization in minority families focuses on three themes: (1) understanding one's culture, (2) getting along in mainstream society, and (3) dealing with racism (Boykin and Toms, 1985). Although ethnic socialization by parents may speed up the process of ethnic identity development, it does not appear to lead adolescents to an ultimately stronger sense of ethnic identity (Phinney and Chavira, in press).

Do members of ethnic minorities have more difficulty than white adolescents in resolving the identity crisis, however? Researchers are just now beginning to examine this question, and the answer is still not known. The little research that has been done suggests more similarities than differences in the *process* through which identity development occurs. One difference, though, appears to be quite important, if perhaps not very surprising: Having a strong ethnic identity is associated with higher self-esteem and stronger self-efficacy among minority youngsters, especially among African-American and Hispanic-American youth, but this is not the case among white youth (Blash and Unger, 1992; Phinney and Alipuria, 1987; Reviere and Bakeman, 1992; Smith, Walker, Fields, and Seay, 1994). It would seem, therefore, that establishing a sense of ethnic identity is more important to individuals who are part of an ethnic minority than for those who are part of a majority.

As one recent review of research on minority adolescent development noted, the task of developing a coherent sense of identity is much more complicated for minority adolescents than for their majority counterparts (Spencer and Dornbusch, 1990). Because identity development is profoundly influenced by the social context in which the adolescent lives, the development of the minority adolescent must be understood in relation to the specific context that nonmajority youngsters face in contemporary society. All too often, this context includes racial stereotypes, a limited number of role models, and mixed messages about the costs and benefits of identifying too closely with the majority culture. Not surprisingly, a number of studies suggest that the incidence of identity foreclosure is more prevalent among minority youth (e.g., Hauser and Kasendorf, 1983).

Alternative Orientations to Ethnic Identity

According to Phinney and her colleagues (Phinney, Devich-Navarro, DuPont, Estrada, and Onwughala, 1994), minority youth have four possibilities open to them for dealing with their ethnicity: **assimilation** (i.e., trying to adopt the majority culture's norms and standards while rejecting those of one's own group); **marginality** (i.e., living within the majority culture but feeling estranged and outcast); **separation** (i.e., associating only with members of one's own culture and rejecting the majority culture); and **biculturalism** (i.e., maintaining ties to both the majority and the minority cultures) (see Figure 8.5). In the past, minority youth were encouraged by majority society to assimilate as much as possible. Assimilation, however, has not proven to be as simple as many nonminority individuals imagine. First, although minority youth are told to assimilate, they may be tacitly excluded from majority society on the basis of their physical appearance or language. This leads to a situation of marginality, in which the minority youth is on the edge of majority society but is never really accepted as a full-status member.

Second, minority youth who do attempt to assimilate are often scorned by their own communities for trying to "act white"—as captured in the array of pejorative terms minority youth have for their friends who have tried

FIGURE 8.5 *A two-dimensional model of identification with two cultures.* (Phinney, Devich-Navarro, DuPont, Estrada, and Onwughala, 1994)

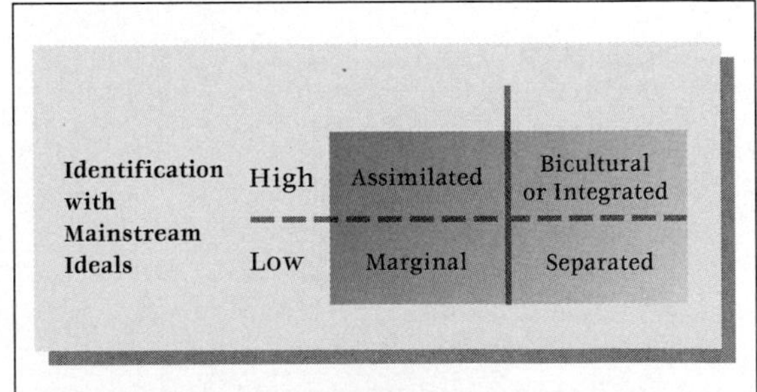

too hard to assimilate: Asian-Americans who act white are "bananas"; Hispanic-Americans are "coconuts"; and African-Americans are "Oreos" (Spencer and Dornbusch, 1990, p. 132). Partly in reaction to this, many minority youth are adopting a strategy of separation. This seems especially common among African-American adolescents, who may be the victims of especially intense discrimination and prejudice (Phinney, Devich-Navarro, DuPont, Estrada, and Onwughala, 1994).

Some writers argue that a more viable alternative to assimilation or separation is biculturalism. Bicultural adolescents "shuttle successfully between their primary or familial culture and the dominant culture" (Spencer and Dornbusch, 1990, p. 133). One writer has proposed a flexibility model, in which minority youth have open to them the norms of both cultures and select between them depending on the situation, a process called **code switching.** At a majority-controlled school, for example, it may be more adaptive to "act white" when being evaluated by white teachers but also more adaptive to conform with the minority group's own norms and standards when in one's neighborhood.

One recent study compared the ethnic identity orientations of Asian, black, Hispanic, and white adolescents (Rotherham-Borus, 1990). As expected, white youngsters were more likely to characterize themselves as assimilated (or "mainstream") than were minority students, who were more likely to characterize themselves as bicultural (between 40 and 50 percent) than as either mainstream or embedded solely within their ethnic group. In this, and other studies, black and Puerto Rican adolescents are relatively more likely to be ethnically embedded,

Having a strong sense of ethnic identity is an important part of the adolescent's psychosocial development, especially among young people who are in the minority within their society. (Rogers/Monkmeyer)

whereas Mexican and Asian adolescents are more likely to be bicultural (e.g., Phinney, DuPont, Espinosa, Revill, and Sanders, 1994). More interesting, however, was the finding that although adolescents' ethnic attitudes differed among the mainstream, bicultural, and strong ethnic groups, their mental health did not. Adolescents with all three orientations had equal self-esteem, grades in school, and feelings of social competence. Similar findings have been reported in a study that further separated bicultural adolescents into groups that differed in the ways they expressed their bicultural orientation (e.g., having a strong "American" identity with recognition of one's ethnic heritage versus having a strong ethnic orientation with recognition of one's American citizenship); in this study, bicultural adolescents with different types of orientations scored similarly on measures of personality and adjustment (Phinney, Devich-Navarro, DuPont, Estrada, and Onwughalu, 1994). Interestingly, foreign-born ethnic minority adolescents tend to express more positive feelings about mainstream American ideals than do their counterparts whose families have been in the United States longer. One interpretation of this is that ethnic minority immigrants arrive in America idealistic about the "melting pot" society, only to discover that they are objects of prejudice and discrimination. This realization may prompt a strengthening of ethnic identity, a desire for separatism, and cynicism about endorsing mainstream American values (Phinney, DuPont, Espinosa, Revill, and Sanders, 1994).

RECAP

In recent years, several researchers have turned their attention to the study of identity development among ethnic minority youth and, in particular, to the study of ethnic identity. Although adolescents from ethnic minorities benefit from having a strong ethnic identity, there are a variety of ways in which this can be positively expressed. Many experts believe that an especially successful approach is biculturalism, in which minority youth have open to them the norms of both the majority and the minority cultures and they select between them, depending on the situation.

SEX-ROLE DEVELOPMENT

Gender is a critical component of one's identity. From birth, boys and girls are socialized to behave in "sex-appropriate" ways—that is, to conform to society's standards for acceptable masculine and acceptable feminine behavior. In American society, strong sex-role stereotypes prevail among children, adolescents, and adults. Traits such as logical, independent, ambitious, and aggressive are considered masculine; and traits such as gentle, sociable, empathic, and tender are considered feminine (Broverman, Vogel, Broverman, Clarkson, and Rosenkrantz, 1972).

Individuals vary in their degrees of masculinity and femininity. Some are decidedly more masculine than feminine, and others are decidedly more feminine than masculine. But some people have a high degree of both masculinity and femininity. For instance, some people are both highly ambitious (a trait usually considered masculine) and highly sensitive (a trait usually considered feminine). Individuals who are both highly masculine and highly feminine are said to be **androgynous** (Bem, 1975).

Researchers have begun to take an interest in the relation between sex-role stereotypes and adolescent identity development. Are teenagers, for example, pressured more than

THE SEXES

ARE THERE SEX DIFFERENCES IN THE ROUTE TO A SENSE OF IDENTITY?

Many writers have argued that male and female adolescents approach the crisis of identity from different perspectives and resolve it through different means. Some theorists have gone so far as to say that although Erikson's framework (which places the crisis of identity development earlier than the crisis of intimacy) is a reasonable model of psychosocial development for males, it does not adequately account for development among girls (Gallatin, 1975). They argue that girls are much more interpersonally oriented than boys and that, as a consequence, girls are likely to face the challenge of intimacy before they deal with the crisis of identity—or at the very least that girls pursue their sense of identity through their relationships with others. Girls learn about themselves, it is argued, in the context of friendships and close relationships, whereas boys forge a sense of identity by being autonomous and independent (Douvan and Adelson, 1966).

There is undoubtedly some truth to the idea that males and females approach and resolve the psychosocial issues of adolescence differently; how could they help but do so, given the strong pressures on them to adhere to two different sets of behavioral standards? But linking male identity development to autonomy and independence and female identity development to intimacy and other interpersonal pursuits is no longer as useful as it once was. Although one classic study of adolescents that was conducted during the early 1960s (Douvan and Adelson, 1966) concluded that "there is not one adolescent crisis, but two major and clearly distinctive ones—the masculine and the feminine" (p. 350), research during the 1980s has pointed to similarities rather than to differences in the ways in which males and females struggle with the task of self-definition (Adams and Fitch, 1982; Archer, 1989; Grotevant and Thorbecke, 1982). Were the early descriptions of sex differences in identity development erroneous, or are these more recent studies off the mark?

In answering this question, we must bear in mind that sex differences—or, for that matter, similarities—in identity development can be understood only against the backdrop of the social context in which development takes place. Assessing the studies in a historical context sheds some light on the controversy. For many adolescent girls, particularly twenty-five or thirty years ago, the roles of adulthood open to them were primarily interpersonal in nature, so

children to behave in stereotypically masculine or feminine ways? If so, to what extent does a person's compliance with prevailing sex-role stereotypes affect his or her self-image?

Sex-Role Socialization during Adolescence

There is some thought that pressures to behave in "sex-appropriate" ways intensify during adolescence, especially for girls (Huston and Alvarez, 1990). This idea, called the **gender intensification hypothesis** (Hill and Lynch, 1983), is that many of the sex differences observed between adolescent boys and girls result not from biological differences but from an acceleration in their socialization to act in stereotypically masculine and feminine ways.

Psychologists John Hill and Mary Ellen Lynch (1983) have summarized some of the that it comes as no surprise that the crisis of identity manifested itself for these young women through their relationships with others. After all, in Erikson's model, identity is pursued with one eye toward the future. But today, as new generations of adolescent girls face a society that presents them with greater and more diverse options for the future, especially in terms of occupation, their identity explorations are likely to extend further into the realms of autonomy and independence than they did in the past.

Changes in the broader social context of adolescence have continued to minimize sex differences in the process of identity development. For instance, whereas a review of research conducted during the 1960s and 1970s concluded that adolescent males move through the process of identity development faster than females (Marcia, 1980), more recent studies suggest that this is no longer the case (Archer, 1989). If young women in the past took more time resolving the crisis of identity than young men did, perhaps it was because the options and alternatives open to women in society at that time were more confusing, more complicated, and more rapidly changing than they were for men. As noted earlier, the length of a moratorium needed to experiment with enough roles is linked to the complexity of the choices the young person faces.

This is not to say that the outcomes of the identity development process are the same for males and females, however, or that the similarities that may characterize identity development during adolescence persist into adulthood. Society has still not fully come to terms with women's interest in careers, and, consequently, the task of integrating occupational and interpersonal commitments into a coherent and satisfying sense of self is likely to be more difficult for women than men. Accordingly, even though boys and girls may go through similar struggles in establishing a sense of identity in adolescence, the consequences of resolving the crisis may have clearer and more immediate advantages for men than women. Thus, for example, achieving a coherent sense of identity during adolescence is a strong predictor of life satisfaction and of becoming married as an adult for men, but for women it predicts neither (Kahn, Zimmerman, Csikszentmihalyi, and Getzels, 1985). Whatever similarities exist between boys and girls in their search for identity as adolescents, the structure of adult experience introduces important differences into the outcome.

research that bears on this issue. They note that, at adolescence, girls become more self-conscious and experience more disruptions in self-image than boys; that achievement behavior becomes more sex-stereotyped, with girls beginning to disengage from math and science; and that girls become more invested in and more competent at forming intimate friendships. One study has found that sex differences in sex-role attitudes and in the expression of masculinity do, in fact, increase in early adolescence, although these increases seem more tied to chronological age than to the onset of puberty (Galambos, Almeida, and Petersen, 1990). The entry into early adolescence may mark the emergence of new behaviors, which in turn may elicit more sex-differentiated behavior. As teenagers begin to date, for example, it may become more important for them to act in ways that are consistent with sex-role expectations and that meet with approval in the peer group. Boys who do not act masculine enough and girls who do not act feminine enough may be less popular and may be less accepted by their same- and opposite-sex peers.

In many respects, sex-role identity—already an important part of the self-concept during childhood—may become an even more important aspect of identity during adolescence. As we shall see in Chapters 10 through 12, which examine intimacy, sexuality, and achievement, the intensification of sex-role socialization during adolescence has important implications for understanding sex differences in a range of different issues. For example, girls' achievement in high school may be lower than boys' because doing well in school is not perceived as appropriately feminine, and so girls who earn high grades may pay a price in popularity.

According to psychologists Carol Gilligan (Gilligan, Lyons, and Hanmer, 1990) and Annie Rogers (1993), who have argued that adolescence is a critical turning point in female psychological development, the mixed messages that adolescent girls receive about desirable behavior are confusing and not easily reconciled. Girls, they argue, arrive at adolescence more likely than boys to prize intimacy and interpersonal communication. Throughout childhood, they have been rewarded for this more "relational" orientation. At adolescence, however, social cognitive abilities grow, and girls begin to realize that the very traits they have been socialized for are not valued in the male-dominated broader society. As a consequence, girls feel caught between what they have been told is correct for their gender (e.g., caring and nurturance) and what they can see is valued by society at large (e.g., assertiveness and independence). Overwhelmed by ambivalence, many girls become less confident and less sure of themselves. As you will read in Chapter 13, some theorists believe that this conflict may contribute to the greater prevalence of depression among females than males both in adolescence and in adulthood.

Other feminist theorists, such as Jean Baker Miller (1986), have argued that the very ways in which we have defined mental health have forced us into a very one-sided view of psychological development. By defining competence as assertive, independent behavior (even the term "identity achieved" has an assertive ring to it), we may have overlooked the importance of understanding how adolescents' psychological growth is facilitated through the formation of relationships with others. These theorists argue that the study of female adolescent development will reveal different pathways to competence for adolescents in general.

Masculinity, Femininity, and Androgyny

If sex-role socialization becomes more intense during adolescence, we would expect to find that conformity to sex-role expectations is an important influence on the adolescent's self-image. Do more feminine girls and more masculine boys feel better about themselves than do their peers, or are boys and girls both better off being somewhat androgynous—as some psychologists suggest (Bem, 1975; Spence and Helmreich, 1978)?

Recent research on sex-role identity during adolescence suggests that the answer to this question may differ for males and females. The relative benefits of androgyny to youngsters' self-image are likely to be greater for girls than for boys. This is because it is specifically the masculine component of androgyny that is associated with better mental health in adolescence (Markstrom-Adams, 1989). Interestingly, this is not the case during childhood, when aspects of *both* masculinity and femininity are linked to well-being for both sexes (Allgood-Merten and Stockard, 1991), or during young adulthood, when femininity as well as masculinity is predictive of well-being among young women (Stein, Newcomb, and Bentler, 1992).

Although masculinity is predictive of mental health for adolescent males and females, androgynous girls feel better about themselves than either very masculine or very feminine girls, whereas masculine boys (not androgynous boys) show the highest levels of self-acceptance, a finding that has emerged in studies of both Western and non-Western youth (Lau, 1989; Orr and Ben-Eliahu, 1993). This may be because peer acceptance during adolescence is also highest for androgynous girls and masculine boys (Massad, 1981). These findings suggest that it is easier for girls to behave sometimes in masculine ways during adolescence than it is for boys to act occasionally in feminine ways. Consistent with research on younger children (Lynn, 1966), during adolescence—at least in contemporary American society—males who do not conform to traditionally masculine sex-role norms are judged more deviant than are females whose behavior departs from exclusively feminine roles.

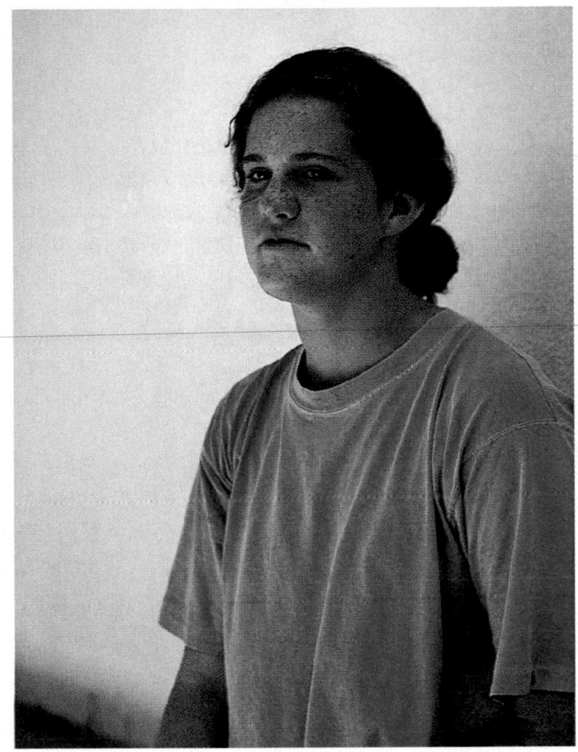

Although masculinity is predictive of mental health for both adolescent males and females, androgynous girls feel better about themselves than either very masculine or very feminine girls. Masculine boys—not androgynous boys—show the highest levels of self-acceptance. (Michael Newman/PhotoEdit)

At first glance, this finding may seem to contradict something we noted earlier—that, during adolescence, pressures to conform with sex-role norms increase more for girls than for boys. If this is so, why is it that boys suffer greater self-image problems when they deviate from what is viewed as appropriate for their gender?

The answer is that although girls may be pressured to adopt (or maintain) certain feminine traits during adolescence, they are not necessarily pressured to relinquish all elements of masculinity. In contrast, boys are socialized from a very early age not to adopt feminine traits and are judged deviant if they show signs of femininity. In other words, girls can be highly pressured during adolescence to behave in feminine ways without necessarily being punished or labeled deviant for exhibiting some masculine traits at the same time; thus, for girls, androgyny is a viable alternative to exclusive femininity. Girls may feel increasingly pressured to dress nicely and to wear makeup when they reach adolescence; but they are not pressured to give up athletics or other typically masculine interests. But boys, from childhood on, are pressured not to behave in feminine ways—even if the femininity is in the context of androgyny. Their gender-role socialization does not intensify during adolescence as much as it does for girls because it is so intense to begin with.

RECAP

An important aspect of adolescent identity is the development of gender identity. Research suggests that adolescence is a time of especially strong socialization for stereotypic gender roles, but that this intensity wanes as individuals move toward young adulthood. In general, among both males and females, many traits traditionally labeled as masculine are associated in adolescence—but not in childhood or young adulthood—with better adjustment and greater peer acceptance. As a result, androgynous females and masculine males report higher self-esteem than their peers do.

KEY TERMS

analysis of variance (ANOVA)
androgynous
assimilation
barometric self-esteem
baseline self-esteem
biculturalism
Big Five
code switching
correlation coefficient
dependent variable
ethnic identity
ethnic socialization
false-self behavior
Five-Factor Model
gender intensification hypothesis
identity diffusion (identity confusion)
identity foreclosure
identity versus identity diffusion
independent variable
marginality
negative identity
psychosocial moratorium
self-conceptions
self-consciousness
self-esteem
self-image stability
sense of identity
separation

FOR FURTHER READING

Adams, G., Gullotta, T., and Montemayor, R. (Eds.). (1992). *Adolescent identity formation.* Newbury Park, Calif.: Sage. A collection of theoretical and empirical articles by the leading researchers in the study of adolescent identity.

Baumeister, R., and Tice, D. (1986). How adolescence became the struggle for self: A historical transformation of psychological development. Pp. 183–201 in J. Suls and A. Greenwald (Eds.), *Psychological perspectives on the self,* Vol. 3. Hillsdale, N.J.: Erlbaum. A thoughtful discussion of the social and historical factors that have made identity development such a salient issue in the study of adolescent development.

Erikson, E. (1968). *Identity: Youth and crisis.* New York: Norton. In this book, Erikson presents his theory of identity development during adolescence.

Gilligan, C., Lyons, N., and Hanmer, T. (Eds.). (1990). *Making connections: The relational worlds of adolescent girls at Emma Willard School.* Cambridge, Mass.: Harvard University Press. An exploration of the challenges faced by young adolescent girls in developing an identity and finding a "voice," by the well-known feminist scholar and her colleagues.

Harter, S. (1990). Identity and self development. Pp. 352–387 in S. Feldman and G. Elliott (Eds.), *At the threshold: The developing adolescent.* Cambridge, Mass.: Harvard University Press. An extensive review of the literatures on self-conceptions, self-esteem, and identity development in adolescence.

Phinney, J. (1990). Ethnic identity in adolescents and adults: A review of research. *Psychological Bulletin, 108,* 499–514. A review and synthesis of the scientific literature on identity development during adolescence and beyond.

CHAPTER 9

AUTONOMY

(Bob Daemmrich/Stock, Boston)

You are about to leave the house:

"Where are you going?"

"Out."

"Out where?"

"Just out."

"Who are you going with?"

"A friend."

"Which friend?"

"Mom, just a friend, okay? Do you have to know everything?"

"I don't have to know everything. I just want to know who you're going out with."

"Debby, okay?"

"Do I know Debby?"

"She's just a friend, okay?"

"Well, where are you going?"

"Out."

SOURCE: Delia Ephron, *Teenage Romance, Or How to Die of Embarrassment* (New York: Viking, 1981).

For most adolescents, establishing a sense of **autonomy** is as important a part of becoming an adult as is establishing a sense of identity. Becoming an autonomous person—a self-governing person—is one of the fundamental developmental tasks of the adolescent years.

Although we often use the words *autonomy* and *independence* interchangeably, in the study of adolescence they mean slightly different things. *Independence* generally refers to individuals' capacity to behave on their own. The growth of independence is surely a part of becoming autonomous during adolescence, but, as you will see in this chapter, *autonomy* has emotional and cognitive as well as behavioral components.

During adolescence, there is a movement away from the dependency typical of childhood toward the autonomy typical of adulthood. But the growth of autonomy during adolescence is often misunderstood. Autonomy is often confused with rebellion, and becoming an independent person is often equated with breaking away from the family. This perspective on autonomy goes hand in hand with the idea that adolescence is inevitably a time of stress and turmoil. But as we have seen in previous chapters, the view that adolescence is a period of "storm and stress" has been questioned repeatedly by recent research. The same sort of rethinking has taken place with regard to the development of autonomy. Rather than viewing adolescence as a time of spectacular and active rebellion, researchers now see the growth of autonomy during adolescence as gradual, progressive, and—although important—relatively undramatic.

Because today's adolescents spend so much time away from the direct supervision of adults, either by themselves or with their peers, learning how to govern their own behavior in a responsible fashion is a crucial task for contemporary youth. As we saw in earlier chapters, with increasing numbers of single-parent and two-career households, more young people are expected to supervise themselves for a good part of the day (Carnegie Council on Adolescent Development, 1992). Many young people feel pressured—by parents, by friends, and by the media—to grow up quickly and to act like adults at an earlier age (Elkind, 1982). One 13-year-old must make plane reservations to fly back and forth between his separated parents' homes. Another is pregnant and, afraid to tell her parents, must seek counseling on her own. A third is expected to take care of his younger siblings each afternoon because both of his parents work. In many regards, the demands on young people to behave independently are greater today than ever before.

There is a curious paradox in all of this, however. At the same time that adolescents have been asked to become more autonomous psychologically and socially, they have become less autonomous economically. Because of the extension of schooling well into the young adult years for most individuals, finan-

The demands on young people to behave independently are greater today than ever before. This adolescent is expected to supervise his younger brothers each day after school. (Mary Kate Denny/PhotoEdit)

cial independence may not come until long after psychological independence has been established. Many young people who are emotionally independent find it frustrating to discover that they have to abide by their parents' rules as long as they are being supported economically. They may feel that the ability to make their own decisions has nothing to do with financial dependence. A 16-year-old who drives, has a part-time job, and has a serious relationship with his girlfriend, for example, may be independent in these respects, but he is nonetheless still dependent on his parents for food and shelter. His parents may feel that as long as their son lives in their home, they should decide how late he can stay out at night. The adolescent may feel that his parents have no right to tell him when he can come and go. This sort of difference of opinion can be a real source of problems and confusion for teenagers and their parents, particularly when they have difficulty agreeing on a level of independence for the adolescent. Disagreements over autonomy-related concerns are at the top of the list of things that provoke quarrels between adolescents and parents (Holmbeck and O'Donnell, 1991; Montemayor, 1986).

AUTONOMY AS AN ADOLESCENT ISSUE

Like identity, autonomy is a psychosocial concern that surfaces and resurfaces during the entire life cycle. The development of independent behavior begins long before puberty. Erik Erikson (1963), whose ideas we examined in the previous chapter, believed that autonomy is the central issue of toddlerhood, just as identity is the central issue of adolescence. Young children, he observed, try to establish an initial sense of autonomy when they begin to explore their surroundings on their own and assert their desire to do as they please. If you spend any time with 3-year-olds, you know that one of their favorite expressions is "No!" In some regards, the early adolescent's behavior that is captured in the excerpt at the beginning of this chapter is quite similar. The toddler who insists on saying "No!" and the young adolescent who insists on keeping her whereabouts secret are both demonstrating their growing sense of independence and autonomy.

Although childhood and adolescence are important periods for the development of autonomy, it is a mistake to suggest that issues of autonomy are resolved once and for all upon reaching young adulthood. Questions about our ability to function independently arise whenever we find ourselves in positions that demand a new degree of self-reliance. Following a divorce, for example, someone who has depended on a spouse over the years for economic support, guidance, or nurturance must find a way to function more autonomously and more independently. During late adulthood, autonomy may become a significant concern of the individual who suddenly finds it necessary to depend on others for assistance and support.

If establishing and maintaining a healthy sense of autonomy is a lifelong concern, why has it attracted so much attention among scholars interested in adolescence? When we look at the development of autonomy in relation to the biological, cognitive, and social changes of adolescence, it is easy to see why. Consider first the impact of puberty. Some theorists (for example, A. Freud, 1958) have suggested that the physical changes of early adolescence trigger changes in the young person's emotional relationships at home (Holmbeck and Hill, 1991). Adolescents' interest in turning away from parents and toward peers for emotional support—a development that is part of establishing adult independence—may be sparked by their emerging interest in sexual relationships and by their concerns over such things as dating and intimate friendships. In some senses, puberty drives the adolescent away from exclusive emotional dependence on the family. Furthermore, the changes in stature and physical appearance occurring at puberty may provoke changes in how much autonomy the young person is granted by parents and teachers. Youngsters who simply look more mature may be given more responsibility by adults around them.

The cognitive changes of adolescence also play an important role in the development of autonomy. Part of being autonomous involves being able to make our own decisions. When we turn to others for advice, we often receive conflicting opinions. For example, if you are deciding between staying home to study for an exam and going out to a party, your professor and the person throwing the party would probably give you different advice. As an adult, you are able to see that each individual's perspective influences his or her advice. The ability to see this, however, calls for a level of intellectual abstraction that is not available until adolescence. Being able to take other people's perspectives into account, to reason in more sophisticated ways, and to foresee the future consequences of alternative courses of action all help the young person to weigh more effectively the opinions and suggestions of others and to reach his or her independent decisions. The cognitive changes of adolescence also provide the logical foundation for changes in the young person's thinking about social, moral, and ethical problems. These changes in thinking are important prerequisites to the development of a system of values that is based on the individual's own sense of right and wrong and not merely on rules and regulations handed down by parents or other authority figures (Mazor, Shamir, and Ben-Mosche, 1990; Mazor and Enright, 1988).

Finally, changes in social roles and activities during adolescence are bound to raise concerns related to independence, as the adolescent moves into new positions that demand increasing degrees of responsibility and self-reliance. Being able to work, to marry, to drive, to drink, and to vote—to name just a few activities that are first permitted during adolescence—all require a certain degree of autonomy, the ability to manage oneself responsibly in the absence of monitoring by parents or teachers. Becoming involved in new roles and taking on new responsibilities place the adolescent in situations that require and stimulate the development of independent decision-making abilities and the clarification of personal values. A teenager might not really think much about the responsibilities associated with taking a job, for example, until he or she actually ends up in one. Choosing whether to drink does not become an important question until the adolescent begins to approach the legal drinking age. And deciding what one's political leanings are becomes a more pressing concern when the young person realizes that he or she will soon have the right to vote.

THREE TYPES OF AUTONOMY

We have talked a great deal thus far about the need to develop a sense of autonomy during adolescence. But what does it really mean to be an autonomous or independent person? One way to approach this question is to begin by thinking about the people whom you would describe as independent. Why do they seem so? Is it because they are able to rely on themselves rather than depending excessively on others for support or guidance? Is it because they can make their own decisions and follow them through, withstanding pressures to go against what they really know is right? Or it is perhaps because they are independent thinkers—people who have strong principles and values that they won't compromise?

Each of these characterizations is a reasonable enough description of what it means to be independent, and yet each describes a different sort of independence. The first characterization involves what psychologists call **emotional autonomy**—that aspect of independence which is related to changes in the individual's close relationships, especially with parents. The second characterization corresponds to what is sometimes called **behavioral autonomy**—the capacity to make independent decisions and follow through with them. The third characterization involves an aspect of independence that is referred to as **value autonomy,** which is more than simply being able to resist pressures to go along with the demands of others; it means having a set of principles about right and wrong, about what is important and what is not. Throughout most of this chapter, we will examine these three aspects of autonomy.

RECAP

Although the development of autonomy is an important psychosocial issue throughout the life span, it is especially salient during adolescence because of the physical, cognitive, and social changes of the period. Psychologists generally differentiate among three types of autonomy in adolescence: emotional autonomy, which refers to emotional independence in relationships with others, especially parents; behavioral autonomy, which refers to the development of independent decision-making abilities; and value autonomy, which concerns the development of independent beliefs.

THE DEVELOPMENT OF EMOTIONAL AUTONOMY

The relationship between children and their parents changes repeatedly over the course of the life cycle. Changes in the expression of affection, the distribution of power, and patterns of verbal interaction, to give a few examples, are likely to occur whenever important transformations take place in the child's or the parents' competencies, concerns, and social roles. By the end of adolescence, individuals are far less emotionally dependent on their parents than they were as children. One can see this in several ways. First, older adolescents do not generally rush to their parents whenever they are upset, worried, or in need of assistance. Second, they do not see their parents as all-knowing or all-powerful. Third, adolescents often have a great deal of emotional energy wrapped up in relationships outside the family; in fact, they may feel more attached to a boyfriend or a girlfriend than to their parents. And finally, older adolescents are able to see and interact with their parents as people—not just as their parents. Many parents find, for example, that they can confide in their adolescent children, something that was not possible when their children were younger, or that their adolescent children can easily sympathize with them when they have had a hard day at work. These sorts of changes in the adolescent-parent relationship all reflect the development of emotional autonomy (Steinberg, 1990).

Emotional Autonomy and Detachment

Early writings about emotional autonomy were influenced by psychoanalytic thinkers such as Anna Freud (1958), who argued that the physical changes of puberty cause substantial disruption and conflict inside the family system. The reason, Freud believed, is that intrapsychic conflicts that have been repressed since early childhood are reawakened at early adolescence by the resurgence of sexual impulses. (These conflicts revolved around the young child's unconscious attraction toward the parent of the opposite sex and ambivalent feelings toward the parent of the same sex.) The reawakened conflicts are expressed as increased tension among family members, arguments, and a certain degree of discomfort around the house. As a consequence of this tension, early adolescents are driven to separate themselves, at least emotionally, from their parents, and they turn their emotional energies to relationships with peers—in particular, peers of the opposite sex. Psychoanalytic theorists call this process of separation **detachment,** because to them it appears as though the early adolescent is attempting to sever the *attachments* that have been formed during infancy and strengthened throughout childhood.

Detachment, and the accompanying storm and stress inside the family, were viewed by Freud and her followers as normal, healthy, and inevitable aspects of emotional development during adolescence. In fact, Freud believed that the absence of conflict between an adolescent and his or her parents signified that the young person was having problems growing up. This view was compatible with the idea that adolescence was an inherently tumultuous time—a perspective that, as you know, dominated ideas about adolescence for many, many years.

Studies of adolescents' family relationships have not supported Freud's idea, however. In

In contrast to the view that adolescent-parent tension is the norm, every major study done to date of teenagers' relations with their parents has shown that most families get along quite well during the adolescent years. (Myrleen Ferguson/PhotoEdit)

contrast to predictions that high levels of adolescent-parent tension are the norm, that adolescents detach themselves from relationships with their parents, and that adolescents are driven out of the household by unbearable levels of family conflict, every major study done to date of teenagers' relations with their parents has shown that most families get along quite well during the adolescent years (Steinberg, 1990). Although parents and adolescents may bicker more often than they did during earlier periods of development, there is no evidence that this bickering significantly diminishes closeness between parents and teenagers (Hill and Holmbeck, 1986). One team of researchers, for example, who asked adolescents and children of different ages to rate how close they were to their parents, found that 19-year-old college students reported being just as close as fourth-graders (Hunter and Youniss, 1982).

The psychic and interpersonal tension believed to arise at puberty does not show up in markedly strained family relationships. Although adolescents and their parents undoubtedly modify their relationships during adolescence, their emotional bonds are by no means severed. This is an important distinction, for it means that emotional autonomy during adolescence involves a *transformation,* not a breaking off of family relationships. Adolescents can become emotionally autonomous from their parents *without* becoming detached from them (Collins, 1990; Hill and Holmbeck, 1986; Steinberg, 1990).

Emotional Autonomy and Individuation

As an alternative to the classic psychoanalytic perspective on adolescent detachment, some theorists have suggested that the development of emotional autonomy be looked at in terms of the adolescent's developing sense of **individuation.** One such theorist is the noted psychoanalyst Peter Blos, who writes, "Individuation implies that the growing person takes increasing responsibility for what he does and what he is, rather than depositing this responsibility on the shoulders of those under whose influence and tutelage he has grown up" (1967, p. 168). The process of individuation, which begins during infancy and continues well into late adolescence, involves a gradual, progressive sharpening of one's sense of self as autonomous, as competent, and as separate from one's parents. Individuation, therefore, has a great deal to do with the development of a sense of identity, in that it involves changes in how we come to see and feel about ourselves. The process does not involve stress and turmoil. Rather, individuation entails relinquishing childish dependencies on parents in favor of more mature, more responsible, and less dependent relationships. Adolescents who have been successful in establishing a sense of individuation can accept responsibility for their choices and actions instead of looking to their parents to do it for them (Josselson, 1980). For example, rather than rebelling against her parents' midnight curfew by deliberately staying out later, a girl who has a healthy sense of individuation might take her parents aside before going out and say: "This party tonight may last longer than midnight. If it does, I'd like to stay a bit longer. Suppose I call you at eleven o'clock and let you know when I'll be home. That way, you won't worry as much if I come home a little later."

Several studies of the growth of emotional autonomy have appeared in recent years. These studies indicate that the development of emotional autonomy is a long process, beginning early in adolescence and continuing well into young adulthood. In one (Steinberg and Silverberg, 1986), a questionnaire measuring four aspects of emotional autonomy was administered to a sample of 10- to 15-year-olds. The four components were (1) the extent to which adolescents' *de-idealized* their parents ("My parents sometimes make mistakes"); (2) the extent to which adolescents were able to *see their parents as people* ("My parents act differently with their own friends than they do with me"); (3) *nondependency,* or the degree to which adolescents depended on themselves, rather than on their parents, for assistance ("When I've done something wrong, I don't always depend on my parents to straighten things out"); and (4) the degree to which the adolescent felt *individuated* within the relationship with his or her parents ("There are some things about me that my parents do not know"). As you can see in Figure 9.1, scores on three of the four scales—all except "perceives parents as people"—increased over the age period studied.

Similar findings have emerged in other studies. In one, for example, the researchers found that as adolescents aged, the number of their friends whom their parents knew declined significantly, reflecting greater individuation and privacy on the part of the adolescent (Feiring and Lewis, 1993). In another study, in which adolescents were interviewed about their family relationships, the researchers found that older adolescents were also more likely to de-idealize their parents. For example, one adolescent said about his father: "I used to listen to everything. I thought he was always right. Now I have my own opinions. They may be wrong, but they're mine and I like to say them" (Smoller and Youniss, 1985, p. 8).

FIGURE 9.1 *Age differences in four aspects of emotional autonomy.* (Steinberg and Silverberg, 1986)

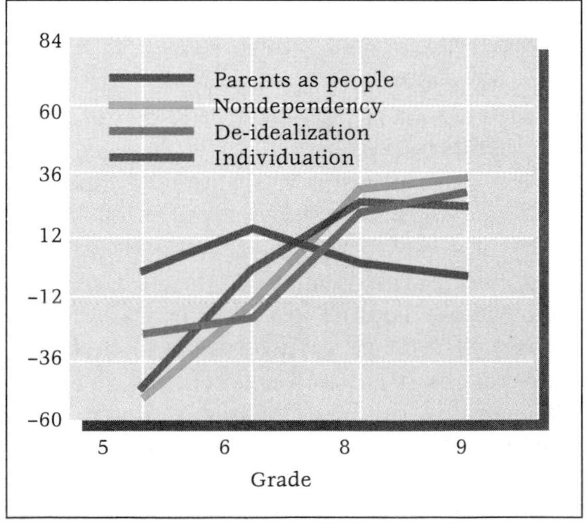

De-idealization may be one of the first aspects of emotional autonomy to develop, because adolescents may shed their childish images of their parents before replacing them with more mature ones. Although middle adolescents are less likely than young adolescents to hold on to idealized pictures of their parents, when it comes to seeing their parents as individuals, 15-year-olds are no more emotionally autonomous than are 10-year-olds. Even during the high school years, adolescents appear to have some difficulty in seeing their parents as individuals beyond their roles as parents. This aspect of emotional autonomy may not develop until much later—perhaps not until young adulthood (Smollar and Youniss, 1985; White, Speisman, and Costos, 1983). This aspect of emotional autonomy appears to develop later in adolescents' relations with their fathers than with their mothers, because fathers seem to interact less often with their adolescents in ways that permit them to be seen as individuals (Youniss and Smollar, 1985).

Interestingly, and in contrast to the old view that adolescents needed to sever their ties with their parents in order to grow up healthily, a number of studies find that the development of emotional autonomy may have different psychological effects on the adolescent depending on whether his or her parent-child relationship is a close one. Adolescents who become emotionally autonomous, but who also feel distant or detached from their parents, score poorly on measures of psychological adjustment; whereas adolescents who demonstrate the same degree of emotional autonomy, but who still feel close and attached to their parents, are more psychologically adjusted than their peers (Frank, Poorman, and Charles, in press; Lamborn and Steinberg, 1993; Ryan and Lynch, 1989). In essence, whereas detachment has negative effects on adolescents' mental health, individuation has positive ones.

Several writers have explored the ways in which the process of developing autonomy may differ for adolescents whose parents have divorced (Feldman and Quatman, 1988; Sessa and Steinberg, 1991; Wallerstein and Kelly, 1974; Weiss, 1979). These writers argue that having divorced parents prompts the adolescent to grow up "faster"—to de-idealize parents at an earlier age. As a consequence, adolescents from divorced homes may begin the process of individuation somewhat earlier than their peers. Whether this has positive or negative consequences, however, is not known.

What triggers the process of individuation? Two different models have been suggested. According to several researchers, puberty is the main catalyst (e.g., Bulcroft, 1991; Holmbeck and Hill, 1991; Steinberg, 1989). Changes in the adolescent's physical appearance provoke changes in the way that adolescents are viewed—by themselves and by their parents—which, in turn, provoke changes in parent-child interaction. As we saw in Chapter 4, shortly after puberty most families experience an increase in bickering and squabbling. Some writers have suggested that this increase in conflict helps adolescents to see their parents in a different light and to develop a sense of individuation (Cooper, 1988; Holmbeck and Hill, 1991; Steinberg, 1990).

Other authors believe that adolescents' movement toward higher levels of individuation is stimulated by their social-cognitive development (Collins, 1990; Smetana, 1988a). As you read in Chapter 2, *social cognition* refers to the thinking we do about ourselves and our relationships with others. The development of emotional autonomy in adolescence may be provoked by young people's development of more sophisticated understandings of themselves and their parents. Prior to adolescence, individuals accept their parents' views of themselves as accurate (e.g., "My parents think I am a good girl, so I must be"). But as individuals develop more differentiated self-conceptions in early and middle adolescence (recall the discussion of this in Chapter 8), they come to see that their parents' view is but one of many—and one that may not be entirely accurate ("My parents think I am a good girl, but they don't know what I am really like"). By late adolescence, individuals are able to see that these apparent discrepancies between their self-conceptions and the views of their parents are perfectly understandable ("There are sides of me that have been influenced by my parents and sides of me that have not") (see Mazor and Enright, 1988).

This is not to suggest that the process of individuation is always a smooth one. Some writers have suggested that as adolescents begin to de-idealize their parents, they may begin to feel both more autonomous and more insecure—what one research team labeled a "double-edged sword" (Frank, Pirsch, and Wright, 1990; Frank et al., in press). That is, even though our childish images of our parents as being all-knowing and all-powerful may be inaccurate, they still provide a certain degree of emotional comfort. Leaving such images behind can be both liberating and frightening. Indeed, some researchers have found that emotional autonomy is associated not only with insecurity for the adolescent but also with increased feelings of rejection for the parents (Ryan and Lynch, 1989).

RECAP

Formerly, adolescence was viewed as a time during which individuals need to break away from and rebel against their parents. More recent research indicates, however, that the growth of emotional autonomy is typically more peaceful and less tumultuous. Instead of emphasizing the young person's need for detachment, therefore, contemporary psychologists stress the process of individuation, which is set in motion in early adolescence by the physical and cognitive changes of the period.

Emotional Autonomy and Parenting Practices

Whether provoked by puberty or by the development of more advanced cognitive skills, and whether approached with confidence or with trepidation, according to most theorists healthy individuation is fostered by close, not distant, family relationships (Grotevant and Cooper, 1986). Tense family relationships during adolescence indicate problems, not positive development. Researchers have found, for example, that adolescents who feel the most autonomous—that is, those who are most likely to feel that they have been granted "enough" freedom by their parents—are not the ones who have severed relationships at home. In fact, just the opposite is the case: Autonomous adolescents report that they are quite close to their parents, enjoy doing things with their families, have few conflicts with their mothers and fathers, feel free to turn to their parents for advice, and say they would like to be like their parents (Kandel and Lesser, 1972). Rebellion, negativism, and excessive involvement in the peer group are more common among psychologically immature adolescents than among mature ones (Josselson, Greenberger, and McConochie, 1977a, 1977b). Even during the college years, students who live away from home (which is in its own way a type of autonomy)—as opposed to remaining in their parents' home and commuting to school—report more affection for their parents, better communication, and higher levels of satisfaction in the relationship (Sullivan and Sullivan, 1980). Strained family relationships appear to be associated with a lack of autonomy during adolescence, rather than with its presence.

Emotional autonomy develops best under conditions that encourage both individuation and emotional closeness. This can be seen quite clearly in the work of Stuart Hauser and his colleagues, who have studied videotapes of parents and adolescents in discussion and have examined whether certain types of interaction are more or less facilitative of healthy adolescent development (Hauser, Powers, and Noam, 1991). The tapes were coded for two specific types of behavior: enabling behavior and constraining behavior. Parents who use a lot of *enabling behavior* accept their adolescent while at the same time helping the teenager to develop and state his or her own ideas, through questions, explanations, and the tolerance of differences of opinion. In contrast, parents who use *constraining behavior* have difficulty accepting their child's individuality and react to expressions of independent thinking with remarks that are distracting, judgmental, or devaluing. After hearing an adolescent's opinion that differs from his own, for example, an enabling father might ask for more clarification or might genuinely probe the adolescent's logic, whereas a constraining father might cut off further discussion by saying that the adolescent is wrong or ignorant.

Not surprisingly, Hauser has found that adolescents whose parents use a great deal of enabling and relatively little constraining are more likely to develop in healthy ways: They are more individuated and score higher on measures of ego development and psychosocial competence. This is in line with other research showing that healthy identity development is more likely to occur within families in which adolescents are encouraged both to be "connected" to their parents and to express their own individuality (Cooper, Grotevant, and Condon, 1983; Grotevant and Cooper, 1986).

As we saw in Chapter 4, adolescents' development is affected differently by different styles of parenting. In particular, independence, responsibility, and self-esteem are all fostered by parents who are authoritative (friendly, fair, and firm), rather than authoritarian (excessively harsh), indulgent (excessively lenient), or indifferent (excessively aloof to the point of neglectful). Let us now look more closely at these findings in light of what we know about the development of emotional autonomy.

In authoritative families, guidelines are established for the adolescent's behavior, and standards are upheld, but they are flexible and open to discussion. Moreover, these standards and guidelines are explained and implemented in an atmosphere of closeness, concern, and fairness. Although parents may have the final say when it comes to their child's behavior, the decision that is reached usually comes after consultation and discussion—with the child included. In discussing an adolescent's curfew, for example, authoritative parents would sit down with their child and explain how they arrived at their decision and why they picked the hour they did. They would also ask the adolescent for his or her suggestions and would consider them carefully in making a final decision.

It is not difficult to see why the sort of give-and-take that is found in authoritative families is well suited to the child's transition into adolescence. Because standards and guidelines are flexible and adequately explained, it is not hard for the family to adjust and modify them as the child matures emotionally and intellectually (Smetana and Asquith, 1994). At some point, for example, a teenager may ask his or her parents to consider establishing a later curfew, and authoritative parents would think about the request seriously and would discuss it openly. Gradual changes in family relations that permit the young person more independence and encourage more responsibility but that do not threaten the emotional bond between parent and child—in other words, changes that promote increasing emotional autonomy—are relatively easy to make for a family that has been flexible and has been making these sorts of modifications in family relationships all along (Baumrind, 1978).

In authoritarian households, where rules are rigidly enforced and seldom explained to the child, adjusting to adolescence is more difficult for the family. Authoritarian parents may see the child's increasing emotional independence as rebellious or disrespectful, and they may resist their adolescent's growing need for independence, rather than reacting to it openly. Authoritarian parents, on seeing that their daughter is becoming interested in boys, may implement a rigid curfew in order to restrict her social life. Instead of encouraging autonomy, authoritarian parents may inadvertently maintain the dependencies of childhood by failing to give their child sufficient practice in making decisions and being responsible for his or her actions. In essence, authoritarian parenting may interfere with adolescent individuation.

When closeness is absent as well, the problems are compounded. In families in which excessive parental control is accompanied by extreme coldness and punitiveness, the adolescent may rebel against parents' standards explicitly, in an attempt to assert his or her independence in a visible and demonstrable fashion (Hill and Holmbeck, 1986). Adolescents whose parents refuse to grant reasonable curfews are the ones who typically stay out the latest. Such rebellion is not indicative of genuine emotional autonomy, though; it is more likely to be a demonstration of the adolescent's frustration with his or her parents' rigidity and lack of understanding. And, as noted earlier, when adolescents attempt to establish emotional autonomy within the context of a cold or hostile family, the effects on the young person's mental health are likely to be negative (Lamborn and Steinberg, 1993).

In both indulgent families and indifferent families, a different sort of problem arises. These kinds of parents do not provide sufficient guidance for their children, and, as a result, youngsters who are raised permissively do not acquire adequate standards for behavior. Someone who has never had to abide by his parents' rules as a child faces tremendous difficulty learning how to comply with rules as an adult. In the absence of parents' guidance and rules, permissively reared teenagers often turn to their peers for advice and emotional support—a practice that can be problematic when the peers are themselves still relatively young and inexperienced. Not surprisingly, adolescents whose parents have failed to provide sufficient guidance are likely to become psychologically dependent on their friends—emotionally detached from their parents, perhaps, but not genuinely autonomous. The problems of parental permissiveness are exacerbated by a lack of closeness, as is the case in indifferent families.

Some parents who have raised their children permissively until adolescence are caught by surprise by the consequences of not having been stricter earlier on. The greater orientation toward the peer group of permissively raised adolescents may involve the young person in behavior that his or her parents disapprove of. As a consequence, some parents who have been permissive throughout a youngster's childhood shift gears when he or she enters adolescence and become autocratic, as a means of controlling the youngster over whom they feel they have lost control. For instance, parents who have never placed any restrictions on their daughter's afternoon activities during elementary school suddenly begin monitoring her teenage social life once she enters junior high school. Shifts like these are extremely hard on adolescents—just at the time when they are seeking greater autonomy, their parents become more restrictive. Having become accustomed to relative leniency, adolescents whose parents change the rules in the middle of the game may find it difficult to accept standards that are being strictly enforced for the first time.

RECAP

Healthy individuation is fostered by close, not distant, family relationships. Adolescents who are raised in authoritative homes in which their parents are both accepting and tolerant of the young person's individuality enjoy many psychological advantages over their peers, including a more fully developed sense of emotional autonomy.

THE DEVELOPMENT OF BEHAVIORAL AUTONOMY

One of the most popular misconceptions about adolescent development is that adolescents demonstrate autonomy by rebelling against the wishes of their parents. But in many instances, rebelling against one's parents or other authorities is done not out of independence but in the service of conforming to one's peers. One recent study indicated, in fact, that during early adolescence individuals become more emotionally autonomous from their parents but less autonomous from their friends (Steinberg and Silverberg, 1986). Merely substituting one source of influence (the peer group) for another (the family), though, is hardly evidence of growth toward independence. Excessive adherence to the pressures of one's friends is not more autonomous than is excessive adherence to the pressures of one's parents. Moreover, as we saw earlier in this chapter, rebellion is associated with immaturity, not with healthy development. Just what is meant, then, by behavioral autonomy?

All individuals—at any age—are susceptible to the pressures of those around them. The opinions and advice of others, especially people whose knowledge and judgment we respect, are, and should be, important influences on our choices and decisions. Surely, then, we would not want to say that the behaviorally autonomous adolescent is entirely free from the influence of others. Rather, an individual who is behaviorally autonomous is able to turn to others for advice when it is appropriate, can weigh alternative courses of action based on his or her own judgment and the suggestions of others, and can reach an independent conclusion about how to behave (Hill and Holmbeck, 1986). Let's look more closely at why and how changes in behavioral autonomy occur during adolescence. Researchers have looked at this in three domains: changes in decision-making abilities, changes in susceptibility to the influence of others, and changes in feelings of self-reliance.

Changes in Decision-Making Abilities

The more sophisticated reasoning processes employed by the adolescent permit him or her to hold multiple viewpoints in mind simultaneously, allowing comparisons among the viewpoints to be drawn—an ability that is crucial for weighing the opinions and advice of others. In addition, because adolescents are better able than children to think in hypothetical terms, they are more likely to consider the possible long-term consequences of choosing one course of action over another. And the enhanced role-taking capabilities of adolescence permit the teenager to consider another person's opinion while taking into account that person's perspective. This is important in determining whether someone who gives advice has special areas of expertise, particular biases, or vested interests that one should keep in mind. Taken together, these cognitive changes result in improved decision-making skills and, consequently, in the individual's greater ability to behave independently.

A study by Catherine Lewis (1981b) sheds a good deal of light on these issues. She presented over 100 adolescents ranging in age from 12 to 18 with a series of "problems" that they were to help another teenager solve. The problems concerned such things as becoming involved in different sorts of risky situations, revising an opinion of someone who had previously been respected, or reconciling different pieces of advice from two "experts." One of the problems, for example, focused on a teenager's indecision about whether to have cosmetic surgery.

Lewis looked at adolescents' responses along five dimensions: whether they were aware of risks; whether they were aware of likely future consequences; whether parents, peers, or outside specialists were recommended as consultants; whether attitudes were revised in light of new information; and whether the adolescent recognized and cautioned against the vested interests of people giving advice. The adolescents were grouped by grade level, with seventh- and eighth-graders forming one group, tenth-graders a second group, and twelfth-graders a third group. The results of the study are shown in Figure 9.2.

The age groups differed along four of the five dimensions studied, with older adolescents demonstrating more sophisticated decision-making abilities. The older adolescents were more likely to be aware of risks, more likely to consider future consequences, more likely to turn to an independent specialist as a consultant, and more likely to realize when vested interests existed and to raise cautions about accepting advice from people who might be biased.

Decision-making abilities improve over the course of the adolescent years, with gains continuing well into the later years of high school. These developments provide the cognitive tools for behavioral autonomy: being able to look ahead and assess risks and likely outcomes of alternative choices, being able to recognize the value of turning to an independent "expert," and being able to see that someone's advice may be tainted by his or her own interests.

The recognition that individuals' decision-making skills improve over the course of adolescence has prompted numerous debates about young people's abilities to make decisions concerning their own health care, such as whether they may seek the care of physicians for contraceptive services, counseling, or medical treatment without their parents' consent or knowledge. Although experts agree that adolescents' decision-making tools improve with age, there is little consensus about whether the improvement is sufficient to permit adolescents to seek such services and, if so, at what specific age such independence should be permitted. As a consequence, laws governing adolescents' independent health care behavior are often inconsistent and highly variable from state to state (Gittler, Quigley-Rick, and Saks, 1990).

RECAP

One of the main ways in which the development of behavioral autonomy during adolescence is evident is in the growth of decision-making abilities. As individuals mature, they become better able to seek out and weigh the advice of individuals with different degrees of expertise and to use this information in making independent decisions. One controversy

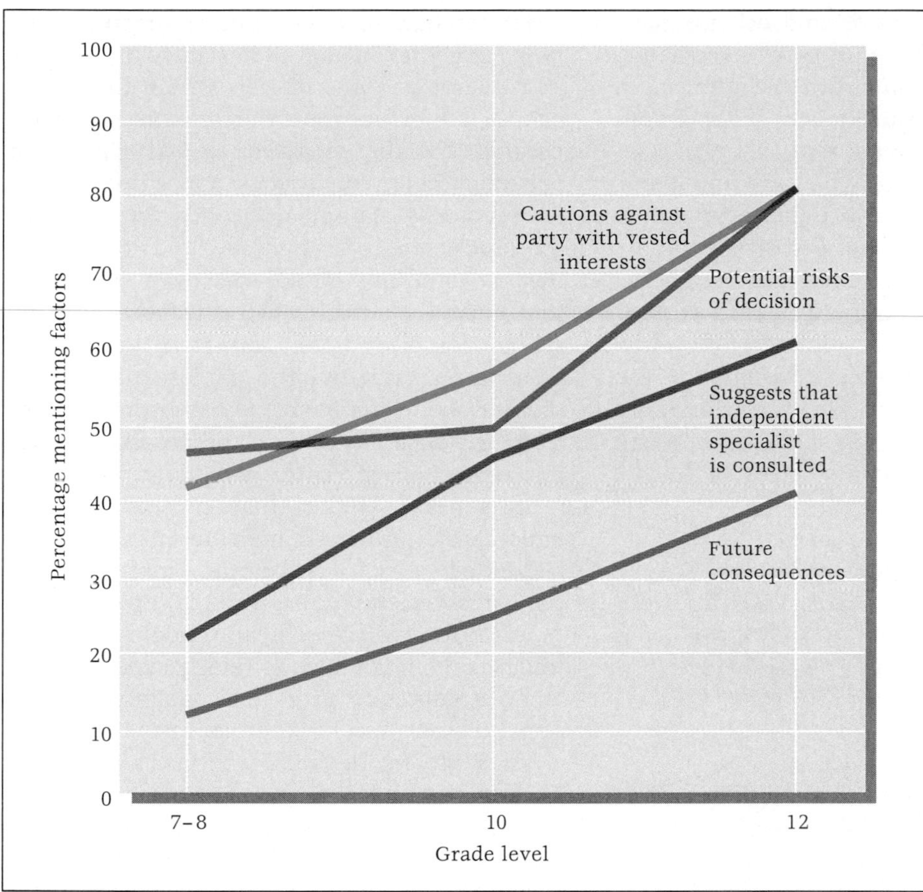

FIGURE 9.2 *Decision-making abilities improve during adolescence.* (Derived from Lewis, 1981b)

that has been debated is whether adolescents' decision-making abilities are mature enough to permit them to make independent decisions about their own health care.

Changes in Conformity and Susceptibility to Influence

As the adolescent comes to spend more time outside the family, the opinions and advice of others—not only peers but adults as well—become more important. At a certain point, for example, adolescents seek the advice of friends, rather than of their parents, concerning how to dress. They may turn to a teacher or guidance counselor for advice about what courses to take in school, instead of bringing such questions home. Understandably, a variety of situations arise in which adolescents may feel that their parents' advice may be less valid than the opinions of others.

And there are issues that might be talked over with more than one party. For example, a teenage girl who is trying to decide whether to take a part-time job after school might discuss the pros and cons with her parents, but she might also turn to friends and ask for their advice. When friends and parents disagree, adolescents must reconcile the differences of opinion and reach their own, independent conclusions.

In situations in which parents and peers give conflicting advice, do teenagers tend to follow one group more often than the other? Adolescents are often portrayed as being extremely susceptible to the influence of **peer pressure**—more so than children or young adults—and as stubbornly resistant to the influence of their parents. But is peer pressure really more potent during adolescence than during other times in the life cycle?

Adolescents are more likely to conform to their peers' opinion when it comes to short-term, day-to-day, and social matters such as styles of dress. But when it comes to long-term questions or issues concerning basic values, parents remain more influential than peers. (Shirley Zeiberg)

Researchers have studied conformity and peer pressure during adolescence by putting adolescents in situations in which they must choose either between the pressures of their parents and the pressures of their peers or between their own wishes and those of others—typically, parents or friends. For example, an adolescent boy might be told to imagine that he and his friends discover something that looks suspicious on the way home from school. His friends tell him that they should keep it a secret. But the adolescent tells his mother about it, and she advises him to report it to the police. He then would be asked by the researcher to say what he would do.

In general, studies that contrast parents' and peers' influences indicate that, in some situations, peers' opinions are more influential; in other situations, parents' opinions are more influential. Specifically, adolescents are more likely to conform to their peers' opinions when it comes to short-term, day-to-day, and social matters—styles of dress, tastes in music, choices among leisure activities, and so on. This is particularly true during junior high school and the early years of high school. When it comes to long-term questions concerning educational or occupational plans, however, or to questions of values, religious beliefs, or ethics, teenagers are primarily influenced by their parents (Brittain, 1963; Young and Ferguson, 1979). Some studies also have looked at adolescents' willingness to seek advice from adults outside their family. These studies indicate that in situations calling for objective information (such as facts about getting admitted to a particular college) rather than opinion (such as whether the college is supposed to be a friendly place), teenagers are likely to turn to outside experts such as their teachers (Young and Ferguson, 1979).

Similar findings emerge from studies of the consultants adolescents turn to when they have problems (Wintre, Hicks, McVee, and Fox, 1988). In general, when the adolescent's problem centers on a relationship with a friend, he or she chooses to turn to a peer, and this preference becomes stronger with age. But adolescents' willingness to turn to an adult for advice with problems—especially problems that involve adolescents and their parents—remains very strong and increases as individuals move toward late adolescence. This suggests that older adolescents are quite willing to turn to adult experts whose advice they consider valuable.

Considered together, these findings are consistent with some of the findings we looked at earlier regarding changes in adolescents' decision-making abilities. With age, adolescents become increasingly likely to turn to "experts" for advice. On social matters, the "experts" are friends; on issues requiring specific objective information, teachers and other adults likely to have the necessary knowledge are the authorities; and on questions of values, ethics, and plans, parents remain the advisers of choice. More important, the results of these studies indicate that peer pressure—or, for that matter, parental pressure—is likely to be ineffective in some situations and powerful in others.

Studies that contrast the influence of peers and adults do not really get to the heart of peer pressure, however, because most peer pressure operates when adults are absent from the scene—when adolescents are at a party, on the way home from school, or on a date. In order to get closer to this issue, researchers have studied how adolescents respond when placed between the pressure of their friends and their own opinions of what to do. For example, an adolescent boy might be asked whether he would go along with his friends' pressure to vandalize some property even though he did not want to do so (Berndt, 1979).

In general, most studies using this approach show that conformity to peers is higher during early and middle adolescence than during preadolescence or later adolescence (Berndt, 1979; Brown, 1990; Krosnick and Judd, 1982; Steinberg and Silverberg, 1986). This is especially true when the behavior in question is antisocial—such as cheating, stealing, or trespassing—and it is especially true for boys. These findings are in line with studies of delinquent acts, which are often committed by boys in groups and is more common during middle adolescence (Berndt, 1979). Several studies indicate that, compared with their more autonomous friends, adolescents who are more susceptible to peer pressure to engage in delinquent activity actually are more likely to misbehave (Brown, Clasen, and Eicher, 1986).

Although we know that conformity to peer pressure is greater during early adolescence than before or after, it is not exactly clear just why this is so. One interpretation is that adolescents are more susceptible to peer influence during this time because of their heightened orientation toward the peer group. Because they care more about what their friends think of them, they are more likely to go along with the crowd to avoid being rejected (Brown et al., 1986). It is possible that this heightened conformity to peer pressure during early adolescence is a sign of a sort of emotional "way station" between becoming emotionally autonomous from parents and becoming a genuinely autonomous person (Steinberg and Silverberg, 1986). In other words, the adolescent may become emotionally autonomous from parents before he or she is emotionally ready for this degree of independence and may turn to peers to fill this void. Each of these accounts suggests that susceptibility to peer pressure increases as youngsters move into early adolescence, peaks at around age 14, and declines thereafter (Brown et al., 1986; Steinberg and Silverberg, 1986).

A different version of the same story focuses on the strength of peer pressure. It

Conformity to peers—especially in situations involving antisocial or delinquent behavior—is higher during early and middle adolescence than during other points in the lifespan. According to some theorists, some forms of delinquency may result from youngsters' heightened susceptibility to the influence of their friends. (Joel Gordon)

may be, for instance, that individuals' *susceptibility* to peer pressure remains constant over adolescence but that the peer pressure itself *strengthens* and then weakens over the period. Early adolescent peer groups may exert more pressure on their members to conform than do groups of younger or older individuals, and the pressure may be strong enough to make even the most autonomous teenagers comply. Although this is an attractive alternative explanation—particularly to adolescents who appeal to their parents by saying, "No one will talk to me if I don't do it!"—studies have not borne it out. In fact, it appears that peer pressure to misbehave increases steadily throughout adolescence, beyond the age at which it would be expected to diminish (Brown et al., 1986).

Thus, when we put together the research about peer pressure, peer conformity, and parental conformity, the following picture emerges. During childhood, boys and girls are highly oriented toward their parents and far less oriented toward their peers; peer pressure is not especially strong. As they approach adolescence, children become somewhat less oriented toward their parents and more oriented toward their peers, and peer pressure begins to escalate. As a result, during preadolescence, there is little net gain in behavioral autonomy—overall levels of conformity do not change, but the source of influence shifts. During early adolescence, conformity to parents continues to decline, and both conformity to peers and peer pressure continue to rise—again, there is little change in overall behavioral autonomy. It is not until middle and late adolescence, therefore, that genuine increases in behavioral autonomy occur, for it is during this time period (between the ninth and twelfth grades) that conformity both to parents and to peers declines even though peer pressure continues to increase (see Figure 9.3).

FIGURE 9.3 *During adolescence, susceptibility to peer pressure increases and then falls, while susceptibility to parental pressure decreases. Perceptions of the strength of peer pressure increase throughout the period.*

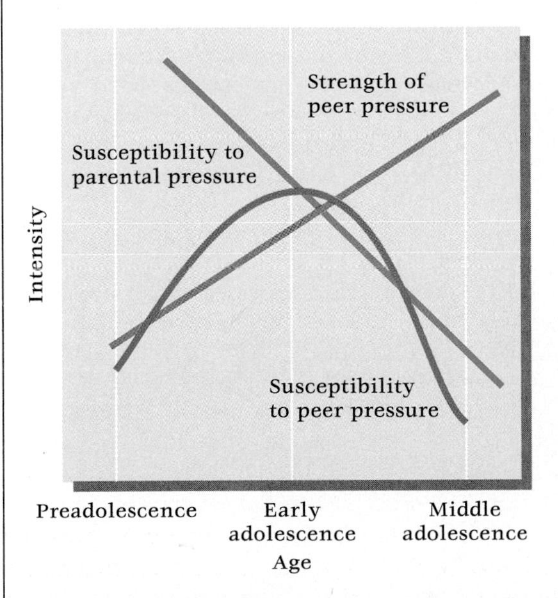

Within a group of teenagers of the same age, of course, there are some who are highly autonomous, others who are easily influenced by their peers, others who are oriented toward their parents, and still others who are swayed by both peers and parents, depending on the situation. In general, autonomous youngsters and adult-oriented youngsters are likely to have come from homes in which their parents were warm and moderately controlling—the typical authoritative household. Peer-oriented children are likely to have parents who were less nurturant and either extremely controlling or extremely permissive. Like emotional autonomy, then, behavioral autonomy appears to be associated with authoritative, rather than with permissive, autocratic, or neglectful, parenting (Devereux, 1970) (see accompanying box).

Although it is tempting to conclude from these studies that authoritative parenting fosters the development of autonomy, we must be careful about drawing this conclusion, since the direction of effects could work just as plausibly the other way around. Perhaps responsible, independent children elicit warm and democratic behavior from their parents, whereas less autonomous youngsters invoke harsher discipline or parental nonchalance. In all likelihood, both processes are at work—children are affected by their parents, and parents are affected by their children. Authoritative parenting probably leads to adolescent autonomy, which in turn leads to more authoritative parenting.

Interestingly, the development of behavioral autonomy varies across cultures because of differences in the age expectations that adolescents and parents have for independent behavior. Psychologist Shirley Feldman and her colleagues have examined this issue by asking parents and adolescents from both Asian and Anglo cultural groups to fill out a "teen timetable"—a questionnaire that asks at what age one would expect an adolescent to

THE SCIENTIFIC STUDY OF ADOLESCENCE

PARENT-CHILD RELATIONS AND ADOLESCENTS' PEER ORIENTATION

Until fairly recently, social scientists who were interested in adolescent development studied young people in one setting at a time. Researchers looked at family relations *or* at peer relations, at school *or* at work, and at home *or* in the community. Increasingly, however, researchers have begun to acknowledge the linkages among the different contexts of adolescence, and they are beginning to ask questions about the nature of these connections. Instead of asking how adolescents are affected in the home environment, for example, studies might ask how events in the home environment affect events in the peer group.

This change in orientation reflects, in part, the increased importance of a perspective called the **ecology of human development.** From this perspective, one focuses not only on the developing individual but also on the interrelations between the individual and his or her contexts and on the interconnections among the contexts themselves. The most important proponent of this view has been psychologist Urie Bronfenbrenner (1979, 1989).

According to Bronfenbrenner, the ecology of adolescent development can be thought of as having four distinct levels: each of the immediate settings in which adolescents live (e.g., the family, the school), which he calls **micro-systems;** the system of relations *between* these immediate settings (e.g., the family–peer group link, the home-school link), which he calls the **meso-system;** the settings that do not contain the adolescent but that affect him or her indirectly (e.g., the parent's workplace), which he calls the **exo-system;** and the broader context of culture and historical time (e.g., the country and era in which an adolescent lives), which he calls the **macro-system.** Most research on adolescent development has focused on either the micro-system or the macro-system, and far less attention has been paid to the meso-system and to the exo-system.

A nice illustration of a study of adolescent development at the level of the meso-system is found in the literature on adolescent peer orientation. Psychologists Andrew Fuligni and Jacquelynne Eccles (1993) were interested in studying whether the ways in which adolescents are treated by their parents affect the ways in which they behave with their friends—a meso-system question, in Bronfenbrenner's model, because it focuses on the link between two settings (the home and the peer group). The researchers hypothesized that authoritatively reared adolescents should be less peer oriented than other young people, because adolescents in authoritative homes have more opportunities to practice independent decision making. This practice, the researchers reasoned, should translate into greater independence outside the home environment.

Fuligni and Eccles administered a series of questionnaires to young adolescents over a one-year period. The questionnaires measured such family variables as parental strictness and decision-making opportunity and such peer-group variables as peer advice-seeking and peer orientation. The researchers found that adolescents who were the most strongly peer oriented—both in terms of healthy advice-seeking and in terms of less healthy, excessive peer orientation—were more likely to come from families in which they were granted few opportunities for decision making and in which parents were especially strict (Fuligni and Eccles, 1993). Moreover, the adolescents whose parents became even more authoritarian (i.e., stricter and less likely to permit the adolescent to make decisions) over the one-year period were the most peer oriented of all (see figure).

Although many parents clamp down on their teenagers' independence out of fear that not doing so will allow them to fall under the "evil" influence of the peer group, this strategy often backfires. Evidently, having one's parents limit one's autonomy at just the time when more independence is desired and expected makes adolescents turn away from the family and toward their friends.

SOURCE: Fuligni, A., and Eccles, J. (1993). Perceived parent-child relationships and early adolescents' orientation toward peers. *Developmental Psychology, 29,* 622–632.

Effects of changes in parental strictness and family decision making on adolescents' orientation toward their peers. (Fuligni and Eccles, 1993)

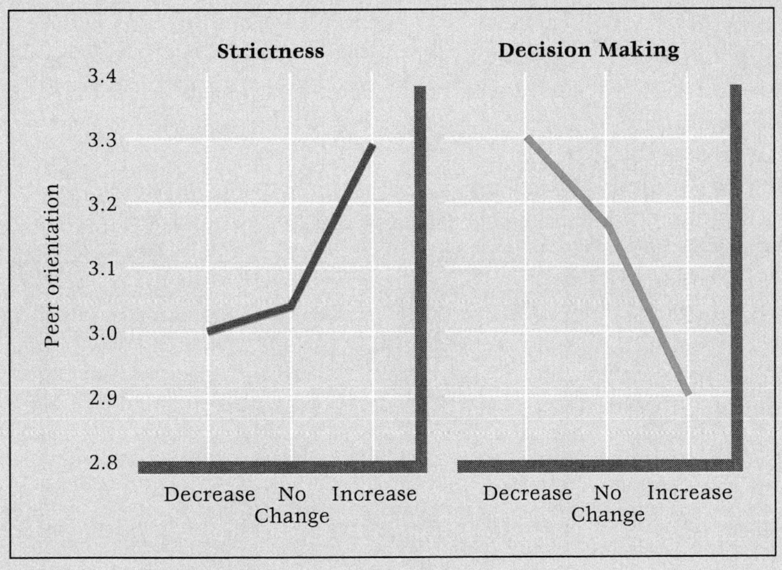

be permitted to engage in various behaviors that signal autonomy (e.g., "spend money however you want," "go out on dates," "go to rock concerts with friends"). In general, she has found that Anglo adolescents and their parents living in America, Australia, or Hong Kong have earlier expectations for adolescent autonomy than do Asian adolescents and parents from these same countries (Feldman and Quatman, 1988; Rosenthal and Feldman, 1991). Because of this, adolescents from Asian families may be less likely to seek autonomy from their parents than are their Anglo counterparts.

Surprisingly, in these studies there were neither sex nor birth-order differences in age expectations for autonomy—contrary to the popular beliefs that boys expect more autonomy than girls and that later-born adolescents are granted earlier freedom because their older siblings have paved the way. Interestingly, the autonomy-granting timetable of families who have emigrated from a culture that is relatively slower to grant adolescents autonomy to a culture where autonomy is granted sooner falls somewhere between the two extremes; this has been found in studies both of Chinese immigrants in America and Australia (Rosenthal and Feldman, 1990) and of East German immigrants in the former West Germany (Silbereisen and Schmitt-Rodermund, in press). It is also the case that adolescents who "feel" older seek more independence than their same-aged peers who "feel" younger (Galambos, Kolaric, and Maggs, 1994).

Changes in Feelings of Self-Reliance

A third approach to the study of behavioral autonomy focuses on adolescents' own judgments of how autonomous they are. When adolescents of different ages are asked to complete standardized tests of **self-reliance,** for example, the results show that subjective feelings of autonomy increase steadily over the adolescent years and, contrary to stereotypes, that adolescent girls report feeling more self-reliant than adolescent boys do (Greenberger, 1982; Steinberg and Silverberg, 1986). This is especially interesting in light of the findings concerning susceptibility to peer pressure, discussed earlier, since it indicates that adolescents may describe themselves as gaining in self-reliance during a period when their susceptibility to peer pressure may be increasing (see Figure 9.4). Although adults may view adolescents' giving in to peer pressure as a sign of diminished autonomy, adolescents may not see their own behavior in this light.

RECAP

Although adolescence is, in general, a time of advances in decision-making abilities, there is

FIGURE 9.4 *Age differences in three types of autonomy.* (Steinberg and Silverberg, 1986)

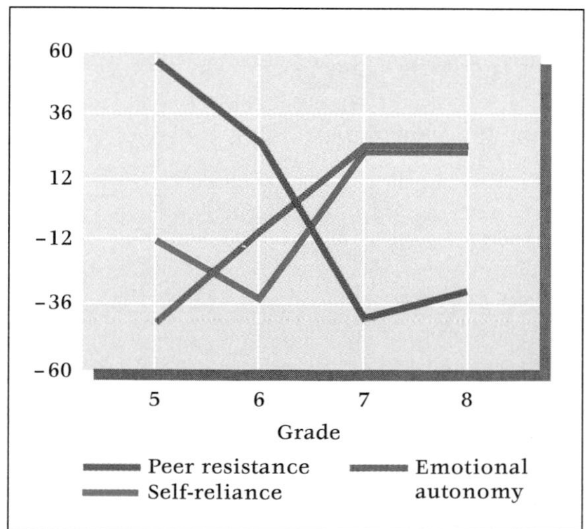

a temporary period, during early adolescence, when individuals are particularly susceptible to peer pressure, especially on issues concerning day-to-day activities. Susceptibility to peer pressure increases between childhood and early adolescence, and then it decreases over the high school years. Generally speaking, adolescents whose parents are extremely authoritarian or extremely permissive are the most easily influenced by their friends.

THE DEVELOPMENT OF VALUE AUTONOMY

The development of value autonomy entails changes in the adolescent's conceptions of moral, political, ideological, and religious issues. Three aspects of the development of value autonomy during adolescence are especially interesting. First, adolescents become increasingly abstract in the way they think about these sorts of issues. Take the example of an 18-year-old man who is deciding whether to participate in a disruptive demonstration at his state capital against policies that he believes indirectly support racial discrimination. Instead of looking at the situation only in terms of the specifics of discrimination, he might think about the implications of knowingly violating the law in general. Second, during adolescence, beliefs become increasingly rooted in general principles that have some ideological basis. So an 18-year-old might say that demonstrating against discrimination is acceptable because promoting racial equality is more important than living in accord with the law, and so breaking a law is legitimate when the status quo maintains inequality. Finally, beliefs become increasingly founded in the young person's own values and not merely in a system of values passed on by parents or other authority figures. Thus an 18-year-old may look at the issue of discrimination in terms of what he himself believes, rather than in terms of what his parents have told him to do.

Much of the growth in value autonomy can be traced to the cognitive changes characteristic of the period. With the adolescent's enhanced reasoning capabilities and the further development of hypothetical thinking comes a heightened interest in ideological and philosophical matters and a more sophisticated way of looking at them. The ability to consider alternative possibilities and to engage in thinking about thinking allows for the exploration of differing value systems, political ideologies, personal ethics, and religious beliefs.

But the growth of value autonomy is encouraged by the development of emotional and behavioral independence as well. As we shall see in a moment, there is some evidence that the development of value autonomy occurs later (between ages 18 and 20) than does the development of emotional or behavioral autonomy, which takes place during early and middle adolescence. As young people gain increasing distance from the emotional dependencies of childhood, they rely less on their parents' beliefs and values. The establishment of emotional autonomy provides adolescents with the ability to look at their parents' views more objectively. When young people no longer see their parents as omnipotent and infallible authorities, they may seriously reevaluate the ideas and values that they accepted without question as children. Not surprisingly, individuals with a stronger sense of value autonomy show more maturity in other psychological domains as well, such as in the realm of ego development (Hart and Chmeil, 1992).

And as adolescents begin to test the waters of independence behaviorally, they may experience a variety of cognitive conflicts caused by having to compare the advice of parents and friends and having to deal with competing pressures to behave in given ways. These conflicts may prompt the young person to consider, in more serious and thoughtful terms, what it is that he or she really believes. This struggle to clarify values, provoked in part by the exercise of behavioral autonomy, is a large part of the process of developing a sense of value autonomy.

Moral Development during Adolescence

Moral development has been the most widely studied aspect of value autonomy during adolescence. The dominant theoretical viewpoint for some time now has been a perspective that is grounded in Piaget's theory of cognitive development. As you will recall from the discussion in Chapter 2 of changes in thinking processes during adolescence, the emphasis within the Piagetian view, or *cognitive-developmental* perspective, is on changes in the structure and organization of thought rather than on changes in its content. Theories of morality that stem from the cognitive-developmental viewpoint similarly emphasize shifts in the type of reasoning that individuals use in making moral decisions, rather than changes in the content of the decisions they reach or the actions they take as a result. Although the initial formulation of the cognitive-developmental perspective on morality was presented by Piaget himself, the theory was subsequently expanded by Lawrence Kohlberg, and it is Kohlberg's work that is more relevant to the study of value autonomy during adolescence.

Moral Reasoning. Consider the following dilemma:

> In Europe, a woman was near death from a very bad disease, a special kind of cancer. There was one drug that the doctors thought might save her. It was a form of radium that a druggist in the same town had recently discovered. The drug was expensive to make, but the druggist was charging ten times what the drug cost him to make. He paid $200 for the radium and charged $2,000 for a small dose of the drug. The sick woman's husband, Heinz, went to everyone he knew to borrow the money, but he could only get together about $1,000, which was half of what it cost. He told the druggist that his wife was dying, and asked him to sell it cheaper or let him pay later. But the druggist said, "No, I discovered the drug and I'm going to make money from it." Heinz got desperate and broke into the man's store to steal the drug for his wife.
>
> Should the husband have done that? Was it right or wrong? (Kohlberg and Gilligan, 1972)

According to Kohlberg, whether or not you think that Heinz should have stolen the drug is less important than the reasoning behind your answer. Kohlberg suggested that there are three levels of moral reasoning: **preconventional moral reasoning,** which is dominant during most of childhood; **conventional moral reasoning,** which is usually dominant during late childhood and early adolescence; and **postconventional moral reasoning** (sometimes called *principled moral reasoning*), which emerges sometime during the adolescent or young adult years.

Researchers assess individuals' levels of moral thinking by examining their responses to a series of moral dilemmas, such as the story about Heinz and the drug. These dilemmas are presented either in an interview, in which case the adolescents' responses are recorded, transcribed, and coded (Kohlberg and Gilligan, 1972); or in a questionnaire, in which adolescents respond to the dilemmas in a sort of multiple-choice format (Rest, Davison, and Robbins, 1978). The responses of individuals are classified as falling into one of the three levels described above.

Preconventional thinking is characterized by reference to external and physical events.

The ways in which individuals think about moral dilemmas change during adolescence. (Tom McCarthy/Unicorn Stock Photos)

Preconventional moral decisions are not based on society's standards, rules, or conventions (hence the label *pre*conventional). Children at this stage approach moral dilemmas in ways that focus on the rewards and punishments associated with different courses of action. One preconventional child might say that Heinz should not have stolen the drug because he could have gotten caught and sent to jail. Another might say that Heinz was right to steal the drug because people would have been angry with him if he had let his wife die.

Conventional thinking about moral issues focuses not so much on tangible rewards and punishments but on how an individual will be judged by others for behaving in a certain way. In conventional moral reasoning, special importance is given to the roles people are expected to play and to society's rules, social institutions, and conventions. One behaves properly because, in so doing, one receives the approval of others and helps to maintain the social order. The correctness of society's rules is not questioned, however—one "does one's duty" by upholding and respecting the social order. A conventional thinker might say that Heinz should not have stolen the drug because stealing is against the law. But another might counter that Heinz was right to steal the drug because it is what a good husband is expected to do. According to most studies of moral reasoning, the majority of adolescents and adults think primarily in conventional terms.

Postconventional reasoning is relatively rare. At this level of reasoning, society's rules and conventions are seen as relative and subjective rather than as authoritative. One may have a moral duty to abide by society's standards for behavior—but only insofar as those standards support and serve human ends. Thus occasions arise in which conventions ought to be questioned and when more important principles—such as justice, fairness, or the sanctity of human life—take precedence over established social norms. For instance, a postconventional response might be that Heinz should not have stolen the drug because in doing so he violated an implicit agreement among members of society—an agreement that gives each person the freedom to pursue his or her livelihood. However, another principled thinker might respond that Heinz was right to steal the drug because someone's life was at stake and because preserving human life is more important than preserving individual freedoms. Whereas conventional thinking is oriented toward society's rules, postconventional thinking is founded on more broadly based moral principles and is oriented toward the individual's personal conscience. For this reason, it is the development of postconventional reasoning that is especially relevant to the discussion of value autonomy.

Kohlberg's theory and its derivatives (for example, Gilligan, 1982) have generated a wealth of research and have for the past thirty years dominated the study of moral development during adolescence. An important alternative to Kohlberg's model was proposed in the late 1970s by psychologist Carol Gilligan (1982), who argued that Kohlberg's view of morality placed too much emphasis on a type of moral orientation characteristically employed by men. Gilligan's perspective is discussed in the box on pages 354–355.

Studies have confirmed Kohlberg's suggestion that moral reasoning becomes more principled over the course of childhood and adolescence (Hoffman, 1980). Moreover, development appears to proceed through the sequence described in Kohlberg's theory (Colby, Kohlberg, Gibbs, and Lieberman, 1983). Preconventional reasoning dominates the responses of children; conventional responses begin to appear during preadolescence, and they continue into middle adolescence; and postconventional reasoning does not appear until late adolescence.

Advanced levels of moral reasoning are more common among children raised in authoritative families in which parents encourage their child to participate in family discussions, in which the level of conflict in family discussions is neither extremely low nor extremely high, and in which parents expose the adolescent to moral arguments that are fashioned at a higher stage than his or her own (Boyes and Allen, 1993; Haan, Smith, and Block, 1968; Holstein, 1972; Walker and Taylor, 1991b). As in other cognitive-developmental theories, such as Piaget's (see Chapter 2), according to Kohlberg's theory, development to higher stages of moral reasoning occurs when the adolescent is developmentally "ready"—when his or her reasoning is predominantly at one stage but partially at the next higher one—and when he or she is exposed to the more advanced type of reasoning by other people, such as parents (Walker and Taylor, 1991a).

Kohlberg's idea that individuals become more principled in their thinking during adolescence is especially relevant to our discussion of value autonomy. Although individuals may not enter a stage of postconventional thinking during adolescence, they do begin to place greater emphasis on abstract values and moral principles during the adolescent years. Studies by James Rest and his colleagues (Rest et al., 1978) have shown this to be true. Their studies indicate that the appeal of postconventional moral reasoning increases over the course of adolescence, while the appeals of preconventional and of conventional reasoning both decline. During the high school years, the proportion of postconventional responses given by individuals increases from about 25 percent to about 33 percent. Over the course of late adolescence and early adulthood, the proportion increases further, to about 45 percent. (The appeal of postconventional thinking appears to increase both with age and with schooling; most adults reach a plateau after completing their formal education.) Thus Rest's studies provide support for the idea that value autonomy grows during adolescence, particularly during the late adolescent years.

● ***Moral Reasoning and Moral Behavior.*** It is one thing to reason about moral problems in an advanced way, but it is another thing to *behave* consistently with one's reasoning. Some critics have argued that although Kohlberg's theory may provide a window on how people think about abstract and hypothetical dilemmas of life and death, it does not tell us very much about the ways people reason about day-to-day problems or the ways people behave when they find themselves in situations that might evoke moral considerations. As it turns out, research on Kohlberg's theory has answered these criticisms fairly well. As for the first of these concerns, for example, research indicates that people reason about life-and-death dilemmas in ways parallel to their reasoning about moral dilemmas that they actually encounter in their everyday life (Walker, de Vries, and Trevethan, 1987). And as for the second of these concerns, many studies indicate that individuals' behavior *is* related to the way in which they reason about hypothetical moral dilemmas. For example, individuals who are capable of reasoning at higher stages of moral thought are less likely to commit antisocial acts, less likely to cheat, less likely to conform to the pressures of others, more likely to engage in political protests, and more likely to assist others in need of help (Rest, 1983).

Of course, moral behavior and moral reasoning do not *always* go hand in hand. Most of us have found ourselves in situations where we have behaved "less morally" than we would have liked to act. According to one writer, however, we would not expect that moral behavior would follow exactly from moral reasoning, because other factors enter into moral decision making that complicate matters (Rest, 1983). In tests measuring moral reasoning, assessments are made in a social vacuum, but such vacuums rarely exist in the real world. For example, you may realize in the abstract that complying with highway speed limits is important because such limits prevent accidents, and you may obey these limits most of the time when you drive. But you may have found yourself in a situation in which you weighed your need to get somewhere in a hurry (perhaps you were late for an important job interview) against your moral belief in the importance of obeying speeding laws, and you decided that in this instance you would behave in a way inconsistent with your belief. Situational factors influence moral choices, and they also influence moral reasoning. When individuals perceive that they will be severely hurt by behaving in a morally advanced way (for example, if standing up for someone will lead to severe punishment), they are less likely to reason at a higher moral level (Sobesky, 1983). Moral reasoning is an important influence on moral behavior, but it cannot be considered out of context.

RECAP

Most of the research to date on the development of value autonomy has focused on moral development in particular. According to Lawrence Kohlberg's theory, which is the dominant perspective on the development of moral reasoning, adolescence is a time of potential shifting from a morality that defines right and wrong in terms of society's rules to one that defines right and wrong on the basis on one's

DO A MAN AND A WOMAN SPEAK ABOUT MORAL PROBLEMS "IN A DIFFERENT VOICE"?

Few theories have generated as much controversy among psychologists as Lawrence Kohlberg's theory of the development of moral reasoning. In particular, critics have argued that his view of what constitutes "more advanced" moral reasoning is oriented to how men typically view moral problems and that it underrepresents an equally valid approach to morality which women happen to use more often. The most compelling argument in this spirit was made by psychologist Carol Gilligan in her widely cited book *In a Different Voice* (1982).

Essentially, Gilligan argues that Kohlberg's scheme places great weight on what she calls a **justice orientation.** This is an orientation toward problems of inequality or oppression that holds out as its ideal a morality of reciprocity and equal respect. From this perspective—or "voice," as Gilligan would call it—the most important consideration in making a moral decision is whether the individuals involved are treated "fairly" by the ultimate decision.

An equally valid alternative to the justice orientation, says Gilligan, is a **care orientation.** From this perspective, the focus is on problems of abandonment and detachment, and the ideal is a morality of attention to others and responsiveness to human need. As opposed to the justice orientation, which is rooted in the premise that moral decisions are best made from a detached position of "objectivity" ("rules are rules," "fair is fair"), the caring orientation is rooted in the belief that our moral decisions should be shaped by our attachments and our responsiveness to others.

An example may help to clarify the distinction. In responding to the Heinz dilemma, discussed on page 350, individuals with a justice orientation cast the problem as a conflict between Heinz's desire to save his wife and the druggist's right to engage in his business—a conflict between the abstract values of life and property. Individuals with a caring orientation, in contrast, see the dilemma in entirely different terms: as a dilemma of responsiveness. The question is not whether the druggist has a right to property that outweighs other rights but rather why the druggist is not being responsive to the needs of another person. Rather than seeing society as functioning with a system of rules or abstract principles, individuals with a caring orientation view society as functioning through the interconnection of human relationships.

Theories of morality and of human development in general, argues Gilligan, have emphasized the sort of intellectual, individualistic, and detached reasoning characteristic of the justice orientation as the index of mental health and have given short shrift to emotional, interpersonal, and attachment concerns. Gilligan criticizes most theories of psychological adjustment for holding up as the pinnacle of psychological health the individual who can function independently, rather than the person who can function *inter*dependently. We see this not only in abstract theories of development but also in the way in which children are socialized to emphasize competition over cooperation, and assertiveness over concern for others. In Kohlberg's theory, this bias toward detached individualism is reflected in the elevation to the highest level of morality of a view that places abstract principles of individual rights over all other considerations. In her book, Gilligan presented evidence that women are likely to approach moral problems from a caring orientation, rather than from the justice orientation idealized in Kohlberg's theory.

In more recent studies, Gilligan and others have found that *both* men and women are capable of approaching moral problems from the perspectives of justice and caring but that women may be more likely to give caring-oriented responses before justice-oriented ones, whereas men are more likely to follow the opposite pattern (Ford and Lowery, 1986; Galotti, 1989; Galotti, Kozberg, and Farmer, 1991; Gilligan, 1986; Walker et al., 1987). When individuals are prompted to hear a moral problem in a different voice, they appear to be able to do so—regardless of their gender. In other words, men are capable of viewing a moral problem from a caring orientation, and women are capable of viewing a problem from a justice orientation. (Recall the competence-performance distinction discussed in Chapter 2.)

Although men and women are more similar than different in the types of responses they give to moral dilemmas, at least one study indicates that the *process* of moral development may differ between the sexes (Boldizar, Wison, and Deemer, 1989). In a longitudinal study that followed individuals from high school into young adulthood, these researchers found that both men's and women's moral development was correlated with the amount of education they had completed but that the relation between moral development and both work and marriage differed for males and females. The moral development of males, but not females, was associated with their feelings of career fulfillment; men who were more satisfied in their careers scored higher on the test of moral reasoning. In contrast, moral development among females, but not males, was associated with marriage; young adult married women scored lower on the test of moral reasoning than did their single counterparts. Of course, we must be careful not to infer a causal connection between moral reasoning and work or marriage: It could simply be the case that more advanced moral thinkers were able to find satisfying careers (in the case of men) or chose to delay marriage (in the case of women). But this study suggests that even though men and women may reach similar moral endpoints, they may follow different routes in getting there.

Gilligan's work suggests that there are two distinct voices to be heard in moral debates and that society—especially a society governed primarily by men—may be more inclined to listen to one voice than another. The fact that most of the major theories of human development have been constructed by men—Freud, Piaget, Erikson—also has biased our views of what mental health is. But while Gilligan's studies suggest that there may be gender differences in our tendencies to prefer one or the other orientation, her work also indicates that both men and women can adopt either perspective. By helping children to hear and speak with both voices, we may encourage the development of more complete—and more moral—people.

own basic moral principles. This shift does not tend to occur until late in adolescence, however, suggesting that the development of value autonomy occurs later than the development of either emotional or behavioral autonomy. One important critic of Kohlberg's theory has been Carol Gilligan, who has argued that Kohlberg's theory, like most developmental theories, overemphasizes traditional conceptions of morality (which emphasize justice) and underemphasizes conceptions that are more likely to be espoused by females (which emphasize care).

Political Thinking during Adolescence

Less is known about the development of political thinking during adolescence than about moral development, but research on this topic is generally consistent with the view that beliefs become more principled, more abstract, more informed, and more independent during the adolescent years. This pattern is linked in part to the general cognitive development of the adolescent and in part to the growth of specific expertise as the adolescent is exposed to more political information and ideas (Torney-Purta, 1992).

Between the sixth and twelfth grades, political thinking becomes more conceptual and more principled and less simplistic and less pragmatic (Torney-Purta, 1990). A researcher who has studied the development of political ideology during adolescence extensively is Joseph Adelson (1972). He suggests that political thinking changes during adolescence in several important ways. First, it becomes more abstract. In response to the question "What is the purpose of laws?" for example, 12- and 13-year-olds are likely to reply with concrete answers—"So people don't kill or steal," "So people don't get hurt," and so on. Older adolescents, in contrast, are likely to respond with more abstract and more general statements—"To ensure safety and enforce the government" and "They are basically guidelines for people. I mean, like this is wrong and this is right and to help them understand" (Adelson, 1972, p. 108).

Second, political thinking during adolescence becomes increasingly less authoritarian and less rigid. Young adolescents are inclined toward obedience, toward authority, and toward an uncritical, trusting, and acquiescent stance toward government. For example, when asked what might be done in response to a law that is not working out as planned, the young

Whereas younger adolescents believe in autocratic rule and support existing laws, older adolescents are more likely to challenge authority and argue that laws should be reexamined. These Massachusetts students are protesting against an initiative that would lower property taxes and cut school budgets. (Sandra Johnson/Picture Cube)

adolescent will "propose that it be enforced more rigorously." An older teenager may suggest, instead, that the law needs reexamination and perhaps amendment. In contrast to older adolescents, younger adolescents are "more likely to favor one-man rule as [opposed to] representative democracy; . . . [show] little sensitivity to individual or minority rights; [and are] indifferent to the claims of personal freedom" (Adelson, 1972, p. 108).

Of special significance is the development during middle and late adolescence of a roughly coherent and consistent set of attitudes—a sort of ideology—which does not appear before this point. This ideology is, in Adelson's words, "more or less organized in reference to a more encompassing . . . set of political principles" (1972, p. 121).

Shifts in all three of these directions—increasing abstraction, decreasing authoritarianism, and increasing use of principles—are similar to the shifts observed in studies of moral development, and they support the idea that value autonomy begins to emerge during the late adolescent years. The movement away from authoritarianism, obedience, and unquestioning acceptance of the rulings of authority is especially interesting because it suggests, further, that an important psychological concern for adolescents revolves around questioning the values and beliefs emanating from parents and other authority figures and trying to establish one's own priorities.

As is the case with moral development, there may be gaps between adolescents' political thinking in hypothetical situations and their political attitudes and behavior. In general, the most important influences on the political behavior of young people tends to be the social context in which they come of age (Torney-Purta, 1990). This context includes the adolescent's immediate community as well as the larger social and historical environment. Thus, for example, minority adolescents, especially those living in environments in which there are limited economic opportunities, tend to be more cynical about politics than their white counterparts. Similarly, a recent study of German youth indicates that adolescents were more likely to develop right-wing (excessively authoritarian) attitudes when they were raised by authoritarian parents within a broader context that promoted anti-foreigner and antidemocratic attitudes (Noack, Kracke, and Hofer, 1994). Finally, studies of adolescents' political attitudes over historical periods show quite clearly that young people's political attitudes and level of political participation (voting, demonstrating, letter writing, etc.)—like those of adults—fluctuate and change in relation to current events (Torney-Purta, 1990).

Religious Beliefs during Adolescence

Religious beliefs, like political beliefs, also become more abstract and more principled during the adolescent years. Specifically, adolescents' beliefs become more oriented toward spiritual and ideological matters and less oriented toward rituals, practices, and the strict observance of religious customs (Wuthnow and Glock, 1973). For example, although 87 percent of all adolescents pray, and 95 percent believe in God, 60 percent of all young people feel that organized religion does not play a very important role in their lives (Farel, 1982). Compared with children, adolescents place more emphasis on the internal aspects of religious commitment (such as what an individual believes) and less on the external manifestations (such as whether an individual goes to church) (Elkind, 1978).

Generally speaking, the stated importance of religion—and especially of participation in an organized religion—declines somewhat during the adolescent years. More high school students than older adolescents attend church regularly, and, not surprisingly, more of the younger adolescents state that religion is important to them (Benson, Donahue, and Erickson, 1989; Johnston, O'Malley, and Bachman, 1986). Interestingly, several studies have indicated that the decline in the importance of religion during late adolescence appears to be more noteworthy among college than noncollege youth (Yankelovich, 1974), suggesting that college attendance may play some part in shaping (or, as the case may be, in *un*shaping) young people's religious beliefs. As we saw in Chapter 8, studies of identity development during the college years have indicated that, over the course of college, students' traditional religious commitments are shaken but are not replaced with alternative beliefs (Waterman, 1982). Late adolescence appears to be a time when individuals reexamine and reevaluate many of the beliefs and values they have grown up with.

Although some parents may interpret this transformation as indicating a sort of "rebellion" against the family's values, the development of religious thinking during late adolescence might be better understood as part of the overall development of value autonomy. As the adolescent develops a stronger sense of independence, he or she may leave behind the unquestioning conventionality of earlier religious behavior as a first step toward finding a truly personal faith. According to one writer, an adolescent who continues to comply with his or her parents' religious beliefs without ever questioning them may actually be showing signs of immature conformity or identity foreclosure, rather than spiritual maturity (Hill, 1986).

Although individuals generally become less involved in formal religion during the adolescent years, there are differences among adolescents in their degree of religiosity. Approximately 35 percent of high school seniors report weekly attendance at religious services; another 30 percent report that religion is "very important to them," even though they do not worship regularly; and about 10 percent of high school seniors report no religious preference at all. The remaining 25 percent report having a religious preference but do not feel that religion is very important to them (Johnston et al., 1986). Some, but not all, research suggests that religious adolescents are less depressed than other adolescents, significantly less likely than their peers to engage in premarital sexual intercourse, and somewhat less likely to engage in deviant or delinquent behavior, such as drug use (Benson et al., 1989; Donahue, 1994; Wright, Frost, and Wisecarver, 1993). Not only does religious participation affect other aspects of adolescent behavior, however, but certain behaviors themselves also affect religious participation. For example, more frequent sexual activity leads to less frequent church attendance, just as the reverse is true (Thornton and Camburn, 1989).

All in all, studies of the development of religious beliefs during adolescence indicate many parallels with the development of moral and political reasoning. According to a widely cited stage theory of religious development, during late adolescence individuals enter into a stage in which they begin to form a system of personal religious beliefs, rather than relying solely on the teachings of their parents (Fowler, 1981). This is reminiscent, of course, of the adolescent's transition to principled moral reasoning or to the development in middle to late adolescence of a coherent political ideology. In all likelihood, developments in all three domains—moral, political, and religious—probably reflect the underlying growth of cognitive abilities and the shift from concrete to abstract reasoning that characterizes the adolescent transition. As you now understand, this fundamental shift in cognitive ability affects adolescents' thinking across a wide variety of topics.

RECAP

Although far less studied than the development of moral reasoning, changes in the domains of political and religious thinking during adolescence also reflect the individual's growing sense of value autonomy. As with moral reasoning, political and religious thinking become more abstract, more principled, and more independent, especially during late adolescence. Indeed, late adolescence is often a time during which individuals question many of the political and religious teachings they were exposed to during childhood, as they search to find belief systems that reflect their own values, not simply the values of their parents.

A CONCLUDING NOTE

Popular theories of adolescent development in Western societies have tended to emphasize the goals of self-definition (i.e., identity) and independent functioning (i.e., autonomy) (Baumeister and Tice, 1986). It is important to keep in mind, however, that healthy adolescent development involves not only the ability to be a successful individual but also the ability to maintain healthy and satisfying attachments with others. Put another way, experts think of positive psychological development in terms of the adolescent's capacity to function both independently and *inter*dependently (Ford, 1987; Greenberger and Sorensen, 1974).

These dual goals—what some writers have called *agency* and *communion* (e.g., Bakan, 1972)—define the psychosocial agenda during adolescence. In this chapter, about autonomy, and in the previous chapter, about identity, we emphasized the development of agency. In the next two chapters, covering intimacy and sexuality, we will focus on communion.

KEY TERMS

autonomy
behavioral autonomy
care orientation
conventional moral reasoning
detachment
ecology of human development
emotional autonomy
exo-system
individuation
justice orientation
macro-system
meso-system
micro-systems
peer pressure
postconventional moral reasoning
preconventional moral reasoning
self-reliance
value autonomy

FOR FURTHER READING

Fowler, J. (1981). *Stages of faith.* New York: Harper & Row. The dominant theoretical viewpoint in the study of the development of religious thought.

Gilligan, C. (1982). *In a different voice.* Cambridge, Mass.: Harvard University Press. A highly readable presentation of Gilligan's ideas about how the genders differ in their moral orientations.

Gittler, J., Quigley-Rick, M., and Saks, M. (1990). *Adolescent health care decision making: The law and public policy.* Washington, D.C.: Carnegie Council on Adolescent Development. A discussion of many of the issues related to adolescents' abilities and rights to make decisions about their own health care.

Hauser, S., Powers, S., and Noam, G. (1991). *Adolescents and their families.* New York: Free Press. A series of studies of family interaction during adolescence, with an emphasis on the ways in which parents enable or constrain the development of healthy autonomy.

Steinberg, L. (1990). Autonomy, conflict, and harmony in the family relationship. Pp. 255–276 in S. Feldman and G. Elliott (Eds.), *At the threshold: The developing adolescent.* Cambridge, Mass.: Harvard University Press. A review of the literature on the development of autonomy within the family context.

Torney-Purta, J. (1990). Youth in relation to social institutions. Pp. 457–477 in S. Feldman and G. Elliott (Eds.), *At the threshold: The developing adolescent.* A review of research and theory on political socialization in adolescence.

CHAPTER 10

INTIMACY

(Nancy Sheehan/Picture Cube)

One of the most remarkable things about adolescence is the way in which close relationships change during these years. Think about the friendships you had as a child and compare them with those you had as a teenager. Think about the boyfriends or girlfriends that children have and the boyfriends or girlfriends of adolescents. And think about relationships between parents and their children, and about how these relationships change during adolescence. In all three cases, adolescents' relationships are closer, more personal, more involved, and more emotionally charged. During adolescence, in short, relationships become more intimate.

At the outset, it is necessary to draw a distinction between *intimacy* and *sexuality*. The concept of **intimacy**—at least as it is used in the study of adolescence—does not have a sexual or physical connotation. Rather, an intimate relationship is an emotional attachment between two people that is characterized by concern for each other's well-being; a willingness to disclose private, and occasionally sensitive, topics; and a sharing of common interests and activities. Two individuals can therefore have an intimate relationship without having a sexual one. And by the same token, two people can have a sexual relationship without being especially intimate.

The development of intimacy during adolescence involves changes in the adolescent's *need* for intimacy, changes in the *capacity* to have intimate relationships, and changes in the extent to which and the way in which this capacity to be intimate is *expressed*. Although the development of intimacy during adolescence is almost always studied in relation to friendships with peers, adolescents' intimate relationships are by no means limited to other teenagers. Parents often have intimate relationships with their adolescents, especially when their children have reached a sufficient level of maturity. Siblings, even with many years between them, are often close confidants. Sometimes young people even form intimate relationships with adults who are not in their immediate family.

Obviously, one of the central issues in the study of intimacy during adolescence is the onset of dating. Although the young person's initiation into opposite-sex relationships is undoubtedly important, it is not the only noteworthy change that occurs in close relationships during adolescence. Adolescence is also an important time for changes in what we look for in friends, in our capacity to be intimate with people of *both* sexes, and in the way we express our closeness with friends.

INTIMACY AS AN ADOLESCENT ISSUE

Intimacy is an important concern throughout most of the life span. Friends and confidants provide support when we are feeling emotionally vulnerable, assistance when we need it, and companionship in a variety of activities and contexts (Weiss, 1974). During childhood, not having friends is associated with a range of psychological and social problems (Hartup, 1983). And during adulthood, having at least one intimate friendship is beneficial to an individual's health: People who have others to turn to for emotional support are less likely to suffer from psychological and physical disorders (Myers, Lindentthal, and Pepper, 1975). Without question, close relationships are extremely important to people of all ages. Why, then, is the development of intimacy especially important during adolescence?

One reason is that it is not until adolescence that truly intimate relationships—relationships characterized by openness, honesty, self-disclosure, and trust—first emerge. Although children certainly have important friendships,

Children's friendships center around shared activities. Not until adolescence are friendships based on the sorts of bonds that are formed between individuals who care about, know, and understand each other in a special way. (David Wells/Image Works)

their relationships are different from those formed during adolescence. Children's friendships are activity oriented, for example; they are built around games and shared pastimes. To a child, a friend is someone who likes to do the same things he or she does. But teenagers' close friendships are more likely to have a strong emotional foundation; they are built on the sorts of bonds that form between people who care about and know and understand each other in a special way.

Another reason for the importance of intimacy during adolescence concerns the changing nature of the adolescent's social world: during early adolescence, the increasing importance of peers and, during late adolescence, the increasing importance of opposite-sex peers. In Chapter 9 we looked at the young person's growing orientation toward peers as part of the development of emotional autonomy. In this chapter we look at changes in adolescent peer relations again but in a different light—as part of the development of intimacy.

Why do such important changes take place in close relationships during adolescence? Several theorists have answered this question by pointing to significant links between the development of intimacy during adolescence and the biological, cognitive, and social changes of the period (Berndt, 1982; Savin-Williams and Berndt, 1990). Puberty and its attendant changes in sexual impulses often raise new issues and concerns requiring serious, intimate discussion. Some young people feel hesitant to discuss sex and dating with their parents, and so they turn instead to relationships outside the family. But sexual maturation may also provoke intimacy between adolescents and their parents, as when young people turn to their mothers or fathers for advice, information, and guidance (Kandel and Lesser, 1972).

Advances in thinking—especially in the realm of social cognition—are also related to the development of intimacy during adolescence (Hill and Palmquist, 1978). The growth of social cognition during adolescence, as we saw in Chapter 2, is reflected in the young person's more sophisticated conceptions of social relationships and in improvements in interpersonal understanding and communication. These changes permit adolescents to establish and maintain far more mature relationships that are characterized by higher levels of empathy, self-disclosure, and responsiveness to each other's thoughts and feelings. The limitations in preadolescents' ability to look at things from another person's point of view may make intimate interpersonal relationships a cognitive impossibility (Beardslee, Schultz, and Selman, 1987; Selman, 1980). It is hard to be an intimate friend to someone when you are unable to empathize with that person. Improvements in social competence and gains in intimacy during adolescence, therefore, are partly attributable to improvements in social cognition (Ford, 1982).

We can also point to changes in the adolescent's social roles as potentially affecting the development of intimacy. Perhaps most simply, the behavioral independence that often accompanies the transition from childhood into adolescence provides greater opportunities for adolescents to be alone with their friends, engaged in intimate discussion. Adolescents spend more time talking to their friends than in any other activity (Csikszentimihalyi and Larson, 1984). Moreover, the recognition of adolescents as "near adults" may prompt their parents and other adults to confide in them and turn to them for support. Shared experiences, such as working, as well as the development of emotional autonomy, may help give young people and their parents more of a basis for friendship and communication (Youniss and Smollar, 1985). Finally, changes in the structure of schools during early adolescence—often giving younger teenagers more contact with older ones—may promote new types of peer relationships (Blyth, Hill, and Smyth, 1981).

During the course of preadolescence and adolescence, relationships are gradually transformed from the friendly but activity-oriented friendships of childhood to the more self-conscious, more analytical, and more intimate relationships of adulthood. In the next section, we examine why and how this transformation occurs.

RECAP

Most writers draw a distinction between intimacy and sexuality. In adolescence, the development of intimacy refers to the development of relationships that are characterized by self-disclosure, trust, and concern. There are a number of reasons that intimacy becomes an important psychosocial concern in adolescence. Chief among them are the changes of puberty, which draw young people together around common concerns; the cognitive changes of the period, which allow for a more sophisticated understanding of relationships; and the social changes of the period, which provide for more opportunities for adolescents to be alone with each other.

THEORETICAL PERSPECTIVES ON ADOLESCENT INTIMACY

The most important theoretical perspectives on the development of intimacy during adolescence are those of Harry Stack Sullivan (1953a), Erik Erikson (1968), and, more recently, a group of writers who have studied attachment relationships in adolescence, using models that initially had been developed for the study of attachment in infancy (e.g., Greenberg, Siegel, and Leitch, 1983; Kobak and Sceery, 1988; Rice, 1990). Let's look at each of these views in turn.

Sullivan's Theory of Interpersonal Development

Like Erikson, whose theory of adolescent identity development was discussed at length in Chapter 8, Sullivan took a far less biological view of development than other psychoanalytic thinkers, such as Anna Freud, had taken. Instead, Sullivan emphasized the social aspects of growth, suggesting that psychological development can be best understood when looked at in interpersonal terms. Specifically, Sullivan's theory focuses on transformations in the adolescent's relationships with others. In particular, the challenges of adolescence (and, indeed, according to Sullivan, of the entire life cycle) revolve around trying to satisfy our changing interpersonal needs.

As the child develops, different interpersonal needs surface that lead either to feelings of security (when the needs are satisfied) or to feelings of anxiety (when the needs are frustrated). Sullivan charted a developmental progression of needs, beginning in infancy and continuing through adolescence (see Table 10.1): the *needs for contact and for tenderness* (infancy), the *need for adult participation* (early childhood), the *need for peers and for peer acceptance* (middle childhood), the **need for intimacy** (preadolescence), the **needs for sexual contact and for intimacy with a peer of the opposite sex** (early adolescence), and the **need for integration into adult society** (late adolescence) (Sullivan, 1953b). These changing interpersonal needs define the course of interpersonal development through different phases of the life span. During middle childhood, for example, youngsters need to be accepted into peer groups, or else they feel rejected and ostracized.

In Sullivan's view, the security that is derived from having satisfying relationships with others is the "glue" which holds together a sense of self. Identity and self-esteem are gradually built up through interpersonal relationships. Like Erikson, Sullivan viewed psychosocial development as cumulative: The frustrations and satisfactions we experience during earlier periods affect our later relationships and developing sense of identity. The child who as an infant has his or her need for

TABLE 10.1 INTERPERSONAL NEEDS ASSOCIATED WITH DIFFERENT DEVELOPMENTAL ERAS: SULLIVAN'S THEORY

Developmental Epochs	Interpersonal Needs
Infancy (0 to 2–3 yrs.)	Need for contact with people Need for tenderness from the mothering one
Childhood (2–3 to 6–7 yrs.)	Need for adult participation in the child's play
Juvenile era (6–7 to 8–10 yrs.)	Need for peer playmates Need for acceptance into peer society groups
Preadolescence (8–10 to 12–14 yrs.)	Need for intimacy and consensual validation in same-sex chumships
Early adolescence (12–14 to 17–18 yrs.)	Need for sexual contact Need for intimacy with an opposite-sex peer
Late adolescence (17–18 yrs. to adult)	Need for integration into adult society

SOURCE: Sullivan, 1953b.

contact or tenderness frustrated will approach interpersonal relationships in subsequent eras with greater anxiety, a more intense need for security, and a shakier sense of self.

When important interpersonal transitions arise (for example, during childhood, when the social world is broadened to include significant relationships with peers), having a solid foundation of security in past relationships will aid in the successful negotiation of the transition. An individual who is very anxious about forming relationships with others is likely to have trouble forming new types of relationships, because they threaten an already-shaky sense of security. A child who does not have a strong sense of security may have many friends in elementary school but may be too afraid to form intimate friendships upon reaching preadolescence. She or he may try to continue having friendships like those of childhood—friendships that focus on playing games, for example, rather than talking—long after friends have outgrown getting together to "play." As a result, that youngster may be rejected by peers and may feel lonely and isolated.

● ***Sullivan's View of Interpersonal Development during Adolescence.*** Looking back at the progression of interpersonal needs that Sullivan mapped out, we see that he distinguished between intimacy and sexuality and, perhaps more important, that he suggested that the need for intimacy—which surfaces during preadolescence—precedes the development of heterosexual relationships, which do not emerge until adolescence. In other words, Sullivan believed that the capacity for intimacy first develops before adolescence and in the context of same-sex, not opposite-sex, relationships. One of the main challenges of adolescence, according to Sullivan, is making the transition from the nonsexual, intimate, same-sex friendships of preadolescence to the sexual, intimate, opposite-sex friendships of late adolescence.

Sullivan divided the years between childhood and adulthood into three periods: *preadolescence, early adolescence,* and *late adolescence.* During preadolescence, children begin to focus their attention on relationships with a few close friends, generally of the same sex. It is through these friendships—"chumships," as Sullivan called them—that the need for intimacy is first satisfied. With chums, the young person learns to disclose and receive intimate, private information and to build a close, mutual friendship that is based on honesty, loyalty, and trust. Sullivan believed that these relationships could even have a corrective influence, helping to repair interpersonal problems that might have developed during childhood. A good preadolescent friend, for example, can help one overcome feelings of insecurity that have developed as a result of poor family relationships.

Not all youngsters feel secure enough as preadolescents, however, to forge these more mature, intimate friendships. The feelings of insecurity are so strong for some that anxiety holds them back. As a result, some youngsters never fully develop the capacity to be intimate with others, a limitation that takes its toll on relationships throughout adolescence and adulthood. In other words, Sullivan felt that forming intimate friendships during preadolescence is a perquisite to forming close relationships as an adolescent or young adult.

According to Sullivan, the preadolescent era comes to an end with the onset of puberty. Early adolescence is marked by the emergence of sexuality, in the form of a biologically based, powerful sex drive. As a consequence of this development, a change in the preferred "target" of the adolescent's need for intimacy takes place. He or she must begin to make a shift from intimate relationships with members of the same sex to intimate relationships with members of the opposite sex.

Like all interpersonal transitions, the movement from same-sex into opposite-sex relation-

Generally, intimacy develops first within same-sex friendships. Only later in adolescence are emotionally intimate relationships between males and females common. (Spencer Grant/Picture Cube)

ships can be fraught with anxiety. For adolescents who do not have a healthy sense of security, it can be scary to leave the safety of nonsexual same-sex friendships and venture into the world of opposite-sex relationships, dating, and sexuality.

The chief challenge of adolescence, according to Sullivan, is to integrate the individual's established need for intimacy with the emerging need for sexual contact in a way that does not engender an excessive degree of anxiety. Just as Erikson viewed adolescence as a time of experimentation with different identities, Sullivan saw adolescence as a time of experimentation with different types of interpersonal relationships. Some adolescents choose to date many different people to try to find out what they are looking for in a relationship with someone else. Others get involved very deeply with a boyfriend or girlfriend in a relationship that lasts throughout their entire adolescence. Others may have a series of serious relationships. And still others keep intimacy and sexuality separate. They may develop close platonic relationships with opposite-sex peers, for example, or they may have sexual relationships without getting very intimate with their sex partners. And just as Erikson viewed role experimentation as a healthy part of the adolescent's search for identity, Sullivan viewed the adolescent's experimentation with different types of relationships as a normal way of handling new feelings, new fears, and new interpersonal needs. For many young people, experimentation with sex and intimacy continues well into late adolescence.

If the interpersonal tasks of adolescence have been negotiated successfully, the young person enters late adolescence able to be intimate, able to enjoy sex, and, most critical, able to experience intimacy and sexuality in the same relationship. This accomplished, the adolescent turns to the interpersonal needs of late adolescence: carving a niche in adult society. This latter task, in some senses, is reminiscent of the adolescent identity crisis described by Erikson.

RECAP

The three main theoretical approaches to the study of intimacy in adolescence are those of Sullivan, Erikson, and the attachment theorists. According to Sullivan, the need for intimacy emerges in preadolescence and is typically satisfied through same-sex friendships. During adolescence, this need is integrated with sexual impulses and desires, and the focus of the adolescent's interpersonal concerns are redirected toward opposite-sex peers. According to Sullivan, the chief challenge of adolescence is to integrate an already-established need for intimacy with the emerging need for sexual contact in a way that does not engender an excessive degree of anxiety.

Erikson's View of Intimacy

Erik Erikson (1968) argued that development during the adolescent and young adult years revolves around two psychosocial crises: the crisis of **identity versus identity diffusion,** prominent during adolescence (see Chapter 8), and the crisis of **intimacy versus isolation,** prominent during early adulthood. Erikson's ideas about the subject of intimacy are far less developed than his ideas about the issue of identity. Nonetheless, his view of the relationship *between* intimacy and identity is important to understand and provides somewhat of a contrast to Sullivan's perspective.

Erikson believed that, in a truly intimate relationship, two individuals' identities become fused in such a way that neither person's identity is lost. Together, two people who are in love form a couple that has its own life, its own future, and its own identity. Yet the partners do not lose their own sense of individuality. When two people marry, for example, becoming a part of a couple becomes an important part of each person's identity, but it doesn't erase the sense of self that each person had before the marriage.

It follows, Erikson reasoned, that adolescents must establish a sense of identity before they are capable of real intimacy. Without a secure sense of identity, people are afraid and unwilling to make serious commitments to others: They fear that they will lose their identity in the relationship. A young woman who is struggling to establish an occupational identity, for example, may feel that getting seriously involved with someone may impede her progress toward discovering who *she* really is as an individual.

Relationships between individuals who have not yet established a sense of identity may look intimate, but generally they are not. Adolescents who throw themselves into going steady often display a sort of "pseudointimacy." On the surface, their relationship may seem to be close, but a more careful examination usually reveals a sort of shallow, superficial intimacy. The couple may proclaim their faith in each other, for instance, but deep down they may be mistrustful or afraid to voice their concerns. They may say that they are open with each other, but they may not disclose what they are really feeling, for fear of losing the relationship. They may say that they will stay together forever, but they have trouble making any concrete plans for the future that include each other. According to Erikson, this type of pseudointimacy is to be expected during adolescence. After all, it is difficult to commit yourself to someone else before you yourself know who you are.

● ***Erikson and Sullivan: Conflicting Views?*** It may appear that there is a disagreement between Erikson and Sullivan about the relation between intimacy and identity. Sullivan viewed the development of intimacy as occurring primarily during preadolescence. He suggested that the development of the capacity for intimacy is a precedent to the development of a coherent sense of identity, which does not occur until late adolescence. Erikson, on the other hand, argued that the establishment of a coherent sense of identity necessarily occurs prior to the development of intimacy, since one must have a clear sense of who one is in order to avoid becoming lost in a relationship with someone else. What are we to make of this difference? Which comes first, the development of identity or the development of intimacy?

A number of studies have attempted to answer this question by assessing individuals on separate measures of identity and intimacy and examining the relation between the two scores (e.g., Dyk and Adams, 1990; Levitz-Jones and Orlofsky, 1985; Orlofsky, Marcia, and Lesser, 1973). If Erikson's view is correct, only individuals who have achieved a sense of identity should score high in intimacy, and no individuals who are high in intimacy should be low in identity. If Sullivan's view is correct, only individuals who have achieved intimacy in their relationships should score high in identity, and no individuals who score high in identity should score low in intimacy.

Unfortunately, none of the studies of the relation between identity and intimacy provide clear support for one theory over the other. Although scores on measures of identity and intimacy are generally correlated (that is, individuals who have a coherent sense of identity are more likely to have intimate interpersonal relationships, and vice versa), it has been difficult to determine whether development in one domain actually *leads to* development in another. Rather, it seems that individuals follow different developmental routes, with some establishing a sense of identity first and then advancing in the realm of intimacy, and others following the reverse pattern.

One hypothesis along these lines concerns sex differences in patterns of psychological development. As we shall see later in this chapter, many theorists have argued that intimacy is a far more fundamental concern for adolescent girls than for adolescent boys and that the psychosocial "crises" of identity and intimacy may even be merged for female adolescents (Josselson, Greenberger, and McConochie, 1977b). For adolescent boys—actually, for males at all ages—intimacy is perhaps a more distant concern that is less important in the process of self-definition (Maccoby, 1990). In essence, Sullivan's view may be more applicable to girls, whereas Erikson's may be more applicable to boys (Bakken and Romig, 1992; Dyk and Adams, 1990).

Rather than debating which comes first—identity or intimacy—it seems more sensible to suggest that the development of intimacy and the development of identity go hand in hand throughout adolescence, with changes in one realm of psychosocial development affecting changes in the other. One reason for the apparent disagreement between Erikson and Sullivan is that the two theorists focus on different aspects of intimacy. Whereas Sullivan's concern was primarily with the adolescent's need and *capacity* for intimacy (hence, his focus on early adolescence), Erikson's has been with the *expression* of intimacy and commitment (hence, his focus on late adolescence). Close relationships are used as a safe context in which adolescents confront difficult questions of identity; yet, at the same time, the development of an increasingly coherent and secure sense of self provides the foundation upon which adolescents build and strengthen intimate relationships with others. Although we may speak of them as though they are independent processes, the development of intimacy and identity—along with the development of autonomy, sexuality, and achievement—are highly interrelated.

RECAP

In Erikson's theory, the psychosocial crisis of late adolescence is labeled "intimacy versus isolation." According to this viewpoint, individuals must first develop a coherent sense of identity before they are able to develop genuinely intimate relationships with others. This position contrasts somewhat with that of Sullivan, who argues that the development of intimacy precedes the development of a coherent sense of self. There is some evidence (1) that Erikson's model may be more true for males than for females and (2) that for females the tasks of identity and intimacy may be somewhat merged.

Attachment in Adolescence

In recent years, a new perspective on intimacy during adolescence has emerged, one that draws on theories of the development of the attachment relationship during infancy (e.g., Ainsworth, Blehar, Waters, and Wall, 1978; Bowlby, 1969; Sroufe, 1979). In these theories of infant development, an **attachment** is defined as a strong emotional bond that is enduring and persistent. Virtually all infants form attachment relationships with their mothers (and most do with their fathers and other caregivers, as well), but not all infants have attachment relationships of the same quality. Psychologists differentiate among three types of attachment: **secure attachment, anxious-avoidant attachment,** and **anxious-resistant attachment.** A secure attachment between infant and caregiver is characterized by trust, an anxious-avoidant attachment is characterized by indifference on the part of the infant toward the caregiver, and an anxious-resistant attachment by ambivalence. The security of the early attachment relationship is important, because studies show that infants who have had a secure attachment are more likely to grow into psychologically and socially skilled children (Matas, Arend, and Sroufe, 1978).

Many theorists who study adolescent development believe that the nature of the individual's attachment relationships during infancy continues to have an influence on his or her capacity to form satisfying intimate relationships during adolescence and adulthood, for two reasons. First, some theorists have argued that the initial attachment relationship forms the basis for a more general model of interpersonal relationships that we employ throughout life. This so-called **internal working model** determines to large measure whether we feel trusting or apprehensive in relationships with others and whether we see ourselves as worthy of others' affection. According to the theory, individuals who had enjoyed a secure attachment relationship during infancy will have a more positive and healthy internal working model of relationships during adolescence, whereas individuals who had been anxiously attached as infants will have a less positive model (e.g., Kobak and Sceery, 1988).

A second reason for the continued importance of early attachment relationships during adolescence is cumulative. Although few longitudinal studies of infant attachment have followed individuals into and through adolescence, a number of studies have followed infants well into the childhood years (e.g., Erickson, Sroufe, and Egeland, 1985; Lewis,

Feiring, McGuffog, and Jaskir, 1984; Renken, Egeland, Marvinney, Mangelsdorf, and Sroufe, 1989). These studies quite convincingly show that anxiously attached infants are more likely to develop psychological and social problems during childhood, including poor peer relationships. These problems in peer relations during childhood, in turn, likely affect the development of social competence during adolescence, forming a link between early experience and later social relations. Interestingly, several studies indicate that the benefits of positive relations with peers extend beyond adolescence: Individuals who establish healthy intimate relationships with agemates during adolescence are more psychologically healthy and more satisfied with their lives as middle-aged adults (Hightower, 1990; Willits, 1988). Taken together, these studies suggest an orientation toward the study of intimate relationships that examines the development of close relationships over the entire life span, as emphasized in the theoretical models of both Erikson and Sullivan.

In addition to employing the three-way attachment classification scheme to study the links among infancy, childhood, and adolescence, attachment theorists have also applied these classifications to the study of adolescents' attachments to others (e.g., Armsden and Greenberg, 1987; Greenberg et al., 1983; Kenny, 1987) as well as to adolescents' internal working models (Kobak, Cole, Ferenz-Gillies, Fleming, and Gamble, 1993; Kobak and Sceery, 1988). In some of these studies, adolescents' current relationships with parents and peers are assessed, whereas in other studies adolescents are asked to recount their childhood experiences through the use of a procedure called the **Adult Attachment Interview** (see the accompanying box). In general, individuals who have secure attachments during adolescence (or who describe their earlier attachments as having been secure) are more socially competent and better adjusted than their insecure peers (Benson, Harris, and Rogers, 1992; Finnegan and Perry, 1993; Kerns, 1994; Kobak and Cole, 1994; Rice, 1990).

RECAP

According to attachment theorists, intimacy during adolescence must be examined in relation to the individual's history of close relationships and, in particular, of the individual's infant attachments. There is evidence that individuals who enjoyed a secure attachment to their caregiver during infancy develop a healthier or more secure internal working model of relationships: more healthy ideas about relationships, more advanced social competencies, and a more positive view of themselves in relationships with others. A secure internal working model permits the individual to enter into more satisfying intimate relationships during adolescence and adulthood.

RESEARCH ON THE DEVELOPMENTAL COURSE OF INTIMACY

Changes in the Nature of Friendship

"How do you know that someone is your best friend?" When this question is posed to children and adolescents of different ages, younger and older respondents give different sorts of answers. Consider, for example, the

THE SCIENTIFIC STUDY OF ADOLESCENCE

CHARACTERIZING ADOLESCENT ATTACHMENT USING THE Q-SORT PROCEDURE

Once limited to research on infants, the study of attachment has now established a strong presence in research on adolescents. But whereas infants' attachments to their parents are studied by observing babies interacting with their caregivers, adolescents' attachments are usually studied by interviewing young people about their early family relationships. The Adult Attachment Interview, developed by psychologist Mary Main and her colleagues (Main, Kaplan, and Cassidy, 1985), is designed to yield insight into the individual's internal working model of him- or herself in relation to others. The internal working model that an individual has during adolescence or adulthood is presumed to have been influenced significantly by the individual's early attachment experiences.

Gathering information through interviews can provide rich, detailed insight into an individual's life, and interviewing is often preferable to collecting data through questionnaires or observations, especially when one is interested in the person's subjective recollections. But analyzing information that is collected through an interview can be extremely difficult and time-consuming: Interviews usually are transcribed and then coded before being used in research. Fortunately, there is an extremely useful method for analyzing interviews or, for that matter, any data for which you would like to have raters give their evaluations, such as a videotaped observation.

This method, called a **Q-Sort,** asks raters to read the interview transcript and then to sort a certain number of cards with statements potentially describing the interview into piles ranging from "extremely characteristic" to "extremely uncharacteristic." What is different in the Q-Sort from other rating procedures is that raters are forced to place a specific number of items in each pile. Sometimes, raters must place equal numbers of items in each pile, but more often they are asked to make the piles form a bell curve by placing more items in the middle piles than in the outer piles. This procedure makes it impossible for a rater to overuse one of the categories (e.g., by placing most of the items in the pile marked "somewhat characteristic"), which frequently happens if raters are not instructed otherwise.

Psychologist Roger Kobak has developed a Q-Sort specifically for rating adolescents' responses to the Adult Attachment Interview (Kobak, Cole, Ferenz-Gillies, Fleming, and Gamble, 1993). In his studies, raters read the interview transcripts and then sort 100 different items potentially

following two responses—the first from a kindergarten child, the second from a sixth-grader (from Berndt, 1981, p. 180):

> I sleep over at his house sometimes. When he's playing ball with his friends, he'll let me play. When I slept over, he let me get in front of him in four-squares [a playground game]. He likes me.

> If you can tell each other things that you don't like about each other. If you get into a fight with someone else, they'd stick up for you. If you can tell them your phone number and they don't give you crank calls. If they don't act mean to you when other kids are around.

These two examples illustrate the most important trend in the development of chil-

describing the respondent into nine piles, using a forced bell-curve distribution. The distribution of items obtained for an individual's interview are then compared with what experts say that different prototypic profiles should look like. On the basis of the similarities between an adolescent's Q-Sort and those suggested by the experts, adolescents are characterized as *secure* (e.g., among the most characteristic items are "Is generally trusting in his or her relationships" and "Is generous, forgiving of faults in self and parents"); *dismissing* (e.g., "Demeans or plays down the need to rely on others" and "Seems detached or uninfluenced by childhood experiences"); or *preoccupied* (e.g., "Relies on others in a frustrated or dissatisfied way" and "Is confused or overwhelmed with information about relationships").

Kobak has found that secure, dismissing, and preoccupied adolescents differ in interesting ways. Compared with dismissing or preoccupied adolescents, for example, secure adolescents interact with their mothers with less unhealthy anger and more appropriate assertiveness, suggesting that they may experience fewer difficulties in establishing emotional autonomy (Kobak et al., 1993). In a study of college students, a lack of security was associated with depression (especially among preoccupied women) and with higher rates of eating disorders (especially among dismissing women) (Kobak and Cole, 1994; Kobak, Sudler, and Gamble, 1992). Individuals who are judged to be secure also have more stable romantic relationships than their insecure counterparts (Davis and Kirkpatrick, in press).

One final note: In one of his studies (Dozier and Kobak, in press), Kobak used a fascinating approach to make sure that the individuals who were classified as dismissing based on their interview responses were actually insecure and were genuinely avoiding the subject of relationships during the interview, rather than simply being forgetful. The researchers measured individuals' physiological responses both before and during the interview, using standard measures such as skin conductance. Elevations in skin conductance have been shown in previous research to occur when individuals are being deceptive and when they deliberately attempt to inhibit their emotions in the presence of emotionally powerful or disturbing material. Kobak found that individuals who were classified as dismissing showed marked increases in skin conductance when asked to recall experiences of separation and rejection by their parents.

SOURCE: Kobak, R., Cole, H., Ferenz-Gillies, R., Fleming, W., and Gamble, W. (1993). Attachment and emotion regulation during mother-teen problem-solving: A control theory analysis. *Child Development, 64*, 231–245.

dren's conceptions of friendship: It is not until early adolescence that such features as self-disclosure and loyalty are mentioned as important dimensions of friendship. Thomas Berndt (1981), for example, compared how kindergarten children, third-graders, and sixth-graders responded to questions about their conceptions of close friendship. The children's responses were classified into one of eight categories, including play or association ("He calls me all the time"), prosocial behavior ("She helps me do things"), intimacy or trust ("I can tell her secrets"), and loyal support ("He'll stick up for me when I'm in a fight"). In general, responses mentioning prosocial behavior and association were equally frequent across all age groups—in fact, they were among the most frequent types of responses at all ages. But answers mentioning intimacy and loyalty, which were virtually absent among the kindergarten students, increased dramatically between the third and sixth grades.

A similar study revealed comparable results (Bigelow and LaGaipa, 1975). Not until seventh grade did individuals mention intimacy, and not until this time did children mention "common interests" or "similar attitudes and values" (see Figure 10.1). As in Berndt's study, the researchers found that responses mentioning prosocial behavior and common activities were high at all age levels. One team of writers suggests that it may be important to differentiate between companionship, which appears much before adolescence, and intimacy, which may not emerge until considerably later (Buhrmester and Furman, 1987).

That conceptions of friendship come to place greater weight on such dimensions as intimacy, loyalty, and shared values and attitudes during early adolescence is consistent with Sullivan's theory (Savin-Williams and Berndt, 1990). As adolescents' needs for intimacy increase, so might the emphasis that they place on intimacy as an important component of friendship. The findings are also consistent with what we know about other cognitive changes characteristic of early adolescence. As you will recall from Chapter 2, adolescents have greater facility than children in thinking about abstract concepts, such as intimacy and loyalty. And adolescents' judgments of others are more sophisticated, more psychological, and less tied to concrete attributes than are those of children.

Several studies indicate that the importance of intimacy as a defining feature of friendship continues to increase throughout early and middle adolescence (Berndt and Perry, 1990). But an interesting pattern of change occurs around age 14. During middle adolescence (between ages 13 and 15), particularly for

FIGURE 10.1 *Children and adolescents have different conceptions of "friendship." Some sorts of conceptions do not appear until the fifth or sixth grade.* (Derived from Bigelow and LaGaipa, 1975)

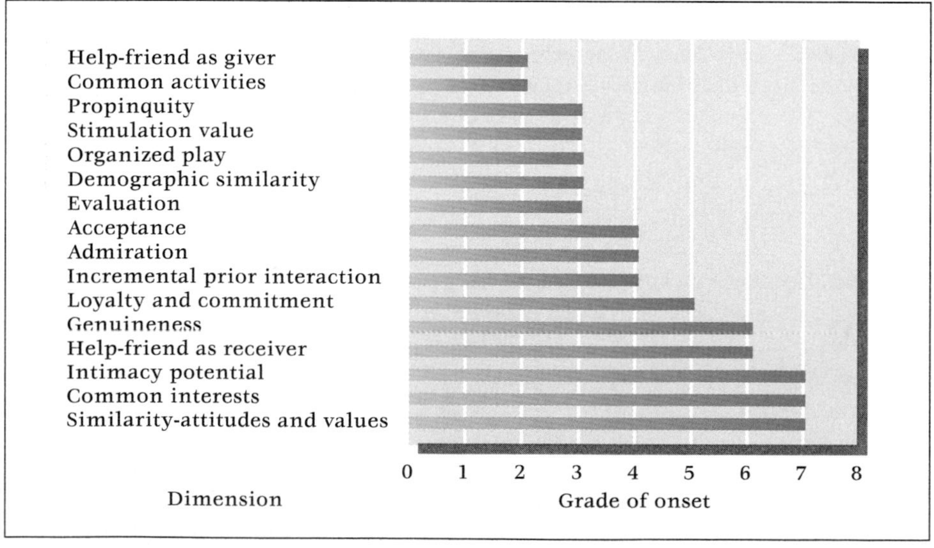

girls, concerns about loyalty and anxieties over rejection become more pronounced and may temporarily overshadow concerns about intimate self-disclosure (Berndt and Perry, 1990; Douvan and Adelson, 1966). As two writers explain:

> The girls in this age group [ages 14 to 16] are unique in some respects, that is, different from both older and younger girls. What stands out in their interviews is the stress placed on security in friendships. They want the friend to be loyal, trustworthy, and a reliable source of support in any emotional crisis. She should not be the sort of person who will abandon you or who gossips about you behind your back. . . . With so much invested in the friendship, it is no wonder that the girl is so dependent on it. . . . The girl is likely to feel like the [patient] in that famous *New Yorker* cartoon, who, getting up from the couch, takes a pistol from her purse and says [to her psychoanalyst]: "You've done me a world of good, Doctor, but you know too much." (Douvan and Adelson, 1966, pp. 188–189)

How might Sullivan have explained this pattern? Why might loyalty become such a pressing concern for girls during the middle adolescent years? One possible answer is that, at this age, girls may feel more anxious about their relationships because they are beginning to make the transition into opposite-sex relationships. These transitions, as Sullivan noted, can sometimes make us feel insecure. Perhaps it is anxiety over dating and heightened feelings of insecurity that cause adolescent girls temporarily to place a great deal of emphasis on the trust and loyalty of their close friends.

Changes in the Display of Intimacy

In addition to placing greater emphasis on intimacy and loyalty in defining friendship than children do, teenagers are also more likely actually to display intimacy in their relationships. For example, one team of researchers examined age differences in the degree to which youngsters had intimate knowledge about their best friends (Diaz and Berndt, 1982). Although fourth- and eighth-graders had comparable degrees of knowledge about nonintimate characteristics of their best friends (such as the friend's telephone number or birth date), eighth-graders knew significantly more things about their friends that could be classified as intimate (such as what their friends worry about or what they are proud of) (see also Jones and Dembo, 1989). Along similar lines, another study showed that, between the fifth and eleventh grades, increasingly more adolescents agree with such statements as "I know how [my friend] feels about things without his [or her] telling me" and "I feel free to talk to [my friend] about almost everything" (Sharabany, Gershoni, and Hofman, 1981). Consistent with Sullivan's viewpoint, then, during preadolescence and early adolescence, youngsters' friendships become more personal.

Individuals also become more responsive toward close friends during adolescence (Berndt, 1982; Berndt and Perry, 1990). This can be interpreted as another indicator of their increased capacity for intimacy. Before preadolescence, for example, children are actually less likely to help and share with their friends than with other classmates (perhaps because children are more competitive with their friends than with other youngsters and do not want to feel inferior). By about fourth grade, children treat their friends and other classmates similarly when it comes to sharing and cooperation. But by the time they have reached eighth grade, one team of researchers found, friends are "more generous and more helpful toward each other than toward other classmates" (Berndt, 1982, p. 1452). Interestingly, adolescents are also *physically and physiologically* responsive to their friends: One recent study found that the behaviors and emotional states of pairs of friends were more frequently synchronized, or "on the same wavelength," than were those of acquaintances, even when the pairs were engaged in the same task (Field, Greenwald, Morrow, Healy, Foster, Guthertz, and Frost, 1992). Evidently, there may be something genuine about "chemistry" between close friends!

Finally, during the course of adolescence, individuals become more interpersonally sensitive—they show greater levels of empathy and social understanding—in situations in which they are helping or comforting others. Compared with children, adolescents are more likely to understand and acknowledge how their friends feel when those friends are having problems. For instance, one researcher asked children and adolescents how they would help a younger friend who had been scared by a horror movie on television. The children were more likely to deny their friend's feelings, whereas the adolescents were more likely to respond sensitively and supportively (Burleson, 1982).

RECAP

Research on the development of intimacy in adolescence points to changes in individuals' conceptions about friendship and in the display of intimacy. With development, adolescents place more emphasis on trust and loyalty as defining features of friendship, they become more self-disclosing in their relationships, and they become more responsive to their friends.

Changes in the "Targets" of Intimacy

According to Sullivan, adolescence is a time of noteworthy changes in the "targets" of intimate behavior. During preadolescence and early adolescence, intimacy with peers is hypothesized to replace intimacy with parents, and during late adolescence, intimacy with peers of the opposite sex is thought to take the place of intimacy with same-sex friends. Actually, this view appears to be only somewhat accurate. As we shall see, new targets of intimacy do not *replace* old ones. Rather, new targets are *added* to old ones.

Parents and Peers as Targets of Intimacy. The increasing intimacy between teenagers and their friends during the course of adolescence is generally not accompanied by a decrease in intimacy toward parents. Declines in intimacy between adolescents and their parents, which appear to occur during early adolescence, are temporary. By the end of adolescence, young people and their parents are quite close. One study, for example, compared levels of intimacy between adolescents and their best friends, their mothers, and their fathers (Hunter and Youniss, 1982). Thirty adolescents in each of four different age groups—9, 12, 15, and 19—were asked to rate the three relationships along four measures of intimacy: (1) their willingness to discuss problems with the other person, (2) their ability to talk through disagreements, (3) feelings of companionship, and (4) the degree of intimate knowledge possessed by the other person. Ratings across these measures were summed to form overall intimacy scores for each of the three relationships (see Figure 10.2).

As expected, intimacy between adolescents and their best friends increased across the four groups. And from age 12 on, adolescents described their relationships with their best friends as more intimate than those with their mothers or fathers. But this difference between parent and peer intimacy reflected increases in intimacy with peers, not decreases in intimacy with parents. Intimacy between adolescents and their mothers was

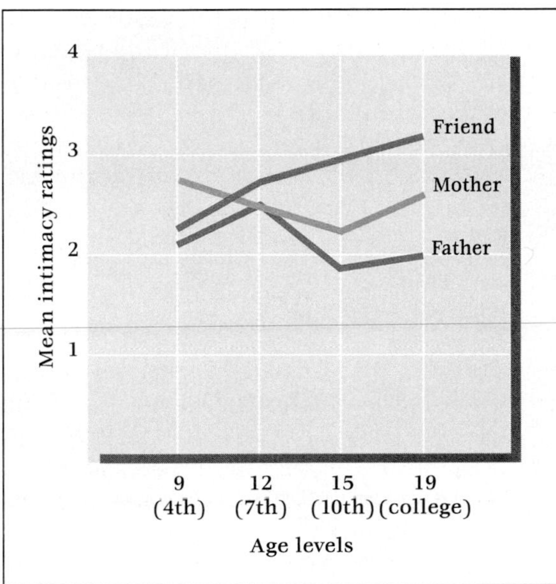

FIGURE 10.2 *Age differences in intimacy in three relationships.* (Adapted from Hunter and Youniss, 1982)

equal across the four groups, and intimacy between adolescents and their fathers appeared to increase slightly between ages 9 and 12, to decrease slightly between ages 12 and 15 (returning to the level at 9 years of age), and to remain steady between ages 15 and 19.

Findings consistent with these were obtained when nearly 2,500 students in a large Midwestern school district were asked to list the important people in their lives—people they cared about, went to for advice, or did things with (Blyth, Hill, and Thiel, 1982). The number of peers listed increased over the course of the age range studied (from grades 7 through 10). But no changes were found across this same age range in the percentage of adolescents listing their mothers or fathers—in each grade, for both boys and girls, about 93 percent of the adolescents who were sampled listed their parents. It is important to note that these patterns may vary across cultures, however: One study found that Japanese adolescents (and Japanese boys, in particular) were less likely than American adolescents to list their parents—and were more likely to list their peers—as significant others (Darling, Hamilton, and Matsuda, 1990).

Studies of adolescents' preferences for social support similarly show that the likelihood of turning to a peer during a time of trouble increases during adolescence but that the likelihood of turning to a parent remains constant (Kneisel, 1987). In a recent study of African-American, Hispanic-American, and European-American youth, the researchers found that, between ages 7 and 14, the amount of support received from one's immediate family remained fairly constant, while the amount of support received from friends increased—a pattern seen in all three ethnic groups (Levitt, Guacci-Franci, and Levitt, 1993). In other words, even though adolescents begin to see their friends as increasingly important sources of emotional support, they do not cease needing or using their parents for the same purpose. Interestingly, adolescents may feel freer to express anger during arguments with family members than during arguments with friends, presumably because anger may lead to the end of a friendship but not to the end of a family relationship (Laursen, 1993).

There are important differences between adolescents' relationships with their mothers and fathers, however. In general, adolescents interact much more often with their mother than with their father, and this is true for males as well as females. Of their two parents, adolescents see their mothers as being more understanding, more accepting, and more willing to negotiate; they view their mothers as less judgmental, less guarded, and less defensive. The difference between perceptions of mothers and fathers is especially large for girls: As a rule, the mother-daughter relationship tends to be the closest and the father-daughter relationship the least intimate, with mother-son and father-son relationships falling in between (Monck, 1991; Noller and Callan, 1990; Youniss and Smollar, 1985).

There are also important differences among ethnic groups in the expression of intimacy between adolescents and parents. One recent study of late adolescents found, for example, that Vietnamese-American and Chinese-American individuals felt less comfortable talking to their parents about such intimate matters as sex or dating than did Filipino-Americans or Mexican-Americans, who in turn felt less comfortable than European-Americans. The researchers speculated that these differences reflected ethnic differences in norms of formality in family relationships, especially in relationships between adolescents and their fathers (Cooper, Baker, Polichar, and Welsh, in press).

An important transition in intimate relationships appears to take place sometime between the fifth and eighth grades. During this period, peers become the most important source of companionship and intimate self-disclosure—surpassing parents and, interestingly, other family members, such as siblings, as well (Buhrmester and Furman, 1987; Larson and Richards, 1991). Peers may become increasingly important as targets of intimacy not simply because they are similar in age but also because they do not share the same family with the adolescent. As adolescents begin the process of individuation, they may need to seek intimacy outside the family as a means of establishing an identity beyond their family role.

In general, adolescents interact much more often with their mother than with their father, and this is true for males as well as females. Compared to their fathers, adolescents see their mothers as more understanding, accepting, and willing to negotiate, and less judgmental, guarded, and defensive. (Hinton/Monkmeyer)

Adolescents also have very different sorts of intimate relationships with parents and peers, and these differences point to different ways in which mothers, fathers, and friends may contribute to the social development of the young person. Even in close families, parent-adolescent relations are characterized by an imbalance of power, with parents as nurturers, advice givers, and explainers whom adolescents turn to because of their experience and expertise. Adolescents' interactions with their friends, in contrast, are more mutual and more balanced and are more likely to provide adolescents with opportunities to express alternative views and engage in an equal exchange of feelings and beliefs (Hunter, 1984). Rather than viewing one type of relationship as more or less intimate than the other, it seems wiser to say that both types of intimacy are important, for each influences a different aspect of the adolescent's developing character in important ways. Intimacy with parents provides opportunities to learn from someone older and wiser; intimacy with friends provides opportunities to share experiences with someone who has a similar perspective and degree of expertise.

The different functions of intimacy with parents and peers are also illustrated in a study of social support during a transition into a new school (Dunn, Putallaz, Sheppard, and Lindstrom, 1987). As you recall from Chapter 6, changing schools during adolescence can sometimes be stressful, and **social support**—emotional assistance from others—can help buffer adolescents against the potential negative effects of stress (Hauser and Bowlds, 1990). The study found that support from family members was more predictive of adaptation to the demands of the new school, as indexed by grades and attendance, but that support from peers was more predictive of low psychological distress, as indexed by measures of depression and anxiety. The absence of peer support was especially critical for boys. One reason: Girls may be more likely than boys to seek out other sources of support when their peers do not provide it. Interestingly, a lack of support from parents *or* from friends in school is associated with low self-worth in early adolescence; having support from parents, siblings, or nonschool friends does not fully compensate for a lack of support from classmates, and having support from siblings, classmates, or others does not compensate at all for a lack of support from parents (East and Rook, 1992). Although more research on social support among minority adolescents is sorely needed, at least one study indicates that parental support is more strongly related to self-esteem among white than black adolescents (Levitt et al., 1993).

A recent study of the differential uses of parents and peers as sources of support indicates that whom adolescents turn to is likely to be highly dependent upon the specific issue at hand. This particular study asked adolescents whom they would turn to if they had a substance-abuse problem; the respondents could name as many different people as desired (Windle, Miller-Tutzauer, and Barnes, 1991). Among the early adolescents surveyed, only 43 percent listed their parents among people they would turn to for help, whereas 60 percent listed friends; among the middle adolescents, the proportions were 39 percent and 70 percent, respectively (see Figure 10.3). More interestingly, 10 percent of all early adolescents and almost that proportion of middle adolescents said that they would turn to no one at all—a far more common response among boys than girls. There also were interesting ethnic differences in adolescents' responses, with black and Hispanic youngsters being *twice* as likely as white adolescents to report being socially isolated (i.e., having no one to turn to).

In general, the results of research on changes in intimacy with parents and peers as an individual ages are similar to the findings discussed in Chapter 9, regarding autonomy: Although the importance of peer relationships undoubtedly increases during adolescence, the significance of family relationships does not decline so much as it narrows in focus. Parents do not cease to be important sources of influence or, as we see here, targets of intimacy. Throughout adolescence, parents and adolescents remain close; parents—especially mothers—remain important confidants; and both mothers and fathers continue to be significant influences on the young person's behavior and decisions. Indeed, even in adolescence being close to one's parents has a more positive impact on psychological health than being close to one's friends does (Greenberg, Siegel, and Leitch, 1983), and studies

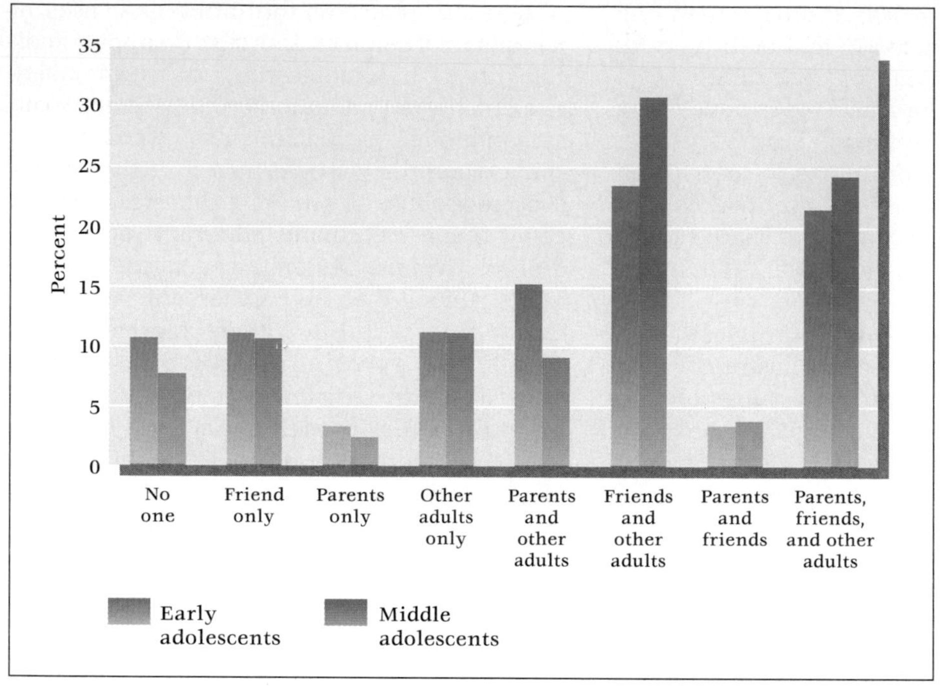

FIGURE 10.3 *Percentages of early and middle adolescents who would turn to various sources of support for help with a drug problem.* (Windle et al., 1991)

show that the quality of the relationship which adolescents have with their parents may have an influence on the quality of the relationship which they have with close friends (Cooper, Carlson, Keller, Koch, and Spradling, 1993; Gold and Yanof, 1985). Increasingly, psychologists are coming to see family relationships and peer relationships as influencing, rather than competing with, each other. Nevertheless, it seems clear that peers take on an increasingly important role in the individual's social life over the course of adolescence. Although peers do not *replace* parents, they clearly contribute to the adolescent's social development in a unique and beneficial way.

Other Family Members as Targets of Intimacy. Comparatively little is known about adolescents' relationships with siblings and with members of their extended family. In the Midwestern survey discussed above, only about 10 percent of the adolescents who had a brother or a sister failed to list a sibling as an important person in their life. Furthermore, more than two-thirds of the adolescents with brothers or sisters listed all of their siblings as significant (Blyth, Hill, and Thiel, 1982). Adolescents typically rate their relationship with their "favorite" brother or sister as having about the same level of intimacy as their relationship with their best friend (Greenberger, Steinberg, Vaux, and McAuliffe, 1980). When researchers do not specify that the sibling be a "favorite" brother or sister, however, the relationship is usually described as less intimate than the adolescent's relationship with parents or friends (Buhrmester and Furman, 1987).

Approximately 80 percent of adolescents list at least one member of their extended family (grandparents, aunts, uncles, and cousins) as significant in their lives, with extended family members constituting about one-fifth of all people listed as important (Blyth, Hill, and Thiel, 1982). Contact with extended family is infrequent, however, either through actual visits or via the telephone, because extended family members often live outside the adolescent's area (Feiring and Lewis, 1991). One might suspect, therefore, that although adolescents consider grandparents, aunts, uncles, and cousins to be important, these relatives rarely serve as targets of intimacy. There appears to be a slight increase in intimacy with extended family members during childhood, but an especially steep drop-off in intimacy with grandparents and other extended family members occurs between childhood and adolescence (Buhrmester and Furman, 1987; Levitt et al., 1993).

Although a decline in intimacy with grandparents is often observed during adolescence, this may not be as common among adolescents who are living with a single, divorced mother (Clingempeel, Colyar, Brand, and Hetherington, 1992). Indeed, divorce may be associated with *increased* contact between adolescents and their grandparents, especially between the adolescent and his or her maternal grandfather. Interestingly, puberty seems to increase the intimacy between adolescent boys from divorced homes and their grandfathers (perhaps to compensate for diminished contact with their father), whereas it seems to distance adolescent girls from their grandfathers (perhaps because of discomfort about the girl's sexuality).

Same-Sex versus Opposite-Sex Friendships

It is not until late adolescence that intimate friendships with opposite-sex peers begin to be important. Consistent with Sullivan's theory, studies of preadolescents and young teenagers point to a very strong sex cleavage in adolescents' friendships, with boys rarely reporting friendships with girls, and girls rarely reporting friendships with boys (Hallinan, 1981). Indeed, gender is the single most important determinant of friendship during preadolescence, playing a considerably more powerful role than, for example, race or socioeconomic background (Schofield, 1981). (Age is also an important determinant of preadolescents' friendships, but it is difficult to study, since the organization of most elementary schools—at least in America—makes it hard for children to develop friendships with older or younger peers.)

The schism between boys and girls during early adolescence results from various factors. First, despite whatever changes may have taken place in American society with regard to sex-role socialization during the past twenty-five years, it is still the case that preadolescent and early adolescent boys and girls have different interests, engage in different sorts of peer activities, and perceive themselves to be different from each other (Schofield, 1981). In one study, for example, an interviewer asked a young adolescent boy why boys and girls sit separately in the school lunchroom. "So they can talk," the boy replied. "The boys talk about football and sports and the girls talk about whatever they talk about" (Schofield, 1981, p. 68). The sex cleavage in adolescent friendships results more from adolescents' preferring members of the same sex—and the activities they engage in—than from their actually disliking members of the opposite sex (Bukowski, Gauze, Hoza, and Newcomb, 1993).

But perhaps a more interesting reason for the low frequency of cross-sex friendships during early adolescence is the concern of some adolescents that contact with members of the opposite sex will be interpreted as a sign of romantic involvement (Schofield, 1981). As one girl put it, "If you talk with boys they [other girls] say that you're almost going with him." Another girl from the same class remarked that boys and girls rarely work together on class projects "because people like to work with their friends. . . . When you're working on a project . . . your friend has to call and come over to your house. If it's a boy, it can be complicated" (Schofield, 1981, p. 69).

The discomfort that younger adolescents feel about cross-sex relationships is vividly illustrated in the following observation of three preadolescent boys in an amusement park:

> The boys seem very interested in the girls they see, and there is considerable whispering and teasing about them. Tom had received a small coin bank as a prize which he decides that he no longer wishes to keep. At this time we are standing in line for a roller coaster directly behind three girls—apparently a year or two older than these twelve-year-olds—one of whom is wearing a hooded jacket. Frank tells Tom to take the bank and "stuff it in her hood," which Tom does to the annoyance of his victim. When she turns around, Tom and Hardy tell her that Frank did it, and of course Frank denies this, blaming Tom. The girls tell the boys to shut up and leave them alone. As things work out, Hardy has to sit with one of these girls on the ride and he clearly appears embarrassed, while Tom and Frank are vastly amused. After the ride Tom and Frank claim that they saw Hardy holding her. Frank said that he saw them holding hands, and Tom said: "He was trying to go up her shirt." Hardy vehemently denies these claims. A short while later we meet these girls again, and Frank turns to Hardy, saying "Here's your honey." The girl retorts as she walks away, "Oh, stifle it." (Fine, 1981, p. 43)

Friendly interactions between early adolescent boys and girls, when they do occur, typically involve "overacting attraction or romantic interest in such a pronounced or playful way that the indication of interest can be written off as teasing or fooling around" (Schofield, 1981, p. 71).

The transitional period—between same-sex nonsexual relationships and opposite-sex sexual ones—appears to be a somewhat trying time for adolescents. This period usually coincides with the peer group's shift from same-sex cliques to mixed-sex crowds, which we examined in Chapter 5. The interpersonal strains and anxieties inherent in the transition show up in the high levels of teasing, joking around, and overt discomfort young adolescents so often display in situations that are a little too close to being romantic or sexual. As one researcher put it, intimacy between boys and girls before middle adolescence appears to be "impeded at least partly because . . . children are aware that they are approaching the age when they may begin to become deeply

As mixed-sex relationships begin to develop, adolescents may mask their anxieties by teasing and joking around with members of the opposite sex. (Glass/Monkmeyer)

involved with each other in a romantic or sexual way" (Schofield, 1981, pp. 69–71).

These observations support Sullivan's claim that intimacy between adolescent boys and girls is relatively slow to develop and generally is tinged with an air of sexuality. Contrary to his notion that cross-sex intimacy comes to replace intimacy with peers of the same sex, however, researchers have found that intimate relationships between adolescents of the same sex continue to develop throughout adolescence. They clearly are not displaced by the eventual emergence of intimacy between adolescent males and females (Connolly and Johnson, 1993; Sharabany et al., 1981). Although researchers find that the likelihood of opposite-sex peers appearing on adolescents' lists of people who are important to them increases during early and middle adolescence, the number of same-sex peers listed also increases or remains constant (Blyth et al., 1982; Feiring and Lewis, 1991).

Although intimacy between the sexes increases during early adolescence (Buhrmester and Furman, 1987), many adolescents do not list a single opposite-sex peer as a significant person in their lives. In middle school, only 8 percent of adolescents' friendships are with members of the opposite sex; by high school, this figure has risen only to 13 percent (Degirmencioglu and Urberg, 1994). When females do include opposite-sex peers, the boys they list are often older and often from another school, suggesting that opposite-sex intimacy occurs primarily in the context of dating—again, this is consistent with predictions derived from Sullivan's theory. Similarly, when boys list girls as important friends, they generally are of the same age or younger (Blyth et al., 1982). Boys and girls who have opposite-sex friends are more integrated into the social networks and more socially competent (Degirmencioglu and Urberg, 1994; Feiring and Lewis, 1991). Interestingly, having an intimate relationship with an opposite-sex peer is more strongly related to boys' general level of interpersonal intimacy than it is to girls' (Buhrmester and Furman, 1987). This suggests that opposite-sex relationships may play a more important role in the development of intimacy among adolescent boys than girls.

RECAP

Adolescence is also a time during which adolescents broaden their circle of confidants. In general, new types of relationships are added to the adolescent's social world without replacing previous ones. Whereas in childhood the primary targets of intimacy are parents and, to a lesser extent, siblings, beginning in preadolescence the network of intimates widens to include peers as well as family members. It is not until relatively late in adolescence, however, that intimacy with opposite-sex peers develops: Cross-sex friendships are relatively rare before adolescents begin dating.

INTIMACY AND PSYCHOSOCIAL DEVELOPMENT

The Function of Close Relationships

Intimate friendships during adolescence play an important role in the young person's overall psychological development, particularly in the realms of identity and sexuality. Both Sullivan and Erikson have stressed the role of friendship in helping the adolescent establish a coherent sense of identity. Close friends serve as a sounding board for adolescents' fantasies and questions about the future. Adolescents often talk to their friends about the careers they hope to follow, the people they hope to get involved with, and the life they expect to lead after they leave home. Friends provide advice on a range of identity-related matters—from how to act in different situations to what sorts of occupational and educational paths to pursue. At least one study finds that having an intimate friendship is more central to adolescents' mental health than it is to children's (Buhrmester, 1990), and, not surprisingly, adolescents who report having at least one close friendship report higher levels of self-esteem than their peers who do not. It also has been found that intimacy with same-sex friends and intimacy with romantic partners make distinct contributions to adolescents' self-esteem (Connolly and Konarski, 1994). However, it is not clear whether intimacy leads to self-esteem or whether adolescents with already high self-esteem are more likely to develop close friendships (Savin-Williams and Berndt, 1990).

Peers also play an extremely important part in socializing adolescents into the roles of adulthood. This is especially the case when it comes to sex roles. The pressure adolescents exert on each other to behave in ways they deem as sex-appropriate is often remarkably strong (Fine, 1981, 1987; Schofield, 1981). It is not necessarily the case, however, that as adults individuals demonstrate the same level of intimacy in their relationships as they did as adolescents; intimacy is in some regards a skill that continues to develop well after adolescence and that may be displayed in different ways within different contexts (Sharabany and Wiseman, 1993).

As we shall see in Chapter 11, friends are also important agents of sexual socialization during adolescence: Teenagers are far more likely to discuss sex with their friends than with their parents. Through close friendships, adolescents learn a great deal about sex and about ways of dealing with members of the opposite sex—lessons that are less likely to be learned from parents or other adults.

These positive aspects of close relationships notwithstanding, it is important to recognize that intimate relationships can have negative as well as beneficial effects on the young person's development. According to one theorist, frequent conversations with friends about personal problems and difficulties may lead to too much introspection and self-consciousness in the young person (Mechanic, 1983). Adolescent friendships may be beneficial precisely because they are *not* like those envisioned by Sullivan, but because they involve young people in exciting activities that distract them from being preoccupied with themselves (Savin-Williams and Berndt, 1990).

We should also keep in mind that the effects of having an intimate friendship with someone depend on who that someone is and what takes place in the relationship. Friendships often provide for positive things like self-disclosure, intimacy, and companionship, but they also may give rise to insecurity, jealousy, and mistrust (Rubin, 1980). And, as we saw in Chapter 5, adolescents who are intimate with peers who have antisocial values or habits are themselves more likely to develop similar patterns of behavior. It is easy to forget, but it goes without saying, that not all close relationships foster positive developmental outcomes.

RECAP

Adolescents who have intimate friendships typically have better mental health than peers who do not. We do not know which comes first, however, intimacy or psychological health: Although it seems likely that intimacy, and the social support it provides, enhances adolescents' well-being, it is also likely that psychologically healthy adolescents are better able to make and maintain close relationships with others. Nonetheless, experts agree that close peer relationships are an essential part of healthy social development during adolescence.

Adolescent Loneliness

According to several surveys of high school and college students, late adolescence is one of the loneliest times in the life span. Although we often think of the elderly as being lonely, most studies show that the highest levels of loneliness are reported not by older adults but by adolescents and youth (Cutrona, 1982). Because adolescents may have developed strong needs for intimacy but may not yet have forged the social relationships necessary to satisfy these needs, they may be especially prone to feelings of social isolation. Being with other people who have active social lives can also be hard. Feelings of loneliness are intensified when we feel that the people around us are happier and more socially active than we are. The college student who remains in his room while his suitemates are out on a weekend evening is likely to feel lonelier than the student who is in his room but knows that the student next door is having an equally uneventful night.

The potential for feeling lonely increases over the adolescent years, as the large cliques and crowds that are common in early and middle adolescence begin to break down. In addition, changing conditions in the school setting during the adolescent years—such as moving to a new school or having a daily class schedule that is different from one's friends—make it difficult for high school students to maintain as many close friends as had been the case in junior high school or elementary school (Berndt and Perry, 1990), although changing schools is easier for adolescents who have better social skills than for their less adept peers (Vernberg, Ewell, Beery, and Abwender, 1994). In surveys about friendship, the number of best friends named by individuals typically peaks in early adolescence at about four to six and then begins to decline. By adulthood, most individuals name only one best friend, a few close friends, and numerous acquaintances (Savin-Williams and Berndt, 1990).

If the transition from junior high school to high school can take a toll on the adolescent's intimate social network, the transition from high school to college can be devastating. Most young people report a steep decline in their satisfaction with their high school friendships over the course of the transition into college (Shaver, Furman, and Buhrmester, 1985). And, unfortunately, many students in their first year of college do not immediately find replacements for this loss of intimacy.

According to an extensive study of loneliness among students at UCLA (Cutrona, 1982), nearly half of all students experience great loneliness during the first months of college. Leaving behind the familiarity of one's family, high school friends, and a hometown boyfriend or girlfriend and entering a large, impersonal institution can be a very difficult transition. In Chapter 6, we noted that half of all students who drop out of college do so during their first year. Loneliness is a contributing factor in many cases. Researchers find that loneliness is equally likely to be experienced by male and by female students, by students from all the various ethnic groups, and by students living in dormitories as well as those in off-campus housing (Cutrona, 1982). Although many students experience severe loneliness during their first year in college, these feelings subside somewhat for most people by the end of the year. However, a significant number of students never overcome their initial feelings of social isolation and continue to feel lonely throughout college. This has led researchers to

THE SEXES

ARE THERE SEX DIFFERENCES IN INTIMACY?

When asked to name the people who are most important to them, adolescent girls—particularly in the middle adolescent years—list more friends than boys do, and girls are more likely to mention intimacy as a defining aspect of close friendship. In interviews, adolescent girls express greater interest in their close friendships, talk more frequently about their intimate conversations with friends, and express greater concern about their friends' faithfulness and greater anxiety over rejection (Berndt, 1982; Feiring and Lewis, 1991). Girls are more likely than boys to make distinctions in the way they treat intimate and nonintimate friends, and girls appear to prefer to keep their friendships more exclusive, being less willing to include other classmates in their cliques' activities (Berndt, 1982; Bukowski, Sippola, Gauze, Hoza, and Newcomb, 1993). Intimacy with same-sex friends increases markedly between childhood and early adolescence among girls but does not show a similar increase among boys. Indeed, when self-disclosure is taken as the measure of intimacy, it is clear that boys' friendships with other boys do not approach girls' friendships with other girls until late in adolescence, if at all (Buhrmester and Furman, 1987; Savin-Williams and Berndt, 1990). Girls also appear to develop intimate relationships with boys earlier than boys do with girls (see figure). And girls appear to be more sensitive and empathic than boys, especially when comforting friends who are distressed (Berndt, 1982; Blyth, Hill, and Thiel, 1982; Burleson, 1982; Eisenberg, Miller, Shell, McNalley, and Shea, 1991; Sharabany, Gershoni, and Hofman, 1981). In these very numerous—and very important—respects, the expression of intimacy certainly appears to be more advanced among adolescent girls than among boys.

Yet on some measures, adolescent boys and girls show similar degrees of intimacy in their interpersonal relationships. Although girls are more likely to mention self-disclosure when asked to define close friendship, boys and girls report similar levels of actual self-disclosure in their same-sex friendships and have equivalent degrees of intimate knowledge about their best friends (Diaz and Berndt, 1982; Sharabany, Gershoni, and Hofman, 1981). In group situations, boys and girls are equally likely to help their friends (Zeldin, Small, and Savin-Williams, 1982). Boys and girls report comparable levels of intimacy with their mothers, and the majority of adolescents feel closer to their mothers than to their fathers; but boys report greater intimacy with fathers than girls do (Kandel and Lesser, 1972; Youniss and Smollar, 1985).

On the face of it, it appears that intimacy is a more conscious concern for adolescent girls than for boys. But this does not mean that intimacy is *absent* from boys' relationships. "Boys may spend less time in conversations about their emotions and ideas than girls, but they may [nevertheless] acquire a deep understanding of each other by spending time together" (Berndt, 1982, p. 1450). It is important to recognize, therefore, that boys and girls have different *types* of friendships. Consequently, they express intimacy in somewhat different ways. In general, boys' friendships are more oriented toward shared activities than toward the explicit satisfaction of emotional needs—as is often the case in girls' friendships; and the development of intimacy between adolescent males may be a quieter, more subtle phenomenon.

Many theorists have suggested that these sex differences in intimacy are the result of different patterns of socialization, with females being more strongly encouraged to develop and express intimacy—especially verbal intimacy—than males. Consistent with this, research shows that an individual's *sex role* (how masculine, feminine, or androgynous he or she is) is a better predictor of the person's capacity for intimate friendship than his or her *sex* (Jones and Costin, 1993). For instance, androgynous males (males who are both masculine and feminine) report levels of intimacy in their friendships that are comparable to females' levels of intimacy (Jones and Dembo, 1989).

Other factors could be at work, however, that lead to the greater expression of certain types of intimacy between females than between males. Social pressures on males and females during adolescence are quite different and may lead to differences in expressions of intimacy in certain types of relationships. For instance, theorists have noted that **homophobia**—the fear of homosexuality—is stronger among adolescent males than among adolescent females and leads to suppressed intimacy in relationships between boys (Kite, 1984). One reason that male adolescents may not be as intimate in their friendships as female adolescents may be that boys are nervous that expressions of intimacy—even without sexual contact—will be taken as a sign of their sexual orientation.

Although much research to date has led to the conclusion that girls experience more intimacy in their relationships than boys do (Maccoby, 1990), it is important to bear in mind that thcsc studies have been based mainly on samples of white youngsters. Several recent studies of nonwhite youth, however, suggest that there may not be sex differences in intimacy in some ethnic groups. In particular, African-American males report as much intimacy in their friendships as do African-American females, and sex differences in intimacy among Mexican-American adolescents appear far less consistently than they do among their white counterparts (DuBois and Hirsch, 1990; Jones, Costin, and Ricard, 1994). Sanctions against intimate disclosure may be especially strong among *white* males, but they may be far less so among their minority counterparts.

Age differences in reported intimacy in same- and opposite-sex relationships. In general, intimacy is reported by girls at an earlier age than by boys. (Adapted from Sharabany, Gershoni, and Hofman, 1981)

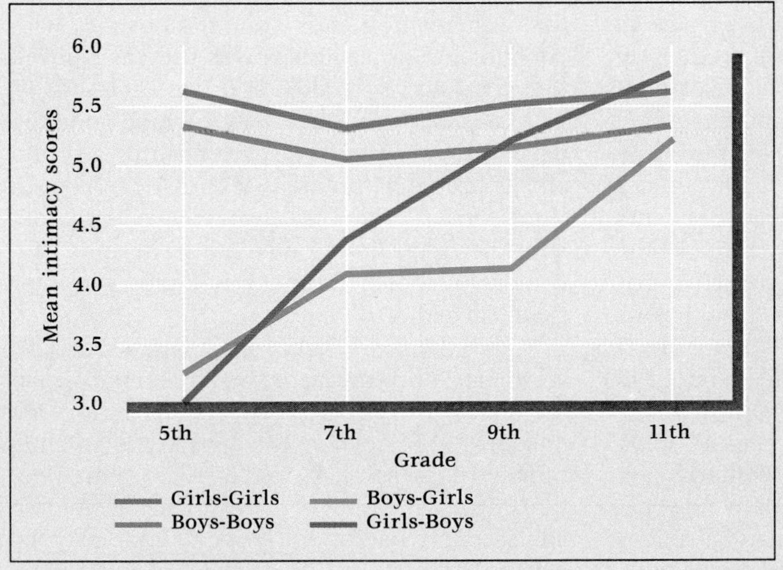

ask what enables some students to adjust to the transition into college and eventually form friendships whereas other students remain lonely.

The results of the UCLA study indicate that the likelihood of overcoming loneliness is strongly related to students' attitudes. Students who remain lonely do many of the same things as students who eventually overcome their loneliness. Both groups are equally likely to go to parties, join clubs, and strike up conversations with strangers in class. Although the groups' behaviors do not differ, their attitudes do. Students who eventually form friendships are more likely to have high initial expectations for their social life and to maintain them even though they may be lonely when they first arrive on campus. In contrast, students who remain lonely are likely to adjust their expectations and lower their initial goals. They are more likely to tell themselves that they do not need friends or that their schoolwork is far more important than their social lives. By rationalizing about their loneliness, they may increase their chances of staying lonely. Research also indicates that lonely individuals are less likely to engage in intimate self-disclosure and are frequently poor judges of how intimate their relationships actually are, often believing that they have achieved more intimacy than they actually have (Rotenberg and Whitney, 1992).

College counselors can help lonely students overcome their feelings, not only by teaching them how to be more socially assertive but also by helping them to change their beliefs and expectations about social relationships. It may not be sufficient, for example, simply to encourage lonely students to join campus organizations or to participate in activities that are likely to bring them into contact with potential friends. Even though they may get out and meet people, the pessimistic attitudes that many lonely students have in social situations may impede their social adjustment.

RECAP

A transition from one school to another often disrupts adolescents' intimate social networks. As a result, loneliness tends to increase during the adolescent years and is quite common in the early years of college. Research indicates that relatively few high school friendships and romances survive the transition into college.

OPPOSITE-SEX RELATIONSHIPS

Dating and Romantic Relationships

Opposite-sex relationships during middle and late adolescence may play an important role in furthering the development of intimacy, although there are surprisingly few studies of how adolescents are affected by their boyfriends or girlfriends. Sullivan believed that establishing intimate relationships with peers of the opposite sex was the chief developmental task of middle and late adolescence. The capacity for intimacy, which initially develops out of same-sex friendships, eventually is brought into cross-sex relationships. In some senses, then, Sullivan viewed relationships between boyfriends and girlfriends as a context in which intimacy is *expressed* rather than learned.

Some theorists have speculated that this view may be more accurate for females than for males. In American society, boys are not encouraged to develop the capacity to be emotionally expressive, particularly in their relationships with other males. During middle adolescence, as we have seen, girls may be better than boys at certain types of intimacy—self-disclosure and interpersonal understand-

The capacity for intimacy, which initially develops out of same-sex friendships, eventually is brought into opposite-sex relationships. Relationships between boyfriends and girlfriends more often than not are contexts in which intimacy is expressed rather than learned. (Richard Hutchings/Photo Researchers)

ing, for example. Girls, therefore, are more likely than boys upon entering a relationship to be capable of being intimate and eager for emotional closeness. Some studies of early sexual relationships confirm this idea: For adolescent girls, early sexual relationships are far more likely to involve love, emotional involvement, and intimacy. For this reason, some writers have suggested that girls play an important role in teaching boys how to be more open, more sensitive, and more caring (Simon and Gagnon, 1969). In other words, whereas for girls cross-sex relationships may provide a context for further *expression* of intimacy, for boys they may provide a context for the further *development* of intimacy. This notion is consistent with the finding, discussed earlier, that opposite-sex relationships may play a more important role in the development of intimacy among boys than among girls, who may develop and experience intimacy earlier with same-sex friends (Buhrmester and Furman, 1987).

There is a big difference between the sort of learning that takes place in a long-term, intimate relationship between two people and the lessons that are learned through casual dating, however. Dating is a well-established social institution in American adolescent life. Today, adolescent girls begin dating around age 12 or 13, and most boys between ages 13 and 14, earlier than was the case in previous decades (McCabe, 1984). Although early maturers begin dating somewhat earlier than late maturers (Simmons and Blyth, 1987), age norms within the adolescents' school are more important in determining the age at which dating begins than is the adolescent's level of physical development. In other words, a physically immature 14-year-old who goes to school where it is expected that 14-year-olds date is more likely to date than a physically mature 14-year-old who lives in a community where dating is typically delayed until 16 (Dornbusch, Carlsmith, Gross, Martin, Jennings, Rosenberg, and Duke, 1981). *Sexual* behavior, however, as we shall see in Chapter 11, is more strongly influenced by biological development (Udry, Billy, Morris, Gruff, and Raj, 1985). By the age of 16, more than 90 percent of adolescents of both sexes have had at least one date, and, during the later years of high school, more than half of all students average one or more dates weekly. Only 15 percent of high school students date less than once a month. About 75 percent of high school students have been steadily involved with someone else by the end of high school (Dickenson, 1975; Feiring, 1993).

Given the prevalence of dating among contemporary adolescents, it is almost embarrassing to say that we know very little about the impact or significance of dating relationships for adolescent development (Savin-

Williams and Berndt, 1990). In particular, the role of dating in the development of intimacy is not at all clear. Some young people—especially boys—may learn how to be more intimate through dating. But for the majority of young people, dating appears more likely to foster superficiality, rather than self-disclosure; shallow sociability, rather than genuineness; and the avoidance of real closeness (Douvan and Adelson, 1966). All in all, "pseudointimacy" is as likely an outcome of dating as is intimacy. It is not until late adolescence that dating relationships begin to be characterized by a level of emotional depth and maturity that can be described as intimate and not until late adolescence that individuals develop genuine attachments to individuals other than their parents (Douvan and Adelson, 1966; Hazan, 1994). Over the course of adolescence, the importance of one's romantic partner—relative to other relationships—increases, and, by college, individuals typically name their romantic partner first on a list of significant others (up from fourth in grade 7 and third in grade 10) (Furman and Wehner, in press).

"Dating" can mean a variety of different things, of course, from group activities that bring males and females together (without much actual contact between the sexes); to group dates, in which a group of boys and girls go out jointly (and spend part of the time in couples and part of the time in large groups); to casual dating in couples; to serious involvement with a steady boyfriend or girlfriend. Generally speaking, casual socializing with opposite-sex peers and experiences in a mixed-sex social network generally occur before the development of romantic relationships (Connolly and Johnson, 1993). As a consequence, more adolescents have experience in mixed-sex group activities like parties or dances than dating, and more have experience in dating than in having a serious boyfriend or girlfriend (Tobin-Richards, 1985).

There are also age and sex differences in what adolescents look for in a romantic partner: During middle adolescence, boys are more likely to mention physical attractiveness and girls are more likely to mention interpersonal qualities, such as support or intimacy. By late adolescence, however, both sexes emphasize interpersonal qualities, and the ingredients of a satisfying relationship are very similar for males and females (and quite similar to those mentioned by adults): passion, communication, commitment, emotional support, and togetherness (Feiring, 1993; Levesque, 1993). Interestingly, adolescents' satisfaction with their romantic relationships are not as negatively affected by such qualities as conflict or possessiveness as is the case among adults (Levesque, 1993).

There is some evidence that, especially for girls, it may be important to differentiate between group versus couple activities in examining the impact of dating on adolescents' psychological development. Participating in mixed-sex activity in group situations—going to parties or dances, for example—may have a positive impact on the psychological well-being of young adolescent girls, while serious dating in couples may have a more negative effect (Tobin-Richards, 1985). The reasons for this are not entirely clear, but researchers believe that pressures on girls to engage in sexual activity when they are out alone on dates or involved with a steady boyfriend may have a negative impact on their mental health (Simmons and Blyth, 1987). Although boys may feel peer pressure to become sexually active, this may be a very different sort of pressure—with very different consequences—from what girls feel. Because boys generally begin dating at a later age than girls—and date people who are younger rather than older—beginning to date in couples may be less anxiety-provoking for boys, who have the advantage of a few additional years of "maturity."

Given the generally high level of superficiality operating in most adolescents' dating relationships, it comes as no surprise that early and intensive dating—for example, becoming "seriously involved" before age 15—has a somewhat stunting effect on interpersonal development. This is probably true for both sexes, but researchers have focused primarily on girls, because boys are less likely to begin serious dating quite so early. Compared with their peers, girls who begin serious dating early are less mature socially, less imaginative, and more superficial (Douvan and Adelson, 1966). (Interestingly, in one study, the most frequently mentioned negative aspect of romantic relationships was "too much commitment" [Feiring, 1993].) In addition, adolescents of different ages date for different reasons—younger adolescents are more likely than older ones to date because it enhances their own status (Roscoe et al., 1987).

This is not to say that dating is not a valuable interpersonal experience for the adolescent. Adolescent girls who do not date at all show signs of retarded social development, excessive dependency on their parents, and feelings of insecurity (Douvan and Adelson, 1966), and adolescents who date and go to parties regularly are more popular, have a stronger self-image, and report greater acceptance by their friends (Connolly and Johnson, 1993; Long, 1989; Tobin-Richards, 1985). It is not clear, of course, whether a moderate degree of dating *leads* to higher levels of social development or whether more socially advanced and confident adolescents are simply more likely to date and go to parties. Nonetheless, it does seem that for girls, in particular, *early and intensive involvement* with a boyfriend may do more harm than good. All in all, a moderate degree of dating—and delaying serious involvement until middle adolescence—appears to be the most potentially valuable pattern. Perhaps adolescents need more time to develop the capacity to be intimate through same-sex friendships and less pressured group activities before they enter intensively into the more highly ritualized and not very intimate relationships that are encouraged through dating.

We also know that adolescents behave in a variety of ways within dating relationships and that these patterns of behavior may be learned at home. One recent study, for example, looked at the relationship between the type of conflict behavior that adolescents saw their parents engage in, the level of conflict they experienced with their parents, and the type of conflict behavior the adolescents engaged in with their dating partners (Martin, 1990). In general, adolescents' ways of dealing with conflict in their romantic relationships were linked to the models they had been exposed to at home, especially for daughters. For example, girls who had witnessed a great deal of conflict between their parents reported higher levels of verbal aggression, physical aggression, and relationship difficulties with their boyfriends. This study, along with those discussed earlier about adolescent attachment, suggest that variations in adolescents' romantic relationships may have their origins—at least in part—in the adolescents' family experiences.

Dating plays a very different role in adolescents' lives today than it did in previous times (Gordon and Miller, 1984). In earlier eras, dating during adolescence was a part of the process of courtship and mate selection: Individuals would date in order to ready themselves for marriage, and they would "play the field" before settling down. As you will see in the next section, during the mid-1950s, the *average* age at first marriage in the United States was 20 among women and 22 among men—which means that substantial numbers of individuals were marrying during their late adolescent years. Because of this, in the mid-1950s dating during the high school years was clearly a prelude to settling down.

Now, however, the average age at which people marry is considerably later—nearly 25 for women and nearly 27 for men (Holmes, 1994). This, of course, gives high school dating a whole new meaning, since it is clearly divorced from its courtship function. One sign of this is that, over the past two decades, dating appears to have become more informal, less competitive, and less rigidly structured by traditional sex-role stereotypes (Miller and Gordon, 1986). Adolescent dating is now an end in itself, especially for the majority of young people who are headed toward college (Long, 1989; McCabe, 1984). All in all, most adolescents date because it is fun—although what constitutes "fun" varies from one adolescent to the next: In one high school newspaper, one girl was quoted as saying that her "favorite way to have a good time is going to church or to Bible study and praising the Lord," while a male classmate of hers said that one of his "favorite ways to have a good time is to go out to eat with my girlfriend, stop at the store to get a couple of beers, and go back to my house to make sweet, beautiful love when nobody is there" (Glenbard East Echo, 1984, pp. 90–91).

RECAP

Despite the fact that almost all adolescents date by the time they are 16, far less is known about the nature and consequences of romantic relationships during adolescence than about adolescent friendships. Because the age at which individuals marry has become considerably later over the past half-century, dating during adolescence has lost its significance for courtship. In general, social activities with the opposite sex begin in early adolescence as group activities that bring males and females together, proceed to casual dating in couples, and, later in adolescence, progress to serious involvement with a steady romantic partner. A moderate degree of dating, without any serious involvement until late in adolescence, is associated with better mental health and well-being than either early, intense dating or no dating at all.

Breaking Up

As is the case with friendships during the move from high school to college, young people are likely to report dissatisfaction with their high school romances during this transition as well. In one study, which followed a sample of students from the summer before their first year in college through the first three semesters of college, about one-half of all high school romances ended, and those that did not end became much less satisfying when one of the partners began college. Males were far more likely than females to report feeling lonely and dissatisfied with their older relationships (Shaver et al., 1985).

The evidence, then, suggests that high school romances are not especially durable. Are the prospects any better for dating relationships that are formed during college? Although it is now nearly twenty years old, the best data on this issue come from a study that followed 231 college couples in the Boston area over a period of two years (Hill, Rubin, and Peplau, 1979). Questionnaires covering a wide range of psychological and social topics were completed by both members of each couple several times over the course of the study. By the end of the two-year period, 103 couples (45 percent of the original group) had broken up; the average amount of time that these relationships had lasted was 16 months.

On the basis of the questionnaires completed at the beginning of the study, could the breakups have been predicted in advance? According to the results of this study, a variety of factors considered together could significantly predict which relationships would eventually break up and which ones would remain intact. Couples who remained together reported higher levels of intimacy and love to begin with, were equally committed to each other (rather than one person's being significantly more involved than the other), and were highly similar on such characteristics as age, educational plans, SAT scores, and physical attractiveness. Similarity of attitudes, religion, and social class (as assessed by parents' education levels) were not good predictors of staying together.

Breakups were most likely to occur at three times of the year, reflecting the sensitivity of students' social relationships to the school calendar: May–June, September, and December–January. Evidently, having to make vacation plans, changes in living arrangements, and changes in school plans prompt many couples to reevaluate the status of their relationship.

As the authors point out, there are two sides to every breakup. Although, in the majority of cases, it was possible to identify a "breaker-upper" and a "broken-up-with"—in the sense of who was primarily responsible for ending things—couples did not always agree on who wanted to end the relationship: Respondents were biased toward saying that "they themselves, rather than their partners, were the ones who wanted to break up." Moreover, members of a couple often had different perceptions of why the relationship ended. The factors typically mentioned were boredom, differences in interests, and the woman's desire to be independent. Less often mentioned was that one of the partners had a romantic interest in someone else.

Contrary to beliefs about women being more romantic than men, this and previous studies provide some evidence that men fall in love more readily than women and that women fall out of love more easily than men. For example, it was more often the woman who ended the relationship, frequently because she had become the less involved partner. And rejected men took breaking up harder than did rejected women—they often could not reconcile themselves to the fact that they were no longer loved and that the relationship had ended. Men also found it more difficult than women to stay friends after the relationship ended.

Incidentally, although the song says that "breaking up is hard to do," it is harder on the person being broken up with: "Breaker-uppers" feel considerably less depressed, less lonely, and happier—albeit guiltier—even one year after the breakup.

Adolescent Marriage and Divorce

Most Americans marry for the first time in their middle twenties, with men, on the average, marrying at a somewhat later age than women. In 1993, the median age at first marriage was 26.5 for men and 24.5 for women—the oldest it has been in more than 100 years (Holmes, 1994). Generally, from the late 1950s on, and particularly during the past twenty years, the average age at which American men and women first marry has risen steadily, no doubt reflecting the increasing labor force involvement of young women, the increasing acceptance of cohabitation, higher rates of college enrollment among women, and the increasing availability of contraception (see Figure 10.4). As a consequence, the percentage of married teenagers has diminished substantially in recent decades. In 1960 and 1970, 1 in 10 teenage women was married. In 1986, this had declined to 1 in 20 (Wetzel, 1987).

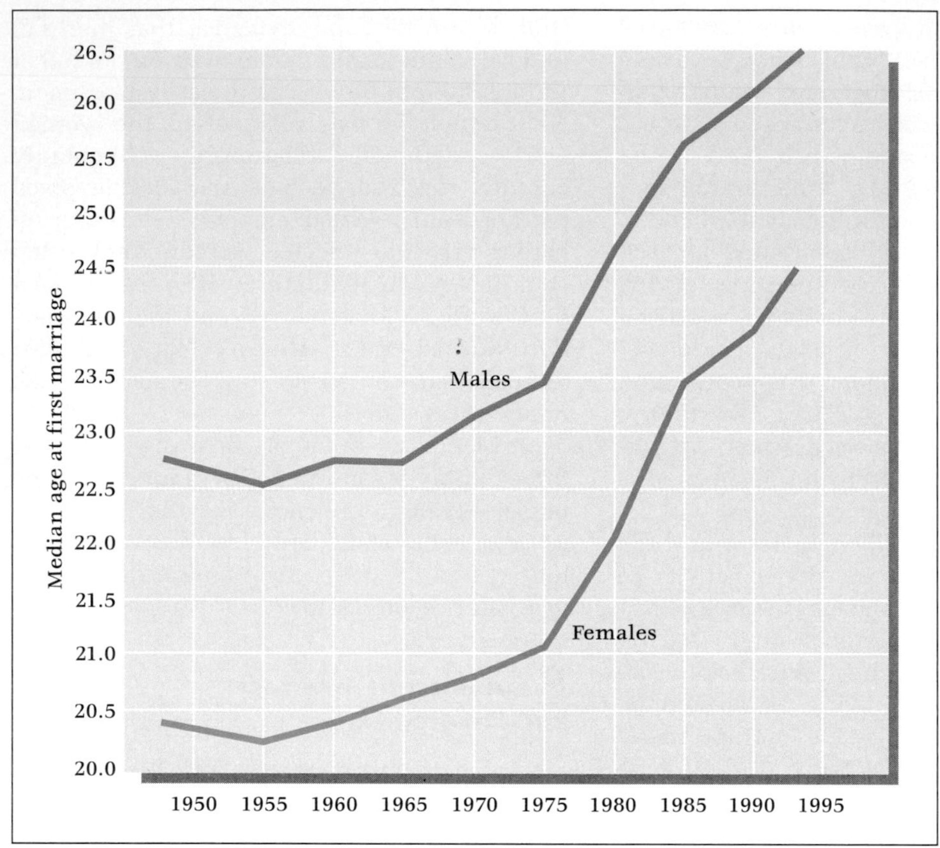

FIGURE 10.4 *First marriage occurs at a much later age today than it did forty years ago.*

The trend toward delayed marriage is probably for the better. The younger people are when they marry, the greater their chances of experiencing marital problems and divorce (Teti, Lamb, and Elster, 1987). Indeed, the divorce rate among men who marry in their teens is three times that of men who marry in their late twenties, and the divorce rate of women who marry before turning 18 is four times that of women who marry in their late twenties (Lewis and Spanier, 1979).

The higher rate of marital instability among the young is not surprising, given the array of other factors often characteristic of early marriage. Teenagers are more likely than adults to marry because of premarital pregnancy (the most common reason for marriage during adolescence); they are more likely to be under economic stress; and they are more likely to have low levels of education and, therefore, poor job prospects. (Teti et al., 1987). On several counts, teenagers who marry are likely to begin married life with problems that require a tremendous degree of coping and that, consequently, do not bode well for marital success. Premarital pregnancy, economic stress, and low levels of education are associated with higher divorce rates at all ages. In other words, teenagers' marriages are more likely to end in divorce because teenagers who marry are more likely to have the problems that lead to divorce among couples of all ages.

Not all adolescents who marry get divorced, of course. Adequate financial resources, a long-standing relationship before marriage, having completed high school, and delaying pregnancy until at least one year into married life are among the factors most predictive of marital success. Not surprisingly, these same factors—education, income, long engagement, and delayed childbearing—are also highly predictive of marital success among adults.

RECAP

The average age at which individuals marry has increased considerably since 1955, and, as a consequence, teenage marriage is quite uncommon today. Overall, the trend toward later marriage is a positive one, since marriage during adolescence is associated with a greater risk for marital unhappiness and for divorce. Among teenagers who do marry, having adequate financial resources, a long-standing relationship before marriage, completing high school, and delaying pregnancy are all predictive of marital success.

KEY TERMS

Adult Attachment Interview
anxious-resistant attachment
anxious-avoidant attachment
attachment
homophobia
identity versus identity diffusion
internal working model
intimacy
intimacy versus isolation
need for intimacy
need for integration into adult society
need for sexual contact
need for intimacy with a peer of the opposite sex
Q-Sort
secure attachment
social support

FOR FURTHER READING

Kobak, R., and Cole, H. (1994). Attachment and meta-monitoring: Implications for adolescent autonomy and psychopathology. In D. Cicchetti and S. Toth (Eds.), *Rochester symposium on developmental psychopathology,* Vol. 5: *Disorders and dysfunctions of the self.* Rochester, N.Y.: University of Rochester Press. A thoughtful demonstration of the application of attachment theory to the study of adolescent development.

Montemayor, R. (Ed.). (in press). *Advances in adolescent development,* Vol. 3: *Relationships in adolescence.* Newbury Park, Calif.: Sage. A collection of articles on the nature and function of various types of relationships in adolescence.

Savin-Williams, R., and Berndt, T. (1990). Friendship and peer relations. Pp. 277–307 in S. Feldman and G. Elliott (Eds.), *At the threshold: The developing adolescent.* Cambridge, Mass.: Harvard University Press. A review of the literature on friendship and intimacy during adolescence.

Sullivan, H. S. (1953a). *The interpersonal theory of psychiatry.* New York: Norton. Sullivan's most extensive statement of his theory of interpersonal development.

Youniss, J., and Smollar, J. (1985). *Adolescent relations with mothers, fathers, and friends.* Chicago: University of Chicago Press. A study of the different roles played by mothers, fathers, and friends in the development of the adolescent.

CHAPTER 11

SEXUALITY

(Perlstein/Jerrican/Photo Researchers)

Have teenagers' attitudes towards sex changed in recent decades? Should society be worried about sexual activity among young adolescents, or is teenage sex no more troublesome than many of the other adult-like activities that young people engage in? Does sex education prevent unwanted pregnancies, or does it encourage young people to begin sexual activity earlier? Should adolescents have access to contraceptives, and, if so, should their parents be told? Have adolescents changed their sexual behavior in response to the threat of AIDS?

In this chapter, we examine adolescent sexuality in contemporary society with an eye toward dedramatizing and demystifying an aspect of adolescent behavior that has received a great deal more media attention than systematic research investigation. In order to present a more accurate picture of adolescent sexuality, we will need to step back and look at sexual behavior and development during adolescence in context—in the context of society and how it has changed, and in the context of adolescence as a period in the life cycle and how *it* has changed.

SEXUALITY AS AN ADOLESCENT ISSUE

Like other aspects of psychosocial development, sexuality is not an entirely new issue that surfaces for the first time during adolescence. Young children are curious about their sex organs and at a very early age derive pleasure (if not what adults would label orgasm) from genital stimulation—as both Sigmund Freud and the famous sex researcher Alfred Kinsey pointed out long ago (Kinsey, Pomeroy, and Martin, 1948). And, of course, sexual activity and sexual development continue long after adolescence. Although sexual development may be more dramatic and more obvious before adulthood, it by no means ceases at the end of adolescence.

Nonetheless, most of us would agree that adolescence is a fundamentally important time—if not *the* most important time in the life cycle—for the development of sexuality. There are several reasons for this. Perhaps most obvious is the link between adolescent sexuality and puberty. There is an increase in the sex drive in early adolescence as a result of hormonal changes (Udry, 1987). Moreover, it is not until puberty that individuals become capable of sexual reproduction. Before puberty, children are certainly capable of kissing, petting, masturbating, or even having sexual intercourse. But it is not until puberty that males can ejaculate semen or females begin to ovulate, and the fact that pregnancy is a possible outcome of sexual activity changes the nature and meaning of sexual behavior markedly—for the adolescent and for others. What had previously been innocuous sex play becomes serious business when pregnancy is a genuine possibility. Finally, as we saw in Chapter 1, not until puberty do individuals develop the secondary sex characteristics that serve as a basis for sexual attraction and as dramatic indicators that the young person is no longer physically a child.

But the increased importance of sexuality at adolescence is not solely a result of puberty. The cognitive changes of adolescence play a part in the changed nature of sexuality as well. One obvious difference between the sexual play of children and the sexual activity of adolescents is that children are not especially introspective or reflective about sexual behavior. Sex during adolescence is the subject of sometimes painful conjecture ("Will she or won't she?"), decision making ("Should I or shouldn't I?"), hypothetical thinking ("What if he wants to do it tonight?"), and self-conscious concern ("Am I good-looking enough?"). As we saw in Chapter 10, one of the chief tasks of

Although sexuality is undoubtedly an important psychosocial issue during adolescence, sexual concerns do not surface for the first time at this stage in the life span. It is normal for children to be curious about sex and about their sex organs at an early age. (Fredrick D. Bodin/Stock, Boston)

adolescence is to figure out how to deal with sexual desires and how to incorporate sex successfully and appropriately into social relationships. Much of this task is cognitive in nature, and much of it is made possible by the expansion of intellectual abilities that takes place during the period.

In addition to how the physical changes of puberty and the growth of sophisticated thinking capabilities influence sexuality during adolescence, the new social meaning given to sexual and dating behavior at this time in the life cycle makes sexuality an especially important psychosocial concern. As we shall see, the main influences on adolescents' sexual behavior are social, not biological.

You may have played "doctor" with your friends when you were a little child, but—as you well know—the game meant something quite different then from what it would if you were to play it now. Although younger children may engage in sex play, and although even infants may experience sexual arousal, it is not until adolescence that sexual activity begins to take on the social meaning it will continue to have throughout adulthood. With all due respect to Freud and Kinsey, one must place the sex play of children in proper perspective. Indeed, Sullivan (1953a), whom you read about in Chapter 10, believed that sex play before adolescence had more to do with simple curiosity than with true sexuality. Adolescence is a turning point in the development of sexuality because it marks the onset of deliberate sexually motivated behavior that is recognized, both by oneself and by others, as primarily and explicitly sexual in nature.

According to two experts, there are four distinct developmental challenges concerning sexuality in adolescence (Brooks-Gunn and Paikoff, 1993). First, the adolescent needs to come to feel comfortable with his or her maturing body—its shape, size, and attractiveness. Second, the individual should accept having feelings of sexual arousal as normal and appropriate. Third, healthy sexual development in adolescence involves feeling comfortable about choosing to engage in—or choosing *not* to engage in—various sexual activities; that is, healthy sexual development involves understanding that sex is a voluntary activity for oneself and for one's partner. Finally, healthy sexual development, at least for those who are sexually active, includes understanding and practicing safe sex—sex that avoids pregnancy and sexually transmitted diseases.

RECAP

Adolescence is a fundamentally important time in the life cycle for the development of sexuality, reflecting the physical and hormonal changes of puberty, the increased capacity for the individual to understand and think about sexual feelings, and the new social meaning given to sexual behavior by society and its institutions. Four developmental challenges of adolescence are accepting one's changing body, accepting one's feelings of sexual arousal, understanding that sexual activity is voluntary, and practicing safe sex.

HOW SEXUALLY PERMISSIVE IS CONTEMPORARY SOCIETY?

It is impossible to understand sexuality as a psychosocial phenomenon without taking into account the social milieu in which adolescents learn about and first experience sexuality. Although we tend to think of sex as something that adolescents are inevitably anxious or concerned about, it is no more true to suggest that sexuality is always riddled with problems during adolescence than it is to say that all adolescents have problems in establishing a sense of identity or in developing a sense of autonomy. Like any other aspect of psychosocial growth, the development of sexuality is determined largely by its context. Of particular importance is the way in which adolescents and children are exposed to and educated about sexuality—a process called **sexual socialization.**

When did you first learn about sex? How much were you exposed to as a child? Was it something that was treated casually around your house or something that had an air of mystery to it? Was your transition into adult sexual activity gradual or abrupt?

As you know from previous chapters, the passage of adolescents into adulthood is believed to be easier and less stressful when transitions between the two eras are gradual, or continuous (Benedict, 1934). One aspect of the adolescent passage that anthropologists have examined extensively from this perspective is the transition of young people into adult sexual roles. In *Patterns of Culture* (1934), Ruth Benedict observed that anxiety about sex—which was thought to be common among teenagers in contemporary society—was absent in many traditional cultures. Margaret Mead's observations of young people in Samoa and New Guinea (1928/1978) provided evidence that sexual development during adolescence was calm, not stressful, in societies where sexual experimentation was treated openly and casually during childhood and where special attention was not drawn to the adolescent's changed sexual status.

Think about some of the things you learned gradually and casually as a child—learning your way around the kitchen, for example—and imagine how different things would have been had this learning been handled the way most families handle sexual socialization. Suppose that early in your childhood your parents had treated cooking food as though the activity had special, mysterious significance. Suppose that you had never been permitted to see anyone actually cooking food, that you had been prohibited from seeing movies in which people cooked food, and that you had been excluded from any discussions of cooking. Nevertheless, imagine that you knew that something went on in the kitchen and that there was some special activity that adults did there which you would be permitted, even expected, to do when you grew up. Perhaps you even overheard other kids at school talking about cooking, but you still weren't sure just what the activity was or what one was supposed to do (or not do). Imagine how confused and ambivalent and anxious you would feel.

In some respects, this is how many families in contemporary society handle sexual socialization. By being so secretive about sex when children are young and so worried about it when they are adolescents, Mead and Benedict argued, contemporary societies may have turned sexuality into a problem for young people.

Mead's and Benedict's observations of sexual socialization in traditional societies also indicated that cultures vary considerably in the ways in which they handle the sexual development of children and adolescents. Their observations were further borne out in *Patterns of Sexual Behavior* (Ford and Beach, 1951), perhaps the most extensive study to date of sexual behavior in different cultural contexts. In this enormous undertaking, the authors catalogued the sexual socialization and activity of children and adolescents in over two hundred societies. Drawing on hundreds of studies undertaken by cultural anthropologists over the years, Ford and Beach categorized societies into three groups: restrictive societies, semirestrictive societies, and permissive societies.

Sexual Socialization in Restrictive Societies

In **restrictive societies,** the adolescent's transition into adult sexual activity is highly discontinuous. Pressure is exerted on youngsters to refrain from sexual activity until they either have undergone a formal rite of passage or have married. In many restrictive societies,

In restrictive societies, sexual activity before marriage is explicitly discouraged.
(Nickelsberg/Gamma-Liaison)

adolescents pursue sex in secrecy. Within the broad category of restrictive societies, of course, there are wide variations in the degree of restrictiveness and in the methods used to discourage sexual activity before marriage. For example, in some societies, the sexual activity of young people is controlled by separating the sexes throughout childhood and adolescence. Boys and girls are not permitted to play together and never associate with each other before marriage in the absence of chaperons. In other societies, sexual activity before the attainment of adult status is restricted through the physical punishment and public shaming of sexually active youngsters (Ford and Beach, 1951).

Sexual Socialization in Semirestrictive Societies

In **semirestrictive societies,** "adult attitudes toward . . . premarital affairs in adolescents are characterized by formal prohibitions that are . . . not very serious and in fact are not enforced" (Ford and Beach, 1951, p. 187). For example, sexual activity among youngsters may be formally prohibited, but children playing together may imitate the sexual behavior of their elders, and unless this play is brought explicitly to the attention of adults, little is done about it. In other semirestrictive societies "premarital promiscuity is common, and the parents do not object as long as the love affairs are kept secret" (Ford and Beach, 1951, p. 187). It is premarital pregnancy, rather than premarital sex, that is objectionable, and unmarried adolescents whose sexual activity has resulted in pregnancy are often forced to marry.

Generally speaking, the sexual socialization of children and adolescents in America and other industrialized societies has followed either a restrictive or a semirestrictive pattern, depending on the particular historical period and social group in question. At the time of the publication of *Patterns of Sexual Behavior* more than four decades ago, Ford and Beach classified America as "restrictive." And some would argue that this classification is still valid today. For the most part, for example, American children are likely to be discouraged from—or even punished for—masturbation; sexual exploration is frowned upon; and sex play is discouraged. Adults rarely mention sexual matters in the presence of children, and there even are regulations prohibiting children from being exposed to sexual activity on television or in the movies. Adults openly try to discourage young people—especially young women—from becoming sexually active by lecturing to them about the virtues of virginity, by not openly discussing matters of sex and pregnancy, and by making it difficult for young people to obtain contraception.

At the same time, however, some aspects of sexual socialization appear to place contemporary America more in the "semirestrictive" category. Adolescent boys and girls are not typically segregated, boys and girls usually date without chaperons present, and premarital sex is not generally punished with public humiliation. Adolescents are encouraged to date, even though adults know that dating provides a context for sexual activity. And it does seem at times as though we attempt only halfheartedly to enforce prohibitions against premarital sexual activity. Many parents are well aware that young people are sexually active, and they prefer to look the other way rather than restrict children's activities.

Sexual Socialization in Permissive Societies

In **permissive societies,** the transition of young people into adult sexual activity is highly continuous and usually begins in childhood. Whether contemporary America is restrictive or semirestrictive may be subject to debate, but by no stretch of the imagination is it a permissive society—at least in comparison with many of the cultures described by Ford and Beach. Consider, for example, these descriptions of sexual socialization in some of the societies they categorized as permissive:

> Among the Pukapukans of Polynesia, where parents simply ignore the sexual activities of young children, boys and girls masturbate freely and openly in public. . . . Young Trobriand children engage in a variety of sexual activities. In the absence of adult control, typical forms of amusement for Trobriand girls and boys include manual and oral stimulation of the genitals and simulated coitus. Young Seniang children publicly simulate adult copulation without being reproved . . . Lesu children playing on the beach give imitations of adult sexual intercourse, and adults in this society regard this to be a natural and normal game. . . . Sexual life begins in earnest among the Trobrianders at six to eight years for girls, ten to twelve for boys. Both sexes receive explicit instruction from older companions whom they imitate in sex activities. . . . At any time a couple may retire to the bush, the bachelor's hut, an isolated yam house, or any other convenient place and there engage in prolonged sexual play with full approval of their parents. (Ford and Beach, 1951, pp. 188–191)

RECAP

Although we tend to think of contemporary industrialized society as being sexually permissive, there are many societies around the world that are far more lenient about sex. By most indications, Americans' attitudes toward adolescent sex are neither restrictive nor permissive—but ambivalent. Many experts believe that the mixed messages adolescents receive about sexuality in the United States contribute to the high incidence of problems such as teenage pregnancy and sexually transmitted diseases.

ADOLESCENTS' SEXUAL ATTITUDES AND BEHAVIOR

Adolescents' Attitudes toward Sex

Most social scientists agree that American adolescents' attitudes toward sex—and toward premarital sex in particular—became more liberal during the late 1960s and 1970s and have become only slightly more conservative since then (Chilman, 1986). But the meaning of this change in attitudes is often misunderstood. Three points must be kept in mind. First, while it is certainly true that teenagers became more tolerant of sexual relations before marriage, it is also true that adults themselves became more permissive of premarital sex during the same time period (Clayton and Bokemeier, 1980). In other words, American society as a whole—not simply young people—changed its views toward sex.

Second, the changes in attitudes toward premarital sex among adolescents during the late 1960s and early 1970s, and the trend toward greater conservatism during the 1980s, cannot be understood apart from many other attitudinal changes that took place during these decades. Although attitudes toward premarital sex changed, many other attitudes also shifted (for example, attitudes toward racial equality and women's rights). Thus trends in sexual attitudes are best understood as a part of a larger attitudinal shift.

Finally, although adolescents become more permissive of premarital intercourse, they did not become proponents of promiscuity, "free love," or casual sex. Being emotionally involved, rather than being legally married, became the important criterion for judging the acceptability of sexual involvement. It is important to keep in mind, however, that adolescents as a group are as varied in their attitudes toward sex as adults are (Katchadourian, 1990).

Although young people have become more permissive over the past three decades, adolescents clearly do not favor sexual promiscuity or sexual exploitation. Surveys indicate that the majority of adolescents believe that openness, honesty, and fidelity are important elements of a sexual relationship. Although an adolescent may have a series of sexual partners over a period of time, he or she is likely to be monogamous within each relationship, a pattern known as **serial monogamy.**

Another important trend in young people's changing attitudes toward sex has been the decline in popularity of the double standard. In past eras, many people believed that premarital sex was permissible for men but not for women. But most adolescents today believe that males and females should follow the same standards for premarital sexual behavior (Ferrell, Tolone, and Walsh, 1977; King, Balswick, and Robinson, 1977). This shift toward a single standard of sexual conduct, which began during the late 1960s and accelerated during the early 1970s, was related, no doubt, to other large-scale attitudinal shifts in matters related to women's rights and sexual equality. Although the double standard has waned, it has not disappeared: Aggressive sexual behavior is still more accepted among adolescent males than females (Goodchilds and Zellman, 1984).

It appears, then, that what has taken place—not only in sexual values and attitudes, but across a range of topics—has been a shift away from conformity to institutionalized norms and toward a perspective that places greater emphasis on the individual's personal judgment and values (Conger, 1975). Television sitcoms and parents' concerns to the contrary, today's adolescents are neither preoccupied with sex nor anxious about it. Indeed, as we shall see, being sexually active during adolescence—and being comfortable about it—has become part of the normal adolescent experience.

RECAP

Important changes in attitudes toward adolescent premarital sex occurred during the 1970s and have continued since that time. Most teenagers today believe that it is acceptable to have intercourse before marriage as long as it takes place within the context of a loving, intimate relationship. Another important trend in young people's changing attitudes toward sex has been the decline in acceptance of the double standard.

Sexual Activity during Adolescence

Because of the controversies surrounding premarital intercourse, most of the research conducted into the sexual behavior of adolescents has focused on this single activity. Although this is undoubtedly an important topic of concern, it is also wise to remember that a good deal of the sexual activity of adolescents—even sexually experienced adolescents—involves activities other than sexual intercourse, such as necking and petting. Moreover, because most individuals do not begin their sexual experiences with intercourse but progress toward it through stages of gradually increasing intimacy, it is important to view intercourse as one activity in a long progression, rather than as an isolated behavior (Brooks-Gunn and Paikoff, 1993).

Stages of Sexual Activity. Most adolescents' first experience with sex falls into the category of **autoerotic behavior**—sexual behavior that is experienced alone (Katchadourian, 1990). The most common autoerotic activities reported by adolescents are having erotic fantasies (about three-quarters of all teenagers report having sexual fantasies, mainly about television figures or movie stars) and masturbation (reported by about half of all adolescent boys and one-fourth of all adolescent girls) (Koch, 1993). In addition, many boys have wet dreams, or **nocturnal orgasms,** during adolescence, although they generally are infrequent (Katchadourian, 1990).

By the time most adolescents have reached high school, they have "crossed the line from autoerotic to sociosexual behaviors" (Katchadourian, 1990, p. 335). **Sociosexual behaviors** are those involving another person. Interestingly, the developmental progression of sexual behaviors, from less intimate to more intimate, has not changed very much over the past thirty-five years, and the sequence in which males and females engage in various sexual activities is remarkably similar. Necking and petting above the waist occur earlier than genital touching through clothing, which occurs before direct genital contact, which in turn occurs earlier than intercourse or oral sex. There is some evidence that teenagers are engaging in oral sex at an earlier age today than in the past, and among adolescents oral sex is actually more common than intercourse (Newcomer and Udry, 1985). Although boys engage in these activities at a somewhat earlier age than girls, the similarities in age of first experience and in prevalence are far more striking than the differences between genders.

There is some evidence that the orderly progression of sexual activity described above is more common among white adolescents than among African-Americans, however (Smith and Udry, 1985). White adolescents are likely to follow a more predictable pattern that includes more petting and takes longer to move toward intercourse. African-Americans, in contrast, are more likely to move toward intercourse at an earlier age and without as many intervening steps. This difference has an important implication for our understanding of adolescent pregnancy. Virtually all adolescents who are virgins find themselves unprepared for contraception when they begin necking, but the more gradual progression of sexual activity among whites is less likely to be affected by this lack of preparation than is the case among African-Americans. Faster progression of sexual activity may place young African-American adolescents at greater risk for pregnancy.

● ***Premarital Intercourse during Adolescence.*** Estimates of the prevalence of premarital intercourse among contemporary adolescents vary considerably from study to study, depending on the nature of the sample surveyed, the year and region in which the study was undertaken, and the reliability of the data gathered. Some studies suggest that adolescents do not always report their sexual activity honestly or accurately, with males tending to overstate their level of activity and females tending to understate it (Alexander, Somerfield, Ensminger, Johnson, and Kim, 1993; Newcomer and Udry, 1988). Nevertheless, the following paragraph summarizes what social scientists have concluded.

Overall, about 12 percent of boys and 6 percent of girls report having intercourse by age 13 (Katchadourian, 1990). There are vast regional and ethnic differences in the prevalence of sexual activity during the junior high school years, however. For example, although only 12 percent of white males are sexually active by this age, 19 percent of Hispanic males and 42 percent of African-American males are (Hayes, 1987). The comparable figures for girls are 5 percent, 4 percent, and 10 percent, respectively. There are also large regional differences in the prevalence of early sexual intercourse, with sexual activity occurring earlier in rural and inner-city communities than in the suburbs. One study, for example, found that more than half of all eighth-graders living in rural Maryland reported having had sexual intercourse—about twice the rate found in studies of nationwide samples of adolescents from this age group (Alexander, Ensminger, Kim, Smith, Johnson, and Dolan, 1989). In this study of rural youth, and in studies of inner-city Baltimore teenagers (e.g., Zabin, et al., 1986b), about 85 percent of African-American 14-year-old males reported having had sexual intercourse.

Although these regional and ethnic variations make it difficult—if not misleading—to generalize about the "average" age at which American adolescents initiate sexual intercourse, national surveys of young people indicate that far more adolescents are sexually active at an earlier age today than in the recent past (Brooks-Gunn and Paikoff, 1993). (One recent study of San Francisco youth found that one-fifth of the adolescents surveyed were sexually active by eighth grade [Millstein, Irwin, Adler, Cohn, Kegeles, and Dolcini, 1992]). The best estimates we have are that, by age 15, about one-third of boys and 25 percent of girls have had intercourse; by age 19, the percentages of sexually experienced individuals are 86 percent among boys and 80 percent among girls (see Figure 11.1) (Miller and Moore, 1990). Whatever one feels about these figures, one conclusion is inescapable: Sexual intercourse during high school is now a part of the normative experience of adolescence in America.

As you can see from Figure 11.2, however, there are substantial ethnic differences in age of sexual initiation. African-American adolescents are more likely to begin sexual activity earlier than other adolescents and to progress toward intercourse more quickly. This is readily apparent from Figure 11.2, which shows the cumulative percentage of sexually active adolescents at each age, separately for white, African-American, and Hispanic youth. These data indicate that African-American adolescents are much more likely to have had sexual intercourse at each age, and that ethnic differences in the ages at which sex

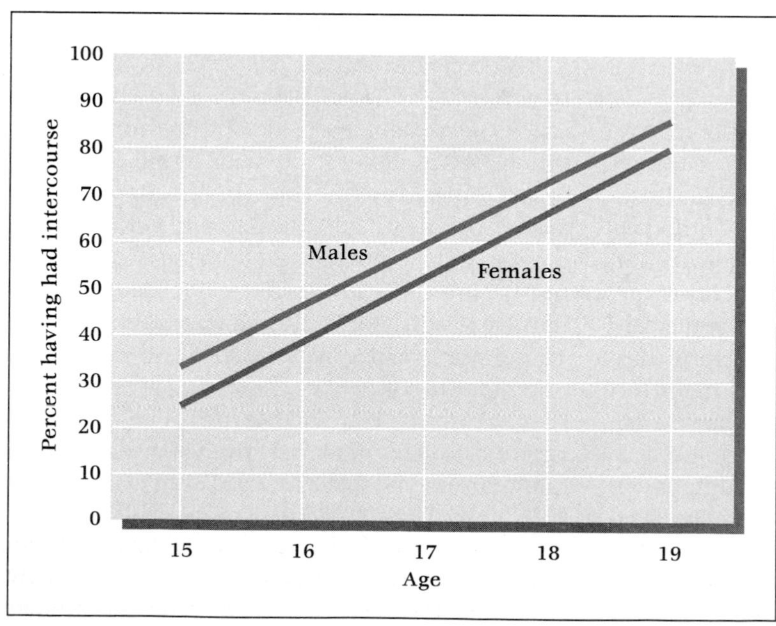

FIGURE 11.1 *About one-third of all American males and one-fourth of American females have had sexual intercourse by age 15. By age 19, the vast majority of males and females are sexually experienced.*
(Miller and Moore, 1990)

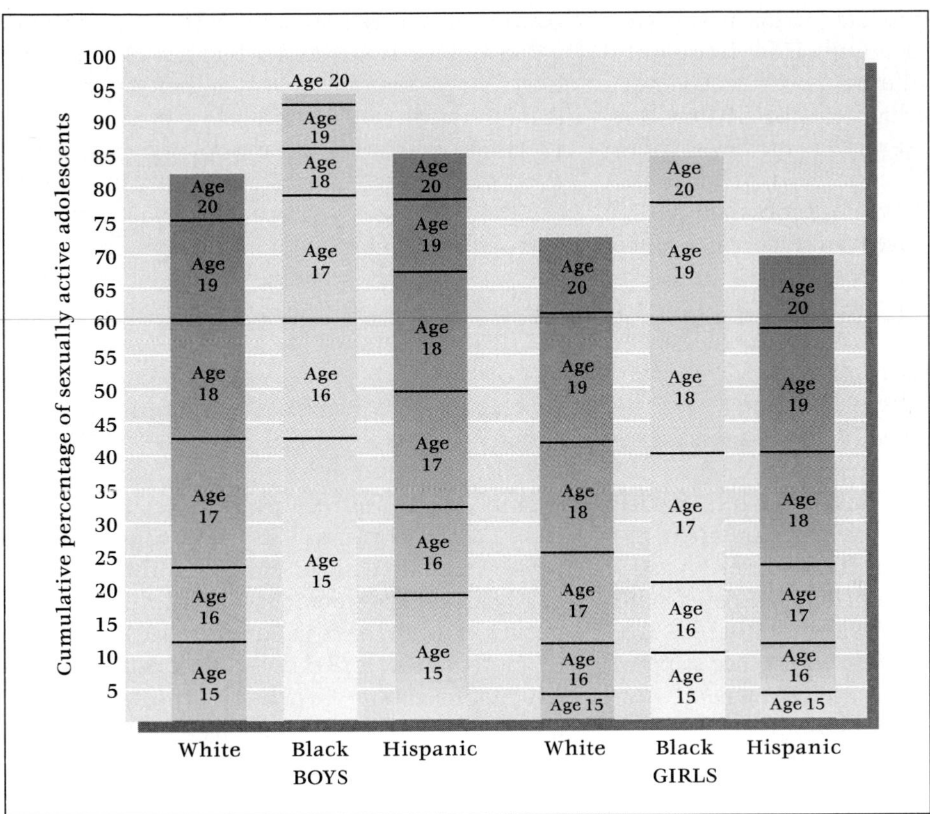

FIGURE 11.2 *This chart shows the cumulative percentage of sexually active adolescents at various ages, by sex and ethnicity.* (Hayes, 1987)

begins are most dramatic early in adolescence. One reason for the relatively high rate of early sexual activity of African-American adolescents is the higher proportion of black youth who grow up in single-parent homes and in poor neighborhoods, both of which, as you will read later in this chapter, are risk factors for early sexual activity (Lauritsen, 1994). In general, Mexican-American youngsters who were born in Mexico are less likely to be sexually active at an early age than are their counterparts who are American-born, reflecting differences in norms between the two countries (Aneshensel, Becerra, Fielder, and Schuler, 1990). Studies also indicate that, among all ethnic groups, rates of sexual activity are higher among economically disadvantaged youth. Interestingly, early sexual activity is more common among African-American youth attending all-black schools than among their peers in integrated schools (Furstenberg, Morgan, and Allison, 1987), indicating the importance of the social context in which teenagers live as an influence on their sexual behavior.

There is a large difference, of course, between having intercourse once and being sexually active on a regular basis—a distinction that seems to get lost in discussions of sexual activity among youth. How frequently do teenagers have intercourse? The average sexually experienced high school girl has sexual intercourse between two and three times each month. However, about 15 percent of the high school–aged girls who report having had sexual intercourse have done so only once (Zelnick, Kantner, and Ford, 1981). Interestingly, although African-American youngsters generally begin sexual activity at an earlier age than their peers, sexually active African-American teenagers have intercourse less frequently than other sexually active adolescents (Hayes, 1987).

Most teenagers who have had intercourse have had only one sexual partner; about 20 percent have had four or more different partners; and about 10 percent have had sex with six or more partners (Miller and Moore, 1990; Washington Post, 1994). As with other aspects of sexual behavior, there are ethnic and gender variations in the number of sexual partners adolescents report having had: Black males are more than twice as likely as white males to have had six or more partners; black females and white females are about equally likely to have had multiple partners, however (Miller and Moore, 1990).

● ***Changes in Patterns of Adolescent Premarital Intercourse over Time.*** We noted earlier that attitudes toward premarital intercourse during adolescence became more liberal during the mid-1960s and became especially so during the early 1970s. Not surprisingly, accompanying this shift in attitudes was an equally noteworthy shift in the prevalence of adolescent premarital sex. The major changes have not been in behaviors such as necking and petting but in the incidence and prevalence of intercourse among teenagers (Vener and Stewart, 1974). Presumably, teenagers have long distinguished between intercourse and other sexual activities in their values and actions, and what has shifted during the past three decades has been their stance specifically toward intercourse.

Three trends are of special interest. First, the overall percentage of American adolescents—of all ages—who have engaged in premarital sex accelerated markedly during the early 1970s but stabilized somewhat during the 1980s (Hayes, 1987; Ventura, 1984). For example, the proportion of high school youth who have had premarital intercourse rose from about 20 percent before the mid-1960s, to about 35 percent during the early 1970s, to approximately 50 percent in the late 1970s, to slightly more than 50 percent today (Hayes, 1987; Katchadourian, 1990; Washington Post, 1994). Among college students, the increase has been equally notable, but it occurred primarily during the period from 1966 to 1973, when the prevalence rate rose from about 40 percent to about 75 percent; changes in the prevalence of premarital sex among college students since then have been less dramatic (Dreyer, 1982).

Second, the median age at which adolescents first engage in intercourse has declined. For example, in 1971, the average age at first intercourse was 16.4 years. By 1976, this had declined to 16.1 years, and it is slightly lower today, with nearly one-third of adolescents having intercourse for the first time before age 15 (Scales, 1991). As we shall see in a later section, these figures are important to consider in discussions of sex education, because they indicate that programs which do not begin until the later years of high school are probably too late for a substantial number of young people.

Finally, the greatest increase in the prevalence of premarital intercourse has been among females. Before 1965, there were substantial gaps between the proportions of sexually active boys and girls. As Figure 11.3

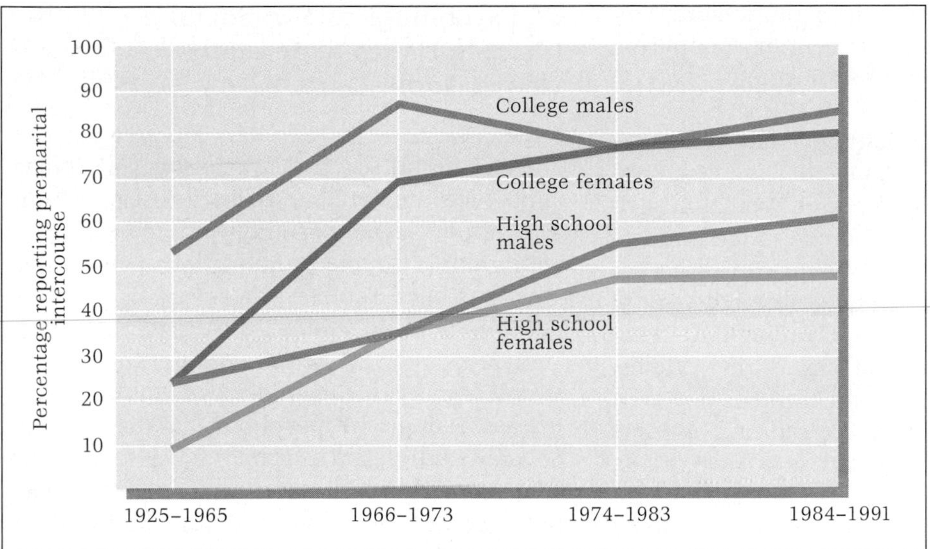

FIGURE 11.3 *Changes in the percentage of high school and college males and females who have experienced sexual intercourse in four historical eras.* (Derived from Dreyer, 1982; Hayes, 1987; Vrazzo, 1990; and Washington Post, 1994)

shows, since about 1965 the proportion of sexually experienced high school males has nearly tripled, but the proportion of sexually experienced high school females is nearly five times higher today than thirty years ago. Among college students, the proportion of males who have had premarital intercourse has increased by 60 percent since 1965; among females, the increase has been greater than 300 percent. As you can see from the figure, sex differences in rates of premarital intercourse today—among high school or college youth—are not large at all.

A similar, though less dramatic, picture of change emerges when we look at the prevalence of premarital intercourse among African-American versus white teenage women. Between 1971 and 1976, the prevalence of premarital intercourse among African-American 15- to 19-year-old females increased by 19 percent. But during this same time period, there was a 41 percent increase in the proportion of sexually experienced white girls of the same age (Zelnick et al., 1981). Between 1976 and 1982, however, the percentage of sexually experienced African-American 15- to 19-year-olds declined, while the comparable percentage among white teenagers continued to increase. Thus rates of premarital intercourse in different subgroups of American adolescents have converged with the passing of time.

● ***Adolescent Sexual Behavior in Perspective.*** Whether adults approve or not, then, sexual activity has become a part of the normal American teenager's life. However, although many parents, educators, and other adults are alarmed and concerned about sexual activity among the young, for most adolescents, sexual involvement is accompanied by affection, emotional involvement, and commitment to a relationship. By no stretch of the imagination can the majority of today's young people be described as promiscuous or morally lax in matters of sex.

Although it is interesting to speculate on the causes of these changes in adolescents' sexual behavior—the increased availability of the birth control pill, the overall liberalization of social attitudes, and the earlier age of puberty have all been suggested—the more pressing issue is how society ought to react to the changed nature of sex during adolescence. Premarital sex is not limited to males, to minority youngsters, or to adolescents with emotional problems. It is a part of life for the *average* teenager. The longer we ignore this—by failing to provide adequate sex education, by limiting the accessibility of effective contraception, and by not dealing with the issue squarely—the more difficulties society, and young people in particular, will face.

RECAP

Sexual intercourse, once delayed until early adulthood, is clearly now a part of the typical adolescent's experience. More than half of all teenagers have sexual intercourse before graduating from high school, although there are wide ethnic and regional differences in the age of onset of sexual activity. In general, African-American adolescents are more likely to begin sexual activity earlier than other adolescents and to progress toward intercourse more quickly. The most dramatic change during the past two decades in the incidence of premarital sex has been among white females, however. Over the past twenty-five years, rates of premarital intercourse in different subgroups of American adolescents have converged.

Psychological and Social Characteristics of Sexually Active Adolescents

For many years, researchers studied the psychological and social characteristics of adolescents who engaged in premarital sex with the assumption that sexually active teenagers were more troubled than their peers. This view has been replaced as sexual activity has become more prevalent.

Indeed, several recent studies show that sexual activity during adolescence is decidedly *not* associated with psychological disturbance. Several studies, for example, have shown that adolescents who become sexually active earlier than their peers have levels of self-esteem and life satisfaction similar to the levels of other adolescents (Billy, Landale, Grady, and Zimmerle, 1988; Bingham and Crockett, 1994; Jessor, Costa, Jessor, and Donovan, 1983). Another study indicated that unmarried girls who became pregnant were more likely to have high self-esteem and strong feelings of efficacy, rather than the reverse (Robbins, Kaplan, and Martin, 1985). Thus, both the prejudice that only "troubled" adolescents have sex and the belief that sexual activity during adolescence leads to later psychological disturbance are false.

It does seem to be the case, however, that *early* sexual activity (i.e., having intercourse before age 16) is associated with a more general attitudinal and behavioral profile that includes experimentation with drugs and alcohol, a low level of religious involvement, tolerance of deviant behavior, a lower interest in academic achievement, and a higher orientation toward independence (Miller and Moore, 1990). Although many studies have found this link between early sexual activity and minor deviance, the nature of the causal chain is not entirely clear. Some studies show that involvement in minor deviance (especially alcohol and drug use) precedes early involvement with sex (Rosenbaum and Kandel, 1990). Others show that deviance follows earlier sexual activity (Elliott and Morse, 1989). And still others suggest that experimentation with deviant activity and early sex occur simultaneously and may reflect some common underlying factor (e.g., Dorius, Heaton, and Steffen, 1993; Orr, Beiter, and Ingersoll, 1991; Rowe, Rodgers, Meseck-Bushey, and St. John, 1989). As you will read in Chapter 13, many (but not all) experts believe that a more general inclination toward problem behavior is behind an overarching pattern that combines minor delinquency, precocious sex, disengagement from school, and drug and alcohol use. It is important to bear in mind, however, that studies of adolescents who become sexually active *after* age 16 do not find major differences between these youth and their virginal counterparts. One consistent finding that has emerged from research, however, is that young adolescents who are sexually active are less likely than older teenagers to protect themselves against pregnancy and sexually transmitted diseases.

Researchers also have asked whether adolescents who become sexually active earlier than their peers have different family histories than other adolescents. Studies generally have not supported the widely held view that vigilant monitoring by parents and open communication between parents and children have a strong impact on adolescent sexual behavior (Casper, 1990; Moore, Peterson, and Furstenberg, 1986; Newcomer and Udry, 1984; but see Small and Luster, 1994). Adolescents whose parents keep close tabs on them or who discuss sex with them are neither more nor less likely to be sexually active (Miller and Moore, 1990). Not surprisingly, the effect of parent-child communication about sex on adolescent sexual behavior depends on who is doing the communicating and what is being communicated. Communication between adolescents (both boys and girls) and their mothers about sex is associated with less sexual activity, but communication between fathers and sons about sex is associated with *increased* sexual activity—presumably because fathers tacitly encourage their sons to become sexually active (Brooks-Gunn and Furstenberg, 1989). Not surprisingly, parental attitudes may make a difference, especially for girls: Among girls with liberal parents, talking about sex is associated with more sexual activity; this is not true among girls with conservative parents, however (Fisher, 1989).

Overall, however, most studies find that the impact of parent-adolescent communication on adolescent's sexual behavior is very small, especially compared with other factors (Casper, 1990). One family factor that does appear to make a difference, however—especially for girls—is household composition. In general, adolescents whose parents are in the process of divorcing as well as girls who live in single-parent households—regardless of when (or if) a divorce took place—are more likely to be sexually active than their peers (Crockett and Bingham, 1994; Flewelling and Bauman, 1990; Miller and Bingham, 1989; Miller and Moore, 1990; Newcomer and Udry, 1987). One hypothesis, consistent with what we saw in Chapter 4 about the family, is that parental divorce temporarily disrupts the adolescent's behavior, leading him or her into early involvement with drugs, alcohol, and minor delinquency, which, according to some studies, increases the likelihood of sex.

But why should growing up in a single-parent home affect girls' sexual behavior more than that of boys? At least three possibilities exist. One is that social influences on girls' sexual behavior are in general stronger and more varied than are the influences on boys' behavior. Boys' parents may not attempt to exert great control over their sexual activity, regardless of whether the household has one parent or two. Consequently, boys from one- and two-parent homes may be equally likely to be sexually active. Girls' sexual behavior, in contrast, may be more subject to parents' controls. Single-parent homes are typically more permissive than two-parent homes (Dornbusch, Carlsmith, Bushwall, Ritter, Leiderman, Hastorf, and Gross, 1985), and this difference in control may be enough to make a difference in girls' sexual activity.

An alternative possibility is that single-parent mothers are more likely to be dating than married mothers and, in so doing, may inadvertently be role models of sexual activity to their adolescents (Miller and Moore, 1990). To the extent that this modeling effect is stronger between parents and children of the same sex, we would expect to find a more powerful effect of growing up in a single-parent home on the sexual behavior of daughters than sons. Yet a third possibility is that girls are more likely than boys to respond to problems at home by turning outside the family for alternative sources of warmth and support; if their family environment is not satisfying, girls (whether in divorced homes or not) may be more likely than boys to seek the affection and attention of a romantic partner (Whitbeck, Hoyt, Miller, and Kao, 1992).

Other studies have examined the influence of people other than parents on adolescents' sexual behavior—in particular, the influence of peers and siblings. Generally speaking, adolescents are more likely to be sexually active when their peers are (DiBlasio and Benda, 1992; East, Felice, and Morgan, 1993; Udry, 1987); when they *believe* that their friends are sexually active, whether or not their friends actually are, (Brooks-Gunn and Furstenberg, 1989); and when they have older siblings who model more sexually advanced behavior (East et al., 1993; Rodgers and Rowe, 1988). There are age and ethnic differences in the relative importance of parental and peer influence, however. As one would expect, peers become increasingly more influential with age (Treboux and Busch-Rossnagel, 1990). In addition, African-American adolescents report relatively less familial influence over their sexual behavior than do white adolescents, whereas Hispanic adolescents report relatively more (Scott and Owen, 1990).

Peer influences on adolescents' sexual activity appear to operate in two different, but compatible, ways. First, when an adolescent's peers are sexually active, they establish a normative standard that having sex is acceptable (Dornbusch et al., 1981; Furstenberg et al., 1987; Miller and Moore, 1990). Interestingly, one of the reasons that minor drug use may lead to earlier involvement in sexual activity is that drug use may lead an adolescent to form friendships with a different group of friends, a group that is sexually more permissive (Whitbeck, Conger, Simons, and Kao, 1993).

Second, peers influence each other's sexual behavior directly, either through communication among friends ("You haven't done it *yet*! What's the matter with you?") or, more commonly, between potential sex partners. Along these lines, several studies show that sexual activity spreads within a community of adolescents much like an "epidemic," with sexually experienced adolescents initiating their less experienced partners into increasingly more advanced sex (Rodgers and Rowe, 1993). Once they become sexually experienced, previously inexperienced adolescents then "infect" other adolescents in turn. Over time, then, the percentage of sexually experienced adolescents within a community grows and grows.

Finally, several studies have examined the role of the broader environment in influencing adolescent sexual behavior. Adolescents growing up in poor neighborhoods, for example, are more likely to engage in early sexual activity than adolescents from more affluent communities (Brewster, Billy, and Grady, 1993; Brooks-Gunn, Duncan, Klebanov, and Sealand, 1993; Crane, 1991). When adolescents grow up in poverty, they may see little hope for the future, and they therefore may be more likely to risk their occupational and economic future by becoming sexually active (Lauritsen, 1994). To a young person who believes that the chances of getting a good job are slim, an early pregnancy does not seem as costly as it might seem to someone who hopes to complete high school, attend college, and secure a good job. Studies also show that adolescents who watch a lot of sexually oriented television are themselves more likely to be sexually active, although it is not clear whether television viewing leads to sexual activity or vice versa (Brown and Newcomer, 1991).

RECAP

Sexual activity during adolescence does not carry the psychological risks that many adults associate with it. In general, adolescents who are sexually active have psychological profiles that are similar to, rather than different from, their nonactive peers. There is evidence, however, that early sexual activity (having intercourse before age 16) is more common among teenagers growing up in single-parent households and is associated with higher rates of problem behaviors, such as drug and alcohol use. Adolescent sexual behavior is influenced not only by the family but also by peers, siblings, and forces in the broader community.

Sex Differences in the Meaning of Sex

Any discussion of the psychosocial significance of sexual experience during adolescence must be sensitive to the very substantial sex differences in the way in which early sexual activity is experienced. Despite the convergence of males' and females' *rates* of sexual activity, the early sexual experiences of adolescent boys and girls are usually very different in nature and, as a consequence, are imbued with very different *meanings* (Brooks-Gunn and Paikoff, 1993). In other words, the sexual behavior of males and females may be similar, but the sexual socialization of males and females is quite different.

As noted earlier, the typical adolescent boy's first sexual experience is in early adolescence, through masturbation (Gagnon, 1972). At the outset, then, the sexual socialization of the adolescent boy typically places sex outside of an interpersonal context. Before adolescent boys begin dating, they have generally already experienced orgasm and know how to arouse themselves sexually. For males, the development of sexuality during adolescence revolves around efforts to integrate the capacity to form close relationships into an already-existing sense of sexual capability.

Yet, at the time of first intercourse, boys are likely to keep matters of sex and intimacy separate. Boys often have as their first partner someone they describe as a "casual date" (Carns, 1973). Generally, it is the male partner of a couple who is likely to initiate sex, and, interestingly, the typical male reports more love for a woman who lost her virginity with him than for a woman who lost her virginity with a previous partner. His own loss of virginity, however, has no impact on his feelings of affection in a relationship (Peplau, Rubin, and Hill, 1977). These findings suggest that the early sexual experiences of males are often interpreted not in terms of intimacy and emotional involvement but in terms of recreation (Hendrick and Hendrick, 1994). And males typically report that the people to whom they describe their first sexual liaison—generally, male peers—are overwhelmingly approving (Carns, 1973; Miller and Simon, 1980). It is little surprise, when looked at in light of these findings, that the most common immediate reactions among adolescent males

THE INFLUENCES OF HORMONES AND FRIENDS ON ADOLESCENT SEXUAL BEHAVIOR

We noted earlier that increased interest in sex at adolescence is likely to have both biological and social causes. Specifically, adolescents are thought to become interested in sex in part because of increases in sex hormones at puberty and in part because sexual activity becomes accepted—even encouraged—in their peer group. But is one set of factors more important than the other? One recent series of studies, by J. Richard Udry and his colleagues (Smith, Udry, and Morris, 1985; Udry, 1987; Udry, Talbert, and Morris, 1986), suggests that a fuller understanding of adolescent sexual behavior necessitates looking at biological and social influences in interaction rather than at either set of influences alone. However, the way in which hormones and friends interact to influence sexual behavior appears to be different for males than for females.

According to Udry's studies, boys' and girls' initial interest in sex is influenced primarily by the surge in certain hormones—**testosterone,** to be specific—at puberty. Adolescents with higher levels of **androgens** (testosterone is an androgen) are more likely than their peers to report masturbating, thinking about sex, and planning to have sexual intercourse within the next year. This hormonal change appears to increase adolescents' interest in sex and in their arousal when exposed to sexual stimuli.

Motivation to have sex is one thing; becoming sexually active is another. How important is the rise in testosterone levels at puberty in determining the onset of sexual intercourse? The answer appears to differ in boys and girls. Among boys, but not girls, the increased level of androgens is directly related to the likelihood of their being sexually active. Younger boys who are more mature biologically are more likely to be sexually active than older boys whose hormone levels are lower. Boys' sexual behavior is not entirely dependent on their hormone levels, however. Boys who are more popular with girls in their school are more likely to initiate sex early than are boys who are less popular with girls. Although there is also some evidence that boys whose friends are sexually active are themselves more likely to be involved in sex, this seems more to do with the influence of hormones than with the influence of friends: Boys tend to have friends who are at a similar level of pubertal development and who therefore are likely to have similar testosterone levels and rates of sexual activity. All in all, the evidence provided in Udry's studies indicates a very strong biological influence on the sexual behavior of adolescent boys.

As you know from the discussion in Chapter 1 concerning biological development during ado-

to having intercourse for the first time are excitement, satisfaction, exhilaration, and happiness (Gordon and Gilgun, 1987; Oswald, Bahne, and Feder, 1994; Sorensen, 1973).

The typical girl's first experience is likely to be very different and likely to leave her feeling very differently as well. Although the majority of adolescent girls masturbate, masturbation is a far less prevalent activity among girls than among boys, and it is far less regularly practiced. Thus the typical adolescent girl, in contrast to the typical boy, is more likely to experience sex for the first time with another person. For her, the development of sexuality involves the integration of sexual activity into an existing capacity for intimacy lescence, androgens, including testosterone, contribute to increases in boys' sex drive as well as to the development of secondary sex characteristics like facial hair. Because of this, it is difficult to determine whether increases in androgens lead to increased sexual activity because of the increased sex drive (which may make boys with higher testosterone levels want to have sex more) or because of changes in their physical appearance (which may make them more attractive to girls). In girls, however, although androgens are responsible for increases in the sex drive, a different set of hormones—**estrogens**—is primarily responsible for changes in appearance, including breast development, and for changes in females' receptivity to males' sexual advances. Because of this, it is possible to study whether the increased interest in sex among girls after puberty is more influenced by increases in their sex drive or by changes in their receptivity and physical appearance (both of which, presumably, influence their sexual attractiveness to boys). Thus far, the answer appears to point mostly to the impact of estrogen on girls' receptivity to boys' sexual overtures (Udry, Halpern, and Campbell, 1991).

Despite these effects of hormones on girls' sexual behavior, though, Udry's studies show that social factors are far more important in influencing girls' involvement in sexual intercourse than boys', especially among white girls (Udry and Billy, 1987). Although increases in androgens lead to increased interest in sex among girls, whether this interest is translated into behavior depends on the social environment. Among girls with high levels of androgens, those who have sexually permissive attitudes and friends who are sexually active are more likely to engage in intercourse. But girls whose social environment is less encouraging of sex—even girls with high levels of androgens—are unlikely to be sexually active. In other words, whereas hormones seem to have a direct and powerful effect on the sexual behavior of boys, the impact of hormones on the sexual behavior of girls seems to depend on the social context in which they live.

To what can we attribute this sex difference? Udry hypothesizes that boys develop in an environment that is more uniformly tolerant and encouraging of sexual behavior than girls do. In this environment, all that boys need to become sexually active is the jolt which the increase in androgens provides. For girls, however, the environment is more varied. Some girls develop within a context that permits or even encourages sexual activity; others do not. Although the increase in androgens also provides a jolt to the sexual motivation of the adolescent girl, if she develops within a context that places social controls on sexual activity, this hormonal awakening will not be translated into sexual experience.

and emotional involvement. The girl's sexual script is one that, from the outset, tinges sex with romance, love, friendship, and intimacy (Aitken and Chaplin, 1990; Hendrick and Hendrick, 1994).

Boys and girls also encounter very different social attitudes about sex: Society still is much more discouraging of sexual activity outside the context of emotional involvement among adolescent girls than boys (Goodchilds and Zellman, 1984; Gordon and Gilgun, 1987). Because of the possibility of pregnancy, the potential adverse consequences of premarital sexual activity are far more serious for girls than for boys. For this reason, society monitors the sexual activity of girls more carefully,

There are substantial gender differences in the way in which early sexual activity is experienced psychologically. For adolescent boys, early sexual relationships are often brief, impersonal, and associated with a sense of achievement. (Rick Smolan/Stock, Boston)

and girls are more likely to be encouraged to approach sex cautiously (Rosenthal, 1994). Girls' feelings of sexual desire—which may be just as strong as boys'—are "tempered by their knowledge that girls are not supposed to be sexual or that if they are, they will be marked as bad and unlovable" (Tolman, 1993, p. 4).

Not surprisingly, then, at the time of first intercourse, the adolescent girl's first sexual partner is likely to be a person she describes as someone she was "in love with" at the time (Kallen and Stephenson, 1982). There is a social meaning to losing one's virginity that is still today very different for young women and for young men, and women typically report feeling more love for a man if he was their first sexual partner (Peplau et al., 1977). After having intercourse for the first time, the typical adolescent girl is more likely to encounter disapproval or mixed feelings on the part of others in whom she confides (generally speaking, peers) than is the typical boy (Carns, 1973). And she is likely to report feeling afraid, guilty, and worried, as well as happy or excited about the experience (Gordon and Gilgun, 1987; Oswald et al., 1994; Sorensen, 1973). For the adolescent girl, then, early sexual experience is more tied to emotional involvement and, more often than not, is complicated by fears of becoming pregnant (Gordon and Gilgun, 1987). Although young women are more likely today than they were twenty years ago to admit to their friends that they have lost their virginity soon after the event has occurred, boys still are more likely than girls to tell their friends soon after having intercourse for the first time because it is easier to do so when the act has not been accompanied by emotional involvement (Kallen and Stephenson, 1982).

RECAP

Any discussion of the psychological aspects of adolescent sexuality must differentiate between the experiences of males and females. Early sexuality for males is tinged with elements of recreation, whereas for females it is more linked to feelings of intimacy and closeness. Because of the risks of pregnancy, adolescent girls are more likely than boys to be socialized to view sex with caution and are therefore more likely to feel ambivalent, rather than uniformly positive, about engaging in sex.

Homosexuality during Adolescence

Much discussion about homosexuality during adolescence is muddied with confusion and misinformation about the nature and antecedents of homosexuality. In attempting to separate fact from myth, we need to keep in mind several important distinctions.

First, there is an important distinction between engaging in homosexual activity or having homosexual feelings, on the one hand, and having an exclusive and enduring preference for sexual activity with people of the same sex, on the other. It is not uncommon, for example, for young adolescents to engage in sex play with members of the same sex or to have questions about the nature of their feelings for same-sex peers. Indeed, one study indicated that, by age 16, over 20 percent of adolescent boys had engaged in homosexual activity to the point of orgasm (Kinsey, Pomeroy, and Martin, 1948). But even though many adolescents have such homosexual experiences, nearly all young people—over 90 percent, in fact—develop an exclusive preference for heterosexual relationships by the end of adolescence. And contrary to myths about the increasing prevalence of homosexuality in contemporary American society, the proportion has remained at or near this level since the mid-1940s, when researchers began studying the phenomenon (Hunt, 1974).

A second distinction to be made is the one between homosexuality as an exclusive preference and homosexuality as an interest that may exist simultaneously with strong heterosexual interests. Many people mistakenly view sexual preference as an "either-or" attribute, with individuals being either exclusively heterosexual or exclusively homosexual. In fact, however, of the 8 percent of Americans who do not develop an exclusive preference for heterosexual relationships, only one-third are exclusively homosexual in their orientation. Nearly twice as many describe themselves as bisexual—having both heterosexual *and* homosexual interests (Conger, 1977).

Finally, a great deal of confusion about homosexuality results because people tend to confuse **sexual preference** (the extent to which someone prefers heterosexual activity, homosexual activity, or both), **sex-role behavior** (the extent to which an individual behaves in traditionally "masculine" or "feminine" ways), and **gender identity** (which gender an individual believes he or she is psychologically). There is no connection between an adolescent's sexual preference and his or her sex-role behavior. Individuals with strong, or even exclusive, preferences for homosexual relationships exhibit the same range of masculine and feminine behaviors that is seen among individuals with strong or exclusive heterosexual interests. In other words, exclusively gay men (like exclusively heterosexual men) may act in very masculine, very feminine, or both masculine and feminine ways; and the same holds true for exclusively lesbian and exclusively heterosexual women. Along similar lines, individuals with homosexual interests are generally not confused about their gender identity—or, at least, they are no more confused than are individuals with heterosexual interests.

Studies of the antecedents of homosexuality generally have focused on two sets of factors: biological influences, such as hormones, and social influences, such as the parent-child relationship. More is known about the development of homosexuality among men than among women—the prevalence of homosexuality is much greater among men than among women—but the weight of the evidence thus far suggests that an adolescent's sexual preference is likely to be shaped by a complex interaction of social and biological influences (Green, 1980, 1987; Paul, 1993; Savin-Williams, 1988).

Support for the contention that homosexuality is determined at least partly by biological

THE SCIENTIFIC STUDY OF ADOLESCENCE

RISK FACTORS FOR SEXUAL ACTIVITY

If you keep up with reports on health in the popular media, you have probably heard the term *risk factor* used in discussions of heart disease or cancer. A **risk factor** is an individual or environmental hazard that increases a person's vulnerability to a negative outcome, such as a disease (Werner and Smith, 1982). The presence of a risk factor does not guarantee that the negative outcome will occur, but it increases the probability of the outcome. Thus, someone who smokes cigarettes (a risk factor for lung cancer) will not necessarily develop lung cancer, but the smoker has a higher probability of doing so than a nonsmoker does, all other factors being equal. Risk factors also operate in a cumulative fashion: Individuals who have several risk factors have a greater probability of developing the outcome than do those with only one of the risk factors. For instance, someone with multiple risk factors for cancer (e.g., cigarette smoking, a familial history of cancer, a high-fat diet) has a much greater probability of developing the disease than does a person with only one of the risk factors.

Social scientists have applied cumulative risk factor models to the study of adolescent behavior, asking, for example, which adolescents are at risk for developing substance abuse problems or for contracting AIDS. Such models can be extremely informative when the outcome in question has multiple causes. Instead of searching for *the* cause of drug use, a researcher might acknowledge that drug use is multiply determined and might ask, instead, how a diverse set of potential causes might work together. In so doing, the researcher may be able to discover which adolescents are most at risk for developing the problem (that is, which adolescents have the most risk factors); then preventive interventions can be designed and aimed specifically at the most vulnerable population.

A nice illustration of this approach comes from a recent study of adolescent sexual activity by human ecologists Stephen Small and Tom Luster (1994). **Human ecology** is a branch of social science that is devoted to studying development in context. Thus Small and Luster began their investigation by acknowledging that adolescent sexual activity is multiply determined and is influenced by factors at the individual, familial, and extrafamilial levels (see the accompanying figure). Previous research had shown, for example, that drug use (an individual factor), household composition (a familial factor), and peer norms (an extrafamilial factor) all contribute independently to an adolescent's sexual behavior. But how do these factors operate together? Is an adolescent who uses drugs *and* who comes from a divorced home more at risk for involvement in sexual activity than one who uses drugs *or* who comes from a divorced home?

Small and Luster surveyed a sample of approximately 2,200 adolescents and collected information about their sexual behavior (that is, whether they were sexually experienced or not) and about fourteen factors that were hypothesized to place adolescents at risk for involvement in sexual activity. Among the factors studied were alcohol use, school performance, having a steady boyfriend or girlfriend, parental values, and self-esteem. The researchers then looked at the relation between each of the potential risk factors and sexual activity to see which risk factors were independent predictors of sexual activity. Among the most important predictors of sexual activity were having a steady boyfriend or girlfriend, using alcohol regularly, having parents with permissive values about sex, and being worried about one's future occupational chances. As you read earlier in this chapter, these variables had been found in previous studies to be predictive of adolescent sexual activity. Small and Luster found—also consistent with earlier research (e.g., O'Beirne, 1994; Lauritsen, 1994)—that there were more predictors of girls' sexual activity than of boys'; for instance, not having parental support was a risk factor for females but not for males.

Once the risk factors were identified, Small and Luster gave each adolescent a score of 1 for each factor that was present in his or her life. They then looked to see whether adolescents with higher scores were indeed more likely to be sexually active. The results are presented in the accompanying figure.

As you can see, there is a clear relation between adolescents' sexual behavior and the number of risk factors they report. Among girls, for example, only 1 percent of those with no risk factors were sexually active, in comparison

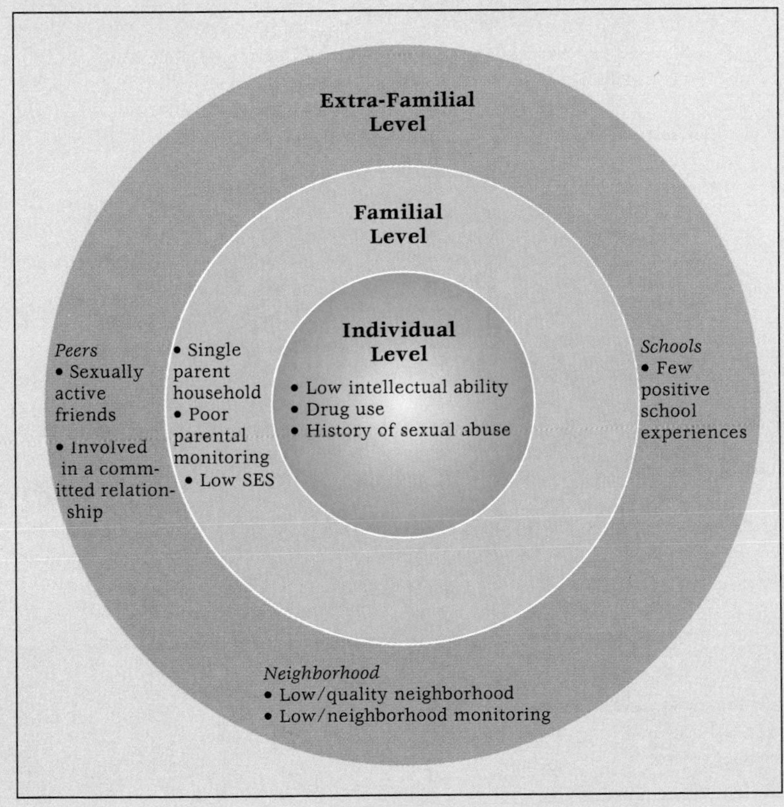

An ecological model of selected risk factors for adolescent sexual activity. (Small and Luster, 1994)

with 22 percent of those with two risk factors, 50 percent with four risk factors, and 80 percent with eight or more risk factors. Among boys, 15 percent of those with no risk factors were sexually active, as opposed to 39 percent of those with one risk factor, 55 percent with two risk factors, and 93 percent with five or more risk factors. The graph shows quite clearly that the percentage of sexually experienced adolescents rises steadily as a function of the number of risk factors present.

What are the implications of these findings? According to the researchers, the most important implication is that efforts aimed at preventing adolescent sexual activity must focus on more than one factor. In their words, "Programs should try to reduce the number of risk factors adolescents are exposed to at various levels of the human ecology, and they need to try to help teens deal successfully with the risks they are exposed to" (Small and Luster, 1994, p. 191).

Source: Small, S., and Luster, T. (1994). Adolescent sexual activity: An ecological, risk-factor approach, *Journal of Marriage and the Family, 56,* 181–192.

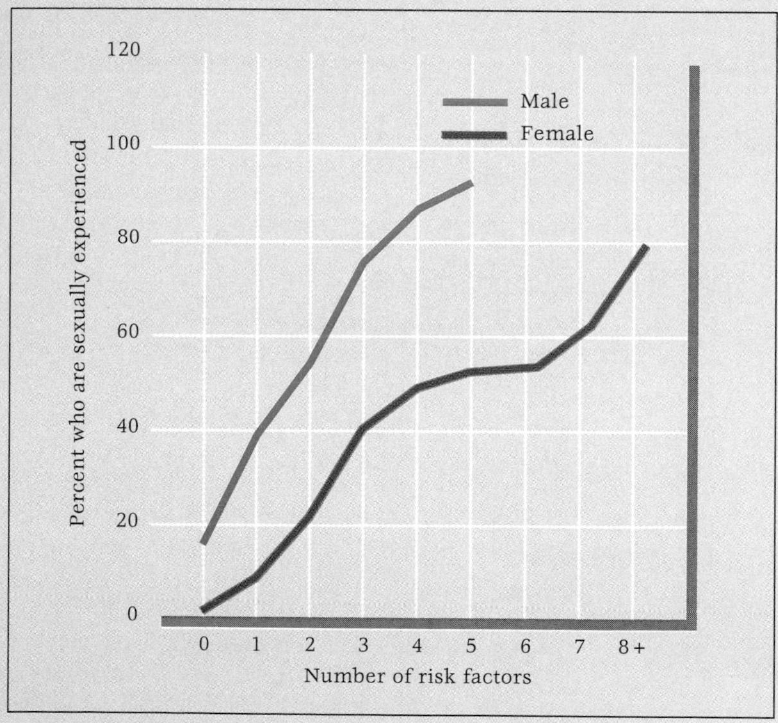

Sexual experience status as a function of number of risk factors.

There is no connection between an adolescent's sexual preference and his or her sex-role behavior. Individuals with strong, or even exclusive, preferences for homosexual relationships exhibit the same range of masculine and feminine behaviors seen among individuals with strong or exclusive heterosexual interests. (Paula Lerner/Woodfin Camp)

factors comes from two sources. You may recall that, in Chapter 1, we drew a distinction between the organizational and the activational roles of hormones on behavior. The hormonal changes of puberty activate sexual behavior, but the particular pattern of sexual behavior that is activated may depend on the way in which hormonal pathways in the brain were organized early in life. There is suggestive evidence that gay and lesbian adults may have been exposed prenatally to certain hormones that, in theory, could affect sexual orientation through their effects on early brain organization (Savin-Williams, 1988). Second, there is some evidence that homosexuality has a strong genetic component, since sexual orientation is more likely to be similar among close relatives than distant relatives and between identical twins than fraternal twins (Savin-Williams, 1988). Although environmental explanations for this similarity cannot be ruled out, chances are that at least some of the predisposition to develop a homosexual orientation is inherited.

One popular theory of biological-environmental interaction is that early biological predispositions may channel some youngsters into patterns of play and social relationships that can lead to the development of homosexuality. Studies suggest that sex hormones may influence preferences for aggressive activities, which, consequently, may be related to preferences for stereotypic masculine or feminine behavior. Thus, for example, boys who are biologically predisposed toward timidity may avoid rough play as young children and gradually may come to prefer activities that are more typical of young girls.

These early behavioral preferences may come to affect the parent-child relationship in ways that increase the likelihood of an individual's developing a homosexual orientation. Several studies suggest that a higher proportion of homosexuals than heterosexuals report having had problems in their early family relationships and, specifically, in their relationship with their father. The stereotype of the homosexual's father as cold and distant once was rejected as an artifact of popular stereotype and poor research designs. But more carefully designed studies have offered at least partial confirmation of this notion. Both gay and lesbian adults are more likely than heterosexuals to describe their fathers as distant and rejecting. Whereas gay men are more likely than heterosexuals to report having had close and generally positive relationships with their mothers, lesbians are more likely than heterosexuals to describe their mothers as cold and unpleasant (Bell, Weinberg, and Hammersmith, 1981).

It is difficult to conclude that these disruptions in the parent-child relationship are the primary cause of homosexuality, however. Researchers now believe that, at least for many gay men, early biologically influenced preferences for feminine behavior may have alienated these boys from their fathers and from other boys and that these youngsters may have grown up seeking the affection from males that they did not receive as children. One recent study, for example, showed that the majority of young boys who behave like girls grow up to be gay adults (Green, 1987). Several other studies also suggest that nonconformity with gender roles during early childhood is an important predictor of adult homosexuality (Bell et al., 1981).

Although these studies point to certain factors that appear more often than not in the early histories of homosexuals, the research evidence does not indicate that *all* individuals who show patterns of gender nonconformity or who have distant relations with their fathers inevitably become homosexual. Nor does research show that all homosexuals have identical developmental histories. For example, although it is true that homosexuals are more likely than heterosexuals to describe their parents in negative terms, not all gay and lesbian individuals feel this way. Indeed, only about half do, suggesting that a large number of homosexuals had quite positive family relationships growing up. And, of course, many heterosexuals describe their parents in exceedingly negative terms. Similarly, although the majority of boys with persistently feminine behavior preferences may grow up to be gay, a substantial number of boys with this preference do not.

Regardless of its origins, it is important to bear in mind that homosexuality is not considered by mental health experts to be a form of psychopathology, an indicator of an underlying psychological disturbance, or a condition warranting psychological treatment. Perhaps as we begin to understand more about the interplay among biological and social factors that contribute to the development of a homosexual orientation, our attitudes toward homosexuality will change for the better. Indeed, as one expert noted, "Society tends to treat . . . homosexuals as if they had a choice about their sexual orientation, when in fact they have no more choice about how they develop than heterosexuals do" (Marmor, quoted in Brody, 1987, p. 17).

Indeed, prejudice and ignorance about homosexuality may cause significant psychological distress for gay and lesbian adolescents, especially if they encounter hostility from those around them. As you know by now, the developmental tasks in the domains of identity, intimacy, and sexuality present formidable challenges for many teenagers. These challenges may be exacerbated for gay and lesbian adolescents, who may be forced to resolve these issues without the same degree of social support as their heterosexual peers. Indeed, a recent review of the literature found that a very substantial number of gay and lesbian adolescents had been harassed, physically abused, or verbally abused by peers or adults while growing up (Savin-Williams, 1994; Telljohann and Price, 1993). Abuse of this sort may account for the relatively higher rates of suicide, substance abuse, running away from home, and school difficulties reported by gay and lesbian adolescents (Savin-Williams, 1994).

RECAP

Approximately 8 percent of the adolescent and young adult population is either partially or exclusively gay or lesbian. Current theories of the origins of homosexuality suggest a complex interaction of genetic and environmental influences. Experts agree that homosexuality is not a form of psychopathology, an indicator of an underlying psychological disturbance, or a condition warranting psychological treatment. Indeed, many difficulties experienced by gay and lesbian youth result from their being harassed by peers and adults.

Rape and Sexual Abuse during Adolescence

Although most research on adolescent sexual activity has focused on voluntary sexual behavior between consenting individuals, there is growing public awareness that a significant minority of teenagers are forced to have sex against their will (Moore, Nord, and Peterson, 1989). This includes adolescents who have been the victims of forcible rape by a stranger, sexual abuse within the family, or **date rape**—when a young person, typically a woman, is forced by a date to have sex against her will. Date rape continues to be a serious problem on college campuses as well as within the younger adolescent population.

Because both perpetrators and victims of sexual assaults are often reluctant to admit their experience, it is difficult to obtain accurate estimates of the numbers of adolescents who have been sexually victimized. We do know that adolescent victims of sexual abuse are disproportionately female and poor (Cappelleri, Eckenrode, and Powers, 1993). According to one team of researchers, however, more than 10 percent of white females, and more than 5 percent of African-American females, report having had nonvoluntary sexual intercourse before age 18 (Moore et al., 1989). Women who were most likely to have been raped during adolescence were those who lived apart from their parents before age 16; who were physically, emotionally, or mentally limited; who were raised at or below the poverty level; or whose parents abused alcohol or used other drugs. Indeed, two-thirds of all women who had three or more of these risk factors were raped as adolescents. In contrast to popular perception, adolescents are abused (sexually, physically, and emotionally) and neglected at a higher rate than are younger children (Cappelleri et al., 1993).

The figures on sexual abuse do not include adolescents who have been forced to engage in sexual activity other than intercourse and, as such, clearly underestimate the proportion of teenagers who have been sexually abused. Other estimates, which include all forms of nonvoluntary sex, however, suggest that about 25 percent of all females and close to 10 percent of all males have been victimized sexually before reaching adulthood (Camarena and Sarigiani, 1994; Nagy, Adcock, and Nagy, 1994).

Several studies have examined the psychological consequences of having been the victim of sexual abuse during adolescence. Adolescents who have been sexually abused show higher than average rates of poor self-esteem, anxiety, fear, and depression (Calverley and Fischer, 1993; Williamson, Borduin, and Howe, 1991); are more likely to engage in risky behavior (Hibbard, Ingersoll, and Orr, 1990; Nagy et al., 1994); and are more likely to become pregnant as teenagers (Butler and Burton, 1990). There is also some evidence that sexual abuse prior to adolescence may lead to precocious (i.e., very early) puberty (Herman-Giddens, Sandler, and Friedman, 1988).

RECAP

A significant minority of teenagers, mainly females, are forced to have sex against their will. Living apart from one's parents, having physical or psychological problems, being raised in poverty, and having parents who abuse alcohol or other drugs are all risk factors for sexual abuse. Adolescents who have been sexually abused show higher than average rates of poor self-esteem, anxiety, fear, and depression; are more likely to engage in risky behavior; and are more likely to become pregnant as teenagers.

Contraceptive Use

One reason for the great concern among adults over the sexual activity of adolescents is the failure of many sexually active young people to use birth control measures regularly. Among late adolescent males, 40 percent reported using either no contraception or an ineffective method (i.e., withdrawing before ejaculating) the first time they had sex (Miller and Moore, 1990). Only half of all young women reported having used some method of birth control regularly during their first year of having intercourse, and nearly one-sixth of all 15- to 19-year-old sexually active women reported never having used any contraception at all (Chilman, 1990; Hayes, 1987). In one large study, 20 percent of 17- to 19-year-old males had not used contraception the last time they had sex (Miller and Moore, 1990). About 40 percent of sexually active teenagers reported using birth control sporadically. Only one-third of sexually active adolescents always used birth control (Hayes, 1987).

Although these figures are worrisome, there has been a clear improvement in adolescent contraceptive behavior during the last decade. In 1976, for example, nearly two-thirds of sexually active young women reported that they had not used contraception during their first intercourse (as opposed to about half today), and more than 35 percent reported never using birth control (as opposed to about 15 percent today). During the late 1980s, partly in response to the threat of AIDS, condom use among older teenagers more than doubled (Miller and Moore, 1990).

Among adolescents who do use contraception, the most popular method by far is the birth control pill, which is used by approximately 60 percent of sexually active teenage girls. About 20 percent of girls report that their partner uses condoms, and an additional 5 percent report using a diaphragm. Withdrawal, a highly ineffective method of preventing pregnancy, unfortunately is still used by a large number of teenagers, as is the rhythm method—a method of birth control that requires more regular menstrual cycling than many teenagers have and more careful monitoring of menstrual cycling than most teenagers are capable of. Other methods, such as the intrauterine device (IUD), are not widely used by teenagers (Hayes, 1987).

Why do so few adolescents use contraception regularly? Social scientists point to several factors. First, for a sizable minority of adolescents, contraceptives are not readily available—or, if they are, young people may not know where to get them. Approximately 15 percent of adolescent girls and 25 percent of adolescent boys reported that they did not use contraceptives when they had sex for the first time because they could not get them (Hayes, 1987). This is likely to be an especially important barrier among younger adolescents, who may feel uncomfortable discussing their sexual activity with parents or other adults whose help or consent may be necessary in order to obtain birth control. Having ready access to a free, confidential family planning service that does not require parents' consent is a strong predictor of whether adolescents will use contraceptives at

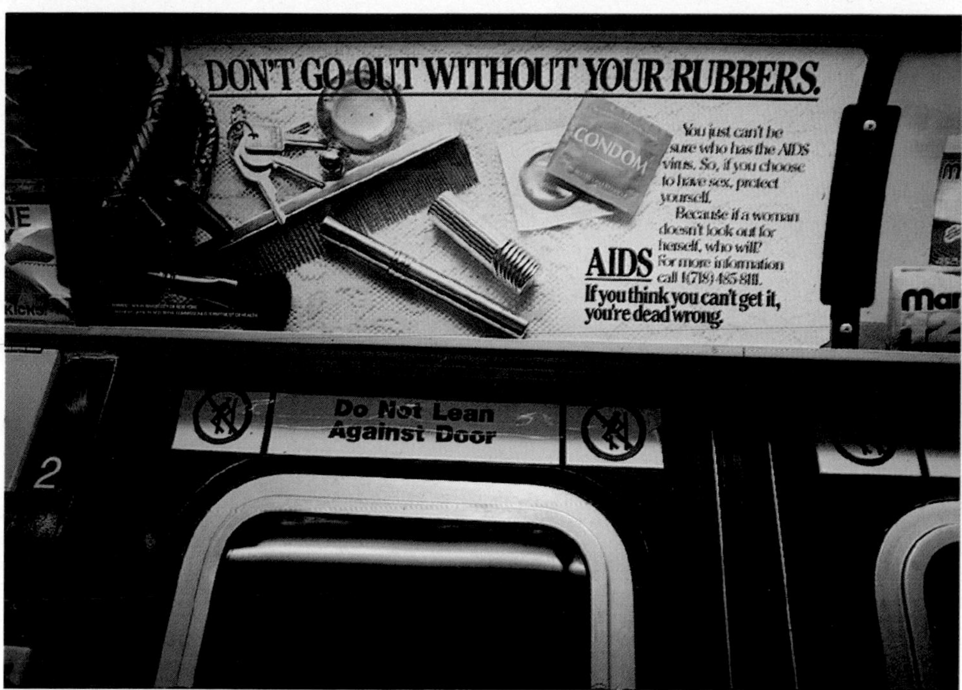

One of the reasons for the great concern of adults over the sexual activity of adolescents is the failure of many sexually active young people to use birth control measures regularly. Forty percent of late adolescent males report having used either no contraception or an ineffective method the first time they had sex. (Goodwin/Monkmeyer)

all or will use them consistently (Brooks-Gunn and Furstenberg, 1989).

Second, many young people are insufficiently educated about sex, contraception, and pregnancy (Trussell, 1989). Many young people do not fully understand that the likelihood of pregnancy varies over the course of a woman's menstrual cycle, and more than half mistakenly believe that it is during menstruation that the risk of pregnancy is greatest (Zelnick and Kantner, 1973). At the time of first intercourse, about one-third of all teenagers who do not use contraception fail to do so because they don't know about contraception or don't think about using contraceptives (Hayes, 1987). Among sexually active teenagers, 20 percent of all girls and more than 40 percent of all boys usually "just trust to luck" that pregnancy will not result from intercourse (Sorensen, 1973). Unfortunately, few sexually active adolescents who fail to use contraception remain lucky for very long.

Psychological factors also play a role in adolescents' failure to use contraception. Many young people do not recognize the seriousness of pregnancy and take the possibility lightly (Hayes, 1987). More than 25 percent of nonusers of contraception report that they or their partners simply did not want to use birth control. From a cognitive perspective, the limited ability of young adolescents to engage in long-term hypothetical thinking, and their occasionally egocentric tendency to believe that they are immune from the forces that affect others, may impede their consideration of pregnancy or a sexually-transmitted disease as a likely outcome of sexual activity. Perhaps most important, many adolescents fail to use birth control because doing so would be tantamount to admitting that they are planfully and willingly sexually active (Miller and Moore, 1990). Going on the pill or purchasing a condom requires an adolescent to acknowledge that he or she is having sexual relations. For many young people, this is an extremely difficult admission to make. This may be especially true for young women who feel ambivalent and guilty about sleeping with someone for the first time. And many teenagers do not anticipate having intercourse (Trussell, 1989).

Given all these reasons, it comes as no surprise to learn that one of the best predictors of contraceptive use is the adolescent's age: Older teenagers are better informed, less guilty about having sex, and better able to see and understand the potential negative consequences of an unwanted pregnancy (Miller and Moore, 1990). It is also important for adolescents to understand the need to use contraception every time they have sex. One recent study found that a very large proportion of teenagers who have had sex with contraception have also had sex *without* contraception (Arnett and Balle-Jensen, 1993).

One recent study nicely illustrates the role that emotional factors play in influencing contraceptive use. Individuals who feel very guilty about having sex are less likely to be sexually active, but when they are, they are also less inclined to use effective contraception—perhaps because their guilt inhibits their ability to plan for sex (Gerrard, 1987). When sexual standards become more permissive, many individuals who would otherwise feel guilty about having sex are drawn into sexual relationships. Unfortunately, their feelings of guilt are not changed by the aura of permissiveness, and, as a consequence, they have sex without using effective contraception. Along these lines, studies indicate that religious adolescents are less likely to be sexually active but also are less likely to use birth control if they do have sex (Studer and Thornton, 1987).

More interesting, perhaps, is research indicating that the rate of adolescent pregnancy is substantially higher in the United States than in other industrialized countries—despite the fact that the rate of teenage sexual activity in the United States is comparable to that in other countries (Jones et al., 1987). For numerous reasons, American teenagers are less likely than their counterparts in other industrialized countries to use contraception *regularly* and effectively (Arnett and Balle-Jensen, 1993). According to one widely cited study, this is because nonmarital sex is portrayed in the United States as "romantic, exciting, and titillating . . . [while] at the same time, young people get the message that good girls should say no" (Jones et al., 1987, p. 239). As yet another expert wrote, "Sex saturates American life—in television programs, movies, and advertisements—yet the media generally fail to communicate responsible attitudes toward sex, with birth control remaining a taboo subject" (Westoff, 1988, p. 254). One result of this set of mixed messages is that the rates of both teenage childbearing and teenage abortion are substantially higher here than in many industrialized nations (Westoff, 1988).

Taken together, this evidence suggests that there is a great deal that adults can do to improve the contraceptive behavior of adolescents. First, adults can see that contraceptives are made accessible to the young people who feel they need them. Second, adults can provide sex education at an early enough age to instruct young people in the fundamentals of contraceptive use before, rather than after, adolescents have become sexually active. Third, parents and teachers can make adolescents feel more free to talk about their sexual interests and concerns, so that young people will be more apt to look at their own behavior seriously and thoughtfully. Finally, the mass media need to portray sex in a more responsible fashion, showing contraception use along with sexual activity. When, for instance, was the last time you saw a couple in a film or on television interrupt sex in order to discuss birth control?

RECAP

Adolescents are infamously poor users of contraception, especially in the United States. Most experts agree that the reasons so few adolescents use birth control regularly are that contraceptives are not as accessible as they might be, that adolescents are insufficiently educated about pregnancy and contraception, that adolescents seldom anticipate having intercourse until they become sexually active on a regular basis, and that using birth control requires the sort of long-term planning that many young people are reluctant or unable to engage in.

TEENAGE PREGNANCY AND CHILDBEARING

The Nature and Extent of the Problem

Given the high rate of sexual activity and poor record of contraceptive use among contemporary adolescents, it comes as little surprise to learn that many young women become pregnant before the end of adolescence. Each year, approximately one million American adolescents become pregnant—the highest rate of teen pregnancy in the industrialized world (Schellenbach, Whitman, and Borkowski, 1992).

Recent statistics indicate that nearly one-fourth of American young women experience pregnancy before the age of 18, and the number increases to about 45 percent before the age of 21. Among black youth, over 40 percent experience pregnancy by age 18 and nearly two-thirds by age 21. These rates are actually slightly lower than they were in the 1970s, not because rates of sexual activity have declined but primarily because of more effective contraceptive use among sexually active teenagers (Furstenberg, Brooks-Gunn, and Chase-Landsdale, 1989; Hayes, 1987). In 1988, however, the rate of teenage childbearing increased, either because of increased sexual activity, decreased use of contraceptives, decreased access to abortion, or some combination of these factors (Barringer, 1990). Indeed, between 1983 and 1993, the rate of childbearing among unwed women (most of whom were teenagers or young adults) soared by 70 percent (Holmes, 1994).

It is important to keep in mind that not all adolescent pregnancies result in childbirth. About 40 percent of all teenage pregnancies are aborted, and slightly more than 10 percent end in miscarriage. Among women who carry their pregnancy full term, the vast majority—over 90 percent—keep and raise the infant, while 1 in 10 chooses to have the child adopted. Thus, of the approximately one million pregnancies recorded among teenage women each year, approximately half end in abortion or miscarriage, about 45 percent result in the birth of an infant who will be raised by his or her mother (with or without the help of a spouse or other family members), and about 5 percent result in the birth of an infant put up for adoption (Hayes, 1987) (see Figure 11.4).

It is important to distinguish between pregnancies and actual births—a distinction that seems often to get lost in debates over the consequences of teenage pregnancy. Because of the many pregnant adolescents choosing

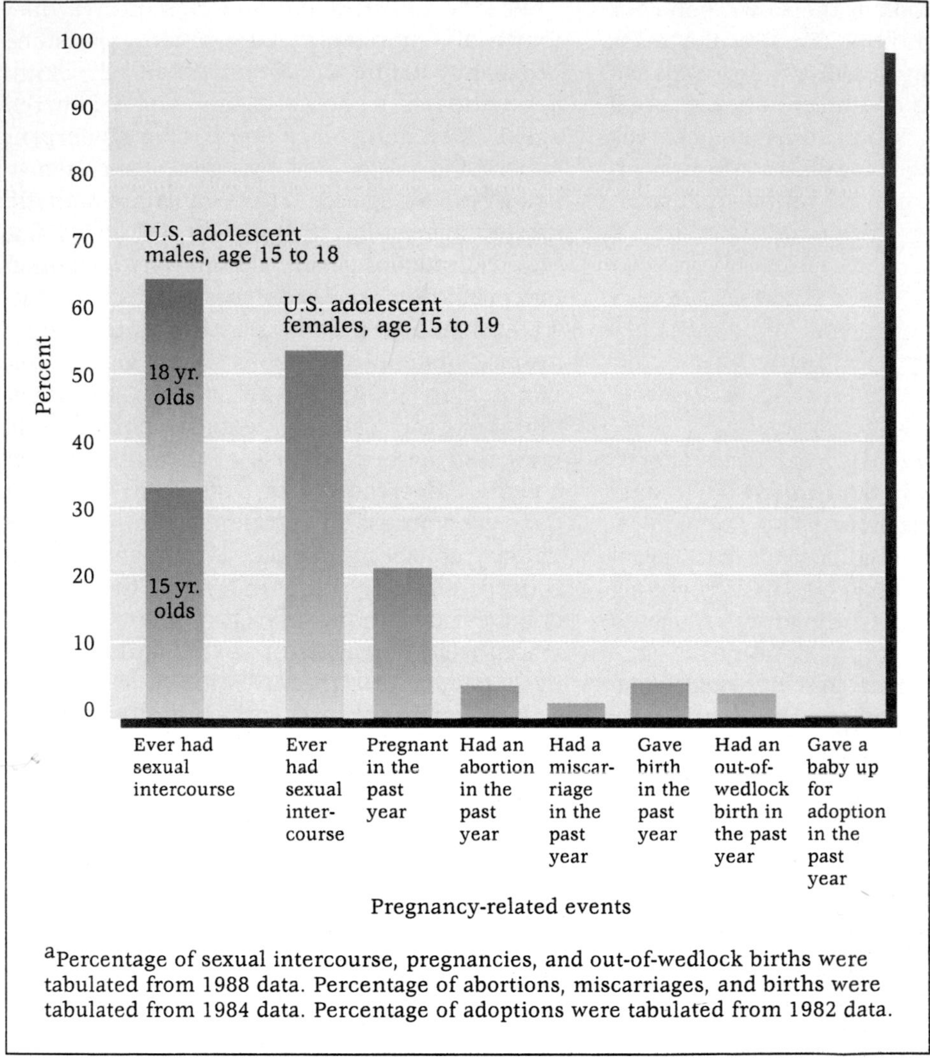

FIGURE 11.4 *An overview of adolescent pregnancy and parenting in the United States.* (Office of Technology Assessment, 1991)

abortion, the birth rate among teenage women is far lower than it would otherwise be, and it may surprise you to learn that the birth rate among adolescent women today is considerably lower than it was in previous eras. Contrary to the popular idea that teenage childbearing has reached epidemic proportions in this country is the truth of the matter: Relatively more women gave birth to an infant before reaching adulthood in previous decades than today—by a large margin. For example, in 1955 the rate of childbearing among women between the ages of 15 and 19 was 90 births per 1,000 women. Today, by contrast, it is about 50 births per 1,000 women (Miller and Moore, 1990).

If teenage childbearing is less prevalent today than in earlier eras, why does the issue receive so much attention in the popular press? First, although the rate of childbearing may be lower today than before, the proportion of teenage childbearing that occurs *out of wedlock* is much higher. In earlier eras, adolescents who became pregnant were much more likely to marry before the child was born. Their pregnancy and childbearing did not cause as much concern, because they were "legitimized" by marriage. One source estimates that about half of all adolescent women who married during the late 1950s were pregnant at the time of marriage (Furstenberg, Brooks-Gunn, and Morgan, 1987). As recently as 1955, out-of-wedlock births accounted for only about 14 percent of all births to young women. But by 1988, this figure had skyrocketed to 66 percent and has continued to climb rapidly since (Furstenberg, 1991; Furstenberg et al., 1987; Holmes, 1994).

Society is now more tolerant of single parenthood and of nonmarital pregnancy than it was forty years ago, and many more women choose this option today than did so in the past. Nonetheless, one reason for the special concern about teenage childbearing in the popular press is that such a high proportion of it occurs outside of marriage. Whether this should be a concern, however—setting issues of morality aside for the moment—is still hotly debated, as we shall see in a moment. Indeed, there is some evidence that the fates of a large group of adolescent mothers are worsened, not bettered, by marrying the father of their child.

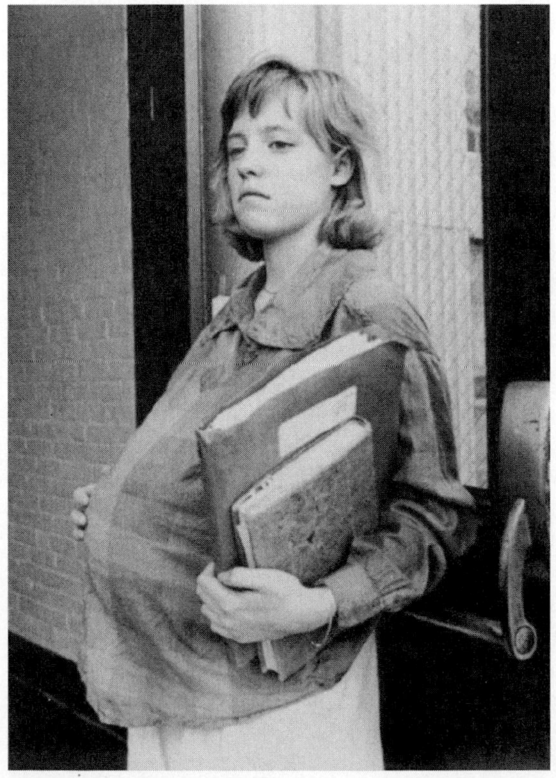

Nearly one-fourth of American young women become pregnant before their 18th birthday. About half of these pregnancies result in the birth of a baby. (Gale Zucker/Stock,Boston)

A second reason for widespread concern is that rates of teenage childbearing vary markedly across ethnic and socioeconomic groups. Middle-class women are far more likely to abort their pregnancies than are poor women, and, as a consequence, the problem of teenage childbearing is densely concentrated among economically disadvantaged youth (Miller and Moore, 1990). And because minority adolescents are more likely to grow up poor, teenage childbearing is especially high in nonwhite communities. Among white adolescents, nearly two-thirds of all births occur outside of marriage; among African-American adolescents, the percentage is close to 100 (Schellenbach et al., 1992). The rate for Hispanic teenagers falls somewhere in between; interestingly, young Mexican-American women are more likely to bear their first child within marriage (the pattern similar to white adolescents), whereas young Puerto Rican women are more likely to bear children out of wedlock (the pattern similar to African-Americans) (Darabi and Ortiz, 1987). Because minority youth are more likely to experience problems such as school failure or unemployment, early childbearing is likely to take place in the context of limited social and economic resources. Indeed, the main reason for the high rate of nonmarital childbearing among African-Americans is the higher proportion of adolescents growing up in single-parent homes (Bumpass and McLanahan, 1987), which experience more stress.

Contributing Factors

Many myths permeate discussions of the causes of adolescent pregnancy and complicate what is actually a fairly simple matter. The most important differences between young women who do and do not become pregnant during adolescence are in their sexual activity and contraceptive use. As you have read, sexual activity among American young people is high, and contraceptive use is sporadic and inadequate. Studies of adolescent contraceptive use, as we have seen, suggest that misinformation about sex and pregnancy, a lack of access to contraceptives, and adherence to the "personal fable" that unprotected intercourse is not going to result in conception all contribute to teenage pregnancy.

Do adolescents who become pregnant actually *want* to have a baby? This has been an extremely difficult question for social scientists to answer. According to national surveys, 85 percent of births to women aged 15 to 19 are unintended—that is, unwanted or mistimed—a figure suggesting that the vast majority of adolescent mothers did not become pregnant intentionally. Yet, studies that plumb the issue a bit deeper find that many young women who say they do not want to become pregnant are actually ambivalent, not unequivocally negative, about the prospect of having a child. More important, those who are ambivalent about childbearing are less likely to use contraception effectively (Zabin, Astone, and Emerson, 1993). Thus, it seems safe to say that while the vast majority of sexually active teenagers do not actively wish to become pregnant, a significant minority feel less troubled by the prospect of early parenthood than do their peers, and that these youngsters are more likely to risk pregnancy by having unprotected sex. Research indicates that the younger sisters of adolescent mothers may be more likely to become adolescent parents themselves, in part because their older sister may communicate some acceptance of early motherhood (East, 1994; East and Felice, 1992).

There are important differences between pregnant teenagers who do, and do not, seek abortion. Although studies show that teenagers can make well-reasoned decisions about abortion, this option is not chosen equally often within all segments of the adolescent population: Unplanned pregnancies are much more likely to be terminated by abortion among young women who are academically successful and ambitious; who come from middle- or upper-class families; whose parents are well-educated; and whose significant others support the decision to terminate the pregnancy (Hayes, 1987; Miller and Moore, 1990). An important factor accounting for the racial and socioeconomic differences in adolescent childbearing, therefore, is that white and middle-class adolescent women perceive themselves as having more to lose—economically and in terms of their careers—by having a child so early in life than do their minority and poor counterparts. With expanded educational and occupational opportunities for poor and minority women, a greater number may realize that delaying childbearing may be preferable (Hayes, 1987).

Several studies have examined whether teenagers who choose to abort an unwanted pregnancy are harmed psychologically by the experience. The consensus among experts is that they are not (Hayes, 1987). Indeed, one recent study indicates that pregnant teenage women who abort their pregnancy are significantly better off two years later, psychologically as well as socially and economically, than comparable women who choose to give birth to their child (Zabin, Hirsch, and Emerson, 1989). Among the most important differences between the groups was that the young women who had terminated their pregnancy by abortion were less likely over the next two years to experience a subsequent pregnancy and were more likely to practice contraception. Given the apparent psychological and economic benefits of terminating an unwanted adolescent pregnancy, it is easy to understand why many social scientists have questioned the wisdom of recent court decisions designed to restrict adolescents' access to abortion services (Blum, Resnick, and Stark, 1990). Studies show that laws requiring parental notification or limiting access to legal abortion do, in fact, result in fewer terminated pregnancies among pregnant adolescents (Joyce and Mocan, 1990; Rogers, Boruch, Stoms, and DeMoya, 1991).

Less research has examined pregnant adolescents who choose adoption. In general, formal adoption, like abortion, is selected by adolescents from more affluent backgrounds and with higher educational aspirations; yet informal adoption—in particular, having one's child raised by one's own mother—is widely practiced within the poor, African-American community (Resnick, Blum, Bose, Smith, and Toogood, 1990; Sandven and Resnick, 1990). Like adolescents who choose to abort their pregnancy, those who choose to have their infant adopted (formally or informally) show no negative psychological effects of the decision. In fact, in terms of occupational and educational attainment, adolescents who select adoption are better off than those who choose to rear their child (Kalmuss, Namerow, and Bauer, 1992; Sandven and Resnick, 1990).

The Role of the Father

Relatively little is known about the male partners of pregnant adolescents. Research indicates, however, that this group of males may share a number of distinguishing characteristics that differentiate them from their peers who do not impregnate adolescent women. Most important has been the discovery that the sexual partners of adolescent girls are less likely to be adolescents themselves than to be young adults, and they are more likely than their peers to have had problems with school, with work, with drugs and alcohol, and with the law and to have fathered a child previously (Elster, Lamb, Peters, Kahn, and Tavare, 1987; Hardy, Duggan, Masnyk, and Pearson, 1989; Marsiglio, 1987; Rivara, Sweeney, and Henderson, 1987; Vera Institute of Justice, 1990). These higher rates of problem behavior among the male partners of pregnant adolescents help to explain why marriage may not be the best response to pregnancy for teenage women, as we shall see in a few pages.

The problematic profiles of teenage fathers notwithstanding, research indicates that young men's educational development and mental health are hurt by fathering a child early in life, even if they do not marry the child's mother (Buchanan and Robbins, 1990; Furstenberg et al., 1989; Vera Institute of Justice, 1990). Men who impregnate adolescent women are more likely to drop out of school and to report feeling anxious and depressed as young adults than their peers. The adverse effects of teenage fatherhood appear to be greater among white and Hispanic men than among African-American men, however, perhaps because teenage fatherhood is more disruptive and is seen as less acceptable within the white and Hispanic communities (Buchanan and Robbins, 1990). In general, however, teenage fathers receive little in the way of supportive services or assistance in becoming responsible parents (Kiselica and Sturmer, 1993).

Consequences for Mother and Child

Because teenage childbearing tends to go hand in hand with a variety of other problems—the most critical of which is poverty—it is extremely difficult to know whether any problems of teenage mothers or their children result from the mother's young age or from other, correlated factors. Separating the effects of early childbearing from poverty is a matter of more than theoretical importance: If early childbearing is in fact a problem in and of itself, it would be important to direct preventive programs at deterring adolescent pregnancy (either by discouraging sexual activity or by encouraging effective contraceptive use) and childbearing (by encouraging adoption and abortion). But if *poverty,* not the mother's age, is the key, an entirely different set of strategies would be called for, aimed not at youngsters' sexual behavior but at all individuals' economic circumstances. It is extremely important, therefore, to ask whether and in what ways a mother's age at the time she gives birth affects her and her child's well-being.

The prevailing wisdom until fairly recently was that children born to teenage mothers were at great risk for a range of health and behavioral problems in the short and long term, including low birth weight, conduct problems, hyperactivity, and achievement difficulties. New and more sophisticated studies, however, temper this conclusion. These new studies indicate that many of the problems that are believed to plague children born to adolescent mothers result primarily from the environment of poverty and single parenthood in which these children are raised, rather than from the mother's age (e.g., Moore and Snyder, 1991; Schellenbach et al., 1992; Wasserman, Rauh, Brunelli, Garcia-Castro, and Necos, 1990). In general, children born to middle-class adolescents differ little from their counterparts born to older mothers, and children born to poor adolescents are similar to children born to equally poor adults. One important exception to this general similarity between the children of adolescent and adult mothers is that adolescent mothers—even of similar socioeconomic origin—may perceive their babies as being especially difficult and may interact with their infants less often in ways that are known to be beneficial to the child's cognitive and social development (Coll, Hoffman, and Oh, 1987; Furstenberg et al., 1989; Miller and Moore, 1990; Schellenbach et al., 1992; Sommer, Whitman, Borkowski, Schellenbach, Maxwell, and Keogh, 1993). To what extent this directly jeopardizes the child's development is not known with any certainty, although studies suggest that children born to adolescent mothers are more likely to have school problems, more likely to be involved in misbehavior and delinquent activity, and more likely themselves to be sexually active at an early age (Furstenberg et al., 1987). There is also some evidence that children of adolescent mothers may be at greater risk for abuse and neglect (Stier, Leventhal, Berg, Johnson, and Mezger, 1993).

We know from other studies that many of the problem behaviors seen among children of adolescent mothers are prevalent among poor children growing up in single-parent homes. Because adolescent mothers are more likely than adult mothers to be both unmarried and poor, their children are at greater risk of developing a variety of psychological and social problems. In other words, the greater incidence of problems among offspring of adolescent mothers may reflect the overall environment in which their children grow up, rather than the ways in which they are raised by their mothers.

Studies of the long-term consequences of adolescent parenthood indicate that serious problems associated with it directly involve the teenage mother, however (Furstenberg et al., 1989). In general, women who bear children early are likely to suffer disruptions in their educational and occupational careers, and these disruptions can have dire long-term consequences (Hayes, 1987). Not only are adolescent mothers more likely to come from a poor background, but they are also more likely to remain poor than their equally disadvantaged peers who delay childbearing until after their schooling is completed (Moore, Myers, Morrison, Nord, Brown, and Edmonston, 1993). Adolescent childbearing, then, can contribute to a vicious cycle of welfare dependency: Individuals who grow up in families dependent on welfare are more likely to have children early in life, which generally means that their economic opportunities will be limited by having to change educational and occupational plans. The result often is continued dependence on public assistance by the adolescent mother and, therefore, by her child—who, like the mother, grows up with welfare as a part of life. Although we can in theory separate the effects of poverty on children from the effects of adolescent childbearing, in reality the two usually go together, and the end result is that children born to adolescent mothers are more likely than other children to suffer the effects both of malnutrition—in the womb as well as in the world—and of environmental deprivation.

Yet the news is not always bad, and having a child early in life does not cast in concrete a life of poverty and misery for the mother and her youngster. Studies show that there is considerable diversity among teenage mothers in the routes that their adult lives take. Some research suggests that the long-term consequences of early childbearing may not be as negative among African-Americans as among whites or Hispanic-Americans, especially among African-Americans living in communities in which early childbearing is accepted as normative (Moore et al., 1993; Smith and Zabin, 1993).

In general, however, young women who remain in high school and delay subsequent childbearing fare a great deal better over the long run—as do their children—than their counterparts who drop out of school or have more children relatively early on (Furstenberg et al., 1987; Upchurch and McCarthy, 1990). Marriage tends to be a "high-risk" strategy (Furstenberg et al., 1987). In some cases, when a stable relationship is formed and economic resources are available, marriage improves the mother's and the child's chances for life success; this seems to be especially true for women who marry somewhat later. In other cases, however, a hasty decision to marry in the absence of a stable relationship and economic security actually worsens many other problems (Teti and Lamb, 1989).

Prevention and Programs

Although there are stories of young women whose lives are not devastated by early childbearing, in general, studies suggest that there are not many such successes. The statement, nearly thirty years ago, that "the girl who has an illegitimate child at the age of 16 suddenly has 90 percent of her life's script written for her" (Campbell, 1968, p. 238) is still more often than not true today. In general, the "successes" are young women who have avoided dire poverty, rather than those who have achieved great economic success. Although the picture of adolescent parenthood appears less uniform or dire than typically painted in the popular press, there is still consensus among experts that it is important to try to prevent teenage pregnancy and childbearing. Unfortunately, this task is more easily said than done. To date, few strategies have proven effective on a large scale. One approach that we can be cautiously optimistic about involves a combination of school-based sex education and school-based health clinics through which adolescents can receive information about sex and pregnancy as well as contraception. Evaluations indicate that this combination of sex education and clinic actually diminishes the rate of teen pregnancy, even within inner-city communities characterized by high rates of adolescent pregnancy and childbearing (Zabin et al., 1986a). Unfortunately, as you might suspect, many parents have objected to such programs in their community, fearing that they will stimulate teenage sexual activity. However, most studies indicate that these fears—however intuitively reasonable—are unwarranted (Furstenberg et al., 1987).

Research on the consequences of adolescent childbearing also suggests that many of the negative effects of having children early can be prevented or at least minimized by lessening the disruptive economic impact of teenage parenthood on young women's lives. What do we know about the factors that work toward this end? First, it is clear that marrying the father of the child may place the adolescent mother at greater risk if the father is not capable of supporting himself economically, much less his family. Studies show, in contrast, that if the father is able to find a good job and remain employed, he can be an important source of psychological and economic support and a healthy influence on the mother and child. Given the characteristic problems of male partners of adolescent mothers that we discussed earlier, however, it is all too likely that marriage may diminish, rather than enhance, an adolescent mother's economic circumstances. In addition, marriage places the adolescent mother at greater risk of having another child relatively soon, which further jeopardizes her already-precarious economic situation. One of the factors most likely to worsen the problems of teenage mothers is having yet another child (Furstenberg et al., 1987). Moreover, teenage marriage, as you know, is very likely to end in divorce (see Chapter 10), which itself is an additional stressor on the mother and child.

Adolescent mothers therefore cannot always look to the father of the child to help break the cycle of poverty that afflicts young parents. However, they can, in many cases, look to their own parents for support, and this may be an effective strategy for some (Stevens, 1988). Teenage mothers who move in with their own family for a short time—a practice far more common among African-Americans than among Hispanic-Americans or white adolescents—are more likely to enjoy educational and occupational success than their counterparts who live on their own, studies show (Miller and Moore, 1990). The family's help allows the young mother to return to school or find employment. Without this help, many young mothers must drop out of school and find and pay for child care, which often is more costly than the income their low-paying jobs generate. Without a high school diploma, these women have little chance of improving their economic situation and, consequently, of improving the opportunities for their child.

Although having the support of one's own family is important for adolescent mothers' development and well-being, actually living with one's family of origin after having a baby is not uniformly beneficial, as several recent studies of three-generational African-American families show. On the negative side, when adolescent mothers live with their own mother, the living arrangement may undermine the development of their own parenting skills (Chase-Lansdale, Brooks-Gunn, and Zamsky, 1994; Spieker and Bensley, 1994), and problems in the relationship between the adolescent and her mother can adversely affect the teen parent's mental health (Davis and Rhodes, 1994; Musick, 1994). On the positive side, living with one's mother is associated with continued schooling, which confers long-term economic advantages (Spieker and Bensley, 1994). Interestingly, one recent study of a sample of predominantly white three-generational families found that support from the adolescent mother's *father* may be especially beneficial (Oyserman, Radin, and Benn, 1993). One fact is certain, though: Adolescent mothers who receive social support fare better, are better parents, and have healthier children than do adolescent mothers who lack support (Leadbeater and Bishop, 1994). Studies suggest that a lack of support is an especially dire problem among poor Hispanic adolescent mothers (Wasserman et al., 1990).

Because it is so important for young mothers to have an adequate income and the chance for adequate employment, many policy makers have called for changes in the ways that schools treat pregnant students and for changes in the provision of day care (Seitz and Apfel, 1993, 1994). Among the most important are adaptations in school schedules and the development of school-based child care centers, so that pregnant students can remain in school after the birth of their child; the expansion of subsidized child care for young mothers who are out of school, so that the economic benefits of having a job are not outweighed by the costs of suitable child care during the workday; and the expansion of family planning services to adolescent mothers so that they can prevent yet another pregnancy.

RECAP

There are approximately one million teenage pregnancies each year in the United States, about half of which are carried full term. Research on the consequences of teenage childbearing indicates that the problems for the teenage mother are typically much greater than are those for her child. Although there are occasional success stories, teenage parents are more likely than their peers to experience disruptions in their educational and occupational development. Adolescent mothers who have social support from family or friends and who are able to complete high school fare far better than those who do not. Research shows that teenagers are not harmed psychologically by aborting their pregnancy or by placing their infant up for adoption.

AIDS AND OTHER SEXUALLY TRANSMITTED DISEASES

Helping youngsters understand sex, pregnancy, and contraception is an important goal of sex education programs for adolescents.

Helping them avoid the risks of **sexually transmitted diseases,** or *STDs,* is another. Once called "venereal diseases," STDs are caused by viruses, bacteria, or parasites that are transmitted through sexual contact (Mahoney, 1983). According to the American Medical Association, 2.5 million adolescents contract a sexually transmitted disease each year, and 1 in 4 teenagers contracts a sexually transmitted disease before graduating from high school (Gans, 1990). Some of the most common STDs among adolescents are **gonorrhea** (caused by a bacterium), **chlamydia** (caused by a bacterium), and **herpes** (caused by a virus). These diseases pose a significant health risk to young people, because they are associated with increased rates of cancer and infertility.

During the 1980s, a new and far more serious STD commanded the world's attention: **AIDS,** or *Acquired Immune Deficiency Syndrome.* AIDS is transmitted through bodily fluids, especially semen, during sexual intercourse, or blood when drug users share needles. Before information was available about the transmission of AIDS, some individuals were infected through blood transfusions in hospitals. Now hospitals routinely screen blood for the AIDS virus—HIV, or human immunodeficiency virus—and this means of transmission is extremely rare today.

AIDS itself has no symptoms, but HIV attacks the body's immune system, interfering with the body's ability to defend itself against life-threatening diseases like pneumonia or cancer. About 25 percent of all individuals who are infected with the virus develop complications within five years; about half of all people in the United States known to have AIDS have died as a result.

Although the incidence of AIDS in the United States was initially concentrated within two groups, gay men and drug users who use needles, recent surveys indicate that the transmission of AIDS through heterosexual activity is a clear danger within the adolescent community, particularly among inner-city minority youngsters (D'Angelo, Getson, Luban, and Gayle, 1991), among homeless youth (Rotheram-Borus, Koopman, and Ehrhardt, 1991), and among high school dropouts (St. Louis, Conway, Hayman, Miller, Petersen, and Dondero, 1991). Among infected females, the major source of infection is heterosexual intercourse (Futterman, Hein, Reuben, Dell, and Shaffer, 1993). Because there is a long period of time between HIV infection and the actual manifestation of illness, however—sometimes, as long as ten years—many more adolescents are likely to be asymptomatic carriers of the HIV virus who may develop AIDS in young adulthood (Hein, 1988b), and the number of HIV-infected adolescents is doubling almost every year (Centers for Disease Control, cited in Meyer, 1994). You should be aware that HIV infection is not limited to poor, inner-city adolescents, however: In 1990 it was estimated that 1 in 500 college students (and 1 in 200 male college students) would test HIV-positive (Gayle, Keeling, Garcia-Tunon, Kilbourne, Narkunas, Ingram, Rogers, and Curran, 1990).

The chances of contracting HIV are greatest among individuals who use intravenous drugs, have unprotected sex, have many sexual partners, and already have another sexually transmitted disease (such as gonorrhea). Because these risk factors are more common among young people than adults, the risk of HIV infection among adolescents is substantial. Accordingly, in recent years numerous efforts have been made to develop AIDS education programs specifically aimed at teenagers (e.g., Hausser and Michaud, 1994; Jemmott, Jemmott, and Fong, 1992; St. Lawrence, 1993).

Unfortunately, despite the existence of many programs designed to reduce the prevalence of HIV infection among adolescents, many young people, especially minority youth, remain confused and misinformed about AIDS (DiClemente, Boyer, and Morales, 1988; Goodman and Cohall, 1989). One recent study of urban Hispanic-American adolescents estimated that 42 percent were at high or moderate risk for HIV infection, based on their sexual behavior (Smith, McGraw, Crawford, Costa, and McKinlay, 1993).

Most experts believe that, short of abstinence, the best way for teenagers to protect themselves against contracting HIV and many other STDs is by using condoms during sex. Educating young people about the risk factors associated with AIDS is important, because studies show that adolescents who believe that they are at risk for HIV infection, and who are motivated to avoid the risk, are more likely to take precautions during intercourse (DiClemente, Durbin, Siegel, Krasnovsky, Lazarus, and Comacho, 1992; Hausser and Michaud, 1994; Jemmott et al., 1992; Orr and Langefeld, 1993; Rotheram-Borus and Koopman, 1991). Adolescents are less likely to protect themselves when they feel negatively about using condoms and when their friends are actively engaged in risky sex (Pleck, Sonenstein, and Ku, 1991; Walter, Vaughan, Gladis, Ragin, Kasen, and Cohall, 1992). It is important to remember that adolescents' sexual behavior is as much, if not more, influenced by their perceptions of benefits (e.g., the fun of having different partners) as it is by their perceptions of costs (e.g., the risks of having different partners) (Levinson, Jaccard, and Beamer, in press).

While most adolescents are now aware of the risk of HIV infection, it has been difficult to convince teenagers to translate this knowledge into safer behavior (Kegeles, Adler, and Irwin, 1988). Indeed, there are signs that initial progress made in fostering safer behaviors among adolescents during the late 1980s has slowed considerably in recent years (Ku, Sonenstein, and Pleck, 1993). As one team of authors concluded, "dissemination of information, in and of itself, is unlikely to deter the spread of AIDS significantly" (Shayne and Kaplan, 1988, p. 199). For this reason, sex education programs that combine AIDS information with the distribution of condoms hold the most promise. Contrary to widespread public opinion, such programs do not increase the likelihood of adolescents becoming sexually active (Furstenberg, Moore, and Peterson, 1985; Hanson, Myers, and Ginsburg, 1987).

SEX EDUCATION

Many adolescents receive some sort of classroom instruction about sexual matters—whether through high school health classes, biology classes, classes designated exclusively for the purpose of sex education, or educational programs administered through youth or religious organizations. Such classes and programs, if they are available, are likely to be targeted toward adolescents rather than toward children and preadolescents (Kirkendall, 1981).

Until recently, most evaluations of formal sex education programs administered through schools rated them remarkably disappointing (Stout and Rivara, 1989). The consensus among experts was that most sex education programs failed because they emphasized the biological over the emotional aspects of sex (and thus did not prepare adolescents for making decisions about sexual involvement); because they came too late in high school (and thus did not reach adolescents before they became sexually active); and because they focused primarily on changing students' knowledge rather than their behavior (and thus did not directly affect patterns of sexual activity or contraceptive use).

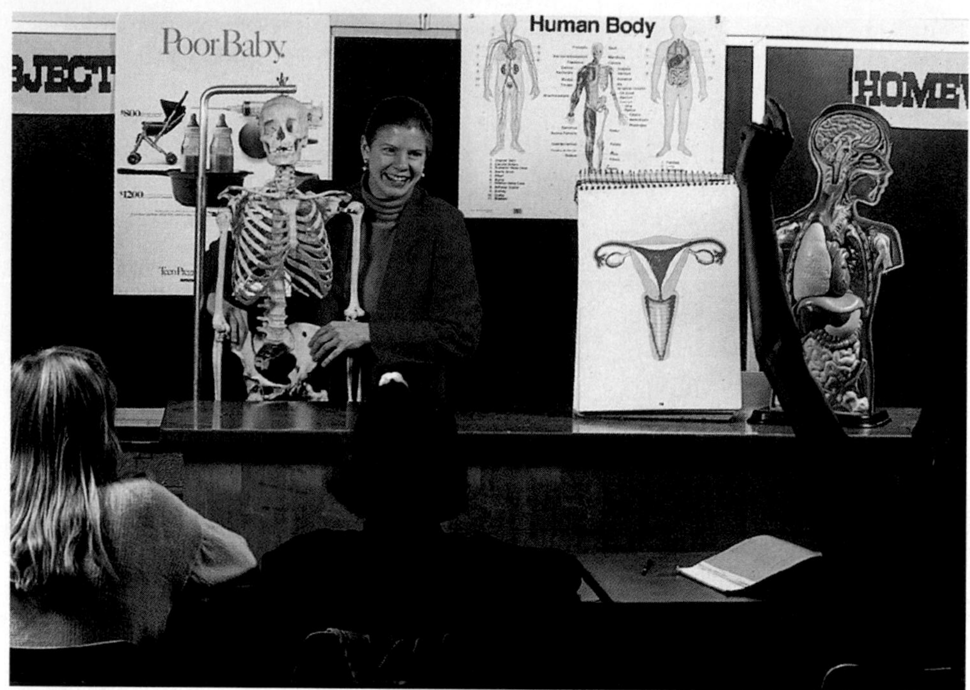

Sex education courses that focus on increasing youngsters' knowledge about sex, contraception, and pregnancy should begin early and should be combined with courses designed to teach decision-making skills and interpersonal assertiveness. (Will & Deni McIntyre/Photo Researchers)

A new wave of sex education programs has been developed, and initial evaluations of these programs have been more encouraging, however. According to a recent review of these programs by a panel of the National Academy of Sciences, sex education courses that focus on increasing youngsters' knowledge about sex, contraception, and pregnancy should begin early and should be combined with courses designed to teach decision-making skills and interpersonal assertiveness. They should teach adolescents the skills they need to resist peer pressure to become sexually active. In addition, the panel recommended that the media take a more socially responsible position and portray sexual relationships and the responsibilities of parenthood more accurately on television and in movies (Hayes, 1987).

The panel also recommended that contraceptive services be expanded for teenagers. Noting that adolescents are often reluctant to seek contraceptives from their physicians and are more inclined to use the services of clinics, the experts recommended that sex education programs include clear information about how to obtain and use contraceptives and that communities consider developing school-based clinics in which adolescents can receive information about contraception and obtain contraceptives. Research suggests that the combination of sex education and school-based clinics is more effective in deterring adolescent pregnancy than sex education programs alone (Zabin et al., 1986a). Indeed, studies show that increasing adolescents' knowledge about sex has little impact—positive or negative—on their sexual behavior (Hanson et al., 1987; Kirby, Harvey, Claussenius, and Novar, 1989).

During the mid-1980s, the emphasis in sex education shifted from encouraging "responsible" sex to encouraging sexual abstinence. In addition to sessions about sexual decision making and values and exercises designed to enhance students' self-esteem, such programs taught adolescents to "just say no" to sexual intercourse. It was hoped that by encouraging sexual abstinence these programs would also have the effect of reducing teenage pregnancy. Unfortunately, careful evaluations of these programs have shown that they are not at all successful, either in changing adolescents' sexual behavior or in reducing rates of nonmarital pregnancy (Christopher and Roosa, 1990; Roosa and Christopher, 1990). To date, the only clear successes in decreasing the rate of adolescent pregnancy are programs that combine education about sexuality and contraception with referrals for contraceptive services (e.g., Zabin et al., 1986a).

RECAP

Sex education programs that combine information with contraceptive services appear to hold the most promise in reducing unintended pregnancy and the prevalence of sexually transmitted disease, including AIDS—a rapidly growing problem in the adolescent population, especially among poor, inner-city adolescents. While most adolescents are now aware of the risk of AIDS, it has been difficult to convince teenagers to translate this knowledge into safer behavior. Programs that simply advocate abstinence have not been successful, and information alone appears to do little to change adolescents' sexual behavior.

KEY TERMS

AIDS (Acquired Immune Deficiency Syndrome)
androgens
autoerotic behavior
chlamydia
date rape
estrogens
gender identity
gonorrhea
herpes
human ecology
nocturnal orgasms
permissive societies
restrictive societies
risk factor
semirestrictive societies
serial monogamy
sex-role behavior
sexual socialization
sexual preference
sexually transmitted diseases (STDs)
sociosexual behavior
testosterone

FOR FURTHER READING

Boxer, A., Cohler, B., Herdt, G., and Irvin, F. (1993). Gay and lesbian youth. Pp. 249–280 in P. Tolan and B. Cohler (Eds.), *Handbook of clinical research and practice with adolescents.* New York: Wiley. A good overview of the scientific literature on the development of gay and lesbian youth.

Brooks-Gunn, J., and Paikoff, R. (1993). "Sex is a gamble, kissing is a game": Adolescent sexuality and health promotion. Pp. 180–208 in S. Millstein, A. Petersen, and E. Nightingale (Eds.), *Promoting the health of adolescents: New directions for the twenty-first century.* New York: Oxford University Press. A recent review of the literature on adolescent sexuality, with an emphasis on the promotion of healthy sexual development.

Furstenberg, F., Jr. (1991). As the pendulum swings: Teenage childbearing and social concern. *Family Relations, 40,* 127–138. A prominent social scientist examines facts and fallacies about teenage pregnancy.

Gordon, S., and Gilgun, J. (1987). Adolescent sexuality. In V. Van Hasselt and M. Hersen (Eds.), *Handbook of adolescent psychology.* New York: Pergamon. An extensive discussion of the psychological aspects of sexual development during adolescence.

Hayes, C. (Ed.). (1987). *Risking the future: Adolescent sexuality, pregnancy, and childbearing.* Washington, D.C.: National Academy Press. The comprehensive report of the National Academy of Sciences on sexuality and pregnancy among American youth.

CHAPTER 12

ACHIEVEMENT

(Alan Odie/PhotoEdit)

Because adolescence typically is a time of preparation for the roles of adulthood, considerable attention has been paid to the development and expression of achievement during these years. Broadly defined, **achievement** concerns the development of motives, capabilities, interests, and behavior that have to do with performance in evaluative situations. More specifically, the study of achievement during adolescence has focused on young people's performance in educational settings and on their hopes and plans for future scholastic and occupational careers. Since most young people form their first realistic educational and vocational plans during adolescence, researchers have long been interested in the factors that appear to play the greatest role in influencing individuals' futures.

Achievement is a particularly important consideration in the study of adolescence in contemporary society. Industrialized societies place an extraordinary emphasis on achievement, competition, and success—more so than on cooperation, for example, or on the development of satisfying interpersonal relationships (McClelland, 1961). During childhood and adolescence, youngsters are continually tested to determine how they stand scholastically in relation to their peers. In most industrialized societies, the amount of education a person has completed and the job he or she holds—two of the most important indicators of achievement—provide a basis for individuals' self-conceptions and their image in the eyes of others (Featherman, 1980).

A second reason for the importance of achievement in the study of adolescence in contemporary society concerns the range and rapidly changing nature of the choices faced by today's young people. Unlike youth in most traditional cultures, adolescents in modern societies are confronted with a phenomenally wide array of difficult occupational and educational decisions before they turn 25. Beyond such fundamental questions as what type of career to follow and whether to continue with schooling after high school, there are other difficult issues to ponder: what specific sorts of jobs should be pursued within a particular career path, what kind of educational preparation would be most appropriate, and how entry into the labor force is best negotiated. For the college student contemplating a career in business, for instance, is it better to major in business administration, or is it better to follow a liberal arts course of study? How early is it necessary to decide which aspects of business to specialize in? Is it necessary to go to graduate school, or do employers prefer applicants with work experience in place of an advanced degree? These are all difficult questions to answer. And they are made more difficult because the nature of education and work changes so rapidly in contemporary society.

Finally, achievement is a particularly important issue in the study of adolescence in contemporary society because of wide variation in levels of educational and occupational success. By the end of high school, many adolescents demonstrate a high enough level of academic achievement to enter selective colleges and universities; yet a sizable number of their peers enter adulthood unable even to read a newspaper or understand a bus schedule. Although the majority of adolescents today complete high school and go on to college, a substantial number leave high school before graduating. Similar disparities exist in the occupational achievements of young people: Most youth make the transition from school to work without a great deal of difficulty, but a significant number experience long bouts of unemployment. Even within the population of young people who enter the labor force, there is considerable variation in earnings and in occupational status. Many important questions in the study of adolescent achievement, therefore, concern factors that distinguish between young people who are successful—however success is defined—and those who are not.

ACHIEVEMENT AS AN ADOLESCENT ISSUE

As noted above, in contemporary society, achievement is a lifelong concern. Educational institutions—even for young children—stress performance, competition, and success on tests of knowledge and ability. Concerns over achievement continue throughout adulthood as well. Like their younger counterparts, adults for the most part place a premium on success. Work and occupational attainment play an important role in shaping the adult's values, self-concept, and self-esteem (Featherman, 1980). Development in the realm of achievement neither begins nor ends during adolescence.

Achievement during the adolescent years, though, merits special attention for several reasons. First, the fact that adolescence is a time of preparation for adult work roles raises questions about the nature of the preparation that young people receive and the processes through which they sort themselves (or are sorted) into the occupational roles that may influence the remainder of their lives. Many of the factors that narrow an individual's educational options and vocational alternatives are prominent during the high school and college years, and it is important to ask how such options are defined and at what age educational and occupational decisions are made.

Second, although differences in school performance and achievement are apparent as early as the first grade, not until adolescence do individuals begin to appreciate fully the implications of these differences for immediate and future success. During childhood, for example, children's occupational plans are made to a large extent on the basis of fantasy and passing interests, without any realistic assessment of their practicality or feasibility. Not until adolescence do individuals begin to evaluate their occupational choices in light of their talents, abilities, and opportunities.

Third, it is clear that the educational and occupational decisions made during adolescence are more numerous, and that the consequences of such decisions are more serious, than the decisions characteristic of childhood. For example, in most elementary schools, although children may be grouped by ability—groupings that have implications for subsequent achievement—they generally are all exposed to fairly similar curricula and have few opportunities to veer from the educational program established by their school system. In high school, however, students can select how much science and math they want to take, whether they wish to study a foreign language, whether they want to pursue an academic or vocational track—even whether they want to remain in school once they have reached the legal age for leaving school. Moreover, it is during adolescence that most individuals decide whether they want to pursue postsecondary education or enter a full-time job directly from high school. All these decisions have important implications for the sort of choices and plans the adolescent will make in the future, which in turn will influence his or her earnings, lifestyle, identity, and subsequent psychosocial development.

It is neither surprising nor coincidental that many achievement-related issues surface for the first time during adolescence. One major reason for this relates to the social transition of adolescence. In virtually all societies, adolescence is the period when important educational and occupational decisions are made, and society has structured its educational and work institutions accordingly. In America, for example, it is not until adolescence that individuals attain the status necessary to decide whether they will continue or end their formal education. And it is not until adolescence that people are allowed to enter the labor force in an official capacity, since child labor regulations typically prohibit the employment of youngsters under the age of 14 or so. The transition from school to work—one of the central issues in the study of achievement during adolescence—is a *socially* defined transition, a passage that society has determined will be negotiated during adolescence.

The special significance of achievement in adolescence does not derive solely from the transitional nature of the period, however. The intellectual changes of the period are important as well. Not until adolescence are individuals cognitively capable of seeing the long-term consequences of educational and occupational choices or of realistically considering the range of scholastic and work possibilities open to them. Thus a second reason for the prominence of achievement-related issues during adolescence relates to the advent of more sophisticated forms of thinking. The ability to think in hypothetical terms, for example, raises new achievement concerns for the individual ("Should I go to college after I graduate, or should I work for a while?"); it also permits the young person to think through such questions in a logical and systematic fashion ("If I decide to go to college, then . . .).

Finally, the emergence of many achievement concerns during adolescence is tied to the biological changes of puberty. As noted in Chapter 2, not until early adolescence do sex differences in achievement test performance begin to emerge, with boys scoring higher on tests of mathematics, and girls outscoring boys on tests of verbal skills. As we shall see, sex differences in achievement-related motives and beliefs appear around puberty as well. These sex differences are related primarily to the differential responses that boys and girls receive from others as a result of changes in their appearance at puberty and as a result of differences in how adolescent boys and girls view themselves. Boys may be encouraged to pursue coursework (and, by implication, careers) in math and science, whereas girls may be encouraged to study the arts and humanities. This differential treatment may have important implications for sex differences in educational and occupational attainment.

In this chapter, we look at the nature of achievement during the adolescent years. As you will see, the extent to which an adolescent is successful in school and in preparing for work is influenced by a complex array of personal and environmental factors. In addition, we shall find that development in the realm of achievement is cumulative, in that youngsters who are successful early are likely to reap the benefits of the educational system, to continue to succeed in school, and to complete more years of education than their peers. This success, in turn, gives them an advantage in the labor market, since the prestige and status of individuals' entry-level jobs are largely dependent on their educational background.

If there is a theme to this chapter, it is that, at least with respect to achievement during adolescence, the rich get richer, and the poor get poorer. More often than not, personal and environmental influences on achievement complement rather than correct each other, in the sense that individuals who bring personal advantages to the world of achievement—talent, a motive to succeed, high aspirations for the future—are also likely to grow up in an environment that supports and maintains achievement success. We begin with a look at one set of factors that may differentiate the "rich" from the "poor" early in their schooling—long before adolescence, in fact: their motives to succeed and their beliefs about the causes of their successes and failures.

RECAP

Achievement is an important issue during adolescence because society typically designates adolescence as a time for preparation for adult work roles; because individuals now can understand the long-term implications of their educational and career decisions; and because, during adolescence, schools begin making distinctions among individuals that potentially have profound effects on their long-term occupational development. Because educational and occupational achievement are so cumulative, during adolescence the "rich" tend to get richer, while the "poor" get poorer.

ACHIEVEMENT MOTIVES AND BELIEFS

The Motive to Achieve

One of the oldest notions in the study of achievement is that individuals differ in the extent to which they strive for success and that this differential striving—which can be measured independently of sheer ability—helps to account for different degrees of actual achievement. Two students may both score 100 on an intelligence test, but if one student simply *tries* much harder than the other to do well in school, their actual grades may differ. The extent to which an individual strives for success is referred to as his or her **need for achievement** (McClelland, Atkinson, Clark, and Lowell, 1953). Need for achievement is an intrinsically motivated desire to perform well that operates even in the absence of external rewards for success. A student who works very hard on an assignment that is not going to be graded probably has a very strong need for achievement. All other factors being equal, a student who tries hard to succeed in school is, in fact, more likely to succeed than one who tries less (Wentzel, 1989).

Generally, researchers have found that adolescents who have a strong need for achievement come from families in which parents have set high performance standards, have rewarded achievement success during childhood, and have encouraged autonomy and independence (Rosen and D'Andrade, 1959; Winterbottom, 1958). Equally important, however, this training for achievement and independence generally takes place in the context of warm parent-child relationships in which the child forms close identifications with his or her parents (Shaw and White, 1965). Put most succinctly, authoritative parenting, coupled with parents' encouragement of success, is likely to lead to the development of a strong need for achievement.

One psychological factor that interacts with an adolescent's need for achievement is a related and, in some senses, complementary motive—**fear of failure.** Fear of failure, which is often manifested in feelings of anxiety in test-taking or other evaluative situations, can interfere with successful performance. Generally speaking, when the achievement situation involves an easy task, and when a little anxiety helps to focus attention (if, for example, the task is boring), a moderate amount of fear of failure may improve performance by increasing one's concentration. Usually, however, the anxiety generated by a strong fear of failure interferes with successful performance. This is often the case in situations in which the task involves learning something new or solving a complex problem—like many tasks faced by adolescents in school settings. Individuals with a high fear of failure often come from family environments in which parents have set unrealistically high standards for their children's achievement and react very negatively to failure (rather than simply reacting positively to success) (Spielberger, 1966).

PATTERNS OF ACHIEVEMENT IN ADOLESCENT BOYS AND GIRLS

We noted in Chapter 2 in discussing cognitive development that sex differences in cognitive skills during adolescence are trivial. On standardized tests of intellectual abilities, girls and boys perform at about the same level; and when sex differences are observed, they are small—too small, indeed, to make a meaningful difference in adolescents' school performance. Despite this absence of sex differences in ability, girls in general are less likely than boys to pursue advanced courses in math and science, and those girls who do so are more likely to drop out before finishing (Kavrell and Petersen, 1984). Studies of college students show that women are exceedingly underrepresented among graduates whose degrees are in math, engineering, and the physical sciences and are overrepresented among graduates whose degrees are in the humanities and education (Smith, 1992). Because high school preparation undoubedly influences college course choices—which, in turn, affect career choices—educators have been interested in understanding why sex differences in math achievement emerge during adolescence. In essence, if adolescent girls and adolescent boys have equal math ability, why do they show different patterns of math and science achievement during high school?

Psychologists have offered several explanations. The first concerns sex differences in the social consequences of succeeding in school and, particularly, of succeeding in math and science classes. Most notably, fear of success may be more prevalent among females than among males during early and middle adolescence than during childhood or adulthood (Butler and Nissan, 1975; Hoffman, 1977; Ishiyama and Chabassol, 1985). This finding and other research on achievement-related conflicts among adolescent girls (Rosen and Aneshensel, 1975) suggest that the social world of adolescent peer groups may make it difficult for adolescent girls to integrate positive feelings toward achievement—especially toward achievement in stereotypically masculine subject areas—into their sense of identity (Douvan and Adelson, 1966).

Of special importance for girls is the relation between academic achievement, the development of a feminine identity, and social relations with boys. As psychologists Judith Bardwick and Elizabeth Douvan (1971) explain: "Until adolescence the idea of equal capacity, opportunity, and life style [for men and women] is held out to [girls]. But sometime in adolescence the message becomes clear that one had better not do too well, that competition is aggressive and unfeminine, that deviation threatens the heterosexual relationship" (p. 152).

In other words, adolescent girls may not fear "success" per se, but they may be wary of other consequences—not necessarily negative consequences, but often merely complicated consequences—that may befall them as a result of their achievement. Girls are more likely to have been socialized to believe that their achievement is out of their control, and they are consequently more likely to feel helpless in response to failure (Dweck and Light, 1980). During adolescence, when concerns over dating and socializing may be paramount and when the sense of self is shaky and the view of the future cloudy, achievement may carry a different connotation for girls than it does for boys. Actually, one study indicated that *both* males and females had negative feelings about women's occupational success, suggesting that females' fear of success may be just as much a result of cultural bias against women's succeeding as it is a reflection of an achievement-related motive prevalent among females (Monahan, Kuhn, and Shaver, 1974).

A second account focuses on sex differences in attitudes toward mathematics. Although girls and boys are equally likely to report liking math, girls are less likely than boys to believe that taking math classes will be useful to their future careers, and, by high school, there are clear sex differences in course selection and preference (Kavrell and Petersen, 1984; Klebanov and Brooks-Gunn, 1992). As a result, girls may place less value on achievement in math classes and may be less inclined to continue a math curriculum and more inclined to drop out of advanced math classes (Smith, 1992). Thus, it appears that sex differences in career expectations may influence early attitudes toward math classes, which, in turn, influence math attainment. As we shall see later in this chapter, sex differences in adolescents' occupational ambitions are still quite marked. Unfortunately, to the extent that young adolescent girls opt out of advanced math classes, they limit their chances of moving into occupations that require preparation in math and thus contribute to perpetuating occupational sex stereotypes. Interestingly, the finding that boys are more positive about math and science than girls are, and that girls are more positive about language arts than boys are, is not limited to the United States, as the accompanying figure illustrates.

Psychologist Jacquelynne Eccles and her colleagues have argued that these sex differences in course selection may be related to sex differences in achievement attributions and beliefs. Parents, in particular, may pass on different expectations to sons and daughters, regardless of similarities in sons' and daughters' actual achievement. Parents of sons are more likely to believe that their child's

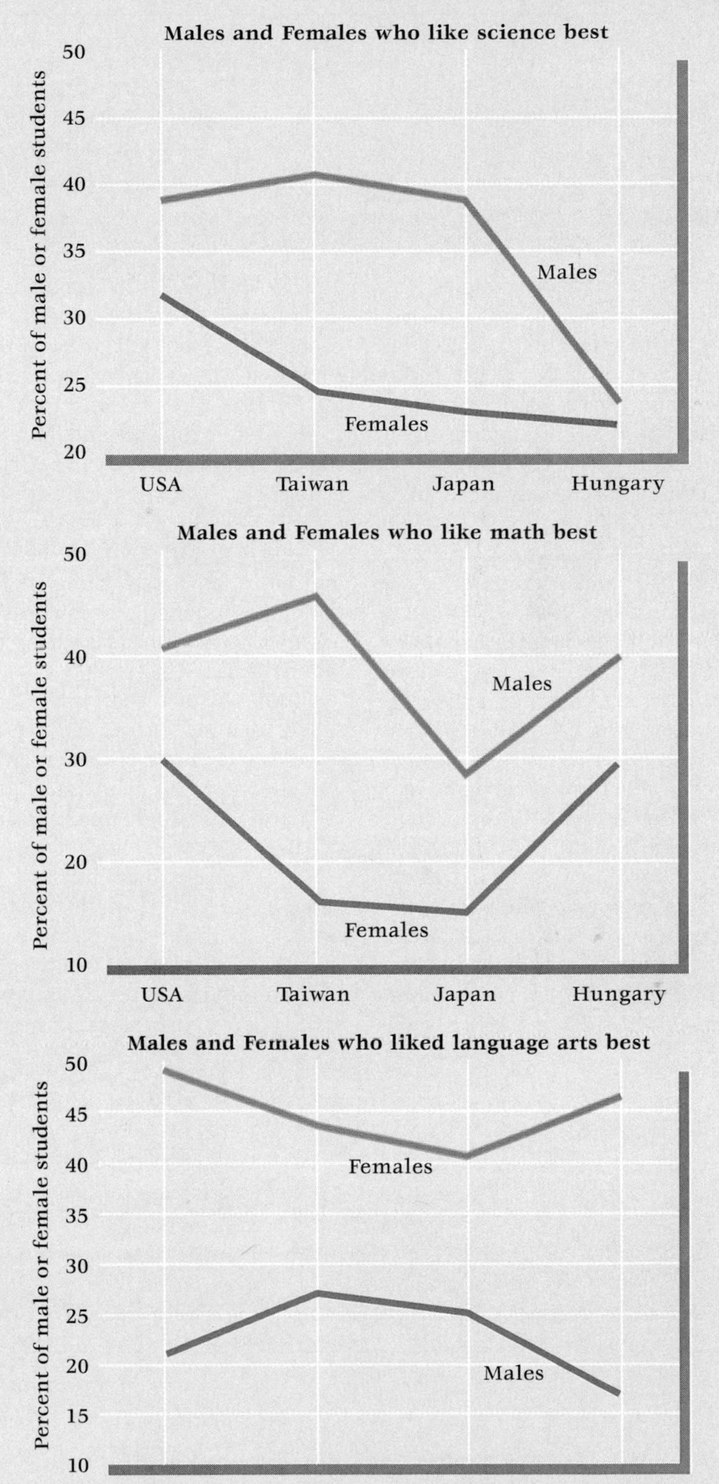

Cross-cultural differences in males' and females' favorite classes. (Evans, 1992)

success in math reflects his intrinsic math ability, whereas parents of daughters are more likely to attribute their child's math success to hard work. Parents of sons are also more likely than parents of daughters to think that taking advanced math courses is important (Parsons [Eccles], Adler, and Kaczala, 1982). To make matters worse, studies indicate that school counselors and teachers also endorse views that support math achievement among boys but discourage it among girls (Kavrell and Petersen, 1984).

Overall, then, research indicates that parents' beliefs about their child's abilities—which are in part determined by the parents' *own* stereotypes about gender—influence the child's academic self-conceptions, which in turn influence performance in school (Eccles, 1993; Jacobs, 1991; Jacobs and Eccles, 1992) (see accompanying figure). This seems to be especially important during the middle-school years, when adolescents' self-conceptions are relatively more malleable and perhaps more susceptible to their parents' influences (Klebanov and Brooks-Gunn, 1992). It also is the case that girls from divorced homes are more adversely affected by parental gender stereotyping than are their peers from nondivorced homes (Smith, 1992).

Studies show that grades in school decline during early adolescence, for both boys and girls. This decline has been attributed to harder grading practices by teachers (Kavrell and Petersen, 1984) and to the declining importance of achievement to adolescents as they approach high school (Elmen, 1991). But the decline in grades in math and science may evoke very different responses in boys and girls. Boys, who have been told that they are good at math and science and that these subjects are important, may simply try harder to do better. Girls, who receive less support for achievement in math and science both from adults (who may inadvertently socialize them to believe that these subjects are difficult and not very useful) and peers (who may convey the message that success in these subjects is not attractive), may respond by avoiding math and science entirely. This response is easy to understand: By the time an adolescent girl has reached the point in high school that she is able to choose among electives, she has been socialized to believe that math and science are difficult, that these classes are not especially worthwhile, and that success in them is inconsistent with being popular and attractive.

How parents contribute to sex differences in math and science achievement. (Adapted from Eccles, 1993)

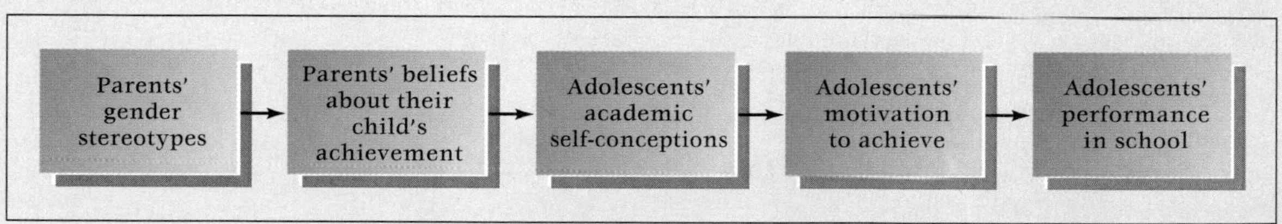

An adolescent's need for achievement and his or her fear of failure work together simultaneously to pull the individual toward, and repel the individual from, achievement situations. Individuals with a relatively strong need for achievement and a relatively weak fear of failure are more likely to actively approach challenging achievement situations—by taking more difficult classes, for example—and to look forward to them. In contrast, those whose fear of failure is relatively intense and whose need for achievement is relatively weak will dread challenging situations and will do what they can to avoid them. Many students who have trouble persisting at tasks and who fear failure become **underachievers**—students' whose grades are far lower than one would expect, based on their intellectual ability (McCall, in press).

Several studies indicate that at least some components of adolescents' drive for achievement may have their origins not only in the family but also in youngsters' inborn **temperament.** (Psychologists use *temperament* to refer to an individual's characteristic style of responsiveness and mood, which is present early in infancy and remains reasonably stable throughout childhood.) Individuals who are rated as more persistent and less distractible as children are, as adolescents, more likely to achieve well in school (Guerin, Gottfried, Oliver, and Thomas, in press). Other studies show that the sort of hard-driving behavior thought to be associated with heart disease in adulthood—so-called **Type-A behavior**—has its beginnings in a "hard-driving" temperament as well (Steinberg, 1985).

The Importance of Beliefs

In recent years, researchers have questioned the usefulness of asserting the existence of global achievement-related motives that are expressed equally in a variety of situations. The relation between an individual's internal needs and his or her actual effort and performance varies in different situations. Someone who has a strong need for achievement might express this need to different degrees in academic and in social situations—or even in different sorts of academic and different sorts of social situations—depending on past experiences and the individual's perception of the specific situation. Because of this, individuals' actual performance in achievement situations may not be strongly related to their general achievement motives. Some students who want very much to succeed, for example, are susceptible to feelings of anxiety and helplessness in performance settings.

The newer research indicates that adolescents make judgments about their likelihood of succeeding or failing and that they exert different degrees of effort accordingly. Consider, for instance, the different ways that two individuals might approach a card game. Someone who believes that the outcome of the game is based on luck rather than on skill will not try as hard as someone who feels that how he or she plays the game makes a difference.

A number of studies indicate that students' beliefs about their abilities exert a strong influence on their motivation and effort, which in turn influences their scholastic performance (Harter, Whitesell, and Kowalski, 1991; Marsh, 1990; Mac Iver, Stipek, and Daniels, 1991). In order to understand this process, it is necessary to draw a distinction between **intrinsic motivation** and **extrinsic motivation.** Individuals who are intrinsically motivated strive to achieve because of the pleasure they get out of learning and mastering the material. Individuals who are extrinsically motivated strive to achieve because of the rewards they get for performing well and the punishments they receive for performing poorly. Early theories of achievement motivation did not draw this distinction and, as a consequence, may have grouped together students who—while highly motivated to do well in achievement situations—may have been motivated for very different reasons.

We all know individuals who are genuinely interested in what they learn in school, and we know others whose main concern is really just their grade-point average. These two approaches to achievement have very different psychological consequences for the individual adolescent. Adolescents who believe that they are competent are more likely to be intrinsically motivated and are more likely to maintain their efforts to do well in school. In contrast, adolescents who have doubts about their abilities are more likely to be extrinsically motivated and to be more susceptible to feelings of anxiety and hesitation in the face of challenge. That is, although extrinsically motivated adolescents want to do well in school, the source of their motivation puts them on shaky ground.

Individuals who are intrinsically motivated strive to achieve because of the pleasure they get out of mastering the material. (Spencer Grant/Stock, Boston)

You read earlier that adults—parents and teachers, for instance—can affect adolescents' *degree* of achievement motivation. It is also true that adults affect the extent to which an adolescent's achievement motives are intrinsic or extrinsic. When adults attempt to control an adolescent's achievement behavior through rewarding good grades (e.g., by giving prizes or money), punishing bad grades (e.g., by restricting privileges), or excessively supervising their performance (e.g., by constantly checking up on their homework), adolescents are more likely to develop an extrinsic orientation and, as a result, are less likely to do well in school. In contrast, adolescents whose parents encourage their autonomy and are supportive of school success (without rewarding it concretely) tend to perform better in the classroom (Deci and Ryan, 1985; Ginsburg and Bronstein, 1993). Girls, especially, are negatively affected by overcontrolling parents or teachers, perhaps because girls tend to be more susceptible to adult influence than boys are (Boggiano, Main, and Katz, 1991).

Other studies suggest that the way in which adolescents view intelligence in general also enters into the achievement equation. Three factors interact to predict students' behavior: whether the student believes that intelligence is fixed or malleable; whether the student is oriented more toward extrinsic rewards (performance) or more toward intrinsic rewards (mastery); and whether the student is confident about his or her abilities (Ames and Archer, 1988; Henderson and Dweck, 1990).

Students who believe that intelligence is fixed tend to be oriented toward their performance and are greatly affected by their degree of confidence. If they are confident about their abilities, they tend to work hard and seek out challenges. If they are insecure, however, they tend to give up easily and feel helpless.

Students who believe that intelligence is malleable, in contrast, approach achievement situations from a different perspective. These students are more likely to have learning goals than performance goals; for them, satisfaction comes from mastering the material, not simply from gaining a good evaluation. Students who have this orientation are far less affected by their level of confidence, because they are less concerned about their performance. Whether assured or insecure, these students exert effort and seek out challenges, because they are motivated by learning rather than by performing.

When conditions change such that performance becomes more important than learning, students' motives and beliefs change as a result. You have probably experienced this when you have enrolled in a course in which the instructor stressed grades, rather than mastery of the material. This sort of emphasis brings out the worst in students—literally. Performance goals make students more extrinsically motivated, more insecure about their abilities, and more hesitant to challenge themselves.

One of the most interesting applications of this viewpoint has been in studies of changes in adolescents' academic motivation during the transition from elementary school to junior high school (Eccles, Midgley, Wigfield, Buchanan, Reuman, Flanagan, and Mac Iver, 1993). It has been widely reported that students' motivation and school performance decline when they move into secondary school (Elmen, 1991). Why might this be? Among the other important changes that take place during this school transition (see Chapter 6) is a shift, on the part of teachers, toward a more performance-oriented style of instruction and evaluation. During secondary school, students discover that more of an emphasis is placed on grades than had been the case in elementary school. This shift in emphasis undermines many students' intrinsic motivation and their self-confidence, which diminishes their performance.

These newer models of the psychological aspects of achievement during adolescence suggest that students' beliefs (about the nature of ability in general and the nature of *their* ability in particular) influence their motivation, which in turn influences their performance. One additional factor involves the way in which students interpret their successes and failures. Researchers who are interested in **achievement attributions** (Dweck and Wortman, 1980) have studied how the attributions that individuals make for their success or failure influence their performance. According to these theorists, individuals attribute their performance to a combination of four factors: ability, effort, task difficulty, and luck. When individuals succeed and attribute their success to "internal" causes, such as their ability or effort, they are more likely to approach future tasks confidently and with self-assurance. If, however, individuals attribute their success to "external" factors outside their control, such as luck or having an easy task, they are more likely to remain unsure of their abilities. Not surprisingly, scholastically successful individuals, who tend to be high in achievement motivation, are likely to attribute their successes to internal causes (Carr, Borkowski, and Maxwell, 1991; Powers and Wagner, 1984).

How youngsters interpret their failures is also important in influencing their subsequent behavior. Some youngsters try harder in the face of failure, whereas others withdraw and exert less effort. According to psychologist Carol Dweck (Dweck and Light, 1980), when individuals attribute their failures to a lack of effort, they are more likely to try harder on future tasks. But individuals who attribute their failure to factors that they feel cannot be changed (bad luck, lack of intelligence, task difficulty) are more likely to feel helpless and to exert less effort in subsequent situations.

Suppose, for instance, a student takes the Scholastic Aptitude Test and receives a score of 500. He then is told by his guidance counselor that the SAT is a measure of intelligence and that his score reflects how smart he is. The counselor tells the student that he can retake the test if he wants to but that he should not expect to score much higher than 500. Now imagine a different student, who also scored 500 on the test. She is told by her guidance counselor that effort has a great deal to do with scores on the SAT and that she can raise her score by trying harder. In all likelihood, the next time these students take the test, the first student would not try as hard as the second student would, because the first student is more likely to feel helpless.

Students who are led to believe that their efforts do not make a difference—by being told, for example, that they are stupid or that the work is too difficult for them—develop **learned helplessness:** the belief that failure is inevitable (Dweck and Light, 1980). As a result of learned helplessness, some students try less hard than their peers, and they do not do as well as they might. Research on adolescents' attributions for success and failure suggests that, instead of dismissing low-achieving students as having "low needs for achievement" or "low intelligence," teachers and other school personnel can help students achieve more by helping them learn to attribute their performance to factors that are under their own control (Wilson and Linville, 1985).

RECAP

Early theories of the development of achievement stressed individual differences in achievement motivation: Some individuals were believed to have a stronger "need for achievement" than others, and individuals were thought to differ as well in the extent to which they are afraid of failure. Although it is surely true that adolescents who strive for success expend more effort in school and achieve more there, contemporary theories tend to stress the interaction of motives, beliefs, attributions, and goals as influencing adolescents' achievement orientation. Adolescents who believe that ability is malleable (rather than fixed); who are motivated by intrinsic, rather than extrinsic, rewards; who are confident about their abilities; and who attribute their successes and failures to effort (rather than to ability or luck) achieve more in school than their peers.

ENVIRONMENTAL INFLUENCES ON ACHIEVEMENT

Ability, beliefs, and motivation may play a large role in influencing individual performance, but opportunity and situational factors also have a great deal to do with achievement (Featherman, 1980). Many of the differences in academic or occupational achievement that are observed among adolescents result not from differences in adolescents' abilities, motives, or beliefs but from differences in the environments where abilities and motives are expressed.

School environments differ markedly—in physical facilities, in opportunities for pursuing academically enriched programs, and in classroom atmospheres. For example, students are more engaged and achieve more in schools that are more personal, less departmentalized, and less rigidly tracked and in which team-teaching is used more frequently

Adolescents who attend schools in which there are ample resources—such as computers—have a distinct advantage over their peers who attend schools in impoverished communities. (Spencer Grant/The Picture Cube)

(Gamoran, 1992; Lee and Smith, 1993). Unfortunately, many school districts, plagued with shrinking tax bases, are characterized by decaying school buildings, outdated equipment, and textbook shortages. In some schools, problems of crime and discipline have grown so overwhelming that attention to these matters has taken precedence over learning and instruction. Many young people who genuinely want to succeed are impeded not by a lack of talent or motivation but by a school environment that makes academic success virtually impossible.

The school, of course, is not the only environment that makes a difference in adolescents' achievement, and few would argue that schools should accept full responsibility for adolescents who do not succeed at a level consonant with their abilities. If anything, the evidence suggests that important aspects of the home environment are better predictors of adolescents' academic achievement (Coleman, Campbell, Hobson, McPartland, Mood, Weinfeld, and York, 1966).

The Influence of the Home Environment

Researchers have focused on three ways in which the adolescent's home may influence his or her level of achievement. First, as you now know from studies of parental influences on sex difference in achievement, studies have shown that adolescents' achievement is directly related to the level of achievement that their parents *expect* them to attain. Adolescents whose parents expect them to go to college are more likely to do so than are adolescents of equal ability whose parents expect less of them (Featherman, 1980). Parental encouragement of academic success may be manifested in a number of ways, all of which have been shown to be beneficial to adolescents' school performance.

First, parents who encourage school success set higher standards for their child's school performance and homework completion and have higher aspirations for their child, which in turn contributes to school success (Entwistle and Hayduk, 1988; Natriello and McDill, 1986; Wilson and Wilson, 1992). Second, parents who encourage school success support values that are consistent with doing well in school, and they structure the home environment to support academic pursuits so that the messages children receive from their teachers are echoed at home (Hanson and Ginsburg, 1988; Kurdek and Sinclair, 1988). Third, parents who encourage success are likely to be more involved in their child's education—more likely to attend school programs, to help in course selection, to maintain interest in school activities and assignments, and the like—all of which contribute to students success (Astone and McLanahan, 1991; Baker and Stevenson, 1986; Grolnick and Slowiaczek, 1994; Steinberg, Lamborn, Dornbusch, and Darling, 1992; Stevenson and Baker, 1987). Parental involvement in schooling may make academics seem both more important and more conquerable to the adolescent, which may enhance the young person's academic self-conceptions (Grolnick and Slowiaczek, 1994). In contrast, parental disengagement from school may make students themselves more likely to disengage and do poorly (Roeser, Lord, and Eccles, 1994).

Studies also have shown that authoritative parenting—parenting that is warm, firm, and fair—is linked to school success during adolescence (Dornbusch, Ritter, Liederman, Roberts, and Fraleigh, 1987; Steinberg, Lamborn, Darling, Mounts, and Dornbusch, 1994). In contrast, parenting that is especially punitive, harsh, strict, or inept is associated with lower school engagement and diminished achievement (DeBaryshe, Patterson, and Capaldi, 1993). In one study, for example, sociologist Sanford Dornbusch and his colleagues (Dornbusch et al., 1987) demonstrated that adolescents whose parents were authoritative consistently performed better in school than did peers whose parents were indulgent or authoritarian. Interestingly, the poorest school performance was observed among adolescents whose parents were inconsistent in their child rearing. That is, even though adolescents whose parents were autocratic received lower grades than did students whose parents were authoritative, adolescents whose parents used a mixture of authoritarian and indulgent techniques performed even worse. Underachievers have also been found to come from homes in which the mother and father are inconsistent with each other (McCall, in press). Interestingly, extreme parental *permissiveness* (rather than authoritarianism) is associated with higher rates of dropping out of school (Rumberger, Ghatak, Poulos, Ritter, and Dornbusch, 1990).

Why do adolescents achieve more in school when they come from authoritative homes? One reason is that authoritative parenting promotes the development of a healthy achievement orientation—including an emphasis on intrinsic motivation—which in turn facilitates adolescent school performance (DeBaryshe et al., 1993; Lamborn, Mounts, Steinberg, and Dornbusch, 1991; Steinberg, Elmen, and Mounts, 1989). This is in part because authoritative parents are more likely to hold healthier beliefs about their child's achievement and less likely to be overly controlling—two factors that strengthen adolescents' work orientation and intrinsic motivation (Arbeton, Eccles, and Harold, 1994; Grolnick and Slowiaczek, 1994; Pratt, Filipovich, and Bountrogianni, in press). Having a strong work orientation enhances achievement both directly, as we saw earlier, and indirectly, through the positive impression it makes on teachers (Farkas, Grobe, and Shuan, 1990). In general, these findings are in line with a good deal of research suggesting that consistent, authoritative parenting is associated with a wide array of benefits to the adolescent, including higher achievement motivation, greater self-esteem, and enhanced competence (Maccoby and Martin, 1983). Authoritative parents also tend to be more involved in school, which benefits adolescents through that pathway (Paulson, 1994; Steinberg, Dornbusch, and Brown, 1992).

Finally, studies have shown that the quality of an adolescent's home environment—as measured simply in terms of the presence of such items as a television set, dictionary, encyclopedia, newspaper, vacuum cleaner, and other indicators of family income—is more strongly correlated with youngsters' level of academic achievement than is the quality of the physical facility of the school they attend, or the background and training of their teachers, or the level of teachers' salaries paid by the school district (Armor, 1972). A number of researchers have also shown that the extent to which the adolescent's parents provide the youngster with **cultural capital**—by exposing the adolescent to art, music, literature, and so forth—exerts a positive impact on achievement, above and beyond the effects of the parents' own level of education (DiMaggio, 1982).

With this in mind, it is important to point out that a disheartening number of young people in this country live in overcrowded, inadequate housing and come from families that are under severe economic and social stress—so much so, that parental encouragement and involvement are often undermined by neighborhood conditions. These obstacles to success disproportionately afflict youngsters from minority backgrounds. Put succinctly, many American youngsters do not grow up in an atmosphere that is conducive to academic achievement.

The Influence of Friends

There is also evidence that friends influence adolescents' achievement, in addition to parental influences. Indeed, some studies suggest that friends, not parents, are the most salient influences on adolescents' day-to-day school behaviors, such as doing homework and exerting effort in class (Kurdek, in press; Steinberg et al., 1992). When most of us think about the influence of adolescents' peers on achievement, we tend immediately to think of the ways in which peers *undermine* academic success. But contrary to the notion that the influence of the peer group is always negative, recent studies suggest that the impact of friends on adolescents' school performance depends on the academic orientation of the peer group. Having friends who earn high grades and aspire to further education appears to enhance adolescents' achievement, whereas having friends who earn low grades or disparage school success may interfere with it (Natriello and McDill, 1986). As they move into middle school, adolescents become increasingly worried about their friends' reactions to success in school; one study found, for example, that by eighth grade, students did not want their classmates to know that they worked hard in school, even though they knew that it would be helpful to convey this impression to their teachers (Juvonen and Murdock, 1993). Adolescents with an extremely high orientation toward peers tend to perform worse in school, on average (Fuligni and Eccles, 1992).

For example, according to one extensive study of friends in school (Epstein, 1983a), students' grades changed over time in relation to the grades of their friends. Students with best friends who achieved high grades in school were more likely to show improvements in their own grades than were students who began at similar levels of achievement but whose friends were not high achievers. Peers also exerted a small but significant influence on each other's college plans. Among low-achieving adolescents, for example, those with high-achieving friends were more likely to plan to continue their education than were those with low-achieving friends.

The potential negative impact of friends on achievement is vividly seen in a widely reported study of African-American male peer groups in an inner-city school (Fordham and Ogbu, 1986). These researchers found that bright students in this school had to live down the "burden of acting white" and face criticism from their peers, who referred to them as "brainiacs." When a small group of these students were placed in an environment in which all their peers were high achievers, the derision and negative labeling did not occur, however.

Recently, a number of researchers have begun to study how the influences of parents and peers operate together to affect adolescents' achievement (Fletcher, Darling, Steinberg, and Dornbusch, 1995; Kurdek, in press; Steinberg et al., 1992). The family environment has an effect on adolescents' choice of friends, and this in turn can influence school achievement. In addition, having friends who value school can positively affect academic achievement, even among teenagers who do not come from nonauthoritative homes. By the same token, having friends who disparage school success may offset the benefits of authoritative parenting. Rather than asking whether family *or* friends influence adolescents' school performance, then, it may make more sense to ask how these two forces—along with the influence of the school itself—work together.

Situational factors can affect occupational attainment as well. In the opinion of some social critics, strong institutional barriers impede the occupational attainment of women and members of ethnic minorities (Ogbu, 1978). These barriers may be especially strong during adolescence, when young people are steered away from some educational and occupational pursuits and toward others—not on the basis of ability or interest but because of gender, socioeconomic background, or ethnicity. As we saw in Chapter 6, the ways in which schools determine which students are exposed to which curricula restrict the opportunities of those students who are placed in the slower tracks and perpetuate these students' academic disadvantages. The courses they encounter are likely to be less stimulating and less intellectually enriching than those taken by their peers. And students who are placed in the slower tracks tend to come disproportionately from minority groups and to be economically disadvantaged—partly because their academic test scores warrant remedial placement, but partly as a consequence of their social background (Featherman, 1980).

Thus, although psychological factors play an important role in determining occupational and scholastic success, it is impossible to examine achievement during adolescence thoroughly without taking into account the broader environment in which individuals pursue their educational and occupational careers. Moreover, distinguishing between motivational and environmental factors is hard: They typically go hand in hand. Living in an environment that offers few opportunities for success induces feelings of learned helplessness, which in turn leads individuals to feel that exerting any effort to succeed is futile. Attending school in an environment where achievement is not encouraged engenders attitudes and beliefs inconsistent with striving for achievement. Rather than viewing achievement during adolescence as being determined by one single factor, such as ability, it is more accurate to say that patterns of achievement are the result of a cumulative process that includes a long history of experience and socialization in school, in the family, at work, and in the peer group.

Having friends who value school can positively affect academic achievement; by the same token, having friends who disparage school success can depress school performance. (Antman/The Image Works)

RECAP

In addition to the influence of beliefs, motives, attributions, and goals, individuals' levels of achievement are also affected by the social context in which they develop, including conditions in the school, the family, and the peer group. A good deal of research indicates that adolescents perform better and are more engaged in school when they come from authoritative homes in which their parents are highly involved in their education. In addition, adolescents whose friends support academic achievement perform better in school than do peers whose friends disparage academic achievements.

EDUCATIONAL ACHIEVEMENT

Educational achievement is usually defined in one of three ways: **school performance** (the grades students earn in school), **academic achievement** (performance on standardized tests), or **educational attainment** (the number of years of schooling completed). These different measures of educational achievement are, not surprisingly, interrelated, but they are less tied to each other than one would expect.

No single factor adequately accounts for differences in adolescents' levels of educational achievement. Generally speaking, mental ability—as assessed by IQ tests—is highly correlated with performance on achievement tests (not surprisingly, since IQ tests and achievement tests are designed to tap similar abilities); mental ability is moderately correlated with school grades and only mildly correlated with educational attainment (Featherman, 1980).

Grades in school—and to an even greater extent, educational attainment—are influenced by a wider range of factors than simply an adolescent's intellectual abilities. Grades, for example, are influenced by teachers' judgments of students' mastery of the material, and these judgments may be influenced by teachers' evaluations of students' efforts and behaviors in the classroom (Farkas et al., 1990). How many years of school an adolescent completes is likely to be influenced by his or her family background as well as by school performance. Two adolescents may have similar grade-point averages, but if one comes from a poor family and cannot afford to go to college, the two will have different levels of educational attainment. In the words of sociologist David Featherman, "High intelligence begets good grades, and both assist one in acquiring above-average education, but . . . it is obvious that some persons fail to achieve their educational potentials while others ultimately obtain degrees and certification in spite of more modest accomplishments in school or average mental ability" (1980, p. 696). Educational attainment has important implications for subsequent earnings: As Figure 12.1 shows, although wages have dropped across the board, the gap in earnings between high school graduates and college graduates is wide and *growing*. When they enter the labor force, individuals with a college degree earn nearly twice as much per hour as do individuals with only a high school diploma (Economic Policy Institute, 1994).

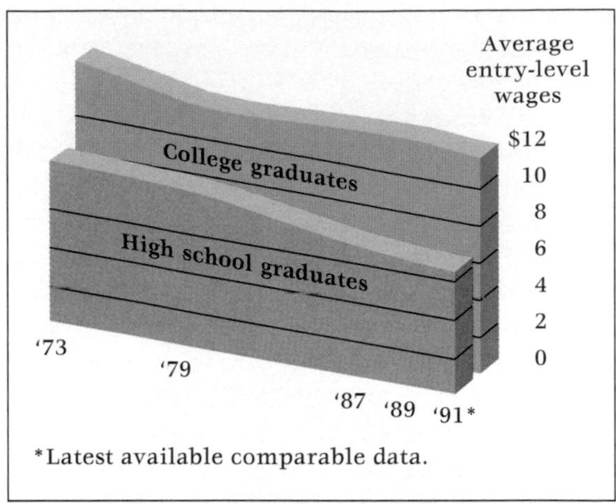

FIGURE 12.1 *Average entry-level wages for high school and college graduates over time.* (Economic Policy Institute, 1994)

The Importance of Socioeconomic Status

One of the most powerful influences on educational achievement is the socioeconomic status of the adolescent's family. Middle-class adolescents score higher on basic tests of academic skills, earn higher grades in school, and complete more years of schooling than their working-class and lower-class peers (Sewell and Hauser, 1972). Although some of the socioeconomic gaps in school achievement appear to be closing, many disparities between the social classes remain strong, and the importance of socioeconomic status in determining educational achievement remains substantial (Featherman, 1980).

Adolescents who come from lower socioeconomic levels are more likely to score lower than their more advantaged peers on standardized tests of achievement, and youngsters who come from higher socioeconomic levels are more likely to score higher. Similarly, youngsters whose parents have gone to college are more likely to attend college themselves than are those whose parents did not attend college. And youngsters whose parents completed high school are also more likely to attend college than are youngsters whose parents did not complete high school (Johnson, 1975). Socioeconomic status, therefore, influences both achievement and attainment and, as a consequence, influences occupational achievement as well. However, you should bear in mind that variations *within* socioeconomic categories are often as substantial as differences *between* categories. Not all youngsters from affluent backgrounds have higher levels of educational achievement than adolescents from poorer families, and many youngsters from economically disadvantaged households go on to receive college and postcollege degrees.

One reason that family background is related to educational achievement is that children from lower socioeconomic levels are more likely to enter elementary school scoring low on tests of basic academic competence. These initial differences reflect both genetic and environmental factors. Middle-class adults generally have higher IQs than lower-class adults, and this advantage is passed on to middle-class children—both through inheritance and through the benefit that middle-class youngsters receive from growing up under more favorable environmental conditions (Featherman, 1980). Affluent youngsters receive better health care and better nutrition, for example, both of which contribute to their higher performance on intelligence tests. The disadvantages of poorer youngsters in achievement test scores persist—and may even increase—throughout elementary and secondary school (Coleman et al., 1966; Entwisle and Hayduk, 1988). Because progress in high school depends so heavily on having a solid foundation of basic academic competence, adolescents who enter secondary school without having mastered basic academic skills quickly fall behind. Many then leave high school before graduating.

One bit of encouraging news on this front comes from recent long-term evaluations of an intervention designed to improve the academic achievement of very poor youngsters who, by virtue of their poverty, were at high risk for academic failure (Campbell and Ramey, 1993). The researchers compared a group of adolescents who had participated in an intensive educational program during their preschool and elementary school years with matched samples of adolescents who had had the preschool intervention only, the elementary school intervention only, or no educational intervention at all. The interventions were targeted at improving the children's school skills and at strengthening the links between parents and their child's school.

The researchers found that the individuals who had participated in the preschool intervention (with or without the elementary school intervention) were performing significantly better in school than those who had not. Interestingly, adolescents who had been in the elementary school intervention only had no advantages over those who had been in no intervention at all. These findings suggest that intervention *prior* to entering first grade may be extremely important in preventing long-term academic problems among impoverished youngsters.

A second reason for the relatively poorer school performance of disadvantaged youth is stress, both before and during adolescence. Adolescents who come from lower-class backgrounds experience more stressful live events, report more daily hassles, and attend schools with more negative climates (Felner et al., in press). Stress has been shown to adversely affect adolescents' mental health, well-being, and school performance (DuBois, Felner, Brand, Adan, and Evans, 1992; Felner et al., in press) (see accompanying box).

STRESS AS THE LINK BETWEEN SOCIOECONOMIC STATUS AND ACHIEVEMENT

Social scientists have long known that, on average, adolescents from lower-class families achieve less in school and complete fewer years of schooling than their counterparts from middle-class homes. This achievement gap has been attributed to differences in the early family environments of poor and well-to-do youngsters, to differences in their parents' expectations and aspirations, and to differences in youngsters' academic capabilities. A new study on this topic demonstrates, however, that yet another factor—stress—may play an important role in explaining socioeconomic differences in educational achievement.

Psychologist Robert Felner and his colleagues (Felner et al., 1995) have been studying a sample of African-American and white young adolescents living in a poor rural community. One-third of the parents in the sample were employed in unskilled occupations, and more than one-third of the parents studied had not graduated from high school. Thus, in terms of two of the most widely used indexes of social class—occupation and education—the sample had a high proportion of lower-class families. The study is especially interesting because it focuses on the rural poor—most of our knowledge about adolescent development in poverty comes from studies of inner-city families (McLoyd, 1990).

As in previous studies, Felner found that youngsters from the lower-class homes (whether defined by parental education or by occupation) perform more poorly in school and on tests of achievement than their counterparts from higher-class homes. Interestingly, adolescents' achievement is affected by *both* parental education and occupation, indicating that each component of social class contributes to achievement independently. The negative effects of low socioeconomic status on achievement were apparent among both African-American and white youngsters. Once this pattern was established, Felner than asked *why* this was so.

Psychologists use the term **mediating variable** to refer to a variable that helps explain the link between an independent variable, such as social class, and scores on a dependent variable, such as educational achievement. In Felner's study, the researchers hypothesized that stress was a mediating variable that linked social class and school achievement. They looked at several different types of stressors, including **stressful life events** (such as the death of a loved one), daily hassles (such as having nagging parents), family conflict, and an alienating school climate.

In order to establish that a mediating variable is, in fact, at work, the researcher attempts to demonstrate four things: (1) that scores on the dependent variable are linked to scores on the independent variable (in this case, educational achievement and social class); (2) that scores on the mediating variable are linked to the independent variable (e.g., that stress was related to social class); (3) that scores on the dependent variable are also linked to the mediating variable (e.g., that educational achievement was linked to stress); and (4) that the link between the independent variable and the dependent variable is significantly weakened when the mediating variable is taken into account (in this case, that once stress was taken into account, the link between social class and educational achievement would diminish) (see figure).

As noted above, Felner first established that educational achievement was in fact linked to social class, satisfying the first condition listed in the preceding paragraph. He then examined whether scores on the measures of stress used in the research were in fact correlated with social class, and found that they were: Students from lower-class homes were more likely to be exposed to stress than were their more advantaged counterparts. This satisfied the second condition listed above. Next, Felner looked to see whether the third condition was met, by examining the relation between stress and achievement. Sure enough, the researchers found that scores on most of the indexes of stress were significantly correlated with students' school performance and with math and reading achievement test scores. Students who had experienced more negative life events or daily hassles, for example, earned lower grades, were absent from school more often, and scored lower on standardized tests of achievement. The pattern of correlations satisfied the third condition.

Finally, Felner turned to the fourth condition—that taking stress into account would diminish the link between social class and educational achievement. In order to do this, the researchers reexamined the link between social class and achievement after controlling for stress. There are a number of ways of doing this statistically, but, in essence, what the researchers did was to ask whether individuals from different social classes who report *the same amount of stress* still have different achievement scores. If they do, this would mean that stress did not account for the social class differences in achievement. If they do not, however, this would indicate that stress is a significant mediating variable.

As the researchers hypothesized, once they took stress into account, the social class differences in school grades and in math achievement disappeared. This indicated that stress was a significant mediating variable linking social class and these two outcomes. In the case of reading scores, however, the researchers found that the link between social class and achievement remained significant, even after taking stress into account. This finding suggested that something other than stress—not measured in this study—accounts for the link between social class and reading achievement.

In many social science studies comparing groups of adolescents—for example, males and females, poor and affluent youth, or blacks and whites—the researcher is content merely to document that the groups differ on some outcome of interest, such as achievement. Although this sort of research can be a good starting point, it rarely adds much to our understanding of adolescent development, since the studies invariably leave open the question of *why* the difference exists. Without understanding the underlying processes that led to group differences, it is difficult, if not impossible, to design efforts to influence patterns of development, if that is a researcher's ultimate goal. Thus, if we are interested in helping lower-class youngsters achieve more in school, we need to know not only that they do in fact achieve less than their more affluent peers but also the reasons for the difference. Felner's research suggests that at least one step we can take would involve reducing the amount of stress in poor adolescents' lives.

SOURCE: Felner, R., et al. (1995). Poverty and educational disadvantage: Environmental mediators of socioemotional and academic achievement in early adolescence. *Child Development*.

Direct and indirect effect of social class on educational achievement. Part of the effect results from stress. (Felner et al., in press)

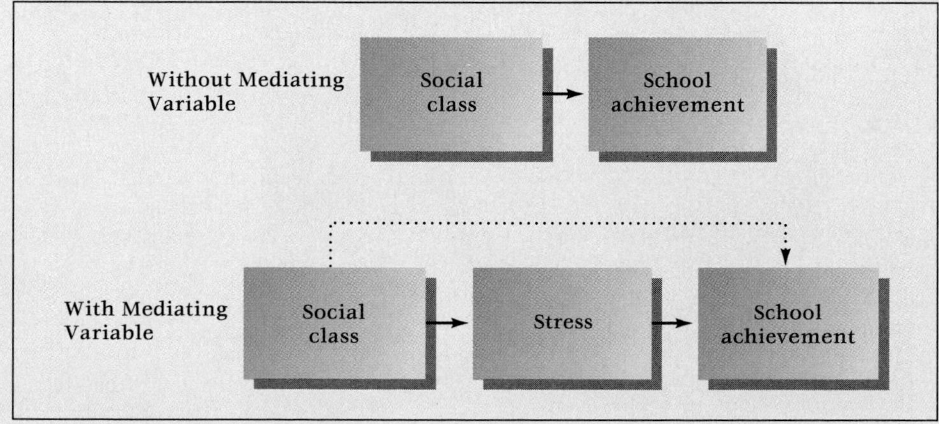

Studies also suggest that parents from higher social classes are more likely to be involved in their adolescent's education, through formal parent-teacher organizations, like the PTA or PTO, and through conferences with their child's teachers (Stevenson and Baker, 1987). They are also more likely to have information about their child's school and to be responsive to their child's school problems and to help select more rigorous courses for their child to take (Baker and Stevenson, 1986). As we noted earlier, since adolescents whose parents are involved in their schooling perform better than adolescents whose parents are not involved, youngsters from higher social classes may achieve more in school than their less advantaged peers (Stevenson and Baker, 1987).

Socioeconomic differences in school achievement—however measured—obviously reflect the cumulative and combined effects of a variety of influences, and it is simplistic to explain group differences in achievement without considering these factors simultaneously. What is perhaps more interesting—and more worthy of scientific study—is to ask what it is about the many youngsters from economically disadvantaged backgrounds who are successful that accounts for their overcoming the tremendous odds against them. Although more research on this subject is sorely needed, several findings suggest that what might be most important is the presence of warm and encouraging parents who raise their children authoritatively, take an interest in their children's academic progress, and hold high aspirations for their children's educational attainment (Bachman, 1970; Simpson, 1962). In other words, positive family relations and parents' encouragement can, in some circumstances, overcome the negative influence of socioeconomic disadvantage.

Adolescents whose parents are involved in their schooling perform better than adolescents who parents are not. Parents from higher social classes are more likely to be involved in their adolescent's education. (Michael Newman/ PhotoEdit)

RECAP

Socioeconomic status is an extremely important influence on educational achievement. Generally, adolescents from higher social classes perform better in school and complete more years of schooling than do their less advantaged counterparts. One reason for this difference is that the home environment of more affluent adolescents is more supportive of school success: Middle-class adolescents are better nourished, more consistently encouraged, and less exposed to stress than are their less affluent peers.

Ethnic Differences in Educational Achievement

Among the most controversial—and intriguing—findings in research on adolescents' achievement are those concerning ethnic differences in school success. On average, the educational achievement of African-American and Hispanic-American students—virtually however indexed—lags behind that of white students, and all three groups achieve less in school than do Asian-American students. Although some of these differences can be attributed to socioeconomic differences among these ethnic groups, the group disparities persist even after socioeconomic factors are taken into account (Brandon, 1991; Call and McNall, 1992; Humphries, 1988; Mickelson, 1990; Steinberg, Dornbusch, and Brown, 1992; Sue and Okazaki, 1990). The academic superiority of Asian-American students tends to emerge during the transition into junior high school—when most other students' grades typically decline (Fuligni, 1994).

Several theories have been advanced to explain these differences. One set of theories involves the perceptions that adolescents have about the likely payoff of hard work in school. For example, urban anthropologist John Ogbu (1974) has argued that many minority youth do not believe that educational success will have substantial occupational payoff for them, because of a prejudicially imposed "job ceiling" on the career development of African-American and Hispanic-American individuals. Consistent with this, African-American adolescents who believe they have been victims of discrimination achieve less in school than do peers who do not hold this belief (Taylor, Casten, Flickinger, Roberts, and Fulmore, 1994). In contrast, Asian-American youngsters not only believe in the value of school success but also are very anxious about the possible negative repercussions of not doing well in school, both in terms of occupational success and in terms of their parents' disappointment (Chung and Walkey, 1989; Steinberg et al., 1992). Moreover, Asian youth believe that the only way that they can succeed in mainstream American society is through educational achievement (Sue and Okazaki, 1990).

An alternative, and complementary, view stresses differences in ethnic groups' beliefs about ability. We noted earlier that adolescents who believe that intelligence is malleable are more likely to be intrinsically motivated, mastery oriented, and, as a consequence, academically successful. It is therefore interesting to note that Asian cultures tend to place more emphasis on effort than on ability in explaining school success and are more likely to believe that all students have the capacity to succeed (Hess, Chih-Mei, and McDevitt, 1987; Holloway, 1988; Stevenson and Stigler, 1992). It is also important to note that Asian students—both in the United States and in Asia—spend significantly more time each week on homework and other school-related activities, and significantly less time socializing and watching television, than do other youth, as Figure 12.2 clearly illustrates (Caplan, Choy, and Whitmore, 1992; Fuligni and Stevenson, in press; Steinberg et al., 1992). Moreover, and contrary to popular belief, Asian students do not pay a price for their superior achievement in terms of

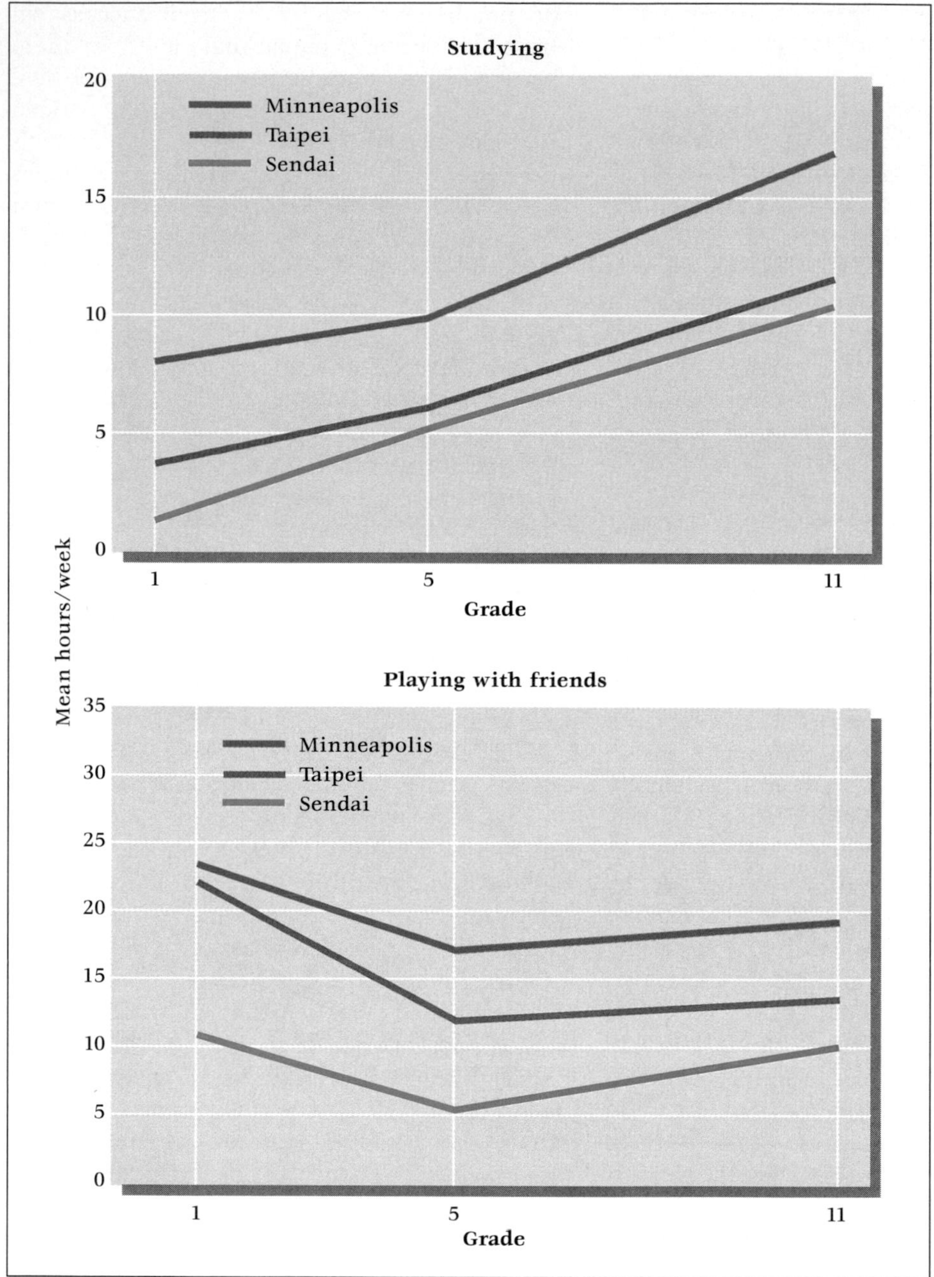

FIGURE 12.2 *Cross-cultural differences in the time adolescents spend studying and playing with friends.* (Fuligni and Stevenson, in press)

increased anxiety, depression, or stress (Crystal, Chen, Fuligni, Stevenson, Hsu, Ko, Kitamura, and Kimura, 1994).

One explanation for ethnic differences in performance, then, is that parents and teachers in Asian communities are more likely to socialize adolescents into believing that their success is in their own hands, whereas parents and teachers in African-American and Hispanic-American communities are more likely to communicate the message that, although education is important, there is little that minority individuals can do to succeed within a discriminatory society (Mickelson, 1990). Unfortunately, this latter message simply is not true: Not only does educational achievement matter for minority youth, but it also may make more of a difference for minority youngsters than for their majority counterparts (Wetzel, 1987).

Of course, as is the case with research on socioeconomic differences in educational achievement, research on ethnic differences indicates that there are wide variations *within* as well as between ethnic groups. First, there are differences in educational achievement among youngsters from different countries of origin that may be classified together into the same larger ethnic group (e.g., differences among Chinese-, Filipino-, and Vietnamese-American adolescents, all of whom are classified as Asian, and differences among Puerto Rican, Cuban-, and Mexican-American adolescents, all of whom are classified as Hispanic) (Fletcher and Steinberg, 1994; Velez, 1989). Second, studies of ethnic minority youngsters show that recent immigrants tend to achieve more in school than do American-born minority youngsters, suggesting that part of becoming acculturated to American society—at least among teenagers—may be learning to devalue academic success (Spencer and Dornbusch, 1990). Third, and most important, studies indicate that, within all ethnic groups, students achieve more when they feel a sense of belonging to their school, when they see the connection between academic accomplishment and future success, when their friends and parents value and support educational achievement, and when their parents are effective monitors of their children's behavior and schooling (Alva, 1993; Connell, Spencer, and Aber, 1994; Falbo, in press; Goodenow, 1992; Luthar, 1994; Murdock, 1994; Reyes and Jason, 1993; Steinberg et al., 1992).

RECAP

Recent studies indicate that there are ethnic differences in educational achievement above and beyond those attributable to socioeconomic status. In general, Asian-American adolescents outperform Anglo-American students, who in turn do better in school than African-American or Hispanic-American students. One reason for the superior performance of Asian students is that they are more likely to hold beliefs about achievement that are predictive of success in school. In contrast, parents and teachers in African-American and Hispanic-American communities are more likely to communicate the message that, although education is important, there is little that minority individuals can do to succeed within a discriminatory society. These different messages may lead students from different backgrounds to devote different degrees of effort to their studies.

Changes in Educational Achievement over Time

As noted in Chapter 6, more students are going on to postsecondary education today than ever before. In other words, levels of educational attainment in America have risen substantially over the past six decades. For example, whereas in 1937 only 15 percent of the students enrolled in the fifth grade eventually entered college, by 1982, this figure had risen to well over 50 percent. Today, between 50 and 60 percent of recent high school graduates enroll in postsecondary programs (Wetzel, 1987).

These overall trends are encouraging, but several variations from this pattern have drawn the concern of educators in recent years. Notably, although high school graduation rates have increased in recent years among African-American youth, college enrollment rates among minorities have actually declined (De Parle, 1991). Thus, for example, whereas one-third of African-American high school graduates enrolled in college in 1976, only one-fourth did so in 1988, and only slightly more did so in 1991. Similarly, the proportion of Hispanic-American high school graduates enrolling in college dropped from 36 percent in 1976, to 27 percent in 1985, and to 24 percent in 1991 (Fiske, 1987; U.S. Bureau of the Census, 1993). Most experts attribute the decline to cutbacks in financial aid.

Trends in academic achievement, however, have not paralleled trends in educational attainment. Thus, although more students are staying in school, they are not necessarily learning more. For example, as Figure 12.3 indicates, between 1970 and 1980, average scores on the Scholastic Aptitude Test (SAT) declined by about fifty points, rose by about fifteen points between 1980 and 1984, and then declined somewhat between 1984 and 1991 (U.S. Bureau of the Census, 1993).

The relatively poor showing of American adolescents on standardized tests of achievement was carefully documented in a series of reports based on the National Assessment of Educational Progress (NAEP) (Mullis, Dossey, Campbell, Gentile, O'Sullivan, and Latham,

FIGURE 12.3 *SAT scores declined between 1970 and 1980, increased between 1980 and 1984, and then began to decline again in 1987.* (U.S. Bureau of the Census, 1993)

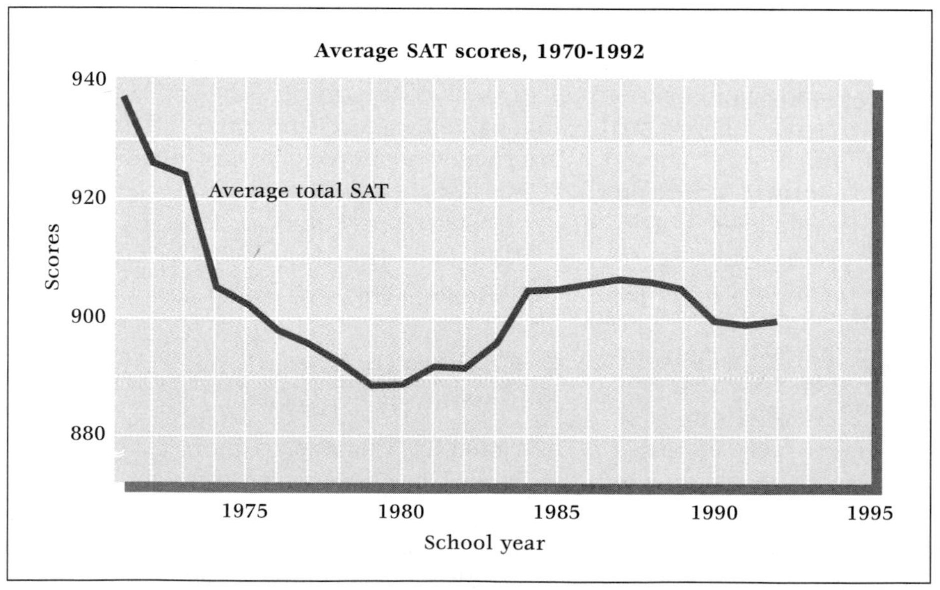

1994). This national assessment of student achievement is conducted by the federal government, in order to track trends in educational achievement over time. Because the NAEP tests have been administered regularly over the past twenty-five years, it is possible to compare the achievement levels of today's adolescents with their counterparts two decades ago.

According to recent NAEP reports, student achievement in reading, writing, and math has not improved significantly over the past twenty-five years, despite massive national efforts at educational reform (see Figure 12.4). Student achievement in science has risen somewhat during the past decade, but this gain has merely offset the decline that took place during the 1970s, and student achievement in science today is no better than it was in 1969.

Perhaps more important, most analyses of the NAEP data indicate that the modest gains

FIGURE 12.4 *Over-time changes in adolescents' scores on standardized tests of achievement.* (National Assessment of Educational Progress, 1994)

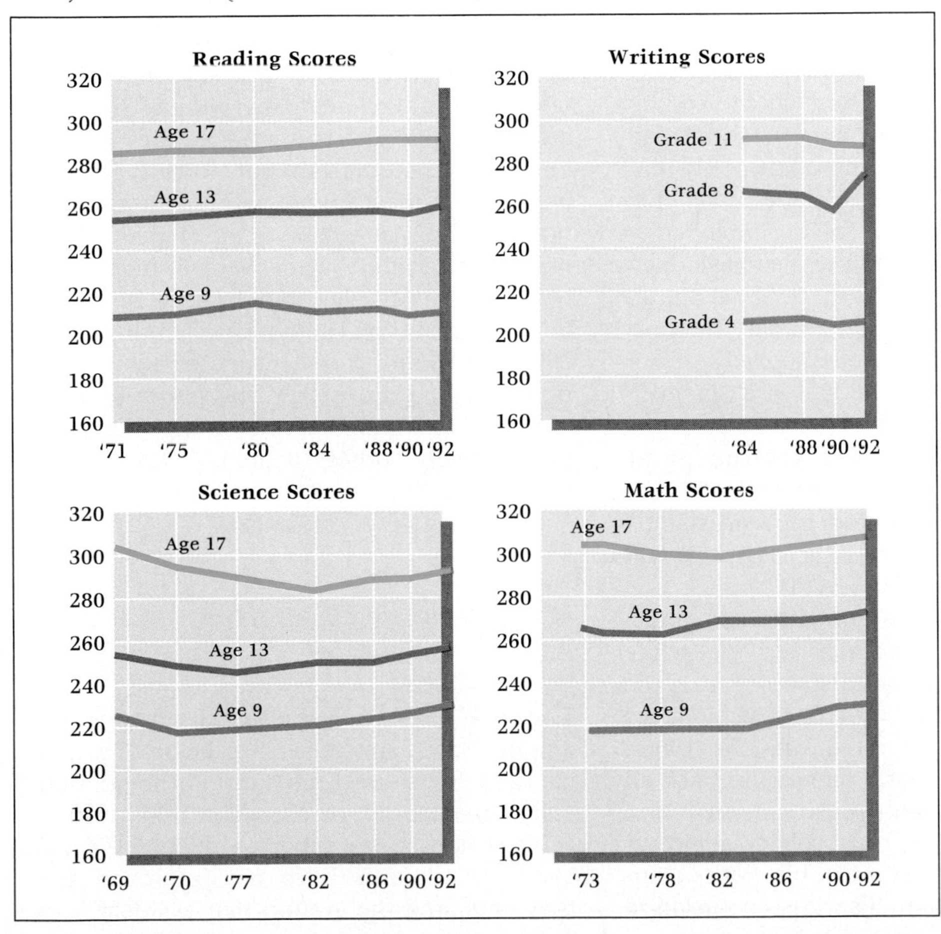

in achievement that have occurred during the past decade or so have been in relatively simple skills. In reading and writing, for example, although more than half of all American 13-year-olds today can read well enough to be able to search for specific information and can make generalizations from reading material, only 10 percent can understand and summarize relatively complicated information. Fewer than half of all students are able to write a simple report (e.g., on a book or television show) at their grade level, and fewer than one-third are able to write a persuasive essay. Only 2 percent of eleventh-graders, and only 1 percent of eighth-graders, are able to write a reasonably sophisticated report that is able to interest and inform a reader (Mullis et al., 1994).

Levels of achievement in math and science show a similar pattern. Thus, while virtually all 17-year-olds can add, subtract, multiply, and divide using whole numbers, only half can perform computations with decimals, fractions, and percents and solve simple equations, and only 6 percent can use basic algebra. Nearly all 17-year-olds have some simple knowledge about plants and animals, but only 40 percent have any detailed knowledge of science, and only 7 percent can use scientific knowledge to draw conclusions. As one expert put it, virtually all adolescents can "read, write, add, subtract and count their change. But as one moves up the scale toward slightly more complicated tasks, success falls off rapidly" (Manegold, 1994, p. A14).

As is the case in rates of high school graduation, the gap in achievement between white and minority youngsters narrowed during the 1970s; but a wide disparity still exists, and the gap did not shrink at all during the 1980s. According to NAEP data, across virtually all subject areas, the average African-American or Hispanic-American high school senior is performing at a level comparable to the average white eighth-grader. There is no reason to be sanguine about the performance of white students, however—since the 1970s, their test scores have remained stagnant, and U.S. scores on standardized tests of math and science are among the lowest in the industrialized world (Stevenson and Stigler, 1992). Three-fourths of all college faculty believe that entering students lack basic skills, and colleges have reported a significant increase in demand for remedial coursework for incoming freshmen (Mullis, Owen, and Phillips, 1990).

If more American students are remaining in high school, and so many are going on to college, why are their achievement test scores so low? The NAEP report suggests several reasons—among them, that teachers are not spending enough time on basic instruction in the classroom; that students are not taking advanced courses when they are offered, especially courses in math and science; that parents are not encouraging academic pursuits at home; and that students are not spending sufficient time on their studies outside of school. The average high school senior, for example, spends only about one hour per day on homework (Mullis et al., 1990). Perhaps not surprisingly, students report feeling more unhappy, more lethargic, and less interested while doing homework than during other activities (Leone and Richards, 1989).

RECAP

The low level of educational achievement among American youth has been a national concern for some time now. Although some gains in scores on standardized tests of achievement were reported during the mid-1980s, test scores have not improved since that time, and the ground that was lost in the late 1960s and early 1970s has not been recovered. Among the reasons given for this pattern are that teachers are not spending enough time on basic instruction, that students are not taking advanced courses when they are offered, that parents are not encouraging academic pursuits at home, and that adolescents are not spending sufficient time on their studies outside of school.

Dropping Out of High School

There was a time when leaving high school before graduating did not have the dire consequences that it does today. With changes in the labor force, however, have come changes in the educational requirements for entry into the world of work. Today educational attainment is a powerful predictor of adult occupational success and earnings. Not surprisingly, high school dropouts are far more likely than graduates to live at or near the poverty level, to experience unemployment, to depend on government-subsidized income maintenance programs, and to be involved in delinquent and criminal activity.

Although dropping out of high school is less prevalent now than it was thirty-five years ago, a substantial number of today's adolescents leave high school before graduating. The national dropout rate declined from more than 30 percent in 1960 to 20 percent in 1970, but the rate began to increase in the late 1970s, and since then it has remained around 25 percent. There are huge variations in dropout rates from region to region, however, with average rates varying from around 10 percent (in Minnesota) to nearly 40 percent (in Florida) (Fitzpatrick and Yoels, 1992); indeed, in some urban areas, *more than half* of all students leave school prematurely (Bryk and Thum, 1989). It is important to point out, however, that more than half of all youngsters who do not graduate on time eventually complete their high school education by returning to school or through a General Education Development (GED) program. The proportion of individuals who have not completed a high school degree by age 24 is only 14 percent (U.S. Bureau of the Census, 1993).

When dropout rates are examined for different ethnic groups, we find that African-American youngsters drop out of high school at a rate only slightly greater than that among white youngsters (both are near the national average) but that Hispanic youngsters drop out at more than twice the rate of other youth (U.S. Bureau of the Census, 1993) (see Figure 12.5). One reason for this is the large proportion of Hispanic youth who are not English-speaking; a lack of proficiency in English is a major determinant of dropping out (Steinberg, Blinde, and Chan, 1984).

Given the findings on educational achievement discussed earlier, the research evidence on the other correlates of dropping out comes as no surprise. In addition to the prevalence of

FIGURE 12.5 *Percent of the population aged 18 to 24 who have dropped out of school, as of 1991.* (U.S. Bureau of the Census, 1993)

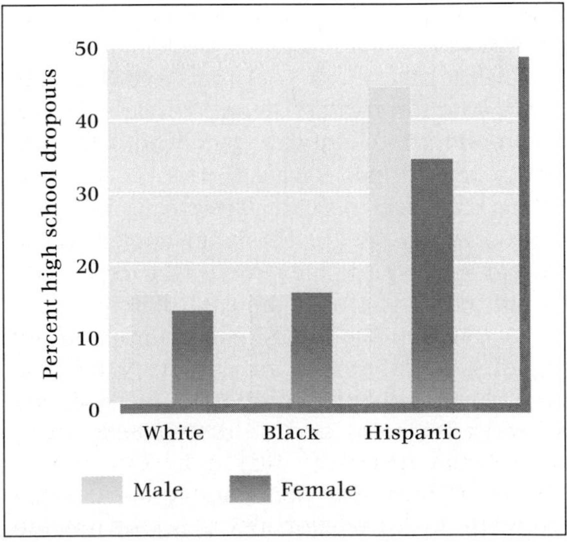

dropping out among Hispanic youngsters and among youngsters who are not fluent in English, adolescents who leave high school before graduating are more likely to come from lower socioeconomic levels, poor communities, large families, single-parent families, nondemanding families, and households where little reading material is available. In short, adolescents who drop out of school are more likely to come from socially and economically disadvantaged backgrounds (Entwisle, 1990; Rumberger, 1983; Zimiles and Lee, 1991).

Coupled with this socioeconomic disadvantage, adolescents who drop out of high school also are more likely to have had a history of poor school performance, low school involvement, poor performance on standardized tests of achievement and intelligence, negative school experiences, and a variety of behavioral problems, such as excessive aggression (Cairns, Cairns, and Neckerman, 1989). Many high school dropouts have had to repeat one or more grades in elementary school. By the time youngsters have reached the ninth grade, for example, it is possible to predict—with over 90 percent accuracy—which adolescents will complete high school simply by knowing each individual's age (which indicates whether he or she has been held back in school), IQ, socioeconomic background, and achievement test scores (Walters and Kranzler, 1970). More remarkably, one researcher was able to identify youngsters who would become high school dropouts with 75 percent accuracy at the time the individuals were in the third grade, solely on the basis of family background variables, achievement test scores, elementary school grades, and IQ scores (Lloyd, 1978). Students who ultimately drop out of school generally have an especially difficult time during the transition into high school, when their grades decline dramatically (Roderick, 1991).

The picture that emerges, then, is that dropping out of high school is not so much a decision that is made during the adolescent years but, like other aspects of adolescent achievement, the culmination of a long process. For the dropout, this process is characterized by a history of repeated academic failure and increasing alienation from school.

Although most research on the causes of dropping out has focused on characteristics of adolescents who leave school prematurely, a number of studies have focused on the schools that dropouts leave. In general, dropping out is less likely from schools where the environment is orderly, where academic pursuits are emphasized, and where the faculty is committed. Dropout rates are also higher in larger schools that group students according to ability (Bryk and Thum, 1989). Consistent with this, some research suggests that dropout rates may be reduced in some cases by permitting students who are having educational difficulties to change schools, rather than leaving school altogether (Lee and Burkam, 1992).

RECAP

About 25 percent of adolescents leave high school before graduating, although a fair number return to school in young adulthood and earn their diploma at a later date. There are wide ethnic and regional differences in dropout rates, however, and dropping out of school is an especially serious problem among Hispanic youth. Dropouts are more likely than their peers to come from economically disadvantaged backgrounds, to come from single-parent homes, and to have had a poor record of educational achievement throughout their school years. Studies also suggest that the schools from which students drop out are larger, more disorderly, and less focused on academics than other schools.

OCCUPATIONAL ACHIEVEMENT

During early and middle adolescence, school is the setting in which achievement is most often expressed. During late adolescence, the focus shifts to the world of work and careers. Although we often think of school and work as separate domains, achievement is one aspect of psychosocial development during adolescence that links them together. Rather than thinking of educational achievement and occupational achievement as separate, it is more useful to think of them as different manifestations of the same basic psychosocial phenomena.

The number of years of schooling an individual completes is the single best indicator of his or her eventual occupational success. It is not simply that adolescents benefit in the labor force by having a high school diploma or a college degree. Although these credentials matter, research shows that each year of education—even without graduating—adds significantly to occupational success. In other words, individuals who have completed three years of college earn more money, on average, than individuals who have completed only one year, even though neither group has a college degree in hand. You may be surprised to learn, however, that grades in high school and college are virtually unrelated to occupational success. A few years after graduation, A students and C students hold similarly prestigious jobs and earn comparable amounts of money (Garbarino and Asp, 1981).

Researchers who are interested in occupational achievement during adolescence have examined several issues, including the ways in which young people make decisions about their careers and the influences on their occupational aspirations and expectations. We begin with a look at the development of adolescents' occupational plans.

The Development of Occupational Plans

The development of occupational plans during adolescence can be viewed in many respects as paralleling, or even as part of, the identity development process. As with developing a coherent sense of identity, the development of occupational plans follows a sequence that involves an examination of one's traits, abilities, and interests; a period of experimentation with different work roles; and an integration of influences from one's past (primarily, identification with familial role models) with one's hopes for the future. And as is also the case with identity development, occupational role development is profoundly influenced by the social environment in which it takes place.

For the past thirty years, the dominant theoretical viewpoint in the study of the development of occupational plans has been that of Donald Super (1967). Super suggests that occupational plans develop in stages, with adolescence as an important time for the crystallization of plans that are more realistic, less based on fantasy, and more grounded in the adolescent's assessment of his or her talents. Before adolescence, individuals express occupational interests, but these are much like fantasies and have little to do with the plans they will eventually make. When children are asked what they want to be when they grow up, they are likely to respond with occupations that are exciting, glamorous, or familiar—a teacher, a police officer, a baseball player, a movie star.

With the advent of more sophisticated thinking capabilities during early adolescence, however, and as the economic and practical realities of adulthood become imminent, young people begin to consider career alternatives in a more systematic fashion. They plan educational and work activities to suit their career interests, and they evaluate career decisions in terms of long- as well as short-term consequences. Instead of merely being attracted to glamorous or exciting jobs, adolescents think about such mundane realities as the need to earn a living.

According to Super, between ages 14 and 18 individuals first begin to crystallize a vocational preference. During this period of **crystallization,** individuals begin to formulate ideas about appropriate work and begin to develop occupational self-conceptions that will guide subsequent educational decisions. Although adolescents may not settle on a particular career at this point, they do begin to narrow their choices according to their interests, values, and abilities. One adolescent may decide that she wants a career in which she works with people. Another may decide that he wants a career in which he can earn a great deal of money. A third may think about a career in science. During this period, the adolescent begins to seek out information on his or her tentative choice and make plans for the future (Osipow, 1973). The process is reminiscent of the sort of role experimentation described by Erik Erikson (1968) in his theory of adolescent identity development (see Chapter 8). In both cases, during middle adolescence, alternative identities are considered and evaluated on the basis of exploration, experimentation, and self-examination (Crites, 1989).

Following the period of crystallization is a period of **specification,** occurring roughly between the ages of 18 and 21. During this period, the young person recognizes the need to specify his or her vocational interests and begins to seek appropriate information to accomplish this. In many regards, a similar process is followed during the stage of specification as during the stage of crystallization: Alternatives are considered, information is sought, decisions are made, and preferences are consolidated. The chief difference, however, is that during the period of specification, more narrowly defined career pursuits within a general career category are considered (rather than general career categories themselves). For example, during the period of crystallization, a young person may decide to pursue a career in the field of mental health, without being able to specify a vocational preference within this general category. During the specification stage, he or she might begin to consider and compare a variety of careers within the mental health profession—social work, educational counseling, clinical psychology, psychiatry, and so on—and make choices among them.

Although the chronological ages given in Super's theory must be taken as only rough guidelines, his perspective is an influential one, and it has shaped the way in which career counselors advise young people. Perhaps most important, Super's perspective reminds us that vocational development comes relatively late during adolescence and that a good deal of growth in this arena takes place during the young adult years. This has become increasingly true in contemporary society, as more and more young people have chosen to continue their education in college and postpone their entrance into a career until their midtwenties. Changes in the broader environment in which adolescents develop—in this case, changes in the accessibility of higher education—can exert a powerful influence on the developmental course of occupational planning.

Influences on Occupational Choices

What makes one individual choose to become an attorney and another decide to be a teacher? Why do some students pursue careers in psychology while others major in computer science? Researchers have long been interested in the reasons that individuals end up in certain careers. While Super's developmental theory has helped us understand the general stages of career planning, it does not shed light on why certain careers appeal to some individuals but not to others. In other words, Super's theory focuses on how and when individuals make career choices, rather than on why they make the career choices they do.

● ***The Role of Personality.*** Many theorists who are interested in why people enter different occupational fields have examined the role of personality factors—traits, interests, and values—in the process of career selection. They believe that individuals select careers that match, in one way or another, certain elements of their personality. Perhaps the most widely cited perspective of this sort is that of John Holland (1985).

After years of extensive analysis of jobs and the people who select them, Holland determined that career choices can be viewed as a reflection of basic personality styles. Certain occupational environments are well suited to individuals with certain personalities, and others are not. Successful career choice, in Holland's model, entails the matching of a particular personality type—a given set of interests and personality characteristics—with a vocation that allows the expression of these traits. By answering questions on a standardized personality inventory, an individual can determine which basic personality dimensions are characteristic of himself or herself and can then examine directories in which occupations have been classified according to the same typology.

After completing Holland's personality inventory—called the **Self-Directed Search**—an individual better understands his or her vocational profile (which of the personality dimensions are dominant and which are less important). Because different occupations typically offer different degrees of opportunity to express different traits, a good career choice in Holland's view is one that provides the best fit between a person's personality and a vocation's characteristics. Someone who is artistic, social, and enterprising, for example, would be better suited to a career in acting than in accounting. Other theoretical frameworks focusing on the fit between individual personality characteristics and work environments are popular as well.

There are important limitations to theories of career choice that are based solely on personality traits, however. First, it is clear that interests and abilities are not fixed during adolescence and young adulthood (Mortimer and Lorence, 1979). They continue to develop and change during the adult years. Indeed, one of the most important influences on personality development during adulthood is work itself! Thus, through working in a job that emphasizes certain personality characteristics, requires certain abilities, or reinforces certain values, individuals begin to change in these directions. Consequently, a job that may seem like a bad match during early adulthood may, over time, become a good match, as the adult employee grows and changes in response to the work environment. For example, an individual may not be especially interested in social interactions but may, because of a tight job market, end up in a teaching position after graduating from college. Over time, the more he or she interacts with students, the more appealing the interpersonal aspects of the job may become. Eventually, this person may come to feel that having opportunities for social interaction on the job is very important.

A second problem with theories of career choice that emphasize personality dimensions is that they may underestimate the importance of other factors that influence and shape vocational decisions. Many career decisions are influenced more by individuals' beliefs about what sorts of jobs are "appropriate" for them rather than by interests and preferences. It is all well and good, for example, for an adolescent to discover that he or she is well suited for a career in medicine; but the realization is of little value if the young person's family cannot afford the cost of college or medical school. An adolescent girl may discover, through taking a vocational preference inventory, that she is well suited for work in the area of construction or building, but she may find that her parents, peers, teachers, and potential employers all discourage her from following this avenue of employment. Put most simply, career choices are not made solely on the basis of individual preference; they are the result of an interaction among individual preference, social influence, and important forces in the broader social environment. It is to these influences and forces that we now turn.

● ***The Influence of Parents and Peers.*** Adolescents' occupational ambitions and achievements are highly correlated with the ambitions and achievements of those around them (Duncan, Featherman, and Duncan, 1972). Youngsters from middle-class families are more likely than their less advantaged peers to aspire to and enter middle-class occupations. In addition, apart from their own socioeconomic status, youngsters who have many friends from middle-class backgrounds are more likely than those who have many friends from lower socioeconomic levels to aspire to high-status occupations (Simpson, 1962).

A variety of explanations have been offered for the fit between adolescents' ambitions and the socioeconomic status of those around them. First, and perhaps most important, **occupational attainment**—the prestige or status an individual achieves in the world of work—depends strongly on educational attainment (Alexander and Eckland, 1975). As we saw earlier, educational attainment is greatly influenced by socioeconomic status. Thus, because middle-class adolescents are likely to complete more years of schooling than their lower-class peers, economically advantaged adolescents are more likely to seek and enter higher-status occupations.

Second, middle-class parents, as we noted earlier, are more likely to raise their children in ways that foster the development of strong needs for achievement (Rosen, 1956) and interest in career exploration (Grotevant and Cooper, 1988). The development of achievement motivation, which has an impact on school performance, also has an impact on youngsters' occupational ambitions—both directly (in that individuals with strong needs for achievement will express these needs by aspiring to occupations that provide opportunities to achieve status or wealth) and indirectly, through the effects of achievement motivation on academic achievement (in that youngsters who are successful in school are likely to be encouraged to seek higher-status occupations and engage in identity exploration).

Third, the same opportunities that favor economically advantaged youngsters in the world of education—better facilities, more opportunities for enrichment, greater accessibility of higher education—also favor middle-class youngsters in the world of work. Because their parents, for example, are more likely to work in positions of power and leadership, middle-class youngsters often have important family connections and sources of information about the world of work that are less available to youngsters from poorer families. In addition, coming from a family that is economically well off may provide an adolescent with more time to explore career options and to wait for an especially desirable position rather than having to take the first job that becomes available, out of economic necessity.

Fourth, parents, siblings, and other important sources of influence serve as models for adolescents' occupational choices (Barber and Eccles, 1992; Grotevant and Cooper, 1988). Although it is true that some young people establish career choices through the explicit rejection of their parents' careers, the weight of the evidence suggests that adolescents' and parents' vocations are more similar than different, particularly when the adolescent's family relationships have been warm and close and when strong identifications have formed. As

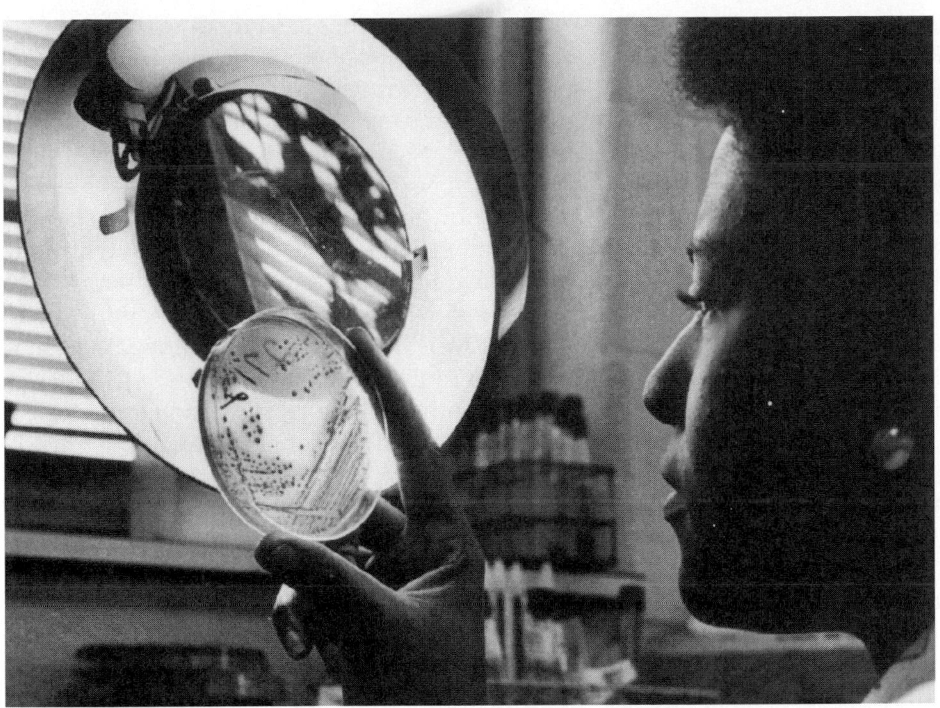

Although some young people establish career choices by rejecting their parents' occupations, the majority of adolescents select careers that are similar to, rather than different from, those of their parents. Parents-child similiarity in occupational choices is greatest in families with warm, close relationships. (Guy Gillette/Photo Researchers)

we saw in our discussion of mothers' employment in Chapter 4, adolescents are especially influenced by the work roles of the parent of the same sex. This finding has become increasingly important as growing numbers of women enter the labor force and hold high-status occupations. Daughters of women who are happily employed outside the home are far more likely themselves to seek careers in addition to marriage and family responsibilities than are adolescent girls whose mothers are not employed (Leslie, 1986). Young women whose mothers occupy high-status occupations are more likely to do so themselves when they enter the labor force (Hoffman, 1974). And both sons and daughters are less likely to have sex-stereotyped attitudes about work and more likely to prefer a dual-career arrangement if they come from dual-career families themselves (Barber and Eccles, 1992).

Finally, parents—and to a lesser extent peers—influence adolescents' occupational plans by establishing a value context in which certain occupational choices are encouraged and others are discouraged. According to sociologist Melvin Kohn (1977), middle-class families and middle-class schools encourage children to value autonomy, self-direction, and independence—three features that are more likely to be found in middle-class than in working-class jobs. The children are told, implicitly and explicitly, how important it is to have freedom, power, and status. Adolescents who have been raised to value attributes that are characteristic of middle-class jobs will, not surprisingly, seek those attributes when they plan their careers. They will look for jobs that offer independence and power. In working-class families, in contrast, children are more likely to be raised to value obedience and conformity—two characteristics that are highly valued in most working-class jobs. For youngsters from this socioeconomic background, jobs that appeal to these values will be relatively more attractive. They will have been raised to value such things as job security and not having to worry too much about making high-pressured decisions. Indeed, to many working-class youngsters, the high-stress world of the business executive is not at all an attractive career possibility.

● ***The Broader Context of Occupational Choice.*** Adolescents' occupational choices are made, of course, in a broader context that profoundly influences the nature of their plans. At different times, different employment opportunities arise, and young people—particularly by the time they reach the end of their formal schooling—are often very aware of the prospects for employment in different fields. Understandably, they often tailor their plans in response to what they perceive as the needs and future demands of the labor market, and the acceptability of given occupational choices within their community. One recent study found, for example, that many rural adolescents experience great conflicts between wanting to pursue a career that would take them away from their rural community and wanting to remain close to their roots (Hektner, 1994).

Unfortunately, adolescents also tailor their plans based on their beliefs regarding which jobs are "acceptable" for individuals of particular social class, ethnicity, or gender. Despite the liberalization in sex-role stereotypes that occurred during the past thirty years, for example, it is still the case that adolescent girls' vocational choices tend to be concentrated among jobs that have historically been occupied by women, such as secretarial work, teaching, and nursing, and they are more oriented toward occupations that involve working with people. In contrast, relatively fewer adolescent girls plan to enter jobs in science or engineering—occupational sectors that typically have been dominated by men—and their preferences lean toward occupations that involve working with things, rather than people (Jozefowicz, Barber, Eccles, and Mollasis, 1994). Moreover, many more adolescent girls than boys express concern about having to balance family and work demands in adulthood, and this further affects their occupational decision making, since they may be reluctant to pursue careers that they believe will interfere with family life (Astin, 1984). This task may vary between daughters who grow up in divorced versus nondivorced households, since they probably have been exposed to very different models of how to balance work and family obligations (Barber and Eccles, 1992).

One problem faced by all young people in making career plans is obtaining accurate information about the labor market needs of the future and the appropriate means of pursuing positions in various fields. The majority of young people do not have educational plans that are consistent with the educational requirements of the jobs they hope to enter. Even among high school seniors who perceived themselves as having "considerable" knowledge of the fields they planned to enter, approximately one-fifth were planning on too little education and nearly one-third were planning too much education, given the requirements of the careers to which they aspired (Grotevant and Durrett, 1980). One goal of career educators is to help adolescents make more informed choices about their careers and to free them from stereotypes that constrain their choices.

RECAP

Adolescence is a time for the development of realistic occupational plans. In general, research indicates that adolescents' career choices are influenced by a number of factors, including their personality, their social background, and their perceptions of the labor market and their potential place within it. As is the case with educational achievement, occupational achievement is strongly influenced by socioeconomic status.

KEY TERMS

academic achievement
achievement attributions
achievement
crystallization
cultural capital
educational attainment
extrinsic motivation
fear of failure
fear of success
intrinsic motivation
learned helplessness
mediating variable
need for achievement
occupational attainment
school performance
Self-Directed Search
specification
stressful life events
temperament
Type-A behavior
underachievers

FOR FURTHER READING

Elmen, J. (1991). Achievement orientation in early adolescence: Developmental patterns and social correlates. *Journal of Early Adolescence, 11,* 125–151. A review of the literature on the development of achievement motives in adolescence.

Explaining the school performance of minority students. (1987). Special issue of the *Anthropology and Education Quarterly, 18.* An interesting collection of theoretical articles and case studies exploring school performance among minority students.

Featherman, D. (1980). Schooling and occupational careers: Constancy and change in worldly success. In O. Brim, Jr., and J. Kagan (Eds.), *Constancy and change in human development.* Cambridge, Mass.: Harvard University Press. An extensive review of the cumulative process of educational and occupational attainment during childhood, adolescence, and adulthood.

Henderson, V., and Dweck, C. (1990). Motivation and achievement. Pp. 308–329 in S. Feldman and G. Elliott (Eds.), *At the threshold: The developing adolescent.* Cambridge, Mass.: Harvard University Press. A discussion of the role of achievement beliefs and attributions in adolescent school performance.

Steinberg, L., Dornbusch, S., and Brown, B. (1992). Ethnic differences in adolescent achievement: An ecological perspective. *American Psychologist, 47,* 723–729. A study of how family and peer influences operate to jointly influence achievement in different ethnic groups.

CHAPTER 13

PSYCHOSOCIAL PROBLEMS IN ADOLESCENCE

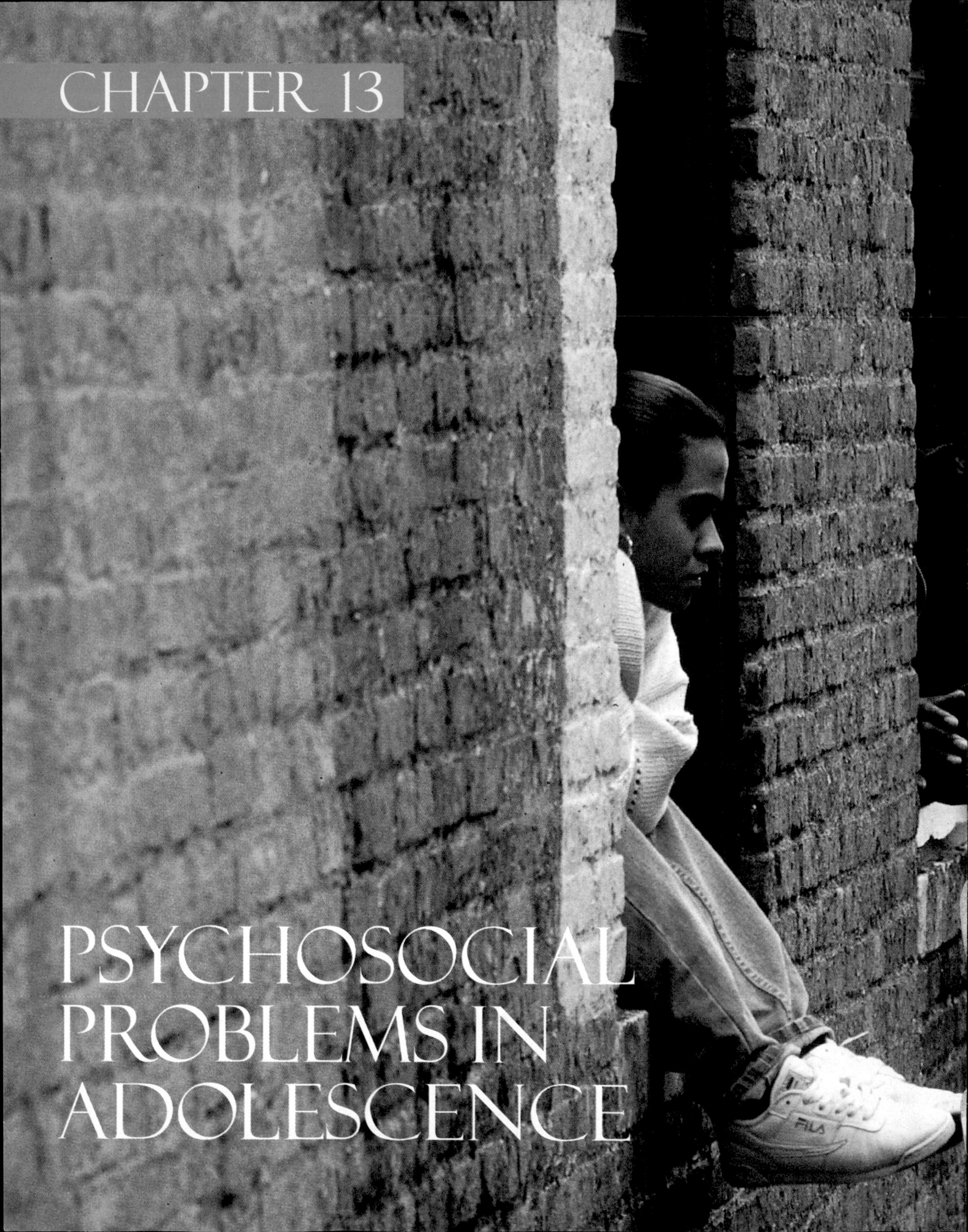

(Goldberg/Monkmeyer)

Although the vast majority of young people move through the adolescent years without experiencing major difficulty, some encounter serious psychological and behavioral problems that disrupt not only their lives but also the lives of those around them. Problems such as substance abuse, depression and suicide, eating disorders, and disorders of conduct (including crime and delinquency)—while certainly not the norm during adolescence—do affect a worrisome number of teenagers (Kazdin, 1993). Moreover, these problems indirectly touch the lives of all of us, either through the personal contact we may have with a troubled young person or indirectly, through increased taxes for community services or heightened anxiety about the safety of our neighborhoods. The young person who drops out of school before graduation, for example, not only jeopardizes his or her own occupational career—reason enough to discourage dropping out of school—but also runs the risk of falling into the welfare system and becoming dependent on public assistance.

In the previous chapters, which examined normative aspects of adolescents psychosocial development, the more problematic aspects of adolescent behavior and development were deliberately deemphasized, in order to dispel the erroneous stereotype of adolescence as an inherently troubled time. As you now know from reading these chapters, research shows that most individuals emerge from adolescence with positive feelings about themselves and their parents; with the ability to form, maintain, and enjoy close relationships with same- and opposite-sex peers; and with the basic capabilities needed to take advantage of a range of educational and occupational opportunities. Most settle into adulthood relatively smoothly and begin establishing their work and family careers with little serious difficulty. Although the transition into adulthood may appear forbidding to the young adolescent approaching many weighty decisions about the future, statistics tell us that, for a remarkably high proportion of youth, the transition is relatively peaceful. Among adolescent girls, 1 in 5 gets pregnant before she is 18, but 4 in 5 do not. Although 20 percent of students do not complete high school by the societally expected age, 80 percent do, and more than half of young people who leave school prematurely later receive a high school diploma. And despite popular media portrayals otherwise, the majority of minority youth are *not* poorly adjusted (Barbarin, 1993).

This is not to gloss over the fact that many healthy adolescents at one time or another experience bouts of self-doubt, periods of family squabbling, academic or vocational setbacks, or broken hearts. But it is important to keep in mind as we look at psychosocial problems during adolescence that there is an important distinction between the normative, and usually transitory, difficulties that are encountered by many, many young people—and by many adults, for that matter—and the serious psychosocial problems that are experienced by a relatively small minority of youth.

SOME GENERAL PRINCIPLES

The mass media like nothing more than to paint extreme pictures of the world in which we live. One way in which this exaggerated view of the world is most obvious is in the presentation of teenage problem behavior. Rarely are portrayals of sex, psychological difficulty, drug use, or delinquency accurate: On television, one experiment with marijuana inevitably leads to drug addiction and school failure. A breakup with a boyfriend is followed by a suicide attempt. An after-school prank develops into a life of crime. A couple's passionate necking session on the beach fades into a commercial, and when the program returns, the adolescent girl is on her way to a life of single parenthood and welfare dependency. Those of you for whom adolescence was not that long ago know that these "facts" about adolescent problem behavior are rarely true; but we are so often bombarded with images of young people in trouble, that it is easy for all of us to get fooled into believing that adolescence equals problems.

One of the purposes of this chapter is to put these problems in perspective. It is therefore helpful, before we look at several problems in detail, to lay out some general principles about adolescent psychosocial problems that apply to a range of issues. First, we need to distinguish between occasional experimentation and enduring patterns of dangerous or troublesome behavior. Research shows that rates of occasional, usually harmless, experimentation far exceed rates of enduring problems. For example, the majority of adolescents experiment with alcohol sometime before high school graduation, and the majority will have been drunk at least once; but, as we shall see, relatively few teenagers will develop drinking problems or will permit alcohol to adversely affect their school or personal relationships.

It is important to differentiate between occasional experimentation and enduring patterns of troublesome behavior. (David Young-Wolff/Tony Stone Images)

Second, we need to distinguish between problems that have their origins and onset during adolescence and those that have their roots during earlier periods of development. It is true, for example, that some teenagers fall into patterns of criminal or delinquent behavior during adolescence, and for this reason we tend to associate delinquency with the adolescent years. But studies suggest that most teenagers who have recurrent problems with the law had problems at home and at school from an early age; in some samples of delinquents, the problems were evident as early as preschool (Moffitt, 1993). In other words, simply because a problem may be displayed *during* adolescence does not mean that it is a problem *of* adolescence.

Third, it is important to remember that some, although not all, of the problems experienced by adolescents are relatively transitory in nature and are resolved by the beginning of adulthood, with few long-term repercussions in most cases. Substance abuse, delinquency, and unemployment are three good examples of problems that tend to follow this pattern: Rates of drug and alcohol use, unemployment, and delinquency are all higher within the adolescent and youth population than in the adult population, but most individuals who have abused drugs and alcohol, been unemployed, or committed delinquent acts as teenagers grow up to be sober, employed, law-abiding adults. Individuals for whom problem behavior persists into adulthood are likely to have had a problematic childhood as well as a problematic adolescence. The fact that some of the problems of adolescence seem to disappear on their own with time does not make their prevalence during adolescence any less significant, but it should be kept in mind when rhetoric is hurled back and forth about the "inevitable" decline of civilization at the hands of contemporary youth.

Finally, as should be evident, problem behavior during adolescence is virtually never a direct consequence of going through the normative changes of adolescence itself. Popular theories about "raging hormones" causing oppositional or deviant behavior have no scientific support whatsoever, for example, nor do the widely held beliefs that problem behaviors are manifestations of an inherent need to rebel against authority, or that bizarre behavior results from having an "identity crisis." As you learned in previous chapters, the hormonal changes of puberty have only a modest direct effect on adolescent behavior; rebellion during adolescence is atypical, not normal; and few adolescents experience a tumultuous identity crisis. When a young person exhibits a serious psychosocial problem, such as depression, the worst possible interpretation is that it is a normal part of growing up. It is more likely to be a sign that something is wrong.

RECAP

Although the vast majority of individuals do not develop serious psychological or social problems during the adolescent years, a significant minority do. In thinking about problem behavior during adolescence, it is important to distinguish between experimentation and enduring patterns of behavior, between problems that have their origins during adolescence and those that do not, and between problems that are transitory and those that persist into adulthood.

PSYCHOSOCIAL PROBLEMS: THEIR NATURE AND CO-VARIATION

Clinical psychologists and other experts on the development and treatment of psychosocial problems during adolescence typically distinguish between two broad categories of problems: internalizing disorders and externalizing disorders (Achenbach and Edelbrock, 1987). **Internalizing disorders** are those in which the young person's problems are turned inward and are manifested in emotional and cognitive symptoms such as depression, anxiety, or in psychosomatic disturbances. (**Psychosomatic disorders** are physical problems that are at least partially psychological in origin, such as bulimia or anorexia.) **Externalizing disorders,** in contrast, are those in which the young person's problems are turned outward and are manifested in behavioral problems (some writers use the expression "acting out" to refer to this set of problems). Common externalizing problems during adolescence are delinquency, drug and alcohol abuse, and truancy. In general, externalizing problems tend to be correlated with extreme parental permissiveness or disengagement, whereas internalizing problems tend to be associated with excessive parental psychological control (Barber, Olsen, and Shagle, 1994). Interestingly, the prevalence of externalizing problems is higher in cultures that tend to treat children (and aggression) more permissively (such as the United States), whereas the prevalence of internalizing problems is higher in cultures in which parents exercise high psychological control over children (such as Thailand) (Weisz, Suwanlert, Chaiyasit, Weiss, Achenbach, and Eastman, 1993).

One of the reasons it is helpful to differentiate between internalizing and externalizing disorders is that the specific problems within each broad category are often highly intercorrelated. That is, drug and alcohol abuse is often associated with problems such as delinquency, truancy, defiance, sexual promiscuity, and violence (Donovan and Jessor, 1985; Elliott, Huizinga, and Menard, 1989; Farrell, Danish, and Howard, 1992; Gilmore, Hawkins, Catalano, Day, Moore, and Abbott, 1991; McGee and Newcomb, 1992; Newcomb and Bentler, 1989; Osgood, Johnston, O'Malley, and Bachman, 1988). All these problems are different sorts of manifestations of a lack of impulse control, and adolescents who engage in these behaviors are often described as "undercontrolled."

There is also a good deal of co-variation in internalizing disorders, although this has been less well studied than co-variation among externalizing problems. Nevertheless, it is the case that depressed adolescents are more likely to experience anxiety, panic, suicidal ideation, eating disorders, and other psychosomatic disturbances (Attie and Brooks-Gunn, 1989; Brady and Kendall, 1992; Cantwell and Baker, 1991; Colten, Gore, and Asettine, 1991; Kandel, Raveis, and Davies, 1991; Petersen, Compas, Brooks-Gunn, Stemmler, Ey, and Grant, 1993). All these disorders are manifestations of distress.

Although the distinction between internalizing disorders and externalizing disorders is useful for organizing information about psychosocial problems during adolescence, it is important to bear in mind that some adolescents experience problems in both domains simultaneously. That is, some adolescents who engage in delinquency also suffer from depression (Cantwell and Baker, 1991; Capaldi, 1991, 1992), and many depressed adolescents also abuse drugs and alcohol (Henry, Feehan, McGee, Stanton, Moffitt, and Silva, 1993; Kandel et al., 1991). Many researchers believe that it is important to distinguish among adolescents who exhibit one specific problem without any others (e.g., depressed adolescents who do not have other internalizing or externalizing problems); adolescents who exhibit more than one problem within the same general category (e.g., drug-abusing delinquent youth); and adolescents who exhibit both internalizing and externalizing problems (e.g., depressed delinquents). These adolescents may have followed very different pathways to deviance and may require very different types of treatment (Capaldi, 1991, 1992; Colten et al., 1991; Ensminger, 1990; McCord, 1990). In general, studies show that multiproblem teenagers have had far worse family experiences than those with one problem (Aseltine and Gore, 1994; Capaldi, 1992; Ge, Best, Conger, and Simons, 1994).

It is also true that the clustering of different problem behaviors is seen more often in some populations than others. Generally, it is seen more often in studies of adolescents than in studies of children or young adults (Gillmore et al., 1991; McGee and Newcomb, 1992). In addition, some studies find that two factors which often are correlated with other externalizing problems such as delinquency and drug use—disengagement from school and early sexual intercourse—may not be part of a problematic syndrome among inner-city African-American youth (Darling and Brown, 1992; Ensminger, 1990; Stanton, Romer, Ricardo, Black, Feigelman, and Galbraith, 1993)

Problem Behavior Syndrome

Researchers have devoted a great deal of attention to studying the co-variation among problems during adolescence, and a number of theories about the origins of what some experts call "problem behavior syndrome" have been proposed. The most widely cited perspective comes from the work of social psychologist Richard Jessor and his colleagues (Donovan and Jessor, 1985; Jessor and Jessor, 1977). According to **problem behavior theory,** the underlying cause of externalizing problems during adolescence is unconventionality in both the adolescent's personality and social environment (Donovan and Jessor, 1985). Unconventional individuals are tolerant of deviance in general, are not highly connected to school or to religious institutions, and are very liberal in their social views. Unconventional environments are those in which a large number of individuals share these same attitudes. According to Jessor's research, unconventional individuals are more likely to engage in a wide variety of **risk-taking behavior,** including experimentation with illegal drugs, having sex without contraception, delinquent activity, and even risky driving (Jessor, 1987). Thus the reason that so many behavior problems appear to go hand in hand is that unconventional individuals in unconventional environments are likely to engage in all sorts of risky activities.

Although Jessor's theory does not specifically hypothesize what the origins of unconventionality are, a number of possibilities have been proposed. One set of theories, for example, emphasizes the biological underpinnings of risk-taking or unconventionality and argues that a predisposition toward deviance may actually be inherited (e.g., Mednick, Gabrielli, and Hitchings, 1987; Rowe, Rodgers, Meseck-Bushey, and St. John, 1989). A second view stresses biologically based differences among individuals in arousal and in sensation-seeking (e.g., Zuckerman, 1983). Yet a third viewpoint emphasizes the early family context in which deviance-prone children are reared and presents problem behavior as a sort of "adaptive" response to a hostile environment (Belsky, Steinberg, and Draper, 1991).

An alternative to the view that there is an underlying trait has been proposed by sociologist Denise Kandel. Kandel and her associates argue that different types of deviance have distinctly different origins, but that involvement in a given problem behavior may itself lead to involvement in a second one. For example, the use of illicit drugs other than marijuana (e.g., cocaine, heroin) increases the chances that an adolescent will become premaritally pregnant (Elliott and Morse, 1989; Yamaguchi and Kandel, 1987) or suicidal (Kandel et al., 1991). Thus, problem behaviors may cluster together not only because of an underlying trait such as unconventionality, but also because some activities—drug use, in particular—lead to involvement in other problem behaviors.

According to a third view, **social control theory** (Gottfredson and Hirschi, 1990; Hirschi, 1969), individuals who do not have strong bonds to society's institutions—such as the family, the school, or the workplace—will be likely to deviate and behave unconventionally in a variety of ways. This view suggests that the apparent clustering of different problem behaviors may stem from an underlying weakness in the attachment of these youngsters to society. This underlying problem leads to the development of an unconventional attitude, to membership in an unconventional peer group, or to involvement in one or several problem behaviors that may set a chain of problem activities in motion. Social control theory helps to explain why behavior problems are not just clustered together but also far more prevalent among poor, inner-city, minority youngsters.

Finally, a number of researchers stress that we should be careful about overstating the

According to problem behavior theory, *the underlying cause of behavior problems in adolescence is unconventionality. Unconventional individuals, who are tolerant of deviance in general, not highly connected to school or to religious institutions, and very liberal in their social views, are more likely to engage in a wide variety of risk-taking behavior, including experimentation with illegal drugs.* (Collins/Monkmeyer)

case for a problem behavior "syndrome" (McCord, 1990; Osgood et al., 1988). They note that, although engaging in one type of behavior problem increases the likelihood of engaging in another, the overlap among behavior problems is far from perfect. Indeed, in one study, it was found that the vast majority of delinquents are *not* serious drug users (Elliott et al., 1989). Such evidence makes it difficult to embrace a theory that identifies a *single* cause of problem behavior. Like other types of behavior, problem behavior has multiple and complex causes that vary from one individual to the next. It may be just as erroneous to generalize about the "troubled" adolescent as it is to generalize about young people overall.

RECAP

Psychologists distinguish between internalizing and externalizing problems. There is a great deal of co-variation among different psychosocial problems during adolescence within the broad internalizing and externalizing disorder categories. Adolescents who engage in delinquency, for example, are more likely than their peers to be truant, to use and abuse drugs, to engage in precocious sexual behavior, and to commit acts of aggression—a pattern that has been termed *problem behavior syndrome.* Conversely, adolescents who suffer from depression are more likely than their peers to feel anxiety and other symptoms of negative affectivity.

Stress and Coping

According to recent studies, nearly half of all adolescents report difficulty in coping with stressful situations at home or at school (Gans, 1990). These stressors include major life changes (e.g., parental divorce, changing schools, having someone in the family suddenly become seriously ill); chronically stressful conditions (e.g., poverty, a disabling illness, constant family conflict); and day-to-day hassles (e.g., school exams, being teased by friends, and arguments with siblings and parents) (Compas, 1987).

For some teenagers, these stressors can lead to internalized disorders, such as anxiety, depression, headaches, and indigestion. For others, the consequences of these stressors are externalized, in behavior and conduct problems or in drug and alcohol abuse. These links between stress and psychosocial problems have been documented in studies of youngsters from all ethnic groups and family backgrounds (Dornbusch, Mont-Reynaud, Ritter, Chen, and Steinberg, 1991). Yet, for some adolescents, the very same sources and levels of stress do not seem to be associated with psychological or physical upset at all. Thus, although we tend to think of stress as having negative effects on our well-being, the connection between stress and dysfunction is not clear-cut.

What makes some adolescents more vulnerable to the effects of stress than others? Psychologists point to three sets of factors. First, the effect of any one stressor is exacerbated if it is accompanied by other stressors. Studies show that stress tends to have a multiplicative effect: An adolescent who faces two stressors at the same time (the parents' divorce and having to change schools, for example) is more than twice as likely to experience psychological problems than is someone who has experienced only one of the two same stressors (Rutter, 1978).

Second, adolescents who have other resources—either internal, such as high self-esteem, healthy identity development, or strong feelings of competence; or external, such as social support from others—are less likely to be adversely affected by stress than their peers (Hauser and Bowlds, 1990; Kliewer and Sandler, 1992; Luthar, 1991). For example, an adolescent who has high self-esteem and warm and close family relationships is less likely to be distressed by a stressful experience in school or with close friends than is a teenager who has the same stressful experience but less support at home or a poorer self-image. Similarly, adolescents with close friends and good social skills seem to be better able to handle stressors such as parental divorce or starting junior high school than are teenagers who lack close friendships or have fewer interpersonal resources.

Finally, some adolescents use more effective coping strategies than do others. Specialists who study coping strategies distinguish between problem-focused coping and emotion-focused coping (Compas, Malearne, and Fondacaro, 1988; Lazarus and Folkman, 1984). **Problem-focused coping** involves taking steps to change the source of the stress, whereas **emotion-focused coping** involves efforts to change one's emotional response to the stress. For instance, if you were feeling very worried about an upcoming exam in this course, a problem-focused strategy might be to form a study group with other students in order to review the material, whereas an emotion-focused strategy might be to go out to a movie or to a party in order to take your mind off the test. More often than not, problem-focused coping involves active mastery of the stressor (treatment of the problem), whereas emotion-focused coping involves passive avoidance or distraction (treatment of the symptom).

There are some situations in which emotion-focused coping is quite effective. These tend to be stressful situations that are clearly uncontrollable, such as getting an injection or having to have painful dental work done. In these instances, trying to distract and calm oneself may help alleviate some of the stress. But, in general, research shows that adolescents who employ problem-focused coping strategies are less vulnerable to the detrimental health consequences of stress, especially if the source of the stress is controllable. Adolescents who use problem-focused strategies are better adjusted, less depressed, and less likely to have behavioral problems (Compas et al., 1988; Ebata and Moos, 1994).

In this chapter, we examine the nature, prevalence, consequences, and amelioration of four sets of problems typically associated with adolescence. Two sets of problems are externalizing disorders—*drug and alcohol use* and *antisocial behavior;* and two sets of problems are internalizing disorders—*depression and suicide* and *eating disorders.* In each case, we ask three central questions: How many, and which, young people have problems in this domain? What do we know about factors that contribute to problems in this area? And, finally, what approaches to prevention and intervention appear to have the most promise?

ADOLESCENT DRUG AND ALCOHOL USE

Our society sends young people mixed messages about drugs and alcohol. Television programs aimed at preadolescents urge viewers to "Just Say NO!" but the televised football games and adult situation comedies that many of these same viewers watch tell them, no less subtly, that having a good time with friends is virtually impossible without something alcoholic to drink. Many celebrities who are idolized by teenagers speak out against cocaine and marijuana, but many equally famous stars admit to using these same drugs.

The mixed signals sent to young people about drugs and alcohol reflect, no doubt, the inconsistent way that we view these substances as a society: Some drugs (like alcohol or Prozac) are fine, as long as they are not abused, but others (like cocaine or LSD) are not; some drinking (enough to relax at a party) is socially appropriate, but too much (enough to impair an automobile driver) is not; some people (those over 21) are old enough to handle drugs, but others (those under 21) are not. It is easy to see why teenagers do not follow the dictates of their elders when it comes to alcohol and drugs. How then, should we view drug and alcohol use among teenagers, when our backdrop is a society that much of the time tolerates, if not actively encourages, adults to use these same substances?

As with most of the problem behaviors that are common during adolescence, discussions of teenage drug and alcohol use are often filled more with rhetoric than with reality. The popular stereotype of contemporary young people is that they use and abuse a wide range of drugs more than their counterparts did previously, that the main reason adolescents use drugs and alcohol is peer pressure, and that the "epidemic" level of drug and alcohol use among American teenagers is behind many of the other problems associated with this age group—including academic underachievement, early pregnancy, suicide, and crime. The simplicity of these assertions is certainly tempting—after all, what could be more reassuring than to identify the "real" culprit (drugs) and the "real" causes (peers) of all the maladies of young people? And what could be even more comforting than the belief that, if we simply teach young people to "say no" to their peers, these problems will all disappear?

Unfortunately, what we would like to believe about adolescent drug and alcohol use is not necessarily identical to what the facts are. As we shall see in this section, although there are grains of truth to many of the popular claims about the causes, nature, and consequences of teenage alcohol and drug use, there are many widely held misconceptions about this subject, too.

Prevalence of Drug and Alcohol Use

Each year since 1975, a group of researchers from the University of Michigan has surveyed a nationally representative sample of over 16,000 American high school seniors on several aspects of their lifestyle and values, including their use and abuse of a variety of drugs. Because of the size and representativeness of the sample of respondents, this survey, called *Monitoring the Future* (Johnston, Bachman, and O'Malley, 1994), is an excellent source of information about patterns of adolescent drug and alcohol use, at least among young people who have not dropped out of school.

The surveys consistently indicate that the two major "legal" drugs—alcohol and cigarettes—are by far the most commonly used substances, both in terms of prevalence (the percentage of teenagers who have *ever* used the drug) and in terms of recency of use (the percentage of teenagers who have used the drug *within the last month*). Nearly all teenagers have tried alcohol, and two-thirds have tried cigarettes. Nearly half of all seniors have tried marijuana, and about one-fourth have smoked marijuana at least once within the last year. After marijuana, however, the percentage of young people who have tried various other drugs drops precipitously, and the percentage of seniors who have used any of the other drugs within the last month is small (Johnston et al., 1994). And, notwithstanding all the media attention given to cocaine, the category of drug that is fourth in popularity among adolescents (after alcohol, cigarettes, and marijuana) is inhalants (see Figure 13.1). In general, although alcohol use among adolescents in most other industrialized countries is comparable to that in the United States, illicit drug use by adolescents is less prevalent abroad (Silbereisen, Robins, and Rutter, in press).

Prevalence statistics, especially those that tap whether an individual has *ever* tried the substance in question, tell us little about the nature and extent of drug use from the standpoint of adolescents' health and well-being. It is one thing to have tried alcohol or marijuana, but it is something else to use either of these substances so often that one's life and behavior are markedly affected. One of the best ways to examine this issue is to look at the percentage of young people who report using any of these substances daily or nearly

FIGURE 13.1 *Percentages of American high school seniors who have ever used various drugs.* (Monitoring the Future, 1994)

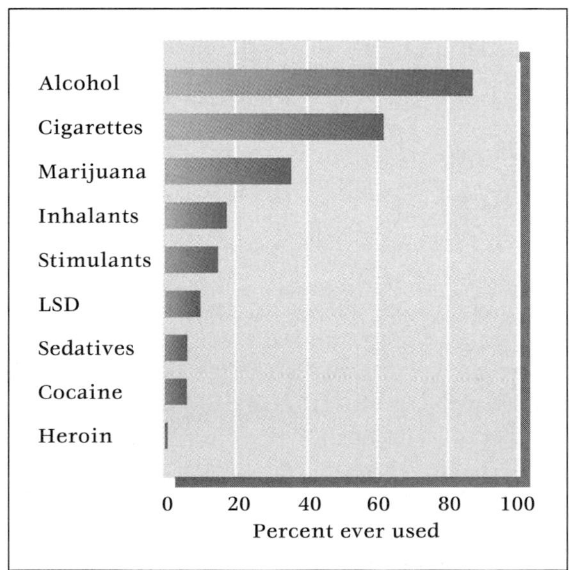

daily. When we do so, we find that cigarettes are the only drugs used by a substantial number of high school seniors daily (about one-fifth smoke daily) and that, of the remaining drugs, only alcohol and marijuana are used daily by even a modest percentage of teenagers (marijuana and alcohol are both used daily by about 2 or 3 percent of seniors). Many adults welcome these statistics and find them reassuring—and in some senses they are. More disquieting, however, is that 28 percent of all seniors, 23 percent of all tenth-graders, and 14 percent of all eighth-graders report having abused alcohol (had more than five drinks in a row) at least once during the past two weeks (Johnston et al., 1993).

Taken together, the findings from these surveys cast doubt on some of the most fervently held stereotypes about adolescent drug use. It is true that many adolescents smoke cigarettes, which is certainly cause for concern, and that many adolescents who drink do so in excess. But the data also indicate that only a very small proportion of young people have serious drug dependency problems (which would lead to daily use) or use hard drugs at all. Moreover, it is very unlikely that drug and alcohol use lurk behind the wide assortment of adolescent problems for which they are so frequently blamed. Rather, the pattern suggests that most adolescents have experimented with alcohol and marijuana, that many have used one or both of these drugs regularly, that alcohol is clearly the drug of choice among teenagers (some of whom drink to excess), and that most teenagers have not experimented with other drugs. From a health and safety standpoint, therefore, education about alcohol and cigarette use and abuse is more urgently needed and may potentially affect a larger percentage of young people than education about any other drug type.

The *Monitoring the Future* study has also been used to chart changes over time in adolescent drug use, and the most recent administrations of the survey have given experts cause for concern. Marijuana use, which had been on a steady decline since the late 1970s, rose quite sharply in 1993, as was the case for LSD (acid, or "drop"), stimulants (such as speed), and inhalants (paint thinner, glue). Patterns for alcohol and cigarettes were different: Alcohol use continued to decline among high school seniors, extending a trend that began in the early 1980s, while cigarette use increased somewhat. Cocaine use, which had peaked during the mid-1980s, continued to drop dramatically and is virtually nonexistent among high school seniors (see Figure 13.2).

The sharp rise in marijuana use, coupled with increases in the use of stimulants and LSD, troubles many observers, because it is reminiscent of the pattern observed during the mid-1970s, when adolescent drug use was at an all-time high. Some experts attributed the increase in drug use during the early 1990s to a weakening of anti-drug messages during the final years of the Bush administration (Treaster, 1994). The continuing decline in alcohol use among adolescents likely reflects the increased public awareness of alcohol-related problems, such as drunk driving.

Several researchers have studied the sequence through which adolescents experiment with different drugs. In general, young people experiment with beer and wine before cigarettes or hard liquor, which precede marijuana use, which in turn precedes the use of other illicit drugs (cocaine, stimulants, LSD) (Kandel, 1980). But although experimentation may follow this sequence, this does not mean that alcohol use invariably leads to marijuana use, or that marijuana use necessarily leads to experimentation with harder drugs. In fact, there is little evidence to support the idea that marijuana is an inevitable "stepping-stone" to hard drug use (whether it is depends on how frequently marijuana is used) (Treaster, 1994). The fact that such a sequence does exist, however, suggests that virtually all users of hard

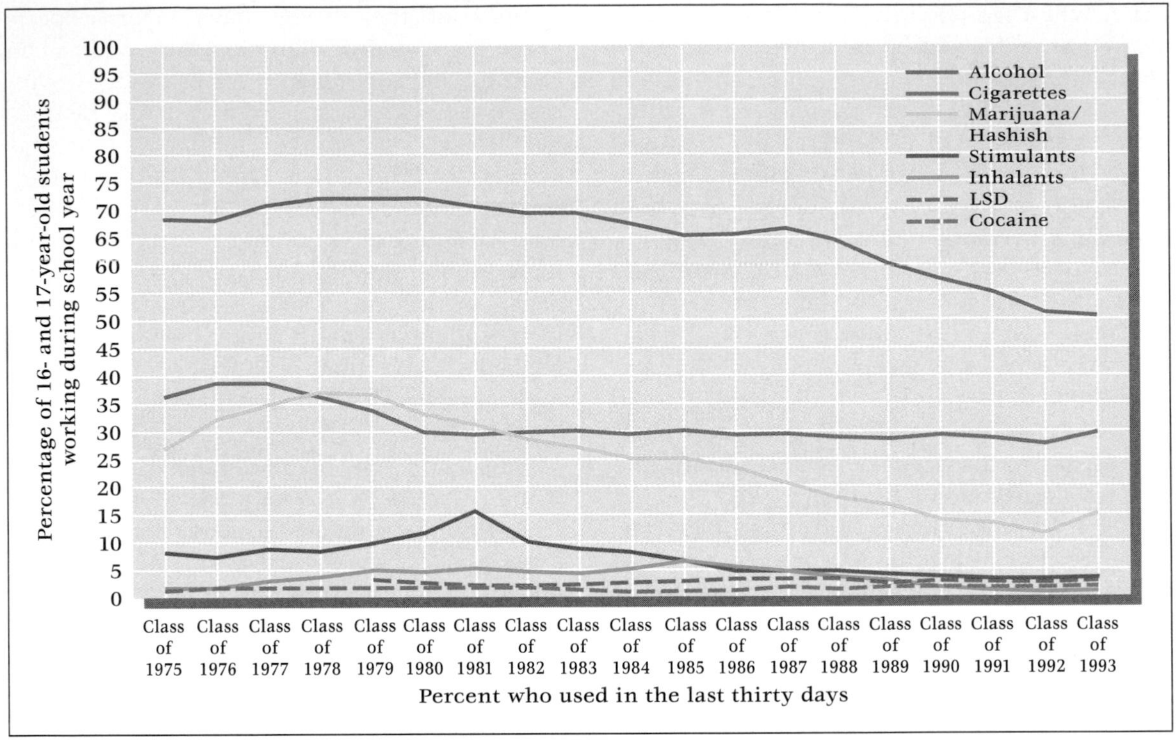

FIGURE 13.2 *Over-time trends in the proportion of high school seniors who report having used various drugs in the thirty days preceding the survey.* (Monitoring the Future, 1994)

drugs have also tried alcohol, cigarettes, and marijuana and, moreover, that one way to prevent adolescents from experimenting with more serious drugs is to stop them from experimenting with alcohol and marijuana. In fact, studies show that adolescents who have not experimented with alcohol or marijuana by the time they are 21 are unlikely ever to use these or other drugs (Kandel and Logan, 1984). For this reason, alcohol and marijuana are considered **gateway drugs,** in the sense that they form a "gate" through which individuals pass before using harder drugs. Whether an individual passes through the gate, however, is influenced by many other factors beyond his or her previous patterns of drug use.

What to make of this mass of numbers, figures, and trends is not entirely clear. Perhaps the most worrisome finding to emerge in recent surveys is that experimentation with drugs begins at an earlier age now than previously, so that the problem may not be the prevalence of drug use among high school seniors but, instead, early experimentation with drugs among their younger counterparts. In fact, more adolescents begin smoking cigarettes, drinking alcohol, and using marijuana before high school than during high school itself (Johnston, O'Malley, and Bachman, 1986). For example, in one recent national survey, more than one-fourth of all eighth-graders reported drinking alcohol regularly, and

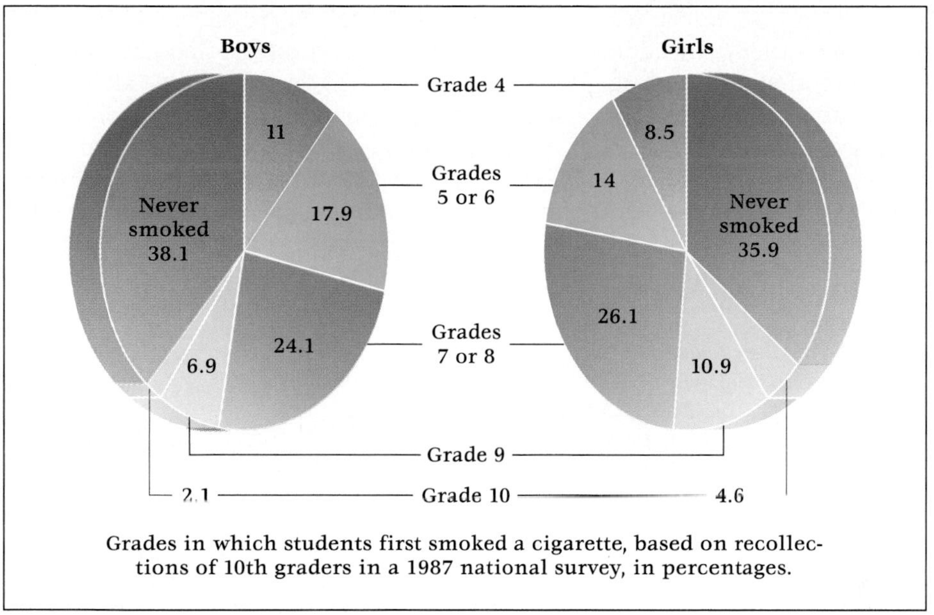

FIGURE 13.3 *Most teenagers who begin smoking do so well before high school.* (National Adolescent Student Health Survey, Department of Health and Human Services, cited in New York Times, 1990)

nearly 10 percent of *sixth-graders*—11- and 12-year-olds—had consumed five or more drinks consecutively at least once during the previous two weeks (Matza, 1990). Nearly 20 percent of eighth-graders have tried inhalants, and 15 percent report having tried marijuana (Johnston et al., 1994). And the typical adolescent who smokes cigarettes begins in grades 7 or 8 (see Figure 13.3).

The early initiation of drug use among young teenagers and preadolescents is especially disturbing and, unfortunately, has been on the rise (see Figure 13.4) (Matza, 1990). Many psychologists believe that early experimentation with drugs is more harmful than experimentation at a later age. Younger adolescents may lack the psychological maturity of judgment necessary to use drugs in moderation or under safe circumstances, and younger adolescents may face unique devel-

FIGURE 13.4 *Drug use among younger adolescents has increased markedly during the past four decades.* (Gans, 1990; Matza, 1990)

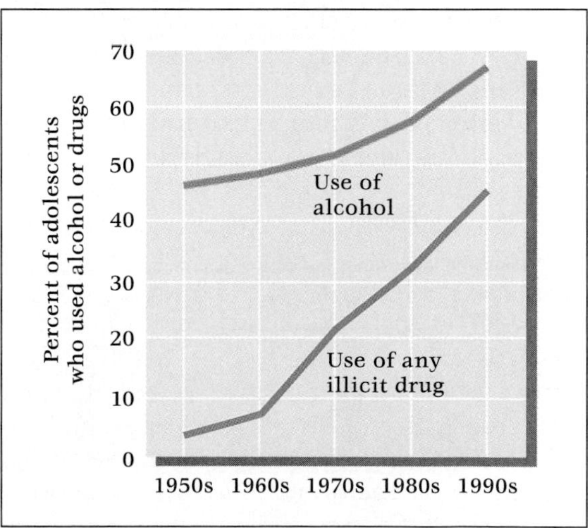

opmental challenges that drug use interferes with (Baumrind and Moselle, 1985). In addition, there is some evidence that heavy drug use may "hurry" adolescents through the psychosocial tasks of adolescence at too fast a pace, thereby interfering with the normal developmental timetable (Newcomb and Bentler, 1988).

Several national surveys have examined ethnic differences in rates of adolescent drug use and abuse. In general, white adolescents are more likely to use drugs and alcohol than minority youngsters, especially African- and Asian-American youth (see Figure 13.5). Rates of drug use among Hispanic adolescents are comparable to those of white youngsters,

FIGURE 13.5 *Monthly and daily use of various drugs among males and females from different ethnic groups.* (Bachman et al., 1991)

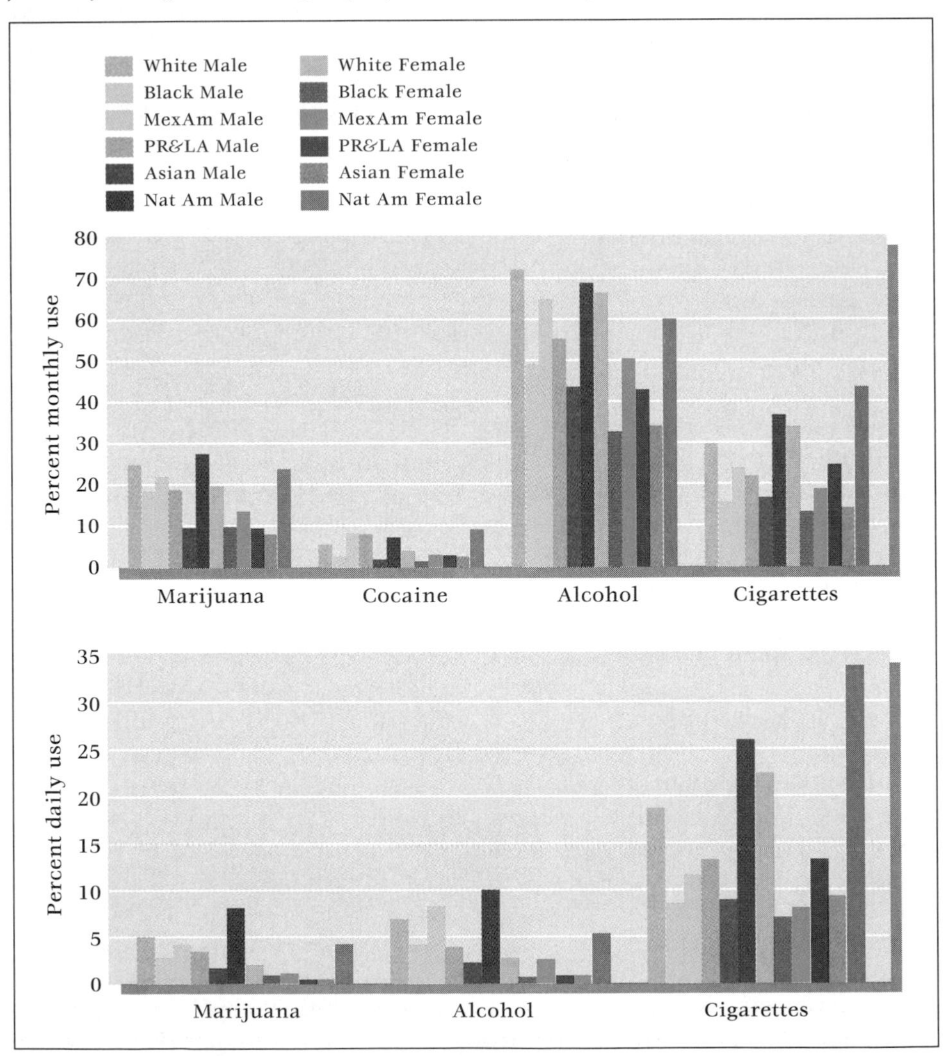

whereas use among American Indian adolescents is the highest (Bachman, Wallace, O'Malley, Johnston, Kurth, and Neighbors, 1991). In general, foreign-born minority youngsters use drugs at a lower rate than do American-born minority youth, suggesting, unfortunately, that part of becoming an "American" teenager means experimenting with drugs (Vega, Gil, and Zimmerman, 1993).

Causes and Consequences of Adolescent Drug and Alcohol Use

In looking at the causes of drug and alcohol use, it is especially important to keep in mind the distinction between occasional experimentation and regular, problematic use. Because the majority of adolescents have experimented with alcohol and marijuana, one can speculate that occasional alcohol and marijuana use has become normative among American high school students and, consequently, that there are plenty of normal, healthy young people who have used these drugs at least once.

Several studies, in fact, indicate that adolescents who experiment with alcohol and marijuana are as well-adjusted as—if not somewhat better adjusted than—their peers who abstain completely from alcohol and marijuana (e.g., Baumrind, 1991; Shedler and Block, 1990). This body of research shows quite clearly that it is important to differentiate among adolescents who are frequent drug users (e.g., at least once a week) or hard drug users (i.e., drugs other than alcohol, tobacco, or marijuana); those who experiment with marijuana and alcohol but who do not use them frequently (i.e., no more than once a month); those who abstain out of irrational fear; and those who abstain out of rational choice (Baumrind, 1991; Hughes, Power, and Francis, 1992). Experimenters and rational abstainers score higher on measures of psychological adjustment than either frequent users or irrational abstainers. Longer-term follow-up studies also show that *moderate* alcohol use during adolescence does not have negative long-term effects (Newcomb and Bentler, 1988). Indeed, cigarette use during adolescence has more harmful long-term health consequences than does experimentation with alcohol or marijuana.

These results do not mean that occasional experimentation with drugs during adolescence *leads to* better adjustment, of course. In fact, research shows that the psychological advantages observed among adolescents who experiment with alcohol and marijuana were evident when these individuals were younger children (Shedler and Block, 1990). Taken together, the studies suggest that moderate alcohol and marijuana use has become normative in contemporary society (however troublesome some adults may find this), that these substances are typically used in social situations, and that better adjusted and more interpersonally competent young people are likely to participate in social activities in which alcohol and drugs are present (Burda and Vaux, 1988; Shedler and Block, 1990). Relative to experimenters, abstainers—and "irrational" abstainers, in particular—tend to be overcontrolled, narrow in their interests, anxious, and inhibited (Shedler and Block, 1990).

Excessive alcohol or drug use, or, more precisely, **substance abuse,** is a different matter. Adolescents who are frequent users of drugs score lower on measures of psychological adjustment as teenagers and were more likely to be maladjusted as children (Shedler and Block, 1990). Indeed, a team of researchers who had followed a sample of individuals from preschool into young adulthood report that, at age 7, individuals who would later become frequent drug users as adolescents were described as "not getting along well with other children, not showing concern for moral issues . . . not planful or likely to think ahead, not trustworthy or dependable . . . [and] not self-reliant or confident" (Shedler and Block, 1990, p. 618). As 11-year-olds, these individuals were described as deviant, emotionally labile, stubborn, and inattentive. This study suggests that drug and alcohol abuse during adolescence is probably a symptom of prior psychological disturbance.

During adolescence itself, of course, drug and alcohol abuse is associated with a host of other problems. Young people who abuse drugs and alcohol are more likely to experience problems at school, to experience psychological distress and depression, to engage in unprotected sexual activity, to abuse alcohol as young adults, and to become involved in dangerous or deviant activities, including crime, delinquency, and truancy (Andersson, Bergman, and Magnusson, 1989; Mensch and Kandel, 1988; Newcomb and Bentler, 1989). Alcohol and drugs are typically implicated in adolescent automobile crashes, the leading cause of death and disability among American teenagers (Gans, 1990), and in other fatal and nonfatal accidents, such as drownings, falls, and burns (Irwin, 1986; Wintemute, Kraus, Teret, and Wright, 1987). Adolescent substance abusers also expose themselves to the long-term health risks of excessive drug use that stem from addiction or dependency; in the case of cigarettes, alcohol, and marijuana, these risks are substantial and well documented—among them, cancer, heart disease, and kidney and liver damage.

Generally, three sets of **risk factors**—psychological, interpersonal, and contextual—for substance abuse have been identified, and the more risk factors that are present for an individual, the more likely he or she is to use and abuse drugs (Hawkins, Catalano, and Miller, 1992; Newcomb and Felix-Ortiz, 1992; Petraitis, Flay, and Miller, 1995). Psychologically, individuals with certain personal-

Alcohol and drugs are typically implicated in adolescent automobile crashes, the leading cause of death and disability among American teenagers. (Bob Daemmrich/Stock, Boston)

ity characteristics—which typically are present before adolescence—are more likely to develop drug and alcohol problems than their peers. These characteristics include anger, impulsivity, depression, and achievement problems (Brook, Whitman, Gordon, and Cohen, 1986; Shedler and Block, 1990). Individuals who have more tolerant attitudes about drug use (and about deviance in general) are also at greater risk for drug abuse (Petraitis et al., 1995).

Interpersonally, individuals with distant, hostile, or conflicted family relationships are more likely to develop substance abuse problems than are their peers who grow up in close, nurturing families (Barnes and Farrell, 1992; Flewelling and Bauman, 1990; Needle, Su, and Doherty, 1990). Drug-abusing youngsters are also more likely than their peers to have parents who are excessively permissive (perhaps to the point of neglect), uninvolved, or rejecting (Baumrind, 1991; Block, Block, and Keyes, 1988; Shedler and Block, 1990), and they are more likely to come from homes in which one or more other family members uses drugs or is tolerant of drug use (Brook, Whiteman, and Gordon, 1983; Brook, Whiteman, Gordon, and Brook, 1984; Conger, Reuter, and Conger, in press; Newcombe, Huba, and Bentler, 1983; Peterson, Hawkins, Abbott, and Catalano, 1994). In addition, individuals with drug and alcohol problems are more likely to have friends who also use and tolerate the use of drugs, both because they are influenced by these friends and because they are drawn to them (Coombs, Paulson, and Richardson, 1991). As you read in Chapter 5, whether and how often adolescents use drugs is an important defining characteristic of peer groups—abstainers tend to have other abstainers as friends, and users tend to be friends with other users. Drug-using adolescents seek drug-using peers, and drug-using peers encourage even more drug use among their friends (Kandel, 1978; Steinberg, Fletcher, and Darling, 1994).

Finally, adolescents who become substance abusers are more likely to live in a social context that makes drug use easier. Important contextual factors are the availability of drugs, the community's norms regarding drug use, the degree to which drug laws are enforced, and the ways in which drug use is presented via the mass media (Petraitis et al., 1995). All other factors being equal, adolescents who have easy access to drugs, who believe that there are ample opportunities to use drugs, and who are exposed to messages that tolerate or even encourage drug use are more likely to use and abuse drugs.

Researchers have also identified important **protective factors** that *decrease* the likelihood of adolescents' engaging in substance abuse. Among the most important protective factors are positive mental health (including high self-esteem and the absence of depressive symptoms), high academic achievement, close family relationships, and involvement in religious activities (Newcomb and Felix-Ortiz, 1992). These protective factors appear to operate over and above the effects of the risk factors listed above. Moreover, most of the risk and protective factors identified operate similarly among adolescents from different ethnic groups (Barnes and Farrell, 1992; Flannery, Vazsonyi, Torquati, and Rowe, 1993; Peterson et al., 1994). One of the reasons for the lower rate of drinking among African-American youth, for example, is that their parents are less likely to drink and to tolerate adolescent drinking (Peterson et al., 1994).

Because one of the most important risk factors for adolescent substance abuse is having a parent who abuses drugs or alcohol, researchers are beginning to look closely at the psychological development of adolescents with an alcoholic parent. Among the most important studies on this topic is one directed by psychologist Laurie Chassin and her colleagues (Chassin and Barrera, 1993; Chassin, Pillow, Curran, Molina, and Barrera, 1993; Chassin,

Rogosch, and Barrera, 1991). As suspected, Chassin finds that adolescents with an alcoholic parent are, on average, more likely to use alcohol and other drugs than other youth (Chassin et al., 1993). In addition, although virtually all adolescents experiment with alcohol (as you now know), adolescents with an alcoholic parent move from experimentation to more frequent and heavier drinking and drug use more rapidly (Chassin and Barrera, 1993). At the same time, Chassin's research shows that only a minority of children of alcoholics develop substance abuse problems of their own—suggesting that parental alcoholism is a risk factor for substance abuse but by no means a guarantee of it. What differentiates children of alcoholics who develop substance abuse problems from those who do not? The answer has to do with the extent to which the alcoholism interferes with family functioning. When the alcoholism diminishes parental monitoring, increases family stress, and heightens family conflict, the adolescent is at much greater risk for developing substance abuse problems (Chassin et al., 1993; Reuter and Conger, 1994). In families where this does not occur, however, the risk is much lower. Not surprisingly, adolescents with an alcoholic parent who continues to abuse alcohol are at much greater risk than those whose alcoholic parent is recovering.

● Prevention and Treatment of Drug and Alcohol Problems

Efforts to prevent drug and alcohol use among teenagers focus on one of three factors: the supply of drugs, the environment in which teenagers may be exposed to drugs, and characteristics of the potential drug user (Newcomb and Bentler, 1989). Although a good deal of government spending and media publicity have been devoted to the first of these approaches—that is, to attempts to control or limit the availability of drugs—the consensus among experts is that it is more realistic to try to change adolescents' motivation to use drugs and the environment in which they live, since it has proven virtually impossible to remove drugs totally from society. In addition, the two most commonly used and abused drugs are both legal—cigarettes and alcohol. Research does show, however, that raising the price of these legal substances does reduce adolescents' use of them (Grossman, Chaloupka, Saffer, and Laixuthai, 1994).

Five different types of drug abuse prevention interventions have been tried, either alone or in combination. In two types of programs, drug use is targeted indirectly, by affecting adolescents' psychological development in general or by helping adolescents to develop alternative activities and interests. The idea behind these sorts of efforts is that adolescents who have high self-esteem, for example, or who are gainfully employed, will be less likely to use drugs. Neither of these approaches has been successful, however.

In other programs, the intervention is more directly aimed at preventing drug use. These programs include information-based efforts (in which adolescents are educated about the dangers of drugs), social skills training (in which adolescents are taught how to turn down drugs), and some combination of informational and general psychological intervention (in which adolescents are educated about drug abuse and exposed to a program designed to enhance their self-esteem, for instance) (Newcomb and Bentler, 1989).

Generally speaking, the results of research designed to evaluate these different approaches have not been especially encouraging (Dielman, 1994; Leventhal and Keeshan, 1993). Experts are now fairly confident that drug education alone, whether based on rational information or "scare tactics," does not prevent drug use. This is reminiscent of research on sex education, which, as we saw in Chapter 11, shows that informational programs are not effective on their own. Educational programs change individuals' knowledge, but they rarely affect their behavior.

The most encouraging results have been found in programs that combine some sort of social competence training with a community-wide intervention aimed not only at adolescents but also at their peers, parents, and teachers (Dielman, 1994; Leventhal and Keeshan, 1993). These multifaceted efforts have been shown to be effective in reducing adolescents' use of alcohol, cigarettes, and other drugs, especially if the programs begin when youngsters are preadolescents and continue well into high school (Bruvold, 1993; Dielman, 1994; Ellickson, Bell, and McGuigan, 1993). Overall, most experts agree that efforts designed simply to change the potential adolescent drug user without transforming the environment in which the adolescent lives are not likely to succeed. Despite their intuitive appeal, efforts to help adolescents "Just Say No" have been remarkably unsuccessful.

One of the problems with all prevention programs is that they often do not distinguish between drug use and drug abuse. As noted earlier, it is abuse, and not occasional use, that is the serious problem. In the words of two leading researchers:

> Although it is important to delay the onset of regular drug use as long as possible to allow time for the development of adaptive and effective personal and interpersonal skills, it may be less important to prevent the use of drugs than the abuse, misuse, and problem use of drugs (which place a tremendous burden on the individual and society). It is in this area that prevention programs have been less successful and are in need of continued development. (Newcomb and Bentler, 1989, p. 246)

A similar problem—that is, failing to distinguish between drug use and drug abuse—has plagued treatment efforts aimed at adolescents who are believed to be drug abusers. Indeed, some experts worry that adolescents who are mistakenly enrolled in treatment programs (because their parents have overreacted to the adolescent's normative and probably harmless experimentation with drugs) may end up more alienated and more distressed—and more likely to become drug abusers—as a result of the "treatment." Evaluations of treatment programs for adolescents who are genuine drug abusers suggest that efforts which involve the adolescent's family, not just the teenager, are most likely to be successful (Dielman, 1994; Newcomb and Bentler, 1989).

RECAP

Among contemporary adolescents, alcohol and cigarettes are still the drugs of choice, although a substantial number of young people have experimented with marijuana as well. Research indicates a clear need to distinguish between experimentation with alcohol and marijuana (which has not been shown to be harmful) and regular or heavy use (which has). Adolescents who abuse alcohol and other drugs are more likely to come from hostile family environments, to have friends who use drugs, and to have other problems, in school as well as in interpersonal relationships. The most promising interventions for substance abuse problems in adolescence are those that target the adolescent's social environment as well as the individual.

ANTISOCIAL BEHAVIOR

Although social scientists disagree about the causes and treatment of antisocial behavior during adolescence—delinquency, crime, aggression, and other conduct problems—there is one point on which there is tremendous agreement: Violations of the law are far more common among adolescents and young adults than among any other age segment of the population. Part of this pattern stems from the fact that certain violations, called **status offenses,** are by definition limited to minors. Status offenses—such as truancy, running away from home, or using alcohol—are behaviors that are not against the law for adults but that nevertheless violate established codes of conduct for juveniles. Even if we discount status offenses, however, research shows that both violent crimes (such as assault, rape, and murder) and property crimes (such as robbery, theft, and arson) increase in frequency between the preadolescent and adolescent years, then peak during the high school years, and finally decline somewhat during young adulthood. One out of every six arrests for murder, rape, robbery, or assault involves a suspect under 18 (Wilkerson, 1994). Individuals under the age 24 account for *well over half* of all violent crimes in the United States (Federal Bureau of Investigation, 1993).

The Prevalence of Antisocial Behavior during Adolescence

Between 1950 and 1980, roughly speaking, there were steady increases in juvenile arrests for virtually all classes of misbehavior. In the early 1980s, the rate of youthful criminal activity leveled off, and it has risen only slightly since then (FBI, 1993). Because such a large proportion of arrests of juveniles are for property crimes, looking at changes in overall arrest rates over time can be misleading. In fact, when we look specifically at violent crimes, a different, and far more troublesome, picture emerges (see Figure 13.6). Between 1965 and 1988, and especially since 1984, the arrest rates for aggravated assault (an attack on another person for the purpose of inflicting severe injury, typically with a weapon) and for murder and nonnegligent manslaughter increased substantially among young people (FBI, 1993). As Figure 13.6 indicates, the increase in the rate of violent crimes among adolescents has been especially dramatic among African-American youth. Observers have also noted that the average age at which individuals are arrested has been falling steadily, as criminal behavior becomes increasingly prevalent among younger boys and girls (Steffensmeier and Streifel, 1991).

Increases in violent crime among young people are significant sources of worry to adults, of course. But they also are significant sources of worry to adolescents themselves, who are the age group most likely to be *victims* of crimes such as theft, robbery, rape, and assault. Indeed, although adolescents under age 18 account for only 10 percent of the population, they constitute nearly one-fourth of all victims of crime (New York Times, 1994). Black and Hispanic adolescents living in the inner city are disproportionately likely to be the victims of violent crime (Hutson, Anglin, and Pratts, 1994). Indeed, for far too many young adolescents growing up in the inner city, gang violence and victimization are chronic problems. One young adolescent living in a poor Chicago neighborhood told an interviewer:

> Many people in the night in my building wait for someone to come and visit. Just wait for someone in the building to open the door so they can go in and show them a knife for money and beat them and someone got killed and all the blood was on the floor of the elevator and everybody got scared about going in the night. So they just stay in their houses. (Richards, Suleiman, Sims, and Sedeño, 1994, p. 9).

In light of the escalating rate of violence among inner-city adolescents, researchers have focused special attention on the problem. Most researchers agree that violence and aggression among youth are strongly linked to

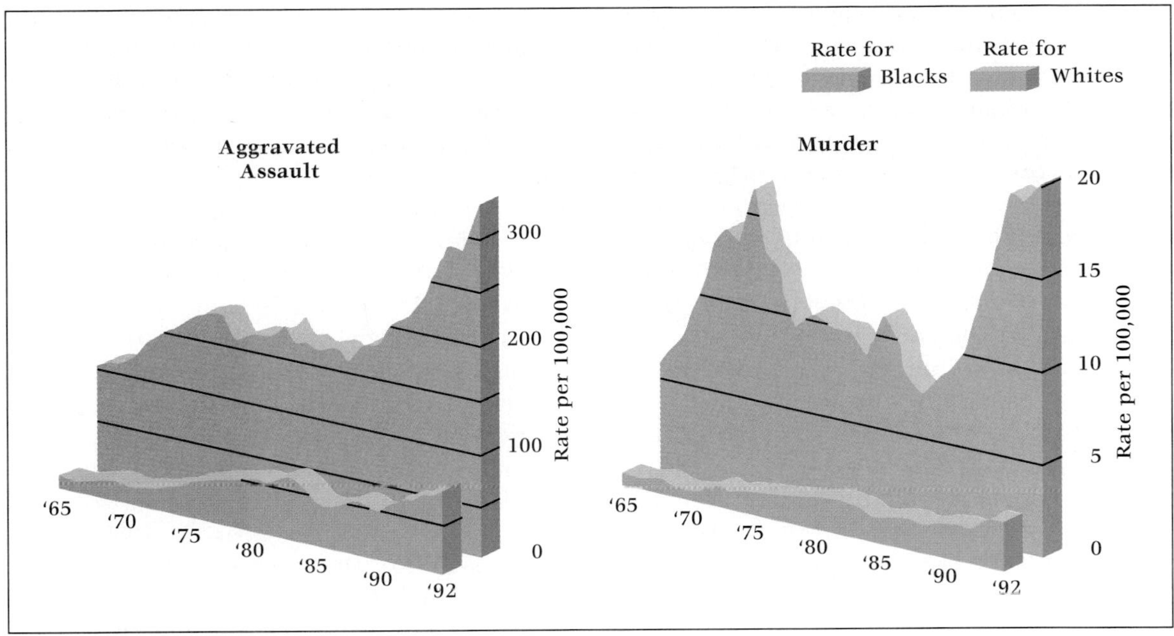

FIGURE 13.6 *Over-time trends in arrests of individuals under 18 for aggravated assault and murder.* (Federal Bureau of Investigation, 1993)

poverty, for a number of reasons. First, when families live in impoverished neighborhoods, parents are less effective in nurturing and monitoring their children, and this diminished effectiveness leads to increased aggression and crime (Sampson and Laub, 1994). Second, concentrated poverty upsets the social fabric of a neighborhood, making it more difficult for adults and social institutions to provide the guidance and supervision that adolescents need (Sampson, 1992; Sampson and Groves, 1989). Third, in many inner-city communities devastated by unemployment, aggression is used by males to demonstrate their standing and power—features which are typically demonstrated in middle-class communities through occupational success (Wilson and Daley, 1985). Finally, repeated exposure to violence—whether in the home or in the neighborhood—breeds violence itself (DuRant, Cadenhead, Pendergrast, Slavens, and Linder, 1994).

Most of the data we have regarding adolescent misbehavior comes from official arrest records. Consequently, it is important to keep in mind that the "official" figures about adolescent crime may both underreport and selectively report rates of misbehavior. Underreporting results from the fact that many adolescents commit offenses that are undetected by authorities or that are handled outside official reporting procedures—for example, when an adolescent who is caught shoplifting is reprimanded by the storekeeper instead of being referred to the police. (Only about one-third of crimes are ever reported to the police [Krisberg, Schwartz, Fishman, Eisikovits, and Guttman, 1986].) Selective reporting results from the fact that lower-class and minority youngsters are more likely both to be arrested and to be treated more harshly than are other youngsters who commit similar offenses, so that official statistics may artificially inflate the proportion of crimes committed by poor, minority youth.

An alternative to relying on official records is to go to adolescents directly and ask them about their involvement in various criminal or status offenses. Several researchers have done this, promising the respondents anonymity and confidentiality. The results of these surveys have been surprising, to say the least. They do not necessarily provide a more accurate picture of juvenile crime, but they certainly provide a different one. Three conclusions are especially interesting. First, the surveys indicate that a very large proportion of adolescents—between 60 percent and 80 percent, depending on the survey sample—have engaged in delinquent behavior at one time or another (Huizinga and Elliot, 1985). Most of these behaviors were not serious crimes, but they nevertheless were genuine status or criminal offenses.

Second, in contrast to official records, which indicate a disproportionate involvement of minority youth in delinquent activities, the surveys indicate that *once social class is taken into account,* there are relatively few ethnic or racial differences in the prevalence of delinquent activity—in either minor or serious misbehavior. According to data from the 1980 National Youth Survey, for example, nearly equal proportions of white, African-American, and Hispanic-American youth admitted to having committed some type of delinquent activity (65 percent among whites, 72 percent among African-Americans, and 59 percent among Hispanics); and equal proportions admitted having committed a serious crime—about 13 percent in each group. Moreover, there are no racial differences in the prevalence of chronic, or repeat, offenders (Krisberg et al., 1986). There are social class differences in serious criminal activity, however, and since minority youth are overrepresented among the poor, they are also overrepresented among those who commit crimes.

Finally, the surveys indicate that, even though minority youth do not commit more delinquent behavior than white youth from the same socioeconomic background—and do not commit more serious delinquent behavior than comparably poor white youth, either—minority youth are far more likely to be arrested and far more likely to be treated harshly by the juvenile justice system. African-American adolescents are seven times more likely to be arrested than white adolescents for minor offenses and twice as likely to be arrested for serious crimes (Krisberg et al., 1986). Minority youth in general are more likely to be sent to correctional facilities than are white youth who commit similar offenses (Krisberg et al., 1986). Thus the reason for the stereotype of the nonwhite juvenile offender is the higher proportion of arrests in this group, not the higher proportion of delinquent and criminal activity. And, of course, the disproportionate number of nonwhite youth living in poverty contributes to racial differences in criminal activity.

Although studies indicate that most adolescents—regardless of their social backgrounds—do something that violates the law at one time or another, the vast majority of teenagers who violate the law do so only once. Thus, although most adolescents have violated the law, a relatively small number of adolescents account for a relatively high proportion of serious criminal activity; one estimate indicates that fewer than 10 percent of adolescents account for about *two-thirds* of all recorded offenses (Yoshikawa, 1994). It is important, therefore, in thinking about the causes of delinquent behavior, to distinguish between delinquent behavior that is serious and chronic and delinquent behavior that is less worrisome. As you will see momentarily, these two sets of delinquent behavior have very different antecedents (Moffitt, 1993).

Surveys indicate that a very large proportion of adolescents—between 60 and 80 percent, depending on the survey sample—have engaged in delinquent behavior at one time or another. Most of these behaviors were not serious crimes, but nevertheless they were chargeable offenses. (Dorothy Littell/Stock, Boston)

Causes of Antisocial Behavior

In general, the earlier an adolescent's "criminal career" begins, the more likely he or she is to become a chronic offender, to commit serious and violent crimes, and to continue committing crimes as an adult (Moffitt, 1993). The older an adolescent is when the delinquent activity first appears, the less worrisome his or her behavior is likely to become. For purposes of discussion, therefore, it is helpful to distinguish between youngsters who begin misbehaving before adolescence and those whose delinquent activity first appears during adolescence. The causes and the consequences of delinquency that begins during preadolescence are quite different from those of delinquency that begins—and typically ends—during adolescence or young adulthood.

In general, youngsters whose problems with the law begin before adolescence are very psychologically troubled. Most of these delinquents are male, many are poor, and a disproportionate number come from homes in which divorce has occurred. More important, however, chronic delinquents typically come from disorganized families with hostile, inept, or neglectful parents who have mistreated their children and failed to instill in them proper standards of behavior or the psychological foundations of self-control (Dishion, Patterson, Stoolmiller, and Skinner, 1991; Farrington and West, 1991; Feldman and Weinberger, 1994; Miller, Cowan, Cowan, Hetherington, and Clingempeel, 1993; Moffitt, 1993). The idea that family factors may underlie chronic delinquency—because of genetic factors, environmental influences, or both—is supported by observations that preadolescent delinquency tends to run in families. Many adolescents who have been in trouble with the law from an early age have siblings who have had similar problems (Loeber and Stouthamer-Loeber, 1986; Rowe, Rodgers, and Meseck-Bushey, 1992). And because antisocial behavior in the child typically provokes further parental ineffectiveness and association with other antisocial children, aggressive children often get caught up in a vicious cycle (Patterson and Yoerger, 1993; Vuchinich, Bank, and Patterson, 1992). As a consequence, early involvement in antisocial activity tends to escalate and become self-perpetuating over time.

There is also considerable evidence that, apart from family factors, there are individual characteristics that distinguish potential delinquent youngsters from their peers, at a relatively early age. First, and most important, children who become delinquent have histories of aggressive and violent behavior—histories that were identifiable as early as age 8 (Farrington and West, 1991; Kupersmidt and Coie, 1990; Loeber, Wung, Keenan, Giroux, Stouthamer-Loeber, Van Kammen, and Maughan, 1993; Stattin and Magnusson, 1989). Second, studies show that children who become delinquents are more likely than their peers to suffer from hyperactivity, or as it is officially known, **attention deficit/hyperactivity disorder (ADHD)** (Farrington, 1989; McGee, Williams, and Feehan, 1992; Moffitt, 1993; Stanger, Achenbach, and McConaughy, 1993); this syndrome is believed to be primarily biological in origin and is characterized by impulsivity, inattentiveness, restlessness, and inappropriately high levels of activity, especially in learning situations. Third, children who become delinquent are more likely than their peers to score low in standardized tests of intelligence and to perform poorly in school (Farrington, 1989; Moffitt and Silva, 1988; White, Moffitt, and Silva, 1989). Fourth, aggressive adolescents often have a prior history of poor peer relations (Coie, Lochman, Terry, and Hyman, 1992; Lyon, Henggeler, and Hall, 1992; Stattin and Magnusson, 1994).

Research by psychologist Kenneth Dodge and his colleagues, into the cognitive aspects of antisocial behavior, indicates that especially aggressive youngsters are likely to suffer from a tendency toward what has been called a **hostile attributional bias** (Dodge, Price, Bachorowski, and Newman, 1990; Lochman and Dodge, 1994). Individuals with a hostile attributional bias are more likely than their peers to interpret ambiguous interactions with other children as deliberately hostile and to react aggressively in order to retaliate. What might be viewed by the average adolescent as an innocent and accidental bump on the basketball court might be interpreted as an intentional shove by someone with a biased viewpoint, and it might lead to a fight. Such problematic information processing has been linked to aggression among white, African-American, and Hispanic-American youngsters alike (Graham, Hudley, and Williams, 1992).

Because aggressiveness, hyperactivity, and intelligence are relatively stable traits over childhood, there is a great deal of continuity in behavior problems over time. Studies that have followed individuals from childhood through adolescence and into adulthood find very high correlations between behavior problems at one point in time and antisocial behavior later in life (Farrington, 1991; Robins, 1986). It is possible, therefore, to identify at a relatively early age individuals who have what might be termed an **antisocial tendency.** Contrary to popular belief, there is no evidence that antisocial individuals uniformly have low self-esteem or that raising their self-esteem does anything to diminish their propensity toward misbehavior (McCord, 1990). As you will read, the prognosis for change in this group of adolescents is very grim. Many antisocial adolescents grow up to be adults who are diagnosed as suffering from antisocial personality disorder.

In contrast to youngsters who begin their delinquent behaviors before adolescence, those who begin after adolescence do not always show signs of psychological abnormality or severe family pathology (Moffitt, 1993). Typically, the offenses committed by these youngsters do not develop into serious criminality, and typically these individuals do not violate the law after adolescence. Much of their delinquent activity occurs with peers. In general, these individuals have learned the norms and standards of society and are far better socialized than their antisocial peers are.

Current research indicates that some family factors may be associated with this type of "socialized delinquency." In particular, there is some evidence that these youngsters are less carefully monitored by their parents (Dornbusch, Carlsmith, Bushwall; Ritter, Hastorf, and Gross, 1985; Patterson and Stouthamer-Loeber, 1984; Steinberg, Lamborn, Darling, Mounts, and Dornbusch, 1994). But there also is evidence that the role of the peer group may be very important (Dishion et al., 1991). Specifically, studies show that much of this kind of delinquent activity occurs in group situations in which adolescents are pressured by their friends to go along with the group. In Chapter 9, you read about studies of age differences in susceptibility to peer pressure, which show that susceptibility increases between preadolescence and middle adolescence and then declines. It comes as no surprise, therefore, to discover that much socialized delinquency follows the same pattern: Rates are low during preadolescence, reach a peak during middle adolescence, and drop off as adolescence ends (Berndt, 1979).

An interesting series of studies by Gerald Patterson and his colleagues (Patterson, 1986; Patterson, DeBaryshe, and Ramsey, 1989; Dishion et al., 1991) indicates how family and peer influences may work together in the development of delinquency. Specifically, these researchers have found that poor parental discipline—discipline that is harsh, inconsistent, and lax—during the early elementary school years leads to the association with deviant or antisocial peers, which in turn leads to delinquent behavior. Dysfunctional child rearing may contribute to the process in two ways. First, adolescents who have distant relationships with their parents are generally more susceptible to peer pressure than other youngsters (Steinberg and Silverberg, 1986). Second, individuals who are raised in dysfunctional ways may develop personality traits that lead children to dislike them—such as aggression—and they may find themselves with few options for friends other than equally disliked and aggressive agemates (Dishion et al., 1991).

● ***Runaways.*** Despite a good deal of attention in the popular media, little empirical research has focused on adolescent runaways. And the little research that has been done paints a different picture than is portrayed in television melodramas in many significant respects. First, the "epidemic" of teenage runaways is grossly overstated. Nationally representative samples of adolescents suggest that between 4 percent and 10 percent of adolescents have *ever* run away from home (running away is more common among poor adolescents) and that fewer than half of all runaways have done so more than once. Second, in contrast to images of teenage runaways traveling across the country, surveys indicate that half of all runaways stay within their community, with relatives or friends. Finally, despite frequent portrayals of "long-lost" runaways, half of all runaways return home within a few days, and from 75 percent to 80 percent return home within a week. Public concern about runaways is high not because the numbers are large but because of the dangers faced on the streets by the 20 percent who do not return home promptly. These young people are exposed to numerous psychological and physical risks, including prostitution and other criminal behaviors, AIDS and other sexually transmitted diseases, and drug and alcohol abuse (McCarthy and Hagen, 1992; Windle, 1989).

Running away from home is typically considered as another manifestation of problem behavior in general, along with delinquency, aggression, truancy, precocious sexuality, and drug and alcohol use. Consistent with this view, runaways—and repeat runaways, in particular—are more likely than other adolescents to be delinquent, to drop out of school, to be aggressive, and to use drugs. The antecedents of running away are similar to those for deviance in general: poverty, low scores on intelligence tests, and family conflict (Garbarino, Wilson, and Garbarino, 1986; Windle, 1989).

Prevention and Treatment of Antisocial Behavior

Given the important differences between the causes of chronic antisocial behavior and socialized delinquency, one would expect that these two groups of adolescents would be best served by different sorts of preventive and after-the-fact interventions. In order to lower the rate of chronic antisocial behavior, we would need mainly to prevent disruption in early family relationships and to head off early academic problems, through a combination of family support and preschool intervention (Yoshikawa, 1994). These strategies are easier proposed than done, however. Our society is hesitant to intervene to prevent family disruption, because we typically wait until we see a sign of trouble in a family before acting. Unfortunately, waiting until after family disruption has occurred before intervening may have little benefit, for research shows that the outlook for delinquents who have begun criminal careers early is not very good. Various attempts at therapy and other sorts of treatment have not, by and large, proven successful. This is the case for treatment approaches that employ individual psychotherapy, group therapy, and diversion programs designed to remove delinquents from the juvenile justice system (to avoid the harmful effects of being labeled "delinquent") and to provide them with alternative opportunities for productive behavior (McCord, 1990). Programs that attempt to change delinquents' beliefs about the value of aggression as a means of solving problems and to teach socially acceptable alternatives to aggression have shown some promise (e.g., Guerra and Slaby, 1990; Lochman, 1992), but even these programs have been only modestly successful in changing offenders' actual behavior (McCord, 1990). Most chronic delinquents go on to commit serious and violent crimes and to continue criminal behavior into adulthood. There is some evidence that family-based interventions (such as parent training or family therapy) may be more successful than interventions that focus on the individual adolescent, but these programs tend to be extremely expensive and time consuming (Bank, Marlowe, Reid, Patterson, and Weinrott, 1991; Henggeler, Melton, and Smith, 1992).

The prognosis for socialized delinquents is considerably better. Because they have internalized a basic foundation of norms and moral standards, it is easier to help them control their own behavior and stop misbehaving. Three types of strategies have been proposed. First, by helping youngsters learn to resist peer pressure, we can give them the necessary psychological tools to avoid being drawn into misbehavior simply to go along with the crowd (Kaplan, 1983). Second, by training parents to monitor their children more effectively, we can minimize the number of opportunities adolescents have to engage in peer-oriented misbehavior (Loeber and Stouthamer-Loeber, 1986). Finally, by treating delinquency seriously when it occurs—by making sure that an adolescent knows that misbehavior has definite consequences—we can deter an adolescent from doing the same thing again in the future.

RECAP

Adolescents account for a disproportionately high number of crimes, including violent crimes. Research shows that chronic offenders are more likely than other adolescents to come from poor families, to have had childhood histories of aggressive behavior, to have been diagnosed as hyperactive, and to score low on standardized tests of intelligence and achievement. Because few approaches to the treatment of chronic offenders have proven successful, many efforts today are being directed at prevention, through early intervention and parent education.

DEPRESSION AND SUICIDE

Most individuals emerge from adolescence confident, with a healthy sense of who they are and where they are headed. But in some instances, the changes and demands of adolescence may leave a teenager feeling helpless, confused, and pessimistic about the future. Although minor fluctuations in self-esteem during early adolescence are commonplace—as you read in Chapter 8—it is not normal for adolescents (or adults, for that matter) to feel a prolonged or intense sense of hopelessness or frustration. Such young people are likely to be psychologically depressed and in need of professional help.

In its mild form, **depression** is probably the most common psychological disturbance among adolescents. Although we typically associate depression with feelings of sadness, there are other symptoms that are important signs of the disturbance, and sadness alone, without any other symptoms, may not indicate depression in the clinical sense of the term. One way of thinking about depression is to consider its four sets of symptoms (Chartier and Ranieri, 1984). Depression has *emotional manifestations,* including dejection, decreased enjoyment of pleasurable activities, and low self-esteem. It has *cognitive manifestations,* such as pessimism and hopelessness. Depressed individuals also have *motivational symptoms,* including apathy and boredom. Finally, depression usually has *physical symptoms,* such as a loss of appetite, difficulties sleeping, and loss of energy.

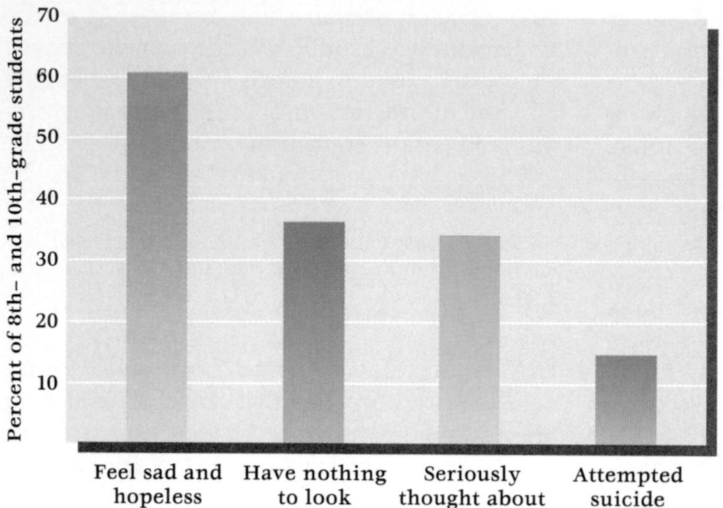

FIGURE 13.7 *Although only 3 percent of adolescents are severely depressed according to standard diagnostic criteria, well over half of all teenagers have felt sad and hopeless at one time or another.* (National Adolescent Student Health Survey, U.S. Department of Health and Human Services, cited in Gans, 1990)

It is helpful to distinguish among depressed mood, depressive syndromes, and depressive disorder (Compas, Ey, and Grant, 1993; Petersen et al., 1993). All individuals experience periods of sadness or depressed mood at one time or another. According to one large-scale survey, more than half of all adolescents occasionally feel sad and hopeless, and more than one-third say they "have nothing to look forward to" (Gans, 1990) (see Figure 13.7). According to other surveys, about 25 percent of adolescents regularly have depressive feelings (Compas et al., 1993).

Fewer individuals report a pattern of depressive symptoms that includes a wider range of symptoms than sadness alone. At any one point in time, about 5 percent of adolescents have the symptoms of a depressive syndrome, and approximately 3 percent meet the diagnostic criteria for clinical depression (Compas et al., 1993; Lewinsohn, Hops, Roberts, Seeley, and Andrews, 1993). Depressed mood, depressive syndrome, and depressive disorder all become more common over the adolescent period, in part because of the increasing prevalence of stressful events during the adolescent years (Larson and Ham, 1993). Although most adolescents are able to cope with these challenges, some are not.

There is a dramatic increase in the prevalence of depressive feelings around the time of puberty; depression is half as common during childhood as it is during adolescence (Compas et al., 1993). Interestingly, whereas depressive feelings are more common among boys than girls prior to adolescence, depression is much more common among females than males after puberty. This sex difference in the prevalence of depression persists throughout most of adulthood (Compas et al., 1993). Some studies indicate that there have been historical increases in the prevalence of depression, especially among adolescents (Lewinsohn, Rohde, Seeley, and Fischer, 1993).

The Nature of Adolescent Depression

Depression during adolescence is often accompanied by other psychosocial or behavioral problems, which occasionally lead to difficulties in diagnosis or treatment (Brady and Kendall, 1992). As we noted earlier in the chapter, various types of internalizing disorders—including depression, anxiety, psychosomatic complaints, and eating disorders—tend to co-vary during adolescence. Just as different externalizing problems are hypothesized to reflect an underlying antisocial syndrome, various indicators of internalized distress may be thought of as different manifestations of an underlying factor. This factor is referred to as **negative affectivity** (Watson and Kendall, 1989).

Diagnosing and studying depression among adolescents has been a tricky business for two very different reasons. On the one hand, professionals have been tempted to attribute nearly *all* observable difficulties to unseen depression. In the past, behaviors such as school phobia, running away from home, or anorexia nervosa were thought to hide the "real" problem—depression. Now, however, it is widely recognized that not all adolescents with behavior problems are necessarily depressed but, as we saw earlier, that depression and other problems can coexist in some cases (Cantwell and Baker, 1991; Compas et al., 1993). In cases in which the main problem seems not to be depression, a careful clinician would certainly want to probe to see whether depressive symptoms were present but would not necessarily jump to the conclusion that depression and behavior problems always go hand in hand.

On the other hand, the popular stereotype of adolescents as "normally disturbed" leads many parents and teachers to fail to recognize genuine psychological problems when they appear. You can probably imagine a parent's description of an adolescent daughter who is critical of herself (which can be an emotional manifestation of depression), unduly negative (a possible cognitive manifestation), bored with everything (a possible motivational manifestation), and not very interested in eating (a possible physical manifestation). It would be easy for this parent to overlook a potentially very real problem and dismiss the daughter's mood and behavior as normal. Obviously, not all instances of self-criticism or apathy reflect psychological disturbance. But a good rule of thumb is that an individual who displays three or more of the signs of depression for two weeks should probably consult a professional (see Table 13.1).

TABLE 13.1 DIAGNOSTIC CRITERIA FOR MILD DEPRESSIVE DISORDER

1. Depressed or irritable mood for most of the day, for more days than not, for at least 1 year.
2. The presence, while depressed, of at least two of the following:
   a. Poor appetite or overeating
   b. Insomnia or hypersomnia (sleeping too much)
   c. Low energy or fatigue
   d. Low self-esteem
   e. Poor concentration or difficulty making decisions
   f. Feelings of hopelessness
3. The symptoms cause clinically significant distress or impairment in social, school, or other important areas of functioning.

SOURCE: *Diagnostic and Statistical Manual of the American Psychiatric Association (DSM-IV)*. Washington, D.C.: American Psychiatric Association, 1994, p. 349.

Adolescent Suicide

According to a recent survey, 15 percent of American tenth-graders attempted suicide in 1987. Fortunately, the vast majority of these attempts—over 98 percent—were not successful. Nevertheless, the fact that 1 of 3 adolescents has contemplated suicide, and 1 in 6 has

THE SEXES

WHY ARE THERE SEX DIFFERENCES IN RATES OF TEENAGE DEPRESSION?

Before adolescence, boys are somewhat more likely to exhibit depressive symptoms than girls, but after puberty the sex difference in prevalence of depression reverses significantly. From early adolescence until very late in adulthood, females report far more depression than males. Why might adolescence mark a turning point in this pattern?

Psychologists do not have a clear answer at this time. Although the fact that the emergence of a strong sex differential coincides with puberty suggests a biological explanation, there actually is little evidence that the sex difference in depression is directly attributable to sex differences in hormonal changes (Rutter and Garmezy, 1983). More likely, changes in social relationships around the time of puberty may leave girls more vulnerable than boys to some forms of psychological distress, and depression may be a stereotypically feminine way of manifesting it.

Social scientists speculate that the emergence of sex differences in depression has something to do with the social role that the adolescent girl may find herself in as she enters the world of boy-girl relationships (Petersen et al., 1993). As you read in previous chapters, this role may bring conflict over achievement, because of fears that success will be perceived as unattractive; heightened self-consciousness over physical appearance; and increased concern over popularity with peers. Since many of these feelings may provoke helplessness, hopelessness, and anxiety, adolescent girls may be more susceptible to depressive feelings. To make matters worse, pressures on young women to behave in sex-stereotyped ways, which intensify during adolescence (Hill and Lynch, 1983), may lead girls to adopt some behaviors and dispositions—passivity, dependency, and fragility, for example—that they have been socialized to believe are part of the feminine role. Consistent with this, studies show that depression in females is significantly correlated with having a poor body image and with having low scores on measures of masculinity (Allgood-Merten, Lewinsohn, and Hops, 1990).

The gender intensification hypothesis is only one explanation for sex differences in the prevalence of depression during adolescence. Two other accounts focus on sex differences in the degree to which adolescence is stressful and on sex differences in the ways that boys and girls cope

attempted suicide, is frightening and distressing (Gans, 1990). The suicide rate is especially high among American Indian and Alaskan Native adolescents (Grossman, Milligan, and Deyo, 1991).

Contrary to myth, adolescents' suicide attempts are rarely impulsive reactions to immediate distress, such as breaking up with someone. Rather, adolescents who attempt to kill themselves usually have made appeals for help and have tried but have not found emotional support from family or friends. Common warning signs of a suicide attempt are shown in Table 13.2, and advice about how to respond is shown in Table 13.3.

You may have read that suicide is a leading cause of death among young people, but this is primarily because very few young people die from other causes, such as disease. Although the rate of suicide rises rapidly dur-

with stress (Nolen-Hoeksema and Girgus, 1994). With respect to the first of these explanations, it is important to note that the link between stress and depression during adolescence is well documented (Petersen et al., 1993). Of interest, then is evidence that early adolescence is generally a more stressful time for girls than boys (Allgood-Merten et al., 1990; Petersen et al., 1991). This is because girls are more likely than boys to experience multiple stressors at the same time (e.g., going through puberty while making the transition into junior high school); because girls are likely to experience more stressful life events than boys; and because the bodily changes of puberty, especially when they occur early in adolescence, are more likely to be stressful for girls than boys—as we saw in Chapter 1. In addition, girls are much more likely than boys to have been sexually abused during childhood, which is a very strong risk factor for depression during adolescence (Cutler and Nolen-Hoeksema, 1991).

Second, there is evidence that girls are more likely than boys to react to stress by turning their feelings inward—for instance, by ruminating about the problem and feeling helpless—whereas boys are more likely to respond either by distracting themselves or by turning their feelings outward, in aggressive behavior or in drug and alcohol abuse (Gjerde, Block, and Block, 1988; Nolen-Hoeksema and Girgus, 1994). As a result, even when exposed to the same degree of stress, girls are more likely to respond to the stressors by becoming depressed (Ge, Lorenz, Conger, Elder, and Simons, 1994). This difference in the ways that boys and girls react to stress helps explain why the prevalence of externalizing disorders is higher in boys, while the prevalence of internalizing disorders is higher in girls.

Interestingly, one study that followed children from preschool into adolescence found that the childhood precursors of adolescent depression were different for boys and girls. Girls who would subsequently become depressed were vulnerable, anxious, and low in self-esteem. Boys who would subsequently become depressed, however, were hostile and antisocial (Gjerde and Block, 1991). These writers have suggested that the idea that depression should be viewed as an internalizing disorder may apply to females but not necessarily to males. Even when males and females suffer from the same underlying problem—such as depression—they may show it in very different ways.

ing the middle adolescent years, it continues to rise throughout adulthood, and suicide is a much more common cause of death among adults than it is among young people (Rutter and Garmezy, 1983; Weiner, 1980). Completed suicide is more common among older adults than adolescents and more common among men than women. Attempted suicide, however, is more common during adolescence than during adulthood and is far more common among adolescent girls than boys (Rutter and Garmezy, 1983).

Although the rate of suicide among adults has increased only slightly in recent decades, the adolescent suicide rate has increased alarmingly during the past forty years—among 15- to 19-year-olds suicide *quadrupled* between 1955 and the end of the 1970s, and it increased again during the late 1980s (Garland and Zigler, 1993). More than half a million

TABLE 13.2 SUICIDE AMONG ADOLESCENTS: EARLY WARNING SIGNS

1. Direct suicide threats or comments such as "I wish I were dead." "My family would be better off without me." "I have nothing to live for."
2. A previous suicide attempt, no matter how minor. Four out of five people who commit suicide have made at least one previous attempt.
3. Preoccupation with death in music, art, and personal writing.
4. Loss of a family member, pet, or boy/girl friend through death, abandonment, break-up.
5. Family disruptions such as unemployment, serious illness, relocation, divorce.
6. Disturbances in sleeping and eating habits and in personal hygiene.
7. Declining grades and lack of interest in school or hobbies that had previously been important.
8. Drastic changes in behavior patterns, such as a quiet, shy person becoming extremely gregarious.
9. Pervasive sense of gloom, helplessness, and hopelessness.
10. Withdrawal from family members and friends and feelings of alienation from significant others.
11. Giving away prized possessions and otherwise "getting their affairs in order."
12. Series of "accidents" or impulsive, risk-taking behaviors. Drug or alcohol abuse, disregard for personal safety, taking dangerous dares.

SOURCE: From "Living with 10- to 15-Year-Olds," A Parent Education Curriculum. © 1984 Center for Early Adolescence, Suite 223, Carr Mill Mall, Carrboro, NC 27510. Reprinted by permission.

young Americans attempt suicide each year, and 60 percent of teenagers say that they personally know another teenager who has attempted suicide (Ackerman, 1993).

A variety of explanations have been given for the increase in suicide among American youth, including pressures to grow up earlier, increasing rates of divorce, less contact with adults, high rates of residential mobility, and having to face an unpredictable job market (Bronfenbrenner, 1974; Rutter, 1980). The recent increase in suicide has been especially pronounced among African-American adolescents (Summerville and Kaslow, 1993).

Efforts to prevent suicide among adolescents have focused on identifying sets of risk factors. Risk factors are characteristics of individuals or their environments that increase the likelihood of their suffering from a particular problem or engaging in a particular behavior—in this case, attempting suicide. Here are the four established sets of risk factors for attempting suicide during adolescence: having a psychiatric problem, especially depression or substance abuse; having a history of suicide in the family; being under stress (especially in the areas of achievement and sexuality); and experiencing parental rejection, family disruption, or extensive family conflict (Blumenthal and Kupfer, 1988; Rubenstein, Heeren, Housman, Rubin, and Stechler, 1989; Wagner and Cohen, in press). Adolescents who have one of these risk factors are significantly more likely to attempt suicide

TABLE 13.3 WHAT TO DO, WHAT NOT TO DO WHEN YOU SUSPECT THE DANGER OF SUICIDE

What to do

1. Ask direct, straightforward questions in a calm manner. "Are you thinking about hurting yourself?"
2. Assess the seriousness of the suicidal intent by asking questions about feelings, important relationships, who else the person has talked with, and the amount of thought given to the means to be employed. If a gun, pills, rope, or other means has been procured and a specific plan has been developed, the situation is very dangerous. Stay with the person until help arrives.
3. Listen and be supportive, without giving false reassurance.
4. Encourage the young person to get professional help and assist the person in doing so.

What not to do

1. Do not ignore warning signs.
2. Do not refuse to talk about suicide if a young person approaches you.
3. Do not react with horror, disapproval, or repulsion.
4. Do not offer false reassurances ("Everything will be all right.") or platitudes and simple answers ("You should be thankful for . . .").
5. Do not abandon the young person after the crisis has passed or after professional counseling has begun.

SOURCE: From "Living with 10- to 15-Year-Olds," A Parent Education Curriculum. © 1984 Center for Early Adolescence, Suite 223, Carr Mill Mall, Carrboro, NC 27510. Reprinted by permission.

than their peers, and adolescents who have more than one risk factor arc dramatically more likely to try to kill themselves. It is also the case that adolescents who have attempted suicide once are at risk for attempting it again (Lewinsohn, Rohde, and Seely, 1994).

Causes and Treatment of Adolescent Depression

A variety of theories have been proposed to account for the onset of depression during adolescence, and current consensus is that depression is likely to be a result of interacting environmental conditions and individual predispositions rather than a result of either set of factors alone. Depression may occur when individuals who are predisposed toward it are exposed to chronic or acute circumstances that precipitate a depressive reaction. Individuals who are not predisposed toward depression are able to withstand a great deal of stress, for instance, without developing any psychological problems. Other individuals, who have strong predispositions toward the disorder, may become depressed in the face of circumstances that most of us would consider to be quite normal.

Research has focused both on individual predispositions toward depression and on the

Contrary to myth, adolescents' suicide attempts are rarely impulsive reactions to immediate distress, such as breaking up with someone. Rather, adolescents who attempt to kill themselves usually have made appeals for help and have tried to seek—but have not found—emotional support from family or friends. (Nancy Hays/Monkmeyer)

environmental circumstances likely to precipitate the disorder. Because depression has been found to have a strong genetic component, it is believed that at least some of the predisposition toward depression is biological and may be related to problematic patterns of neuroendocrine functioning (*neuroendocrine* refers to hormonal activity in the brain and nervous system). Other researchers have focused more on the cognitive set of depressed individuals, suggesting that people with tendencies toward hopelessness, pessimism, and self-blame are more likely to interpret events in their lives in ways that lead to the development of depression. Research suggests that these sorts of cognitive sets develop during childhood and play a role in the onset of depression during adolescence (Garber, Weiss, and Shanley, 1993; Nolen-Hoeksema, Girgus, and Seligman, 1992).

Researchers who have been more concerned with the environmental determinants of depression have focused on three factors (Petersen et al., 1993). First, depression is more common among adolescents from families characterized by high conflict and low cohesion, and it is higher among adolescents from divorced homes. Second, depression is more prevalent among adolescents who are unpopular or who have poor peer relations. Third, depressed adolescents report more stress—both chronic and acute—than nondepressed adolescents do.

You read earlier that the prevalence of depression increases during adolescence. Can these various theories about the causes of depression account for this? For the most part, they can. Biological theorists can point to the hormonal changes of puberty, which are likely to have implications for neuroendocrine activity. Two recent studies, for example, show that depression and negative affect in both boys and girls are correlated with various hormones known to change at puberty (Paikoff, Brooks-Gunn, and Warren, 1991; Susman, Dorn, and Chrousos, 1991). Cognitive theorists can point to the onset of hypothetical thinking at adolescence, which may result in new (and perhaps potentially more depressing) ways of viewing the world (Keating, 1990). And theorists who emphasize environmental factors draw attention to the new environmental demands of adolescence, such as changing schools, beginning to date, or coping with transformations in family relationships—all of which may lead to heightened stress (Algood-Merten et al., 1990). Thus there are many good reasons to expect that the prevalence of depression would increase as individuals pass from childhood into adolescence.

The treatment of depression during adolescence is very similar to its treatment at other points in the life span. Clinicians use a wide range of approaches, including biological therapies employing antidepressant medication (these address the neuroendocrine problem, if one exists); psychotherapies designed to help depressed adolescents understand the roots of their depression, to increase the degree to which they experience reinforcement in their daily activities, or to change the nature of their cognitive set; and family therapies, which focus on changing patterns of family relations that may be contributing to the adolescent's symptoms (Petersen et al., 1993).

Efforts are also made to *prevent* adolescent depression on a larger scale, since this strategy may be more effective than delivering treatment to individuals once they have become depressed. **Primary prevention** approaches emphasize teaching *all* adolescents social competencies and life skills that will help them cope with stress (Weissberg, Caplan, and Harwood, 1991). **Secondary prevention** approaches aim at adolescents who are believed to be at high risk for developing depression, such as teenagers with a depressed parent (who are at risk because of the genetic and environmental risks associated with this) (e.g., Beardslee, Hoke, Wheelock, Rothberg, van de Velde, and Swatling, 1992) or adolescents who are under stress (e.g., Grych and Fincham, 1992).

RECAP

Depression is the most common internalizing disorder of adolescence, afflicting about 3 percent of the adolescent population in its most severe form, but some 25 percent of adolescents in more minor forms. More remarkably, surveys show that 1 of every 6 adolescents has attempted suicide. Although males are more likely to suffer from depression during childhood, depression is much more common among females after puberty—a sex difference that persists into adulthood. The current consensus is that depression is the result of an interacting set of environmental conditions (especially stress and loss) and individual predispositions. Depression during adolescence is treated through a combination of biological, psychological, and family therapies.

EATING DISORDERS

Depression is the most common internalizing disorder observed during adolescence, but it is not the only one. A small, but significant, number of adolescents also suffer from eating disorders. The most common eating disorders among young people are anorexia nervosa, bulimia, and obesity. In this final section of this chapter, we examine each of these problems.

Anorexia Nervosa and Bulimia

In contemporary America, as the expression goes, one can never be too rich or too thin. Unfortunately, not everyone is genetically or metabolically meant to be as thin as fashion magazines tell people they should be. Some adolescents, especially young women, become so concerned about gaining weight that they take drastic—and dangerous—measures to remain thin. Some go on eating binges and then force themselves to vomit to avoid gaining weight, a pattern associated with an eating disorder called **bulimia.** In the more severe cases, young women who suffer from an eating disorder called **anorexia nervosa** actually

THE SCIENTIFIC STUDY OF ADOLESCENCE

TIME-SPACE CLUSTERING OF TEENAGE SUICIDE

When the lead singer of the popular grunge-rock band Nirvana, Kurt Cobain, committed suicide in 1994, many parents and teachers worried that his act might provoke a wave of suicide attempts among Cobain's fans. Their fears were founded on the belief that many adolescent suicides occur during outbreaks, or epidemics, when an unusually high number of suicides occurs within a limited time period or a small geographic area. When such **cluster suicides** do occur, they typically receive a great deal of publicity in the popular press, which may draw a disproportionate amount of attention to suicide outbreaks. Until recently, social scientists did not actually know whether adolescent suicides do occur in clusters with any regularity, or whether we just believe that they do because of the media's attention to them.

A recent study by epidemiologist Madelyn Gould and her colleagues demonstrates, however, that the time-space clustering of adolescent suicide is, in fact, a real phenomenon (Gould, Wallenstein, and Kleinman, 1990). **Epidemiology,** which derives its name from the word *epidemic,* is a branch of medicine devoted to the study of how health problems are spread and distributed within communities. Although we might think of epidemiology as most relevant to the study of physical health problems (such as tracking the spread of a viral infection in a community or monitoring rates of cancer across communities' as a function of levels of cancer-producing agents in their environments), its tools have been applied to the study of psychological and behavioral problems as well. Research into the clustering of adolescent suicides is a case in point.

We know from media reports that *some* adolescent suicides occur in clusters. But these single case studies (a newspaper report about multiple suicides in a particular high school, for example) do not necessarily indicate that clustering is a genuine phenomenon. The problem in relying on single case studies is that some clusters are bound to occur by chance alone. Determining whether adolescent suicides do, indeed, cluster in time and space requires demonstrating that the number of suicides that occur in clusters actually exceeds the number expected by chance.

By analogy, imagine flipping a coin and having heads come up six times in a row. You know that the probability of this happening is exceedingly small. But suppose you knew nothing about coin-flipping probabilities and just happened to hit a six-in-a-row sequence on the first six flips you tried. You might easily draw the incorrect conclusion that it was quite common for a coin to land on the same side six times in a row. By the same token, without hard sta-

starve themselves in an effort to keep their weight down. Adolescents with these sorts of eating disorders have an extremely disturbed body image. They see themselves as overweight when they are actually underweight. Some anorectic youngsters may lose between 25 percent and 50 percent of their body weight. As you would expect, bulimia and anorexia, if untreated, lead to a variety of serious physical problems; in fact, nearly 20 percent of anorectic teenagers inadvertently starve themselves to death.

Anorexia and bulimia each began to receive a great deal of popular attention during the 1980s, because of their dramatic nature, their concentration in the higher social classes, and their association with celebrity. (The singer Karen Carpenter died from anorexia, for tistical evidence, it might be easy to conclude that adolescent suicides occur in clusters on the basis of undue media attention.

In order to examine the hypothesis that adolescent suicides do occur in clusters more than we would expect by chance alone, Gould compiled data about all completed suicides among 15- to 19-year-olds during the period from 1978 to 1984 in the United States, classifying each one by its date and the county in which it occurred. She defined a suicide pair as a cluster if the two suicides occurred in the same county during the same time period. (The researchers examined the data for one-week, two-week, and one-month clustering and found similar results each way.) Since some suicides will occur in the same county within the same time period by chance alone, it was necessary to compare the *observed* number of suicide clusters in each county with the number that would be *expected* by chance. If the observed number were significantly greater than the expected number, that would be evidence of a genuine phenomenon.

Gould's analyses showed quite clearly that adolescent suicides cluster more often than would be expected by chance alone. According to her analyses, about 2 percent of adolescent suicides occur in clusters, after taking chance occurrences into account, with considerable variation by state, sampling unit, and year. (This estimate is probably lower than what one would find if one examined *attempted*—rather than completed—suicide, but data about suicide attempts are not collected systematically enough to analyze in this fashion.) Moreover, other analyses showed that the incidence of clustering increases immediately following stories about suicide in the media. Thus, there was legitimate reason for parents and teachers to be concerned about an increase in adolescent suicide attempts following publicity about Kurt Cobain's death.

Epidemiological research on cluster suicides raises concerns about the advisability of publicizing adolescent suicides and suicide attempts. It was initially thought that publicity surrounding suicide would help increase community awareness of the problem and that such news coverage ultimately would lower the suicide rate. Because a number of studies now demonstrate that publicity increases the likelihood of further suicide attempts, however, this strategy is being reconsidered. Instead, efforts are more likely to be aimed at diminishing the pressures, drug problems, and family difficulties believed to lead adolescents to consider taking their life.

SOURCE: Gould, M., Wallenstein, S., and Kleinman, M. (1990). Time-space clustering of teenage suicide. *American Journal of Epidemiology, 131,* 71–78.

instance, and several Hollywood stars, including actress Jane Fonda, revealed histories of bulimia as adolescents or young adults.) Perhaps because of this attention, initial reports characterized these eating disorders as being of "epidemic" proportion. In fact, careful unbiased studies indicate that the incidence of genuine anorexia and genuine bulimia is small (Kolata, 1988). Fewer than one-half of 1 percent of adolescents are anorexic, and only about 3 percent are bulimic (American Psychiatric Association, 1994). Anorexia and bulimia are far more common among females than males. Indeed, anorexia is almost unheard of among males, and when it is diagnosed in males, it typically is seen as a consequence of some other disorder. Both eating disorders are more common in North American and West-

Although it is far less glamorous and less well-publicized than anorexia or bulimia, obesity is the more common eating disorder. According to recent national surveys, nearly 20 percent of adolescents in the United States are overweight, and about 5 percent of adolescents are obese. (Bob Daemmrich/Stock, Boston)

ern Europe than in other parts of the world, and both are more common among the affluent and better educated (Condit, 1990). Anorexia and bulimia are rarely seen before puberty.

Although the incidence of anorexia and bulimia is small, the proportion of adolescents who are unhappy with their body shape or weight is not. This is especially the case among female adolescents, which no doubt accounts for the greater incidence of anorexia and bulimia among young women than young men. In one recent study, for example, more than one-third of girls whose weight was considered normal by medical and health standards believed that they were overweight—including 5 percent who actually were *underweight* by medical criteria. (Less than 7 percent of normal-weight boys, and no underweight boys, described themselves as being overweight.) In this study, more than 70 percent of the girls reported that they would like to be thinner than they are (as opposed to one-third of the boys), and more than 80 percent said that being thinner would make them happier, more successful, and more popular (Paxton et al., 1991). Not surprisingly, dissatisfaction with one's body is likely to lead to the development of eating problems (Attie and Brooks-Gunn, 1989).

Several theories have been proposed to account for the onset of anorexia and bulimia during adolescence (see Condit, 1990). One perspective emphasizes the biological basis for anorexia, in particular, since there is strong evidence that anorexia is both genetically and hormonally influenced (Holland, Sicotte, and Treasure, 1988; Leibowitz, 1983). Unfortunately, it is difficult in hormonal studies to separate cause and effect: Changes in hormone levels can effect weight loss, but starvation and dieting also affect hormone levels.

A second view emphasizes psychological factors. Some theorists have proposed that anorexia is related to the adolescent's attempts to assert her autonomy within an overly controlling family system (Bruch, 1973; Minuchin, Rosman, and Baker, 1978). Others have suggested that anorexia is a sort of "avoidance" mechanism that reflects the young woman's fears of entering adulthood (Crisp, 1983). (One of the consequences of starvation during early adolescence is that pubertal development is severely delayed [Surbey, 1987].) Still others have pointed to links between anorexia and other internalized disorders, such as depression, since many anorectic women display depressive symptoms (Munoz and Amado, 1986). The suggestion here is that anorexia may simply be a specific manifestation of internalized distress. In addition, there is some evidence that the same medications that are successful in treating depression are useful in treating anorexia (Condit, 1990).

Finally, because anorexia and bulimia are ten times more common in females than males and far more common in some societies and social classes than others, it is likely that broader social forces are a main factor in the development of these eating disorders (Brumberg, 1988). Research indicates, for example, that girls who are early maturers and early daters are likely to report greater dissatisfaction with their body and to be at greater risk for disordered eating (Smolak, Levine, and Gralen, 1993); and that girls who turn to popular magazines, such as *Seventeen, Sassy,* and *Glamour* for information about dieting and appearance are more likely to have a high drive for thinness and disturbed patterns of eating (Levine, Smolack, and Hayden, 1993). One interesting study showed, for example, how bulimia became socially "contagious" in a college sorority (Crandall, 1988). This researcher found that over the course of the academic year, women's eating behavior became more and more like that of their sorority friends—even in a sorority in which binge eating was the norm.

Just because cultural conditions contribute to the development of anorexia nervosa doesn't mean that individual characteristics do not play a role as well. It may be the case that cultural conditions predispose females more than males toward these eating disorders and that, within the population of adolescent women, those who have certain psychological traits (proneness to depression, for example) or familial characteristics (overcontrolling parents, for example) may be more likely to develop problems. The onset of eating disorders, like so many aspects of adolescent development, cannot be understood apart from the context in which young people live.

A variety of therapeutic approaches have been employed successfully in the treatment of anorexia and bulimia, including individual psychotherapy and cognitive-behavior modification, group therapy, family therapy, and, more recently, the use of antidepressant medication (Agras, Schneider, Arnow, Raeburn, and Telch, 1989; Condit, 1990; Vigersky, 1977). The treatment of anorexia often requires hospitalization initially in order to ensure that starvation does not progress to fatal or near-fatal levels (Mitchell, 1985).

Obesity

Although it is far less glamorous and less well-publicized than anorexia or bulimia, obesity is a more common eating disorder. According to recent national surveys, nearly 20 percent of adolescents in the United States are overweight, and about 5 percent of adolescents are **obese**—that is, they are more than 20 percent over the maximum recommended weight for their height—and an additional 15 percent are seriously overweight (Gans, 1990). Current research indicates that obesity is a result of an interplay of genetic and environmental factors.

Because adolescence is a time of dramatic change in physical appearance, the young person's self-image is very much tied to his or her body image. Deviation from the "ideal" physique can lead to loss of self-esteem and other problems in the adolescent's self-image. In particular, being overweight can be a painful source of embarrassment to teenagers, who are unusually self-conscious about their appearance. In addition, obesity during adolescence places the individual at much higher risk for other health problems, including hypertension (high blood pressure), high cholesterol levels, and diabetes (Must, Jacques, Dallal, Bajema, and Dietz, 1992). Nearly 80 percent of obese adolescents will be obese adults and will suffer the disadvantages associated with obesity.

Although a variety of nutritional and behavioral factors can lead to weight gains during adolescence, gaining weight can sometimes result directly from the physical changes of puberty. Not only does the ratio of body fat to muscle increase markedly during puberty, but the body's **basal metabolism rate** also drops about 15 percent. The basal metabolism rate is the minimal amount of energy one uses when resting. A person's weight is partly dependent on this rate.

Do you know people who seem to be able to eat as much as they want without gaining weight? Adolescents whose basal metabolism rate is high can eat more during the course of a day without gaining weight than their peers whose rate is low, because individuals with high metabolic rates naturally burn off more calories. Because basal metabolism normally decreases during adolescence, many individuals who are not overweight as children develop weight problems as teenagers. In fact, obesity is about three times more common during adolescence than during childhood (Paulsen, 1972). Often, a program of intense physical exercise combined with proper nutrition can help youngsters lose weight (Brody, 1987).

RECAP

Eating disorders compose a second set of internalizing disorders seen during adolescence. The most life threatening—anorexia nervosa—fortunately is quite rare. Bulimia, a disorder characterized by binge eating and self-induced vomiting, is more common. Both anorexia and bulimia are far more common in Western societies, among females and among females from affluent and well-educated families. Many young women who do not have anorexia or bulimia nevertheless diet unnecessarily. Obesity is a more prevalent eating disorder than either anorexia or bulimia that also has important psychological and physical health implications. The causes of eating disorders are, like depression, both biological and environmental.

KEY TERMS

anorexia nervosa
antisocial tendency
attention deficit/hyperactivity disorder (ADHD)
basal metabolism rate
bulimia
cluster suicides
depression
emotion-focused coping
epidemiology
externalizing disorders
gateway drugs
hostile attributional bias
internalizing disorders
negative affectivity
obese
primary prevention
problem-focused coping
problem behavior theory
protective factors
psychosomatic disorders
risk factors
risk-taking behavior
secondary prevention
social control theory
status offenses
substance abuse

FOR FURTHER READING

Brumberg, J. (1988). *Fasting girls: The emergence of anorexia as a modern disease.* Cambridge, Mass.: Harvard University Press. A historical look at the social origins and "invention" of anorexia.

Compas, B., Ey, S., and Grant, K. (1993). Taxonomy, assessment, and diagnosis of depression during adolescence. *Psychological Bulletin, 114,* 323–344. A recent review of the literature on adolescent depression.

Jessor, R. (1984). Adolescent development and behavioral health. In J. Matarazzo, S. Weiss, J. Herd, N. Miller, and S. Weiss (Eds.), *Behavioral health: A handbook of health enhancement and disease prevention.* New York: Wiley. An excellent summary of problem behavior theory, by the theory's author.

Moffitt, T. (1993). Adolescence-limited and life-course persistent antisocial behavior: A developmental taxonomy. *Psychological Review, 100,* 674–701. A thorough examination of antisocial behavior during adolescence, with an emphasis on the distinction between chronic and transitory antisocial activity.

Petraitis, J., Flay, B., and Miller, T. (1995). Reviewing theories of adolescent substance use: Organizing pieces in the puzzle. *Psychological Bulletin 117,* 67–103. A comprehensive review of theories of adolescent alcohol and drug use.

APPENDIX

THEORETICAL PERSPECTIVES ON ADOLESCENCE

It is useful to organize theoretical perspectives on adolescence around an issue that has long dominated discussions about the nature of this period of the life span: To what extent is adolescence shaped by the fundamental biological changes of the period, and to what extent is it defined by the environment in which the individual develops? Whereas some theories construe adolescence as a biologically defined period, others view it as contextually determined. Still others fall somewhere between the two extremes of this continuum. The purpose of this brief overview is not to argue for one approach over another but, rather, to demonstrate how each of these views has helped us gain a better understanding of the nature of adolescence.

Biological Theories

The fact that biological change during adolescence is noteworthy is not a matter of dispute. How important this biological change is in defining the psychosocial issues of the period is, however, in dispute. Theorists who have taken a biological, or more accurately, biosocial view of adolescence stress the hormonal and physical changes of puberty as driving forces. The most important biosocial theorist was G. Stanley Hall (1904), considered the "father" of the scientific study of adolescence.

Hall, who was very much influenced by the work of Charles Darwin, the author of the theory of evolution, believed that the development of the individual paralleled the development of the human species, a notion referred to as his theory of **recapitulation.** Infancy, in his view, was equivalent to the time during our evolution when we were primitive, like animals. Adolescence, in contrast, was seen as a time that paralleled the evolution of our species into civilization. For Hall, the development of the individual through these stages was determined primarily by instinct—by biological and genetic forces within the person—and hardly influenced by the environment.

The most important legacy of Hall's view of adolescence is the notion that adolescence is inevitably a period of **storm and stress.** He believed that the hormonal changes of puberty cause upheaval, both for the individual and for those around the young person. Because this turbulence was biologically determined, it was unavoidable. The best that society could do was to find ways of managing the young person whose "raging hormones" would invariably lead to difficulties.

Although scientists no longer believe that adolescence is an inherently stressful period, much contemporary work continues to emphasize the role that biological factors play in shaping the adolescent experience. Indeed, the study of the impact of puberty on adolescent psychosocial development has been, and continues to be, a central question for the field. In addition, current work from the biosocial tradition explores the genetic bases of individual differences in adolescence as well as the sociobiological bases of adolescent behavior.

Organismic Theories

Our next stop on the continuum is in the domain of organismic theorists. Like biosocial theorists, **organismic theorists** also stress the importance of the biological changes of adolescence. But unlike their biosocial counterparts, organismic theories also take into account the ways in which contextual forces interact with and modify the impact of these biological imperatives.

If you have had previous coursework in developmental psychology, you have encountered the major organismic theorists, since they have long dominated the study of development. Three of these theorists, in particular, have had a great influence over the study of adolescence: Sigmund Freud (1938), Erik Erikson (1968), and Jean Piaget (Inhelder and

Piaget, 1958). Although each of these theorists is classified as organismic, the theories they developed emphasized different aspects of individual growth and development.

For Freud, development was best understood in terms of the **psychosexual conflicts** that arise at different points in development. In **psychoanalytic theory,** adolescence is also seen as a time of upheaval—as was the case in Hall's view. According to Freud, the hormonal changes of puberty upset the psychic balance that had been achieved during the prior psychosexual stage, called "latency." Because the hormonal changes of puberty were responsible for marked increases in sexual drive, the adolescent was temporarily thrown into a period of intrapsychic crisis, and old psychosexual conflicts, long buried in the unconscious, were revived. Freud and his followers believed that the main challenge of adolescence was to restore a psychic balance and resolve these conflicts. Although the process was driven by the hormonal changes of puberty, the specific conflicts faced by the young person were seen as dependent on his or her early experiences in the family.

Freud himself actually had very little to say specifically about adolescence. But his daughter, Anna Freud (1958), extended much of her father's thinking to the study of development during the second decade of life. Today, this work is carried on by **neo-Freudians,** such as Peter Blos (1979), whose theories of adolescent development we explore in detail in Chapter 9.

In Erikson's theory, the emphasis was on the **psychosocial crises** characteristic of each period of growth. Like Freud, Erikson also believed that internal, biological developments moved the individual from one developmental stage to the next. But unlike Freud, Erikson stressed the psychosocial, rather than the psychosexual, conflicts faced by the individual at each point in time. Whereas Freud emphasized the development of the **id**—that part of the psyche believed to be dominated by instinctual urges, Erikson emphasized the development of the **ego**—that part of the psyche believed to regulate thought, emotion, and behavior.

Erikson proposed eight stages in psychosocial development, each characterized by a specific "crisis" that arose at that point in development because of the interplay between the internal forces of biology and the unique demands of society. In Erikson's theory, which we look at in detail in Chapter 8, adolescence is seen as a period that revolves around the crisis of identity versus identity diffusion, a crisis that is shaped both by the changes of puberty and by the specific demands that society places on young people. According to Erikson, the challenge of adolescence is to resolve the identity crisis successfully and to emerge from the period with a coherent sense of who one is and where one is headed.

Freud and Erikson both emphasized emotional and social development. For Piaget, development could best be understood by examining changes in the nature of thinking, or cognition. Piaget believed that, as children mature, they pass through stages of cognitive development, and in each stage, from birth to adolescence, their ways of thinking are qualitatively distinct. According to his view, understanding the distinctive features of thought and reasoning at each stage can give us insight into the overall development of the individual at that point in time.

In Piaget's theory, which is discussed in detail in Chapter 2, adolescence marks the transition from concrete to abstract thought. According to this model, adolescence is the period in which individuals become capable of thinking in hypothetical terms, a development which permits a wide expansion of logical abilities. As you will see, many of the familiar changes in behavior that we associate with adolescence have been attributed to these changes in cognitive abilities. Piaget's views have been applied to the study of moral development, social development, and education.

As is the case with the other organismic theories, Piaget's theory of cognitive development emphasizes the interplay between biological and contextual forces. The development of higher-order thinking in adolescence, for example, is influenced both by the internal biological changes of the developmental period and by changes in the intellectual environment encountered by the individual.

Learning Theories

As we move across the theoretical continuum from extreme biological views to extreme environmental ones, we encounter a group of theories that shift the emphasis from biological forces to contextual ones. Whereas organismic theorists tend to emphasize the interaction between biological change and environmental demand, **learning theorists** stress the context in which behavior takes place. The capacity of the individual to learn from experience is assumed to be a biological given. What is of interest to learning theorists is the content of what is learned.

Learning theorists are not especially developmental in their approach and, as a consequence, have little to say specifically about adolescence as a developmental period. Indeed, for learning theorists, the basic processes of human behavior are the same during adolescence as they are during other periods of the life span. But learning theorists have been extremely influential in the study of adolescent development because they have helped us understand how the specific environment in which an adolescent lives can shape the individual's behavior.

There are two general categories of learning theorists. One group, called **behaviorists,** emphasizes the processes of reinforcement and punishment as the main influences on adolescent behavior. The main proponent of this view was B. F. Skinner (1953), whose theory of **operant conditioning** has had a tremendous impact on the entire field of psychology. Within an operant conditioning framework, **reinforcement** is defined as the process through which a behavior is made more likely to occur again, whereas **punishment** is defined as the process through which a behavior is made less likely to occur again. From this vantage point, adolescent behavior can be seen as nothing more or less than the product of the various reinforcements and punishments to which the individual has been exposed. An adolescent who strives to do well in school, for example, does so because she or he has been reinforced for this behavior, or has been punished for not behaving this way, in the past.

A related approach is taken by **social learning theorists.** Social learning theorists, such as Albert Bandura (Bandura and Walters, 1959), also emphasize the ways in which adolescents learn how to behave. But in contrast to behaviorists, social learning theorists place more weight on the processes of **modeling** and **observational learning.** That is, adolescents learn how to behave not simply by being reinforced and punished by forces in the environment but also by watching and imitating those around them. As is clear throughout the text, social learning approaches to adolescence have been very influential in explaining how adolescents are affected by the child-rearing methods employed by their parents and by the influence, or pressure, of their peers.

Sociological Theories

The emphasis within the biosocial, organismic, and learning theories is mainly on forces within the individual, or within the individual's specific environment, in shaping his or her development and behavior. In contrast, sociological theories of adolescence attempt to understand how adolescents, as a group, come of age in society. Instead of emphasizing differences among individuals in their biological makeups or their experiences in the world, sociological theorists emphasize the factors that all adolescents, or groups of adolescents—by virtue of their sharing age, ethnicity, gender, or some other demographic feature—have in common.

Sociological theories of adolescence have often focused on relations between the generations and have tended to emphasize the difficulties young people have in making the transition from adolescence into adulthood, especially in industrialized society. Two themes have dominated these discussions. One theme, concerning the **marginality** of young people, emphasizes the difference in power that exists between the adult and the adolescent generations. Two important thinkers in this vein are Kurt Lewin (1951) and Edgar Friedenberg (1959). Although the view that adolescents are "second-class citizens" was more influential forty years ago than today, contemporary applications of this viewpoint stress the fact that many adolescents are prohibited from occupying meaningful roles in society and therefore experience frustration and restlessness. Some theorists have argued that adults have forced adolescents into occupying one and only one role—that of student—which is an inherently powerless and "infantalizing" position for young people. This was one explanation given for the student movements of the 1960s (e.g., Braungart, 1980).

A modification of this view focuses on differences *within* the adolescent population. According to this viewpoint, the adolescent's **social class,** or socioeconomic status, as it is formally known, structures his or her experience of growing up. Theorists such as August Hollingshead ([1949] 1975) or Robert Havighurst (1952) have emphasized the fact that the experience of adolescence differs markedly as a function of the young person's family background. They argue that it is impossible to generalize about the "nature" of adolescence because it varies so much depending on the resources of the adolescent's family.

The other theme in sociological theories of adolescence concerns intergenerational conflict, or as it is more commonly known, the **generation gap.** Theorists such as Karl Mannheim (1952) and James Coleman (1961) stressed the fact that adolescents and adults grow up under different social circumstances and therefore develop different sets of attitudes, values, and beliefs. As a consequence, there is inevitable tension between the adolescent and the adult generations. Some writers, like Coleman, have gone so far as to argue that adolescents develop a different cultural viewpoint—a **counterculture**—that may be hostile to the values or beliefs of adult society.

Although sociological theories of adolescence clearly place the emphasis on the broader context in which adolescents come of age, there is still a theme of inevitability that runs through their approach. Mannheim, for example, believed that because modern society changes so rapidly, there will always be problems between generations because each cohort comes into adulthood with different experiences and beliefs. Similarly, Lewin believed that marginality is an inherent feature of adolescence because adults always control more resources and have more power than young people.

Historical and Anthropological Approaches

Our final stop on the continuum takes us to the extreme environmental position. Historians and anthropologists who study adolescence share with sociologists an interest in the broader context in which young people come of age, but they take a much more relativistic stance. Historical perspectives, such as those offered by Glen Elder (1980) or Joseph Kett (1977), stress the fact that adolescence as a developmental period has varied considerably from one historical era to another. As a consequence, it is impossible to generalize about such issues as the degree to which adolescence is stressful, the developmental tasks of the period, or the nature of intergenerational relations. Historians would say that these issues all depend on the social, political, and economic forces present at a given time. Even something as "basic" to our view of adolescence as the "identity crisis," they say, is a social invention that arose because of industrialization and the prolongation of schooling. Before the industrial revolution, when most adolescents followed in their parents' occupation, "crises" over identity did not exist.

One group of theorists has taken this viewpoint to its logical extreme. These theorists, called **inventionists,** argue that adolescence is entirely a social invention (Bakan, 1972). Inventionists believe that the way in which we divide the life cycle into stages—drawing a boundary between childhood and adolescence, for example—is nothing more than a reflection of the political, economic, and social circumstances in which we live. They point out that, although puberty has been a feature of development for as long as humans have lived, it was not until the rise of compulsory education that we began treating adolescents as a special and distinct group. This suggests that social conditions, not biological givens, define the nature of adolescent development.

A similar theme is echoed by anthropologists who study adolescence, the most important of whom were Ruth Benedict (1934) and Margaret Mead (1928). Benedict and Mead, whose work is examined in Chapter 3, pointed out that societies vary considerably in the ways in which they view and structure adolescence. As a consequence, these thinkers viewed adolescence as a culturally defined experience—stressful and difficult in societies that saw it this way, but calm and peaceful in societies that had an alternative vision. Benedict, in particular, drew a distinction between continuous and discontinuous societies. In continuous societies (typically, nonindustrialized societies with little social change), the transition from adolescence to adulthood is gradual and peaceful. In discontinuous societies (typically, industrialized societies characterized by rapid social change), the transition into adulthood is abrupt and difficult.

GLOSSARY

academic achievement Achievement that is measured by standardized tests of scholastic ability or knowledge

achievement The psychosocial domain concerning behaviors and feelings in evaluative situations

achievement attributions The beliefs one holds about the causes of one's successes and failures

activational role of hormones The process through which changes in hormone levels, especially at puberty, stimulate changes in the adolescent's behavior, appearance, or growth

adolescent growth spurt The dramatic increase in height and weight that occurs during puberty

adolescent health A new field of study and health care devoted to understanding the health care needs of individuals during the second decade of life

Adult Attachment Interview A structured interview used to assess an individual's past attachment history and "internal working model" of relationships

age of majority The designated age at which an individual is recognized as an adult member of the community

age-grading The process of grouping individuals within social institutions on the basis of chronological age

AIDS (acquired immune deficiency syndrome) A disease, transmitted by means of bodily fluids, that devastates the immune system

analysis of variance (ANOVA) A statistical technique for comparing two or more groups on some variable of interest

androgen One of the sex hormones secreted by the gonads, found in both sexes, but in higher levels among males than among females following puberty

androgynous Possessing both highly masculine and highly feminine traits

anorexia nervosa An eating disorder found chiefly among young women, characterized by dramatic and severe self-induced weight loss

antisocial tendency The presumed psychosocial constellation that underlies various types of externalizing disorders, including delinquency, aggression, and drug use

anxious-avoidant attachment An insecure attachment between infant and caregiver, characterized by indifference on the part of the infant toward the caregiver

anxious-resistant attachment An insecure attachment between infant and caregiver, characterized by distress at separation and anger at reunion

aptitude test A test designed to predict a student's future performance in school, such as the Scholastic Aptitude Test (SAT)

assimilation Trying to adopt the majority culture's norms and standards while rejecting those of one's own ethnic group

asynchronicity of growth The fact that different parts of the body grow at different rates at puberty, which sometimes results in the appearance of gawkiness or awkwardness during early adolescence

attachment The strong affectional bond that develops between an infant and caregiver

attention deficit/hyperactivity disorder (ADHD) A biologically based psychological disorder characterized by impulsivity, inattentiveness, and restlessness, often in school situations

authoritarian parenting A style of parenting characterized by punitive, absolute, and forceful discipline, in which a premium is placed on obedience and conformity

authoritative parenting A style of parenting characterized by warmth, firm control and rational, issue-oriented discipline, in which emphasis is placed on the development of self-direction

autoerotic behavior Sexual behavior that is experienced alone, such as masturbation or sexual fantasizing

automatization The mechanism through which various cognitive processes become automatic, or second nature

autonomy The psychosocial domain concerning the development and expression of independence

baby boom The period following World War II, during which the number of infants born was extremely large

Bar (Bas) Mitzvah In Judiasm, the religious ceremony marking the young person's transition to adulthood

barometric self-esteem The aspect of self-esteem that fluctuates across situations

basal metabolism rate The minimal amount of energy used by the body during a resting state

baseline self-esteem The aspect of self-esteem that is relatively stable across situations and over time

behavioral autonomy The capacity to make independent decisions and follow through with them

behavioral decision theory An approach to understanding adolescent risk-taking, in which behaviors are seen as the outcome of systematic decision-making processes

behaviorists Learning theorists who emphasize the role of concrete stimuli in shaping behavior

biculturalism The successful maintenance of an identification with more than one cultural background

Big Five In the Five-Factor Model of personality, the five critical dimensions: *Extraversion, Agreeableness, Conscientiousness, Neuroticism,* and *Openness to Experience*

brother-sister avoidance The avoidance of any contact or interaction between brothers and sisters from the onset of puberty until one or both persons are married, part of the process of social redefinition at adolescence in many societies

bulimia An eating disorder found chiefly among young women, characterized primarily by a pattern of binge eating and self-induced vomiting

care orientation In Gilligan's theory of moral development, a moral orientation that emphasizes responding to others' needs

child protectionists Individuals who argued, early in the twentieth century, that adolescents needed to be kept out of the labor force in order to protect them from the hazards of the workplace

chlamydia A sexually transmitted disease caused by a bacterium

cliques Small, tightly knit groups of between two and twelve friends, generally of the same sex and age

cluster suicides Outbreaks of suicides, in which an unusually high number of suicides occur within a limited time period or small geographic area

code switching Switching between two different cultural groups' norms for behavior, depending on the situation, a strategy often employed by ethnic minority adolescents

cofigurative cultures Cultures in which the socialization of young people is accomplished not only through contact with elders but also through contact between people of the same age

cognitive-developmental (Piagetian) perspective A perspective on development, based on the work of Piaget, that takes a qualitative, stage-theory approach

cohort A group of individuals born during the same general historical era

community service The involvement of young people in activities that serve some social or economic need of society

competence-performance distinction The distinction between what individuals are capable of and what they actually do, important in the study of cognitive development

componential approach An approach to the study of information processing that divides cognitive processing into its basic components, such as memory or attention

comprehensive high school An educational institution that evolved during the first half of this century, offering a varied curriculum and designed to meet the needs of a diverse population of adolescents

concrete operations The third stage of cognitive development, according to Piaget, spanning the period roughly between age 6 and early adolescence

constraining behavior According to Hauser's model of family processes, interactions that discourage open expression and the exchange of ideas

continuous transition A passage into adulthood in which adult roles and statuses are entered into gradually

conventional moral reasoning According to Kohlberg, the second level of moral development, which develops during late childhood and early adolescence and is characterized by reasoning that is based on the rules and conventions of society

correlation coefficient A measure of the extent to which two factors are related to one another

counterculture A set of values and norms, typically associated with adolescents, that is hostile to the values and norms of adult society

critical thinking Thinking that is in-depth, analytical, and discriminating

cross-sectional study A study that compares two or more groups of individuals at one point in time

crowds Large, loosely organized groups of young people, composed of several cliques and typically organized around a common shared activity

crystallization According to Super, the stage during which individuals, typically between the ages of 14 and 18, first begin to formulate their ideas about appropriate occupations

cultural capital The resources provided within a family through the exposure of the adolescent to art, music, literature, and other elements of "high culture"

culture-fair tests Standardized tests that do not, by virtue of their construction, favor one cultural or ethnic group over another

curvilinear pattern In statistical analyses, a pattern of relation between two variables that resembles a U-shaped or an inverted U-shaped curve

date rape Being forced by a date to have sex against one's will

delayed phase preference A pattern of sleep characterized by later sleep and wake times, which often emerges during puberty

demandingness According to Baumrind, one of the two important dimensions of parenting; *demandingness* refers to the degree to which the parent expects and demands mature, responsible behavior from the child

demographers Social scientists who study large-scale changes in the makeup of the population

dependent variable In a research study, the outcome of interest

depression A psychological disturbance characterized by low self-esteem, decreased motivation, sadness, and difficulty finding pleasure in formerly enjoyable activities

detachment In psychoanalytic theory, the process through which adolescents sever emotional attachments to their parents or other authority figures

discontinuous transition A passage into adulthood in which adult roles and statuses are entered into abruptly

displacement hypothesis The hypothesis that leisure activities displace the more "important" tasks of adolescence

divided attention The process of paying attention to two or more stimuli at the same time

early adolescence The period spanning roughly ages 11 through 14, corresponding approximately to the junior or middle high school years

ecology of human development A perspective on development that emphasizes the broad context in which development occurs

educational attainment The number of years of schooling completed by an individual

effect size In research, the actual magnitude (rather than statistical significance) of a finding

ego In psychoanalytic theory, the part of the psyche that regulates thought, behavior, and emotion

emotional autonomy The establishment of more adult-like and less childish close relationships with family members and peers

emotion-focused coping Reaction to stress in which one attempts to change one's emotional response to the stressor, such as avoidance or distraction; effective in situations in which the source of stress is uncontrollable

enabling behavior According to Hauser's model of family processes, interactions that encourage open expression and the exchange of ideas

endocrine system The system of the body that produces, circulates, and regulates hormones

engagement The extent to which students are psychologically committed to learning and mastering material in school

epidemiology The branch of medicine devoted to the study of how health problems are spread and distributed within communities

epiphysis The closing of the ends of the long bones in the body, which terminates growth in height; one of the markers of the end of puberty

estrogen One of the sex hormones secreted by the gonads, found in both sexes but in higher levels among females than among males following puberty

ethnic identity The aspect of one's sense of identity concerning ancestry or racial group membership

ethnic socialization The process through which individuals acquire knowledge, attitudes, and beliefs about their ethnicity

ethnography A type of research in which individuals are observed in their natural settings

exo-system In the ecological perspective on human development, the layer of the environment that does not directly contain the developing person but affects the settings in which the person lives

Experience Sampling Method (ESM) A method for collecting data about adolescents' emotional states

externalizing disorders Psychosocial problems that are manifested in a turning of the symptoms outward, as in aggression or delinquency

extrinsic motivation Motivation based on the rewards one will receive for successful performance

extrusion The practice of separating children from their parents and requiring them to sleep in other households, part of the process of social redefinition at adolescence in many societies

false-self behavior Behavior that intentionally presents a false impression to others

family life cycle The sequence of phases through which families develop as their needs and concerns change

fear of failure Fear of the consequences of failing in achievement situations

fear of success Fear of the consequences of succeeding in achievement situations

feedback loop A cycle through which two or more bodily functions respond to and regulate each other, such as that formed by the hypothalamus, the pituitary gland, and the gonads

Five-Factor Model A theory that holds that there are five basic dimensions to personality (see *Big Five*)

Forgotten Half The approximately one-half of all American adolescents who do not enroll in college; they have been neglected by researchers and policy-makers

formal operations The fourth stage of cognitive development, according to Piaget, spanning the period from early adolescence through adulthood

functional community According to Coleman, a community in which parents, teachers, and adolescents all share similar values and attitudes

gateway drugs Drugs that, when used over time, lead to the use of other, more dangerous substances

gender identity The aspects of one's sense of self that concern one's masculinity and femininity

gender intensification hypothesis The idea that pressures to behave in sex-appropriate ways intensify during adolescence

generation gap The popular phrase for the alleged conflict between young people and adults over values and attitudes

gifted students Students who are unusually talented in some aspect of intellectual performance

glands Organs that stimulate particular parts of the body to respond in specific ways to particular hormones

gonads The glands that secrete sex hormones: in males, the testes; in females, the ovaries

gonorrhea A sexually transmitted disease caused by a bacterium

health-compromising behaviors Behaviors that place individuals at risk for health problems

health-enhancing behaviors Behaviors that lessen individuals' risk for health problems or that increase well-being

health promotion The attempt to improve adolescent physical and mental well-being by emphasizing healthy behavior and lifestyle choices

herpes A sexually transmitted disease caused by a virus

higher-order thinking Thinking that involves analyzing, evaluating, and interpreting information, rather than simply memorizing it

homophobia The unwarranted fear of homosexuals or homosexuality

hormones Highly specialized substances secreted by one or more endocrine glands

hostile attributional bias The tendency to interpret ambiguous interactions with others as deliberately hostile

human ecology A field of inquiry that focuses on the study of development and behavior in context

hypothalamus A part of the lower brain stem that controls the functioning of the pituitary gland

id In psychoanalytic theory, the part of the psyche dominated by instinctual urges

identity The psychosocial domain concerning feelings and thoughts about the self

identity diffusion (identity confusion) The incoherent, disjointed, incomplete sense of self characteristic of not having resolved the crisis of identity successfully

identity foreclosure The premature establishment of a sense of identity, before sufficient role experimentation has occurred

identity versus identity diffusion According to Erikson, the normative crisis characteristic of the fifth stage of psychosocial development, predominant during adolescence

imaginary audience The belief, often brought on by the heightened self-consciousness of early adolescence, that everyone is watching and evaluating one's behavior

implicit personality theory An intuitive understanding of human behavior and motivation that emerges during early adolescence

independent variable In a research study, the variable presumed to influence the outcome of interest

indifferent parenting A style of parenting characterized by low warmth and low demandingness

individuation The progressive sharpening of one's sense of being an autonomous, independent person

indulgent parenting A style of parenting characterized by high warmth but low demandingness

information processing perspective A perspective on cognition that derives from the study of artificial intelligence and attempts to explain cognitive development in terms of the growth of specific components of the thinking process (for example, memory)

initiation The ceremonial induction of the young person into adulthood

intergenerational conflict Tensions often thought to be inherent in relations between the adolescent and the adult generations; thought by most scholars to have been overestimated

internal working model The implicit model of interpersonal relationships that an individual employs through life, believed to be shaped by early attachment experiences

internalizing disorders Psychosocial problems that are manifested in a turning of the symptoms inward, as in depression or anxiety

intimacy The psychosocial domain concerning the formation, maintenance, and termination of close relationships

intimacy versus isolation According to Erikson, the normative crisis characteristic of the sixth psychosocial stage of development, predominant during young adulthood

intrinsic motivation Motivation based on the pleasure one will experience from mastering a task

inventionists Theorists who argue that the period of adolescence is mainly a social invention

junior high school An educational institution designed during the early era of public secondary education, in which young adolescents are schooled separately from older adolescents

justice orientation In Gilligan's theory of moral development, a moral orientation that emphasizes fairness and objectivity

juvenile justice system A separate system of courts and related institutions developed to handle juvenile crime and delinquency

late adolescence (youth) The period spanning roughly ages 18 through 21, corresponding approximately to the college years

learned helplessness The acquired belief that one is not able to influence events through one's own efforts or actions

learning disability A difficulty with academic tasks that cannot be traced to an emotional problem or sensory dysfunction

learning theories Psychological theories that emphasize the acquisition of behavior through learning

longitudinal study A study following the same group of individuals over time

long-term memory The ability to recall something from a long time ago

macro-system In the ecological perspective on human development, the outermost layer of the environment, containing forces such as history and culture

mainstreaming The integration of adolescents who have educational handicaps into regular classrooms

marginality The situation of being on the margin of the mainstream society, an experience more common among ethnic minority youth

marginal man Lewin's term that refers to the transitional nature of adolescence—poised on the margin of adulthood

median In statistics, a measure of a group's average based on the point above and below which half the members of the group have scored

mediating variable In a research study, a factor presumed to form an intervening link between two variables that are causally connected

menarche The time of first menstruation, one of the important changes to occur among females during puberty

meso-system In the ecological perspective on human development, the layer of the environment formed by the intersection of two or more immediate settings, as in the home-school linkage

meta-analysis A systematic approach to the analysis of a large scientific literature, in which results from different independent studies are pooled

metacognition The process of thinking about thinking itself

micro-systems In the ecological perspective on human development, the immediate settings in which adolescents develop, such as the family or the peer group

middle adolescence The period spanning roughly ages 15 through 18, corresponding approximately to the high school years

middle school An educational institution housing seventh- and eighth-grade students along with adolescents who are one or two years younger

midlife crisis A psychological crisis over identity believed to occur between the ages of 35 and 45, the age range of most adolescents' parents

modeling Imitation

mutual role taking In Selman's theory, the stage of social perspective taking during which the young adolescent can be an objective third party and can see how the thoughts or actions of one person can influence those of another

need for achievement A need that influences the extent to which an individual strives for success in evaluative situations

need for intimacy According to Sullivan, the chief interpersonal need of preadolescence

needs for sexual contact and for intimacy with a peer of the other sex According to Sullivan, the chief interpersonal needs of early adolescence

negative affectivity The presumed underlying cause of internalizing disorders, characterized by high levels of subjective distress

negative identity The selection of an identity that is obviously undesirable in the eyes of significant others and the broader community

neo-Freudians Theorists who have followed in, and expanded on, the psychoanalytic tradition

nocturnal orgasms In males, ejaculations that occur while asleep, sometimes referred to as "wet dreams"

obesity The condition of being more than 20 percent overweight

observational learning The process of learning by watching others

occupational attainment A measure of achievement based on the status or prestige of the job an individual holds

occupational deviance The commission of acts at work that are illegal or unethical

operant conditioning The process by which behavior is shaped through reinforcement and punishment

organismic theories Psychological theories that emphasize the interaction between biological and environmental forces

organizational role of hormones The process through which early exposure to hormones, especially prenatally, organizes the brain or other organs in anticipation of later changes in behavior or patterns of growth

ovaries The female gonads

participant observation A research technique in which the researcher "infiltrates" a group of individuals in order to study their behavior and relationships

particularistic norms Guidelines for behavior that vary from one individual to another; more commonly found in less industrialized societies

peak height velocity The point at which the adolescent is growing most rapidly

peer groups Groups of individuals of approximately the same age

peer pressure The perceived influences of one's agemates or friends to go along with their behavior

permissive societies Societies in which sexual activity during childhood and adolescence is not greatly restrained

personal fable An adolescent's belief that he or she is unique and therefore not subject to the rules that govern other people's behavior

personal responsibility The ability to take responsibility for oneself and manage one's own affairs

pituitary gland One of the chief glands responsible for regulating levels of hormones in the body

postconventional moral reasoning In Kohlberg's theory, the stage of moral development during which society's rules and conventions are seen as relative and subjective rather than as authoritative; also called *principled moral reasoning*

postfigurative cultures Cultures in which the socialization of young people is accomplished almost exclusively through contact between children and their elders

power The ability of a statistical test to detect a genuine effect; power is influenced greatly by the size of one's sample

preconventional moral reasoning According to Kohlberg, the first level of moral development, which is typical of children and is characterized by reasoning that is based on the rewards and punishments associated with different courses of action

prefigurative cultures Cultures in which young people socialize their elders, rather than vice versa

premature affluence Having more income than one can manage maturely, especially during adolescence

preoperational period The second stage of cognitive development, according to Piaget, spanning roughly ages 2 through 5

primary prevention An approach to health promotion that emphasizes teaching all adolescents certain behaviors, values, and information

problem behavior theory A theory that suggests that the co-variation among various types of externalizing disorders results from an underlying trait of unconventionality

problem-focused coping Reaction to stress in which one attempts to change the source of stress, such as attempting to master a difficult challenge; effective in situations in which the source of stress is controllable

propositional logic An abstract system of logic that forms the basis for formal operational thinking

protective factors Factors that lessen individual vulnerability to harm

psychoanalytic theory Freud's theory of development

psychometric A perspective on cognitive development concerned primarily with the measurement of quantitative changes in intelligence through the use of standardized tests

psychosexual conflicts In Freud's theory, the intrapsychic tensions that drive human behavior

psychosocial Referring to aspects of development that are both psychological and social in nature, such as developing a sense of identity or sexuality

psychosocial crises In Erikson's theory, the conflicts that structure the various stages of development

psychosocial moratorium A period of time during which individuals are free from excessive obligations and responsibilities and can therefore experiment with different roles and personalities

psychosomatic disorders Disorders that have both psychological and physical components

puberty The biological changes of adolescence

punishment The process that leads to a decrease in the likelihood that a specific behavior will occur

Q-Sort A research procedure in which raters make their

evaluations by determining how characteristic each of several descriptors is of the person or thing being evaluated

quinceañera An elaborate sort of "coming-out" celebration for adolescent girls that is practiced in many Latino communities

recapitulation In Hall's theory, the notion that individual development parallels the evolution of the species

reference group A group against which an individual compares himself or herself

reinforcement The process that leads to an increase in the likelihood that a specific behavior will occur

responsiveness According to Baumrind, one of the two important dimensions of parenting; *responsiveness* refers to the degree to which the parent responds to the child's needs in an accepting, supportive manner

restrictive societies Societies in which adolescents are pressured to refrain from sexual activity until they have married or undergone a formal rite of passage into adulthood

risk factors Factors that increase individual vulnerability to harm

risk-taking behavior Behavior that is pursued simply because it is risky; risk-taking is thought to be linked to adolescent problem behavior

rite of passage A ceremony or ritual marking an individual's transition from one social status to another, especially marking the young person's transition into adulthood

school-based health centers A new approach to the delivery of health care services to adolescents, which places health care providers in offices located in or adjacent to schools

school climate The overall atmosphere that pervades a school or classroom

school performance A measure of achievement based on an individual's grades in school

school-to-work transition The link between educational institutions and the workplace

secondary prevention An approach to health promotion that is specifically aimed at adolescents who are believed to be at high risk for a particular disease or disturbance

secondary sex characteristics The manifestations of sexual maturation at puberty, including the development of breasts, the growth of facial and body hair, and changes in the voice

secular trend The tendency, over the past two centuries, for individuals to be larger in stature and to reach puberty earlier, primarily because of improvements in health and nutrition

secure attachment A healthy attachment between infant and caregiver, characterized by trust

selective attention The process through which we focus on one stimulus while tuning out another

self-conceptions The collection of traits and attributes that individuals use to describe or characterize themselves

self-consciousness The degree to which an individual is preoccupied with his or her self-image

Self-Directed Search A personality inventory developed by Holland and used to help individuals better understand their vocational interests

self-esteem The degree to which individuals feel positively or negatively about themselves

self-fulfilling prophecy The idea that individuals' behavior is influenced by what others expect of them

self-image stability The degree to which an individual feels that his or her self-image changes from day to day

self-reliance Subjective feelings of one's ability to function autonomously

semirestrictive societies Societies in which pressures against adolescent sexual activity exist but are not vigilantly enforced

sensation-seeking The enjoyment of novel and intense experiences

sense of identity The extent to which individuals feel secure about who they are and who they are becoming

sensorimotor The first stage of cognitive development, according to Piaget, spanning the period roughly between birth and age 2

serial monogamy Having a series of sexual relationships over time in which one is monogamous within each relationship

set point A physiological level or setting (of a specific hormone, for example) that the body attempts to maintain through a self-regulating system

sex cleavage The separation of girls and boys into different cliques, common during late childhood and early adolescence

sex-role behavior Behavior that is consistent with prevailing expectations for how individuals of a given sex are to behave

sexuality The psychosocial domain concerning the development and expression of sexual feelings

sexually transmitted disease (STD) Any of a group of diseases—including gonorrhea, herpes, chlamydia, and AIDS—passed on through sexual contact

sexual preference An individual's preference for same- or opposite-sex sexual partners

sexual socialization The process through which adolescents are exposed to and educated about sexuality

short-term memory The ability to remember something for a very brief period of time

significant others The people most important in an individual's life

social class The social position of an individual or family in society as determined by wealth, power, reputation, or achievement

social cognition The aspect of cognition that concerns thinking about other people, about interpersonal relationships, and about social institutions

social control theory A theory of delinquency that links deviance with the absence of bonds to society's main institutions

social conventions The norms that govern everyday behavior in social situations

social information processing The ways in which individuals think about and use information about social relationships and interpersonal interactions

social learning theorists Learning theorists who emphasize the role of modeling and observational learning

social perspective taking The ability to view events from the perspective of others

social redefinition The process through which an individual's position or status is redefined by society

social responsibility The ability to cooperate with and take responsibility for others

social support The extent to which one receives emotional or instrumental assistance from one's social network

sociosexual behavior The aspect of sexual behavior that is merged with social relationships

specialized structural systems A series of specialized cognitive structures used to solve different types of intellectual problems

specification According to Super, the stage during which individuals, typically between the ages of 18 and 21, first begin to consider narrowly defined occupational pursuits

statistical interaction In research, when the observed effect of an independent variable (e.g., intelligence) on an outcome (e.g., grades) varies as a function of an additional independent variable (e.g., age)

status offenses Violations of the law that pertain to minors but not to adults

storm and stress Hall's phrase that refers to the inevitable turmoil of adolescence

stressful life events Normative and non-normative events presumed to increase individuals' susceptibility to psychological distress

substance abuse The misuse of alcohol or other drugs

Tanner stages A widely used system to describe the five stages of pubertal development

teenager A term popularized about fifty years ago to refer to young people; it connoted a more frivolous and lighthearted image than the term *adolescent*

temperament An individual's characteristic style of responsiveness and mood, present from early infancy

testes The male gonads

testosterone One of the sex hormones secreted by the gonads, found in both sexes but in higher levels among males than females

theory of multiple intelligences Gardner's theory that there are various types of intelligence (e.g., academic, social, athletic) in which individuals differ

tracking The grouping of students, according to ability, into different levels of classes within the same school grade

triarchic theory of intelligence Sternberg's theory of intelligence, in which three different types of intelligence are examined: componential intelligence, experiential intelligence, and contextual intelligence

Type-A behavior A pattern of impatient, hard-driving behavior that is believed to increase individuals' risk for heart disease

underachievers Individuals whose actual school performance is lower than what would be expected on the basis of objective measures of their aptitude or intelligence

universalistic norms Guidelines for behavior that apply to all members of a community; more common in industrialized societies

value autonomy The establishment of an independent set of values and beliefs

youth Today, a term used to refer to individuals between the ages of 18 and 22; it once referred to individuals between the ages of 12 and 24

youth apprenticeship A structured, work-based learning experience that places an adolescent under the supervision of a skilled adult

youth culture The popular culture thought to appeal to and shape the attitudes and behaviors of adolescents and youth

youth unemployment The unemployment of young people, especially 16- to 24-year-olds who are not enrolled in school

REFERENCES

Achenbach, T., and Edelbrock, C. (1987). *The manual for the Youth Self-Report and Profile.* Burlington: University of Vermont.

Ackerman, G. (1993). A congressional view of youth suicide. *American Psychologist, 48,* 183–184.

Adams, G., and Fitch, S. (1982). Ego stage and identity status development: A cross-sequential analysis. *Journal of Personality and Social Psychology, 43,* 574–583.

Adams, G., Gullotta, T., and Montemayor, R. (Eds.). (1992). *Adolescent identity formation.* Newbury Park, Calif.: Sage.

Adams, G., and Jones, R. (1983). Female adolescents' identity development: Age comparisons and perceived child-rearing experience. *Developmental Psychology, 19,* 249–256.

Adegoke, A. (1993). The experience of spermarche (the age of onset of sperm emission) among selected adolescent boys in Nigeria. *Journal of Youth and Adolescence, 22,* 201–209.

Adelson, J. (1972). The political imagination of the young adolescent. In J. Kagan and R. Coles (Eds.), *Twelve to sixteen: Early adolescence.* New York: Norton.

Adelson, J. (1979, January). The generalization gap. *Psychology Today,* pp. 33–37.

Agras, W. S., Schneider, J., Arnow, B., Raeburn, S., and Telch, C. (1989). Cognitive-behavioral and response-prevention treatments for bulimia nervosa. *Journal of Consulting and Clinical Psychology, 57,* 215–221.

Ainsworth, M., Blehar, M., Waters, E., and Wall, S. (1978). *Patterns of attachment.* Hillsdale, N.J.: Erlbaum.

Aitken, D., and Chaplin, J. (1990). Sex miseducation. *Family Therapy Networker, 14,* 24–25.

Alasker, F., and Olweus, D. (1992). Stability of global self evaluations in early adolescence: A cohort longitudinal study. *Journal of Research on Adolescence, 1,* 123–145.

Alexander, C., Ensminger, M., Kim, Y., Smith, B. J., Johnson, K., and Dolan, L. (1989). Early sexual activity among adolescents in small towns and rural areas: Race and gender patterns. *Family Planning Perspectives, 21,* 261–266.

Alexander, C., Somerfield, M., Ensminger, M., Johnson, K., and Kim, Y. (1993). Consistency of adolescents' self-report of sexual behavior in a longitudinal study. *Journal of Youth and Adolescence, 22,* 455–471.

Alexander, J. (1973). Defensive and supportive communications in normal and deviant families. *Journal of Consulting and Clinical Psychology, 40,* 223–231.

Alexander, K., and Cook, M. (1982). Curricula and coursework: A surprise ending to a familiar story. *American Sociological Review, 47,* 626–640.

Alexander, K., and Eckland, B. (1975). School experience and status attainment. In S. Dragastin and G. Elder, Jr. (Eds.), *Adolescence in the life cycle.* Washington, D.C.: Hemisphere.

Alexander, K., Natriello, G., and Pallas, A. (1985). For whom the cognitive bell tolls: The impact of dropping out on cognitive performance. *American Sociological Review, 50,* 409–420.

Allen, J., Hauser, S., Bell, K., and O'Connor, T. (1994). Longitudinal assessment of autonomy and relatedness in adolescent-family interactions as predictors of adolescent ego development and self-esteem. *Child Development, 65,* 179–194.

Allen, J., Hauser, S., Eickholt, C., Bell, K., and O'Connor, T. (in press). Autonomy and relatedness in family interactions as predictors of expressions of negative adolescent affect. *Journal of Research on Adolescence.*

Allen, R., and Mirabell, J. (1990, May). *Shorter subjective sleep of high school students from early compared to late starting schools.* Paper presented at the second meeting of the Society for Research on Biological Rhythms, Jacksonville, FL.

Allgood-Merten, B., Lewinsohn, P., and Hops, H. (1990). Sex differences and adolescent depression. *Journal of Abnormal Psychology, 99,* 55–63.

Allgood-Merten, B., and Stockard, J. (1991). Sex role identity and self-esteem: A comparison of children and adolescents. *Sex Roles, 25,* 129–140.

Allison, P., and Furstenberg, F., Jr. (1989). How marital dissolution affects children: Variations by age and sex. *Developmental Psychology, 25,* 540–549.

Alva, S. (1993). Differential patterns of achievement among Asian-American adolescents. *Journal of Youth and Adolescence, 22,* 407–423.

Amato, P., and Keith, B. (1991a). Parental divorce and the well-being of children: A meta-analysis. *Psychological Bulletin, 110,* 26–46.

Amato, P., and Keith, B. (1991b). Separation from a parent during childhood and adult socioeconomic attainment. *Social Forces, 70,* 187–206.

American Psychiatric Association. (1994). *Diagnostic and Statistical Manual of the American Psychiatric Association (DSM-IV).* Washington, D.C.: American Psychiatric Association.

Ames, C., and Archer, J. (1988). Achievement goals in the classroom: Students' learning strategies and motivation processes. *Journal of Educational Psychology, 80,* 260–267.

Anastasi, A. (1988). *Psychological testing,* 6th ed. New York: Macmillan.

Anderson, E. (1992, March). *Consistency of parenting in stepfather families.* Paper presented at the biennial meetings of the Society for Research on Adolescence, Washington.

Anderson, E., and Starcher, L. (1992, March). *Transformations in sibling relationships during adolescence.* Paper presented at the biennial meetings of the Society for Research on Adolescence, Washington.

Andersson, B. (1994, February). *School as a setting for development—A Swedish example.* Paper presented at the biennial meetings of the Society for Research on Adolescence, San Diego.

Andersson, T., Bergman, L., and Magnusson, D. (1989). Patterns of adjustment problems and alcohol abuse in early adulthood: A prospective longitudinal study. *Development and Psychopathology, 1,* 119–131.

Andersson, T., and Magnusson, D. (1990). Biological maturation in adolescence and the development of drinking habits and alcohol abuse among young males: A prospective longitudinal study. *Journal of Youth and Adolescence, 19,* 33–42.

Aneshensel, C., Becerra, R., Fielder, E., and Schuler, R. (1990). Onset of fertility-related events during adolescence: A prospective comparison of Mexican American and Non-Hispanic White females. *American Journal of Public Health, 80,* 959–963.

Apter, T. (1990). *Altered loves: Mothers and daughters during adolescence.* New York: St. Martin's.

Aquilino, W. (1991). Family structure and home-leaving: A further specification of the relationship. *Journal of Marriage and the Family, 53,* 999–1010.

Arbeton, A., Eccles, J., and Harold, R. (1994, February). *Parents' perceptions of their children's competence: The role of parent attributions.* Paper presented at the biennial meetings of the Society for Research on Adolescence, San Diego.

Archer, S. (1982). The lower age boundaries of identity development. *Child Development, 53,* 1551- 1556.

Archer, S. (1989). Gender differences in identity development: Issues of process, domain, and timing. *Journal of Adolescence, 12,* 117–138.

Armor, D. (1972). School and family effects on black and white achievement: A reexamination of the USOE data. In F. Mosteller and D. Moynihan (Eds.), *On equality of educational opportunity.* New York: Random House.

Armsden, G., and Greenberg, M. (1987). The inventory of parent and peer attachment: Individual differences and their relationship to psychological well-being in adolescence. *Journal of Youth and Adolescence, 16,* 427–453.

Arnett, J., and Balle-Jensen, L. (1993). Cultural bases of risk behavior: Danish adolescents. *Child Development, 64,* 1842–1855.

Aro, H., and Taipale, V. (1987). The impact of timing of puberty on psychosomatic symptoms among fourteen- to sixteen-year-old Finnish girls. *Child Development, 58,* 261–268.

Aseltine, R., Jr., and Gore, S. (1994, February). *The occurrence and co-occurrence of affective disorder and substance abuse during the transition to adulthood.* Paper presented at the biennial meetings of the Society for Research on Adolescence, San Diego.

Asher, S., and Coie, J. (Eds.). (1990). *Peer rejection in childhood.* New York: Cambridge University Press.

Asmussen, L., and Larson, R. (1991). The quality of family time among young adolescents in single-parent and married-parent families. *Journal of Marriage and the Family, 53,* 1021–1030.

Astin, H. (1984). The meaning of work in women's lives: A sociopsychological model of career choice and work behavior. *Counseling Psychologist, 12,* 117–126.

Astone, N., and McLanahan, S. (1991). Family structure, parental practices, and high school completion. *American Sociological Review, 56,* 309–320.

Attie, I., and Brooks-Gunn, J. (1989). The development of eating problems in adolescent girls: A longitudinal study. *Developmental Psychology, 25,* 70–79.

Bachman, J. (1970). *Youth in transition,* Vol. 2, *The impact of family background and intelligence on tenth-grade boys.* Ann Arbor: Institute for Social Research, University of Michigan.

Bachman, J. (1983, Summer). Premature affluence: Do high school students earn too much? *Economic Outlook USA,* 64–67.

Bachman, J., Bare, D., and Frankie, E. (1986). *Correlates of employment among high school seniors.* Paper available from the Institute for Social Research, University of Michigan, Ann Arbor.

Bachman, J., and O'Malley, P. (1986). Self-concepts, self-esteem, and educational experiences: The frog pond revisited (again). *Journal of Personality and Social Psychology, 50,* 35–46.

Bachman, J., and Schulenberg, J. (1993). How part-time work intensity relates to drug use, problem behavior, time use, and satisfaction among high school seniors: Are these consequences or merely correlates? *Developmental Psychology, 29,* 220–235.

Bachman, J., Wallace, J., Jr., O'Malley, P., Johnston, L., Kurth, C., and Neighbors, H. (1991). Racial/ ethnic differences in smoking, drinking, and illicit drug use among American high school seniors, 1976–89. *American Journal of Public Health, 81,* 372–377.

Bakan, D. (1972). Adolescence in America: From idea to social fact. In J. Kagan and R. Coles (Eds.), *Twelve to sixteen: Early adolescence.* New York: Norton.

Baker, D., and Stevenson, D. (1986). Mothers' strategies for school achievement: Managing the transition to high school. *Sociology of Education, 59,* 156–167.

Baker, L., and Brown, A. (1984). Metacognitive skills and reading. In P. Pearson (Ed.), *Handbook of reading research,* Part 2. New York: Longman.

Bakken, L., and Romig, C. (1992, March). *The relationship of intimacy and identity development in middle adolescents.* Paper presented at the biennial meetings of the Society for Research on Adolescence, Washington.

Bandura, A., and Walters, R. (1959). *Adolescent aggression.* New York: Ronald Press.

Bank, L., Marlowe, J., Reid, J., Patterson, G., and Weinrott, M. (1991). A comparative evaluation of parent-training interventions for families of chronic delinquents. *Journal of Abnormal Child Psychology, 19,* 15–33.

Bank, L., Reid, J., and Greenley, K. (1994, February). *Middle childhood predictors of adolescent and early adult aggression.* Paper presented at the biennial meetings of the Society for Research on Adolescence, San Diego.

Barbarin, O. (1993). Coping and resilience: Exploring the inner lives of African-American children. *Journal of Black Psychology, 19,* 478–492.

Barbarin, O., and Soler, R. (1993). Behavioral, emotional, and academic adjustment in a national probability sample of African-American children. *Journal of Black Psychology, 19,* 423–446.

Barber, B. (1992). Family, personality, and adolescent problem behavior. *Journal of Marriage and the Family, 54,* 69–79.

Barber, B. (1994). Cultural, family, and personal contexts of parent-adolescent conflict. *Journal of Marriage and the Family, 56,* 375–386.

Barber, B., and Eccles, J. (1992). Long-term influence of divorce and single parenting on adolescent family- and work-related values, behaviors, and aspirations. *Psychological Bulletin, 111,* 108–126.

Barber, B., Olsen, J., and Shagle, S. (1994). Associations between parental psychological and behavioral control and youth internalized and externalized behaviors. *Child Development, 65,* 1120–1136.

Bardwick, J., and Douvan, E. (1981). Ambivalence: The socialization of women. In V. Gernick and B. Moran (Eds.), *Women in a sexist society: Studies in power and powerlessness.* New York: Basic Books.

Barenboim, C. (1981). The development of person perception in childhood and adolescence: From behavioral comparisons to psychological constructs to psychological comparisons. *Child Development, 52,* 129–144.

Barker, R., and Gump, P. (1964). *Big school, small school: High school size and student behavior.* Stanford, Calif.: Stanford University Press.

Barnes, E. (1980). The black community as the source of positive self-concept for black children: A theoretical perspective. Pp. 106–130 in R. Jones (Ed.), *Black psychology.* New York: Harper & Row.

Barnes, G., and Farrell, M. (1992). Parental support and control as predictors of adolescent drinking, delinquency, and related problem behaviors. *Journal of Marriage and the Family, 54,* 763–776.

Baron, J., and Sternberg, R. (1987). *Teaching thinking skills: Theory and practice.* New York: Freeman.

Barringer, F. (1990, August 17). After long decline, teen births are up. *New York Times,* p. A14.

Barton, P. (1989). *Earning and learning.* Princeton, N.J.: National Assessment of Educational Progress, Educational Testing Service.

Baumeister, R., and Tice, D. (1986). How adolescence became the struggle for self: A historical transformation of psychological development. Pp. 183–201 in J. Suls and A. Greenwald (Eds.), *Psychological perspectives on the self,* Vol. 3. Hillsdale, N.J.: Erlbaum.

Baumrind, D. (1978). Parental disciplinary patterns and social competence in children. *Youth and Society, 9,* 239–276.

Baumrind, D. (1991). The influence of parenting style on adolescent competence and substance use. *Journal of Early Adolescence, 11,* 56–95.

Baumrind, D., and Moselle, K. (1985). A developmental perspective on adolescent drug abuse. *Advances in Alcohol and Substance Abuse, 4,* 41–67.

Bayley, N. (1949). Consistency and variability in the growth of intelligence from birth to eighteen years. *Journal of Genetic Psychology, 75,* 165–196.

Beardslee, W., Hoke, L., Wheelock, I., Rothberg, P., van de Velde, P., and Swatling, S. (1992). Initial findings on preventive interventions for families with parental affective disorders. *American Journal of Psychiatry, 145,* 1335–1340.

Beardslee, W., Schultz, L., and Selman, R. (1987). Level of social-cognitive development, adaptive functioning, and DSM-III diagnoses in adolescent offspring of parents with affective disorders: Implications of the development of the capacity for mutuality. *Developmental Psychology, 23,* 807–815.

Bell, A., Weinberg, M., and Hammersmith, S. (1981). *Sexual preference: Its development in men and women.* Bloomington: Indiana University Press.

Bell, R. (1968). A reinterpretation of the direction of effects in studies of socialization. *Psychological Review, 75,* 81–95.

Belsky, J., Steinberg, L., and Draper, P. (1991). Childhood experience, interpersonal development, and reproductive strategy: An evolutionary theory of socialization. *Child Development, 62,* 647–670.

Bem, S. (1975). Sex-role adaptability: One consequence of psychological androgyny. *Journal of Personality and Social Psychology, 31,* 634–643.

Bence, P. (1992, March). *Patterns of the experience of mood.* Paper presented at the biennial meetings of the Society for Research on Adolescence, Washington.

Benedict, R. (1934). *Patterns of culture.* Boston: Houghton Mifflin.

Bennett, S. (1987). *New dimensions in research on class size and academic achievement.* Madison, Wis.: National Center on Effective Secondary Schools.

Benson, M., Harris, P., and Rogers, C. (1992). Identity consequences of attachment to mothers and fathers among late adolescents. *Journal of Research on Adolescence, 2,* 187–204.

Benson, P., Donahue, M., and Erickson, J. (1989). Adolescence and religion: Review of the literature from 1970–1986. *Research in the Social Scientific Study of Religion, 1,* 153–181.

Berk, L. (1992). The extracurriculum. In P. Jackson (Ed.), *Handbook of research on curriculum.* New York: Macmillan.

Berman, B., Winkleby, M., Chesterman, E., and Boyce, T. (1992). After-school child care and self-esteem in school-age children. *Pediatrics, 89,* 654–659.

Berndt, T. (1979). Developmental changes in conformity to peers and parents. *Developmental Psychology, 15,* 608–616.

Berndt, T. (1981). Relations between social cognition, nonsocial cognition, and social behavior: The case of friendship. In J. Flavell and L. Ross (Eds.), *Social cognitive development: Frontiers and possible futures.* Cambridge, England: Cambridge University Press.

Berndt, T. (1982). The features and effects of friendship in early adolescence. *Child Development, 53,* 1447–1460.

Berndt, T. (1987). *Changes in friendship and school adjustment after the transition to junior high school.* Paper presented at the biennial meetings of the Society for Research in Child Development, Baltimore.

Berndt, T., and Perry, T. (1990). Distinctive features and effects of early adolescent friendships. Pp. 269–287 in R. Montemayor, G. Adams, and T. Gullota (Eds.), *Advances in adolescence research,* Vol. 2. Beverly Hills, Calif.: Sage.

Beyth-Marom, R., Austin, L., Fischoff, B., Palmgren, C., and Jacobs-Quadrel, M. (1993). Perceived consequences of risky behaviors: Adults and adolescents. *Developmental Psychology, 29,* 549–563.

Biafora, F., Jr., Taylor, D., Warheit, G., Zimmerman, R., and Vega, W. (1993). Cultural mistrust and racial awareness among ethnically diverse Black adolescent boys. *Journal of Black Psychology, 19,* 266–281.

Bierman, K., and Furman, W. (1984). The effects of social skills training and peer involvement on the social adjustment of preadolescents. *Child Development, 55,* 151–162.

Bigelow, B., and LaGaipa, J. (1975). Children's written descriptions of friendship. *Developmental Psychology, 11,* 857–858.

Biller, H. (1981). Father absence, divorce, and personality development. In M. Lamb (Ed.), *The role of the father in child development,* 2nd ed. New York: Wiley.

Billy, J., Landale, N., Grady, W., and Zimmerle, D. (1988). Effects of sexual activity on adolescent social and psychological development. *Social Psychology Quarterly, 51,* 190–212.

Bingham, C., and Crockett, L. (1994). Predictors and outcomes of the timing of first sexual intercourse. Manuscript submitted for publication. Department of Psychology, Michigan State University.

Blash, R., and Unger, D. (1992, March). *Cultural factors and the self-esteem and aspirations of African-American adolescent males.* Paper presented at the biennial meetings of the Society for Research on Adolescence, Washington.

Block, J., Block, J., and Keyes, S. (1988). Longitudinally foretelling drug usage in adolescence: Early childhood personality and environmental precursors. *Child Development, 59,* 336–355.

Block, J., and Robins, R. (1993). A longitudinal study of consistency and change in self-esteem from early adolescence to early adulthood. *Child Development, 64,* 909–923.

Bloom, A. (1987). *The closing of the American mind.* New York: Simon & Schuster.

Blos, P. (1967). The second individuation process of adolescence. In R. S. Eissler et al. (Eds.), *Psychoanalytic study of the child,* Vol. 15. New York: International Universities Press.

Blos, P. (1979). *The adolescent passage.* New York: International Universities Press.

Blum, R., Resnick, M., and Stark, T. (1990). Factors associated with the use of court bypass by minors to obtain abortions. *Family Planning Perspectives, 22,* 158–160.

Blumenthal, S., and Kupfer, D. (1988). Overview of early detection and treatment strategies for suicidal behavior in young people. *Journal of Youth and Adolescence, 17,* 1–24.

Blyth, D., Hill, J., and Smyth, C. (1981). The influence of older adolescents on younger adolescents: Do grade-level arrangements make a difference in behaviors, attitudes, and experiences? *Journal of Early Adolescence, 1,* 85–110.

Blyth, D., Hill, J., and Thiel, K. (1982). Early adolescents' significant others: Grade and gender differences in perceived relationships with familial and non-familial adults and young people. *Journal of Youth and Adolescence, 11,* 425–450.

Blyth, D., Simmons, R., Bulcroft, R., Felt, D., Van Cleave, E., and Bush, D. (1980). The effects of physical development on self-image and satisfaction with body image for early adolescent males. In F. G. Simmons (Ed.), *Handbook of community and mental health,* Vol. 2. Greenwich, Conn: JAI Press.

Blyth, D., Simmons, R., and Zakin, D. (1985). Satisfaction with body image for early adolescent females: The impact of pubertal timing within different school environments. *Journal of Youth and Adolescence, 14,* 227–236.

Bogenschneider, K., and Steinberg, L. (1994). Maternal employment and adolescent academic achievement: A developmental analysis. *Sociology of Education, 67,* 60–77.

Boggiano, A., Main, D., and Katz, P. (1991). Mastery motivation in boys and girls: The role of intrinsic versus extrinsic motivation. *Sex Roles, 25,* 511–520.

Bohrnstedt, G., and Felson, R. (1983). Explaining the relations among children's actual and perceived performances and self-esteem: A comparison of several causal models. *Journal of Personality and Social Psychology, 45,* 43–56.

Boldizar, J., Wilso, K., and Deemer, D. (1989). Gender, life experiences, and moral judgment development: A process-oriented approach. *Journal of Personality and Social Psychology, 57,* 229–238.

Boxer, A., Cohler, B., Herdt, G., and Irvin, F. (1993). Gay and lesbian youth. In P. Tolan and B. Cohler (Eds.), *Handbook of clinical research and practice with adolescents.* Pp. 249–280. New York: Wiley.

Borrine, M., Handal, P., Brown, N., and Searight, H. (1991). Family conflict and adolescent adjustment in intact, divorced, and blended families. *Journal of Consulting and Clinical Psychology, 59,* 753–755.

Bourne, E. (1978a). The state of research on ego identity: A review and appraisal, Part I. *Journal of Youth and Adolescence, 7,* 223–251.

Bourne, E. (1978b). The state of research on ego identity: A review and appraisal, Part II. *Journal of Youth and Adolescence, 7,* 371–392.

Bowlby, J. (1969). *Attachment and loss,* Vol. 1: *Attachment.* New York: Basic Books.

Boyer, E. (1983). *High school.* New York: Harper & Row.

Boyer, E. (1986, December). Transition from school to college. *Phi Delta Kappan,* 293–287.

Boyes, M., and Allen, S. (1993). Styles of parent-child interaction and moral reasoning in adolescence. *Merrill-Palmer Quarterly, 39,* 551–570.

Boykin, A., and Toms, F. (1985). Black child socialization: A conceptual framework. In H. McAdoo and J.

McAdoo (Eds.), *Black children: Social, educational, and parental environments.* Newbury Park: Sage.

Braddock, J. (1985). School desegregation and black assimilation. *Journal of Social Issues, 41,* 9–22.

Bradley, L., and Bradley, G. (1977). The academic achievement of black students in desegregated schools: A critical review. *Review of Educational Research, 47,* 399–449.

Brady, E., and Kendall, P. (1992). Comorbidity of anxiety and depression in children and adolescents. *Psychological Bulletin, 111,* 244–255.

Brandon, P. (1991). Gender differences in young Asian Americans' educational attainments. *Sex Roles, 25,* 45–62.

Braungart, R. (1980). Youth movements. Pp. 560–597 in J. Adelson (Ed.), *Handbook of adolescent psychology.* New York: Wiley.

Bray, J., Berger, S., Tiuch, G., and Boethel, C. (1993, March). *Nonresidential parent-child relationships following divorce and remarriage: A longitudinal perspective.* Paper presented at the biennial meetings of the Society for Research in Child Development, New Orleans.

Brewster, K., Billy, J., and Grady, W. (1993). Social context and adolescent behavior: The impact of community on the transition to sexual activity. *Social Forces, 71,* 713–740.

Britner, P., Crosby, C., and Jodl, K. (1994, February). *The death penalty as applied to juvenile offenders: Jurors' perceptions of adolescents' criminal responsibility.* Paper presented at the biennial meetings of the Society for Research on Adolescence, San Diego.

Brittain, C. (1963). Adolescent choices and parent/peer cross-pressures. *American Sociological Review, 28,* 385–391.

Brody, G., Stoneman, Z., Flor, D., McCrary, C., Hatings, L., and Conyers, O. (1994). Financial resources, parent psychological functioning, parent co-caregiving, and early adolescent competence in rural two-parent African-American families. *Child Development, 65,* 590–605.

Brody, J. (1987, June 3). Personal health column. *New York Times.*

Bronfenbrenner, U. (1974). The origins of alienation. *Scientific American, 231,* 53–61.

Bronfenbrenner, U. (1979). *The ecology of human development.* Cambridge, Mass.: Harvard University Press.

Bronfenbrenner, U. (1989). Ecological systems theory. Pp. 187–249 in R. Vasta (Ed.), *Annals of child development,* Vol 6. Greenwich, Conn.: JAI Press.

Bronfenbrenner, U., and Crouter, N. (1982). Work and family through time and space. In S. Kammerman and C. Hayes (Eds.), *Families that work: Children in a changing world.* Washington, D.C.: National Academy Press.

Bronstein, P., Duncan, P., Clauson, J., Abrams, C., Yannett, N., Ginsburg, G., and Milne, M. (1994). Enhancing middle school adjustment for children from lower-income families: A parenting intervention. Manuscript submitted for publication. Department of Psychology, University of Vermont.

Brook, J., Whitman, M., and Gordon, A. (1983). Stages of drug use in adolescence: Personality, peer, and family correlates. *Developmental Psychology, 19,* 269–277.

Brook, J., Whitman, M., Gordon, A., and Brook, D. (1984). Paternal determinants of female adolescent's marijuana use. *Developmental Psychology, 20,* 1032–1043.

Brook, J., Whitman, M., Gordon, A., and Cohen, P. (1986). Dynamics of childhood and adolescent personality traits and adolescent drug use. *Developmental Psychology, 22,* 403–414.

Brooks-Gunn, J. (1987). Pubertal processes and girls' psychological adaptation. Pp. 123–153 in R. Lerner and T. Fochs (Eds.), *Biological-psychosocial interactions in early adolescence: A life-span perspective.* Hillsdale, N.J.: Erlbaum.

Brooks-Gunn, J. (1989). Pubertal processes and the early adolescent transition. Pp. 155–176 in W. Damon (Ed.), *Child development today and tomorrow.* San Francisco: Jossey-Bass.

Brooks-Gunn, J., Boyer, C., and Hein, K. (1988). Preventing HIV infection and AIDS in children and adolescents. *American Psychologist, 43,* 958–964.

Brooks-Gunn, J., Duncan, G., Klebanov, P., and Sealand, N. (1993). Do neighborhoods influence child and adolescent development? *American Journal of Sociology, 99,* 353–395.

Brooks-Gunn, J., and Furstenberg, F., Jr. (1989). Adolescent sexual behavior. *American Psychologist, 44,* 249–257.

Brooks-Gunn, J., and Paikoff, R. (1993). "Sex is a gamble, kissing is a game": Adolescent sexuality and health promotion. Pp. 180–208 in S. Millstein, A. Petersen, and E. Nightingale (Eds.), *Promoting the health of adolescents: New directions for the twenty-first century.* New York: Oxford University Press.

Brooks-Gunn, J., and Petersen, A. (Eds.). (1991). The emergence of depressive symptoms during adolescence. *Journal of Youth and Adolescence, 20* (whole issue).

Brooks-Gunn, J., and Reiter, E. (1990). The role of pubertal processes. Pp. 16–23 in S. Feldman and G. Elliott (Eds.), *At the threshold: The developing adolescent.* Cambridge, Mass.: Harvard University Press.

Brooks-Gunn, J., and Ruble, D. (1979). *The social and psychological meaning of menarche.* Paper presented at the biennial meetings of the Society for Research in Child Development, San Francisco.

Brooks-Gunn, J., and Ruble, D. (1982). The development of menstrual-related beliefs and behaviors during early adolescence. *Child Development, 53,* 1567–1577.

Brooks-Gunn, J., and Warren, M. (1985). The effects of delayed menarche in different contexts: Dance and nondance students. *Journal of Youth and Adolescence, 14,* 285–300.

Brooks-Gunn, J., and Warren, M. (1989). Biological contributions to negative affect in young girls. *Child Development, 60,* 40–55.

Brooks-Gunn, J., Warren, M., and Rosso, J. (1991). The impact of pubertal and social events upon girls' problem behavior. *Journal of Youth and Adolescence.*

Broverman, I., Vogel, S., Broverman, D., Clarkson, F., and Rosenkrantz, P. (1972). Sex-role stereotypes: A current appraisal. *Journal of Social Issues, 28,* 59–78.

Brown, A. (1975). The development of memory: Knowing, knowing about knowing, and knowing how to know.

In H. Reese (Ed.), *Advances in child development and behavior,* Vol. 10. New York: Academic Press.

Brown, B. (1990). Peer groups. Pp. 171–196 in S. Feldman and G. Elliott (Eds.), *At the threshold: The developing adolescent.* Cambridge, Mass.: Harvard University Press.

Brown, B., Clasen, D., and Eicher, S. (1986). Perceptions of peer pressure, peer conformity dispositions, and self-reported behavior among adolescents. *Developmental Psychology, 22,* 521–530.

Brown, B., Freeman, H., Huang, B., and Mounts, N. (1992, March). *"Crowd hopping": Incidence, correlates and consequences of change in crowd affiliation during adolescence.* Paper presented at the biennial meetings of the Society for Research on Adolescence, Washington.

Brown, B., Lamborn, S., and Newmann, F. (1992). "You live and you learn": The place of school engagement in the lives of teenagers. In F. Newmann (Ed.), *Student engagement and achievement in American high schools.* New York: Teachers College Press.

Brown, B., and Lohr, M. J. (1987). Peer group affiliation and adolescent self-esteem: An integration of ego-identity and symbolic interaction theories. *Journal of Personality and Social Psychology, 52,* 47–55.

Brown, B., Mory, M., and Kinney, D. (1994). Casting crowds in a relational perspective: Caricature, channel, and context. In R. Montemayor, G. Adams, and T. Gullotta (Eds.), *Advances in adolescent development,* Vol. 5: *Personal relationships during adolescence.* Newbury Park, Calif.: Sage.

Brown, B., and Mounts, N. (1989, April). *Peer group structures in single versus multiethnic high schools.* Paper presented at the biennial meetings of the Society for Research in Child Development, Kansas City.

Brown, B., Mounts, N., Lamborn, S., and Steinberg, L. (1993). Parenting practices and peer group affiliation in adolescence. *Child Development, 64,* 467–482.

Brown, J. (1994, February). *Adolescents' uses of mass media and bedroom culture.* Paper presented at the biennial meetings of the Society for Research on Adolescence, San Diego.

Brown, J., and Newcomer, S. (1991). Television viewing and adolescents' sexual behavior. *Journal of Homosexuality, 21,* 77–91.

Brown, J., White, A., and Nikopoulou, L. (1993). Disinterest, intrigue, resistance: Early adolescent girls' use of sexual media content. Pp. 177–195 in B. Greenberg, J. Brown, and N. Buerkel-Rothfuss (Eds.), *Media, sex, and the adolescent.* Creskill, N.J.: Hampton Press.

Brubacher, J., and Rudy, W. (1976). *Higher education in transition,* 3rd ed. New York: Harper & Row.

Bruch, H. (1973). *Eating disorders.* New York: Basic Books.

Brumberg, J. (1988). *Fasting girls: The emergence of anorexia as a modern disease.* Cambridge, Mass.: Harvard University Press.

Bruvold, W. (1993). A meta-analysis of adolescent smoking prevention programs. *American Journal of Public Health, 83,* 872–880.

Bryk, A., and Thum, Y. (1989). The effects of high school organization on dropping out: An exploratory investigation. *American Educational Research Journal, 26,* 353–383.

Buchanan, C., Eccles, J., and Becker, J. (1992). Are adolescents the victims of raging hormones?: Evidence for activational effects of hormones on moods and behavior at adolescence. *Psychological Bulletin, 111,* 62–107.

Buchanan, C., and Maccoby, E. (1993, March). *Relationships between adolescents and their nonresidential parents: A comparison of nonresidential mothers and fathers.* Paper presented at the biennial meetings of the Society for Research in Child Development, New Orleans.

Buchanan, C., Maccoby, E., and Dornbusch, S. (1991). Caught between parents: Adolescents' experience in divorced homes. *Child Development, 62,* 1008–1029.

Buchanan, M., and Robbins, C. (1990). Early adult psychological consequences for males of adolescent pregnancy and its resolution. *Journal of Youth and Adolescence, 19,* 413–424.

Buhrmester, D. (1990). Intimacy of friendship, interpersonal competence, and adjustment during preadolescence and adolescence. *Child Development, 61,* 1101–1111.

Buhrmester, D., and Furman, W. (1987). The development of companionship and intimacy. *Child Development, 58,* 1101–1113.

Buhrmester, D., and Furman, W. (1990). Perceptions of sibling relationships during middle childhood and adolescence. *Child Development, 61,* 1387–1396.

Bukowski, W., Gauze, C., Hoza, B., and Newcomb, A. (1993). Differences and consistency between same-sex and other-sex peer relationships during early adolescence. *Developmental Psychology, 29,* 255–263.

Bukowski, W., Peters, P., Sippola, L., and Newcomb, A. (1993, March). *Patterns in the selection of same- and other-sex friends among aggressive and nonaggressive early adolescent boys and girls.* Paper presented at the biennial meetings of the Society for Research in Child Development, New Orleans.

Bukowski, W., Sippola, L., Gauze, C., Hoza, B., and Newcomb, A. (1993, March). *On which aspects of friendship are there differences between boys and girls?* Paper presented at the biennial meetings of the Society for Research in Child Development, New Orleans.

Bulcroft, R. (1991). The value of physical change in adolescence: Consequences for the parent-adolescent exchange relationship. *Journal of Youth and Adolescence, 20,* 89–106.

Bumpass, L., and McLanahan, S. (1987, April). *Unmarried motherhood: A note on recent trends, composition and black-white differences.* Paper presented at the annual meeting of the Population Association of America, Chicago.

Burda, P., and Vaux, A. (1988). Social drinking in supportive contexts among college males. *Journal of Youth and Adolescence, 17,* 165–172.

Burleson, B. (1982). The development of comforting communication skills in childhood and adolescence. *Child Development, 53,* 1578–1588.

Butler, J., and Burton, L. (1990). Rethinking teenage childbearing: Is sexual abuse a missing link? *Family Relations, 39,* 73–80.

Butler, R., and Nissan, M. (1975). Who is afraid of success? And why? *Journal of Youth and Adolescence, 4,* 259–270.

Byrnes, J., and Takahira, S. (1993). Explaining gender differences on SAT-math items. *Developmental Psychology, 29,* 805–810.

Cairns, R., Cairns, B., and Neckerman, H. (1989). Early school dropout: Configurations and determinants. *Child Development, 60,* 1437–1452.

Cairns, R., Cairns, B., Neckerman, H., Gest, S., and Gariepy, J. L. (1988). Social networks and aggressive behavior: Peer support or peer rejection? *Developmental Psychology, 24,* 815–823.

Cairns, R., Leung, M., Buchanan, L., and Cairns, B. (1994). Friendships and social networks in childhood and adolescence: Fluidity, reliability, and interrelations. Unpublished manuscript, Department of Psychology, University of North Carolina, Chapel Hill.

Call, K., and McNall, M. (1992). Poverty, ethnicity, and youth adjustment: A comparison of poor Hmong and non-Hmong adolescents. Pp. 373–392 in W. Meeus, M. de Goede, W. Knox, and K. Hurrelmann (Eds.), *Adolescence, careers, and cultures.* New York: de Gruyter.

Calverley, R., and Fischer, K. (1993, March). *The development of negative core self-representations in maltreated children and adolescents.* Paper presented at the biennial meetings of the Society for Research in Child Development, New Orleans.

Camarena, P., and Sarigiani, P. (1994, February). *Sexual victimization and psychological adjustment across adolescence.* Paper presented at the biennial meetings of the Society for Research on Adolescence, San Diego.

Campbell, A. (1968). The role of family planning in the reduction of poverty. *Journal of Marriage and the Family, 30,* 236–245.

Campbell, B. (1977). The impact of school desegregation: An investigation of three mediating factors. *Youth and Society, 9,* 79–111.

Campbell, E., Adams, G., and Dobson, W. (1984). Familial correlates of identity formation in late adolescence: A study of the predictive utility of connectedness and individuality in family relations. *Journal of Youth and Adolescence, 13,* 509–526.

Campbell, F., and Ramey, C. (1993, April). *Mid-adolescent outcomes for high risk students: An examination of the continuing effects of early intervention.* Paper presented at the biennial meetings of the Society for Research in Child Development, New Orleans.

Campos, R., Raffaelli, M., Ude, W., Greco, M., Ruff, A., Rolf, J., Antunes, C., Halsey, N., Greco, D., and the Street Youth Study. (1994). Social networks and daily activities of street youth in Belo Horizonte, Brazil. *Child Development, 65,* 319–330.

Cantwell, D., and Baker, L. (1991). Manifestations of depressive affect in adolescence. *Journal of Youth and Adolescence, 20,* 121–134.

Capaldi, D. (1991). Co-occurrence of conduct problems and depressive symptoms in early adolescent boys, I: Familial factors and general adjustment at grade 6. *Development and Psychopathology, 3,* 277–300.

Capaldi, D. (1992). Co-occurrence of conduct problems and depressed mood in early adolescent boys, II: A two-year follow-up at grade 8. *Development and Psychopathology, 4.*

Capaldi, D., and Patterson, G. (1991). Relation of parental transitions to boys' adjustment problems, I: A linear hypothesis; II: Mothers at risk for transitions and unskilled parenting. *Developmental Psychology, 27,* 489–504.

Caplan, N., Choy, M., and Whitmore, J. (1992, February). Indochinese refugee families and academic achievement. *Scientific American,* 36–42.

Cappelleri, J., Eckenrode, J., and Powers, J. (1993). The epidemiology of child abuse: Findings from the Second National Incidence and Prevalence Study of Child Abuse and Neglect. *American Journal of Public Health, 83,* 1622–1624.

Carnegie Council on Adolescent Development. (1989). *Turning points: Preparing youth for the 21st century.* New York: Carnegie Corporation of New York.

Carnegie Council Adolescent Development. (1992). *A matter of time: Risk and opportunity in the after-school hours.* Washington, D.C.: Carnegie Council on Adolescent Development.

Carns, D. (1973). Talking about sex: Notes on first coitis and the double sexual standard. *Journal of Marriage and the Family, 35,* 677–688.

Carr, M., Borkowski, J., and Maxwell, S. (1991). Motivational components of underachievement. *Developmental Psychology, 27,* 108–118.

Carskadon, M., Vieria, C., and Acebo, C. (1993). Association between puberty and delayed phase preference. *Sleep, 16,* 258–262.

Case, R. (1985). *Intellectual development: Birth to adulthood.* New York: Academic Press.

Casper, L. (1990). Does family interaction prevent adolescent pregnancy? *Family Planning Perspectives, 22,* 109–114.

Caspi, A., Elder, Jr., G., and Bem, D. (1987). Moving against the world: Life-course patterns of explosive children. *Developmental Psychology, 23,* 308–313.

Caspi, A., Lynam, D., Moffitt, T., and Silva, P. (1993). Unraveling girls' delinquency: Biological, dispositional, and contextual contributions to adolescent misbehavior. *Developmental Psychology, 29,* 19–30.

Caspi, A., and Moffitt, T. (1991). Individual differences and personal transitions: The sample case of girls at puberty. *Journal of Personality and Social Psychology, 61,* 157–168.

Casteel, M. (1993). Effects of inference necessity and reading goal on children's inferential generation. *Developmental Psychology, 29,* 346–357.

Catsambis, S. (1992, March). *The many faces of tracking in middle school grades: Between- and within-school differentiation of students and resources.* Paper presented at the biennial meetings of the Society for Research on Adolescence, Washington.

Cauce, A. (1987). School and peer competence in early adolescence: A test of domain-specific self-perceived competence. *Developmental Psychology, 23,* 287–291.

Chalmers, D., and Lawrence, J. (1993). Investigating the effects of planning aids on adults' and adolescents' organisation of a complex task. *International Journal of Behavioural Development, 16,* 191–214.

Chandler, M. (1987). The Othello effect: Essay on the

emergence and eclipse of skeptical doubt. *Human Development, 30,* 137–159.

Chao, R. (1994). Beyond parental control and authoritarian parenting style: Understanding Chinese parenting through the cultural notion of training. *Child Development, 65,* 1111–1119.

Charner, I., and Fraser, B. (1987). *Youth and work.* Washington, D.C.: William T. Grant Foundation Commission on Work, Family, and Citizenship.

Chartier, G., and Ranieri, D. (1984). Adolescent depression: Concepts, treatments, prevention. In P. Karoly and J. Steffen (Eds.), *Adolescent behavior disorders: Foundations and contemporary concerns.* Lexington, Mass.: Lexington.

Chase-Landsdale, P., Brooks-Gunn, J., and Zamsky, E. (1994). Young African-American multigenerational families in poverty: Quality of mothering and grandmothering. *Child Development, 65,* 373–393.

Chassin, L., and Barrera, M., Jr. (1993). Substance use escalation and substance use restraint among adolescent children of alcoholics. *Psychology of Addictive Behaviors, 7,* 3–20.

Chassin, L., Pillow, D., Curran, P., Molina, B., and Barrera, M., Jr. (1993). Relation of parental alcoholism to early adolescent substance use: A test of three mediating mechanisms. *Journal of Abnormal Psychology, 102,* 3–19.

Chassin, L., Rogosch, F., and Barrera, M., Jr. (1991). Substance use and symptomatology among adolescent children of alcoholics. *Journal of Abnormal Psychology, 100,* 449–463.

Cherlin, A., Furstenberg, F., Jr., Chase-Lansdale, L., Kiernan, K., Robins, P., Morrison, D., and Teitler, J. (1991). Longitudinal studies of effects of divorce on children in Great Britain and the United States. *Science, 252,* 1386–1389.

Children's Defense Fund. (1989). *Service opportunities for youths.* Washington, D.C.: Children's Defense Fund.

Chilman, C. (1986). Some psychosocial aspects of adolescent sexual and contraceptive behaviors in a changing American society. In J. Lancaster and B. Hamburg (Eds.), *School-age pregnancy and parenthood: Biosocial dimensions.* New York: Aldine de Gruyter.

Chilman, C. (1990). Promoting healthy adolescent sexuality. *Family Relations, 39,* 123–131.

Christopher, F. S., and Roosa, M. (1990). An evaluation of an adolescent pregnancy prevention program: Is "Just say no" enough? *Family Relations, 39,* 68–72.

Chung, R., and Walkey, F. (1989). Educational and achievement aspirations of New Zealand Chinese and European secondary school students. *Youth and Society, 21,* 139–152.

Church, R. (1976). *Education in the United States.* New York: Free Press.

Clancy, S., and Dollinger, S. (1993). Identity, self, and personality, I: Identity status and the five-factor model of personality. *Journal of Research on Adolescence, 3,* 227–246.

Clark, R., and Delia, J. (1976). The development of functional persuasive skills in childhood and early adolescence. *Child Development, 47,* 1008–1014.

Clasen, D., and Brown, B. (1985). The multidimensionality of peer pressure in adolescence. *Journal of Youth and Adolescence, 14,* 451–468.

Clayton, R., and Bokemeier, J. (1980, November). Premarital sex in the seventies. *Journal of Marriage and the Family,* 759–775.

Clingempeel, W., Colyar, J., Brand, E., and Hetherington, E. (1992). Children's relationships with maternal grandparents: A longitudinal study of family structure and pubertal status effects. *Child Development, 63,* 1404–1422.

Coe, C., Hayashi, K., and Levine, S. (1988). Hormones and behavior at puberty: Activation or concatenation. Pp. 17–41 in M. Gunnar and W. A. Collins (Eds.), *The Minnesota Symposia on Child Psychology,* Vol. 21. Hillsdale, N.J.: Erlbaum.

Cohen, Y. (1964). *The transition from childhood to adolescence.* Chicago: Aldine.

Coie, J., Lochman, J., Terry, R., and Hyman, C. (1992). Predicting early adolescent disorder from childhood aggression and peer rejection. *Journal of Consulting and Clinical Psychology, 60,* 783–792.

Colby, A., Kohlberg, L., Gibbs, J., and Lieberman, M. (1983). A longitudinal study of moral judgment. *Monographs of the Society for Research in Child Development, 48,* Serial No. 200.

Coleman, J. (1961). *The adolescent society.* Glencoe, Ill.: Free Press.

Coleman, J., Campbell, E., Hobson, C., McPartland, J., Mood, A., Weinfeld, F., and York, R. (1966). *Equality of educational opportunity.* Washington, D.C.: U.S. Government Printing Office.

Coleman, J., and Hoffer, T. (1987). *Public and private high schools: The impact of communities.* New York: Basic Books.

Coleman, J., Hoffer, T., and Kilgore, S. (1982). *High school achievement: Public, Catholic and other private schools compared.* New York: Basic Books.

Coll, C., Hoffman, J., and Oh, W. (1987). The social ecology and early parenting of Caucasian adolescent mothers. *Child Development, 58,* 955–963.

Collins, W. A. (1988). Research on the transition to adolescence: Continuity in the study of developmental processes. Pp. 1–15 in M. Gunnar and W. A. Collins (Eds.), *Minnesota Symposium on Child Psychology,* Vol 21. Hillsdale, N.J.: Erlbaum.

Collins, W. A. (1990). Parent-child relationships in the transition to adolescence: Continuity and change in interaction, affect, and cognition. Pp. 85–106 in R. Montemayor, G. Adams, and T. Gullotta (Eds.), *Advances in adolescent development,* Vol. 2: *The transition from childhood to adolescence.* Beverly Hills, Calif.: Sage.

Collins, W. A., and Russell, G. (1991). Mother-child and father-child relationships in middle adolescence: A developmental analysis. *Developmental Review, 11,* 99–136.

Colten, M., Gore, S., and Aseltine, Jr., R. (1991). The patterning of distress and disorder in a community sample of high school aged youth. Pp. 157–180 in M. Colten and S. Gore (Eds.), *Adolescent stress: Causes and consequences.* New York: Aldine de Gruyter.

Compas, B. (1987). Coping with stress during childhood and adolescence. *Psychological Bulletin, 101,* 393–403.

Compas, B., Ey, S., and Grant, K. (1993). Taxonomy, assessment, and diagnosis of depression during adolescence. *Psychological Bulletin, 114,* 323–344.

Compas, B., Malcarne, V., and Fondacaro, K., (1988). Coping with stress during childhood and adolescence. *Psychological Bulletin, 101,* 393–403.

Conant, J. (1959). *The American high school today.* New York: McGraw-Hill.

Condit, V. (1990). Anorexia nervosa: Levels of causation. *Human Nature, 1,* 391–413.

Conger, J. (1975). Current issues in adolescent development. In *Master lectures on developmental psychology.* Washington, D.C.: American Psychological Association.

Conger, J. (1977). *Adolescence and youth,* 2nd ed. New York: Harper & Row.

Conger, K., Conger, R., and Elder, G., Jr. (1994). Sibling relationships during hard times. Pp. 235–252 in R. Conger and G. Elder, Jr. (Eds.), *Families in troubled times: Adapting to change in rural America.* New York: Aldine.

Conger, R., Conger, K., Elder, G., Jr., Lorenz, F., Simons, R., and Whitbeck, L. (1992). A family process model of economic hardship and adjustment of early adolescent boys. *Child Development, 63,* 526–541.

Conger, R., Conger, K., Elder, G., Jr., Lorenz, F., Simons, R., and Whitbeck, L. (1993). Family economic stress and adjustment of early adolescent girls. *Developmental Psychology, 29,* 206–219.

Conger, R., Ge, X., Elder, G., Jr., Lorenz, F., and Simons, R. (1994). Economic stress, coercive family process, and developmental problems of adolescents. *Child Development, 65,* 541–561.

Conger, R., Reuter, M., and Conger, K. (in press). The family correlates of adolescent vulnerability and resilience to alcohol use and abuse. *Sociological Studies of Children.*

Connell, J., Spencer, M., and Aber, J. (1994). Educational risk and resilience in African-American youth: Context, self, action, and outcomes in school. *Child Development, 65,* 493–506.

Connell, J., and Wellborn, J. (1991). Competence, autonomy, and relatedness: A motivational analysis of self-system processes. Pp. 43–77 in M. Gunnar and A. Sroufe (Eds.), *Minnesota symposium on child development,* Vol. 22. Hillsdale, N.J.: Erlbaum.

Connolly, J., and Johnson, A. (1993, March). *The psychosocial context of romantic relationships in adolescence.* Paper presented at the biennial meetings of the Society for Research in Child Development, New Orleans.

Connolly, J., and Konarski, R. (1994). Peer self-concept in adolescence: Analysis of factor structure and of associations with peer experience. *Journal of Research on Adolescence, 4,* 385–403.

Coombs, R., Paulson, M., and Richardson, M. (1991). Peer vs. parental influence in substance use among Hispanic and Anglo children and adolescents. *Journal of Youth and Adolescence, 20,* 73–88.

Cooper, C. (1988). Commentary: The role of conflict in adolescent parent relationships. Pp. 181–187 in M. Gunnar and W. A. Collins, (Eds.), *Minnesota Symposium on Child Psychology.* Vol 21. Hillsdale, N.J.: Erlbaum.

Cooper, C., Baker, H., Polichar, D., and Welsh, M. (in press). Cultural perspectives on values and communication of adolescents with their fathers, mothers, siblings, and friends. In W. Collins and S. Shulman (Eds.), *New directions for child development: The role of fathers in adolescent development.* San Francisco: Jossey-Bass.

Cooper, C., Carlson, C., Keller, J., Koch, P., and Spradling, V. (1993, March). *Conflict negotiation in early adolescence: Links between family and peer relational patterns.* Paper presented at the biennial meetings of the Society for Research in Child Development, New Orleans.

Cooper, C., and Grotevant, H. (1987). Gender issues in the interface of family experience and adolescents' friendship and dating identity. *Journal of Youth and Adolescence, 16,* 247–264.

Cooper, C., Grotevant, H., and Condon, S. (1983). Individuality and connectedness in the family as a context for adolescent identity formation and role taking skill. In H. Grotevant and C. Cooper (Eds.), *Adolescent development in the family.* San Francisco: Jossey-Bass.

Coulten, C., and Pandey, S. (1992). Geographic concentration of poverty and risk to children in urban environments. *American Behavioral Scientist, 35,* 238–257.

Crandall, C. (1988). Social contagion of binge eating. *Journal of Personality and Social Psychology, 55,* 588–598.

Crane, J. (1991). The epidemic theory of ghettos and neighborhood effects on dropping out and teenage childbearing. *American Journal of Sociology, 96,* 1226–1259.

Crisp, A. (1983). Some aspects of the psychopathology of anorexia nervosa. Pp. 15–28 in P. Darby, P. Garfinkel, D. Garner, and D. Cosina (Eds.), *Anorexia nervosa: Recent developments in research.* New York: Alan R. Liss.

Crites, H. (1989). *Career differentiation in adolescence.* In D. Stern and D. Eichorn (Eds.), *Adolescence and work.* Hillsdale, N.J.: Erlbaum.

Crockett, L., and Bingham, C. (1994, February). *Family influences on girls' sexual experience and pregnancy risk.* Paper presented at the biennial meetings of the Society for Research on Adolescence, San Diego.

Crockett, L., and Dorn, L. (1987). *Young adolescents' pubertal status and reported heterosocial interaction.* Paper presented at the biennial meetings of the Society for Research in Child Development, Baltimore.

Cross, W. (1978). The Thomas and Cook models of psychological nigrescence: A literature review. *Journal of Black Psychology, 4,* 13–31.

Crouter, A., MacDermid, S., McHale, S., and Perry-Jenkins, M. (1990). Parental monitoring and perceptions of children's school performance and conduct in dual- and single-earner families. *Developmental Psychology, 26,* 649–657.

Crystal, D., Chen, C., Fuligni, A., Stevenson, H., Hsu, C., Ko, H., Kitamura, S., and Kimura, S. (1994). Psychological maladjustment and acdemic achievement: A cross-cultural study of Japanese, Chinese, and American high school students. *Child Development, 65,* 738–753.

Csikszentmihalyi, M., and Larson, R. (1984). *Being adolescent.* New York: Basic Books.

Csikszentmihalyi, M., Larson, R., and Prescott, S. (1977). The ecology of adolescent activity and experience. *Journal of Youth and Adolescence, 6,* 281–294

Cummings, E., Ballard, M., El-Sheikh, M., and Lake, M. (1991). Resolution and children's responses to interadult anger. *Developmental Psychology, 27,* 462–470.

Cusick, P. A. (1973). *Inside high school.* New York: Holt, Rinehart and Winston.

Cutler, S., and Nolen-Hoeksema, S. (1991). Accounting for sex differences in depression through female victimization: Childhood sexual abuse. *Sex Roles, 24,* 425–438.

Cutrona, C. (1982). Transition to college: Loneliness and the process of social adjustment. In L. Peplau and D. Perlman (Eds.), *Loneliness: A sourcebook of current theory, research, and therapy.* New York: Wiley.

Damico, R. (1984). Does working in high school impair academic progress? *Sociology of Education, 57,* 157–164.

Damico, S., and Sparks, C. (1986). Cross-group contact opportunities: Impact on interpersonal relationships in desegregated middle schools. *Sociology of Education, 59,* 113–123.

D'Angelo, L., Getson, P., Luban, N., and Gayle, H. (1991). Human immunodeficiency virus infection in urban adolescents: Can we predict who is at risk? *Pediatrics, 88,* 982–986.

Daniels, D., Dunn, J., Furstenberg, F., Jr., and Plomin, R. (1985). Environmental differences within the family and adjustment differences within pairs of adolescent siblings. *Child Development, 56,* 764–774.

Danner, F., and Day, M. (1977). Eliciting formal operations. *Child Development, 48,* 1600–1606.

Darabi, K., and Ortiz, V. (1987). Childbearing among young Latino women in the United States. *American Journal of Public Health, 77,* 25–28.

Darling, N., and Brown, B. (1992, March). *Patterning of academic performance and deviance among African-American and European-American youths in three communities.* Paper presented at the biennial meetings of the Society for Research on Adolescence, Washington.

Darling, N., Hamilton, S., and Matsuda, S. (1990, March). *Functional roles and social roles: Adolescents' significant others in the United States and Japan.* Paper presented at the biennial meetings of the Society for Research on Adolescence, Atlanta.

Davis, A., and Rhodes, J. (1994). African-American teenage mothers and their mothers: An analysis of supportive and problematic interactions. *Journal of Community Psychology, 22,* 12–19.

Davis, K., and Kirkpatrick, L. (in press). Attachment style, gender, and relationship stability: A longitudinal analysis. *Journal of Personality and Social Psychology.*

DeBaryshe, K., Patterson, G., and Capaldi, D. (1993). A performance model for academic achievement in early adolescent boys. *Developmental Psychology, 29,* 795–804.

Deci, E., and Ryan, R. (1985). *Intrinsic motivation and self-determination in human behavior.* New York: Plenum.

Degirmencioglu, S., Tolson, J., and Urberg, K. (1993, March). *Stability of adolescent social networks over the school year.* Paper presented at the biennial meetings of the Society for Research in Child Development, New Orleans.

Degirmencioglu, S., and Urberg, K. (1994, February). *Cross-gender friendships in adolescence: Who chooses the 'other'?* Paper presented at the biennial meetings of the Society for Research on Adolescence, San Diego.

Demetriou, A., Efklides, A., Papadaki, M., Papantoniou, G., and Economou, A. (1993). Structure and development of causal-experimental thought: From early adolescence to youth. *Developmental Psychology, 29,* 480–497.

Demo, D., and Savin-Williams, R. (1983). Early adolescent self-esteem as a function of social class: Rosenberg and Pearlin revisited. *American Journal of Sociology, 88,* 763–774.

Demorest, A., Meyer, C., Phelps, E., Gardner, H., and Winner, E. (1984). Words speak louder than actions: Understanding deliberately false remarks. *Child Development, 55,* 1527–1534.

DeParle, J. (1991, June 9). Without fanfare, Blacks march to greater high school success. *New York Times,* pp. 1 ff.

Devereux, E. (1970). The role of peer group experience in moral development. In J. Hill (Ed.), *Minnesota Symposium on Child Psychology,* Vol. 4. Minneapolis: University of Minnesota Press.

Diaz, R., and Berndt, T. (1982). Children's knowledge of a best friend: Fact or fancy? *Developmental Psychology, 18,* 787–794.

DiBlasio, F., and Benda, B. (1992). Gender differences in theories of adolescent sexual activity. *Sex Roles, 27,* 221–240.

Dickenson, G. (1975). Dating behavior of black and white adolescents before and after desegregation. *Journal of Marriage and the Family, 37,* 602–608.

DiClemente, R. (1990). The emergence of adolescents as a risk group for Human Immunodeficiency Virus infection. *Journal of Adolescent Research, 5,* 7–17.

DiClemente, R., Boyer, C., and Morales, E. (1988). Minorities and AIDS: Knowledge, attitudes, and misconceptions among Black and Latino adolescents. *American Journal of Public Health, 78,* 55–57.

DiClemente, R., Durbin, M., Siegel, D., Krasnovsky, F., Lazarus, N., and Comacho, T. (1992). Determinants of condom use among junior high school students in a minority, inner-city school district. *Pediatrics, 89,* 197–202.

Dielman, T. (1994). School-based research on the prevention of adolescent alcohol use and misuse: Methodological issues and advances. *Journal of Research on Adolescence, 4,* 271–293.

DiMaggio, P. (1982). Cultural capital and school success: The impact of status culture participation on the grades of U.S. high school students. *American Sociological Review, 47,* 189–201.

Dishion, T., Patterson, G., Stoolmiller, M., and Skinner, M. (1991). Family, school, and behavioral antecedents to early adolescent involvement with antisocial peers. *Developmental Psychology, 27,* 172–180.

Dodge, K. (1986). A social information-processing model of social competence in children. Pp. 77–125 in M. Perlmutter (Ed.), *Minnesota Symposium on Child Psychology,* Vol. 18. Hillsdale, N.J.: Erlbaum.

Dodge, K., and Coie, J. (1987). Social information-processing factors in reactive and proactive aggression in children's peer groups. *Journal of Personality and Social Psychology, 53,* 1146–1158.

Dodge, K., Price, J., Bachorowski, J., and Newman, J. (1990). Hostile attributional biases in severely aggressive adolescents. *Journal of Abnormal Psychology, 99,* 385–392.

Doherty, W., and Needle, R. (1991). Psychological adjustment and substance use among adolescents before and after a parental divorce. *Child Development, 62,* 328–337.

Donahue, M. (1994, February). *Positive youth development in religiously-based youth programs.* Paper presented at the biennial meetings of the Society for Research on Adolescence, San Diego.

Donnelly, D., and Finkelhor, D. (1992). Does equality in custody arrangement improve the parent-child relationship? *Journal of Marriage and the Family, 54,* 837–845.

Donovan, J., and Jessor, R. (1985). Structure of problem behavior in adolescence and young adulthood. *Journal of Consulting and Clinical Psychology, 53,* 890–904.

Dorius, G., Heaton, T., and Steffen, P. (1993). Adolescent life events and their association with the onset of sexual intercourse. *Youth and Society, 25,* 3–23.

Dornbusch, S. (1994, February). *Off the track.* Presidential address to the Society for Research on Adolescence, San Diego.

Dornbusch, S., Carlsmith, J., Bushwall, S., Ritter, P., Leiderman, P., Hastorf, A., and Gross, R. (1985). Single parents, extended households, and the control of adolescents. *Child Development, 56,* 326–341.

Dornbusch, S., Carlsmith, J., Gross, R., Martin, J., Jennings, D., Rosenberg, A., and Duke, P. (1981). Sexual development, age, and dating: A comparison of biological and social influences upon one set of behaviors. *Child Development, 52,* 179–185.

Dornbusch, S., Mont-Reynaud, R., Ritter, P., Chen, Z., and Steinberg, L. (1991). Stressful events and their correlates among adolescents of diverse backgrounds. Pp. 111–130 in M. Colten and S. Gore (Eds.), *Adolescent stress: Causes and consequences.* Hawthorne, N.Y.: Aldine de Gruyter.

Dornbusch, S., Ritter, P., Liederman, P., Roberts, D., and Fraleigh, M. (1987). The relation of parenting style to adolescent school performance. *Child Development, 58,* 1244–1257.

Douvan, E., and Adelson, J. (1966). *The adolescent experience.* New York: Wiley.

Dozier, M., and Kobak, R. (in press). Psychophysiology in attachment interviews: Converging evidence for deactivating strategies. *Child Development.*

Dreyer, P. (1982). Sexuality during adolescence. In B. Wolman (Ed.), *Handbook of developmental psychology.* Englewood Cliffs, N.J.: Prentice-Hall.

Dryfoos, J. (1990). *Adolescents at risk: Prevalence and prevention.* New York: Oxford University Press.

Dryfoos, J. (1993). Schools as places for health, mental health, and social services. *Teachers College Record, 94,* 540–567.

Dubas, J., Graber, J., and Petersen, A. (1991). A longitudinal investigation of adolescents' changing perceptions of pubertal timing. *Developmental Psychology, 27,* 580–586.

DuBois, D., Felner, R., Brand, S., Adan, A., and Evans, E. (1992). A prospective study of life stress, social support, and adaptation in early adolescence. *Child Development, 63,* 542–557.

DuBois, D., and Hirsch, B. (1990). School and neighborhood friendship patterns of blacks and whites in early adolescence. *Child Development, 61,* 524–536.

Duncan, O., Featherman, D., and Duncan, B. (1972). *Socioeconomic background and achievement.* New York: Semmar Press.

Duncan, P., Ritter, P., Dornbusch, S., Gross, R., and Carlsmith, J. (1985). The effects of pubertal timing on body image, school behavior, and deviance. *Journal of Youth and Adolescence, 14,* 227–236.

Dunn, S., Putallaz, M., Sheppard, B., and Lindstrom, R. (1987). Social support and adjustment in gifted adolescents. *Journal of Educational Psychology, 79,* 467–473.

Dunphy, D. (1963). The social structure of urban adolescent peer groups. *Sociometry, 26,* 230–246.

Dunphy, D. (1969). *Cliques, crowds, and gangs.* Melbourne: Chesire.

DuRant, R., Cadenhead, C., Pendergrast, R., Slavens, G., and Linder, C. (1994). Factors associated with the use of violence among urban Black adolescents. *American Journal of Public Health, 84,* 612–617.

Dusek, J., and Flaherty, J. (1981). The development of the self-concept during the adolescent years. *Monographs of the Society for Research in Child Development, 46,* Serial No. 191.

Dweck, C., and Light, B. (1980). Learned helplessness and intellectual achievement. In J. Garber and M. Seligman (Eds.), *Human helplessness.* New York: Academic Press.

Dweck, C., and Wortman, C. (1980). Achievement, test anxiety, and learned helplessness: Adaptive and maladaptive cognitions. In H. Krohne and L. Laux (Eds.), *Achievement, stress, and anxiety.* Washington, D.C.: Hemisphere.

Dyk, P., and Adams, G. (1990). Identity and intimacy: An initial investigation of three theoretical models using cross-lag panel correlations. *Journal of Youth and Adolescence, 19,* 91–110.

Earls, F., Cairns, R., and Mercy, J. (1993). The control of violence and the promotion of nonviolence in adolescents. Pp. 285–304 in S. Millstein, A. Petersen, and E. Nightingale (Eds.), *Promoting the health of adolescents: New directions for the twenty-first century.* New York: Oxford University Press.

Early, D., and Eccles, J. (1994, February). *Predicting par-*

enting behavior: The role of SES, neighborhood risk, and parental values. Paper presented at the biennial meetings of the Society for Research on Adolescence, San Diego.

East, P. (1994, February). *The younger sisters of childrearing adolescents: Their sexual and childbearing attitudes, expectations and behaviors.* Paper presented at the biennial meetings of the Society for Research on Adolescence, San Diego.

East, P., and Felice, M. (1992). Pregnancy risk among the younger sisters of pregnant and childbearing adolescents. *Developmental and Behavioral Pediatrics, 13,* 128–136.

East, P., Felice, M., and Morgan, M. (1993). Sisters' and girlfriends' sexual and childbearing behavior: Effects on early adolescent girls' sexual outcomes. *Journal of Marriage and the Family, 55,* 953–963.

East, P., and Rook, K. (1992). Compensatory patterns of support among children's peer relationships: A test using school friends, nonschool friends, and siblings. *Developmental Psychology, 28,* 163–172.

Ebata, A., and Moos, R. (1994). Personal, situational, and contextual correlates of coping in adolescence. *Journal of Research on Adolescence, 4,* 99–126.

Eccles, J. (1993, March). *Parents as gender-role socializers during middle childhood and adolescence.* Paper presented at the biennial meetings of the Society for Research in Child Development, New Orleans.

Eccles, J., Lord, S., and Midgley, C. (1991). What are we doing to early adolescents? The impact of educational contexts on early adolescents. *American Journal of Education, 99,* 521–542.

Eccles, J., Midgley, C., Wigfield, A., Buchanan, C., Reuman, D., Flanagan, C., and Mac Iver, D. (1993). Development during adolescence: The impact of stage-environment fit on young adolescents' experiences in schools and families. *American Psychologist, 48,* 90–101.

Economic Policy Institute. (1994). *The state of working in America, 1992–93.* Washington, D.C.: Economic Policy Institute.

Edelman, P., and Ladner, J. (Eds.). (1991). *Adolescence and poverty: Challenge for the 90s.* Washington, D.C.: Center for National Policy Press.

Eder, D. (1985). The cycle of popularity: Interpersonal relations among female adolescence. *Sociology of Education, 58,* 154–165.

Eder, D., and Parker, S. (1987). The cultural production and reproduction of gender: The effect of extracurricular activities on peer-group culture. *Sociology of Education, 60,* 200–213.

Eggebeen, D., and Lichter, D. (1991). Race, family structure, and changing poverty among American children. *American Sociological Review, 56,* 801–817.

Eisenberg, N., Miller, P., Shell, R., McNalley, S., and Shea, C. (1991). Prosocial development in adolescence: A longitudinal study. *Developmental Psychology, 27,* 849–857.

Eisenstadt, S. (1956). *From generation to generation.* Glencoe, Ill.: Free Press.

Elder, G., Jr. (1974). *Children of the Great Depression.* Chicago: University of Chicago Press.

Elder, G., Jr. (1980). Adolescence in historical perspective. In J. Adelson (Ed.), *Handbook of adolescent psychology.* New York: Wiley.

Elder, G., Jr., and Ardelt, M. (1992, March). *Families adapting to economic pressure: Some consequences for parents and adolescents.* Paper presented at the biennial meetings of the Society for Research on Adolescence, Washington.

Elder, G. H., Jr., Caspi, A., and van Nguyen, T. (1986). Resourceful and vulnerable children: Family influences in stressful times. In R. Silbereisen, K. Eyferth, and G. Rudinger (Eds.), *Development as action in context.* Heidelberg: Springer.

Elder, G., Jr., Conger, R., Foster, E., and Ardelt, M. (1992). Families under economic pressure. *Journal of Family Issues, 13,* 5–37.

Elder, G. H., Jr., van Nguyen, T., and Caspi, A. (1985). Linking family hardship to children's lives. *Child Development, 56,* 361–375.

Elkind, D. (1967). Egocentrism in adolescence. *Child Development, 38,* 1025–1034.

Elkind, D. (1978). Understanding the young adolescent. *Adolescence, 13,* 127–134.

Elkind, D. (1982). *The hurried child.* Reading, Mass.: Addison-Wesley, 1982.

Elkind, D. (1985). Egocentrism redux. *Developmental Review, 5,* 218–226.

Elkind, D., Barocas, R., and Rosenthal, R. (1968). Combinatorial thinking in adolescents from graded and ungraded classrooms. *Perceptual and Motor Skills, 27,* 1015–1018.

Ellickson, P., Bell, R., and McGuigan, K. (1993). Preventing adolescent drug use: Long-term results of a junior high program. *American Journal of Public Health, 83,* 856–861.

Elliott, B., and Richards, M. (1991, July). *Children and divorce: Educational performance and behaviour before and after parental separation.* Paper presented at the meetings of the International Society for the Study of Behavioural Development, Minneapolis.

Elliott, D., Huizinga, D., and Menard, S. (1989). *Multiple problem youth: Delinquency, substance abuse, and mental health problems.* New York: Springer-Verlag.

Elliott, D., and Morse, B. (1989). Delinquency and drug use as risk factors in teenage sexual activity. *Youth and Society, 21,* 32–57.

Elliott, D., and Wofford, S. (1991). *Adolescent employment.* Brief prepared for press release available from the authors. Boulder: Institute of Behavioral Science, University of Colorado.

Ellis, N. (1991). An extension of the Steinberg accelerating hypothesis. *Journal of Early Adolescence, 11,* 221–235.

Elmen, J. (1991). Achievement orientation in early adolescence: Developmental patterns and social correlates. *Journal of Early Adolescence, 11,* 125–151.

Elster, A., Lamb, M., Peters, L., Kahn, J., and Tavare, J. (1987). Judicial involvement and conduct problems of fathers of infants born to adolescent mothers. *Pediatrics, 79,* 230–234.

Enright, R., Levy, V., Harris, D., and Lapsley, D. (1987).

Do economic conditions influence how theorists view adolescents? *Journal of Youth and Adolescence, 16,* 541–560.

Ensminger, M. (1990). Sexual activity and problem behaviors among Black, urban adolescents. *Child Development, 61,* 2032–2046.

Entwisle, D. (1990). Schools and the adolescent. Pp. 197–224 in S. Feldman and G. Elliott (Eds.), *At the threshold: The developing adolescent.* Cambridge, Mass.: Harvard University Press.

Entwisle, D., and Hayduk, L. (1988). Lasting effects of elementary school. *Sociology of Education, 61,* 147–159.

Epstein, J. (1983a). Selecting friends in contrasting secondary school environments. In J. Epstein and N. Karweit (Eds.), *Friends in school.* New York: Academic Press.

Epstein, J. (1983b). The influence of friends on achievement and affective outcomes. Pp. 177–200 in J. Epstein and N. Karweit (Eds.), *Friends in school.* New York: Academic Press.

Erickson, M. F., Sroufe, L. A., and Egeland, B. (1985). The relationship between quality of attachment and behavior problems in preschool in a high-risk sample. *Growing Points of Attachment Theory and Research: Monographs of the Society for Research in Child Development, 50,* 147–193.

Erikson, E. (1959). Identity and the life cycle. *Psychological Issues, 1,* 1–171.

Erikson, E. (1963). *Childhood and society.* New York: Norton.

Erikson, E. (1968). *Identity: Youth and crisis.* New York: Norton.

Evans, D. (1993, March). *A model of structural self-complexity: Its relation to age, symptomatology and self-perception.* Paper presented at the biennial meetings of the Society for Research in Child Development, New Orleans.

Evans, E., Rutberg, J., Sather, C., and Turner, C. (1990, April). *Content analysis of contemporary teen magazines for adolescent females.* Paper presented at the meeting of the American Educational Research Association, Boston.

Evans, M. (1992, March). *Achievement and achievement-related beliefs in Asian and Western contexts: Cultural and gender differences.* Paper presented at the biennial meetings of the Society for Research on Adolescence, Washington.

Eveleth, P., and Tanner, J. (1976). *Worldwide variation in human growth.* New York: Cambridge University Press.

Falbo, T. (in press). *Against the odds: Latino youth and high school graduation.* Austin: University of Texas Press.

Farel, A. (1982). *Early adolescence and religion: A status study.* Carrboro, N.C.: Center for Early Adolescence.

Farkas, G., Grobe, R., and Shuan, Y. (1990). Cultural resources and school success: Gender, ethnicity, and poverty groups within an urban school district. *American Sociological Review, 55,* 127–142.

Farrell, A., Danish, S., and Howard, C. (1992). Relationship between drug use and other problem behaviors in urban adolescents. *Journal of Consulting and Clinical Psychology, 60,* 705–712.

Farrell, M., and Rosenberg, S. (1981). *Men at midlife.* Boston: Auburn House.

Farrington, D. (1989). Early predictors of adolescent aggression and adult violence. *Violence and Victims, 4,* 79–100.

Farrington, D. (1991). Childhood aggression and adult violence: Early precursors and later-life outcomes. Pp. 5–29 in D. Pepler and K. Rubin (Eds.), *The development and treatment of childhood aggression.* Hillsdale, N.J.: Erlbaum.

Farrington, D., and West, D. (1991). The Cambridge Study in Delinquent Development: A long-term follow-up of 411 London males. Pp. 115–138 in H. Kerner and G. Kaiser (Eds.), *Criminality: Personality, behavior, and life history.* New York: Springer-Verlag.

Fauber, R., Forehand, R., McCombs, A., and Wierson, M. (1990). A mediational model of the impact of marital conflict on adolescent adjustment in intact and divorced families: The role of disrupted parenting. *Child Development, 61,* 1112–1123.

Featherman, D. (1980). Schooling and occupational careers: Constancy and change in worldly success. In O. Brim, Jr., and J. Kagan (Eds.), *Constancy and change in human development.* Cambridge, Mass.: Harvard University Press.

Federal Bureau of Investigation. (1993). *Uniform crime reports for the United States.* Washington, D.C.: U.S. Government Printing Office.

Feingold, A. (1988). Cognitive gender differences are disappearing. *American Psychologist, 43,* 95–103.

Feingold, A. (1993). Cognitive gender differences: A developmental perspective. *Sex Roles, 29,* 91–112.

Feiring, C. (1993, March). *Developing concepts of romance from 15 to 18 years.* Paper presented at the biennial meetings of the Society for Research in Child Development, New Orleans.

Feiring, C., and Lewis, M. (1991). The transition from middle childhood to early adolescence: Sex differences in the social network and perceived self-competence. *Sex Roles, 24,* 489–510.

Feiring, C., and Lewis, M. (1993). Do mothers know their teenagers' friends? Implications for individuation in early adolescence. *Journal of Youth and Adolescence, 22,* 337–354.

Feldman, C., Stone, A., and Renderer, B. (1990). Stage, transfer, and academic achievement in dialect-speaking Hawaiian adolescents. *Child Development, 61,* 472–484.

Feldman, S., and Gehring, T. (1988). Changing perceptions of family cohesion and power across adolescence. *Child Development, 59,* 1034–1045.

Feldman, S., and Quatman, T. (1988). Factors influencing age expectations for adolescent autonomy: A study of early adolescents and parents. *Journal of Early Adolescence, 8.*

Feldman, S., and Rosenthal, D. (1994). Culture makes a difference . . . or does it? A comparison of adolescents in Hong Kong, Australia, and the United States. Pp. 25–45 in R. Silbereisen and E. Todt (Eds.), *Adolescence in context: The interplay of family, school, peers, and work in adjustment.* New York: Springer-Verlag.

Feldman, S., and Weinberger, D. (1994). Self-restraint as a mediator of family influences on boys' delinquent behavior: A longitudinal study. *Child Development, 65,* 195–211.

Feldstein, M., and Ellwood, D. (1982). Teenage unemployment: What is the problem? In R. Freeman and D. Wise (Eds.), *The youth labor market problem: Its nature, causes, and consequences.* Chicago: University of Chicago Press.

Felner, R., et al. 1995. Socioeconomic disadvantage, proximal environmental experiences, and socio-emotional and academic adjustment in early adolescence: Investigation of a mediated effects model. *Child Development, 66,* 774–792.

Felson, R., and Zielinski, M. (1989). Children's self-esteem and parental support. *Journal of Marriage and the Family, 51,* 727–735.

Fennema, E., and Peterson, P. (1985). Autonomous learning behavior: A possible explanation of gender-related differences in mathematics. In P. Peterson, L. Wilkinson, and M. Hallinan, (Eds.), *The social context of instruction.* Orlando, Fla.: Academic Press.

Fennema, E., and Sherman, J. (1977). Sex-related differences in mathematics achievement, spatial visualization, and affective factors. *American Educational Research Journal, 14,* 51–71.

Ferrell, M., Tolone, W., and Walsh, R. (1977). Maturational and societal changes in the sexual double-standard: A panel analysis (1967–1971; 1970–1974). *Journal of Marriage and the Family, 39,* 255–271.

Field, T., Greenwald, P., Morrow, C., Healy, B., Foster, T., Guthertz, M., and Frost, P. (1992). Behavior state matching during interactions of preadolescent friends versus acquaintances. *Developmental Psychology, 28,* 242–250.

Fine, G. (1981). Friends, impression management, and preadolescent behavior. In S. Asher and J. Gottman (Eds.), *The development of children's friendships.* Cambridge, England: Cambridge University Press.

Fine, G. (1987). *With the boys.* Chicago: University of Chicago Press.

Fine, G., Mortimer, J., and Roberts, D. (1990). Leisure, work, and the mass media. Pp. 225–252 in S. Feldman and G. Elliott (Eds.), *At the threshold: The developing adolescent.* Cambridge, Mass.: Harvard University Press.

Finnegan, R., and Perry, D. (1993, March). *Preadolescents' self-reported attachments to their mothers and their social behavior with peers.* Paper presented at the biennial meetings of the Society for Research in Child Development, New Orleans.

Fischoff, B. (1988). Judgment and decision making. Pp. 153–187 in R. Sternberg and E. Smith (Eds.), *The psychology of human thought.* New York: Cambridge University Press.

Fisher, T. (1989). An extension of the findings of Moore, Peterson, and Furstenberg [1986] regarding family sexual communication and adolescent sexual behavior. *Journal of Marriage and the Family, 51,* 637–639.

Fiske, E. (1987, November 12). Colleges open new minority drive. *New York Times,* p. 12.

Fitzpatrick, K. (1993). Exposure to violence and the presence of depression among low-income, African-American youth. *Journal of Consulting and Clinical Psychology, 61,* 528–531.

Fitzpatrick, K., and Yoels, W. (1992). Policy, school structure, and sociodemographic effects on statewide high school dropout rates. *Sociology of Education, 65.*

Flanagan, C. (1990). Change on family work status: Effects on parent-adolescent decision making. *Child Development, 61,* 163–177.

Flannery, D., Vazsonyi, A., Torquati, J., and Rowe, D. (1993, March). *Parenting, personality, and school influences on substance use in Caucasian and Hispanic early adolescents.* Paper presented at the biennial meetings of the Society for Research in Child Development, New Orleans.

Fletcher, A., Darling, N., Steinberg, L., and Dornbusch, S. (1995). The company they keep: Relation of adolescents' adjustment and behavior to their friends' perceptions of authoritative parenting in the social network. *Developmental Psychology, 31,* 300–310.

Fletcher, A., and Steinberg, L. (1994, February). *Generational status and country of origin as influences on the psychological adjustment of Asian-American adolescents.* Paper presented at the biennial meetings of the Society for Research on Adolescence, San Diego.

Flewelling, R., and Bauman, K. (1990). Family structure as a predictor of initial substance use and sexual intercourse in early adolescence. *Journal of Marriage and the Family, 52,* 171–181.

Ford, C., and Beach, F. (1951). *Patterns of sexual behavior.* New York: Harper & Row.

Ford, M. (1982). Social cognition and social competence in adolescence. *Developmental Psychology, 18,* 323–340.

Ford, M. (1987). Processes contributing to adolescent social competence. In M. Ford and D. Ford (Eds.), *Humans as self-constructing living systems.* Hillsdale, N.J.: Erlbaum.

Ford, M., and Lowery, C. (1986). Gender differences in moral reasoning: A comparison of the use of justice and care orientations. *Journal of Personality and Social Psychology, 50,* 777–783.

Fordham, C., and Ogbu, J. (1986). Black students' school success: Coping with the burden of "acting white." *Urban Review, 18,* 176–206.

Forehand, R., Thomas, A. M., Wierson, M., Brody, G., and Fauber, R. (1990). Role of maternal functioning and parenting skills in adolescent functioning following parental divorce. *Journal of Abnormal Psychology, 99,* 278–283.

Forehand, R., Wierson, M., Thomas, A., Fauber, R., Armistead, L., Kemptom, T., and Long, N. (1991). A short-term longitudinal examination of young adolescent functioning following divorce: The role of family factors. *Journal of Abnormal Child Psychology, 19,* 97–111.

Forgatch, M., DeGarmo, D., and Knutson, N. (1994, February). *Transitions within transitions: The impact of adolescence and family structure on boys' antisocial behavior.* Paper presented at the biennial meetings of the Society for Research on Adolescence, San Diego.

Fowler, J. (1981). *Stages of faith.* New York: Harper & Row.

Frank, S., Pirsch, L., and Wright, V. (1990). Late adolescents' perceptions of their relationships with their parents: Relationships among deidealization, autonomy, relatedness, and insecurity and implications for adolescent adjustment and ego identity status. *Journal of Youth and Adolescence, 19,* 571–588.

Frank, S., Poorman, M., and Charles, M. (in press). The parenting alliance as a moderator of risks and benefits associated with late adolescent separation processes. *Journal of Research on Adolescence.*

Franklin, K., Janoff-Bulman, R., and Roberts, J. (1990). Long-term impact of parental divorce on optimism and trust: Changes in general assumptions or narrow beliefs? *Journal of Personality and Social Psychology, 59,* 743–755.

Freeman, R., and Wise, D. (Eds.). (1982). *The youth labor market problem: Its nature, causes, and consequences.* Chicago: University of Chicago Press.

Freud, A. (1958). Adolescence. *Psychoanalytic Study of the Child, 13,* 255–278.

Freud, S. (1938). *An outline of psychoanalysis.* London: Hogarth Press.

Fried, M., and Fried, M. (1980). *Transitions: Four rituals in eight cultures.* New York: Norton.

Friedenberg, E. (1959). *The vanishing adolescent.* Boston: Beacon Press.

Friedenberg, E. (1967). *Coming of age in America.* New York: Vintage Books.

Frisch, R. (1983). Fatness, puberty, and fertility: The effects of nutrition and physical training on menarche and ovulation. In J. Brooks-Gunn and A. Petersen (Eds.), *Girls at puberty.* New York: Plenum.

Fuligni, A. (1994, February). *Academic achievement and motivation among Asian-American and European-American early adolescents.* Paper presented at the biennial meetings of the Society for Research on Adolescence, San Diego.

Fuligni, A., and Eccles, J. (1992, March). *The effects of early adolescent peer orientation on academic achievement and deviant behavior in high school.* Paper presented at the biennial meetings of the Society for Research on Adolescence, Washington.

Fuligni, A., and Eccles, J. (1993). Perceived parent-child relationships and early adolescents' orientation toward peers. *Developmental Psychology, 29,* 622–632.

Fuligni, A., and Stevenson, H. (1995). Time-use and mathematics achievement among American, Chinese, and Japanese high school students. *Child Development 66,* 830–842.

Furbey, M., and Beyth-Marom, R. (1992). Risk-taking in adolescence: A decision-making perspective. *Developmental Review, 12,* 1–44.

Furman, W., and Buhrmester, D. (1985). Children's perceptions of the personal relationships in their social networks. *Developmental Psychology, 21,* 1016–1024.

Furman, W., and Wehner, E. (in press). Romantic views: Toward a theory of adolescent romantic relationships. In R. Montemayor, (Ed.), *Advances in adolescent development,* Vol. 3: *Relationships in adolescence.* Newbury Park, Calif.: Sage.

Furstenberg, F., Jr. (1990a). Coming of age in a changing family system. Pp. 147–170 in S. Feldman and G. Elliott (Eds.), *At the threshold: The developing adolescent.* Cambridge, Mass.: Harvard University Press.

Furstenberg, F., Jr. (1990b). *How families manage risk and opportunity in dangerous neighborhoods.* Paper presented at the 84th annual meeting of the American Sociological Association, Washington, D.C., August.

Furstenberg, F., Jr. (1991). As the pendulum swings: Teenage childbearing and social concern. *Family Relations, 40,* 127–138.

Furstenberg, F., Jr., Brooks-Gunn, J., and Chase-Lansdale, L. (1989). Teenaged pregnancy and childbearing. *American Psychologist, 44,* 313–320.

Furstenberg, F., Jr., Brooks-Gunn, J., and Morgan, S. (1987). *Adolescent mothers in later life.* New York: Cambridge University Press.

Furstenberg, F., Jr., Moore, K., and Peterson, J. (1985). Sex education and sexual experience among adolescents. *American Journal of Public Health, 75,* 1331–1332.

Furstenberg, F., Jr., Morgan, S. P., and Allison, P. (1987). Paternal participation and children's well-being after marital dissolution. *American Sociological Review, 52,* 695–701.

Furstenberg, F., Jr., Peterson, J., Nord, C., and Zill, N. (1983). The life course of children of divorce: Marital disruption and parental contact. *American Sociological Review, 48,* 125–129.

Furstenberg, F., Jr., et al. (1987). Race differences in the timing of adolescent intercourse. *American Sociological Review, 52,* 511–518.

Futterman, D., Hein, K., Reuben, N., Dell, R., and Shaffer, N. (1993). Human immunodeficiency virus–infected adolescents: The first 50 patients in a New York City program. *Pediatrics, 91,* 730–735.

Gaddis, A., and Brooks-Gunn, J. (1985). The male experience of pubertal change. *Journal of Youth and Adolescence, 14,* 61–70.

Gagne, E. (1985). *The cognitive psychology of school learning.* Boston: Little, Brown.

Gagnon, J. (1972). The creation of the sexual in early adolescence. In J. Kagan and R. Coles (Eds.), *Twelve to sixteen: Early adolescence.* New York: Norton.

Galambos, N., Almeida, D., and Petersen, A. (1990). Masculinity, femininity, and sex role attitudes in early adolescence: Exploring gender intensification. *Child Development, 61,* 1905–1914.

Galambos, N., and Garbarino, J. (1985). Adjustment of unsupervised children in a rural setting. *Journal of Genetic Psychology, 146,* 227–231.

Galambos, N., Kolaric, G., and Maggs, J. (1994, February). *Adolescents' subjective age: An Indicator of phenomenological maturity.* Paper presented at the biennial meetings of the Society for Research on Adolescence, San Diego.

Galambos, N., and Maggs, J. (1990). Putting mothers' work-related stress in perspective: Mothers and adolescents in dual-earner families. *Journal of Early Adolescence, 10,* 313–328.

Galambos, N., and Maggs, J. (1991). Out-of-school care of young adolescents and self-reported behavior. *Developmental Psychology, 27,* 644–655.

Galambos, N., and Silbereisen, R. (1987). Income change, parental life outlook, and adolescent expectations for job success. *Journal of Marriage and the Family, 49,* 141–149.

Gallatin, J. (1975). *Adolescence and individuality.* New York: Harper & Row.

Galotti, K. (1989). Gender differences in self-reported moral reasoning: A review and new evidence. *Journal of Youth and Adolescence, 18,* 475–488.

Galotti, K., Kozberg, S., and Farmer, M. (1991). Gender and developmental differences in adolescents' conceptions of moral reasoning. *Journal of Youth and Adolescence, 20,* 13–30.

Gamoran, A. (1987). The stratification of high school learning opportunities. *Sociology of Education, 60,* 135–155.

Gamoran, A. (1992). The variable effects of high school tracking. *American Sociological Review, 57,* 812–828.

Gamoran, A. (1993). Alternative uses of ability grouping in secondary schools: Can we bring high-quality instruction to low-ability classes? *American Journal of Education, 102,* 1–22.

Gamoran, A., and Mare, R. (1989). Secondary school tracking and educational inequality: Compensation, reinforcement, or neutrality? *American Journal of Sociology, 94,* 1146–1183.

Gans, J. (1990). *America's adolescents: How healthy are they?* Chicago: American Medical Association.

Garbarino, J., and Asp, C. (1981). *Successful schools and competent students.* Lexington, Mass.: Lexington Books.

Garbarino, J., Burston, N., Raber, S., Russell, R., and Crouter, A. (1978). The social maps of children approaching adolescence: Studying the ecology of youth development. *Journal of Youth and Adolescence, 7,* 417–428.

Garbarino, J., Wilson, J., and Garbarino, J. (1986). The adolescent runaway. Pp. 315–351 in J. Garbarino and J. Sebes (Eds.), *Troubled youth, troubled families.* New York: Aldine.

Garber, J., Weiss, B., and Shanley, N. (1993). Cognitions, depressive symptoms, and development in adolescents. *Journal of Abnormal Psychology, 102,* 47–57.

Gardner, H. (1983). *Frames of mind.* New York: Basic Books.

Gardner, W., and Herman, J. (1990). Adolescents' AIDS risk taking: A rational choice perspective. Pp. 17–34 in W. Gardner, S. Millstein, and B. Wilcox (Eds.), *Adolescents in the AIDS epidemic.* San Francisco: Jossey-Bass.

Gargiulo, J., Attie, I., Brooks-Gunn, J., and Warren, M. (1987). Girls' dating behavior as a function of social context and maturation. *Developmental Psychology, 23,* 730–737.

Garland, A., and Zigler, E. (1993). Adolescent suicide prevention: Current research and social policy implications. *American Psychologist, 48,* 169–182.

Gavin, L., and Furman, W. (1989). Age differences in adolescents' perceptions of their peer groups. *Developmental Psychology, 25,* 827–834.

Gayle, H., Keeling, R., Garcia-Tunon, M., Kilbourne, B., Narkunas, J., Ingram, F., Rogers, M., and Curran, J. (1990). Prevalence of the human immunodeficiency virus among university students. *New England Journal of Medicine, 323,* 1538–1541.

Ge, X., Best, K., Conger, R., and Simons, R. (1994, February). *Parenting behaviors and the occurrence and co-occurrence of adolescent depressive symptoms and conduct problems.* Paper presented at the biennial meetings of the Society for Research on Adolescence, San Diego.

Ge, X., Lorenz, F., Conger, R., Elder, G., Jr., and Simons, R. (1994). Trajectories of stressful life events and depressive symptoms during adolescence. *Developmental Psychology, 30,* 467–483.

Gecas, V., and Seff, M. (1990). Families and adolescents: A review of the 1980s. *Journal of Marriage and the Family, 52,* 941–958.

Gerrard, M. (1987). Sex, sex guilt, and contraceptive use revisited: The 1980s. *Journal of Personality and Social Psychology, 52,* 975–980.

Gilligan, C. (1982). *In a different voice.* Cambridge, Mass.: Harvard University Press.

Gilligan, C. (1986). *Adolescent development reconsidered.* Paper presented at the Invitational Conference on Health Futures of Adolescents, Daytona Beach, Florida.

Gilligan, C., Lyons, N., and Hanmer, T. (Eds.). (1990). *Making connections: The relational worlds of adolescent girls at Emma Willard School.* Cambridge, Mass.: Harvard University Press.

Gillmore, M., Hawkins, J., Catalano, R., Jr., Day, L., Moore, M., and Abbott, R. (1991). Structure of problem behaviors in preadolescence. *Journal of Consulting and Clinical Psychology, 59,* 499–506.

Gilsanz, V., Roe, T., Mora, S., Costin, G., and Goodman, W. (1991). Changes in vertebral bone density in Black girls and White girls during childhood and puberty. *New England Journal of Medicine, 325,* 1597–1600.

Ginsburg, G., and Bronstein, P. (1993). Family factors related to children's intrinsic/extrinsic motivational orientation and academic performance. *Child Development, 64,* 1461–1474.

Ginzberg, E. (1977). The job problem. *Scientific American, 237,* 43–51.

Gittler, J., Quigley-Rick, M., and Saks, M. (1990). *Adolescent health care decision making: The law and public policy.* Washington, D.C.: Carnegie Council on Adolescent Development.

Gjerde, P., and Block, J. (1991). Preadolescent antecedents of depressive symptomatology at age 18: A prospective study. *Journal of Youth and Adolescence, 20,* 217–232.

Gjerde, P., Block, J., and Block, J. (1988). Depressive symptoms and personality during late adolescence: Gender differences in the externalization-internalization of symptom expression. *Journal of Abnormal Psychology, 97,* 475–486.

Glazer, R., and Bassok, M. (1989). Learning theory and the study of instruction. *Annual Review of Psychology, 40.* Palo Alto, Calif.: Annual Reviews.

Glenbard East Echo. (1984). *Teenagers themselves.* New York: Adama Books.

Glover, R., and Marshall, R. (1993). Improving the school-to-work transition of American adolescents. *Teachers College Record, 94,* 588–610.

Gold, M., and Petronio, R. (1980). Delinquent behavior in adolescence. In J. Adelson (Ed.), *Handbook of adolescent psychology*. New York: Wiley.

Gold, M., and Yanof, D. (1985). Mothers, daughters, and girlfriends. *Journal of Personality and Social Psychology, 49,* 654–659.

Goldstein, B. (1976). *Introduction to human sexuality*. Belmont, Calif.: Star.

Good, T., and Brophy, J. (1948). *Looking in classrooms*. New York: Harper & Row.

Goodchilds, J., and Zellman, G. (1984). Sexual signalling and sexual aggression in adolescent relationships. In N. M. Malamuth and E. D. Donnerstein (Eds.), *Pornography and sexual aggression*. New York: Academic Press.

Goodenow, C. (1992, April). *School motivation, engagement, and sense of belonging among urban adolescent students*. Paper presented at the annual meeting of the American Educational Research Association, San Francisco.

Goodlad, J. (1984). *A place called school*. New York: McGraw-Hill.

Goodman, E., and Cohall, A. (1989). Acquired immunodeficiency syndrome and adolescents: Knowledge, attitudes, beliefs, and behaviors in a New York City adolescent minority population. *Pediatrics, 84,* 36–42.

Goossens, L., Seiffge-Krenke, I., and Marcoen, A. (1992, March). *The many faces of adolescent egocentrism: Two European replications*. Paper presented at the biennial meetings of the Society for Research on Adolescence, Washington.

Gordon, M., and Miller, R. (1984). Going steady in the 1980s: Exclusive relationships in six Connecticut high schools. *Sociology and Social Research, 68,* 463–479.

Gordon, S., and Gilgun, J. (1987). Adolescent sexuality. In V. Van Hasselt and M. Hersen (Eds.), *Handbook of adolescent psychology*. New York: Pergamon.

Gore, T. (1987). *Raising PG kids in an X-rated society*. Nashville, Tenn.: Abingdon Press.

Gottfredson, D. (1985). Youth employment, crime, and schooling: A longitudinal study of a national sample. *Developmental Psychology, 21,* 419–432.

Gottfredson, M., and Hirschi, T. (1990). *A general theory of crime*. Stanford, Calif.: Stanford University Press.

Gould, M., Wallenstein, S., and Kleinman, M. (1990). Time-space clustering of teenage suicide. *American Journal of Epidemiology, 131,* 71–78.

Gould, R. (1972). The phases of adult life. *American Journal of Psychiatry, 129,* 521–531.

Graber, J., Brooks-Gunn, J., and Warren, M. (in press). The antecedents of menarcheal age: Heredity, family environment, and stressful life events. *Child Development*.

Graham, C. (1991). Menstrual synchrony: An update and review. *Human Nature, 2,* 293–311.

Graham, E. (1988, January 19). As kids gain power of purse, marketing takes aim at them. *Wall Street Journal,* pp. 1 ff.

Graham, S. (1993, March). *Peer-directed aggression in African-American youth from an attributional perspective*. Paper presented at the biennial meetings of the Society for Research in Child Development, New Orleans.

Graham, S., Hudley, C., and Williams, E. (1992). Attributional and emotional determinants of aggression among African-American and Latino young adolescents. *Developmental Psychology, 28,* 731–740.

Gray, W., and Hudson, L. (1984). Formal operations and the imaginary audience. *Developmental Psychology, 20,* 619–627.

Green, R. (1980). Homosexuality. In H. Kaplan, A. Freedman, and B. Sadock (Eds.), *Comprehensive textbook of psychiatry,* Vol. 2, 3rd ed. Baltimore: Williams & Wilkins.

Green, R. (1987). *The 'Sissy Boy' syndrome and the development of homosexuality*. New Haven, Conn.: Yale University Press.

Greenberg, B., Brown, J., and Buerkel-Rothfuss, N. (Eds.). (1993). *Media, sex, and the adolescent*. Creskill, N.J.: Hampton Press.

Greenberg, M., Siegel, J., and Leitch, C. (1983). The nature and importance of attachment relationships to parents and peers during adolescence. *Journal of Youth and Adolescence, 12,* 373–386.

Greenberger, E. (1982). Education and the acquisition of psychosocial maturity. In D. McClelland (Ed.), *The development of social maturity*. New York: Irvington.

Greenberger, E., and Chen, C. (1994, February). *Family relationships and psychological well-being in early and late adolescence: A comparison of Caucasian- and Asian-Americans*. Paper presented at the biennial meetings of the Society for Research on Adolescence, San Diego.

Greenberger, E., and Sorenson, A. (1974). Toward a concept of psychosocial maturity. *Journal of Youth and Adolescence, 3,* 329–358.

Greenberger, E., and Steinberg, L. (1981). The workplace as a context for the socialization of youth. *Journal of Youth and Adolescence, 10,* 185–210.

Greenberger, E., and Steinberg, L. (1983). Sex differences in early work experience: Harbinger of things to come? *Social Forces, 62,* 467–486.

Greenberger, E., and Steinberg, L. (1986). *When teenagers work: The psychological and social costs of adolescent employment*. New York: Basic Books.

Greenberger, E., Steinberg, L., and Ruggiero, M. (1982). A job is a job is a job . . . Or is it? Behavioral observations in the adolescent workplace. *Work and Occupations, 9,* 79–96.

Greenberger, E., Steinberg, L., and Vaux, A. (1981). Adolescents who work: Health and behavioral consequences of job stress. *Developmental Psychology, 17,* 691–703.

Greenberger, E., Steinberg, L., Vaux, A., and McAuliffe, S. (1980). Adolescents who work: Effects of part-time employment on family and peer relations. *Journal of Youth and Adolescence, 9,* 189–202.

Greenfield, P., Bruzzone, L., Koyamatsu, K., Satuloff, W., Nixon, K., Brodie, M., and Kingsdale, D. (1987). What is rock music doing to the minds of our youth? A first experimental look at the effects of rock music lyrics and music videos. *Journal of Early Adolescence, 7,* 315–329.

Grief, E., and Ulman, K. (1982). The psychological impact of menarche on early adolescent females: A review of the literature. *Child Development, 53,* 1413–1430.

Grolnick, W., and Slowiaczek, M. (1994). Parents' involvement in children's schooling: A multidimensional conceptualization and motivational model. *Child Development, 65,* 237–252.

Grossman, D., Milligan, C., and Deyo, R. (1991). Risk factors for suicide attempts among Navajo adolescents. *American Journal of Public Health, 81,* 870–874.

Grossman, M., Chaloupka, F., Saffer, H., and Laixuthai, A. (1994). Effects of alcohol price policy on youth: A summary of economic research. *Journal of Research on Adolescence, 4,* 347–364.

Grotevant, H., and Cooper, C. (1986). Individuation in family relationships: A perspective on individual differences in the development of identity and role-taking skill in adolescence. *Human Development, 29,* 82–100.

Grotevant, H., and Cooper, C. (1988). The role of family experience in career exploration during adolescence. In P. Baltes, D. Featherman, and R. Lerner (Eds.), *Life-span development and behavior,* Vol. 8. Hillsdale, N.J.: Erlbaum.

Grotevant, H., and Durrett, M. (1980). Occupational knowledge and career development in adolescence. *Journal of Vocational Behavior, 17,* 171–182.

Grotevant, H., and Thorbecke, W. (1982). Sex differences in styles of occupational identity formation in late adolescence. *Developmental Psychology, 18,* 396–405.

Grumbach, M., Roth, J., Kaplan, S., and Kelch, R. (1974). Hypothalamic-pituitary regulation of puberty in man: Evidence and concepts derived from clinical research. In M. Grumbach, G. Grave, and F. Mayer (Eds.), *Control of the onset of puberty.* New York: Wiley.

Grych, J., and Fincham, F. (1992). Interventions for children of divorce: Toward greater integration of research and action. *Psychological Bulletin, 111,* 434–454.

Guerin, D., and Gottfried, A. (in press). Developmental stability and change in parent reports of temperament: A ten-year longitudinal investigation. *Merrill-Palmer Quarterly.*

Guerin, D., Gottfried, A., Oliver, P., and Thomas, C. (in press). Temperament and school functioning during early adolescence. *Journal of Early Adolescence.*

Guerra, N., and Slaby, R. (1990). Cognitive mediators of aggression in adolescent offenders, 2: Intervention. *Developmental Psychology, 26,* 269–277.

Gunnore, M. (1994, February). *Noncustodial mothers' and fathers' contributions to the adjustment of adolescents in stepfamilies.* Paper presented at the biennial meetings of the Society for Research on Adolescence, San Diego.

Haan, N., Smith, M., and Block, J. (1968). Moral reasoning of young adults: Political-social behavior, family background, and personality correlates. *Journal of Personality and Social Psychology, 10,* 183–201.

Hafetz, E. (1976). Parameters of sexual maturity in man. In E. Hafetz (Ed.), *Perspectives in human reproduction,* Vol. 3: *Sexual maturity: Physiological and clinical parameters.* Ann Arbor, Mich.: Ann Arbor Science Publishers.

Hale, S. (1990). A global developmental trend in cognitive processing speed. *Child Development, 61,* 653–663.

Hall, G. S. (1904). *Adolescence.* New York: Appleton.

Hallinan, M. (1981). Recent advances in sociometry. In S. Asher and J. Gottman (Eds.), *The development of children's friendship.* New York: Cambridge University Press.

Hallinan, M. (1992). The organization of students for instruction in the middle school. *Sociology of Education, 65.*

Hallinan, M. (1994). School differences in tracking effects on achievement. *Social Forces, 72,* 799–820.

Hallinan, M., and Sorensen, A. (1987). Ability grouping and sex differences in mathematics achievement. *Sociology of Education, 60,* 63–72.

Hallinan, M., and Teixeira, R. (1987). Opportunities and constraints: Black-white differences in the formation of interracial friendships. *Child Development, 58,* 1358–1371.

Hallinan, M., and Williams, R. (1989). Interracial friendship choices in secondary schools. *American Sociological Review, 54,* 67–78.

Halpern, C., and Udry, J. (1994, February). *Pubertal increases in body fat and implications for dieting, dating, and sexual behavior among Black and White females.* Paper presented at the biennial meetings of the Society for Research on Adolescence, San Diego.

Hamburg, D. (1986). *Preparing for life: The critical transition of adolescence.* New York: Carnegie Corporation of New York.

Hamilton, S. (1990). *Apprenticeship for adulthood.* New York: Free Press.

Hanson, S., and Ginsburg, A. (1988). Gaining ground: Values and high school success. *American Educational Research Journal, 25,* 334–365.

Hanson, S., Myers, D., and Ginsburg, A. (1987). The role of responsibility and knowledge in reducing teenage out-of-wedlock childbearing. *Journal of Marriage and the Family, 49,* 241–256.

Hardy, J., Duggan, A., Masnyk, K., and Pearson, C. (1989). Fathers of children born to young urban mothers. *Family Planning Perspectives, 21,* 159–163.

Hart, D., and Chmiel, S. (1992). Influence of defense mechanisms on moral judgment development: A longitudinal study. *Developmental Psychology, 28,* 722–730.

Hart, D., Fegley, S., and Brengelman, D. (1993). Perceptions of past, present, and future selves among children and adolescents. *British Journal of Developmental Psychology, 11,* 265–282.

Harter, S. (1990). Identity and self development. Pp. 352–387 in S. Feldman and G. Elliott (Eds.), *At the threshold: The developing adolescent.* Cambridge, Mass.: Harvard University Press.

Harter, S., and Monsour, A. (1992). Developmental analysis of conflict caused by oppossing attributes in the adolescent self-portrait. *Developmental Psychology, 28,* 251–260.

Harter, S., Stocker, C., and Robinson, N. (in press). The perceived directionality of the link between approval and self-worth: The liabilities of a looking glass self orientation among young adolescents. *Journal of Research on Adolescence.*

Harter, S., Marold, D., Whitesell, N., and Cobbs, G. (in press). A model of the effects of parent and peer support on adolescent false self behavior. *Child Development.*

Harter, S., Whitesell, N., and Kowalski, P. (1991). The effects of educational transitions on children's perceptions of competence and motivational orientation. Manuscript submitted for publication. Department of Psychology, University of Denver.

Hartup, W. (1977). Adolescent peer relations: A look to the future. In J. Hill and F. Monks (Eds.), *Adolescence and youth in prospect.* Guildford, England: IPC Press.

Hartup, W. (1983). Peer relations. In E. M. Hetherington (Ed.), *Handbook of child psychology: Socialization, personality, and social development,* Vol. 4. New York: Wiley.

Hauser, S., Book, B., Houlihan, J., Powers, S., Weiss-Perry, B., Follansbee, D., Jacobson, A., and Noam, G. (1987). Sex differences within the family: Studies of adolescent and parent family interactions. *Journal of Youth and Adolescence, 16,* 199–220.

Hauser, S., and Bowlds, M. (1990). Stress, coping, and adaptation. Pp. 388–413 in S. Feldman and G. Elliott (Eds.), *At the threshold: The developing adolescent.* Cambridge, Mass.: Harvard University Press.

Hauser, S., and Kasendorf, E. (1983). *Black and white identity formation.* Malabar, Fla.: Robert E. Kreiger.

Hauser, S., Powers, S., and Noam, G. (1991). *Adolescents and their families.* New York: Free Press.

Hausser, D., and Michaud, P. (1994). Does a condom-promoting strategy (the Swiss STOP-AIDS campaign) modify sexual behavior among adolescents? *Pediatrics, 93,* 580–585.

Havighurst, R. (1952). *Developmental tasks and education.* New York: McKay.

Hawkins, J., Catalano, R., and Miller, J. (1992). Risk and protective factors for alcohol and other drug problems in adolescence and early adulthood: Implications for substance abuse prevention. *Psychological Bulletin, 112,* 64–105.

Hayes, C. (Ed.). (1987). *Risking the future: Adolescent sexuality, pregnancy, and childbearing,* Vol. 1. Washington, D.C.: National Academy Press.

Hayward, C., Killen, J., and Taylor, C. (1994, February). *Timing of puberty and the onset of psychiatric symptoms.* Paper presented at the biennial meetings of the Society for Research on Adolescence, San Diego.

Hazan, C. (1994, February). *The role of sexuality in peer attachment formation.* Paper presented at the biennial meetings of the Society for Research on Adolescence, San Diego.

Hechinger, F. (1993). Schools for teenagers: An historic dilemma. *Teachers College Record, 94,* 522–539.

Hein, K. (1988a). *Issues in adolescent health: An overview.* Washington, D.C.: Carnegie Council on Adolescent Development.

Hein, K. (1988b). *AIDS in adolescence: A rationale for concern.* Washington, D.C.: Carnegie Council on Adolescent Development.

Hektner, J. (1994, April). *When moving up implies moving out: How rural adolescents and their parents think about higher education and careers.* Paper presented at the annual meeting of the American Educational Research Association, New Orleans.

Henderson, V., and Dweck, C. (1990). Motivation and achievement. Pp. 308–329 in S. Feldman and G. Elliott (Eds.), *At the threshold: The developing adolescent.* Cambridge, Mass.: Harvard University Press.

Hendrick, S., and Hendrick, C. (1994, February). *Gender, sexuality, and close relationships.* Paper presented at the biennial meetings of the Society for Research on Adolescence, San Diego.

Henggeler, S., Melton, G., and Smith, L. (1992). Family prevention using multisystemic therapy: An effective alternative to incarcerating serious juvenile offenders. *Journal of Consulting and Clinical Psychology, 60,* 953–961.

Henry, B., Feehan, M., McGee, R., Stanton, W., Moffitt, T., and Silva, P. (1993). The importance of conduct problems and depressive symptoms in predicting adolescent substance use. *Journal of Abnormal Child Psychology, 21,* 469–480.

Herman-Giddens, M., Sandler, A., and Friedman, N. (1988). Sexual precocity in girls: An association with sexual abuse? *American Journal of the Diseases of Childhood, 142,* 431–433.

Hess, R., Chih-Mei, C., and McDevitt, T. (1987). Cultural variations in family beliefs about children's performance in mathematics: Comparisons among People's Republic of China, Chinese-American, and Caucasian-American families. *Journal of Educational Psychology, 79,* 179–188.

Hetherington, E. (1981). Children and divorce. In R. Henderson (Ed.), *Parent-child interaction: Theory, research, and prospects.* New York: Academic Press.

Hetherington, E. M. (1991). The role of individual differences and family relationships in children's coping with divorce and remarriage. In P. Cowan and E. M. Hetherington, (Eds.), *Advances in family research,* Vol. 2: *Family transitions.* Hillsdale, N.J.: Erlbaum.

Hetherington, E. M. (1993). An overview of the Virginia longitudinal study of divorce and remarriage with a focus on early adolescence. *Journal of Family Psychology, 7,* 39–56.

Hetherington, E. M., Clingempeel, W., Anderson, E., Deal, J., Hagan, M., Hollier, E., and Lindner, M. (1992). Coping with marital transitions: A family systems perspective. *Monographs of the Society for Research in Child Development, Serial No. 227.*

Hetherington, E. M., Stanley-Hagan, M., and Anderson, E. (1989). Marital transitions: A child's perspective. *American Psychologist, 44,* 303–312.

Heyns, B. (1982). *Summer learning and the effects of schooling.* New York: Academic Press.

Hibbard, R., Ingersoll, G., and Orr, D. (1990). Behavioral risk, emotional risk, and child abuse among adolescents in a nonclinical setting. *Pediatrics, 86,* 896–901.

Higgins, A., and Turnure, J. (1984). Distractibility and concentration of attention in children's development. *Child Development, 44,* 1799–1810.

Hightower, E. (1990). Adolescent interpersonal and familial predictors of positive mental health at midlife. *Journal of Youth and Adolescence, 19,* 257–276.

Hill, C. (1986). A developmental perspective on adolescent 'rebellion' in the church. *Journal of Psychology and Theology, 14,* 306–318.

Hill, C., Rubin, Z., and Peplau, L. (1979). Breakups before marriage: The end of 103 affairs. In G. Levinger and O. Moles (Eds.), *Divorce and separation.* New York: Basic Books.

Hill, J. (1980). The family. In M. Johnson (Ed.), *Toward adolescence: The middle school years (Seventy-ninth yearbook of the National Society for the Study of Education).* Chicago: University of Chicago Press.

Hill, J. (1983). Early adolescence: A framework. *Journal of Early Adolescence, 3,* 1–21.

Hill, J., and Holmbeck, G. (1986). Attachment and autonomy during adolescence. In G. Whitehurst (Ed.), *Annals of child development.* Greenwich, Conn.: JAI Press.

Hill, J., and Holmbeck, G. (1987). Disagreements about rules in families with seventh-grade girls and boys. *Journal of Youth and Adolescence, 16,* 221–246.

Hill, J., and Lynch, M. (1983). The intensification of gender-related role expectations during early adolescence. In J. Brooks-Gunn and A. Petersen (Eds.), *Female puberty.* New York: Plenum.

Hill, J., and Palmquist, W. (1978). Social cognition and social relations in early adolescence. *International Journal of Behavioral Development, 1,* 1–36.

Hingson, R., and Howland, J. (1993). Promoting safety in adolescents. Pp. 305–327 in S. Millstein, A. Petersen, and E. Nightingale (Eds.), *Promoting the health of adolescents: New directions for the twenty-first century.* New York: Oxford University Press.

Hirsch, B., and DuBois, D. (1991). Self-esteem in early adolescence: The Identification and prediction of contrasting longitudinal trajectories. *Journal of Youth and Adolescence, 20,* 53–72.

Hirschi, T. (1969). *Cause of delinquency.* Berkeley: University of California Press.

Hofferth, S. (1992). The demand for and supply of child care in the 1990s. Pp. 3–25 in A. Booth (Ed.), *Child care in the 1990s: Trends and consequences.* Hillsdale, N.J.: Erlbaum.

Hoffman, L. (1974). Effects of maternal employment on the child: A review of the research. *Developmental Psychology, 10,* 204–228.

Hoffman, L. (1977). Fear of success in 1965 and 1974: A follow-up study. *Journal of Consulting and Clinical Psychology, 45,* 310–321.

Hoffman, L. (1991). The influence of the family environment on personality: Accounting for sibling differences. *Psychological Bulletin, 110,* 187–203.

Hoffman, M. (1980). Moral development in adolescence. In J. Adelson (Ed.), *Handbook of adolescent psychology.* New York: Wiley.

Hoge, D., Smit, E., and Hanson, S. (1990). School experiences and predicting changes in self-esteem of sixth- and seventh-grade students. *Journal of Educational Psychology, 82,* 117–127.

Hogue, A., and Steinberg, L. (in press). Homophily of internalized distress in adolescent peer groups. *Developmental Psychology.*

Holland, A., and Andre, T. (1994). Athletic participation and the social status of adolescent males and females. *Youth and Society, 25,* 388–407.

Holland, A., Sicotte, N., and Treasure, L. (1988). Anorexia nervosa: Evidence for a genetic basis. *Journal of Psychosomatic Research, 32,* 561–571.

Holland, J. (1985). *Making vocational choice: A theory of careers,* 2nd ed. Englewood Cliffs, N.J.: Prentice-Hall.

Hollingshead, A. ([1949] 1975). *Elmtown's youth and Elmtown revisited.* New York: Wiley.

Holloway, S. (1988). Concepts of ability and effort in Japan and the United States. *Review of Educational Research, 58,* 327–345.

Holmbeck, G., and Hill, J. (1988). Storm and stress beliefs about adolescence: Prevalence, self-reported antecedents, and effects of an undergraduate course. *Journal of Youth and Adolescence, 17,* 285–306.

Holmbeck, G., and Hill, J. (1991). Conflictive engagement, positive affect, and menarche in families with seventh-grade girls. *Child Development, 62,* 1030–1048.

Holmbeck, G., and O'Donnell, K. (1991). Longitudinal study of discrepancies between maternal and adolescent perceptions of decision-making and desired behavioral autonomy. In R. Paikoff and W. A. Collins (Eds.), *New directions for child development: Shared views of the family during adolescence.* San Francisco: Jossey-Bass.

Holmes, S. (1994, July 20). Birthrate for unwed women up 70% since '83, study says. *New York Times,* pp. 1 ff.

Holstein, C. (1972). The relation of children's moral judgment level to that of their parents and to communication patterns in the family. In R. Smart and M. Smart (Eds.), *Readings in child development and relationships.* New York: Macmillan.

Horan, P., and Hargis, P. (1991). Children's work and schooling in the late nineteenth-century family economy. *American Sociological Review, 56,* 583–596.

Hughes, S., Power, T., and Francis, D. (1992). Defining patterns of drinking in adolescence: A cluster analytic approach. *Journal of Studies on Alcohol, 53,* 40–47.

Huizinga, D., and Elliot, D. (1985). *Juvenile offenders prevalence, offender incidence, and arrest rates by race.* Boulder, Colo.: Institute of Behavioral Science.

Humphries, L. (1988). Trends in levels of academic achievement of blacks and other minorities. *Intelligence, 12,* 231–260.

Hunt, J., and Hunt, L. (1977). Racial inequality and self-image: Identity maintenance as identity diffusion. *Sociology and Social Research, 61,* 539–559.

Hunt, M. (1974). *Sexual behavior in the 1970s.* Chicago: Playboy Press.

Hunter, F. (1984). Socializing procedures in parent-child and friendship relations during adolescence. *Developmental Psychology, 18,* 806–811.

Hunter, F., and Youniss, J. (1982). Changes in functions of three relations during adolescence. *Developmental Psychology, 18,* 806–811.

Huston, A., and Alvarez, M. (1990). The socialization context of gender role development in early adolescence. Pp. 156–179 in R. Montemayor, G. Adams, and T. Gullotta (Eds.), *Advances in adolescent development,* Vol. 2: *The transition from childhood to adolescence.* Beverly Hills, Calif.: Sage.

Huston, A., McLoyd, V., and Garcia Coll, C. (1994). Children and poverty: Issues in contemporary research. *Child Development, 65,* 275–282.

Hutson, H., Anglin, D., and Pratts, M., Jr. (1994). Adolescents and children injured or killed in drive-by shootings in Los Angeles. *New England Journal of Medicine, 330,* 324–327.

Hyde, J., and Linn, M. (1988). Are there sex differences in verbal abilities? A meta-analysis. *Psychological Bulletin, 104,* 53–69.

Hymel, S., Bowker, A., and Woody, E. (1993). Aggressive versus withdrawn unpopular children: Variations in peer and self-perceptions in multiple domains. *Child Development, 64,* 879–896.

Hymel, S., Rubin, K., Rowden, L., and LeMare, L. (1990). Children's peer relationships: Longitudinal prediction of internalizing and externalizing problems from middle to late childhood. *Child Development, 61,* 2004–2021.

Inhelder, B., and Piaget, J. (1958). *The growth of logical thinking from childhood to adolescence.* New York: Basic Books.

Irwin, C., Jr. (1986). Biopsychosocial correlates of risk-taking behavior during adolescence: Can the physician intervene? *Journal of Adolescent Health Care, 7,* 82–96.

Irwin, C., Jr. (1993). Topical areas of interest for promoting health: From the perspective of the physician. Pp. 328–332 in S. Millstein, A. Petersen, and E. Nightingale (Eds.), *Promoting the health of adolescents: New directions for the twenty-first century.* New York: Oxford University Press.

Ishiyama, I., and Chabassol, D. (1985). Adolescents' fear of social consequences of academic success as a function of age and sex. *Journal of Youth and Adolescence, 14,* 37–46.

Jacklin, C. (1989). Female and male: Issues of gender. *American Psychologist, 44,* 127–133.

Jackson, A., and Hornbeck, D. (1989). Educating young adolescents. *American Psychologist, 44,* 831–836.

Jacobs, J. (1991). Influence of gender stereotypes on parent and child mathematics attitudes. *Journal of Educational Psychology, 83,* 518–527.

Jacobs, J., and Eccles, J. (1992). The impact of mothers' gender-role stereotypic beliefs on mothers' and childrens' ability perceptions. *Journal of Personality and Social Psychology, 63,* 932–944.

Jacobsen, T., Edelstein, W., and Hofmann, V. (1994). A longitudinal study of the relation between representations of attachment in childhood and cognitive functioning in childhood and adolescence. *Developmental Psychology, 30,* 112–124.

Jahnke, H., and Blanchard-Fields, F. (1993). A test of two models of adolescent egocentrism. *Journal of Youth and Adolescence, 22,* 313–326.

Jemmott, J., III, Jemmott, L., and Fong, G. (1992). Reductions in HIV risk-associated sexual behavior among Black male adolescents: Effects of an AIDS prevention intervention. *American Journal of Public Health, 82,* 372–377.

Jessor, R. (1984). Adolescent development and behavioral health. In J. Matarazzo, S. Weiss, J. Herd, N. Miller, and S. Weiss (Eds.), *Behavioral health: A handbook of health enhancement and disease prevention.* New York: Wiley.

Jessor, R. (1987). Risky driving and adolescent problem behavior: An extension of problem-behavior theory. *Alcohol, Drugs, and Driving, 3,* 1–11.

Jessor, R., Costa, F., Jessor, L., and Donovan, J. (1983). Time of first intercourse: A prospective study. *Journal of Personality and Social Psychology, 44,* 608–626.

Jessor, R., and Jessor, S. (1977). *Problem behavior and psychosocial development: A longitudinal study of youth.* New York: Academic Press.

John, O., Caspi, A., Robins, R., Moffitt, T., and Stouthamer-Loeber, M. (1994). The "Little Five": Exploring the nomological network of the five-factor model of personality in adolescent boys. *Child Development, 65,* 160–178.

Johnson, E., and Meade, A. (1987). Developmental patterns of spatial ability: An early sex difference. *Child Development, 58,* 725–740.

Johnson, S. (1975). *Update on education: A digest of the National Assessment of Education Progress.* Denver: Education Commission of the States.

Johnston, L., Bachman, J., and O'Malley, P. (1982). *Monitoring the future: Questionnaire responses from the nation's high school seniors, 1981.* Ann Arbor, Mich.: Institute for Social Research.

Johnston, L., Bachman, J., and O'Malley, P. (1993). *Monitoring the future: Questionnaire responses from the nation's high school seniors, 1992.* Ann Arbor, Mich.: Institute for Social Research.

Johnston, L., Bachman, J., and O'Malley, P. (1994). *Monitoring the future: Questionnaire responses from the nation's high school seniors, 1993.* Ann Arbor, Mich.: Institute for Social Research.

Johnston, L., O'Malley, P., and Bachman, J. (1986). *Drug use among American high school students, college students, and other young adults: National trends through 1985.* Washington, D.C.: National Institute on Drug Abuse.

Jones, D., and Costin, S. (1993, March). *Helping orientations, sex role characteristics, and friendship satisfaction during preadolescence and adolescence.* Paper presented at the biennial meetings of the Society for Research in Child Development, New Orleans.

Jones, D., Costin, S., and Ricard, R. (1994, February). *Ethnic and sex differences in best friendship characteristics among African-American, Mexican-American, and European-American adolescents.* Paper presented at the biennial meetings of the Society for Research on Adolescence, San Diego.

Jones, E., et al. (1987). *Teenage pregnancy in industrialized countries.* New Haven, Conn.: Yale University Press.

Jones, G., and Dembo, M. (1989). Age and sex role differences in intimate friendships during childhood and adolescence. *Merrill-Palmer Quarterly, 35,* 445–462.

Jones, H. (1949). Adolescence in our society. In *The fam-*

ily in a democratic society (anniversary papers of the Community Service Society of New York). New York: Columbia University Press.

Jones, M. C. (1957). The later careers of boys who were early- or late-maturing. *Child Development, 28,* 113–128.

Jones, M. C. (1965). Psychological correlates of somatic development. *Child Development, 36,* 899–911.

Jones, M. C., and Bayley, N. (1950). Physical maturing among boys as related to behavior. *Journal of Educational Psychology, 41,* 129–148.

Jones, M. C., and Mussen, P. (1958). Self-conceptions, motivations, and inter-personal attitudes of early- and late-maturing girls. *Child Development, 29,* 491–501.

Jones, N., Pieper, C., and Robertson, L. (1992). The effect of legal drinking age on fatal injuries of adolescents and young adults. *American Journal of Public Health, 82,* 112–115.

Josselson, R. (1980). Ego development in adolescence. In J. Adelson (Ed.), *Handbook of adolescent psychology.* New York: Wiley.

Josselson, R., Greenberger, E., and McConochie, D. (1977a). Phenomenological aspects of psychosocial maturity in adolescence, Part I: Boys. *Journal of Youth and Adolescence, 6,* 25–56.

Josselson, R., Greenberger, E., and McConochie, D. (1977b). Phenomenological aspects of psychosocial maturity in adolescence, Part II: Girls. *Journal of Youth and Adolescence, 6,* 145–167.

Joyce, T., and Mocan, N. (1990). The impact of legalized abortion on adolescent childbearing in New York City. *American Journal of Public Health, 80,* 273–278.

Jozefowicz, D., Barber, B., Eccles, J., and Mollasis, C. (1994, February). *Relations between maternal and adolescent values and beliefs: Gender differences and implications for occupational choice.* Paper presented at the biennial meetings of the Society for Research on Adolescence, San Diego.

Jussim, L., and Eccles, J. (1992). Teacher expectations II: Construction and reflection of student achievement. *Journal of Personality and Social Psychology, 63,* 947–961.

Juvonen, J., and Murdock, T. (1993, March). *Perceived social value of effort and ability accounts: Implications for age-related changes in self-presentation.* Paper presented at the biennial meetings of the Society for Research in Child Development, New Orleans.

Kagan, J., and Coles, R. (Eds.). (1972). *Twelve to sixteen: Early adolescence.* New York: Norton.

Kahn, S., Zimmerman, G., Csikszentmihalyi, M., and Getzels, J. (1985). Relations between identity in young adulthood and intimacy in midlife. *Journal of Personality and Social Psychology, 49,* 1316–1322.

Kahneman, D., Slovic, P., and Tversky, A. (Eds.). (1982). *Judgment under uncertainty: Heuristics and biases.* New York: Cambridge University Press.

Kail, R. (1991a). Processing time declines exponentially during childhood and adolescence. *Developmental Psychology, 27,* 259–266.

Kail, R. (1991b). Developmental change in speed of processing during childhood and adolescence. *Psychological Bulletin, 109,* 490–501.

Kalil, A., and Eccles, J. (1993, March). *The relationship of parenting style and conflict to maternal well-being in single and married mothers of school-aged children.* Paper presented at the biennial meetings of the Society for Research in Child Development, New Orleans.

Kallen, D., and Stephenson, J. (1982). Talking about sex revisited. *Journal of Youth and Adolescence, 11,* 11–24.

Kalmuss, D., Namerow, P., and Bauer, U. (1992). Short-term consequences of parenting versus adoption among young unmarried women. *Journal of Marriage and the Family, 54.*

Kandel, D. (1978). Homophily, selection, and socialization in adolescent friendships. *American Journal of Sociology, 84,* 427–436.

Kandel, D. (1980). Drug and drinking behavior among youth. *Annual Review of Sociology, 6,* 235–285.

Kandel, D., and Lesser, G. (1972). *Youth in two worlds.* San Francisco: Jossey-Bass.

Kandel, D., and Logan, J. (1984). Patterns of drug use from adolescence to young adulthood, I: Periods of risk for initiation, continued use, and discontinuation. *American Journal of Public Health, 74,* 660–666.

Kandel, D., Raveis, V., and Davies, M. (1991). Suicidal ideation in adolescence: Depression, substance abuse, and other risk factors. *Journal of Youth and Adolescence, 20,* 289–310.

Kantor, H., and Brenzel, B. (1992). Urban education and the "truly disadvantaged": The historical roots of the contemporary crisis, 1945–1990. *Teachers College Record, 94,* 278–314.

Kaplan, L. (1983). *Coping with peer pressure.* New York: Rosen.

Katchadourian, H. (1990). Sexuality. Pp. 330–351 in S. Feldman and G. Elliott (Eds.), *At the threshold: The developing adolescent.* Cambridge, Mass.: Harvard University Press.

Katz, M. (1975). *The people of Hamilton, Canada West: Family and class in a mid-nineteenth-century city.* Cambridge, Mass.: Harvard University Press.

Katz, P. (1979). The development of female identity. *Sex Roles, 5,* 155–178.

Kaufman, K., Gregory, W., and Stephan, W. (1990). Maladjustment in statistical minorities within ethnically unbalanced classrooms. *American Journal of Community Psychology, 18,* 757–762.

Kavrell, A., and Petersen, A. (1984). Patterns of achievement in early adolescence. *Advances in Motivation and Achievement, 2,* 1–35.

Kazdin, A. (1993). Adolescent mental health: Prevention and treatment programs. *American Psychologist, 48,* 127–141.

Kazis, R. (1993). *Improving the transition from school to work in the United States.* Washington, D.C.: American Youth Policy Forum, Competitiveness Policy Council, and Jobs for the Future.

Keating, D. (1990). Adolescent thinking. Pp. 54–89 in S. Feldman and G. Elliott (Eds.), *At the threshold: The developing adolescent.* Cambridge, Mass.: Harvard University Press.

Kegeles, S., Adler, N., and Irwin, C., Jr. (1988). Sexually

active adolescents and condoms: Changes over one year in knowledge, attitudes and use. *American Journal of Public Health, 78,* 460–461.

Kelley, J., and de Armaa, A. (1989). Social relationships in adolescence: Skill development and training. In J. Worell and F. Danner (Eds.), *The adolescent as decision-maker.* San Diego: Academic Press.

Keniston, K. (1970). Youth: A "new" stage of life. *American Scholar, 39,* 631–641.

Kenny, M. (1987). The extent and function of parental attachment among first-year college students. *Journal of Youth and Adolescence, 16,* 17–27.

Kerns, K. (1994). Individual differences in friendship quality: Links to child-mother attachment. In W. Bukowski, A. Newcomb, and W. Hartup (Eds.), *The company they keep: Friendship in childhood and adolescence.* New York: Cambridge University Press.

Kett, J. (1977). *Rites of passage: Adolescence in America, 1790 to the present.* New York: Basic Books.

Kilgore, S. (1991). The organizational context of tracking in schools. *American Sociological Review, 56,* 189–203.

King, K., Balswick, J., and Robinson, I. (1977). The continuing premarital sexual revolution among college females. *Journal of Marriage and the Family, 39,* 455–459.

Kinney, D. (1993). From nerds to normals: The recovery of identity among adolescents from middle school to high school. *Sociology of Education, 66,* 21–40.

Kinsey, A., Pomeroy, W., and Martin, C. (1948). *Sexual behavior in the human male.* Philadelphia: Saunders.

Kirby, D., Harvey, P., Claussenius, D., and Novar, M. (1989). A direct mailing to teenage males about condom use: Its impact on knowledge, attitudes and sexual behavior. *Family Planning Perspectives, 21,* 12–18.

Kirkendall, L. (1981). Sex education in the United States: A historical perspective. In L. Brown (Ed.), *Sex education in the eighties.* New York: Plenum.

Kisela, M., and Sturmer, P. (1993). Is society giving teenage fathers a mixed message? *Youth and Society, 24,* 487–501.

Kite, M. (1984). Sex differences in attitudes towards homosexuals: A meta-analytic review. *Journal of Homosexuality, 10,* 69–81.

Klebanov, P., and Brooks-Gunn, J. (1992). Impact of maternal attitudes, girls' adjustment, and cognitive skills upon academic performance in middle and high school. *Journal of Research on Adolescence, 2,* 81–102.

Klerman, L. (1993). The influence of economic factors on health-related behaviors in adolescents. Pp. 38–57 in S. Millstein, A. Petersen, and E. Nightingale (Eds.), *Promoting the health of adolescents: New directions for the twenty-first century.* New York: Oxford University Press.

Kliewer, W., and Sandler, I. (1992). Locus of control and self-esteem as moderators of stress-symptom relations in children and adolescents. *Journal of Abnormal Child Psychology, 20,* 393–413.

Kneisel, P. (1987). *Social support preferences of female adolescents in the context of interpersonal stress.* Paper presented at the biennial meetings of the Society for Research in Child Development, Baltimore.

Kobak, R., and Cole, H. (1994). Attachment and meta-monitoring: Implications for adolescent autonomy and psychopathology. In D. Cicchetti and S. Toth (Eds.), *Rochester symposium on developmental psychopathology,* Vol. 5: *Disorders and dysfunctions of the self.* Rochester NY: University of Rochester Press.

Kobak, R., Cole, H., Ferenz-Gillies, R., Fleming, W., and Gamble, W. (1993). Attachment and emotion regulation during mother-teen problem-solving: A control theory analysis. *Child Development, 64,* 231–245.

Kobak, R., and Sceery, A. (1988). Attachment in late adolescence: Working models, affect regulation, and representations of self and others. *Child Development, 59,* 135–146.

Kobak, R., Sudler, N., and Gamble, W. (1992). Attachment and depressive symptoms during adolescence: A developmental pathways analysis. *Development and Psychopathology, 3,* 461–474.

Koch, P. (1993). Promoting healthy sexual development during early adolescence. Pp. 293–307 in R. Lerner (Ed.), *Early adolescence: Perspectives on research, policy, and intervention.* Hillsdale, N.J.: Erlbaum.

Kohlberg, L. (1976). Moral stages and moralization: The cognitive-development approach. In T. Lickona (Ed.), *Moral development and behavior.* New York: Holt, Rinehart and Winston.

Kohlberg, L., and Gilligan, C. (1972). The adolescent as philosopher: The discovery of the self in a post-conventional world. In J. Kagan and R. Coles (Eds.), *Twelve to sixteen: Early adolescence.* New York: Norton.

Kohn, M. (1977). *Class and conformity,* 2nd ed. Chicago: University of Chicago Press.

Kolata, G. (1988, August 25). Epidemic of dangerous eating disorders may be false alarm. *New York Times,* p. B16.

Kracke, B. (1993, March). *Biopsychosocial influences on male adolescents' initiation and intensification of substance use.* Paper presented at the biennial meetings of the Society for Research in Child Development, New Orleans.

Krisberg, B., Schwartz, I., Fishman, G., Eisikovits, Z., and Guttman, E. (1986). *The incarceration of minority youth.* Minneapolis, Minn.: Hubert H. Humphrey Institute of Public Affairs, National Council on Crime and Delinquency.

Kroger, J. (1993). The role of historical context in the identity formation process of late adolescence. *Youth and Society, 24,* 363–376.

Krosnick, J., and Judd, C. (1982). Transitions in social influence at adolescence: Who induces cigarette smoking? *Developmental Psychology, 18,* 359–368.

Ku, L., Sonenstein, F., and Pleck, J. (1993). Young men's risk behaviors for HIV infection and sexually transmitted diseases, 1988 through 1991. *American Journal of Public Health, 83,* 1609–1615.

Kuhn, D., Langer, J., Kohlberg, L., and Haan, N. (1977). The development of formal operations in logical and moral judgment. *Genetic Psychology Monographs, 95,* 97–188.

Kupersmidt, J., Burchinal, M., Leff, S., and Patterson, C.

(1992, March). *A longitudinal study of perceived support and conflict with parents from middle childhood through adolescence.* Paper presented at the biennial meetings of the Society for Research on Adolescence, Washington.

Kupersmidt, J., and Coie, J. (1990). Preadolescent peer status, aggression, and school adjustment as predictors of externalizing problems in adolescents. *Child Development, 61,* 1350–1362.

Kurdek, L. (in press). School competence of sixth graders: Parenting transitions, family climate, and peer norm effects. *Child Development.*

Kurdek, L., and Fine, M. (1993). The relation between family structure and young adolescents' appraisals of family climate and parenting behavior. *Journal of Family Issues, 14,* 279–290.

Kurdek, L., and Fine, M. (1994). Family acceptance and family control as predictors of adjustment in young adolescents: Linear, curvilinear, or interactive effects. *Child Development, 65,* 1137–1146.

Kurdek, L., and Sinclair, R. (1988). Relation of eighth graders' family structure, gender, and family environment with academic performance and school behavior. *Journal of Educational Psychology, 80,* 90–94.

Kutner, L. (1988, July 14). When young adults head back home. *New York Times,* p. C8.

Lamborn, S., Mounts, N., Brown, B., and Steinberg, L. (1992). Putting school in perspective: The influence of family, peers, extracurricular participation, and part-time work on academic engagement. Pp. 153–181 in F. Newmann (Ed.), *Student engagement and achievement in American secondary schools.* New York: Teachers College Press.

Lamborn, S., Mounts, N., Steinberg, L., and Dornbusch, S. (1991). Patterns of competence and adjustment among adolescents from authoritative, authoritarian, indulgent, and neglectful families. *Child Development, 62,* 1049–1065.

Lamborn, S., and Steinberg, L. (1993). Emotional autonomy redux: Revisiting Ryan and Lynch. *Child Development, 64,* 483–499.

Lapsley, D. (1989). Continuity and discontinuity in adolescent social cognitive development. In R. Montemayor, G. Adams, and T. Gullota (Eds.), *Advances in adolescence research,* Vol. 2. Beverly Hills, Calif.: Sage.

Lapsley, D., Enright, R., and Serlin, R. (1985). Toward a theoretical perspective on the legislation of adolescence. *Journal of Early Adolescence, 5,* 441–466.

Lapsley, D., and Murphy, M. (1985). Another look at the theoretical assumption of adolescent egocentrism. *Developmental Review, 5,* 201–217.

Larkin, R. W. (1979). *Suburban youth in cultural crisis.* New York: Oxford.

Larson, R. (1983). Adolescents' daily experience with family and friends: Contrasting opportunity systems. *Journal of Marriage and the Family, November,* 739–750.

Larson, R. (1990). The solitary side of life: An examination of the time people spend alone from childhood to old age. *Developmental Review, 10,* 155–183.

Larson, R. (1994, February). *Secrets in the bedroom: Adolescents' private music listening.* Paper presented at the biennial meetings of the Society for Research on Adolescence, San Diego.

Larson, R., and Ham, M. (1993). Stress and "storm and stress" in early adolescence: The relationship of negative events with dysphoric affect. *Developmental Psychology, 29,* 130–140.

Larson, R., Kubey, R., and Colletti, J. (1989). Changing channels: Early adolescent media choices and shifting investments in family and friends. *Journal of Youth and Adolescence, 18,* 583–600.

Larson, R., and Lampman-Petraitis, C. (1989). Daily emotional states as reported by children and adolescents. *Child Development, 60,* 1250–1260.

Larson, R., and Richards, M. (Eds.). (1989). The changing life space of early adolescence. *Journal of Youth and Adolescence, 18(6).* A special issue of the journal devoted to a series of studies of how adolescents spend their time.

Larson, R., and Richards, M. (1991). Daily companionship in late childhood and early adolescence: Changing developmental contexts. *Child Development, 62,* 284–300.

Larson, R., and Richards, M. (1994). *Divergent realities: The emotional lives of mothers, fathers, and adolescents.* New York: Basic Books.

Lau, S. (1989). Sex role orientation and domains of self-esteem. *Sex Roles, 21,* 415–422.

Lau, S. (1990). Crisis and vulnerability in adolescent development. *Journal of Youth and Adolescence, 19,* 111–132.

Lauritsen, J. (1994). Explaining race and gender differences in adolescent sexual behavior. *Social Forces, 72,* 859–884.

Laursen, B. (1993). The perceived impact of conflict on adolescent relationships. *Merrill-Palmer Quarterly, 39,* 535–550.

Laursen, B., and Collins, W. (1994). Interpersonal conflict during adolescence. *Psychological Bulletin, 115,* 197–209.

Lazarus, R., and Folkman, S. (Eds.). (1984). *Stress, appraisal, and coping.* New York: Springer-Verlag.

Leadbeater, B., and Bishop, S. (1994). Predictors of behavior problems in preschool children of inner-city Afro-American and Puerto Rican adolescent mothers. *Child Development, 65,* 638– 648.

Lee, V., and Bryk, A. (1988). Curriculum tracking as mediating the social distribution of high school achievement. *Sociology of Education, 61,* 78–94.

Lee, V., and Bryk, A. (1989). A multilevel model of the social distribution of high school achievement. *Sociology of Education, 62,* 172–192.

Lee, V., and Burkham, D. (1992). Transferring high schools: An alternative to dropping out? *American Journal of Education, 100,* 420–453.

Lee, V., Burkham, D., Zimiles, H., and Ladewski, B. (1994). Family structure and its effect on behavioral and emotional problems in young adolescents. *Journal of Research on Adolescence, 4,* 405–437.

Lee, V., Marks, H., and Byrd, T. (1994). Sexism in single-sex and coeducational independent secondary school classrooms. *Sociology of Education, 67,* 92–120.

Lee, V., and Smith, J. (1993). Effects of school restructuring on the achievement and engagement of middle-grade students. *Sociology of Education, 66,* 164–187.

Leibowitz, S. (1983). Hypothalamic catecholamine systems controlling eating behavior: A potential model for anorexia nervosa. Pp. 221–229 in P. Darby, P. Garfinkel, D. Garner, and D. Cosina (Eds.), *Anorexia nervosa: Recent developments in research.* New York: Alan R. Liss.

Leming, J. (1987). Rock music and the socialization of moral values in early adolescence. *Youth and Society, 18,* 363–383.

Lempers, J., Clark-Lempers, D., and Simmons, R. (1989). Economic hardship, parenting, and distress in adolescence. *Child Development, 60,* 25–49.

Leone, C., and Richards, M. (1989). Classwork and homework in early adolescence: The ecology of achievement. *Journal of Youth and Adolescence, 18,* 531–548.

Lerner, J., Castellino, D., and Perkins, D. (1994, February). *The influence of adolescent behavioral and psychosocial characteristics on maternal behaviors and satisfaction.* Paper presented at the biennial meetings of the Society for Research on Adolescence, San Diego.

Lerner, J., Hertzog, C., Hooker, K., Hassibi, M., and Thomas, A. (1988). A longitudinal study of negative emotional states and adjustment from early childhood through adolescence. *Child Development, 59,* 356–366.

Lerner, R. (Ed.). (1993). *Early adolescence: Perspectives on research, policy, and intervention.* Hillsdale, N.J.: Erlbaum.

Leslie, L. (1986). The impact of adolescent females' assessments of parenthood and employment on plans for the future. *Journal of Youth and Adolescence, 15,* 29–49.

Leventhal, H., and Keeshan, P. (1993). Promoting healthy alternatives to substance abuse. Pp. 260–284 in S. Millstein, A. Petersen, and E. Nightingale (Eds.), *Promoting the health of adolescents: New directions for the twenty-first century.* New York: Oxford University Press.

Levesque, R. (1993). The romantic experience of adolescents in satisfying love relationships. *Journal of Youth and Adolescence, 22,* 219–251.

Levine, M., Smolak, L., and Hayden, H. (1993, March). *The relationship of sociocultural factors to eating attitudes and behaviors among middle school girls.* Paper presented at the biennial meetings of the Society for Research in Child Development, New Orleans.

Levinson, D. (1978). *The seasons of a man's life.* New York: Knopf.

Levinson, R., Jaccard, J., and Beamer, L. (in press). Older adolescents' engagement in casual sex: Impact of risk perception and psychosocial motivations. *Journal of Youth and Adolescence.*

Levitt, M., Guacci-Franci, N., and Levitt, J. (1993). Convoys of social support in childhood and early adolescence: Structure and function. *Developmental Psychology, 29,* 811–818.

Levitz-Jones, E., and Orlofsky, J. (1985). Separation-individuation and intimacy capacity in college women. *Journal of Personality and Social Psychology, 49,* 156–169.

Lewin, K. (1948). *Resolving social conflict.* New York: Harper & Row.

Lewin, K. (1951). *Field theory and social science.* New York: Harper & Row.

Lewin-Epstein, N. (1981). *Youth employment during high school.* Washington, D.C.: National Center for Education Statistics.

Lewinsohn, P., Hops, H., Roberts, R., Seeley, J., and Andrews, J. (1993). Adolescent psychopathology, I: Prevalence and incidence of depression and other *DSM-III-R* disorders in high school students. *Journal of Abnormal Psychology, 102,* 133–144.

Lewinsohn, P., Rohde, P., and Seeley, J. (1994). Psychosocial risk factors for future adolescent suicide attempts. *Journal of Consulting and Clinical Psychology, 62,* 297–305.

Lewinsohn, P., Rohde, P., Seeley, J., and Fischer, S. (1993). Age-cohort changes in the lifetime occurrence of depression and other mental disorders. *Journal of Abnormal Psychology, 102,* 110–120.

Lewis, C. (1981a). The effects of parental firm control. *Psychological Bulletin, 90,* 547–563.

Lewis, C. (1981b). How adolescents approach decisions: Changes over grades seven to twelve and policy implications. *Child Development, 52,* 538–544.

Lewis, C. (1987) Minors' competence to consent to abortion. *American Psychologist, 41,* 84–88.

Lewis, M., Feiring, C., McGuffog, C., and Jaskir, J. (1984). Predicting psychopathology in six-year-olds from early social relations. *Child Development, 55,* 123–136.

Lewis, R., and Spanier, G. (1979). Theorizing about the quality and stability of marriage. In W. Burr, R. Hill, I. Nye, and I. Reiss (Eds.), *Contemporary theories about the family.* Glencoe, Ill.: Free Press.

Lieu, T., Newacheck, P., and McManus, M. (1993). Race, ethnicity, and access to ambulatory care among U.S. adolescents. *American Journal of Public Health, 83,* 960–965.

Linn, M. (1987). Establishing a research base for scientific education: Challenges, trends, and recommendations. *Journal of Research in Science Teaching, 24,* 191–216.

Linn, M., and Songer, N. (1991). Cognitive and conceptual change in adolescence. *American Journal of Education, August,* 379–417.

Linn, M., and Songer, N. (1993). How do students make sense of science? *Merrill-Palmer Quarterly, 39,* 47–73.

Linney, J., and Seidman, E. (1989). The future of schooling. *American Psychologist, 44,* 336–340.

Lipsitz, J. (1977). *Growing up forgotten.* Lexington, Mass.: Lexington Books.

Liu, X., Kaplan, H., and Risser, W. (1992). Decomposing the reciprocal relationships between academic achievement and general self-esteem. *Youth and Society, 24,* 123–148.

Livesley, W., and Bromley, D. (1973). *Person perception in childhood and adolescence.* New York: Wiley.

Livson, N., and Peskin, H. (1980). Perspectives on adolescence from longitudinal research. In J. Adelson (Ed.), *Handbook of adolescent psychology.* New York: Wiley.

Lloyd, D. (1978). Prediction of school failure from third-grade data. *Educational Psychological Measurement, 38,* 1193–1200.

Lochman, J. (1992). Cognitive-behavioral intervention with aggressive boys: Three-year follow-up and preventive effects. *Journal of Consulting and Clinical Psychology, 60,* 426–432.

Lochman, J., and Dodge, K. (1994). Social-cognitive processes of severely violent, moderately aggressive, and nonaggressive boys. *Journal of Consulting and Clinical Psychology, 62,* 366–374.

Loeber, R., and Stouthamer-Loeber, M. (1986). Family factors as correlates and predictors of juvenile conduct problems and delinquency. In M. Tonry and N. Morris (Eds.), *Crime and justice,* vol. 7. Chicago: University of Chicago Press.

Loeber, R., Wung, P., Keenan, K., Giroux, B., Stouthamer-Loeber, M., Van Kammen, W., and Maughan, B. (1993). Developmental pathways in disruptive child behavior. *Development and Psychopathology, 5,* 103–133.

Long, B. (1989). Heterosexual involvement of unmarried undergraduate females in relation to self-evaluations. *Journal of Youth and Adolescence, 18,* 489–500.

Louis, K., and Smith, B. (1992). Breaking the iron law of social class: The renewal of teachers' professional status and engagement. In F. Newmann (Ed.), *Student engagement and achievement in American high schools.* New York: Teachers College Press.

Lovitt, T. (1989). *Introduction to learning disabilities.* Boston: Allyn & Bacon.

Luthar, S. (1991). Vulnerability and resilience: A study of high-risk adolescents. *Child Development, 62,* 600–616.

Luthar, S. (1994, February). *Social competence of inner-city adolescents: A six-month prospective study.* Paper presented at the biennial meetings of the Society for Research on Adolescence, San Diego.

Lynn, D. (1966, November). The process of learning parental and sex-role identification. *Journal of Marriage and the Family,* 446–470.

Lyon, J., Henggeler, S., and Hall, J. (1992). The family relations, peer relations, and criminal activities of Caucasian and Hispanic-American gang members. *Journal of Abnormal Child Psychology, 20,* 439–449.

Lyons, J., and Barber, B. (1992, March). *Family environment effects on adolescent adjustment: Differences between intact and remarried families.* Paper presented at the biennial meetings of the Society for Research on Adolescence, Washington.

Maccoby, E. (1988). Gender as a social category. *Developmental Psychology, 24,* 755–775.

Maccoby, E. (1990). Gender and relationships: A developmental account. *American Psychologist, 45,* 513–520.

Maccoby, E., and Jacklin, C. (1974). *The psychology of sex differences.* Stanford, Calif.: Stanford University Press.

Maccoby, E., and Martin, J. (1983). Socialization in the context of the family: Parent-child interaction. In E. M. Hetherington (Ed.), *Handbook of child psychology: Socialization, personality, and social development,* Vol. 4. New York: Wiley.

MacDermid, S., and Crouter, A. (in press). Midlife, adolescence, and parental employment in the family system. *Journal of Youth and Adolescence.*

Mac Iver, D., Stipek, D., and Daniels, D. (1991). Explaining within-semester changes in student effort in junior high school and senior high school courses. *Journal of Educational Psychology, 83,* 201–211.

Magnusson, D., Stattin, H., and Allen, V. (1986). Differential maturation among girls and its relation to social adjustment in a longitudinal perspective. In P. Baltes, D. Featherman, and R. Lerner (Eds.), *Life span development and behavior,* Vol. 7. Hillsdale, N.J.: Erlbaum.

Mahoney, E. (1983). *Human sexuality.* New York: McGraw-Hill.

Main, M., Kaplan, N., and Cassidy, J. (1985). Security in infancy, childhood and adulthood: A move to the level of representation. Pp. 66–106 in I. Bretherton and E. Waters (Eds.), Growing points of attachment theory and research. *Monographs of the Society for Research on Child Development, 50,* 1–2, Serial No. 209.

Manegold, C. (1994, August 18). U.S. students are found gaining only in science. *New York Times,* p. A14.

Mannheim, K. (1952). The problem of generations. In K. Mannheim (Ed.), *Essays on the sociology of knowledge.* London: Routledge & Kegan Paul.

Marcia, J. (1966). Development and validation of ego identity status. *Journal of Personality and Social Psychology, 3,* 551–558.

Marcia, J. (1976). Identity six years after: A follow-up study. *Journal of Youth and Adolescence, 5,* 145–150.

Marcia, J. (1980). Identity in adolescence. In J. Adelson (Ed.), *Handbook of adolescent psychology.* New York: Wiley.

Mare, R. Winship, C., and Kubitschek, W. (1984). The transition from youth to adult: Understanding the age pattern of employment. *American Journal of Sociology, 90,* 326–358.

Marini, M. (1984). The order of events in the transition to adulthood. *Sociology of Education, 57,* 63–84.

Marini, Z., and Case, R. (1994). The development of abstract reasoning about the physical and social world. *Child Development, 65,* 147–159.

Markovits, H., and Valchon, R. (1989). Reasoning with contrary-to-fact propositions. *Journal of Experimental Child Psychology, 47,* 398–412.

Markovits, H., and Valchon, R. (1990). Conditional reasoning, representation, and level of abstraction. *Developmental Psychology, 26,* 942–951.

Markstrom-Adams, C. (1989). Androgyny and its relation to adolescent psychological well-being: A review of the literature. *Sex Roles, 21,* 469–473.

Markstrom-Adams, C., Hofstra, G., and Dougher, K. (in press). The ego-virtue of fidelity: A case for the study of religion and identity formation in adolescence. *Journal of Youth and Adolescence.*

Markus, H., and Nurius, P. (1986). Possible selves. *American Psychologist, 41,* 954–969.

Marsh, H. (1989a). Age and sex effects in multiple dimensions of self-concept: Preadolescence to early adulthood. *Journal of Educational Psychology, 81,* 417–430.

Marsh, H. (1989b). Sex differences in the development of verbal and mathematical constructs: The High School and Beyond Study. *American Educational Research Journal, 26,* 191–225.

Marsh, H. (1990). Causal ordering of academic self-concept and academic achievement: A multiwave, longitudinal panel analysis. *Journal of Educational Psychology, 82,* 646–656.

Marshall, S. (1994, February). *Ethnic socialization of African American children: Implications for parenting, identity development and academic achievement.* Paper presented at the biennial meetings of the Society for Research on Adolescence, San Diego.

Marshall, W. (1978). Puberty. In F. Falkner and J. Tanner (Eds.), *Human growth,* Vol. 2. New York: Plenum.

Marshall, W., and Tanner, J. (1969). Variations in the pattern of pubertal change in girls. *Archive of Disease of Childhood, 44,* 130.

Marsiglio, W. (1987). Adolescent fathers in the United States: Their initial living arrangements, marital experience and educational outcomes. *Family Planning Perspectives, 19,* 240–251.

Martin, B. (1990). The transmission of relationship difficulties from one generation to the next. *Journal of Youth and Adolescence, 19,* 181–200.

Martin, T., and Bumpass, L. (1989). Recent trends in marital disruption. *Demography, 26,* 37–51.

Masnick, G., and Bane, M. (1980). *The nation's families: 1960 1990.* Boston: Auburn House.

Massad, C. (1981). Sex role identity and adjustment during adolescence. *Child Development, 52,* 1290–1298.

Masten, A., Miliotis, D., Graham-Bermann, S., Ramirez, M., and Neemann, J. (1993). Children in homeless families: Risks to mental health and development. *Journal of Consulting and Clinical Psychology, 61,* 335–343.

Matas, L., Arend, R., and Sroufe, L. (1978). Continuity in adaptation in the second year: The relationship between quality of attachment and later competence. *Child Development, 49,* 547–556.

Matza, M. (1990, November 24). More pre-teens drinking, more teens are alcoholics. *Philadelphia Inquirer,* p. 1-A.

Mazor, A., and Enright, R. (1988). The development of the individuation process from a social cognitive perspective. *Journal of Adolescence, 11,* 29–47.

Mazor, A., Shamir, R., and Ben-Moshe, J. (1990). The individuation process from a social-cognitive perspective in kibbutz adolescents. *Journal of Youth and Adolescence, 19,* 73–90.

McCabe, M. (1984). Toward a theory of adolescent dating. *Adolescence, 19,* 159–169.

McCall, R. (in press). Academic underachievers. *Current Directions.*

McCall, R., Applebaum, M., and Hogarty, P. (1973). Developmental changes in mental performance. *Monographs of the Society for Research in Child Development, 38,* Serial No. 150.

McCarthy, B., and Hagen, J. (1992). Mean streets: The theoretical significance of situational delinquency among homeless youth. *American Journal of Sociology, 98,* 597–627.

McCarthy, K., Lord, S., Eccles, J., Kalil, A., and Furstenberg, F., Jr. (1992, March). *The impact of family management strategies on adolescents in high risk environments.* Paper presented at the biennial meetings of the Society for Research on Adolescence, Washington.

McClelland, D. (1961). *The achieving society.* Princeton, N.J.: Van Nostrand.

McClelland, D., Atkinson, J., Clark, R., and Lowell, E. (1953). *The achievement motive.* New York: Appleton-Century-Crofts.

McClintock, M. (1980). Major gaps in menstrual cycle research: Behavioral and physiological controls in a biological context. Pp. 7–23 in P. Komenich, M. McSweeney, J. Noack, and N. Elder (Eds.), *The menstrual cycle,* Vol. 2. New York: Springer.

McCord, J. (1990). Problem behaviors. Pp. 414–430 in S. Feldman and G. Elliott (Eds.), *At the threshold: The developing adolescent.* Cambridge, Mass.: Harvard University Press.

McCrae, R., and John, O. (1992). An introduction to the Five-Factor Model and its applications. *Journal of Personality, 60,* 175–215.

McCullers, C. (1946). *The member of the wedding.* New York: Bantam.

McGee, L., and Newcomb, M. (1992). General deviance syndrome: Expanded hierarchical evaluations at four ages from early adolescence to adulthood. *Journal of Consulting and Clinical Psychology, 60,* 766–776.

McGee, R., Williams, S., and Feehan, M. (1992). Attention deficit disorder and age of onset of problem behaviors. *Journal of Abnormal Child Psychology, 20,* 487–502.

McLanahan, S., and Bumpass, L. (1988). Intergenerational consequences of family disruption. *American Journal of Sociology, 94,* 130–152.

McLoyd, V. (1990). The impact of economic hardship on black families and children: Psychological distress, parenting, and socioemotional development. *Child Development, 61,* 311–346.

McLoyd, V., Jayaratne, T., Ceballo, R., and Borquez, J. (1994). Unemployment and work interruption among African American single mothers: Effects on parenting and adolescent socioemotional functioning. *Child Development, 65,* 562–589.

McNeil, L. (1984). *Lowering expectations: The impact of student employment on classroom knowledge.* Madison, Wis.: Wisconsin Center for Education Research.

Mead, M. (1928). *Coming of age in Samoa.* New York: Morrow.

Mechanic, D. (1983). Adolescent health and illness behavior: Review of the literature and a new hypothesis for the study of stress. *Journal of Human Stress, 9,* 4–13.

Mednick, S., Gabrielli, W., and Hitchings, B. (1987). Genetic factors in the etiology of criminal behavior. Pp. 74–91 in S. Mednick, T. Moffitt, and S. Stack (Eds.), *The causes of crime: New biological approaches.* Cambridge, England: Cambridge University Press.

Medrich, E., Roizen, J., Rubin, V., and Buckley, S. (1982). *The serious business of growing up.* Berkeley: University of California Press.

Mensch, B., and Kandel, D. (1988). Dropping out of high school and drug involvement. *Sociology of Education, 61,* 95–113.

Meyer, L. (1994). *Teenspeak.* Princeton, N.J.: Peterson's.

Mickelson, R. (1990). The attitude-achievement paradox among black adolescents. *Sociology of Education, 63,* 44–61.

Midgley, C., Feldlaufer, H., and Eccles, J. (1988). The transition to junior high school: Beliefs of pre- and post-transition teachers. *Journal of Youth and Adolescence, 17,* 543–562.

Miller, B., and Bingham, R. (1989). Family configuration in relation to the sexual behavior of female adolescents. *Journal of Marriage and the Family, 51,* 499–506.

Miller, B., and Moore, K. (1990). Adolescent sexual behavior, pregnancy, and parenting: Research through the 1980s. *Journal of Marriage and the Family, 52,* 1025–1044.

Miller, J. B. (1986). *Toward a new psychology of women,* 2nd ed. Boston: Beacon Press.

Miller, J., and Yung, S. (1990). The role of allowances in adolescent socialization. *Youth and Society, 17,* 57–63.

Miller, N. (1928). *The child in primitive society.* New York: Bretano.

Miller, N., Cowan, P., Cowan, C., Hetherington, E., and Clingempeel, W. (1993). Externalizing in preschoolers and early adolescents: A cross-study replication of a family model. *Developmental Psychology, 29,* 3–18.

Miller, P., and Simon, W. (1980). The development of sexuality in adolescence. In J. Adelson (Ed.), *Handbook of adolescent psychology.* New York: Wiley.

Miller, R., and Gordon, M. (1986). The decline in formal dating: A study in six Connecticut high schools. *Marriage and Family Review, 10,* 139–156.

Miller-Jones, D. (1989). Culture and testing. *American Psychologist, 44,* 360–366.

Millstein, S. (1989). Adolescent health: Challenges for behavioral scientists. *American Psychologist, 44,* 837–842.

Millstein, S., Irwin, C., Jr., Adler, N., Cohn, L., Kegeles, S., and Dolcini, M. (1992). Health-risk behaviors and health concerns among young adolescents. *Pediatrics, 3,* 422–428.

Millstein, S., Petersen, A., and Nightingale, E. (Eds.). (1993). *Promoting the health of adolescents: New directions for the twenty-first century.* New York: Oxford University Press.

Minuchin, S. (1974). *Families and family therapy.* Cambridge, Mass.: Harvard University Press.

Minuchin, S., Rosman, B., and Baker, L. (1978). *Psychosomatic families: Anorexia nervosa in context.* Cambridge, Mass.: Harvard University Press.

Mitchell, B., Wister, A., and Burch, T. (1989). The family environment and leaving the parental home. *Journal of Marriage and the Family, 51,* 605–613.

Mitchell, E. (Ed.). (1985). *Anorexia nervosa and bulimia: Diagnosis and treatment.* Minneapolis: University of Minnesota Press.

Modell, J., Furstenberg, F., Jr., and Hershberg, T. (1976). Social change and transitions to adulthood in historical perspective. *Journal of Family History, 1,* 7–32.

Modell, J., and Goodman, M. (1990). Historical perspectives. Pp. 93–122 in S. Feldman and G. Elliott (Eds.), *At the threshold: The developing adolescent.* Cambridge, Mass.: Harvard University Press.

Moffitt, T. (1993). Adolescence-limited and life-course persistent antisocial behavior: A developmental taxonomy. *Psychological Review, 100,* 674–701.

Moffitt, T., Caspi, A., Belsky, J., and Silva, P. (1992). Childhood experience and the onset of menarche: A test of a sociobiological model. *Child Development, 63,* 47–58.

Moffitt, T., Caspi, A., Harkness, A., and Silva, P. (1993). The natural history of change in intellectual performance: Who changes? How much? Is it meaningful? *Journal of Child Psychology and Psychiatry, 34,* 455–506.

Moffitt, T., and Silva, P. (1988). IQ and delinquency: A direct test of the differential detection hypothesis. *Journal of Abnormal Psychology, 97,* 330–333.

Moll, R. (1986). *Playing the private college admissions game.* New York: Penguin.

Monahan, L., Kuhn, D., and Shaver, P. (1974). Intrapsychic versus cultural explanations of the "fear of success" motive. *Journal of Personality and Social Psychology, 29,* 60–64.

Monck, E. (1991). Patterns of confiding relationships among adolescent girls. *Journal of Child Psychology and Psychiatry, 32,* 333–345.

Montemayor, R. (1982). The relationship between parent-adolescent conflict and the amount of time adolescents spend alone and with parents and peers. *Child Development, 53,* 1512–1519.

Montemayor, R. (1983). Parents and adolescents in conflict: All families some of the time and some families most of the time. *Journal of Early Adolescence, 3,* 83–103.

Montemayor, R. (1984). Maternal employment and adolescents' relations with parents, siblings, and peers. *Journal of Youth and Adolescence, 13,* 543–557.

Montemayor, R. (1986). Family variation in parent-adolescent storm and stress. *Journal of Adolescent Research, 1,* 15–31.

Montemayor, R. (Ed.). (in press). *Advances in adolescent development,* Vol. 3: *Relationships in adolescence.* Newbury Park, CA: Sage.

Montemayor, R., Brown, B., and Adams, G. (1985). *Changes in identity status and psychological adjustment after leaving home and entering college.* Paper presented at the biennial meetings of the Society for Research in Child Development, Toronto.

Montemayor, R., and Brownlee, J. (1987). Fathers, mothers, and adolescents: Gender-based differences in parental roles during adolescence. *Journal of Youth and Adolescence, 16,* 281–292.

Montemayor, R., and Eberly, M. (in press). Effects of pubertal status and conversation topic on parent and adolescent affective expression. *Journal of Social and Personal Relations.*

Montemayor, R., and Eisen, M. (1977). The development of self-conceptions from childhood to adolescence. *Developmental Psychology, 13,* 314–319.

Moore, K., Myers, D., Morrison, D., Nord, C., Brown, B., and Edmonston, B. (1993). Age at first childbirth and later poverty. *Journal of Research on Adolescence, 3,* 393–422.

Moore, K., Nord, C., and Peterson, J. (1989). Nonvoluntary sexual activity among adolescents. *Family Planning Perspectives, 21,* 110–114.

Moore, K., Peterson, J., and Furstenberg, F., Jr. (1986). Parental attitudes and the occurrence of early sexual activity. *Journal of Marriage and the Family, 48,* 777–782.

Moore, K., and Snyder, N. (1991). Cognitive attainment among firstborn children of adolescent mothers. *American Sociological Review, 56,* 612–624.

Moore, M. (1992). The family as portrayed on prime-time television, 1947–1990: Structure and characteristics. *Sex Roles, 26,* 41–62.

Moos, R. (1978). A typology of junior high and high school classrooms. *American Educational Research Journal, 15,* 53–66.

Morison, P., and Masten, A. (1991). Peer reputation in middle childhood as a predictor of adaptation in adolescence: A seven-year follow-up. *Child Development, 62,* 991–1007.

Morris, N., and Udry, J. (1980). Validation of a self-administered instrument to assess stage of adolescent development. *Journal of Youth and Adolescence, 9,* 271–280.

Mortimer, J., and Finch, M. (1986). The effects of part-time work on adolescent self-concept and achievement. In P. Borman and J. Reisman (Eds.), *Becoming a worker.* Norwood, N.J.: Ablex.

Mortimer, J., Finch, M., Ryu, S., Shanahan, M., and Call, K. (1993, March). *The effects of work intensity on adolescent mental health, achievement and behavioral adjustment: New evidence from a prospective study.* Paper presented at the biennial meetings of the Society for Research in Child Development, New Orleans.

Mortimer, J., Finch, M., Shanahan, M., and Ryu, S. (1990, March). *Work experience, mental health, and behavioral adjustment in adolescence.* Paper presented at the biennial meetings of the Society for Research on Adolescence, Atlanta.

Mortimer, J., Finch, M., Shanahan, M., Ryu, S. (1992). Adolescent work history and behavioral adjustment. *Journal of Research on Adolescence, 2,* 59–80.

Mortimer, J., and Lorence, J. (1979). Work experience and occupational value socialization: A longitudinal study. *American Journal of Sociology, 84,* 1361–1385.

Mory, M. (1992, March). *"Love the ones you're with": Conflict and consensus in adolescent peer group stereotypes.* Paper presented at the biennial meetings of the Society for Research on Adolescence, Washington.

Mory, M. (1994, February). *When people form or perceive sets, they tend to be fuzzy: The case of adolescent crowds.* Paper presented at the biennial meetings of the Society for Research on Adolescence, San Diego.

Moshman, D. (1993). Adolescent reasoning and adolescent rights. *Human Development, 36,* 27–40.

Munoz, R., and Amado, H. (1986). Anorexia nervosa: An affective disorder. Pp. 13–19 in F. Larocca (Ed.), *Eating disorders.* San Francisco: Jossey-Bass.

Mullis, I., Dossey, J., Campbell, J., Gentile, C., O'Sullivan, C., and Latham, A. (1994). *NAEP 1992 trends in academic progress.* Washington, D.C.: U.S. Department of Education.

Mullis, I., Owen, E., and Phillips, G. (1990). *America's challenge: Accelerating academic achievement. A summary of findings from 20 years of NAEP.* Washington, D.C.: U.S. Department of Education.

Munro, G., and Adams, G. (1977). Ego-identity formation in college students and working youth. *Developmental Psychology, 13,* 523–524.

Munsch, J., and Wampler, R. (1993). Ethnic differences in early adolescents' coping with school stress. *American Journal of Orthopsychiatry, 63,* 633–646.

Murdock, T. (1994, February). *Who are you and how do you treat me? Student withdrawal as motivated alienation.* Paper presented at the biennial meetings of the Society for Research on Adolescence, San Diego.

Musick, J. (1994). Grandmothers and grandmothers-to-be: Effects on adolescent mothers and adolescent mothering. *Infancy and Young Children, 6,* 1–9.

Mussen, P., and Jones, M. C. (1957). Self-conceptions, motivations, and interpersonal attitudes of late- and early-maturing boys. *Child Development, 28,* 243–256.

Mussen, P., and Jones, M. C. (1958). The behavior-inferred motivations of late- and early-maturing boys. *Child Development, 29,* 61–67.

Must, A., Jacques, P., Dallal, G., Bajema, C., and Dietz, W. (1992). Long-term morbidity and mortality of overweight adolescents. *New England Journal of Medicine, 327,* 1350–1355.

Myers, J., Lindentthal, J., and Pepper, M. (1975). Life events, social integration, and psychiatric symptomatology. *Journal of Health and Social Behavior, 16,* 421–429.

Nagy, S., Adcock, A., and Nagy, C. (1994). A comparison of risky health behaviors of sexually active, sexually abused, and abstaining adolescents. *Pediatrics, 93,* 570–575.

National Center on Education and the Economy. (1990). *America's choice: High skills or low wages!* Washington, D.C.: National Center on Education and the Economy.

National Commission on Excellence in Education. (1983). *A nation at risk: The imperative for educational reform.* Washington, D.C.: U.S. Department of Education.

National Education Commission on Time and Learning. (1994). *Prisoners of time.* Washington, D.C.: U.S. Government Printing Office.

National Heart, Lung, and Blood Institute Growth and Health Study Research Group. (1992). Obesity and cardiovascular disease risk factors in Black and White girls: The NHLBI Growth and Health Study. *American Journal of Public Health, 82,* 1613–1620.

National Research Council. (1993). *Losing generations.* Washington, D.C.: National Academy Press.

Natriello, G., and McDill, E. (1986). Performance standards, student effort on homework, and academic achievement. *Sociology of Education, 59,* 18–31.

Natriello, G., Pallas, A., and Alexander, K. (1989). On the right track? Curriculum and academic achievement. *Sociology of Education, 62,* 109–118.

Neckerman, H., Cairns, B., and Cairns, R. (1993, March). *Peers and families: Developmental changes, constraints, and continuities.* Paper presented at the Society for Research on Child Development, New Orleans.

Needle, R., Su, S., and Doherty, W. (1990). Divorce, remarriage, and adolescent substance use: A prospective longitudinal study. *Journal of Marriage and the Family, 52,* 157–169.

Neimark, E. (1975). Intellectual development during adolescence. In F. Horowitz (Ed.), *Review of child development research,* Vol. 4. Chicago: University of Chicago Press.

Neugarten, B., and Datan, N. (1974). The middle years. In S. Arieti (Ed.), *American handbook of psychiatry,* 2nd ed., Vol. 1, Part 3. New York: Basic Books.

New York Times. (1991, January 30). Only one U.S. family in four is 'traditional,' p. A19.

New York Times. (1994, July 18). In U.S., crime strikes youth at high rate, p. A16.

Newcomb, M., and Bentler, P. (1988). Impact of adolescent drug use and social support on problems of young adults: A longitudinal study. *Journal of Abnormal Psychology, 97,* 64–75.

Newcomb, M., and Bentler, P. (1989). Substance use and abuse among children and teenagers. *American Psychologist, 44,* 242–248.

Newcomb, M., and Felix-Ortiz, M. (1992). Multiple protective and risk factors for drug use and abuse: Cross-sectional and prospective findings. *Journal of Personality and Social Psychology, 63,* 280–296.

Newcomb, M., Huba, G., and Bentler, P. (1983). Mothers' influence on the drug use of their children: Confirmatory tests of direct modeling and mediational theories. *Developmental Psychology, 19,* 714–726.

Newcombe, N., and Dubas, J. (1987). Individual differences in cognitive ability: Are they related to timing of puberty? Pp. 249–302 in R. Lerner and T. Foch (Eds.), *Biological-psychosocial interactions in early adolescence.* Hillsdale, N.J.: Erlbaum.

Newcomer, S., and Udry, J. (1984, May). Mothers' influence on the sexual behavior of their teenage children. *Journal of Marriage and the Family,* 477–485.

Newcomer, S., and Udry, J. R. (1985). Oral sex in an adolescent population. *Archives of Sexual Behavior, 14,* 41–56.

Newcomer, S., and Udry, J. (1987). Parental marital status effects on adolescent sexual behavior. *Journal of Marriage and the Family, 49,* 235–240.

Newcomer, S., and Udry, J. (1988). Adolescents' honesty in a survey of sexual behavior. *Journal of Adolescence Research, 3,* 419–423.

Newman, B., and Newman, P. (1976). Early adolescence and its conflict: Group identity versus alienation. *Adolescence, 11,* 261–274.

Newmann, F. (1992). Higher order thinking and prospects for classroom thoughtfulness. In F. Newmann (Ed.), *Student engagement and achievement in American high schools.* New York: Teachers College Press.

Nightingale, E., and Wolverton, L. (1993). Adolescent rolelessness in modern society. *Teachers College Record, 94,* 472–486.

Noack, P., Kracke, B., and Hofer, M. (1994, February). *The family context of rightist attitudes among adolescents in East and West Germany.* Paper presented at the biennial meetings of the Society for Research on Adolescence, San Diego.

Nolen-Hoeksema, S., and Girgus, J. (1994). The emergence of gender differences in depression during adolescence. *Psychological Bulletin, 115,* 424–443.

Nolen-Hoeksema, S., Girgus, J., and Seligman, M. (1992). Predictors and consequences of childhood depressive symptoms: A 5-year longitudinal study. *Journal of Abnormal Psychology, 101,* 405–422.

Noller, P., and Callan, V. (1990). Adolescents' perceptions of the nature of their communication with parents. *Journal of Youth and Adolescence, 19,* 349–362.

Nordheimer, J. (1990, October 18). Stepfathers: The shoes rarely fit. *New York Times,* pp. C1 ff.

Nottelmann, E. (1987). Competence and self-esteem during transition from childhood to adolescence. *Developmental Psychology, 23,* 441–450.

O'Beirne, H. (1994, February). *Differential correlates of male and female adolescents' sexual activity.* Paper presented at the biennial meetings of the Society for Research on Adolescence, San Diego.

O'Brien, D., and Overton, W. (1982). Conditional reasoning and the competence-performance issue: A developmental analysis of a training task. *Journal of Experimental Child Psychology, 34,* 274–290.

O'Brien, S., and Bierman, K. (1988). Conceptions and perceived influence of peer groups: Interviews with preadolescents and adolescents. *Child Development, 59,* 1360–1365.

Offer, D., Ostrov, E., and Howard, K. (1981). *The adolescent: A psychological self-portrait.* New York: Basic Books.

Ogbu, J. (1974). *The next generation: An ethnography of education in an urban neighborhood.* New York: Academic Press.

Ogbu, J. (1978). *Minority education and caste.* New York: Academic Press.

Olweus, D. (in press). Victimization by peers: Antecedents and long-term outcomes. In K. Rubin and J. Asendorf (Eds.), *Social withdrawal, inhibition, and shyness in childhood.* Hillsdale, N.J.: Erlbaum.

O'Malley, P., and Bachman, J. (1983). Self-esteem: Change and stability between ages 13 and 23. *Developmental Psychology, 19,* 257–268.

Orlofsky, J., Marcia, J., and Lesser, I. (1973). Ego identity status and the intimacy versus isolation crisis of young adulthood. *Journal of Personality and Social Psychology, 27,* 211–219.

Orr, D., Beiter, M., and Ingersoll, G. (1991). Premature sexual activity as an indicator of psychosocial risk. *Pediatrics, 87,* 141–147.

Orr, D., and Langefeld, C. (1993). Factors associated with condom use by sexually active male adolescents at risk for sexually transmitted disease. *Pediatrics, 91,* 873–879.

Orr, E., and Ben-Eliahu, E., (1993). Gender differences in idiosyncratic sex-typed self-images and self-esteem. *Sex Roles, 29,* 271–296.

Osgood, D. W., Johnston, L., O'Malley, P., and Bachman, J. (1988). The generality of deviance in late adolescence and early adulthood. *American Sociological Review, 53,* 81–93.

Osipow, S. (1973). *Theories of career development,* 2nd ed. New York: Appleton-Century-Crofts.

Oswald, H., Bahne, J., and Feder, M. (1994, February).

Love and sexuality in adolescence: Gender-specific differences in East and West Berlin. Paper presented at the biennial meetings of the Society for Research on Adolescence, San Diego.

Overton, W. (1990). Competence and procedures: Constraints on the development of logical reasoning. Pp. 1–32 in W. Overton (Ed.), *Reasoning, necessity, and logic: Developmental perspectives.* Hillsdale, N.J.: Erlbaum.

Overton, W., Ward, S., Noveck, I., Black, J., and O'Brien, D. (1987). Form and content in the development of deductive reasoning. *Developmental Psychology, 23,* 22–30.

Oyserman, D., and Markus, H. (1990). Possible selves and delinquency. *Journal of Personality and Social Psychology, 59,* 112–125.

Oyserman, D., Radin, N., and Benn, R. (1993). Dynamics in a three-generational family: Teens, grandparents, and babies. *Developmental Psychology, 29,* 564–572.

Pabon, E., Rodriguez, O., and Gurin, G. (1992). Clarifying peer relations and delinquency. *Youth and Society, 24,* 149–165.

Paikoff, R., and Brooks-Gunn, J. (1991). Do parent-child relationships change during puberty? *Psychological Bulletin, 110,* 47–66.

Paikoff, R., Brooks-Gunn, J., and Warren, M. (1991). Effects of girls' hormonal status on depressive and aggressive symptoms over the course of one year. *Journal of Youth and Adolescence, 20,* 191–216.

Paikoff, R., Carlton-Ford, S., and Brooks-Gunn, J. (1993). Mother-daughter dyads view the family: Associations between divergent perceptions and daughter well-being. *Journal of Youth and Adolescence, 22,* 473–492.

Pallas, A., Natriello, G., and McDill, E. (1989). The changing nature of the disadvantaged population: Current dimensions and future trends. *Educational Researcher, 18,* 16–22.

Pantages, T., and Creedon, C. (1978). Studies of college attrition: 1950–1975. *Review of Educational Research, 48,* 49–101.

Parke, R. (1988). Families in life-span perspective: A multilevel developmental approach. Pp. 159–190 In E. M. Hetherington and M. Perlmutter (Eds.), *Child development in life-span perspective.* Hillsdale, N.J.: Erlbaum.

Parker, J., and Asher, S. (1987). Peer acceptance and later personal adjustment. Are low accepted children at risk? *Psychological Bulletin, 102,* 357–389.

Parkhurst, J., and Asher, S. (1992). Peer rejection in middle school: Subgroup differences in behavior, loneliness, and interpersonal concerns. *Developmental Psychology, 28,* 231–241.

Parsons, J. Eccles, Adler, T., and Kaczala, C. (1982). Socialization of achievement attitudes and beliefs: Parental influences. *Child Development, 53,* 310–321.

Parsons, T. (1949). The social structure of the family. In R. Anshen (Ed.), *The family: Its function and destiny.* New York: Harper & Row.

Pasley, K., and Gecas, V. (1984). Stresses and satisfactions of the parental role. *Personnel and Guidance Journal, 2,* 400–404.

Patterson, G. (1986). Performance models for antisocial boys. *American Psychologist, 41,* 432–444.

Patterson, G., DeBaryshe, B., and Ramsey, E. (1989). A developmental perspective on antisocial behavior. *American Psychologist, 44,* 329–335.

Patterson, G., and Stoolmiller, M. (1991). Replications of a dual failure model for boys' depressed mood. *Journal of Consulting and Clinical Psychology, 59,* 491–498.

Patterson, G., and Stouthamer-Loeber, M. (1984). The correlation of family management practices and delinquency. *Child Development, 55,* 1299–1307.

Patterson, G., and Yoerger, K. (1993, March). *Adolescent first arrest: One model or two?* Paper presented at the biennial meetings of the Society for Research in Child Development, New Orleans.

Paul, J. (1993). Childhood cross-gender behavior and adult homosexuality: The resurgence of biological models of sexuality. *Journal of Homosexuality, 24,* 41–54.

Paulsen, E. (1972). Obesity in children and adolescents. In H. Barnett and A. Einhorn (Eds.), *Pediatrics.* New York: Appleton-Century-Crofts.

Paulsen, K., and Johnson, M. (1983). Sex role attitudes and mathematical ability in 4th-, 8th-, and 11th-grade students from a high socioeconomic area. *Developmental Psychology, 19,* 210–214.

Paulson, S. (1994). Relations of parenting style and parental involvement with ninth-grade students' achievement. *Journal of Early Adolescence, 14,* 250–267.

Paxton, S., Wertheim, E., Gibbons, K., Szmukler, G., Hillier, L., and Petrovich, J. (1991). Body image satisfaction, dieting beliefs, and weight loss behaviors in adolescent girls and boys. *Journal of Youth and Adolescence, 20,* 361–380.

Peplau, L., Rubin, Z., and Hill, C. (1977). Sexual intimacy in dating relationships. *Journal of Social Issues, 33,* 86–109.

Peskin, H. (1967). Pubertal onset and ego functioning: A psychoanalytic approach. *Journal of Abnormal Psychology, 72,* 1–15.

Peskin, H. (1973). Influence of the developmental schedule of puberty on learning and ego functioning. *Journal of Youth and Adolescence, 2,* 273–290.

Petersen, A. (1985). Pubertal development as a cause of disturbance: Myths, realities, and unanswered questions. *Genetic, Social, and General Psychology Monographs, 111,* 205–232.

Petersen, A. (1988). Adolescent development. *Annual Review of Psychology, 39,* 583–607.

Petersen, A. (in press). A longitudinal investigation of adolescents' changing perceptions of pubertal timing. *Developmental Psychology.*

Petersen, A., Compas, B., Brooks-Gunn, J., Stemmler, M., Ey, S., and Grant, K. (1993). Depression in adolescence. *American Psychologist, 48,* 155–168.

Petersen, A., Graber, J., and Sullivan, P. (1990, March). *Pubertal timing and problem behavior: Variations in effects.* Paper presented at the biennial meetings of the Society for Research on Adolescence, Atlanta.

Petersen, A., Sarigiani, P., and Kennedy, R. (1991). *Adoles-*

cent depression: Why more girls? Journal of Youth and Adolescence, 20, 247–272.

Petersen, A., and Taylor, B. (1980). The biological approach to adolescence: Biological change and psychological adaptation. In J. Adelson (Ed.), *Handbook of adolescent psychology.* New York: Wiley.

Peterson, P., Hawkins, J., Abbott, R., and Catalano, R. (1994). *Journal of Research on Adolescence, 4,* 203–227.

Petraitis, J., Flay, B., and Miller, T. (1995). Reviewing theories of adolescent substance use: Organizing pieces in the puzzle. *Psychological Bulletin.*

Phinney, J. (1990). Ethnic identity in adolescents and adults: A review of research. *Psychological Bulletin, 108,* 499–514.

Phinney, J., and Alipuria, L. (1987). *Ethnic identity in older adolescents from four ethnic groups.* Paper presented at the biennial meetings of the Society for Research in Child Development, Baltimore.

Phinney, J., and Chavira, V. (in press). Parental ethnic socialization and adolescent outcomes in ethnic minority families. *Journal of Research on Adolescence.*

Phinney, J., Devich-Navarro, M., DuPont, S., Estrada, A., and Onwughala, M. (1994, February). *Bicultural identity orientations of African American and Mexican American Adolescents.* Paper presented at the biennial meetings of the Society for Research on Adolescence, San Diego.

Phinney, J., DuPont, S., Espinosa, Revill, J., and Sanders, K. (1994). Ethnic identity and American identification among ethnic minority adolescents. In F. van de Vijver (Ed.), *Proceedings of 1992 conference of the international association for cross-cultural psychology.* Tilburg, The Netherlands: Tilburg University Press.

Pierce, K. (1993). Socialization of teenage girls through teen-magazine fiction: The making of a new woman or an old lady? *Sex Roles, 29,* 59–68.

Pleck, J., Sonenstein, F., and Ku, L. (1991). Adolescent males' condom use: Relationships between perceived cost-benefits and consistency. *Journal of Marriage and the Family, 53,* 733–745.

Plomin, R., and Daniels, D. (1987). Why are children in the same family so different from one another? *Behavioral and Brain Sciences, 10,* 1–60.

Powell, A., Farrar, E., and Cohen, D. (1985). *The shopping mall high school.* Boston: Houghton Mifflin.

Powers, S., and Wagner, M. (1984). Attributions for school achievement of middle school students. *Journal of Early Adolescence, 4,* 215–222.

Pratt, M., Filipovich, and Boutrogianni, M. (in press). Parenting style and parental beliefs and practices concerning school and home. *Merrill-Palmer Quarterly.*

President's Science Advisory Committee. (1974). *Youth: Transition to adulthood.* Chicago: University of Chicago Press.

Prinsky, L., and Rosenbaum, J. (1987). Leer-ics or lyrics? *Youth and Society, 18,* 384–394.

Pulkkinen, L. (1982). Self-control and continuity from childhood to adolescence. In P. Baltes and O. Brim (Eds.), *Life-span development and behavior,* Vol. 4. New York: Academic Press.

Quadrel, M., Fischoff, B., and Davis, W. (1993). Adolescent (in)vulnerability. *American Psychologist, 48,* 102–116.

Raffaelli, M., and Larson, R. (1987). *Sibling interactions in late childhood and early adolescence.* Paper presented at the biennial meetings of the Society for Research in Child Development, Baltimore.

Renken, B., Egeland, B., Marvinney, D., Mangelsdorf, S., and Sroufe, L. A. (1989). Early childhood antecedents of aggression and passive withdrawal in early elementary school. *Journal of Personality, 57,* 257–282.

Repinski, D., and Leffert, N. (1994, February). *Adolescents' relations with friends: The effects of a psychoeducational intervention.* Paper presented at the biennial meetings of the Society for Research on Adolescence, San Diego.

Resnick, M., Blum, R., Bose, J., Smith, M., and Toogood, R. (1990). Characteristics of unmarried adolescent mothers: Determinants of child rearing versus adoption. *American Journal of Orthopsychiatry, 60,* 577–583.

Rest, J. (1983). Morality. In J. Flavell and E. Markman (Eds.), *Handbook of child psychology,* Vol. III: Cognitive development. New York: Wiley.

Rest, J., Davison, M., and Robbins, S. (1978). Age trends in judging moral issues: A review of cross-sectional, longitudinal, and sequential studies of the Defining Issues Test. *Child Development, 49,* 263–279.

Reubens, B., Harrison, J., and Rupp, K. (1981). *The youth labor force, 1945–1995: A cross-national analysis.* Totowa, N.J.: Allanheld, Osmun.

Reuman, D. (1989). How social comparison mediates the relation between ability-grouping practices and students' achievement expectancies in mathematics. *Journal of Educational Psychology, 81,* 178–189.

Reuter, M., and Conger, R. (1994, February). *Family dysfunction as a mediator in the relationship between parental substance use and adolescent substance use.* Paper presented at the biennial meetings of the Society for Research on Adolescence, San Diego.

Reviere, S., and Bakeman, R. (1992, March). *Measuring multicultural competence: American Whites, American Blacks, and immigrants.* Paper presented at the biennial meetings of the Society for Research on Adolescence, Washington.

Reyes, O., and Jason, L. (1993). Pilot study examining factors associated with academic success for Hispanic high school students. *Journal of Youth and Adolescence, 22,* 57–71.

Rice, K. (1990). Attachment in adolescence: A narrative and meta-analytic review. *Journal of Youth and Adolescence, 19,* 511–538.

Richards, M., Boxer, A., Petersen, A., and Albrecht, R. (1990). Relation of weight to body image in pubertal girls and boys from two communities. *Developmental Psychology, 26,* 313–321.

Richards, M., and Duckett, E. (1994). The relationship of maternal employment to early adolescent daily experience with and without parents. *Child Development, 65,* 225–236.

Richards, M., and Larson, R. (1993). Pubertal development and the daily subjective states of young adolescents. *Journal of Research on Adolescence, 3,* 145–169.

Richards, M., Suleiman, L., Sims, B., and Sedeño, A. (1994, February). *Experiences of ethnically diverse young adolescents growing up in contexts of poverty, violence, and racism.* Paper presented at the biennial meetings of the Society for Research on Adolescence, San Diego.

Richardson, J., Dwyer, K., McGuigan, K., Hansen, W., Dent, C., Johnson, C., Sussman, S., Brannon, B., and Flay, B. (1989). Substance use among eighth-grade students who take care of themselves after school. *Pediatrics, 84,* 556–566.

Richardson, J., Radziszewska, B., Dent, C., and Flay, B. (1993). Relationship between after-school care of adolescents and substance use, risk taking, depressed mood, and academic achievement. *Pediatrics, 92,* 32–38.

Rierdan, J., Koff, E., and Stubbs, M. (1989). Timing of menarche, preparation, and initial menstrual experience: Replication and further analyses in prospective study. *Journal of Youth and Adolescence, 18,* 413–426.

Rigsby, L., and McDill, E. L. (1975). Value orientations of high school students. Pp. 53–74 in H. R. Stub (Ed.), *The sociology of education: A sourcebook,* 3rd ed. Homewood, Ill.: Dorsey.

Riley, T., Adams, G., and Neilsen, E. (1984). Adolescent egocentrism: The association among imaginary audience behavior, cognitive development, and parental support and rejection. *Journal of Youth and Adolescence, 13,* 401–438.

Rivara, F., Sweeney, P., and Henderson, B. (1987). Risk of fatherhood among Black teenage males. *American Journal of Public Health, 77,* 203–205.

Robbins, C., Kaplan, H., and Martin, S. (1985, August). Antecedents of pregnancy among unmarried adolescents. *Journal of Marriage and the Family,* 567–583.

Roberts, D. (1993). Adolescents and the mass media: From "Leave It to Beaver" to "Beverly Hills 90210". *Teachers College Record, 94,* 629–644.

Robins, L. (1986). Changes in conduct disorder over time. Pp. 227–259 in D. Farran and J. McKinney (Eds.), *Risk in intellectual and psychosocial development.* New York: Academic Press.

Robinson, N. (in press). Evaluating the nature of perceived support and its relation to perceived self-worth in adolescents. *Journal of Research on Adolescence.*

Roderick, M. (1991, Fall). The path to dropping out: Evidence and intervention. *Research Bulletin of the Malcom Weiner Center for Social Policy,* pp. 1 ff.

Rodgers, J., and Rowe, D. (1988). Influence of siblings on adolescent sexual behavior. *Developmental Psychology, 24,* 722–728.

Rodgers, J., and Rowe, D. (1993). Social contagion and adolescent sexual behavior: A developmental EMOSA model. *Psychological Review, 100,* 479–510.

Rodgers, R. (1973). *Family interaction and transaction: A developmental approach.* Englewood Cliffs, N.J.: Prentice-Hall.

Rodman, H., Pratto, D., and Nelson, R. (1988). Toward a definition of self-care children: A commentary on Steinberg (1986). *Developmental Psychology, 24,* 292–294.

Roeser, R., Lord, S., and Eccles, J. (1994, February). *A portrait of academic alienation in adolescence: Motivation, mental health, and family experience.* Paper presented at the biennial meetings of the Society for Research on Adolescence, San Diego.

Rogers, A. (1993). Voice, play, and a practice of ordinary courage in girls' and women's lives. *Harvard Educational Review, 63,* 265–295.

Rogers, J., Boruch, R., Stoms, G., and DeMoya, D. (1991). Impact of the Minnesota parental notification law on abortion and birth. *American Journal of Public Health, 81,* 294–298.

Rohner, R., and Pettengill, S. (1985). Perceived parental acceptance-rejection and parental control among Korean adolescents. *Child Development, 56,* 524–528.

Roosa, M., and Christopher, F. S. (1990). Evaluation of an abstinence-only adolescent pregnancy prevention program: A replication. *Family Relations, 39,* 363–367.

Roscoe, B., Dian, M., and Brooks, R. (1987). Early, middle, and late adolescents' views on dating and factors influencing partners' selection. *Adolescence, 22,* 59–68.

Rose, R. (1988). Genetic and environmental variance in content dimensions of the MMPI. *Journal of Personality and Social Psychology, 55,* 302–311.

Rosen, B. (1956). The achievement syndrome: A psychocultural dimension of social stratification. *American Sociological Review, 21,* 203–211.

Rosen, B., and Aneshensel, C. (1975). The chameleon syndrome. *Journal of Marriage and the Family, 38,* 605–617.

Rosen, B., and D'Andrade, R. (1959). The psychosocial origins of achievement motivation. *Sociometry, 22,* 185–218.

Rosenbaum, E., and Kandel, D. (1990). Early onset of adolescent sexual behavior and drug involvement. *Journal of Marriage and the Family, 52,* 783–798.

Rosenbaum, J. (1976). *Making inequality: The hidden curriculum of high school tracking.* New York: Wiley.

Rosenbaum, J., Stern, D., Hamilton, M., Hamilton, S., Berryman, S., and Kazis, R. (1992). *Youth apprenticeship in America: Guidelines for building an effective system.* Washington, D.C.: William T. Grant Foundation Commission on Youth and America's Future.

Rosenberg, M. (1975). The dissonant context and the adolescent self-concept. In S. Dragastin and G. Elder, Jr. (Eds.), *Adolescence in the life cycle.* Washington, D.C.: Hemisphere.

Rosenberg, M. (1986). Self concept from middle childhood through adolescence. In J. Suls and A. Greenwald (Eds.), *Psychological perspectives on the self,* Vol. 3. Hillsdale, N.J.: Erlbaum.

Rosenberg, M., Schooler, C., and Schoenbach, C. (1989). Self-esteem and adolescent problems: Modeling reciprocal effects. *American Sociological Review, 54,* 1004–1018.

Rosenberg, M., and Simmons, R. (1972). *Black and white self-esteem: The urban school child.* Washington, D.C.: American Sociological Association.

Rosenthal, D. (1994, February). *Gendered constructions of adolescent sexuality.* Paper presented at the biennial meetings of the Society for Research on Adolescence, San Diego.

Rosenthal, D. A., and Feldman, S. S. (1990). The acculturation of Chinese immigrants: The effects on family functioning of length of residence in two cultural contexts. *Journal of Genetic Psychology, 151,* 493–514.

Rosenthal, D., and Feldman, S. (1991). The acculturation of

Chinese immigrants: Effects on family functioning of length of residence in two cultural contexts. Unpublished manuscript, Department of Psychology, University of Melbourne, Victoria, Australia.

Rosenthal, R., and Jacobson, E. (1968). *Pygmalion in the classroom.* New York: Holt, Rinehart and Winston.

Rotbart, D. (1981, March 2). Allowances stay flat, candy rises—And kids lose their innocence. *Wall Street Journal,* pp. 1 ff.

Rotenberg, K., and Whitney, P. (1992). Loneliness and disclosure processes in preadolescence. *Merrill-Palmer Quarterly, 38,* 401–416.

Rotheram-Borus, M. (1990). Adolescents' reference group choices, self-esteem, and adjustment. *Journal of Personality and Social Psychology, 59,* 1075–1081.

Rotheram-Borus, M., and Koopman, C. (1991). Sexual risk behaviors, AIDS knowledge, and beliefs about AIDS among runaways. *American Journal of Public Health, 81,* 206–208.

Rotheram-Borus, M., Koopman, C., and Ehrhardt, A. (1991). Homeless youths and HIV infection. *American Psychologist, 46,* 1188–1197.

Rotheram-Borus, M., and Phinney, J. (1990). Patterns of social expectations among black and Mexican-American children. *Child Development, 61,* 542–556.0

Rousseau, J. ([1762] 1911). *Emile* (B. Foxley, trans.). London: Dent.

Rowe, D., Rodgers, J., and Meseck-Bushey, S. (1992). Sibling delinquency and the family environment: Shared and unshared influences. *Child Development, 63,* 59–67.

Rowe, D., Rodgers, J., Meseck-Bushey, S., and St. John, C. (1989). Sexual behavior and nonsexual deviance: A sibling study of their relationship. *Developmental Psychology, 25,* 61–69.

Rowe, D., Vazsonyi, A., and Flannery, D. (1994). No more than skin deep: Ethnic and racial similarity in developmental processes. *Psychological Review, 101,* 396–413.

Rubenstein, J., Heeren, T., Housman, D., Rubin, C., and Stechler, G. (1989). Suicidal behavior in "normal" adolescents: Risk and protective factors. *American Journal of Orthopsychiatry, 59,* 59–71.

Rubin, K., LeMare, L., and Lollis, S. (1990). Social withdrawal in childhood: Developmental pathways to peer rejection. Pp. 217–249 in S. Asher and J. Coie (Eds.), *Peer rejection in childhood.* New York: Cambridge University Press.

Rubin, Z. (1980). *Children's friendships.* Cambridge, Mass.: Harvard University Press.

Ruble, D., and Brooks-Gunn, J. (1982). The experience of menarche. *Child Development, 53,* 1557–1566.

Ruggiero, M., Greenberger, E., and Steinberg, L. (1982). Occupational deviance among first-time workers. *Youth and Society, 13,* 423–448.

Ruggles, S. (1994). The origins of African-American family structure. *American Sociological Review, 59,* 136–151.

Rumberger, R. (1983). Dropping out of high school: The influence of race, sex, and family background. *American Educational Research Journal, 20,* 199–220.

Rumberger, R., Ghatak, R., Poulos, G., Ritter, P., and Dornbusch, S. (1990). Family influences on dropout behavior in one California high school. *Sociology of Education, 63,* 283–299.

Rutter, M. (1978). Protective factors in children's responses to stress and disadvantage. In M. Kent and J. Rolf (Eds.), *Primary prevention of psychopathology,* Vol. 3: *Promoting social competence and coping in children.* Hanover, N.J.: University Press of New England.

Rutter, M. (1980). *Changing youth in a changing society: Patterns of adolescent development and disorder.* Cambridge, Mass.: Harvard University Press.

Rutter, M. (1983). School effects on pupil progress: Research findings and policy implications. *Child Development, 54,* 1–29.

Rutter, M., and Garmezy, N. (1983). Developmental psychopathology. In E. M. Hetherington (Ed.), *Handbook of child psychology,* Vol. IV: *Socialization, personality, and social development.* New York: Wiley.

Rutter, M., Graham, P., Chadwick, F., and Yule, W. (1976). Adolescent turmoil: Fact or fiction? *Journal of Child Psychiatry and Psychology, 17,* 35–56.

Rutter, M., Maugham, B., Mortimore, P., and Ouston, J. (1979). *Fifteen thousand hours: Secondary schools and their effects on children.* London: Open Books.

Ryan, R., and Lynch, J. (1989). Emotional autonomy versus detachment: Revisiting the vicissitudes of adolescence and young adulthood. *Child Development, 60,* 340–356.

Safer, D. (1986). The stress of secondary school for vulnerable students. *Journal of Youth and Adolescence, 15,* 405–417.

Sagar, H., Schofield, J., and Snyder, H. (1983). Race and gender barriers: Preadolescent peer behavior in academic classrooms. *Child Development, 54,* 1032–1040.

St. John, N. (1975). *School desegregation outcomes for children.* New York: Wiley.

St. Lawrence, J. (1993). African-American adolescents' knowledge, health-related attitudes, sexual behavior, and contraceptive decisions: Implications for the prevention of adolescent HIV infection. *Journal of Consulting and Clinical Psychology, 61,* 104–112.

St. Louis, M., Conway, M., Hayman, C., Miller, C., Petersen, L., and Dondero, T. (1991). Human immunodeficiency virus infection in disadvantaged adolescents. *Journal of the American Medical Association, 266,* 2387–2391.

Salinger, J. D. ([1951] 1964). *The catcher in the rye.* New York: Bantam.

Sampson, R. (1992). Family management and child development: Insights from social disorganization theory. In J. McCord (Ed.), *Advances in criminological theory,* Vol. 3. New Brunswick, N.J.: Transaction Publishers.

Sampson, R., and Groves, W. (1989). Community structure and crime: Testing social-disorganization theory. *American Journal of Sociology, 94,* 774–802.

Sampson, R., and Lamb, J. (1994). Urban poverty and the family context of delinquency: A new look at structure and process in a classic study. *Child Development, 65,* 523–540.

Sandefur, G., McLanahan, S., and Wojtkiewicz, R. (1992). The effects of parental marital status during adolescence on high school graduation. *Social Forces, 71,* 103–121.

Sandven, K., and Resnick, M. (1990). Informal adoption among Black adolescent mothers. *American Journal of Orthopsychiatry, 60,* 210–224.

Sang, F., Schmitz, B., and Tasche, K. (1993). Developmental trends in television coviewing of parent-child dyads. *Journal of Youth and Adolescence, 22,* 531–542.

Savin-Williams, R. (1988). Theoretical perspectives accounting for adolescent homosexuality. *Journal of Adolescent Health Care, 9,* 95–104.

Savin-Williams, R. (1994). Verbal and physical abuse as stressors in the lives of lesbian, gay male, and bisexual youths: Associations with school problems, running away, substance abuse, prostitution, and suicide. *Journal of Consulting and Clinical psychology, 62,* 261–269.

Savin-Williams, R., and Berndt, T. (1990). Friendship and peer relations. Pp. 277–307 in S. Feldman and G. Elliott (Eds.), *At the threshold: The developing adolescent.* Cambridge, Mass.: Harvard University Press.

Savin-Williams, R., and Demo, D. (1983). Situational and transituational determinants of adolescent self-feelings. *Journal of Personality and Social Psychology, 44,* 824–833.

Savin-Williams, R., and Demo, D. (1984). Developmental change and stability in adolescent self-concept. *Developmental Psychology, 20,* 1100–1110.

Scales, P. (1991). *A portrait of young adolescents in the 1990s: Implications for promoting healthy growth and development.* Chapel Hill, N.C.: Center for Early Adolescence.

Scales, P., and McEwin, C. (1994). *Growing pains: The making of America's middle school teachers.* Columbus, Ohio: National Middle School Association.

Schellenbach, C., Whitman, T., and Borkowski, J. (1992). Toward an integrative model of adolescent parenting. *Human Development, 35,* 81–99.

Scheer, S., Unger, D., and Brown, M. (1994, February). *Adolescents becoming adults: Attributes for adulthood.* Paper presented at the biennial meetings of the Society for Research on Adolescence, San Diego.

Schiff, A., and Knopf, I. (1985). The effects of task demands on attention allocation in children of different ages. *Child Development, 56,* 621–630.

Schlegel, A., and Barry, H. (1991). *Adolescence: An anthropological inquiry.* New York: Free Press.

Schmitt-Rodermund, E., and Silbereisen, R. (1993, March). *Adolescents' age expectations during acculturation of German families from Eastern Europe.* Paper presented at the biennial meetings of the Society for Research in Child Development, New Orleans.

Schneider, B., Clegg, M., Byrne, B., Ledingham, J., and Crombie, G. (1989). Social relations of gifted children as a function of age and school program. *Journal of Educational Psychology, 81,* 48–56.

Schneider, B., and Shouse, R. (1991, April). *The work lives of eighth graders: Preliminary findings from the National Educational Longitudinal Study of 1988.* Paper presented at the biennial meetings of the Society for Research in Child Development, Seattle.

Schofield, J. (1981). Complementary and conflicting identities: Images and interaction in an interracial school. In S. Asher and J. Gottman (Eds.), *The development of children's friendships.* Cambridge, England: Cambridge University Press.

Schonert-Reichl, K., and Elliott, J. (1994, February). *Rural pathways: Stability and change during the transition to young adulthood.* Paper presented at the biennial meetings of the Society for Research on Adolescence, San Diego.

Scott, C., and Owen, R. (1990, March). *Similarities and differences in sexuality socialization of males in three cultural/ethnic groups.* Paper presented at the biennial meetings of the Society for Research on Adolescence, Atlanta.

Sebald, H. (1986). Adolescents' shifting orientation toward parents and peers: A curvilinear trend over recent decades. *Journal of Marriage and the Family, 48,* 5–13.

Seginer, R. (1983). Parents' educational expectations and children's academic achievements: A literature review. *Merrill-Palmer Quarterly, 29,* 1–23.

Seidman, E., Allen, L., Aber, J., Mitchell, C., and Feinman, J. (1994). The impact of school transitions in early adolescence on the self-system and perceived social context of poor urban youth. *Child Development, 65,* 507–522.

Seitz, V., and Apfel, N. (1993). Adolescent mothers and repeated childbearing: Effects of a school-based intervention program. *American Journal of Orthopsychiatry, 63,* 572–581.

Seitz, V., and Apfel, N. (1994). Effects of a school for pregnant students on the incidence of low-birthweight deliveries. *Child Development, 65,* 666–676.

Selman, R. (1980). *The growth of interpersonal understanding: Developmental and clinical analyses.* New York: Academic Press.

Sessa, F., and Steinberg, L. (1991). Family structure and the development of autonomy in adolescence. *Journal of Early Adolescence, 11,* 38–55.

Sewell, W., and Hauser, R. (1972). Causes and consequences of higher education: Models of the status attainment process. *American Journal of Agricultural Economics, 54,* 851–861.

Sharabany, R., Gershoni, R., and Hofman, J. (1981). Girlfriend, boyfriend: Age and sex differences in intimate friendship. *Developmental Psychology, 17,* 800–808.

Sharabany, R., and Wiseman, H. (1993). Close relationships in adolescence: The case of the kibbutz. *Journal of Youth and Adolescence, 22,* 671–695.

Shaver, P., Furman, W., and Buhrmester, D. (1985). Transition to college: Network changes, social skills, and loneliness. Pp. 193–219 in S. Duck and D. Perlman (Eds.), *Understanding personal relationships: An interdisciplinary approach.* London: Sage.

Shavit, Y., and Featherman, D. (1988). School, tracking, and teenage intelligence. *Sociology of Education, 61,* 42–51.

Shaw, M., and White, D. (1965). The relationship between child-parent identification and academic underachievement. *Journal of Clinical Psychology, 21,* 10–13.

Shayne, V., and Kaplan, B. (1988). AIDS education for adolescents. *Youth and Society, 20,* 180–208.

Shedler, J., and Block, J. (1990). Adolescent drug use and psychological health: A longitudinal inquiry. *American Psychologist, 45,* 612–630.

Shrum, W., Cheek, N., Jr., and Hunter, S. MacD. (1988). Friendship in school: Gender and racial homophily. *Sociology of Education, 61,* 227–239.

Siegler, R. (1988). Individual differences in strategy choices: Good students, not-so-good students, and perfectionists. *Child Development, 59,* 833–851.

Siegler, R., Liebert, D., and Liebert, R. (1973). Inhelder and Piaget's pendulum problem: Teaching adolescents to act as scientists. *Developmental Psychology, 9,* 97–101.

Signorielli, N. (1993). Television and adolescents' perceptions about work. *Youth and Society, 24,* 314–341.

Silbereisen, R., Kracke, B., and Crockett, L. (1990, March). *Timing of maturation and adolescent substance use.* Paper presented at the biennial meetings of the Society for Research on Adolescence, Atlanta.

Silbereisen, R., Petersen, A., Albrecht, H., and Kracke, B. (1989). Maturational timing and the development of problem behavior: Longitudinal studies in adolescence. *Journal of Early Adolescence.*

Silbereisen, R., Robins, L., and Rutter, M. (in press). Secular trends in substance use: Concepts and data on the impact of social change on alcohol and drug abuse. In M. Rutter and D. Smith (Eds.), *Psychosocial disorders in young people: Time trends and their origins.* New York: Wiley.

Silbereisen, R., and Schmitt-Rodermund, E. (1994). German immigrants in Germany: Adaptation of adolescents' timetables for autonomy. Pp. 105–125 in M. Hofer, P. Noack, and J. Youniss (Eds.), *Psychological responses to social change: Human development in changing environments.* Berlin: De Gruyter.

Silbereisen, R., Schwarz, B., Nowak, M., Kracke, B., and von Eye, A. (1993, March). *Psychosocial adversities and timing of adolescent transitions: A comparison of the former East and West Germanies.* Paper presented at the biennial meetings of the Society for Research in Child Development, New Orleans.

Silverberg, S. (1986). Psychological well-being of parents with early adolescent children. Unpublished doctoral dissertation, Department of Child and Family Studies, University of Wisconsin-Madison.

Silverberg, S., and Steinberg, L. (1987). Adolescent autonomy, parent-adolescent conflict, and parental well-being. *Journal of Youth and Adolescence, 16,* 293–312.

Silverberg, S., and Steinberg, L. (1990). Psychological well-being of parents at midlife: The impact of early adolescent children. *Developmental Psychology, 26,* 658–666.

Silverberg, S., Tennenbaum, D., and Jacob, T. (1992). Adolescence and family interaction. Pp. 347–370 in V. Van Hasselt and M. Hersen (Eds.), *Handbook of social development: A lifespan perspective.* New York: Plenum.

Silverstein, B., Perlick, D., Clauson, J., and McKoy, E. (1993). Depression combined with somatic symptomatology among adolescent females who report concerns regarding maternal achievement. *Sex Roles, 28,* 637–654.

Simmons, R., and Blyth, D. (1987). *Moving into adolescence.* New York: Aldine de Gruyter.

Simmons, R., Blyth, D., and McKinney, K. (1983). The social and psychological effects of puberty on white females. In J. Brooks-Gunn and A. Petersen (Eds.), *Girls at puberty.* New York: Plenum.

Simmons, R., Blyth, D., Van Cleave, E., and Bush, D. (1979). Entry into early adolescence: The impact of school structure, puberty, and early dating on self-esteem. *American Sociological Review, 44,* 948–967.

Simmons, R., Brown, L., Bush, D., and Blyth, D. (1978). Self-esteem and achievement of black and white adolescents. *Social Problems, 26,* 86–96.

Simmons, R., Burgeson, R., Carlton-Ford, S., and Blyth, D. (1987). The impact of cumulative change in early adolescence. *Child Development, 58,* 1220–1234.

Simmons, R., and Rosenberg, F. (1975). Sex, sex roles, and self-image. *Journal of Youth and Adolescence, 4,* 229–258.

Simmons, R., Rosenberg, F., and Rosenberg, M. (1973). Disturbance in the self-image at adolescence. *American Sociological Review, 38,* 553–568.

Simon, W., and Gagnon, J. (1969). On psychosexual development. In D. Goslin (Ed.), *Handbook of socialization theory and research.* Chicago: Rand McNally.

Simons, R., Whitbeck, L., Conger, R., and Chyi-In, W. (1991). Intergenerational transmission of harsh parenting. *Developmental Psychology, 27,* 159–171.

Simpson, R. (1962). Parental influence, anticipatory socialization, and social mobility. *American Sociological Review, 27,* 517–522.

Skinner, B. F. (1953). *Science and human behavior.* New York: Free Press.

Slap, G., and Jablow, M. (1994). *Teenage health care.* New York: Pocket Books.

Small, S. (1988). Parental self-esteem and its relationship to childrearing practices, parent-adolescent interaction, and adolescent behavior. *Journal of Marriage and the Family, 50,* 1063–1072.

Small, S., Eastman, G., and Cornelius, S. (1988). Adolescent autonomy and parental stress. *Journal of Youth and Adolescence, 17,* 377–391.

Small, S., and Luster, T. (1994). Adolescent sexual activity: An ecological, risk-factor approach, *Journal of Marriage and the Family, 56,* 181–192.

Small, S., Silverberg, S., and Kerns, D. (1993). Adolescents' perceptions of the costs and benefits of engaging in health-compromising behaviors. *Journal of Youth and Adolescence, 22,* 73–87.

Smetana, J. (1988a). Concepts of self and social convention: Adolescents' and parents' reasoning about hypothetical and actual family conflicts. Pp. 79–122 in M. Gunnar and W. A. Collins (Eds.), *Minnesota Symposium on Child Psychology,* Vol 21. Hillsdale, N.J.: Erlbaum.

Smetana, J. (1988b). Adolescents' and parents' conceptions of parental authority. *Child Development, 59,* 321–335.

Smetana, J. (1989). Adolescents' and parents' reasoning about actual family conflict. *Child Development, 59,* 1052–1067.

Smetana, J., and Asquith, P. (1994). Adolescents' and parents' conceptions of parental authority and personal autonomy. *Child Development, 65,* 1147–1162.

Smetana, J., Yau, J., and Hanson, S. (1991). Conflict resolution in families with adolescents. *Journal of Research on Adolescence, 1,* 189–206.

Smetana, J., Yau, J., Restrepo, A., and Braeges, J. (1991). Adolescent-parent conflict in married and divorced families. *Developmental Psychology, 27,* 1000–1010.

Smith, E., and Udry, J. (1985). Coital and non-coital sexual behaviors of white and black adolescents. *American Journal of Public Health, 75,* 1200–1203.

Smith, E., Udry, J., and Morris, N. (1985). Pubertal development and friends: A biosocial explanation of adolescent sexual behavior. *Journal of Health and Social Behavior, 26,* 183–192.

Smith, E., and Zabin, L. (1993). Marital and birth expectations of urban adolescents. *Youth and Society, 25,* 62–74.

Smith, E., Walker, K., Fields, L., and Seay, R. (1994, February). *The salience of ethnic identity and its relationship to personal identity and efficacy among African American youth.* Paper presented at the biennial meetings of the Society for Research on Adolescence, San Diego.

Smith, K., McGraw, S., Crawford, S., Costa, L., and McKinlay, J. (1993). HIV risk among Latino adolescents in two New England cities. *American Journal of Public Health, 83,* 1395–1399.

Smith, T. (1992). Gender differences in the scientific achievement of adolescents: Effects of age and parental separation. *Social Forces, 71,* 469–484.

Smith, T. (1993, March). *Federal employment training programs for youth: Failings and opportunities.* Paper presented at the biennial meetings of the Society for Research in Child Development, New Orleans.

Smolak, L., Levine, M., and Gralen, S. (1993). The impact of puberty and dating on eating problems among middle school girls. *Journal of Youth and Adolescence, 22,* 355–368.

Smoll, F., and Schutz, R. (1990). Quantifying gender differences in physical performance: A developmental perspective. *Developmental Psychology, 26,* 360–369.

Smollar, J., and Youniss, J. (1985). *Transformation in adolescents' perceptions of parents.* Paper presented at the biennial meetings of the Society for Research in Child Development, Baltimore.

Sobesky, W. (1983). The effects of situational factors on moral judgments. *Child Development, 54,* 575–584.

Sommer, K., Whitman, T., Borkowski, J., Schellenbach, C., Maxwell, S., and Keogh, D. (1993). Cognitive readiness and adolescent parenting. *Developmental Psychology, 29,* 389–398.

Sommers-Flanagan, R., Sommers-Flanagan, J., and Davis, B. (1993). What's happening on Music Television? A gender role content analysis. *Sex Roles, 28,* 745–754.

Sorensen, R. (1973). *Adolescent sexuality in contemporary society.* New York: World Book.

Sorensen, S., Richardson, B., and Peterson, J. (1993). Race/ethnicity patterns in the homicide of children in Los Angeles, 1980 through 1989. *American Journal of Public Health, 83,* 725–727.

Spence, J., and Helmreich, R. (1978). *Masculinity and femininity: Their psychological dimensions, correlates, and antecedents.* Austin: University of Texas Press.

Spencer, M., and Dornbusch, S. (1990). Challenges in studying minority youth. Pp. 123–146 in S. Feldman and G. Elliott (Eds.), *At the threshold: The developing adolescent.* Cambridge, Mass.: Harvard University Press.

Spencer, M., and Markstrom-Adams, C. (1990). Identity processes among racial and ethnic minority children in America. *Child Development, 61,* 290–310.

Spieker, S., and Bensley, L. (1994). Roles of living arrangements and grandmother social support in adolescent mothering and infant attachment. *Developmental Psychology, 30,* 102–111.

Spielberger, C. (1966). The effects of anxiety on complex learning and academic achievement. In C. Spielberger (Ed.), *Anxiety and behavior.* New York: Academic Press.

Sroufe, L. A. (1979). The coherence of individual development. *American Psychologist, 34,* 834–841.

Stanger, C., Achenbach, T., and McConaughy, S. (1993). Three-year course of behavioral/emotional problems in a national sample of 4- to 16-year-olds, 3: Predictors of signs of disturbance. *Journal of Consulting and Clinical Psychology, 61,* 839–848.

Stanton, B., Romer, D., Ricardo, I., Black, M., Feigelman, S., and Galbraith, J. (1993). Early initiation of sex and its lack of association with risk behaviors among African-Americans. *Pediatrics, 92,* 13–19.

Stattin, H., and Magnusson, D. (1989). The role of early aggressive behavior in the frequency, seriousness, and types of later crime. *Journal of Consulting and Clinical Psychology, 57,* 710–718.

Stattin, H., and Magnusson, D. (1994a, February). *Behavioral and interpersonal antecedents behind the age at leaving home, and the future consequences for parent-child relations.* Paper presented at the biennial meetings of the Society for Research on Adolescence, San Diego.

Stattin, H., and Magnusson, D. (1994b, February). *Onset of official delinquency: Its co-occurrence in time with educational, behavioral, and interpersonal problems.* Paper presented at the biennial meetings of the Society for Research on Adolescence, San Diego.

Steffensmeier, D., and Streifel, C. (1991). Age, gender, and crime across three historical periods: 1935, 1960, and 1985. *Social Forces, 69,* 869–894.

Stein, J., Newcomb, M., and Bentler, P. (1992). The effect of agency and communion on self-esteem: Gender differences in longitudinal data. *Sex Roles, 26,* 465–484.

Steinberg, L. (1981). Transformations in family relations at puberty. *Developmental Psychology, 17,* 833–840.

Steinberg, L. (1985). Early temperamental antecedents of Type A behavior. *Developmental Psychology, 22,* 1171–1180.

Steinberg, L. (1986). Latchkey children and susceptibility to peer pressure: An ecological analysis. *Developmental Psychology, 22,* 433–439.

Steinberg, L. (1987a). The impact of puberty on family relations: Effects of pubertal status and pubertal timing. *Developmental Psychology, 23,* 451–460.

Steinberg, L. (1987b, September). Bound to bicker: Pubescent primates leave home for good reasons. Our teens stay with us and squabble. *Psychology Today,* pp. 36–39.

Steinberg, L. (1987c). Single parents, stepparents, and the susceptibility of adolescents to antisocial peer pressure. *Child Development, 58,* 269–275.

Steinberg, L. (1988). Reciprocal relation between parent-child distance and pubertal maturation. *Developmental Psychology, 24,* 122–128.

Steinberg, L. (1989). Pubertal maturation and parent-adolescent distance: An evolutionary perspective. Pp. 71–97 in G. Adams, R. Montemayor, and T. Gullotta (Eds.), *Advances in adolescent development,* Vol. 1. Beverly Hills, Calif.: Sage.

Steinberg, L. (1990). Autonomy, conflict, and harmony in the family relationship. Pp. 255–276 in S. Feldman and G. Elliott (Eds.), *At the threshold: The developing adolescent.* Cambridge, Mass.: Harvard University Press.

Steinberg, L., Blinde, P., and Chan, K. (1984). Dropping out among language-minority youth. *Review of Educational Research, 54,* 113–132.

Steinberg, L., and Cauffman, E. (1995). The impact of employment on adolescent development. In R. Vasta (Ed.), *Annals of Child Development,* Vol. 11. London: Jessica Kingsley Publishers.

Steinberg, L., Darling, N., Fletcher, A., Brown, B., and Dornbusch, S. (in press). Authoritative parenting and adolescent adjustment: An ecological journey. In P. Moen, G. Elder, Jr., and K. Luscher (Eds.), *Linking lives and contexts: Perspectives on the ecology of human development.* Washington, D.C.: American Psychological Association.

Steinberg, L., and Dornbusch, S. (1991). Negative correlates of part-time work in adolescence: Replication and elaboration. *Developmental Psychology, 17,* 304–313.

Steinberg, L., Dornbusch, S., and Brown, B. (1992). Ethnic differences in adolescent achievement: An ecological perspective. *American Psychologist, 47,* 723–729.

Steinberg, L., Elmen, J., and Mounts, N. (1989). Authoritative parenting, psychosocial maturity, and academic success among adolescence. *Child Development, 60,* 1424–1436.

Steinberg, L., Fegley, S., and Dornbusch, S. (1993). Negative impact of part-time work on adolescent adjustment: Evidence from a longitudinal study. *Developmental Psychology, 29,* 171–180.

Steinberg, L., Fletcher, A., and Darling, N. (1994). Parental monitoring and peer influences on adolescent substance use. *Pediatrics, 93,* 1060–1064.

Steinberg, L., Greenberger, E., Garduque, L., Ruggiero, M., and Vaux, A. (1982). Effects of working on adolescent development. *Developmental Psychology, 18,* 385–395.

Steinberg, L., Lamborn, S., Darling, N., Mounts, N., and Dornbusch, S. (1994). Over-time changes in adjustment and competence among adolescents from authoritative, authoritarian, indulgent, and neglectful families. *Child Development, 65,* 754–770.

Steinberg, L., Lamborn, S., Dornbusch, S., and Darling, N. (1992). Impact of parenting practices on adolescent achievement: Authoritative parenting, school involvement, and encouragement to succeed. *Child Development, 63,* 1266–1281.

Steinberg, L., and Levine, A. (1991). *You and your adolescent: A parent's guide for ages 10 to 20.* New York: Harper Perennial.

Steinberg, L., Mounts, N., Lamborn, S., and Dornbusch, S. (1991). Authoritative parenting and adolescent adjustment across various ecological niches. *Journal of Research on Adolescence, 1,* 19–36.

Steinberg, L., and Silverberg, S. (1986). The vicissitudes of autonomy in early adolescence. *Child Development, 57,* 841–851.

Steinberg, L., and Silverberg, S. (1987). Influences on marital satisfaction during the middle stages of the family life cycle. *Journal of Marriage and the Family, 49,* 751–760.

Steinberg, L., and Steinberg, W. (1994). *Crossing paths: How your child's adolescence triggers your own crisis.* New York: Simon & Schuster.

Stern, D., Finkelstein, N., Stone, J., Latting, J., and Dornsife, C. (1994). *Research on school-to-work transition programs in the United States.* Berkeley, Calif.: National Center for Research in Vocational Education.

Sternberg, R. (1977). *Intelligence, information processing, and analogical reasoning: The componential analysis of human abilities.* Hillsdale, N.J.: Erlbaum.

Sternberg, R. (1983). Components of human intelligence. *Cognition, 15,* 1–48.

Sternberg, R. (1988). *The triarchic mind.* New York: Viking Penguin.

Sternberg, R., and Nigro, G. (1980). Developmental patterns in the solution of verbal analogies. *Child Development, 51,* 27–38.

Sternberg, R., and Rifkin, B. (1979). The development of analogical reasoning processes. *Journal of Experimental Child Psychology, 27,* 195–232.

Stevens, J. (1988). Social support, locus of control, and parenting in three low-income groups of mothers: Black teenagers, Black adults, and White adults. *Child Development, 59,* 635–642.

Stevenson, D., and Baker, D. (1987). The family-school relation and the child's school performance. *Child Development, 58,* 1348–1357.

Stevenson, H., and Stigler, J. (1992). *The learning gap: Why our schools are failing and what we can learn from Japanese and Chinese education.* New York: Simon & Schuster.

Stier, D., Leventhal, J., Berg, A., Johnson, L., and Mezger, J. (1993). Are children born to young mothers at increased risk of maltreatment? *Pediatrics, 91,* 642–648.

Stout, J., and Rivara, F. (1989). Schools and sex education: Does it work? *Pediatrics, 83,* 375–379.

Studer, M., and Thornton, A. (1987). Adolescent religiosity and contraceptive usage. *Journal of Marriage and the Family, 49,* 117–128.

Sue, S., and Okazaki, S. (1990). Asian-American educational achievements: A phenomenon in search of an explanation. *American Psychologist, 45,* 913–920.

Sullivan, H. S. (1953a). *The interpersonal theory of psychiatry.* New York: Norton.

Sullivan, H. S. (1953b). *Conceptions of modern psychiatry.* New York: Norton.

Sullivan, K., and Sullivan, A. (1980). Adolescent-parent separation. *Developmental Psychology, 16,* 93–99.

Sum, A., and Fogg, W. (1991). The adolescent poor and the transition to early adulthood. Pp. 37–110 in P. Edelman and J. Ladner, (Eds.), *Adolescence and poverty: Challenge for the 90s.* Washington, D.C.: Center for National Policy Press.

Summerville, M., and Kaslow, N. (1993, March). *Racial differences in psychological symptoms, cognitive style, and family functioning in suicidal adolescents.* Paper presented at the biennial meetings of the Society for Research in Child Development, New Orleans.

Super, D. (1967). *The psychology of careers.* New York: Harper & Row.

Surbey, M. (1987). Anorexia nervosa, amenorrhea, and adaptation. *Ethology and Sociobiology, 8,* 475–515.

Surbey, M. (1990). Family composition, stress, and human menarche. In F. Bercovitch and T. Zeigler (Eds.), *The socioendocrinology of primate reproduction.* New York: Alan R. Liss.

Susman, E., Dorn, L., and Chrousos, G. (1991). Negative affect and hormone levels in young adolescents: Concurrent and predictive perspectives. *Journal of Youth and Adolescence, 20,* 167–190.

Susman, E., Inhoff-Germain, G., Nottlemann, E., Loriaux, D., Cutler, G., Jr., and Chrousos, G. (1987). Hormones, emotional dispositions, and aggressive attributes in young adolescents. *Child Development, 58,* 1114–1134.

Susman, E., Koch, P., Maney, D., and Finkelstein, J. (1993). Health promotion in adolescence: Developmental and theoretical considerations. Pp. 247–260 in R. Lerner (Ed.), *Early adolescence: Perspectives on research, policy, and intervention.* Hillsdale, N.J.: Erlbaum.

Szeszulski, P., Martinez, A., and Reyes, B. (1994, February). *Patterns and predictors of self-satisfaction among culturally diverse high school students.* Paper presented at the biennial meetings of the Society for Research on Adolescence, San Diego.

Tanner, D. (1972). *Secondary education.* New York: Macmillan.

Tanner, J. (1972). Sequence, tempo, and individual variation in growth and development of boys and girls aged twelve to sixteen. In J. Kagan and R. Coles (Eds.), *Twelve to sixteen: Early adolescence.* New York: Norton.

Taylor, R., Casten, R., and Flickinger, S. (1993). The influence of kinship social support on the parenting experiences and psychosocial adjustment of African-American adolescents. *Developmental Psychology, 29,* 382–388.

Taylor, R., Casten, R., Flickinger, S., Roberts, D., and Fulmore, C. (1994). Explaining the school performance of African-American adolescents. *Journal of Research on Adolescence, 4,* 21–44.

Telljohann, S., and Price, J. (1993). A qualitative examination of adolescent homosexuals' life experiences: Ramifications for secondary school personnel. *Journal of Homosexuality, 26,* 41–56.

Teti, D., and Lamb, M. (1989). Socioeconomic and marital outcomes of adolescent marriage, adolescent childbirth, and their co-occurrence. *Journal of Marriage and the Family, 51,* 203–212.

Teti, D., Lamb, M., and Elster, A. (1987). Long-range socioeconomic and marital consequences of adolescent marriage in three cohorts of adult males. *Journal of Marriage and the Family, 49,* 499–506.

Thornton, A., and Camburn, D. (1989). Religious participation and adolescent sexual behavior and attitudes. *Journal of Marriage and the Family, 51,* 641–653.

Thornton, M., Chatters, L., Taylor, R., and Allen, W. (1990). Sociodemographic and environmental correlates of racial socialization by Black parents. *Child Development, 61,* 401–409.

Timmer, S., Eccles, J., and O'Brien, I. (1985). How children use time. In F. Juster and F. Stafford (Eds.), *Time, goods, and well-being.* Ann Arbor: University of Michigan, Institute for Social Research.

Tobin-Richards, M. (1985). *Sex differences and similarities in heterosexual activity in early adolescence.* Paper presented at the biennial meetings of the Society for Research in Child Development, Toronto.

Tolman, D. (1993, March). *"When my body says yes": Adolescent girls' experiences of sexual desire.* Paper presented at the biennial meetings of the Society for Research in Child Development, New Orleans.

Tolson, J., Halliday-Scher, and Mack, V. (1994, February). *Similarity and friendship quality in African-American adolescents.* Paper presented at the biennial meetings of the Society for Research on Adolescence, San Diego.

Torney-Purta, J. (1990). Youth in relation to social institutions. Pp. 457–478 in S. Feldman and G. Elliott (Eds.), *At the threshold: The developing adolescent.* Cambridge, Mass.: Harvard University Press.

Torney-Purta, J. (1992). Cognitive representations of the political system in adolescents: The continuum from pre-novice to expert. Pp. 11–25 in H. Haste and J. Torney-Purta (Eds.), *The development of political understanding.* San Francisco: Jossey-Bass.

Treaster, J. (1994, February 1). Survey finds marijuana use is up in high schools. *New York Times,* pp. A1 ff.

Treboux, D., and Busch-Rossnagel, N. (1990). Social network influences on adolescent sexual attitudes and behaviors. *Journal of Adolescent Research, 5,* 175–189.

Trussell, J. (1989). Teenage pregnancy in the United States. *Family Planning Perspectives, 21,* 262–269.

Tschann, J., Adler, N., Irwin, C., Jr., Millstein, S., Turner, R., and Kegeles, S. (1991, April). *Pubertal timing and negative affect in the initiation of health risk behaviors: A longitudinal study.* Paper presented at the biennial meetings of the Society for Research in Child Development, Seattle.

Turiel, E. (1978). The development of concepts of social structure: Social convention. In J. Glick and K. A. Clarke-Stewart (Eds.), *The development of social understanding.* New York: Gardner.

U.S. Bureau of the Census. (1993). *Statistical Abstract of the United States.* Washington, D.C.: U.S. Bureau of the Census.

U.S. Bureau of the Census. (1994). *Who's minding the kids.* Washington, D.C.: U.S. Bureau of the Census.

U.S. Department of Commerce, Bureau of the Census. (1940). *Characteristics of the population.* Washington, D.C.: U.S. Government Printing Office.

Udry, J. (1987). Hormonal and social determinants of adolescent sexual initiation. In J. Bancroft (Ed.), *Adolescence and puberty.* New York: Oxford University Press.

Udry, J. R., and Billy, J. (1987). Initiation of coitus in early adolescence. *American Sociological Review, 52,* 841–855.

Udry, J., Billy, J., Morris, N., Gruff, T., and Raj, M. (1985). Serum androgenic hormones motivate sexual behavior in boys. *Fertility and Sterility, 43,* 90–94.

Udry, J., Halpern, C., and Campbell, B. (1991, April). *Hormones, pubertal development, and sexual behavior in adolescent females.* Paper presented at the biennial meetings of the Society for Research in Child Development, Seattle.

Udry, J., Talbert, L., and Morris, N. (1986). Biosocial foundations for adolescent female sexuality. *Demography, 23,* 217–230.

Uhlenberg, P., and Eggebeen, D. (1986). The declining well-being of American adolescents. *Public Interest, 82,* 25–38.

United Nations Population Division, (1976). *Population by sex and age for regions and countries, 1950–2000, as assessed in 1973: Median variant.* New York: United Nations Department of Social and Economic Affairs.

Upchurch, D., and McCarthy, J. (1990). The timing of a first birth and high school completion. *American Sociological Review, 55,* 224–234.

Vandell, D., and Corasaniti, M. (1988). The relation between third graders' after-school care and social, academic, and emotional functioning. *Child Development, 59,* 868–875.

Vandell, D., and Ramanan, J. (1991). Children of the National Longitudinal Survey of Youth: Choices in after-school care and child development. *Developmental Psychology, 27,* 637–643.

Vanfossen, B., Jones, J., and Spade, J. (1987). Curriculum tracking and status maintenance. *Sociology of Education, 60,* 104–122.

Varenne, H. (1982). Jocks and freaks: The symbolic structure of the expression of social interaction among American senior high school students. Pp. 213–235 in G. Spindler (Ed.), *Doing the ethnography of schooling.* New York: Holt, Rinehart and Winston.

Vega, W., Gil, A., and Zimmerman, R. (1993). Patterns of drug use among Cuban-American, African-American, and White non-Hispanic boys. *American Journal of Public Health, 83,* 257–259.

Vega, W., Zimmerman, R., Warheit, G., Apospori, E., and Gil, A. (1993). Risk factors for early adolescent drug use in four ethnic and racial groups. *American Journal of Public Health, 83,* 185–189.

Velez, W. (1989). High school attrition among Hispanic and non-Hispanic White youths. *Sociology of Education, 62,* 119–133.

Vener, A., and Stewart, C. (1974). Adolescent sexual behavior in Middle America revisited: 1970–1973. *Journal of Marriage and the Family, 36,* 728–735.

Ventura, S. (1984). Trends in teenage child bearing, United States, 1970–81. *Vital and Health Statistics Series,* Vol. 21. Washington, D.C.: U.S. Government Printing Office.

Vera Institute of Justice. (1990). *The male role in teenage pregnancy and parenting.* New York: Vera Institute of Justice.

Vernberg, E., Ewell, K., Beery, S., and Abwender, D. (1994). Sophistication of adolescents' interpersonal negotiation strategies and friendship formation after relocation: A naturally occurring experiment. *Journal of Research on Adolescence, 4,* 5–19.

Vigersky, R. (Ed.). (1977). *Anorexia nervosa.* New York: Raven Press.

Vrazzo, F. (1990, November 8). More teen girls sexually active, study finds. *Philadelphia Inquirer,* pp. 1 ff.

Vuchinich, S., Bank, L., and Patterson, G. (1992). Parenting, peers, and the stability of antisocial behavior in preadolescent boys. *Developmental Psychology, 28,* 510–521.

Vuchinich, S., Hetherington, E., Vuchinich, R., and Clingempeel, W. (1991). Parent-child interaction and gender differences in early adolescents' adaptation to stepfamilies. *Developmental Psychology, 27,* 618–626.

Vuchinich, S., Vuchinich, R., and Wood, B. (1993). The interparental relationship and family problem solving with preadolescent males. *Child Development, 64,* 1389–1400.

Waber, D. (1977). Sex differences in mental abilities, hemispheric lateralization, and rate of physical growth at adolescence. *Developmental Psychology, 13,* 29–38.

Wagner, B., and Cohen, P. (in press). Adolescent sibling differences in suicidal symptoms: The role of parent-child relationships. *Journal of Abnormal Psychology.*

Wainer, H., and Steinberg, L. (1992). Sex differences in performance on the mathematics section of the Scholastic Aptitude Test: A bidirectional validity study. *Harvard Educational Review, 62,* 323–336.

Waite, L., Goldscheider, F., and Witsberger, C. (1986). Nonfamily living and the erosion of traditional family orientations among young adults. *American Sociological Review, 51,* 541–554.

Walker, L., de Vries, B., and Trevethan, S. (1987). Moral stages and moral orientations in real-life and hypothetical dilemmas. *Child Development, 58,* 842–858.

Walker, L., and Taylor, J. (1991a). Stage transitions in moral reasoning: A longitudinal study of developmental processes. *Developmental Psychology, 27,* 330–337.

Walker, L., and Taylor, J. (1991b). Family interaction and the development of moral reasoning. *Child Development, 62,* 264–283.

Wallace-Broscious, Serafica, F., and Osipow, S. (1994). Adolescent career development: Relationships to self-concept and identity status. *Journal of Research on Adolescence, 4,* 127–149.

Wallerstein, J. S., and Blakeslee, S. (1989). *Second chances.* New York: Ticknor & Fields.

Wallerstein, J., and Kelley, J. (1974). The effects of parental divorce: The adolescent experience. In E. Anthony and A. Koupernik (Eds.), *The child in his family: Children as a psychiatric risk,* Vol. 3. New York: Wiley.

Walter, H., Vaughan, R., Gladis, M., Ragin, D., Kasen, S., and Cohall, A. (1992). Factors associated with AIDS risk behaviors among high school students in an AIDS epicenter. *American Journal of Public Health, 82,* 528–532.

Walters, H., and Kranzler, G. (1970). Early identification of the school dropout. *School Counselor, 18,* 97–104.

Ward, M. (in press). Talking about sex: Common themes about sexuality in the prime-time television programs children and adolescents view most. *Journal of Youth and Adolescence.*

Ward, S., and Overton, W. (1990). Semantic familiarity, relevance, and the development of deductive reasoning. *Developmental Psychology, 26,* 488–493.

Warneke, C., and Cooper, S. (1994). Child and adolescent drownings in Harris County, Texas, 1983 through 1990. *American Journal of Public Health, 84,* 593–598.

Washington Post. (1994, April 24). Specialists, youngsters paint disturbing portrait of teen sex in the '90s, pp. A1 ff.

Wasserman, G., Rauh, V., Brunelli, S., Garcia-Castro, M., and Necos, B. (1990). Psychosocial attributes and life experiences of disadvantaged minority mothers: Age and ethnic variations. *Child Development, 61,* 566–580.

Waterman, A. (1982). Identity development from adolescence to adulthood: An extension of theory and a review of research. *Developmental Psychology, 18,* 341–358.

Waterman, A., Geary, P., and Waterman, A. (1974). A longitudinal study of changes in ego identity status from the freshman to the senior year at college. *Developmental Psychology, 10,* 387–392.

Waterman, A., and Goldman, J. (1976). A longitudinal study of ego identity development at a liberal arts college. *Journal of Youth and Adolescence, 5,* 361–369.

Waterman, A., and Waterman, M. (1971). A longitudinal study of changes in ego identity status during the freshman year at college. *Developmental Psychology, 5,* 167–173.

Watson, D., and Kendall, P. (1989). Understanding anxiety and depression: Their relation to negative and positive affective states. Pp. 3–26 in P. Kendall (Ed.), *Anxiety and depression.* New York: Academic Press.

Webster, D., Gainer, P., and Champion, H. (1993). Weapon carrying among inner-city junior high school students: Defensive behavior vs. aggressive delinquency. *American Journal of Public Health, 83,* 1604–1608.

Weideger, P. (1976). *Menstruation and menopause.* New York: Knopf.

Weiner, I. (1980). Psychopathology in adolescence. In J. Adelson (Ed.), *Handbook of adolescent psychology.* New York: Wiley.

Weiss, R. (1974). The provisions of social relationships. In Z. Rubin (Ed.), *Doing unto others.* Englewood Cliffs, N.J.: Prentice-Hall.

Weiss, R. (1979). Growing up a little faster: The experience of growing up in a single parent household. *Journal of Social Issues, 35,* 97–111.

Weissberg, R., Caplan, M., and Harwood, R. (1991). Promoting competent young people in competence-enhancing environments: A systems-based perspective on primary prevention. *Journal of Consulting and Clinical Psychology, 59,* 830–841.

Weissberg, R., Caplan, M., and Sivo, P. (1989). A new conceptual framework for establishing school-based social competence promotion programs. In L. Bond, B. Compas, and C. Swift (Eds.), *Prevention in the schools.* Menlo Park, Calif.: Sage.

Weisz, J., Suwanlert, S., Chaiyasit, W., Weiss, B., Achenbach, T., and Eastman, K. (1993). Behavioral and emotional problems among Thai and American adolescents: Parent reports for ages 12–16. *Journal of Abnormal Psychology, 102,* 395–403.

Wentzel, K. (1989). Adolescent classroom goals, standards for performance, and academic achievement: An interactionist perspective. *Journal of Educational Psychology, 81,* 131–142.

Wentzel, K., and Erdley, C. (1993). Strategies for making friends: Relations to social behavior and peer acceptance in early adolescence. *Developmental Psychology, 29,* 819–826.

Werner, E., and Smith, R. (1982). *Vulnerable but invincible: A longitudinal study of resilient children.* New York: McGraw-Hill.

Westoff, C. (1988). Unintended pregnancy in America and abroad. *Family Planning Perspectives, 20,* 254–261.

Wetzel, J. (1987). *American youth: A statistical snapshot.* New York: William T. Grant Foundation Commission on Work, Family, and Citizenship.

Whitbeck, L., Conger, R., Simons, R., and Kao, M. (1993). Minor deviant behaviors and adolescent sexuality. *Youth and Society, 25,* 24–37.

Whitbeck, L., Hoyt, D., Miller, M., and Kao, M. (1992). Parental support, depressed affect, and sexual experience among adolescents. *Youth and Society, 24,* 166–177.

White, J., Moffitt, T., and Silva, P. (1989). A prospective replication of the protective effects of IQ in subjects at high risk for juvenile delinquency. *Journal of Consulting and Clinical Psychology, 57,* 719–724.

White, K., Speisman, J., and Costos, D. (1983). Young adults and their parents. In H. Grotevant and C. Cooper (Eds.), *Adolescent development in the family.* San Francisco: Jossey-Bass.

White, L., and Brinkerhoff, D. (1981). The sexual division of labor: Evidence from childhood. *Social Forces, 60,* 170–181.

Whiting, B., and Whiting, J. (1975). *Children of six cultures.* Cambridge, Mass.: Harvard University Press.

Wigfield, A., Eccles, J., MacIver, D., Reuman, D., and Midgley, C. (1991). Transitions during early adolescence: Changes in children's domain-specific self-perceptions and general self-esteem across the transition to junior high school. *Developmental Psychology, 27,* 552–565.

Wilkerson, I. (1994, May 16). Two boys, a debt, a gun, a victim: The face of violence. *New York Times,* pp. A1 ff.

William T. Grant Foundation Commission on Work, Family, and Citizenship. (1988). *The forgotten half: Non-college youth in America.* Washington, D.C.: William T. Grant Foundation Commission on Work, Family, and Citizenship.

Williamson, J., Borduin, C., and Howe, B. (1991). The

ecology of adolescent maltreatment: A multilevel examination of adolescent physical abuse, sexual abuse, and neglect. *Journal of Consulting and Clinical Psychology, 59,* 449–457.

Willits, F. (1988). Adolescent behavior and adult success and well-being. *Youth and Society, 20,* 68–69.

Wilson, F. (1985). The impact of school desegregation programs on white public-school enrollment, 1968–1976. *Sociology of Education, 58,* 137–153.

Wilson, M., and Daly, M. (1985). Competitiveness, risk taking, and violence: The young male syndrome. *Ethology and Sociobiology, 6,* 59–73.

Wilson, P., and Wilson, J. (1992). Environmental influences on adolescent educational aspirations: A logistic transform model. *Youth and Society, 24,* 52–70.

Wilson, T., and Linville, P. (1985). Improving the performance of college freshmen with attributional techniques. *Journal of Personality and Social Psychology, 49,* 287–293.

Wilson, W. (1987). *The truly disadvantaged: The inner city, the underclass, and public policy.* Chicago: University of Chicago Press.

Windle, M. (1989). Substance use and abuse among adolescent runaways: A four-year follow-up study. *Journal of Youth and Adolescence, 18,* 331–344.

Windle, M., Miller-Tutzauer, C., and Barnes, G. (1991). Adolescent perceptions of help-seeking resources for substance abuse. *Child Development, 62,* 179–189.

Wintemute, G., Kraus, J., Teret, S., and Wright, M. (1987). Drowning in childhood and adolescence: A population-based study. *American Journal of Public Health, 77,* 830–832.

Winterbottom, M. (1958). The relation of need for achievement to learning experiences in independence and mastery. In J. Atkinson (Ed.), *Motives in fantasy, action, and society.* Princeton, N.J.: Van Nostrand.

Wintre, M., Hicks, R., McVey, G., and Fox, J. (1988). Age and sex differences in choice of consultant for various types of problems. *Child Development, 59,* 1046–1055.

Wolf, A., Gortmaker, S., Cheung, L., Gray, H., Herzog, D., and Colditz, G. (1993). Activity, inactivity, and obesity: Racial, ethnic, and age differences among schoolgirls. *American Journal of Public Health, 83,* 1625–1627.

Wong, M., and Csikszentmihalyi, M. (1991). Affiliation motivation and daily experience: Some issues on gender differences. *Journal of Personality and Social Psychology, 60,* 154–164.

Wright, L., Frost, C., and Wisecarver, S. (1993). Church attendance, meaningfulness of religion, and depressive symptomatology among adolescents. *Journal of Youth and Adolescence, 22,* 559–568.

Wright, M. R. (1989). Body image satisfaction in adolescent girls and boys: A longitudinal study. *Journal of Youth and Adolescence, 18,* 71–84.

Wuthnow, R., and Glock, C. (1973). Religious loyalty, defection, and experimentation among college youth. *Journal for the Scientific Study of Religion, 12,* 157–180.

Yamaguchi, K., and Kandel, D. (1987). Drug use and other determinants of premarital pregnancy and its outcome: A dynamic analysis of competing life events. *Journal of Marriage and the Family, 49,* 257–270.

Yankelovich, D. (1974). *The new morality: A profile of American youth in the 1970s.* New York: McGraw-Hill.

Yoshikawa, H. (1994). Prevention as cumulative protection: Effects of early family support and education on chronic delinquency and its risks. *Psychological Bulletin, 115,* 28–54.

Young, H., and Ferguson, L. (1979). Developmental changes through adolescence in the spontaneous nomination of reference groups as a function of decision context. *Journal of Youth and Adolescence, 8,* 239–252.

Youniss, J., and Ketterlinus, R. (1987). Communication and connectedness in mother- and father-adolescent relationships. *Journal of Youth and Adolescence, 16,* 265–292.

Youniss, J., and Smollar, J. (1985). *Adolescent relations with mothers, fathers, and friends.* Chicago: University of Chicago Press.

Zabin, L., et al. (1986b). Ages of physical maturation and first intercourse. *Demography, 23,* 595–605.

Zabin, L., Astone, N., and Emerson, M. (1993). Do adolescents want babies? The relationship between attitudes and behavior. *Journal of Research on Adolescence, 3,* 67–86.

Zabin, L., Hirsch, M., and Emerson, M. (1989). When urban adolescents choose abortion: Effects on education, psychological status and subsequent pregnancy. *Family Planning Perspectives, 21,* 248–255.

Zabin, L., Hirsch, M., Smith, E., Streett, R., and Hardy, J. (1986a). Evaluation of a pregnancy prevention program for urban teenagers. *Family Planning Perspectives, 16,* 119–126.

Zeldin, R., Small, S., and Savin-Williams, R. (1982). Prosocial interactions in two mixed-sex adolescent groups. *Child Development, 53,* 1492–1498.

Zelnick, M., and Kantner, L. (1973). Sex and contraception among unmarried teenagers. In C. Westoff et al. (Eds.), *Toward the end of growth: Population in America.* Englewood Cliffs, N.J.: Prentice-Hall.

Zelnick, M., Kantner, J., and Ford, K. (1981). *Sex and pregnancy in adolescence.* Beverly Hills, Calif.: Sage.

Zill, N. (1984). *Happy, healthy and insecure.* New York: Doubleday.

Zima, B., Wells, K., and Freeman, H. (1994). Emotional and behavioral problems and severe aca-demic delays among sheltered homeless children in Los Angeles County. *American Journal of Public Health, 84,* 260–264.

Zimiles, H., and Lee, V. (1991). Adolescent family structure and educational progress. *Developmental Psychology, 27,* 314–320.

Zimring, F. (1982). *The changing legal world of adolescence.* New York: Free Press.

Zuckerman, M. (Ed.). (1983). *Biological basis of sensation seeking, impulsivity, and anxiety.* Hillsdale, N.J.: Erlbaum.

ACKNOWLEDGMENTS

Chapter 1

Figure 1-4
From: N. M. Morris and J. R. Udry, "Validation of a Self-Administered Instrument to Assess Stage of Adolescent Development," *Journal of Youth and Adolescence,* Vol. 9, 1980, pp. 275–276. Reprinted by permission of Plenum Publishing Corporation.

Figure 1-8A
From: *Being Adolescent: Conflict and Growth in the Teenage Years* by Mihaly Csikszentmihalyi and Reed Larson. Copyright © 1984 by Basic Books, Inc. Reprinted by permission of Basic Books, a division of HarperCollins Publishers, Inc.

Figure 1-8B
From: *Being Adolescent: Conflict and Growth in the Teenage Years* by Mihaly Csikszentmihalyi and Reed Larson. Copyright © 1984 by Basic Books, Inc. Reprinted by permission of Basic Books, a division of HarperCollins Publishers, Inc.

Table 1-1
"Patterns of the Experience of Mood." Patricia J. Bence, Ph.D., Thompkins Cortland Community College, 170 North Street, Dryden, NY 13053. Poster presented to the Fourth Biennial Meeting of the Society for Research on Adolescence, Washington, DC, March, 1992. A grant from the School of Human Ecology at Cornell University partially supported this research.

Box, pp. 52–53
From: A. Caspi and T. Moffitt, "Individual differences and personal transitions: The sample case of girls at puberty, *Journal of Personality and Social Psychology,* 61, 157–168. Copyright 1991 by the American Psychological Association. Reprinted by permission.

Table 1-2
From: B. Goldstein, *Introduction to Human Sexuality,* 1976 McGraw-Hill, Inc. Reprinted by permission of Bernars Goldstein.

Chapter 2

Box, pp. 74–75
From: S. Ward and W. Overton, "Semantic familiarity, relevance and the development of deductive reasoning," *Developmental Psychology,* 26, 488–493. Copyright 1990 by the American Psychological Association. Reprinted by permission.

Chapter 3

Box, pp. 124–125
From: H. Stattin and C. Magnusson, (February 1994). "Behavioral and Interpersonal Antecedents Behind the Age at Leaving Home, and the Future Consequences for Parent-Child Relations," Paper presented at the biennial meetings of the Society for Research on Adolescence, San Diego. Reprinted by permission.

Figure 3-1
From: James R. Wetzel, American Youth: A Statistical Snapshot. Washington, DC: Youth and America's Future: The William T. Grant Commission on Work, Family and Citizenship, 1989. Reprinted by permission.

Figure 3-2
"The Adolescent Poor and the Transition to Early Childhod," by A. Sum and W. Fogg, in P. Edelman and J. Ladner (eds.) *Adolescence and Poverty: Challenge for the 90's,* Center for National Policy Press, 1991.

Chapter 4

Box, pp. 142–143
From: P. Amato and B. Keith, "Parental Divorce and the Well-Being of Children: A meta-analysis," *Psychological Bulletin,* 110, 26–46. Copyright 1991 by the American Psychological Association. Reprinted by permission.

Figure 4-4
From: Conger, "Family Economic Stress and Adjustment of Early Adolescent Girls," *Developmental Psychology,* 29, 206–219. Reprinted by permission of the American Psychological Association.

Figure 4-5
From: Maccoby and Martin, "Socialization in the Context of the Family: Parent-Child Interaction," in E. M. Hetherington (ed.) *Handbook of Child Psychology, Socialization, Personality and Social Development,* Vol. 4. Copyright © 1983 by John Wiley & Sons, Inc. Reprinted by permission of John Wiley & Sons, Inc.

Chapter 5

Figure 5-2
From: Larson and Richards, "Daily Companionship in Late Childhood and Early Adolescence: Changing Developmental Contexts," *Child Development,* 62, 284–300. Copyright © 1991 The Society for Research in Child Development. Reprinted by permission.

Figure 5-3
From: Brown, Mory, and Kinney, "Casting Crowds in a Relational Perspective: Caricature, Channel and Context." In R. Montemayor, G. Adams, and T. Gullotta (eds.) *Advances in Adolescent Development, Vol. 5, Personal Relationships during Adolescence.* © 1994 by Sage Publications, Inc. Reprinted by permission of Sage Publications, Inc.

Box, pp. 156–157
From: David A. Kinney, "From nerds to normals: The recovery of identity among adolescents from middle school to high school," *Sociology of Education,* 66, 21–40. Copyright 1990. Reprinted by permission of the American Sociological Association and David A. Kinney.

Figure 5-4
From: B. Bradford Brown, "Peer Groups," in S. Feldman and G. Elliott (eds.) *At the Threshold: The Developing Adolescent,* pp. 171–196. Harvard University Press, 1990. Reprinted by permission of B. Bradford Brown.

Chapter 6

Box, p. 241
From: L. Jussim and J. Eccles, "Teacher Expectations II: Construction and Reflection of Student Achievement," *Journal of Personality and Social Psychology,* 63, 947-961. Reprinted by permission of the American Psychological Association.

Chapter 7

Figure 7-1
From: *Being Adolescent: Conflict and Growth in the Teenage Years* by Mihaly Csikszentmihalyi and Reed Larson. Copyright © 1984 by Basic Books, Inc. Reprinted by permission of Basic Books, a division of HarperCollins Publishers, Inc.; and "How Children Use Time," by S. G. Timmer, J. Eccles, and I. O'Brien (1985). In F. T. Juster and F. B. Stafford (eds.) *Time, Goods, and Well Being.* Reprinted by permission of the Institute for Social Research.

Figure 7-3
From: Riggiero, Greenberge, and Steinberg "Occupational Deviance Among First Time Workers," *Youth and Society,* 13, 423–448. © 1982 by Sage Publications, Inc. Reprinted by permission of Sage Publications, Inc.

Box, pp. 278–279
From: R. Larson and M. Richards (1991) "Daily Companionship in Late Childhood and Early Adolescence: Changing Developmental Contexts," *Child Development,* 62, 284–300. Copyright © The Society for Research in Child Development. Reprinted by permission.

Figure 7-5
From: Ward, "Talking About Sex: Common Themes About Sexuality in the Prime Time TV Programs Children & Adolescents Most View," *Journal of Youth & Adolescence.* Reprinted by permission of Plenum Publishing Corporation.

Chapter 8

Figure 8-1
From: Harter and Monsour, "Developmental analysis of conflict caused by opposing attributes in the adolescent self-portrait," *Developmental Psychology,* 28, 251–260. Copyright 1992 by the American Psychological Association. Reprinted by permission.

Figure 8-2
From: Hirsch and DuBois, (1991) "Self-Esteem in Early Adolescence: The Identification and Predication of Contrasting Longitudinal Trajectories," *Journal of Youth and Adolescence,* Vol 20, pp. 53–72. Reprinted by permission of Plenum Publishing Corporation.

Box, pp. 300–301
From: D. Rowe, A. Vazsonyi, and D. Flannery, "No More Than Skin Deep: Ethnic and Racial Similarity in Developmental Process," *Psychological Review,* 1994, 101, 396–413. Copyright 1994 by the American Psychological Association. Reprinted by permission.

Figure 8.5
From: Phinney, "Ethnic Identity and American Identification Among Ethnic Minority Adolescents," In F. Van de Vijver (ed.) *Proceedings of 1992 Conference of the International Association for Cross Cultural Psychology.* Copyright 1992 Swets & Zeitlinger Publishers. Reprinted by permission.

Chapter 9

Figure 9-1
From: Steinberg and Silverberg, "The vicissitudes of autonomy in early adolescence," *Child Development,* 57, 841–851. Copyright 1986 The Society for Research in Child Development, Inc. Reprinted by permission.

Figure 9-2
From: Lewis, "The effects of parental firm control," *Psychological Bulletin,* 90, 547–563. Copyright 1981 by the American Psychological Association. Reprinted by permission.

Box, pp. 346–347
From: A. Fuligini and J. Eccles, "Perceived parent-child relationships and early adolescents' orientation toward peers," *Developmental Psychology,* 29, 622–632. *Psychology,* 29, 622–632. Copyright 1993 by the American Psychological Association. Reprinted by permission.

Figure 9-1
From: Steinberg and Silverberg, "The Vicissitudes of Autonomy in Early Adolescence, *Child Development,* 57, pp. 841–851. © Copyright 1986 The Society for Research in Child Development. Reprinted by permission.

Figure 9-4
From: Steinberg and Silverberg, "The Vicissitudes of Autonomy in Early Adolescence, *Child Development,* 57, pp. 841–851. © Copyright 1986 The Society for Research in Child Development. Reprinted by permission.

Chapter 10

Table 10-1
Adapted from *Conceptions of Modern Psychiatry* by Henry Stack Sullivan, with the permission of W. W. Norton & Company, Inc. Copyright 1940, 1945, 1947, 1953 by the William Alanson White Psychiatric Foundation.

Box, pp. 374–375
From: R. Kobak, H. Cole, R. Ferenz-Gillies, W. Flemming, and W. Gamble (1993) "Attachment and Emotion Regulation During Mother-Teen Problem-Solving: A Control Theory Analysis," *Child Development,* 64, 231–245. Copyright © The Society for Research in Child Development. Reprinted by permission.

Figure 10-1
From: Bieglow and LaGaipa, "Children's written descriptions of friendships," *Developmental Psychology,* 11, 857–858. Copyright by the American Psychological Association. Reprinted by permission.

Figure 10-3
From: Windle, et. al., "Adolescent Perceptions of Help-Seeking Resources for Substance Abuse," *Child Development,* 62, pp. 179–189. Copyright © 1991 The Society for Research in Child Development. Reprinted by permission.

Figure in Box, p. 389
From: Sharabany, Gershoni, and Hofman, "Girlfriend, boyfriend: Age & sex differences in intimate friendship," *Developmental Psychology,* 17, 800–808. Copyright 1981 by the American Psychological Association. Reprinted by permission.

Chapter 11

Figure 11-1
From: Brent C. Miller and Kirstin A. Moore, "Adolescent Sexual Behavior, Pregnancy, and Parenting Research

Through the 1980's," *Journal of Marriage and Family,* 52, pp. 1025–1044. Copyrighted 1990 by the National Council on Family Relations, 3989 Central Avenue NE, Suite 550, Minneapolis, MN 55421. Reprinted by permission.

Figure 11-2
Reprinted with permission from *Risking the Future: Adolescent Sexuality, Pregnancy, and Childbearing,* Volume 1. Copyright 1987 by the National Academy of Sciences. Courtesy of the National Aca-demy Press, Washington, DC.

Box, pp. 422–424
From: S. Small and T. Luster, "Adolescent Sexual Activity: An Ecological, Risk-Factor Approach," *Journal of Marriage and the Family,* 1994, 56, 181–192. Reprinted by permission.

Chapter 12

Figure #1
Box, p. 453
From: Evans, E. M. (1992) Achievement & achievement-related beliefs in Asian and Western contexts: Cultural and gender differences. In C. Flanagan (Chair) Cross-cultural perspectives on adolescence: Achievements, concerns, norms, and beliefs. (Abstracts) *Society for Research on Adolescence, Fourth Biennial Meeting,* p. 62. Copyright 1995 by E. M. Evans and H. A. Stevenson, University of Michigan. Reprinted by permission.

Figure #2
Box, p. 454
From: J. Eccles (1993) "Parents as Gender-Role Socializers During Middle Childhood, and Adolescence," Paper presented at the biennial meetings of the Society for Research in Child Development, New Orleans. Reprinted by permission of J. Eccles.

Figure 12-1
From: "How a Diploma Pays Off," May 30, 1994, p. A23. Copyright © 1994 by The New York Times Company. Reprinted by permission.

Box, pp. 466–467
From: R. Felner, et. al. (1995) "Poverty and Educational Disadvantage: Environmental Mediators of Socioemotional and Academic Achievement in Early Adolescence," *Child Development.* Copyright © The Society for Research in Child Development. Reprinted by permission.

Figure 12-2
From: Fuligni and Stevenson, "Time Use and Mathematics Achievement Among American, Chinese, and Japanese High School Students," *Child Development,* June 1995, Vol. 66, No. 3, 830–842. © 1995 The Society for Research in Child Development, Inc. Reprinted by permission.

Chapter 13

Figure 13-3
From: "When Youngsters Light Up," *The New York Times,* December 11, 1990. Copyright © 1990 by The New York Times Company. Reprinted by permission.

Table 13-1
From: *Diagnostic and Statistical Manual of Mental Disorders,* Fourth Edition. Washington, DC, American Psychiatric Association, 1994. Reprinted by permission.

Table 13-2
From: "Living with 10 to 15 Year Olds," A Parent Education Curriculum. © 1992 Center for Early Adolescence, University of North Carolina at Chapel Hill, Carrboro, NC. Reprinted with permission.

Table 13-3
From: "Living with 10 to 15 Year Olds," A Parent Education Curriculum. © 1992 Center for Early Adolescence, University of North Carolina at Chapel Hill, Carrboro, NC. Reprinted with permission.

Box, pp. 520–521
From: M. Gould, S. Wallenstein, and M. Kleinman (1990), "Time-space Clustering of Teenage Suicide," *American Journal of Epidemiology,* Copyright © 1990 by The Johns Hopkins University School of Hygiene and Public Health. All rights reserved.

NAME INDEX

SUBJECT INDEX